THE COMMON AGRICULTURAL POLICY

The Common Agricultural Policy

Continuity and Change

ROSEMARY FENNELL

CLARENDON PRESS · OXFORD
1997

Oxford University Press, Great Clarendon Street, Oxford OX2 6DP

Oxford New York

Athens Auckland Bangkok Bogota Bombay
Buenos Aires Calcutta Cape Town Dar es Salaam
Delhi Florence Hong Kong Istanbul Karachi
Kuala Lumpur Madras Madrid Melbourne
Mexico City Nairobi Paris Singapore
Taipei Tokyo Toronto
and associated companies in
Berlin Ibadan

Oxford is a trade mark of Oxford University Press

Published in the United States
by Oxford University Press Inc., New York

British Library Cataloguing in Publication Data
Data available

Library of Congress Cataloging in Publication Data
Fennell, Rosemary.
The Common agricultural policy : continuity and change / Rosemary Fennell.
Includes bibliographical references and index.
1. Agriculture and state—European Union countries. I. Title.
HD1918.F46 1997 338.1'84—dc21 96-52390

ISBN 0-19-828857-3

1 3 5 7 9 10 8 6 4 2

Typeset by BookMan Services, Ilfracombe
Printed in Great Britain by
Bookcraft (Bath) Ltd.,
Midsomer Norton, Avon

PREFACE

I was an undergraduate at university in Dublin when the European Economic Community came into being on 1 January 1958. In 1961 Ireland applied to join this new Community and, a few months later, the Minister for Agriculture set up a series of small teams to investigate the likely impact of membership of the Community on certain key agricultural processing industries. I was a member of the bacon and pigmeat industry team. We submitted our report at the end of 1962 and to the best of my knowledge none of our twenty-two recommendations was implemented: a salutary demonstration early in my career of the impact of economists on policy-makers! I was a member of the academic staff of Wye College in London University when, on 1 January 1973, Denmark, Ireland, and the United Kingdom finally joined the Community.

The existence of the European Community and, in particular of the Common Agricultural Policy, has been a central feature of my working life; similarly someone who entered farming in the 1960s and 1970s in the original six Member States and in the three which joined in 1973 has worked in a sector deeply influenced by the CAP and any previous national policies were, by the 1990s, no more than a distant memory. Indeed, some of the people who entered farming in those early days of the policy may have already handed over the farm to a new generation.

Over its lifetime, the CAP has had more than its fair share of attention—and certainly more than any other policy involved in the process of European integration. Among academic commentators and analysts, interest has been confined very largely to economists and, in particular, to agricultural economists. The only other academic group to show a keen interest in the CAP are lawyers—not surprisingly because so many important decisions in the European Court of Justice have been made on issues arising from the implementation of the CAP.

The neglect by other disciplines is surprising: the CAP is one of the founding policies of the Community. It is also a very interesting policy because it is so comprehensive and touches not only economics and law but politics, history, sociology, international relations, and, no doubt, many more subject areas. One can only speculate as to the reason for this neglect. Perhaps an impression has been created that the CAP is a very technical policy composed of masses of rules and regulations of interest only to those directly involved in its management. Perhaps, because so many of the policy instruments are concerned with markets and the manipulation of price, it has been perceived as an economic policy. Perhaps an increasingly urbanized population which knows little about farming and cares even less feels inhibited from entering an alien world as anything other than a tourist.

Whatever the reason, it is most unfortunate that the analysis of the CAP has been left so largely in the hands of economists who, not unnaturally, have viewed the policy from their own particular perspective. When examining a policy or a

policy proposal, the tendency among economists today is to carry out their analysis within a very theoretical framework and to display considerable reluctance
to discuss the practicality of their arguments and conclusions. This is contrary to
what classical and neoclassical economists in earlier times would have done.
Because the CAP is such a highly politicized policy, not only at the level of the
Council of Ministers, within the Commission, and in the European Parliament,
but also in the Member States, a theoretical discussion is likely to make little
impact when the measure in question is going to be accepted or rejected on its
political feasibility rather than on its economic merits. Economists need to get
involved in the practicality of running a policy. They need to understand the
political parameters of decision-making and take them into account; political
scientists could play a valuable part in elucidating these aspects of policy and it
is to be regretted that they have so largely ignored the CAP.

When one examines the economic literature on the CAP one becomes aware
very quickly that the authors are drawn overwhelmingly from a narrow range of
countries and experience. Without intending to do so, these commentators provide a distorted picture in which the large farm business, northern European,
Atlantic viewpoint is over-represented and the small farm business, Southern
European, Mediterranean viewpoint is hardly expressed at all. This is not just a
matter of publication in English: it is astonishing how little has been published
in, for instance, Italian or French on the CAP.

While having to confess that I too am a northern European, at least I am no
Anglo-Saxon! While being an economist, I have always been more interested in
political economy—a discipline long out of fashion—than in any other aspect of
the subject! Therefore, I hope I may be able to provide a bridge between
disciplines and open the CAP to wider inspection. Technical detail is kept to a
minimum so that the book can provide a base from which those interested in
many aspects of European integration can explore this fascinating policy.
Although written by an academic economist, the book does not draw on the
views of economists to any great extent but rather concentrates on the views
emanating from within the Institutions of the European Community/Union
itself. In other words, it relies very heavily on the policy-makers and, in particular, the European Commission. What were their intentions in the devising and
implementation of the policy; what have they had to say about its effect, and
how has the outcome compared with their intentions?

One useful feature of an overview such as this, which covers almost four decades of policy development, is that it provides an opportunity to appreciate the
extent to which the policy is a mixture of continuity and change. In this regard
it is unfortunate—and ultimately unhelpful—that so much emphasis is placed
on policy reform which carries with it a connotation of revolution rather than
the reality which is much more akin to subtle change. This reality is not unusual:
policy change at a national level is more often incremental than fundamental.
This can be extremely frustrating but within a democratic framework is almost
inevitable. How much more is this the case when an ever-increasing number of
democratic and highly individual countries come together in a common cause!

Within the European Union context, the CAP is one of the best policy areas to illustrate how difficult it is to bring about change and how important it is to have strong institutional structures and decision-making processes at the centre to counteract the fractionist tendencies of the Member States.

Having set the policy in its historic framework, the book then progresses along thematic lines: incomes, price and market policy, structural policy, the wider policy goals introduced in the 1980s, commercial policy—tracing their development over time. The final chapter picks up certain points arising from earlier chapters and outlines issues which still remain to be resolved. Some topics have had to be omitted—or are treated less thoroughly than they deserve—for lack of space. Other topics are omitted or are dealt with rather briefly because they were felt to be of technical or local interest only and therefore not well suited to an overview such as this book is.

A study of this kind is the product of many years of work and many people have helped it on its way. Over the years I have benefited from discussions with officials of the European Commission—past and present—who have taken the time to discuss particular issues with me. The research was supported by the European Commission (DGXII) under the Stimulation Plan for Economic Science (SPES). My insatiable search for documents brought me to the DGVI documentation centre in Brussels where intermittent forays were met with fortitude, good humour, and liberality.

The library of the European Commission office in London has at times felt like a second home. It has been presided over for more years than either of us would care to remember by Marguerite Brenchley who has been such a marvellous support and whose library hospitality I have abused shamelessly.

Also in London, at various stages in the work members of the staff of MAFF have helped in the provision of information and the home of one of them has been a welcoming staging post between the European Commission's office and Oxford.

Annette Morgan of the Civil Service College was kind enough to read the majority of the chapters for an honest view on their intelligibility. Berkeley Hill of London University (Wye College) and George Peters of Oxford University performed the same service for two of the more technical chapters.

The library staff in my own department—the International Development Centre at Queen Elizabeth House—tolerated with a certain bemusement my unorthodox borrowing procedures which bore only a passing resemblance to their own rules.

Marie-Hélène Baneth undertook some critical translations and located certain documents in Paris for me. Rosemarie Francis and Wendy Grist administered the SPES funds with great care.

Denise Watt turned my handwritten text into a series of splendidly presented typed versions through her skilled use of a computer. Throughout the over-long gestation of this book she remained calm and unruffled no matter how many horrible statistical tables I provided by way of a challenge. Roger Crawford produced the diagrams and bar charts on his computer with his usual skill.

Geoffrey Harrison, now retired, but who was Professor of Biological Anthropology at Oxford University very kindly, at a critical juncture in my thinking through this project, provided me for a term with a hideaway in the shape of the visiting academic's workroom in his department.

Many people who should be listed above are not, due to the feebleness of my memory rather than a lack of appreciation. My colleagues and friends are remembered with particular gratitude for their forbearance as I bored them with tales of frustration in the writing of this book.

To all those who have sustained me in whatever way, I dedicate this book with my thanks.

CONTENTS

A NOTE ON LITERATURE CITATION

The *List of References* is divided into two. Books, journal articles, and conference papers are listed by author and grouped together in the first part. European Community/Union documents are listed by Institution by year, and documents in French and English are grouped together in the same list.

Citation of material published in the *Official Journal of the European Communities* and in the *Bulletin of the European Communities* is limited to the main body of the text where the issue number and date of publication are given.

The most commonly cited Commission sources are the documents known as 'COM docs.' and 'SEC docs.'. These are listed by number order by year. This is the most satisfactory procedure, as date of issue within the year follows no logical pattern.

Prior to 1968, the *Official Journal* (*Journal Officiel*) appeared as a single series; after that date, it was divided into the 'C Series' (Communication) and the 'L Series' (Legislation). In the text citation, this is indicated as OJ C . . . or OJ L . . . followed by the issue number and date of publication. (French language citation is indicated by JO . . . .) Reference is also made in the text to the Special Edition of the *Official Journal*. This was published in the early 1970s and brought together in an English language translation all the legislation passed prior to 1973 which was still operative. This source is cited in the text as Sp. OJ . . . .

Some COM docs. contain draft legislation and increasingly these drafts are being published in the C Series of the *Official Journal* as well. However, where possible in this book, draft legislation is cited in its COM doc. form. The reason is that this is the only place in which one can find the accompanying Explanatory Memorandum, which sometimes provides useful insights into the purpose of the proposed legislation, and the Statistical Annex which sometimes provides useful data on the expected impact of the proposed measure.

Frequent reference is made in the text to the Treaty of Rome and to the treaties which amended it: the Single European Act and the Maastricht Treaty. No source is cited for these documents as they are in the public domain.

The citation of material which appears in *Agence Europe* (a commercial daily news briefing) and in *Agra Europe* (a commercial weekly news briefing) is given in the text only, by date of issue.

References to 'the Commission' which are scattered freely throughout the text are based overwhelmingly on the evidence contained in the COM docs. Although these documents are issued in the name of the Commission as a collegiate body and have been formally adopted as the official Commission view, they originate in a particular part of the Commission bureaucracy. In the case of agriculture, this is Directorate-General VI (DGVI). It would be wrong to assume that every other part of the Commission was fully in agreement with every word they contain—and indeed there might well be differences of opinion within DGVI itself. One of the positive aspects of the Commission's work is the fact that these documents while internal are widely available (even when not published subsequently in the *Official Journal*). This allows a much greater insight into policy formation than one gets from a national government department.

The situation with regard to the Council of Ministers is nowhere near as open and, until Council papers become available, one can only guess at the reasons for certain action or inaction, and the position adopted by individual Member States. Clearly contemporary news media are a help—in particular *Agence Europe*—but the application of a thirty-year rule to the release of Council papers is excessively long.

1

The Foundations of the CAP:
Agricultural Policy in Western Europe in the 1950s

Major Policy Preoccupations

When the Common Agricultural Policy (CAP) was devised it was regarded as a major and exciting innovation in the field of agricultural policy. In one sense this was true in that it represented the first successful attempt to create a single policy for an economic sector, implemented in a unified manner over the territory of a number of independent States, and which governed their relationships not only with each other but also with the rest of the world. Despite the novelty of the achievement, it should come as no surprise to find that the CAP was a child of its time and should be seen in the context of agricultural policy in Western Europe in the 1950s. The basic problems which had produced the main elements of post-war agricultural policy did not disappear or change with the advent of the CAP and, as a result, the aims of the new policy and the instruments used to achieve them remained much the same.

The natural conditions of soil, climate, and topography clearly affect the range of agricultural products which any country can produce and policy has to take these into account. The institutional framework (for example, in the sphere of inheritance and taxation legislation) affects the organization of production. The longer-term historical circumstances play their part—for example, the reaction to the Great Depression of the late nineteenth century, the timing and the pace of industrial expansion, the rate of population growth, the emergence of farming as a political weapon and farmers as a political force, and so forth. A whole host of circumstances combine to create a situation which is unique to each country and yet which also has certain similarities with features found elsewhere.

When one looks back on earlier policies with the unfair advantage of hindsight, the feature which is often the most striking is how unsuitable they appear in the light of what is now known was actually happening at the time. This apparent unsuitability is understandable: it takes time to interpret contemporary events, to decide whether they are temporary phenomena or permanent changes, to react correctly to them at the political level, to translate that reaction into policy adjustments, and to persuade farmers to adapt their production patterns accordingly. By the time all the necessary changes have worked their way through the system, the circumstances may well have altered significantly.

Viewed from the troubled 1990s, two of the most outstanding features of the 1950s and 1960s are the sustained level of general economic expansion, which had such a profound effect on agriculture, and the technological revolution within farming itself. However, these events were not so obvious to those living through them. For the most part, they were preoccupied with their immediate past experiences and with current short-term difficulties. As a result, from today's vantage point, the farm policies pursued in the 1950s appear strangely out of tune with what was actually happening.

As a rule, policy-makers—whether bureaucrats or politicians—build on the past and have very short time-horizons. They tend to tinker with what exists already and rarely make bold innovations. Even the CAP, which in some respects can be regarded as a major leap forward in concept, was in practice a distillation of a variety of policies which had been tried already in the countries comprising the Community. It also reflects the earlier plans which had aimed at creating an agricultural policy common to a number of European States.

There is a widely held belief that agricultural policy is intended to be for the benefit of those who work on the land, producing the raw materials of the farming sector. This is not an unreasonable belief but it is only partially true: there are many aspects of agricultural policy which lie well outside the narrow confines of the economic and social well-being of those in farming. The immediate post-World War II period provides good examples of such considerations.

Understandably the main concern of governments in the early 1950s was to improve the food supply for the benefit of the whole population and to raise consumption levels which had fallen below those of the pre-war period. In pursuing these ends, governments had to take account of the severe balance-of-payments difficulties which they faced and their acute shortages of foreign currency, in particular dollars. The farming sector was seen as a means of aiding the balance of payments: at the very least, an increase in domestic farm output reduced the food import bill and, for a few countries, it meant exports and therefore foreign currency.

Linked to the need to raise total supply was a preoccupation with food security. The wartime and early post-war experience of most West European countries was of food shortages, and governments felt it advisable to try to produce at home as much and as wide a range of products as possible. They were strengthened in this resolve by the poor international political climate, as exemplified by the Korean War and the Cold War between the socialist and capitalist blocs. The possibility that increased agricultural output at home might have involved a misallocation of resources was scarcely considered, so overwhelming was the concern with the balance of payments and security.

By the mid-1950s many of the initial difficulties of the post-war period had passed: food supplies were adequate and the level of consumption was satisfactory. Some countries at least had markedly improved their balance-of-payments situation and the world had grown more accustomed to the political tensions between East and West. Significantly, also, production of the main farm commodities, such as cereals, had expanded appreciably in North America and other major supplying regions, with the result that international trading prices had fallen and substantial surpluses were available to buy.

These changed circumstances had little immediate impact on agricultural policy in Western Europe. The balance-of-payments argument for supporting domestic agriculture continued to be used long after its relevance had diminished. Indeed, as Krause (1968, 77) has pointed out it was used to support restrictive policies which were favoured for some other reason. It was a convenient argument 'and necessary to placate domestic nonagricultural interests and to resist pressures from agricultural exporting countries for a more liberal commercial policy'.

With the growth of surpluses outside Europe, security of supply was no real problem but a high level of self-sufficiency was a popular policy, given the recent experience of the war and post-war period. The unreality of such a policy in the European context is revealed when one realizes that 'agricultural output is crucially dependent upon imported animal feed, imported seed, imported fertilizers, imported petroleum, imported spare parts and machinery, and in some cases even imported workers' (Krause 1968, 77). Added to these considerations was the fact that already in the 1950s the possibility of a nuclear war was recognized with its attendant contamination of land and crops—a prospect which made the objective of self-sufficiency as an element within national security 'increasingly meaningless for virtually all individual countries, if not for Western Europe as a whole' (Coppock 1961, 514).

The development of agricultural policy was undoubtedly haphazard, 'with varying stress being laid in different countries and at different times, according to the current political and economic climate, on long-term measures to improve farm structure and marketing and on short-term adjustments to prices' (Butterwick and Rolfe 1968, 4). Within the confused and often contradictory policy framework, the one noticeable shift which did take place was towards giving greater consideration to the income problems being experienced by many farmers. The 'production at any cost' policy had indeed raised the level of self-sufficiency but it had not raised the incomes of the producers relative to those of other sections of society. Farmers were increasingly perceived as a disadvantaged group, especially in the context of the rising prosperity in many of the countries concerned. Once the artificial difficulties of the immediate post-war period began to recede, the underlying long-term natural and man-made problems of agriculture began to re-emerge. Natural difficulties arose from the limited availability of highly productive land, coupled with climatic and topographical shortcomings. In some regions these natural disadvantages were compounded by the inadequacy of the infrastructure.

Even in areas favoured by nature, institutional and organizational inadequacies hindered productivity. Due to the impact of population pressure in times past and the effect of inheritance laws, the predominant characteristic of agriculture over wide areas of Western Europe was the high proportion of small, badly organized farms. For some, specialization in horticulture, tobacco, wine, or intensive livestock production provided a means of counteracting the negative impact of their small size but 'the majority of smallholdings in Europe ... [were] not specialized farms with high yields but subsistence farms producing the bare necessities of life for the farmer and his family with only a very small surplus left over to sell' (ECE/FAO 1954, 18). On such farms the labour was underemployed, sometimes seasonally but more often permanently and, because of low productivity, using 'more time-consuming methods than those employed on farms without a labour surplus' (ibid.).

This situation contrasted strongly with those regions which were dominated by large underutilized estates, with their attendant landless workforce. Whatever the origin, the most important impact of poor land organization was on the farm labour supply. In general, land was scarce and labour plentiful. This resulted in low productivity per person and therefore low incomes in farming, both absolutely and in relation to incomes received in other sectors of the economy. In these circumstances it is not surprising that there was a constant movement of people out of farming to seek alternative job opportunities.

However, the labour market in Western Europe in the 1950s showed a number of contradictory trends, with some rural regions suffering from considerable underemployment and some urban regions suffering from a labour shortage. The coexistence of these two extremes is partly explained by the fact that the excess labour in farming was often unsuited for the employment opportunities on offer or was unwilling to migrate to another region or country. But another factor inhibiting mobility was the policy pursued in the agricultural sector itself. The protection and support afforded to farming had the effect of slowing down the rate of migration to other employment.

This highlights the fact that the attitude of many governments to the rural labour supply was ambivalent. Some positively did not want to see a reduction in the rural population for social or political reasons, others were more neutral but believed that the agricultural workforce would remain fairly constant, because other sectors would do no more than siphon off the natural increase occurring within the farming population.

Whatever the reason why people did not leave farming in greater numbers, the net result was that they could only raise their incomes by increasing output. It is hardly surprising therefore that, by the end of the 1950s, surplus production began to emerge in some countries for certain products and that the levels of self-sufficiency rose for many others. This situation was not helped by the poor standards of market organization and low levels of quality control. Problems of oversupply would not have emerged if demand had been buoyant but farmers faced falling elasticities of demand for many products at home. For those countries which looked to the export trade, the situation was no better; outlets were limited in other markets also, either due to protectionist policies on the part of the importing countries or to the absence of effective demand.

In 1961, the Organization for European Economic Co-operation (OEEC) described the two main problems of the agricultural sector as being 'the disparity between per capita incomes in agriculture and other branches of the economy and the disequilibrium between production and outlets for a number of basic commodities' (OEEC 1961, 63). Thus incomes and surpluses—familiar issues more than thirty years later—were already to the forefront of government thinking, when devising and executing agricultural policies. But in a certain sense the OEEC description of the main problems was misleading: incomes and surpluses only emerged as issues because of the existence of deeper maladjustments in the structure and organization of the sector; because of the inadequacy of investment in agriculture particularly and in rural areas generally; and because of the contradictions in the aims of policy and the instruments used.

By the mid-1950s most governments in Western Europe had adopted the improvement of farm incomes as a major aim of agricultural policy. This aim was usually expressed in the form of a pious hope rather than a legal requirement but, despite the weakness of the formal commitment, this is how governments perceived their intentions when, for instance, participating in policy discussions in OEEC (see for instance, OEEC 1956). Linked with the income aim was that of achieving greater price stability because it was felt that one of the reasons for the poor income level in farming was the extent of price fluctuations. These occurred seasonally, from year to year, and intermittently due to the movements of prices on international markets.

In pursuit of the twin aims of raising incomes and stabilizing prices, theoretically the approach might have been to raise end-prices for agricultural products, while building in some stabilizing elements internally and at the frontier. In practical terms, however, there were significant limits to the extent to which this could be done. Governments had no wish to raise inflation levels and wage demands by excessive increases in food prices, thus a combination of means had to be found which would help farmers achieve better incomes while maintaining price support at politically acceptable levels. The main tools used to supplement price support were measures to raise efficiency by increasing productivity per person; the improvement of quality standards and marketing; and the reorientation of production towards more suitable commodities.

Efficiency in biological and economic terms was pursued through improvements in the organization of land (enlargement of farms, consolidation of fragmented units, development of infrastructure); through the subsidization of inputs (such as fertilizers), which aimed at changing or improving farming practices; and through increased emphasis on research and advisory work. The reorientation of production was undertaken to encourage farmers to make the best use of whatever factors of production and climatic conditions they had. For instance, in some countries where labour was plentiful and land scarce, the emphasis was placed on livestock and horticulture rather than on cereals and other field crops.

The range and complexity of the policies devised by governments and their agents was enormous—despite efforts made under the auspices of OEEC to liberalize policy. Every conceivable aspect of agriculture was affected: the protection of the domestic market from imported supplies; the encouragement of production and its guidance towards certain commodities; the stimulation of exports in the face of other countries' import restrictions; the adjustment of the structure and organization of production and marketing; the protection of consumers through subsidies and quality controls; the promotion of animal health and welfare; the raising of the technical competence of farmers and farm workers, etc. The list is endless.

Among the most commonly used tools were, at the frontier, quantitative restrictions, customs tariffs, minimum import prices, variable levies, and state trading. Internally, the instruments included target, guaranteed, or fixed prices, marketing boards, stockpiling, input and consumer subsidies. However wide the range in individual countries, the favourite approach throughout Western Europe was the manipulation of the prices received by farmers for their products. This steadfast adherence to price support was surprising in view of its recognized shortcomings.

For instance, OEEC (1957) listed five factors which inhibited the efficiency of price support policies. It referred, firstly, to the political character of agricultural prices which required governments to intervene and arbitrate between the rival claims of consumers and producers. Secondly, there were limitations on effectiveness brought about through natural conditions. Thirdly, farmers themselves prevented price policy from achieving its goals because of their unwillingness to change certain practices or to take new risks, and their inability to implement changes individually which required collective effort. Fourthly, there was the inhibiting effect of the inelasticity of consumer demand and inadequate purchasing power, even with food subsidies. Also, tastes were changing and price policies did not respond quickly enough, so that products in declining demand continued to receive more support than was warranted. Lastly, it was quite clear that, although price policy had prevented market collapse during times of oversupply and had undoubtedly helped to maintain or improve farm incomes in absolute terms, it had not been able to stop the deterioration of farm incomes relative to those of other sectors.

One aspect of price policy which received less attention than might have been expected was its unequal impact on different groups of farmers. Natural conditions such as soil, climate, and topography were clearly of importance—as was recognized by OEEC in the second point outlined above—but so too were size of business and the product mix on the farm. Although schemes were introduced in a number of countries to aid disadvantaged farmers specifically, it was not a widespread practice. Thus, for many farmers with an income problem aggravated by natural or institutional factors, little advantage was gained through price support.

For them, the only real solution was to become less dependent on agriculture as their sole means of livelihood. The provision of off-farm job opportunities was therefore of critical importance, both to remove some labour permanently from farming and as a means of providing part-time employment for others who remained in farming. For the older farmers, the solution offered in some countries was a retirement pension.

One can only speculate as to why there was less concern with income differences within farming than between farming and other sectors. Certainly, it was not a matter which governments were likely to raise with farmers, but why did farmers not press for greater recognition of the difficulties some of their number faced? Given the success of the farming lobby generally in Western Europe, one can only conclude that the issue was played down for tactical reasons. Clearly it would have been unwise to adopt a bargaining position which indicated that some farmers were obtaining excessively high price support as a result of policies intended to improve the lot of the average—or even the marginal—farmer. However, the pursuit of undifferentiated price support meant just that, and the benefits which accrued to a minority of rich farmers were at the expense of poorer consumers and taxpayers, which implies a loss in terms of economic welfare and social justice alike.

Throughout the latter half of the 1950s the predominant aim of agricultural policy remained 'the drive to increase income and improve the standard of living for the agricultural population' (OEEC 1961, 31), still without any attempt to distinguish between different types of farmer and their particular income situations. The retention of the income objective at the forefront of policy suggests that little real progress was made in the course of the decade to achieve it. However, at that time one new element did begin to emerge, namely the desire of governments to limit their financial commitment to agriculture in some way. Towards this end, increasing attention was given to developing the type of family farm which would remain viable in the long term.

The effect of this shift in emphasis meant a growth in the importance of structural reform measures, both on the farm and in the marketing of agricultural products. It was recognized that poor structure was a major obstacle to improved incomes and thus it was hoped that the reform measures introduced would lead ultimately to a lessening of the need for income support which, overwhelmingly, was still being provided through the price mechanism.

However, even if a reduction in the financial commitment to agriculture was the long-term goal, the immediate reality for all governments in Western Europe was that the problems which beset the farming sector were no nearer solution. Some had actually got worse—in particular overproduction and export difficulties. Indeed, the extra investments intended to improve structure may well have exacerbated the situation. OEEC (1958) had already warned that structural improvement would raise production as well as productivity and had recommended an adjustment in production patterns. Unfortunately, OEEC was not specific as to how exactly its recommendation should be achieved but rather lamely pointed to the importance of adequate development in other sectors of the economy, in order to facilitate the absorption of some of the surplus labour from farming.

Special Features of the Six

To the general background picture already sketched must be added certain specific characteristics of the agricultural circumstances of the six individual countries which were to form the European Economic Community.

It is true that certain events in the recent past had touched all these countries—

the Depression of the 1930s, the wartime losses and dislocation, the food shortages, the balance-of-payments problems—and these factors influenced the policies which emerged after the war. But the reaction of each country to these events was dictated, in part at least, by much wider considerations.

For instance, in France the agricultural sector was stagnating, drifting aimlessly behind its protective wall with little evidence of a coherent internal policy. The instability of the Fourth Republic was such that the atmosphere was not conducive to the development and application of long-term policies in any sector. The targets for agriculture laid down in successive national plans remained unfulfilled. French farming life was characterized by disappointment and hopelessness. Open rebellion in the form of farmer riots was not unknown. The government was torn between the desire to raise agricultural production so as to save money on imports and to keep down consumer prices, and the fear that increased output might prove unsaleable both at home and abroad, thereby causing excessive price falls, which would have undermined the stability of agricultural incomes which were already very low. The attitude of the government to the size of the farm labour force was also confused.

In commenting on French policy, OEEC (1956, 65) was able to state that 'the present size of the agricultural population and its distribution over a large number of small, non-specialized holdings which in most cases cannot provide the funds for essential investment suggest that no rapid increase in the average level of productivity and no substantial reduction in production costs can be regarded as likely'. In the light of these circumstances, OEEC suggested that it was only through the removal of marginal farmers to other occupations that it would be possible to renovate agricultural structure and production.

However, OEEC was also able to report that 'it is considered in official quarters that employment in agriculture should be kept practically stable over the next few years, and that no important change should occur in the present balance of the urban and rural population' (OEEC 1956, 54). The government recognized that there was some drift from the land but dismissed it as unimportant. Indeed, it believed that the improved social welfare benefits which were being made available to the farming community were likely to slow down this drift from the land. Clearly the desire to maintain the rural population at its existing level—despite the manifest difficulties which this was causing in terms of low incomes—was politically motivated. It may well have been prompted by a belief that the rest of the economy was unable to provide increased off-farm job opportunities for the farming community and that, while the rural population was discontented with its lot, its members would have been even more rebellious if numbered in the ranks of the urban unemployed.

In sharp contrast was the situation in the Federal Republic of Germany (FRG). There, an early objective was an increase in labour productivity in farming. This approach was very largely necessitated by the rapid expansion of the economy which attracted workers from farming to other sectors in large numbers. As in France, the German Government wished to see a situation develop in which the proportion of basic foodstuffs produced at home was as large as possible. However, the motivation was quite different: it was not sought as an aid to the balance of payments but rather as a safeguard of the food supplies for the general population. The German Government had no particular wish to see the country become an agricultural exporter, rather it was attempting to halt the downward trend in self-sufficiency which had declined to 60 per cent of requirements by the end of the decade compared to 75 per cent at the beginning. Farm structure was poor in Germany—indeed it was far worse than in France—but there was a much more positive belief in the possibility of ameliorating the situation than existed in France.

One of the most notable features of the German approach to agriculture was how early the government adopted a stated policy for the sector. In 1955 the Parliament passed a general Agricultural Act which set out the policy objectives. But this statement was in effect a reiteration of principles which had existed in one way or another since the establishment of the Federal Republic in 1949. As expressed in 1955, the main objectives of policy were:

(a) To achieve a reasonable standard of living for the agricultural population working on well-managed farms, and to allow the agricultural sector to participate fully in the general development of the economy.

(b) To increase agricultural productivity by all possible means.

(c) To stabilize agricultural prices as much as possible. This is considered as an essential condition for an optimum utilization of production resources and for achieving agricultural progress.

(d) To secure a regular food supply at prices which allow the lower income groups of the population to buy food products in sufficient quantities. (OEEC 1957, 90)

The link between these German objectives and those subsequently appearing in Article 39 of the Rome Treaty is unmistakable.

The situation faced by the Italian Government was far more daunting than that faced by the French Government and light-years removed from the circumstances of the Federal Republic. The economic revolution in northern Italy was in its infancy and agriculture throughout the country had to contend with enormous problems. For one thing, Italy has a very low percentage of highly productive land—so unlike France. Also unlike France there was considerable overpopulation in rural areas, leading to much pressure on the scanty land resources. The need for land reform was regarded as very great.

The regional disequilibrium between the North and the South, both in terms of natural and of man-made resources, was far more severe than that experienced in more northerly countries. In the agricultural context, OEEC (1957, 152) was able to report that in Italy 'yields are, in general, double in the North what they are in the South and that 65 per cent of the marketable agricultural production is situated in the North . . . a proportion which is not found in the corresponding figures for the population'.

As in France, the government aimed to raise the volume of production so as to reduce the level of imports of certain foodstuffs, but more important still was the desire to promote intensive crops wherever possible—particularly in those areas which were being extensively farmed (mostly in the South). The land reform programme under which many thousands of smallholdings were created was intended, in part at least, to encourage this trend. Butterwick and Rolfe (1968, 5) maintained that the authors of the land reform could not be 'entirely blamed for failing to foresee the industrial development which revolutionized the Italian economy after 1955'. They saw the problem as 'set permanently in a context of mainly subsistence agriculture and widespread under-employment relieved only by migration abroad' (p. 5).

The creation of smallholdings in Italy was in sharp contrast to the aims of land reform in the other founding Member States of the Community. Elsewhere, the aims of policy were to consolidate fragmented farms, and to increase the size of farms regarded as economically viable. By contrast, the Italian approach was necessitated by the high demographic pressure which also led to the imposition of regulations over a large part of the country stipulating how many workers each farmer had to employ. The numbers laid down differed from province to province and depended on the overall level of unemployment in the province concerned. In many cases this meant that farms had an excessive labour supply which clearly resulted in very low levels of productivity per person.

The three smallest countries—Belgium, the Netherlands, and Luxembourg (Benelux)—took a joint decision in 1955 to harmonize their agricultural policies within seven years. This was an ambitious aim in the face of the very different circumstances of their farming sectors. Luxembourg acknowledged that its agriculture was marginal: the climate is severe and soil fertility low, and farms were small and heavily fragmented. But despite these rather hopeless circumstances the government pursued a highly protectionist policy, reserving the domestic market for its own farmers. The government also opposed a rural exodus and with this in mind improved the level of social welfare benefits for the farming population.

Like the French, the Belgians had structural problems which they did not see being alleviated in the near future, despite their known adverse effects on farming progress. Also like the French, the Belgians were concerned with the possible difficulties which an increased output might have in terms of unsaleable products. Their specific worries, however, were concerned not with crops but with the potential surpluses in the livestock sector. As a result, the Belgian Government adopted a policy of high wheat and sugar prices, which were intended to discourage the larger farms from moving out of arable crops and into livestock production.

This policy must have been in contradiction to another official policy which was to encourage the production of labour-intensive commodities. The reason for the latter policy is to be found in the small size of the heavily fragmented farms in Belgium which, in the 1950s, was coupled with abundant manpower and therefore underemployment on farms. Promotion of horticulture was undoubtedly a logical solution to this situation but the expansion of livestock products, which the government so feared, was an equally sensible solution from the farmers' point of view, which is probably why it occurred, despite official opposition.

The Belgian Government appears to have had an ambivalent attitude to the decline in the farming population. It recognized that technical progress resulted in a fall in numbers in farming but regarded a large agricultural population as socially desirable. It also recognized that there was surplus labour in some regions and that the non-farming sector was not able to absorb it. Instead of encouraging the creation of off-farm employment opportunities, the government seems to have responded to the situation by a further drive towards farming intensification and the promotion of products with a high labour content.

Whatever their differences, all the countries considered so far had one feature in common in the 1950s: they were net importers of agricultural products. Not so the Netherlands: unlike the others it was a net agricultural exporter. The Dutch were primarily engaged in the transformation of imported agricultural raw materials (mostly feed and fertilizers) into exportable agricultural products, mainly in the livestock and horticultural sectors. This export orientation made the Dutch especially conscious of the need for high levels of efficiency in production and marketing. A reflection of this is to be found in the use of the 'well-managed farm' as the basis of policy decisions. The need to export also restricted the types of policy which could be pursued: for instance, their dependence on foreign raw materials meant that their import regime was more liberal than those of the other countries.

As in Germany, Italy, and Belgium land was scarce and farms were small, so intensive farming was encouraged. The Dutch waged a constant and losing battle against rising costs and it is hardly surprising therefore that they had no sentimental attachment to the maintenance of a large rural population. On the contrary, the Netherlands was the only country of the Six actively to encourage the movement of people out of farming to other occupations and, indeed, to other countries.

The Launching of the Economic Community

The first important steps towards the launching of the European Economic Community were taken by the Benelux countries when, in May 1955, they presented to the other member governments of the European Coal and Steel Community (ECSC) a memorandum on European integration. This memorandum was discussed at a meeting of Foreign Ministers held in Messina in June of the same year. At that meeting it was agreed that an intergovernmental conference should prepare the texts of treaties on integration, and that the preparatory work needed to bring about such a conference should be entrusted to a Committee of government delegates.

This Committee was presided over by Paul-Henri Spaak, the then Belgian Foreign Minister. Its first act was to set up four subsidiary committees of experts to handle the various topics under discussion. The subcommittee on the common market completed its work during October 1955 and reported to the Spaak Committee. Agriculture, although not discussed in much detail, was already recognized as presenting special problems. In all, the various expert groups produced ten lengthy reports and, in February 1956, the task of compiling one comprehensive document out of the available material was entrusted to Pierre Uri assisted by von der Groeben and Hupperts. Their report—normally referred to as the *Spaak report* (Comité Intergouvernemental 1956)—was discussed by the Committee of government delegates in April and, with some minor amendments, was unanimously recommended to the governments of the Six as the basis for negotiation of a formal treaty. Apart from the provisions concerning the association of overseas territories, the Spaak report foreshadowed the Treaty of Rome in all essentials.

A chapter of the Spaak report is devoted to agriculture. The inclusion of agriculture within the framework of the proposed Community would have come as no great surprise. The early 1950s were an especially prolific period in terms of the number of plans put forward for the transnational organization of agriculture. A succinct outline of these plans is provided by Bourrinet (1964). The first and probably best known was the Pflimlin Plan, also called the 'Green Pool', originally launched in 1950. This was followed by the Charpentier Plan and—boldest of all—by a Dutch plan which was to become the first of many linked to the name of Sicco Mansholt, then Dutch Minister for Agriculture. Although these plans differed in their details, they all shared a supranational and interventionist approach. In contrast was the Eccles Plan, put forward by the British, which rejected supranationalism in favour of a much looser system involving international product agreements and an intergovernmental consultative committee. Discussion of these various plans in a variety of international fora failed to produce agreement among the countries taking part. This was not only due to a rift between what might be called the 'Continental' view and the 'British' view but also because of differences within the 'Continental' camp itself—what Muth (1970, 79) refers to as the 'gradual French' and the 'immediate Dutch' schools of thought.

While the discussions of the early 1950s foundered, there is no doubt that the experience gained was to prove invaluable later in the negotiations which led up to the signing of the Rome Treaty and the devising of the CAP. Indeed, Wallon (1958) indicates that many of the principles in the Treaty and in the CAP as it emerged in detail had their origin in the discussions on the Green Pool. Malgrain (1965) points out that one of the great benefits of the earlier deliberations was that they highlighted the complexity of European unification in the agricultural sector and the need to search for specific solutions adapted to the problems concerned. This is what the Spaak report (Comité Intergouvernemental 1956) tried to do.

It stated bluntly that the establishment of a general European common market which did not include agriculture was inconceivable. It recognized the special problems which resulted from the social structure of agriculture based on the family farm; the fundamental necessity to have stability of supply; and the instability of the market, which arose from weather conditions and the inelasticity of demand for certain products. Because of extensive government intervention in agriculture there could be no expectation that the mere lifting of quotas and tariffs would result in free circulation of goods. The problems which had brought about the organization of particular markets would not disappear because of the creation of a common market but rather a common solution would have to be found for them, and agriculture would require a transitional period during which it could adjust.

It was apparent that the functioning and development of a common market in the agricultural field required the elaboration and application of a common policy. The Spaak report posed a number of fundamental questions which required answers in the working out of the policy. These were:

- Given the importance of security of supply, what was the degree of self-sufficiency which the Community intended to achieve or, alternatively, the degree of specialization which it intended to develop, as a function of the world economy and export circumstances?
- Assuming that agricultural structure continued to be based on family farms rather than on huge enterprises, how—in particular by what type of encouragement to the many forms of agricultural cooperation—was this farm structure to be reconciled with the development of modern methods of production and marketing?
- Recognizing that economic development could bring with it a progressive reduction in the proportion of the active population engaged in agriculture, what was the extent and speed of transfer to other activities which could take place and, in particular, on the assumption that other decentralized activities—either full time or part time—were created to reabsorb them in their own locality, the size of the workforce thus freed?
- Taking account of the fact that for certain products, following the harvest, the free play of the market led to very great fluctuations in price, what was the degree of stabilization which it was intended to achieve and, more particularly, for which products?
- Taking account of the scope for development of consumption for certain products in certain regions of the Community, for which products would efforts be made to hasten this development?

The authors of the Spaak report saw their task as the establishment of a framework within which it would be possible to conceive, formulate, and put into operation an agricultural policy. It was not possible to outline the policy in advance for the totality of products but they did regard it as advisable to establish objectives and procedures with sufficient flexibility so as not to exclude any choice or instrument which might subsequently be proved necessary.

The new Community agricultural policy could not simply be a collation of the divergent policies of the Member States, as these related to another situation and to objectives different from those which would be linked to the creation of a common market. Unity of conception within a Community policy did not exclude diversification of choice and methods which were a function of the circumstances and aptitudes of the different regions—indeed on the contrary this diversity corresponded to the need for internal specialization within the Community which would promote the common market.

Apart from this specialization, the designers of the report assigned to the agricultural policy the following objectives: stabilization of markets; security of supply; maintenance of an adequate level of income for normally productive enterprises; and the gradual nature of the necessary adjustments in the structure of agriculture and of farms.

Remembering the aims of the German Agricultural Act of 1955, referred to above, these objectives have a familiar ring and in turn they and the considerations which prompted them are strikingly reflected in Article 39 of the Rome Treaty which reads in full:

1.   The objectives of the common agricultural policy shall be:
   (a) to increase agricultural productivity by promoting technical progress and by ensuring the rational development of agricultural production and the optimum utilization of the factors of production, in particular labour;
   (b) thus to ensure a fair standard of living for the agricultural community, in particular by increasing the individual earnings of persons engaged in agriculture;
   (c) to stabilize markets;
   (d) to assure the availability of supplies;
   (e) to ensure that supplies reach consumers at reasonable prices.
2.   In working out the common agricultural policy and the special methods for its application, account shall be taken of:
   (a) the particular nature of agricultural activity, which results from the social structure of agriculture and from structural and natural disparities between the various agricultural regions;
   (b) the need to effect the appropriate adjustments by degrees;
   (c) the fact that in the Member States agriculture constitutes a sector closely linked with the economy as a whole.

The Spaak report envisaged that market regimes would be introduced for a limited number of products only. These would be chosen on the basis of their special problems and their importance to farmers' incomes. In discussing the manner in which the market as a whole would be organized, the report specifically warned that, in replacing national regulations by Community measures, it would be necessary to guard against the risk of creating a vast area protected against third countries and aligning its prices on those of marginal domestic producers.

The Foreign Ministers of the Six discussed the Spaak report in May 1956 and, although important issues remained unresolved, drafting of the Economic and Atomic Energy Treaties was agreed. The task was completed by March 1957 and the Treaties were signed later the same month.[1] While the authors of the Spaak report had clearly been convinced of the need to include the agricultural sector within the common market, there were certain hesitations among the Six when it came to the actual negotiations on the Treaty. It was primarily on the insistence of the French that agriculture was indeed included.

Agricultural Provisions of the Rome Treaty

The fundamental disagreements among the Six as to the actual shape of the future agricultural policy are reflected in the vagueness of the provisions in the Treaty. Most of the work on the policy was postponed until after the Treaty came into force. As indicated above, the objectives which were to underlie the CAP were set out in Art. 39.1. Krause (1968, 89) drew attention to the contradictions inherent in these objectives: 'the desired increase in agricultural earnings could come either from increased productivity, which would in practice require a drastic disregard of structural problems in the member countries, or from higher product prices, which would disregard the consumer interest.' In practice, remarkably little attention was paid then or since to this point and, although Art. 39.1 must be one of the most frequently quoted in the entire Rome Treaty, it is repeated more as a kind of mantra than as a serious contribution to the elucidation of the CAP. Indeed, the objectives have been interpreted in such a general way as to rob them of meaning (Fennell 1985).

Article 39.2 lays down three guidelines to be observed in the working out and application of the CAP. These can be interpreted as requiring that special consideration should be taken of:

(a) the social structure of agriculture (i.e. its basis in the family farm);
(b) the disparities between regions;
(c) the need for a gradual approach (i.e. to allow adjustments to take place without dislocation); and
(d) the close links between agriculture and other sectors of the economy (i.e. that failure to create a common agricultural policy would hinder the achievement of the common internal market in general).

The links referred to under (d) above were subsequently interpreted by the Commission as including the influence on agricultural incomes of general living standards, through the medium of disposable income available to spend on food. Of course, the reverse is also true: that the price and quality of agricultural products influence consumption levels and purchasing power. The links also encompass the downstream activities of traders and processors, who bring together producers and consumers; and the upstream activities of the industries and services which provide inputs for agriculture, for whom the purchasing power of farmers is of major importance. The final link is that of trade: imports and exports of agricultural products are significant elements in external trade (Commission 1960).

Nearly twenty years after the Treaty was signed, the Economic and Social Committee (ESC) was able to describe Article 39 as lacking precision and coherence but that, nevertheless, it represented:

at least for farmers, an overall definition not only of the goals to be achieved but also of the basic aspirations of the farming community. It therefore has considerable psychological significance which should not be disregarded in a general appraisal of the results of the CAP and of the attitudes and judgements which this policy has given rise to or may yet give rise to.   (ESC. rapp. Bourel, 1974, 12)

Article 40 indicates that there was to be some form of common organization of markets, brought into being over a transitional period, with a common price policy and a fund to finance it. Camps (1964) draws attention to the rather perfunctory statement concerning the price policy: 'Any common price policy shall be based on common criteria and uniform methods of calculation' (Art. 40.3, third sentence). In the event this was to become the key feature of the CAP. Couched in generalities though this Article is, at least it does exist and therefore provides a secure foundation for the subsequent market and price policy. No similar Article is included in the Treaty to cover the common organization of structural aid.

Structural references are scattered about the Articles dealing with agriculture in a haphazard fashion. The first objective as laid down in Art. 39.1(a) can be interpreted as requiring some kind of structural policy, in order that it be achieved. However, attempts to pursue this objective through structural policy have been inadequate and, in so far as it has been pursued at all, it has been largely through the price policy, with important elements left in the hands of the Member States.

As mentioned above, the existence of structural and natural disparities between regions is specifically recognized in Art. 39.2 but only in the sense of providing general guidelines for policy formulation and implementation. Other Articles with a structural connotation are 41 and 42. Article 41 makes provision for the possible introduction of certain supplementary measures to allow the objectives set out in Art. 39.1 to be achieved. The examples given in the Article are the 'effective co-ordination of efforts in the spheres of vocational training, of research and of the dissemination of agricultural knowledge' and 'measures to promote consumption of certain products'.

Because the agricultural sector was to be managed by means of a common policy rather than to be left to the vagaries of market forces, there was the danger of conflict between the CAP and the rules on competition laid down in the Treaty. For this reason, Article 42 provides that the rules on competition are to apply to production and trade in agricultural products only to the extent determined by the Council, within the framework of the agricultural policy finally agreed. Furthermore, Article 42 specifically allows the Council to authorize the granting of aid:

(a) for the protection of enterprises handicapped by structural or natural conditions;
(b) within the framework of economic development programmes.

This disorganized and vague approach to structural matters is puzzling: Bourrinet (1964) draws attention to the contradiction between the interest in raising productivity (and, therefore, the need to adapt agricultural structure) and the failure of the Treaty to give the Commission instruments and powers comparable to those indicated for the market policy. This omission is all the more surprising in view of the fact that it was recognized at the time that the existing national agricultural policies effectively masked the true extent of structural defects. It was expected that the application of the provisions of the Treaty on the elimination of frontier protection between Member States, the introduction against third countries of the common customs tariff, and the CAP itself would show up as never before the extent of structural maladjustment.

One of the recognized dangers in the creation of a customs union is that, unless the economically weak regions are given special assistance, they will be unable to compete on equal terms with the stronger regions and, as a result, the income divergence between the two will widen. It is undoubtedly true that, in many instances, the regions with the greatest structural problems in agriculture are also regions in which agriculture is disproportionately important as a source of income and employment. It is not surprising, therefore, that their general economic circumstances are also poor.

Article 2 of the Rome Treaty stipulates that the establishment of a common market was—among other things—to 'promote throughout the Community a harmonious development of economic activities, a continuous and balanced expansion, an increase in stability, an accelerated raising of the standard of living.' Given that agriculture was to be included in this common market, it would seem that structural adaptation of weak parts of the sector (often in weak regions) was an obvious means to pursue these aims. Yet no clear guidance was given in the Treaty on the issue.

With regard to the actual working-out in detail of the features of the agricultural policy, the Commission was charged in Article 43 with the task—as soon as the Treaty was operative—of convening 'a conference of the Member States with a view to making a comparison of their agricultural policies, in particular by producing a statement of their resources and needs'. The Treaty establishing the European Economic Community came into force on 1 January 1958; the agricultural conference was held at Stresa, 3–12 July 1958.

The Stresa Conference

The Conference was attended by official delegations from the six Member States led by the Ministers for Agriculture; there was a delegation representing the European Commission led by its President Hallstein and four other Commissioners (including Mansholt and von der Groeben); there were observers from organizations representing various interests in the farming sector, and journalists from all the Member States. The main activity of the Conference centred around three working parties. These examined (a) the main characteristics of and problems posed by the current situation in agriculture, together with the broad outlines of existing agricultural policy in each Member State; (b) the possible repercussions in the short term of the application of the Treaty of Rome on agriculture in the Six; and (c) the long-term goals of a common policy, taking into account relations with third countries (Communautés Européennes 1959).

This first vital step in the process which ultimately led to the creation of the CAP was taken against a background of poor farm structure, low incomes, surplus labour, rising production, export difficulties, and high levels of government support. These issues still have a familiar ring, although the similarity is somewhat more apparent than real and should not be pressed too far. In some important respects, the context was quite different. For instance, Hallstein highlighted the contradictions in a sector which, in social and organizational terms, reflected a pre-industrial revolution era but which faced a completely changed world in terms of farm management. There was a mismatch of land and labour but the attractiveness of off-farm urban employment to the young was leading to a rural exodus which was a matter of concern to the Member States. Hallstein referred to a clash of cultures, in which the way of life and the values of rural people were regarded as inferior.

Another ideological clash was still fresh in people's minds: the Communist take-over in Eastern Europe and, more recently, the Hungarian uprising of 1956. Hallstein did no more than make oblique references to these events but his meaning would have been crystal clear to his audience:

[I]t is the core of Europe's achievements which is under threat: a whole civilization which rests on the inalienable freedom and dignity of the individual. Wherever it takes place, this tragedy of liberty is also a tragedy of the rural class. Let us look around us, and, alas, we have not far to look; the rural class is its first victim.

It is for this reason that we are convinced that the European rural class will count among the most trustworthy pillars of our unified European market. Because its fate is also at stake, and is one of the first threatened. In this room there is no one whose family tree doesn't reach back, sooner or later, to farming roots. We know what the rural class means to Europe, not only through its economic values, but also by its moral and social values. (Communautés Européennes 1959, 35)

Looking to the future, Hallstein warned that problems were not going to be solved purely because of the existence of a common market but it did provide new possibilities for their solution. He raised the prophetic issue of monetary parity: a common agricultural market would be difficult to achieve in the absence of a stable policy on money and credit. He was critical of the vagueness of the Treaty in relation to money, finance, and economic co-ordination—an understandable view from a former professor of economics!

The key address of the Conference was undoubtedly that given by Mansholt, the agricultural Commissioner. It is probably to his speech more than to any other that people have turned in recent times, when they hark back nostalgically to the spirit of Stresa. However, when one reads his speech, one is struck by the range of problems which he highlighted. Little wonder that he was preoccupied: it was he and his small team within the Commission who had to produce a proposal for a common agricultural policy 'within two years of the entry into force of [the] Treaty' (Art. 43.2), i.e. before 1 January 1960.

Mansholt made the interesting—and often overlooked—point that, while the Rome Treaty contained a section devoted exclusively to agriculture, this did not mean that it was some kind of exception, rather it meant that a different approach was being used to achieve the same objectives i.e. those set out in Article 2 (see previous Section).

He drew attention to the frequent confusion of 'increasing production' with the need to 'increase labour productivity'. He warned of the dangers of insulating producers or consumers from market realities: price must retain its role as a regulator of demand and supply. Attention had to be paid to price relationships between different products, regions, and sizes of farms. While the new policy should be flexible, Mansholt recognized that the Community did not start with a blank sheet of paper: the Member States had brought their baggage with them.

Mansholt envisaged the new common policy as being divided into two parts: one for the improvement of the structure of agriculture, the other for the establishment of a common market. Operationally it was not possible to dissociate the problems of structure from those of the common market. The reason was that the creation of a common market would not be feasible unless efforts were made to improve agricultural structure, particularly in those parts of the Community where structure was very backward. Mansholt made it clear that he was referring not only to the structural aspects of production but also to the methods of marketing and processing.

He maintained that, in its turn, the creation of a common market would stimulate the improvement of production and have a favourable effect on labour productivity and on the possibility of achieving meaningful rationalization of the agricultural sector. He pointed out that in the past many measures had been taken which had not stimulated structural improvement and he warned that Community policy-makers needed to be on their guard lest they made the same mistake again, by losing sight of the structural aspects of policy at Community level. If the future market policy was based on the level of costs of inefficient or submarginal farms, all efforts to improve structure would be painfully lost.

The Ministers for Agriculture of the six Member States all made speeches at the Conference. These reflected their national preoccupations and highlighted the differences in approach which were to become more obvious when the Conference split into its working parties. Two of the themes touched upon amply demonstrate aspects of the debate which were particular to the time and which were very quickly forgotten. Lübke, the German Minister for Agriculture, later to become President of the Federal Republic, raised the issue of security of supply not in the usual context but in relation to the debt which Western Europe owed to the USA in the immediate post-war era. He recalled that his country had been obliged to call on:

deliveries made by countries overseas under the heading of aid. Among these States, special mention must be made of the United States which, in the hard years of famine, had provided exemplary aid to the Federal Republic. This aid has created political and commercial ties which should be taken into account, even if they have not been cemented in bilateral commercial agreements. (Communautés Européennes 1959, 46)

The French Minister, Houdet, devoted a considerable portion of his speech to the needs of the French overseas countries and territories. It was at the insistence of the French that the Rome Treaty contained a section on the association of overseas possessions with the Community and, prior to the independence of so many of these countries in the 1960s, there was frequent discussion of their interests and needs in the context of the new agricultural policy.

Given subsequent events, the most incongruous feature of the Conference is the obvious concern which delegates displayed over the structural inadequacies of agriculture, and the need to put them right. Working Party 3 saw the objective of structural policy as being primarily concerned with the creation of modern profitable family farms and with the improvement of the social circumstances of all those who were mainly involved in farming. The Working Party attached particular importance to measures intended to improve the basis of production on and off the farm. It also regarded general and technical education, and retraining for farmers and farm workers as effective means for improving living standards and production.

Both Working Parties 2 and 3 expressed concern at the danger of misguided investment and that, while structural defects should be tackled through the improvement of productivity, it was necessary to avoid stimulating production. It was recognized that technical progress in production and modifications to agricultural structure would be accompanied by a reduction of full-time employment in farming. For this reason, Working Party 3 thought that it would be advantageous if other employment opportunities were created in the country-side for the labour leaving farming. With this in mind, it recommended that structural policy should be combined with other activities such as industrial decentralization and the improvement of communications. Finally, Working Party 3 recorded unanimous recognition of the closeness of the links between structural and market policy and held that, both in the setting of objectives and in the measures to be taken in the two spheres, there should be reciprocal co-ordination.

Reading the reports of the three Working Parties, it is clear that there were strong disagreements on issues such as surpluses, the proportion of the Community's consumption which should be covered by Community production, and the base on which common prices would be calculated. On one issue of subsequent significance, however, there was no more than slight differences of emphasis: in Working Party 3, one of the delegations—it can only have been the French—declared that the Treaty was founded on the principle of preference for Community products. This flowed from the fact that the Community is based on a customs union which, of itself, created such a preference.

The participants at the Conference reached general agreement on a number of points which formed the core of the Final Resolution. They maintained that agriculture should be regarded as an integral part of the economy and as an essential factor in social life. They recognized that the coming into force of the Treaty would lead naturally to the development of trade within the Community but cautioned that, at the same time, it was necessary to maintain commercial links and contractual, political, and economic relationships with third countries, while also making provision for protection against dumping.

The participants advocated a close correlation between the policies for structural adaptation and the market: the former should contribute to a narrowing of the range of production costs and to a rational orientation of production, while the latter should be managed in such a way as to stimulate the improvement of productivity. They recommended that an equilibrium be found between production and market outlets, taking into account possible exports and imports, so that specialization should conform to the economic structure and natural conditions within the Community.

The efforts made to raise productivity should permit the application of a price policy which simultaneously avoided overproduction and allowed farmers to remain or become competitive. At the same time, a policy of aid to disadvantaged regions or farms would make the necessary adaptations possible. The participants considered that the elimination of aids which were contrary to the spirit of the Treaty was essential. They were concerned to ensure that the elaboration of the CAP took into account the development of production and demand in the associated countries and territories.

The participants believed that the improvement of agricultural structure would allow capital and labour to receive a return comparable with that obtained in other sectors of the economy. They agreed that, given the importance of the familial nature of European agriculture and the unanimous wish to safeguard this characteristic, every effort should be made to raise the economic and competitive capacity of such enterprises. Finally, the participants envisaged that retraining available members of the agricultural workforce and industrialization of those rural regions under greatest pressure would allow for a gradual settlement of the problems faced by marginal farms, which were incapable of becoming economically viable.

The psychological significance of Stresa can hardly be overstated: the atmosphere at the Conference was buoyant. Stresa was an extremely important event in the life of the early Community, not only because of the work accomplished there but also because of the spirit in which it was done. It is true that national attitudes and preoccupations are detectable in the text of the speeches and reports but clearly the participants felt that they were on the brink of an exciting new joint adventure. The European Parliament (Assemblée 1958) observed that the Commission had been fearful that Stresa would follow the established pattern of earlier conferences held under the auspices of OEEC, where the participating States had defended their own agricultural policies without aspiring to common solutions. At Stresa the attitude was more open-minded and the delegates had striven to find a common denominator for the future agricultural policy. The new Community was little more than half a year old and yet it was already tackling the issue of a supranational agricultural policy. This was both a leap in the dark and a continuation of the search for such a policy which had eluded policy-makers since the end of World War II.

The Commission spent the remainder of 1958 and almost the whole of 1959 preparing its draft proposals on the CAP. Now that the CAP is such an accepted fact of life, it is hard to comprehend the extent of the task facing Mansholt's team, handicapped as it was by the inadequacy of the statistical base.[2] Parallel exercises were being undertaken by the European Parliament which published a number of reports in 1958 and 1959 on various aspects of agricultural policy, and which had extensive discussions with the Commission. The draft proposals for the working-out and putting into effect of the CAP were ready in November 1959 and appeared in VI/COM(59)140 (Commission 1959). This document contained three sections: an analysis of the situation in agriculture and a brief account of the policies being pursued in the Member States; a discussion of the basic principles on which the CAP should be founded; and an outline of the proposed framework of the individual commodity regimes and their financing. The European Parliament and the Economic and Social Committee commented extensively on the draft but very few of their views were reflected in the final version of the Commission proposals, which appeared in June 1960 in VI/COM(60)105 (Commission 1960), the main features of which are set out in Chapter 2.

NOTES

1. Two Rome Treaties were signed in 1956: one established the European Economic Community (EEC), the other established the European Atomic Energy Community (Euratom). References in this book to the Rome Treaty all relate to the EEC Treaty.
2. An indication of the size and scope of the task can be found in a work plan for the Agricultural Directorate issued in September 1958 (Commission 1958).

2

Scope and Orientation of the CAP in the 1960s

The 1960 Proposals

The general circumstances surrounding agriculture in the 1950s were outlined in Chapter 1 and these formed the backdrop to the Commission's proposals. Farm households were facing a series of interrelated challenges. At a personal level, there was greater exposure than ever before to consumer goods and services originating elsewhere in the economy. On the farm, there was a growing dependence on bought-in inputs. As with the consumer goods, many of the inputs originated in other sectors where prices and wages were rising more rapidly. As a result, the exchange value of agriculture was declining.

The low elasticity of demand for many agricultural products was coupled with a decline in the share of consumer expenditure actually going to the raw material. At the same time, there were warnings of impending or actual market saturation. All these factors combined to create a serious income dilemma for farmers and it remained to be seen whether a new common policy would succeed where national policies had apparently failed.

The Commission was critical of certain aspects of the agricultural policies of the Six. While it acknowledged that price support had helped to slow the rate at which agricultural incomes were lagging behind those in other sectors, it drew attention to the negative consequences, as farmers were insulated from changes in market preferences. In turn, this had resulted in inadequate investment in desirable directions and in the creation of new surpluses. The Commission also considered that the level of financial aid given by the Member States to combat structural deficiencies was inadequate, both in relation to the size of the task and the impact on farm incomes. The Commission was critical of the failure to establish satisfactory links between structural and market policies, and believed that insufficient attention was paid by the Member States to the interdependence of agriculture and general economic development.

The Commission's review of the situation in agriculture in Part I of COM(60) 105 was, in effect, an update of the statistics which had been available at Stresa. On the input side, mechanization was beginning to make a real impact: pre-war there were 107,000 tractors in the six Member States but by 1958 there were 1.6m. The number of draught animals had fallen by one-quarter since 1947. Chemical fertilizer use, which was already quite high in the Netherlands and Belgium at the beginning of the 1950s, was around 2 tonnes/ha. by 1958/59. In France and Italy, however, despite usage virtually doubling over the same period, the rate of application was still only 0.7 and 0.4 tonnes/ha. respectively.

As for production, while the Commission recognized that some of the differences between Member States were due to natural factors or the historical or economic development of the countries concerned, the level of disparity prompted the view that there was still a considerable production reserve. Compared with pre-war, output in 1957/58 was 28 per cent higher overall. Crop yields were appreciably higher on average, although the range from one Member State to another was considerable. Livestock numbers had risen by about one-fifth to one-sixth since pre-war, except for horses, sheep, and goats. Milk yields were also much higher, though again the differences between Member States were striking: despite significant increases in yields in all countries, the Dutch *pre-war* yield was still higher than the yields in the other countries in the late 1950s!

The universal upward trend in production was not matched on the consumption side, with cereals and potatoes in sharp decline, and livestock products showing a marked increase. As a result of the different rates of change in production and consumption, the levels of self-sufficiency had shifted since pre-war, although overall self-sufficiency had increased only slightly from 85 to 87 per cent (average of 1954/55–1958/59). In balance-of-trade terms, the EC-6 was a net exporter of potatoes, vegetables, pigmeat, cheese, and occasionally butter.

On the structural side, the Commission contrasted those regions where farms were highly developed and of adequate size with other regions where structure was very defective, often with a multiplicity of problems superimposed one on another. Over two-thirds of all farms in the EC-6 were under 10 ha. and, unless such farms were growing specialist crops or under very intensive systems, they were not viable: 'their area is . . . less than the minimum needed for the family farms which are to be aimed at as the foundation of agricultural structure. Their social and economic situation also becomes unsatisfactory when the necessary opportunities to earn supplementary income outside agriculture are lacking' (Commission 1960, I/16).

The Commission drew attention to the limited effectiveness in agriculture of the substitution of capital for land and labour, commenting that it often led 'merely to the substitution of the non-rational use of capital for the non-rational use of labour' (Commission 1960, I/17). It also cautioned that 'in farming, increases in the amount of capital employed do not always lead to savings or more profitable operation, but in many cases to easier work' (ibid. I/25). These constraints on the effectiveness of capital substitution were said to be the consequence of the poor institutional structure in agriculture. Its labour force was still very large, amounting to 14.5m. people in 1958—or more than 1/5th of the total workforce.

However, the exodus from farming was well underway: there had been a decline of 18 per cent in the farm workforce since 1950. The Commission identified the pull of off-farm job opportunities as the main factor. This had aggravated the problems in some regions where most of the farm labour force comprised family members rather than hired workers. As the latter group was much more mobile, it meant that the beneficial effects of increased off-farm employment were not evenly spread. In addition, some regions still had a high birth rate so that, even with out-migration, the effect on the total numbers in farming was slight.

To alleviate this situation, the Commission recommended a general improvement in the economic circumstances of the regions in order to facilitate the growth of industry and services. At the same time, measures were needed to make the farm workforce more mobile, including 'advice on the conversion of enterprises and aid for occupational re-adaptation' (Commission, p. I/20). A decade later such ideas were to take on much greater significance in the discussion which followed the Mansholt Plan of 1968.

Trade in agricultural products with non-member countries was considerable. In 1955–7, agricultural imports as a percentage of total imports ranged from 20 in Belgium/Luxembourg to 34 in F. R. Germany. Exports were fewer and more differentiated, with only 3 per cent and 5 per cent respectively originating in F. R. Germany and Belgium/Luxembourg, while in the Netherlands 31 per cent of all exports were agricultural.

The trend in world prices for agricultural commodities was, in general, downward during the 1950s. Only meat had maintained its world market unit value in 1958 compared with 1952/53. Cereals had fallen by 25 per cent. The Commission drew attention to the fact that international prices were not the result of the free play of market forces but were heavily influenced by government action in exporting countries, the oligopolistic nature of the market, agreements between major suppliers, and stockpiling policies. World stocks were rising and, for some commodities, were considerably in excess of annual exports. The USA was the dominant stockholder, with 80 per cent of stocks of major agricultural raw materials and food.

Fundamental to the Commission's review of agriculture was the question of producer price levels in the Member States. It was a daunting task to create a common price structure for six countries with widely differing starting-points. In general, producer prices in France were the lowest, ranging from roughly 70 to 95 per cent of the EC-6 average, followed by the Netherlands (roughly 90–105 per cent of the average). Most Italian prices were in the range 100–14 per cent, with only barley, oats, and milk below the average. All German prices were above the Community average, in general from 101 to 120 per cent but with oats, sugar beet, and, especially, barley (135 per cent) even higher. Luxembourg had the highest price structure, ranging from 99 per cent of the average for barley to 139 per cent for rye.

The second part of Com(60)105 sets out the general principles on which the CAP was to be based. Its components were to include 'the chief fields dealt with by the national agricultural policies' (Commission, p. II/5). These were defined as structural, market, commercial, and social.[1] Under the umbrella of the CAP, these components were intended to complement each other. Structural policy was to reduce costs and streamline them in the different Member States; to guide production in response to market trends; and to raise the competitiveness of the agricultural sector. Market policy[2] was to be based on economically viable enterprises, bearing in mind the need to raise productivity. The purpose of commercial policy was to stabilize and facilitate trade between the Community and the rest of the world. Social policy was to contribute to the improvement of the living and working conditions of the farming population, so that they approximated the levels in comparable occupations.

The object of the proposals on structure was 'the co-ordination and stimulation of the policies of the Member States . . . and the granting of financial aid from the Community designed to stimulate and speed up improvements in the structure of agriculture' (Commission, Pt. III, Gen. Ch., 1). The Commission recognized that a common policy confined to market and price support could not, of itself, achieve the income objective set out in Art. 39.1 of the Rome Treaty, as it would not eliminate the causes of low incomes and would actually make the existing disparities between regions worse. Events were to prove that the Commission was correct in its view; one of the fundamental weaknesses of the CAP is precisely that it did not develop as an integrated policy.

The danger inherent in the creation of a customs union: that the economically weak regions will fall further behind unless special provision is made to enable them to participate in the general economic development, placed a responsibility on the Member States and on the Community to improve the structure of backward areas. It is clear from Com(60)105 that this danger was well understood and, in that regard, it is surprising that the Rome Treaty made no specific provision for a regional policy. The Treaty did, however, make it clear that an increase in agricultural productivity was the key to higher incomes and the Commission recognized that structural changes were necessary to allow the latest technological developments to take place, to have a rational expansion of output, and to make the best use of the factors of production.

The positive influence which structural improvements could have on the success of the CAP prompted the Commission to propose an agricultural structural policy based on three lines of action:

(a) the co-ordination of the agricultural structural policies of the Member States;
(b) the encouragement of the Member States to intensify their efforts and devote adequate funds to the task; and
(c) the provision of financial aid by the Community to supplement the Member States' own activities.

The aid referred to under (c) would be for two purposes: to help regions to adapt to the new common market situation and to assist agriculture in backward regions where there were reasonable prospects for development. The Commission proposed the establishment of the European Fund for Structural Improvements in Agriculture (known by its French acronym FEASA) not later than 1961. The fate of this fund is outlined later in this chapter.

Commercial policy formed the link between the internal support for agriculture and the relations of the Community with the trading world externally, under the provisions of Articles 110–16 of the Rome Treaty. Thus, for instance, commercial policy in agriculture is governed by the requirement under Art. 113.1 that policy 'shall be based on uniform principles, particularly in regard to changes in tariff rates, the conclusion of tariff and trade agreements, the achievement of uniformity in measures of liberalisation, export policy and measures to protect trade such as those to be taken in case of dumping or subsidies.'

All the Member States had international trade obligations and were members of organizations such as OEEC, GATT, and FAO, which aimed at the expansion of multilateral trade. This was part of the inheritance of the Community but that inheritance also included the treatment of agriculture as a special case. In the same way that agriculture internally was the subject of active management by the State, so externally it was not left to the vagaries of the international market.

The market policy (outlined below) was expected to manipulate prices of agricultural products in such a way 'as will maintain the level of agricultural incomes and to seek a balance between production and outlets' (Commission 1960, II/26)—difficult tasks to achieve simultaneously and which, if they were to be fulfilled, would require that agricultural production would not be exposed 'to the full blast of competition from the world market' (ibid.). The Commission explained that an important reason for this protective approach was that conditions of competition were considerably distorted on the world market where 'prices are often very far removed from those applied to production and consumption in numerous regions of the globe' (ibid.).

While supporting efforts to remove distortion in international competition, the agricultural commercial policy had to balance the stimulation of exports, which the CAP was likely to bring about, with the wider trading interests of the Community. It appears that the balance was tipped in favour of agriculture, as the Commission commented: 'in point of fact, the commercial policy requirements of the Community will not be permitted to endanger the vital interests of its agriculture, and agriculture will have to reckon with outside interests which the Community cannot renounce' (Commission 1960, II/27).

The outline of the market policy is the most thoroughgoing and the most specific of the Commission's proposals. Indeed, by far the greater part of COM(60)105 is taken up with an outline of the individual commodity regimes. Within the CAP, the two elements most closely linked in principle and in practice are the commercial and market policies, to the extent that, in some respects, they merge into one another. In summary, the market policy was:

- to aim at a balance between production and potential markets internally and externally;
- to give due weight to specialization, whether in terms of the suitability of economic structure or natural conditions;
- to allow for the development of supply and demand in the associated countries and territories;
- to be mindful of the external trading conditions of the Community;

- to help farmers achieve fair remuneration approaching that in other sectors, through the value allocated to agricultural products; and
- to stabilize markets, so as to prevent excessive price swings disrupting farmers' incomes without, however, completely eliminating risk and undermining adaptation to changed demand.

The intention was to achieve a common institutional price level for the key commodities by 30 June 1967. The attempt to reach this goal was to cause some of the most important crises in the early years of the new Community.

The initial proposal was for the establishment of common regimes to organize the markets in wheat, coarse grain, sugar, dairy products, beef and veal, pigmeat, poultry, eggs, fruit and vegetables, and wine which, combined, accounted for 80–90 per cent of the agricultural production of EC-6. The Commission promised proposals on rice, fats, fish, and tobacco at a later date.

The third part of COM(60)105 is almost entirely devoted to an analysis of the proposed commodity regimes, including a brief statement of the market situation for each commodity, the aims of the proposed regime, and the instruments which needed to be put in place in the preparatory phase, and in the common market phase. Not surprisingly, given its pivotal position, the greatest attention was paid to cereals.

For the major products—wheat, coarse grain, sugar, and dairy products—target and intervention prices internally and variable levies at the Community frontier were to form the basis of market support. Stabilization funds were to be established for all commodities with the exception of fruit and vegetables. These funds were to form part of the European Agricultural Guidance and Guarantee Fund (EAGGF, but best known under its French acronym FEOGA) and were to be used for internal stockpiling and, where appropriate, export payments to neutralize the higher internal price. The primary source of income of these stabilization funds was to be the variable levies on imports of the particular commodity/ies concerned, topped up where necessary by contributions from governments and producers of the commodity in question. Transfers between stabilization funds and to FEASA were to be allowed, except in the case of the contributions from producers which were to be exclusive to the commodity for which they had been raised.

The final element within the CAP—social policy—was, as indicated above, added to the 1959 draft proposals in response to the criticism by the ESC (CES 1960). Its omission had been surprising in view of the fact that, in its review of existing national policies, the Commission had acknowledged that price policy had been influenced by social objectives. This had resulted in instances of overproduction and this unwanted outcome had demonstrated to the Member States the limitations of such a policy. Thus, the Commission could hardly claim to have been unaware of the social dimension. In criticizing the omission, the ESC considered that the structural policy—which admittedly contained certain social features—did not cover all the social aspects of the common policy. Furthermore, it felt that the whole question of improvement to the structure of agriculture was treated by the Commission more from the economic than the social angle.

In its revised 1960 proposals, the Commission made some attempt to meet the ESC's criticisms but its efforts amounted to little more than an enumeration of the basic principles and essential aims of agricultural social policy which the Commission had lifted in paraphrased form from various parts of the ESC report. The wide range of these principles and aims can be reduced to three main headings:

(a) improvement in working conditions (e.g. the contractual relationships between landlords, farmers, and workers; and arrangements concerning wages and social security);

(b) improvement in educational and training facilities (e.g. the promotion of equality of opportunity for rural children; aids to young farmers starting their careers; and better facilities for those who wished to retrain, either inside or outside agriculture);

(c) improvement in the social environment (e.g. better arrangements for those wishing to retire on pension; improved housing; and greater attention to the social and cultural infrastructure in rural areas).

No provision was made to aid any of these goals financially nor did the Commission even go so far as to suggest a co-ordinating role for itself, as it had done in the case of structural aids. It pleaded that it was not in a position to make detailed proposals 'in view of the complexity of the social problems in agriculture and their numerous ramifications and implications' (Commission 1960, Pt. III, Gen. Ch., para. 3).

The only positive step promised by the Commission was the organization of a Consultative Conference to be held during 1960 on the social aspects of the CAP, after which the Commission would 'draw up proposals on a programme for the development of social policy for agriculture integrated into the social policy of the Community' (Commission 1960, Pt. III, Gen. Ch., para. 3). In the event, the conference in question was not held in 1960; this seems to have caused some concern in the European Parliament as, in October 1960, in the course of a Resolution on the orientation of the CAP (JO 71, 16–11–60), it reminded the Commission of the need to call such a conference. This reminder was repeated in April 1961 in a further Resolution (JO 24, 6–4–61), and the Conference was eventually held in Rome on 28 September–4 October of the same year.

The Outcome of the 1960 Proposals:
Market and Commercial Policies

It should not be forgotten that Com(60)105 was no more than a 'White Paper' and therefore only the first small step in a process which would lead to the establishment of the CAP as it exists today. In December 1960, the Council took a decision in favour of the introduction of an import levy system to be applied initially to cereals, sugar, pigmeat, eggs, and poultry. A timetable was also established for the submission of proposals for individual commodity regimes by the Commission to the Council during 1961 (Bull. EC 1–1961, Annex, 82).

This is not the place to recount the tortuous story of the negotiations on the first commodity regimes, the financing of the policy and other related matters, which occupied most of 1961 and ended in the first agricultural marathon which started in mid-December and, after a session of twenty-three days, ended at 5.29 a.m. on 14 January 1962.[3] Suffice to record that the essential mechanisms of the market policy and an agreement on funding were put in place but the drama was by no means over. Most importantly, the Member States still had to agree on the common price level which was to apply once the transition stage was over. Shortly after the 1962 agreement, Mansholt made a speech in which he answered the criticisms of exporting countries, which accused the Community of having a protectionist autarkic policy. He denied this, saying that there was not as yet a policy but still only a mechanism. This latter was, in itself, neutral and allowed for the possibility of applying a liberal policy just as easily as a protectionist one. The price level was still to be decided and Mansholt recognized the role which a high price would play in stimulating production. 'It is for this reason that the price policy will be decisive for our production in relation to consumption' (Mansholt 1962, 9).

The common cereals price was critical, not only because it is a major commodity but also because of the knock-on effect it has in determining the cost of production of livestock. The decision on cereals was taken at the end of another marathon in December 1964 when the common price level for cereals and its dependent livestock products, to come into force in 1967, was agreed. In the event, the price chosen was towards the upper end of the price spectrum of the Member States, a decision reached under intense German pressure.[4] What the Germans had succeeded in doing was not only to maintain their high price structure but to extend it to the other members of the Community. Other common regimes followed and the completed price and market policy effectively dates from 1970.[5]

Certain events on the money markets in the late 1950s and early 1960s made it almost inevitable that the price structure finally agreed would be more protectionist than the designers of the Treaty could ever have imagined. The French franc was devalued in mid-1957 and again at the end of 1958; the German mark was revalued in early 1961; these shifts in exchange rates caused the French and German support prices for the main agricultural products to diverge. It was inevitable, therefore, that the negotiations on prices under the new CAP were bound to be extremely difficult, and that the main protagonists were going to be Germany and France. It is ironic that not only did the most highly industrialized country of the EC-6 provide the objectives of the agricultural policy in Art. 39.1 of the Rome Treaty (see Chapter 1) but it also shaped its future through the common pricing structure. It was abundantly clear by 1964 what kind of policy the neutral 1962 mechanisms had produced.

Table 2.1. Prices for certain agricultural products in the EEC compared with world price levels, 1967/68[a]

Product	EEC common price UC/100kg.(1)	World market[c] price UC/100 kg.(2)	(1) as a % of (2)
Soft wheat	10.7	5.8	185
Hard wheat[b]	16.1	8.1	200
Husked rice	18.0	15.3	117
Barley	9.1	5.7	160
Maize	9.0	5.6	160
White sugar	22.3	5.1	438
Beef	68.0	38.8	175
Pigmeat	56.7	38.6	147
Poultrymeat	72.3	55.0	131
Eggs	51.1	38.7	132
Butter	187.4	47.2	397
Olive oil[b]	115.6	69.8	166
Oilseeds[b]	20.2	10.1	200

[a] reference period differs for various products
[b] including direct production aids
[c] wholesale entry price

Source: Commission 1968(*b*), Annex 12.

It is interesting to compare the common price level agreed for 1967/68 with world prices at that time (see Table 2.1). The Community has often been accused of having a high level of self-sufficiency as an objective. This is not true: the levels of self-sufficiency have been the result of the price structure adopted early in the history of the CAP. So much of the past quarter century has been dominated by the consequences of those early decisions, not only in terms of coping with surpluses but also in attempting to modify the attitudes which high prices have engendered and in living with the size and shape of the agricultural sector which they have created.

The Council Decision of December 1960 concerning the use of import levies (referred to at the beginning of this section) was not only relevant to the future elaboration of a market policy but also to the development of a common commercial policy. Whereas under the market policy, the levy was intended to bridge the gap between the price levels in the various Member States[6] and assist their transition to a common price level, under the commercial policy, the levy governed the relationship between the Member States and the rest of the world. Principle no.7 of the 1960 Decision is important as it established the basis of what subsequently became known as the principle of Community Preference:

The ratio between the levies applied, on the one hand, to trade between member countries and, on the other, to trade with non-member countries should be such as to ensure to Member States the advantages on the Community market provided for in the Treaty, having due regard to the commercial policy aims of the Treaty.[7] (Bull. EC 1–1961, Annex, 82)

The decision to use a levy rather than an *ad valorem* tariff[8] signalled an exceptional approach to external trade regulation brought about by the particular circumstances in agriculture, where frontier protection is only part of the total support mechanism. In this sense, market and commercial policies are intertwined. This exceptional treatment of agriculture had already been recognized in the General Agreement on Tariffs and Trade (GATT) where, in 1955, the USA had obtained a waiver from GATT rules so that it could continue to use frontier protective devices to prevent the undermining of its domestic support arrangements. This was a most important waiver, as it established the principle that in agriculture internal policy arrangements took precedence over international obligations.

The application of the levy to external trade from mid-1962 onwards resulted in the first of many disputes between the Community and the USA, the USA claiming that its poultry exports to Germany were being adversely affected by the switch over to the levy. From the Community point of view, behind this apparently trivial dispute—which became known as the 'chicken war'—lay a fundamental and often recurring issue, namely the position of producers within the Community in relation to those outside. As far back as the Stresa Conference (Communautés Européennes 1959), reference was made to the preferential position of the internal producer which arose from the very existence of the Community, and the need to balance that preference with the establishment and maintenance of external trade links. The issue arose again in the context of the January 1962 marathon, where Community Preference clashed with the desire of some Member States to retain traditional sources of imports—what Mayoux (1962) referred to as 'a battle of principles, a conflict of interests'.

The principle of Community Preference, in embryonic form in the early 1960s, has developed in the intervening years to imply that, in any trade agreement involving agriculture entered into by the Community with third countries, the concession given to the external party must not be of such a nature or such a size as to undermine the position of the domestic producer on the Community's own market. Thus the commercial policy in agriculture must always take into account the arrangements made under the market policy and, certainly until the Uruguay Round of GATT, market policy took precedence over commercial policy. Whether this situation is likely to undergo a radical revision remains to be seen.

The Short Life and Early Death of Social Policy within the CAP

The main issues discussed in the Rome Conference of 1961 on the social aspects of the CAP can be grouped into four general topic areas:

(a) social problems of the family farm;
(b) policy relating to agricultural wage-earners;

(c) occupational mobility, migration, free movement of persons, and *métayage*;[9] and

(d) education and cultural life in rural districts.

Although there was a certain element of disagreement among the participants, numerous social issues were identified which required attention but the Conference gave scant indication as to the tools to be used, the source of finance, and the body to have ultimate responsibility. Among the more positive indications was the role envisaged by the participants for FEASA, which they saw as aiding agricultural education, the retraining of farm personnel, both within farming and for other employment, and the improvement of housing conditions (Commission 1962).

In his closing address, Mansholt made a number of points which linked market and price policy with social policy and stated that 'all market policy which ignored the social problems of agriculture was doomed to failure' (Commission 1962, 85). He maintained that, as with market and price policy, social policy ought to be considered as a function of economically healthy farms which had good standards of labour productivity. Other measures needed to be taken to raise the standard of non-viable farms and he regarded the improvement of agricultural structure as an indispensable means for raising social conditions within agriculture.

Mansholt drew attention to the fact that although (at that time) only 16 per cent of the working population earned their living from agriculture, the problems associated with making rural areas habitable were of interest to the 50 per cent of the total population who lived in the countryside. No argument could be put forward which would justify that half the population of the Community lived in conditions which were so much less favourable than those of the other half, from the viewpoint of culture, education, hospitals, and basic amenities.

In 1963 the Commission submitted a social action programme in agriculture to the Council of Ministers (Commission 1963(*e*)). It is a strange document, the first half being entirely devoted to setting out the history of the interest in agricultural social policy within the Community Institutions since the Stresa Conference, and an account of the various consultations on the proposed policy undertaken by the Commission. It is clear that there were disagreements among the Member States concerning the establishment of such a policy, in terms of the role of the Commission, the relationship between agricultural social policy and general social policy, and the juridical basis of the policy. This last point was answered in a later section of the document in which the Commission set out its understanding of the legal basis.

In its outline of the action programme, the Commission assigned the following goals to social policy in the agricultural sphere:

• the elimination of social conditions which were still below the standards generally accepted as an equitable minimum, and the elimination of social

conditions which constituted a serious impediment to the putting into operation of the CAP; and
- the achievement of social parity for those who work in agriculture, i.e. that they should reach a standard of living equivalent to that enjoyed by workers carrying out comparable work in other sectors, in the same region, and under similar conditions.

The action programme covered eight broad areas of social life: employment; agricultural training; freedom of entry into farming and security of tenure; wages and other working conditions such as hours of work and free time; protection at work in terms of accident prevention, sickness benefit, safety and hygiene, employment of women and children; social legislation; social security; housing; and *métayage*.

The proposals made within these very broad headings were fairly innocuous and consisted mainly of information collection, in-depth studies, and the formulation of minimum acceptable standards. The most positive actions proposed were in the fields of agricultural training—a scheme for the common financing of educational projects and institutions, and housing—a proposal to draw up plans for the improvement of living conditions for farm workers and farmers. There followed various discussions on the action programme in the European Parliament, the ESC, and the Consultative Committees, during which suggestions were made as to the items within the programme which required priority attention. In 1964, the Commission responded by submitting its own list of priority actions to the Council (Commission 1964). This list was not intended to supersede the 1963 action programme but rather to highlight the most urgent issues.

With the exception of *métayage*, which was dropped, exactly the same broad areas were covered but in a different order and, within some of them, the Commission had divided its proposed actions into short and medium term. In general, the emphasis was still on studies, co-ordination, and the setting of minimum standards. One interesting suggestion for the short term was that there should be an advisory service for farmers which would help them improve their farming skills or assist them to find employment in other spheres, by providing counselling on education, further training, and the availability of specialized social services. The Commission promised to make a concrete proposal along these lines to the Council which, in the event, had to wait until the Mansholt Plan of 1968. It also proposed to expand the activities of the Social Fund to include retraining of farmers as well as agricultural workers.

The priority action document was discussed by a Council working party in July 1964 and the lack of enthusiasm is clearly indicated by the extent of the reservations, general and detailed. The Commission was criticized for lack of clarity, on the grounds that its classification of actions into short term and medium term did not establish an order of priority within the former group. To this rather fatuous point, the Commission replied quite reasonably that all short-term actions were of the same importance. Worries were expressed over the legal instruments which the Commission intended to use (i.e. Regulations, Directives, or Recommendations)[10] and on the absence of any indication as to the methods to be used for putting the various measures into effect. Finally the Commission was instructed to prepare a new document listing its short-term proposals in order of priority (Conseil 1964(*a*)). This it did not do: instead it prepared a further note setting out the state of progress on all the proposed actions, repeated the juridical basis, and maintained the equality of importance of all its short-term proposals (Conseil 1964(*b*)).

At this point the trail goes cold and during the course of the 1960s no social action was taken within the framework of the CAP, although the Commission did attempt to reintroduce some social element through its proposals on Community Programmes in 1967 (discussed in Chapter 9) and in the Mansholt Plan of 1968 (discussed in Chapter 8). It was not until the early 1970s that any social element crept back into the CAP, with the provision of retirement aid and socio-economic advice (outlined in Chapter 8). Anything of a social nature which did occur in the 1960s was piecemeal and came under the auspices of the general social policy of the Community—which is outside the scope of the present book. However, it is worth noting in passing that the measures concerned did include some of the items which had appeared in the action programme, such as retraining assistance for those leaving farming, and the extension to agriculture of minimum provisions on conditions of employment and social security.

It is fair to state that at no stage has there been a recognizable social policy within the CAP. However, as will become clear in Chapter 4, social issues underlie the consideration of the income problem of many farmers. It is also true that certain aspects of the price policy (outlined in Chapter 6) contain social elements but it should also be said that there are serious social drawbacks to the price policy itself. The only lasting legacy of the Rome Conference was the establishment of two Consultative Committees in 1963: one to deal with the social problems of agricultural workers, the other to deal with the social problems of farmers (Sp. OJ 1963–1964). These two Committees are still in operation. Introduced into the original proposals as an afterthought, fate was against the policy from the start. Among the Member States, only Italy seems to have had any real interest in it and the continuing questioning of the policy's legality was an ominous sign.

The policy caused problems within the Commission itself occupying, as it did, an uneasy position within the areas of both agricultural and general social policy. As these policies were handled by different directorates-general, there was plenty of room for suspicion and misunderstanding. The neglect of social issues within the CAP as it has developed has been matched in the general social policy field by an orientation which has taken that policy and the Social Fund away from an interest in agriculture. Thus, social issues in agriculture remain very largely in the hands of the Member States which pursue them with varying degrees of commitment. One can only assume that this outcome was precisely what the Member States intended to happen all along.

Early Proposals on
Structural Policy within the CAP

There was extensive discussion at the Stresa Conference of the structural shortcomings of the agricultural sector and the need to take urgent action to remedy the defects (see Chapter 1). The impression given by those parts of the Conference report which touch on structure is that the participants expected a great deal from structural reform. In the circumstances, it is perhaps surprising that there seems to have been no consideration of how slowly it achieves results, especially as the problems were portrayed as being acute, and there is no evidence that anyone enquired why the existing structural measures in Member States had not produced the desired results already. Most important of all, as events were to prove, it was too readily assumed that market and structural policies would go hand in hand.

In this context, there seems to have been some confusion at the Conference as to how exactly structural issues were to be handled in the future and by whom. From remarks made by Mansholt and given at least four of the agreed points in the Final Resolution, it would seem reasonable to conclude that the participants envisaged a Community structural policy, as well as a Community market policy. The validity of this interpretation is strengthened by consideration of some of the statements made in the report of Working Party 3 outlined in Chapter 1. However, doubts begin to emerge when it is realized that specific reference was also made in the same Working Party report to the need to *harmonize national structural policies.* Weight was added to the harmonization call by its repetition by the chairman of the Working Party (the French Minister for Agriculture, Houdet) and by a rather similar statement made by the chairman of Working Party 2—Lübke, the Agricultural Minister of Federal Germany (Communautés Européennes 1959).

Whether participants were aware of these contradictions or not is unclear and it might be argued that the issue is unimportant—anyone who attends conferences can testify to their frequent displays of confusion and inconsistency. This would be an acceptable proposition were it not for three things. Firstly, the confusion at Stresa is consistent with the vagueness of the Treaty of Rome, in which it is not completely clear that a common structural policy was envisaged. Secondly, Stresa was an unusually important conference, both in its terms of reference and in its participants, and therefore confusion on a fairly basic point is interesting and may be significant. Thirdly, the confusion at Stresa was to find an echo in the ambivalence of the Member States to Community structural policy, which was to appear again and again down the years and which is not fully resolved even today.

Among the early discussion documents produced by the European Parliament on the future agricultural policy, was one concerned with structural and social issues—Vredeling being the rapporteur. In the light of the vagueness of the Treaty and the confusion in the Stresa Conference papers, perhaps it is not surprising that the Vredeling report (Assembleé 1959) devotes considerable space to the elaboration of a legal basis for a structural policy and to an enumeration of the reasons why a structural policy was necessary. Some of the ideas expressed in this parliamentary report found an echo in the later proposals of the Commission.

The parliamentary committee clearly saw the need to adopt an integrated approach to the provision of aid for agriculture, stressing that market and price policy, and structural policy were complementary to one another. The committee gave a certain precedence to structural policy because it was concerned with the long-term position of the rural population within the national economy. Price and market policy was regarded as much more short term and the view was that it should always be judged in the context of structural objectives, and adjusted to conform with the long-term improvements thought desirable.

The committee proposed the establishment of a fund for the improvement of rural structure (Fonds européen d'amélioration des structures rurales), analogous to the market organizations being proposed for the management of the major commodities. It was recognized that the Rome Treaty did not explicitly provide for the creation of such a fund but the committee believed that it derived logically from the provisions of the Treaty. It was regarded as essential that the activities of this structural fund should mesh with other measures at Community and national level.

In its proposals on the CAP, the Commission showed an awareness of the interrelationships between structural, regional, and general economic policy issues. It recognized that the establishment of a common market would necessitate the elimination of national protective measures which would reveal structural defects hitherto concealed, and that the integration process might aggravate regional disparities. It admitted that not all farms could be developed and so employment for surplus farm labour would have to be found in other sectors. It saw the need to find alternative uses for marginal land and, in view of the aims of the CAP, counselled the reconsideration of policies which encouraged the ploughing-up of fallow land and the reclamation of new land, fearing that these activities might make it more difficult to achieve an equilibrium between production and market requirements.

Given the emphasis placed on structural issues at Stresa, in the Vredeling report, and in the Commission's own analysis, it is surprising that the concrete proposals for a structural policy in COM(60)105 were so weak—the coordination at Community level of national effort and the provision of a token amount of Community aid through the creation of FEASA (Fonds européen pour l'amélioration des structures agricoles).[11] The explanation provided by the Commission was that structural problems were local or regional and that therefore it was appropriate for the Member States to assume the main responsibility. To say the least: this is a curious reason, particularly in the light of the Commission's own criticisms of the record of the Member States in the structural field. The logic is made even more obscure when one considers that price and market regimes have been introduced for minor commodities which are produced in certain localities and regions only, suggesting that the Commission's inhibitions are not of general application.

The only possible explanation for the disparity between the amount of attention paid to structural issues and the weakness of the concrete proposals is the existence of political pressure from Member States, resisting the idea of a full-blown structural policy at Community level, complete with executive powers analogous to those under the price and market policy. The reason why Member States should have resisted the surrender of control over structural policy when they were apparently willing to do so in the price and market sphere is not hard to find and is closely linked with the whole purpose of the Community.

The agreement to create a customs union meant the abolition of frontier protection between the Member States and the establishment at the Community frontier of a common customs regime to replace the existing national regimes. Once it had been agreed to include agriculture within the common market, it became necessary to decide what to do about the internal price and market controls in agriculture, which were actually more important than the frontier protective systems. As the Community is based on the four economic freedoms—freedom of movement of goods, persons, services, and capital—strictly speaking the controls should have been removed and agriculture allowed to operate in a free market situation.

However, this was regarded as out of the question, because the deep-seated problems which had prompted the controls in the first place would remain and indeed, it was feared, in some instances become worse. Thus, the decision was taken to have a Community-wide managed market in agricultural products. Of necessity, this meant the surrender of national internal price and market support arrangements and their replacement with some form of common system.

The link between the establishment of a customs union and the existence of national structural policies in agriculture is far more tenuous. Certainly, the need to co-ordinate national policies would have been obvious, so as to prevent investments which were contrary to the objectives of the CAP or which led to unfair competition, but to have moved from this position to one in which the Member States agreed to abolish their structural policies in favour of a common policy represented a major step which some at least of the Member States were not willing to take. Their position on this issue was no doubt strengthened by the fact that the Treaty did not specifically call for a common structural policy.

Apart altogether from political considerations, there is a widespread belief that the Commission realized it would be easier to make progress on the price and market policy than on the structural front. Whether this was because of the stronger legal basis for the former policy or whether it was on purely practical grounds is not clear. There is a further point: in human terms the abandonment of national policies on structure would have been very unpopular both to politicians and to civil servants. The Member States had agreed to the institution of a common market and price policy: henceforth they were to be the implementors and not the designers of policy in these areas. To have surrendered yet another policy area must have been an alarming prospect. Little did they realize what a bureaucratic paradise the price and market policy was to become at national level!

Whatever the truth of the situation, the fact remains that the extensive discussion of structural issues in the early days of the Community was followed by years of frustrated attempts to put some form of structural policy in place alongside the market policy. The first task was to fulfil the co-ordinating role proposed by the Commission in 1960. It was not until February 1962—once the agreement on the market policy had been concluded—that the Commission presented a draft Decision on co-ordination to the Council of Ministers. The Decision was enacted the following December (Sp. OJ 1959–1962). It provided for the establishment of a Standing Committee on agricultural structure to study the policies of the Member States and to provide a means of exchanging information between them and the Commission. In carrying out its studies the Committee was required to take into account the interrelationship between structural policy and regional and market policy, and the trends in agricultural markets.

On the basis of information to be provided by the Member States, the Commission was given the task of submitting an annual report to the European Parliament and to the Council on the state of agricultural structure and policy in the Member States, the means being used to pursue the policy, and the effectiveness of the measures taken in relation to the objectives of the CAP, and to the long-term potential outlets for the various agricultural products. In addition, this annual report was to contain information on the steps being taken at Community level to achieve the co-ordination of structural policy and the Council was given power to adopt the measures necessary to achieve the required co-ordination with the aid, if needed, of Community financing.

The Member States were, among other things, required to give the Commission drafts of any measures which related to structural improvement, multi-annual plans, and regional programmes, and the Commission was empowered to express an opinion on any such measures. Finally the Member States were required to provide the Commission with particulars of all measures relating to the improvement of agricultural structure, which were in existence at the time the Decision came into force, and to keep such information up-to-date by providing particulars of all subsequent structural measures immediately they became operative.

The co-ordination exercise had a confused beginning and it is very probable that the Member States did not see it in quite the same light as the Commission. The latter did not regard it as some simple harmonization exercise, i.e. the elimination of differences between national policies, but rather as an attempt to guide and reinforce such policies. This is clear from the definition of co-ordination given by the Commission which was 'to contribute to the realization of objectives of the CAP . . . to define the particular objectives and guidelines of the structural policy at Community level, to make these objectives obligatory and to ensure that the measures taken and instruments put in place by the Member States conform to these objectives' (Commission 1963(*a*), 2).

Its intentions were also made plain in the preamble to the 1962 Decision which refers to the necessity 'both to co-ordinate structural policy with regional development policy and, within the framework of regional development policy, to take additional measures designed to facilitate the adjustment of agriculture to economic and social trends'. The preamble also states that steps should be taken 'within the framework of the Community to stimulate efforts to improve the structure of agriculture and to do everything possible to increase the economic potential and competitiveness of agriculture' (Sp. OJ 1959–1962, 295).

These commitments clearly involved Community financing and this too was recognized in the preamble where it states that :

as part of the co-ordination of structural policies steps should be taken to ensure that adequate and co-ordinated use is made of Community financing facilities for the purpose of benefiting the structure of agriculture, the facilities in question being those afforded by, *principally,* the Guidance and Guarantee Fund . . . by the European Social Fund and by the European Investment Bank.   (italics added)

The wording of this statement gave the Community the option of creating further financial instruments to aid structural reform if so desired. It was in this context that FEASA was proposed.

Dams (1963, 347) described the co-ordination exercise as consisting 'in orientating, harmonising or stimulating the actions of Member States' within the context of Community structural goals which had to be clearly defined. Within this framework, Member States were to be 'free to select ways and means of attaining these obligatory aims'. This seems to be a fair description of the original intention but it most certainly is not what actually happened in practice. The Member States continued to be the primary force in structural policy. Much of the remainder of the 1960s can be typified as a period of failure to define structural objectives or to launch individual structural improvement measures at Community level.

One thing which the Structures Committee did do during the 1960s was to undertake a detailed analysis of national structural legislation, the results of which appeared in a report issued with the Mansholt Plan in 1968 (Commission 1968(f)). While the exercise may have been useful in making all parties concerned aware of the structural measures in force in the various Member States, it is hard to see that anything of a positive nature emerged from it. As for the annual report on structure required under the 1962 Decision: to have undertaken the presentation of such a detailed study on a yearly basis would have been a mammoth task, and no annual report answering to the description set out in Article 2 of the Decision has ever appeared. The first annual agricultural report of any kind was issued in 1968 to accompany the Mansholt Plan (Commission 1968(d)). Since then, a report on the situation in agriculture has become a regular feature, appearing in conjunction with the annual price proposals. However, this document is very largely devoted to a review of the price and market aspects of the CAP, structural affairs playing a very minor role.

The Setting-Up of FEOGA and the Fate of FEASA

Provision was made under Art. 40.4 of the Rome Treaty for the establishment of 'one or more agricultural guidance and guarantee funds'. The 1962 package of agreements on market regimes included one on the financial mechanism through which the common organization of these regimes was to be funded. This was Regulation 25/62 *on the financing of the common agricultural policy* (Sp. OJ 1959–1962). Despite the sweeping nature of its title, this Regulation was firmly limited to the market policy, as was the Fund set up under its authority. This Fund was FEOGA (Fonds Européen d'Orientation et de Garantie Agricole).[12] The intention always had been to introduce the CAP gradually over a period of years, and, in consequence, the life of FEOGA was divided into two stages. The first, or transitional, stage covered those years during which FEOGA gradually assumed the funding of the market and price policy as it applied to certain commodities. The second, or single market, stage provided the legal basis for the time when FEOGA was fully responsible for market and price support.

The original idea of having a series of separate funds for each commodity or group of commodities had been abandoned and FEOGA was to be part of the Community's budget. Its role was to finance refunds on exports to third countries, to intervene domestically to stabilize markets, and to provide funding for 'common measures adopted in order to attain the objectives set out in Art. 39.1(a) of the Treaty, including the structural modifications required for the proper working of the common market, provided that those measures do not encroach upon the work of the European Investment Bank and the European Social Fund' (Art. 2.2(c)).

The types of 'common measure' envisaged were improvements in storage, processing, distribution, and market intelligence; the adaptation of supply to demand, including converting to another product, limiting output, and prolonging the season for seasonal crops, and projects to stimulate consumer demand. The reason for this structural commitment lay in the recognition that the replacement of the national support mechanisms by the common system was bound to lead to difficulties for individual farmers in certain regions and countries, and that it was only reasonable to provide assistance which would make the necessary production adjustments somewhat easier. Art. 5.2 laid down that, in so far as possible, expenditure on structural measures during the transitional stage should amount to a sum equivalent to one-third of the expenditure on price and market support. Put another way: this meant that structural aid on market adjustment should equal one-quarter of total FEOGA expenditure. No provision was made as to the level of structural expenditure when the single market stage was reached.

The Commission took the view that the inclusion of structural aid under FEOGA was limited in scope by the very purpose for which FEOGA was established, which was to finance the movement towards and the operation of the common market in agricultural products. It meant that a major area of structural adjustment remained for which the Community was providing no aid, because the activities of the European Investment Bank (EIB) and the Social Fund were only marginally related to—or indeed suitable for—the farming sector. The Commission was particularly concerned with backward agricultural regions where financial aid was justified on social and economic grounds.

With this in mind and in the context of its co-ordinating role in structural policy, the Commission proceeded with its proposal on FEASA which it presented to the Council in February 1963 in COM(63)19 final (Commission 1963(*a*)).[13] This proposal followed very closely the intentions laid down in the Commission 1959 and 1960 documents discussed above. The fund was to stimulate and guide the efforts of Member States to improve agricultural structure which conformed with the requirements of the CAP, and to contribute to the general socio-economic balance but without altering the conditions of trade in a manner contrary to the common interest.

Projects seeking aid from the fund were to be of interest to the Community; to seek to improve agricultural structure for the benefit of the whole economy; to keep farms viable or to help farms to become viable and to ensure the growth of their competitiveness; and to provide adequate guarantees of the permanence of the structural improvements undertaken. Priority was to be given to projects which either formed part of a programme for regional economic development, or which gave adequate attention to problems of advice and agricultural training, or which contributed to improving the social situation of workers in agriculture.

Aid was to be in the form of interest rate subsidies or assistance to lengthening the repayment period of loans, or a combination of the two. It was made very clear that FEASA was intended as a source of additional aid: it was not to be a substitute for the EIB, the Social Fund, and FEOGA, nor was it to replace the normal national aids. In its original proposals on the CAP, the Commission had envisaged FEASA as being funded by a contribution from the Community's general budget and by FEOGA. However, in 1963, the Commission proposed an even closer link between FEOGA and FEASA, which was that, out of the monies available to FEOGA for structural aid (i.e. one-third of the expenditure on market and price support), one-quarter should be transferred to FEASA. It was only if this proved inadequate that additional funds could be made available from the rest of the Community budget.

FEASA immediately ran into trouble in the Council of Ministers. The Germans objected to it on the grounds that Community legislation (i.e. Reg. 25/62) did not require the Member States to agree to a second fund when they instituted FEOGA. Though technically true, this objection was surely spurious as it is quite clear that Reg. 25/62 was intended to cover the market and price policy only, together with its attendant structural problems, and it had appeared that there was a firm commitment to a more broadly based common policy.

Bourrinet (1964) was probably nearer the real truth when he maintained that the Germans were unwilling to pay for structural improvements in the south of Italy (which region would have been the main beneficiary), at a time when they were already committed to financing the market and price policy in large part, which was mostly for France's benefit. In the context of German attitudes, it is important to bear in mind that the German rural infrastructure was comparatively good, with relatively small differences between regions, but its farm organization was poor and its agricultural prices high.

Although the Germans fought very hard for a high common cereals price, they must have realized at an early stage that some reduction in their national price was inevitable. Equally they must have seen the advantage to themselves of the structural aids provided under FEOGA to cushion the market adjustments which would be necessary. It was unlikely that they would get any significant return from FEASA but their prospects under FEOGA structural aids were much better. Thus, it was in their interest to kill FEASA.

As things have turned out, the Germans have always done remarkably well out of the Community's structural aids and Italy has done remarkably badly. While there are many administrative reasons for the difference, it is also true that the actual aids on offer have frequently been of a kind which are more helpful to German circumstances than to Italian. Part of the reason for this must surely lie in the original design of the Fund providing the aid.

Berger (1965) put forward a further explanation for the rejection of FEASA which was the purely practical one that it was more efficient to have a single fund only, as it facilitated the co-ordination of actions being taken at Community level on the market and price side and in the structural field. Such concern does not sound like the Council of Ministers, although it is true that fears had been expressed quite independently that the use of two funds would diffuse effort and blur the overall view of agricultural policy. Sadly it must be said that even the use of one fund is no guarantee that the desired co-ordination of its various sections is always achieved.

In order to overcome the Council's objections to FEASA, Mansholt indicated in July 1963 that the Commission would be willing to scrap FEASA and to replace it with a single agricultural fund. This is what happened; and later the same year the Council agreed to divide FEOGA into two sections: the Guarantee section providing market and price support; and the Guidance Section providing structural aid. The financial split remained unaltered, i.e. the Guidance Section was to receive a sum equivalent to one-third of the Guarantee expenditure. This agreement was reflected in the legislation early in 1964 which laid down the specific arrangements needed to implement FEOGA, namely Reg. 17/64 *on the conditions for granting aid from the European Agricultural Guidance and Guarantee Fund* (Sp. OJ, 1963–1964).

The Development of the CAP, 1964–1966

With the enactment of the first part of this operationally important Regulation, the Community could truly be said to be operating a common market policy, as it now had in place in Reg. 17/64 (and backdated to 1962/63) a set of rules for calculating export refunds and a definition of the scope and purpose of intervention. It is clear from the wording of the Regulation that the primary control mechanism for the market was the export refund. This followed logically from a requirement laid down in Regulation 25/62 (Art. 3.3): 'the Council shall each year, on the basis of a report from the Commission, examine how the Community financing of export refunds . . . has affected guidance of production and development of outlets' (Sp. OJ 1959–1962, 127).[14]

It was also in keeping with the situation at that time, when surpluses were smaller and related to fewer commodities than became the case in later decades. The export market was seen as a safety-valve on an overheating internal market and the purpose of the export refund was to make trade possible by funding the operation. The irony of the situation was that the only reason why the Community was able to use export refunds as one of its market support mechanisms was that GATT had permitted the use of export subsidies for primary products. This was contrary to its normal rules and had been forced on it under pressure from the USA and other exporting countries. The only condition was that these subsidies should not allow a country to obtain 'more than an equitable share of world trade' (GATT Art. XVI.3).

Intervention on the domestic market was perceived as the internal equivalent of an export refund. It was described as having an aim and function:

identical with that of refunds on exports to third countries, and its scope was to include all actions subject to Community rules within the framework of the common organization of markets which are designed to withdraw from the market those quantities of products which cannot be absorbed by it, provided that appropriate measures are taken to ensure that for the disposal of such products on the domestic market an outlet other than the usual outlet is found, in order to remedy the situation created by the surplus.   (Art. 5.1 of Reg. 17/64) (Sp. OJ 1963–1964, 106)

As Mansholt had said of the variable levy in 1962 (see above), these were merely mechanisms and inherently neutral: what mattered was the level of prices to which they were applied. At the end of 1964 (as indicated above), the die was cast in favour of a high common cereals price to come into force in 1967. This was to set the tone for the future development of the market policy.

The second part of Reg. 17/64 is basically an amalgamation of certain of the proposed arrangements for FEASA with the structural aspects of FEOGA, as originally submitted to the Council in February 1963. The effect of this revision was to narrow the field of application of structural aids from what it would have been with two funds, and to link them more closely with the implementation of the market and price policy. The type of structural aid provided under the Guidance Section of Reg. 17/64 was in the form of a capital subsidy paid either as a lump sum or in instalments. The Community contribution originally did not exceed 25 per cent of the total investment but provision was subsequently made to raise the Community contribution to a maximum of 45 per cent in certain circumstances, the first such derogation being under Reg. 130/66 to be discussed below. The beneficiary had to provide at least 30 per cent of the total investment and the Member State, in which the project took place, also had to make a contribution (Art. 18.1).

In order to qualify for aid a project had to meet three criteria simultaneously:

(1) that it came within the framework of a Community Programme;
(2) that it was for a purpose connected with the adaptation or guidance made necessary by the economic consequences of implementing the CAP, or for the smooth working of that policy; and
(3) that it offered an adequate guarantee as to the lasting effect of the improvement made (Art. 14.1).

It was laid down that, for a period of two years from the entry into force of the Regulation, the first criterion above did not have to apply and that individual projects not part of a Community Programme would be grant-aided. As things turned out, these individual projects were still being grant-aided right up to the end of the 1970s, when Reg. 17/64 was replaced in part with a measure on processing and marketing to be discussed in Chapter 10.

As mentioned in the previous section, Regulation 25/62 had provided funding arrangements for the CAP up to 30 June 1965 and, in March of that year, the Commission proposed a package of measures which, *inter alia*, covered the financing of the policy to the end of the transition period (i.e. the end of 1969). However, in its proposals the Commission had gone much further than was strictly necessary at that time and the package included, not only important matters relating to agricultural funding, but also a proposal on the replacement of the contributions of the Member States to the Community Budget by the Community's own resources, and a proposal on the strengthening of the European Parliament's budgetary powers.

This attempt to anticipate institutional changes, which it is true had to be made at some stage, precipitated probably the worst crisis in the Community's history, culminating in the walk-out by the French at the end of the Council of Ministers meeting in June 1965 and their refusal to participate in Council activities for the remainder of the year. The quarrel was patched up in January 1966 by an agreement reached in Luxembourg which, in effect, allowed the Member States to ignore the requirement under the Rome Treaty to move from a situation where, in certain fields (agriculture being one of them), majority voting in the Council replaced unanimous voting at the end of the transition period.[15] The compromise reached in Luxembourg was to the effect that when majority voting was appropriate and 'very important interests' of one or more Member States were at stake, then the Council would strive, within a reasonable time, to reach a solution agreeable to all (Commission 1966).

This informal agreement (it had no legal status) was to prove disastrous to the development and good management of the Community. It was cynically misused by the Member States down the years and has had the effect at times of paralysing the work of the Council. Needless to remark, agriculture is one of the main areas of the Community's activities to have been handicapped by the Luxembourg compromise.[16]

Once the dust had settled on the political drama, there were important decisions to be taken on agriculture. Despite earlier agreements on the extension of the market policy to cover a wider range of commodities, the timetable for implementation had slipped significantly. There was an added urgency in that the Kennedy Round of GATT was about to open and the Community needed to agree a common position and, of course, there was the matter of funding the policy, left in abeyance a year previously.

The atmosphere during the agricultural negotiations in 1966 seems to have been extremely tense: a heavy price was paid by all for the events leading up to the Luxembourg compromise. The negotiations were very long and very difficult. *Agence Europe* commented:

[T]he times are no longer propitious to consideration of the interests of European agriculture as a whole. It is increasingly clear that each delegation is defending the interests of its own farmers and refusing to think in purely Community terms. Negotiations have thus degenerated into inter-governmental bargaining, the Commission seeking to transpose them to Community level as far as possible.   (*Agence Europe* 24–6–66, 4)

Thirty years later, the situation had not changed.

Despite the atmosphere, agreements were reached on prices under existing commodity regimes and progress was made on the introduction of new regimes, though the Community stored up trouble for itself with some of the arrangements made. A timetable was agreed for a further group of commodities for which proposals had not yet come before the Council. Needless to remark, the timetable slipped here and there but the net result was that, by the end of the 1960s, market regimes had been introduced for cereals, rice, sugar, olive oil, oilseeds, dairy products, beef and veal, pigmeat, eggs, poultry, fresh fruit and vegetables, live plants, processed fruit and vegetables. Fibre flax and hemp, fisheries, tobacco, and table wine were added in 1970.

Most importantly, the future of FEOGA was settled up to the end of 1969 under Regulation 130/66 *on the financing of the common agricultural policy* (Sp. OJ 1965–1966). On FEOGA-Guarantee, it was agreed that, from 1967/68, the fund would cover 100 per cent of eligible market support for all commodities subject to common regimes, and not as previously a rising proportion of the cost. On the structural side, it was agreed that, from 1967/68, expenditure by FEOGA-Guidance would no longer be linked directly to expenditure on the Guarantee Section but rather would be subject to a fixed ceiling each year of 285m. units of account.[17] As Guidance Section expenditure had not yet reached that level, the imposition of the ceiling was not immediately detrimental but in the longer term it clearly was, as it did not allow for regular growth in structural expenditure. Why then was the ceiling imposed?

The reason was German fear of the growing cost of the CAP: the agreement to increase the number of commodities subject to common regimes and the change in the funding arrangements meant a substantial rise in FEOGA-Guarantee expenditure. The automatic one-third link between the Guidance and Guarantee sections meant that spending on structural measures would have risen pro rata. This was more than the Germans were willing to take: as the largest contributors to the Community budget they feared what the effect might be on that contribution and so insisted that the financial arrangements for the Guidance Section be changed.

While German fears were understandable, the episode points to the continuing lack of enthusiasm which the Member States had for structural policy. The actual level of the ceiling was not as important as the principle involved. The Member States showed themselves willing to spend 70–80 per cent of the Community budget on agriculture but no more than about 5 per cent of this sum went on structural improvement. In other words, practically the whole expenditure was—and is—on the alleviation of symptoms and practically nothing on the removal of causes. With the benefit of hindsight it can be seen that Germany's fears were unfounded: Community expenditure on structure took many years to reach the ceiling of 285m. ua. The reason was the slow pace at which structural measures were enacted but, at the time of the 1966 agreement, the Community Programmes required to complete Reg. 17/64 were still being prepared. If they had been accepted, they could have represented a major new element of expenditure.[18]

The 1966 agreement was also important as an early example of the willingness of the Council to make special provision for the individual requirements of some of its members—exceptions to the norm which would allow the overall package to be accepted. Italy had been disadvantaged by the failure to introduce on time market regimes of particular interest to her. Reg. 130/66 made provision for the payment of special lump sums (mostly for structural improvements) for olives, olive oil, fruit and vegetables, and tobacco. Belgium received a payment for sugar, and the structural needs of Italy and Luxembourg received special mention in relation to the possibility of a higher Community contribution to structural projects under Reg. 17/64.

While these derogations were not in themselves of great financial importance, they were an early indicator of the way in which the Luxembourg compromise was to operate. If unanimity is required, then disproportionate power is given to a Member State to seek some special advantage. It is an invitation to exaggerate the importance of a particular need or problem.

Taking Stock of the CAP at the End of the 1960s

The end of the decade is an opportune moment to stop and take stock of the early progress made to launch the CAP. With the 1966 agreement, the scene was set for the completion of the arrangements necessary for the coming into effect in 1967 of the single internal market for agricultural products, a unified price support mechanism, and a single system of protection against third country imports. The one thing which no one had anticipated or made provision for was the gradual breakdown of the fixed exchange rate system on which the common price mechanism was founded—a system which had underpinned the international money markets in the post-war era: but that is another story.

At the completion of the 1966 negotiations, there was tremendous relief that they had been successful. *Agence Europe* commented that, if agreement had not been reached, then the structure of the CAP would have crumbled and the earlier efforts would have been in vain. It quoted Hallstein as saying that the most important step in the whole of the history of the construction of European unity had been accomplished, as what was involved was the completion of the common agricultural policy. The crisis had been ended and the task that now lay ahead was one of consolidation. It was the end of the package deal formula (*Agence Europe* 25–7–66). Little did he know!

However, in the midst of this hyperbole and euphoria, *Agence Europe* added a cautionary comment on the actual content of the agreements reached: 'from a general economic viewpoint, it is clear that they *confirm the fundamental nature of the Community's agricultural policy*. The policy is one of high prices, protection, based on complicated market intervention machinery, costly for the states and in several sectors for consumers' (*Agence Europe* 25–7–66).

Despite unease at the high price structure and despite the warnings, starting with the original proposals in 1960, of the surplus problem which had got worse in the intervening years, there was no doubt that the market and price policy was forging ahead, with the addition of new commodity regimes and the completion of the old ones. It was an amazing achievement that six independent countries had succeeded in less than a decade in uniting their separate market and price policies into one common policy. However, that was only one of the four pillars of the CAP, what of the other three?

Commercial policy had, of necessity, developed alongside market policy although, as indicated above, in a subordinate position. There was a fundamental conflict between the objective of openness to the world which the Community preached and the practice of a common internal policy based on high support prices and a rising production trend. Even the extension of the CAP to the overseas countries and territories had been quietly dropped with the independence of these States.

Social policy had hardly existed at all and, while some of the later measures adopted under the structural policy could be said to have a social content, as a separate part of the CAP social policy cannot really be said to exist. This is not to say that social measures are totally absent: they do exist but they form part of the agricultural policy of the individual Member States. It is sometimes overlooked that large areas of policy—land law, inheritance, social insurance, income and corporate taxation—all remain in the exclusive control of the Member States.

And what of structural policy? It made a very unsure and hesitant start. Later chapters will outline some of the disappointments and outright failures of this policy from the 1960s onwards. It is clear that it was never intended to replace national structural policies in the same way that the common price and market policy replaced its national counterparts. But even given a more limited role, the positive and sensible link between market support and structural improvement envisaged originally in Reg. 25/62 was broken in Reg. 130/66 when the potential for a full-scale Community structural policy was deliberately restricted by the imposition of a financial ceiling. It would seem reasonable to characterize these early years as ones of retreat on the structural front from the sentiments expressed in some of the most fundamental documentation on the CAP. However, as has been indicated above, despite the emphasis on structure at Stresa, both the Treaty and the Commission proposals were vague and weak when they came to the provision of powers to carry structural policy into effect. It is not surprising that these ambiguities were seized upon to delay and weaken the commitment to a common structural policy.

But it was not only narrow self-interest on the part of certain Member States and the jealous guarding of spheres of activity which hindered the development of a Community structural policy—though these played their part—it was also the adherence to old modes of thinking on agricultural policy. Chapter 1 outlined how agricultural policy developed in the 1950s, with a growing concern for the income situation of farmers and dissatisfaction with price policy as a support mechanism, but, despite its failings, its retention as the main instrument of policy, and the recourse to structural measures only as a last resort and in response to the growing anxiety of governments over the cost of agricultural support.

The creation of the Community, hailed as a great innovation, did not change this basic approach. The worries about income were all there: the price and market policy was created as the main instrument to alleviate these difficulties. Concern with the resulting cost was soon to mount but by their actions the Member States indicated their continued preference for price support as the main instrument of policy, thereby perpetuating the well-established and traditional approach. The mould had not been broken.

NOTES

1. The social element did not appear in the original 1959 proposals and was added to take account of the criticisms by the ESC (CES 1960). Most of the references to social policy in COM(60)105 are lifted directly from the ESC report and, as will be seen later in the chapter, it was a short-lived element in the policy.
2. It is more usual to refer to this element of policy as 'price policy' or 'price and market policy'. All three terms are used interchangeably throughout the book.
3. There are various accounts of these events ranging from the dry, factual statements in the *Bulletin* of the EC, to the comments of someone who participated (e.g. Mayoux (1962)), to the synthesis written more than twenty years later by Neville-Rolfe (1984).
4. For a German view of the negotiations, see Hendriks (1991).
5. A few commodities were added in later years either to placate particular Member States or as a result of the Enlargement of the Community.
6. There is an analogy here with the later use of monetary compensatory amounts to

bridge the gap caused by currency fluctuations, particularly in the 1970s and early 1980s.

7. The reference to the Rome Treaty recalls Art. 44.2 and the system of minimum prices which were to be a feature of the first or transitional period. They were not to prevent the development of a natural preference between Member States. Camps (1964, 76) points out that this is 'the only reference in the agricultural articles of the Treaty to the principle of Community preference'.

8. These mechanisms ae discussed more fully in Chs. 6 and 7.

9. The system of sharecropping which used to be prevalent in certain regions and for certain crops most notably in France and Italy. Although regulated by law, the economic circumstances of the *métayer* (sharecropper) were usually inferior to those of owner-occupiers and tenant farmers.

10. Regulations are the strongest form of legislation, as they come into force directly without the necessity for ratification by the national parliaments. Directives are binding on Member States but require national legislation to give them legal effect. Recommendations have no legal standing and are merely what their name suggests.

11. The European Fund for Structural Improvements in Agriculture, referred to earlier in the chapter. Clearly this fund owed something in conception to the proposal made by the agricultural committee of the European Parliament (outlined above), although the fund suggested by the latter body was for rural rather than agricultural structure.

12. European Agricultural Guidance and Guarantee Fund (EAGGF).

13. This formed part of a package which also included proposals on the conditions for granting aid from FEOGA (Commission 1963(*b*)), and on the financing of both FEOGA and FEASA (Commission 1963(*c*)).

14. This quotation illustrates the way in which the meaning of the word 'guidance' changed in the early years of the CAP from manipulation of the market (in 1962) to structural adjustment (by 1964).

15. Under the Treaty, except where specifically stated to the contrary, majority voting is the norm. During the early years of the Community, the Treaty allowed greater use of unanimity.

16. The whole episode in 1965 provides an excellent illustration of the way in which agriculture has become embroiled in the 'high politics' of the Community to the detriment of the good management of the sector and out of all proportion to its importance. (See Neville-Rolfe (1984) for an agricultural perspective of the 1965 dispute.)

17. It will be recalled that, under Reg. 25/62, aid for structural improvement was to equal one-third of the expenditure on market and price support.

18. The Community Programmes are discussed in Ch. 9.

3

The Changing Shape of the Agricultural Sector

The Economy at Large and Agriculture's Place in It

Before embarking on a review of the way in which the CAP has developed over time, it is opportune to pause and examine the main features of the agricultural sector in the Member States and the Community. This chapter relies entirely on the statistical evidence provided by the Community itself and because that Community has changed in size over time the data used reflect that fact. This complicates the picture, as indeed do the changes in the selection of statistics made available. For instance, Table 3.1 provides some basic data on the Community as it was in 1984 and 1993: the first year was chosen purely because that was the earliest occasion on which the data were published in a particular way—which has since been repeated annually. Despite many limitations and concerns about continuity and comparability over time and between Member States, the real problem lies in the overwhelming amount of data now available. The material included in this chapter is but a small selection and has been chosen to highlight certain features of the sector, in particular agriculture's place in the wider economy; aspects of production and human consumption; the place of the Community in world agricultural trade; the physical size of farms and certain features of the people who work on those farms; and finally the cost of the CAP in budgetary terms.

The first indicator in Table 3.1—total area of the Member States in 1993—is self-explanatory, except in one respect: it includes the eastern Länder in Germany and, as a result, the relative size of that country has increased. Previously Germany represented 11 per cent of the total area of EU-12. In a similar manner, its total population has grown so that, whereas previously, Germany, Italy, the UK, and France had roughly comparable populations, since reunification Germany, with nearly one-quarter of the EU total, is by far the most populous Member State. The UK, France, and Italy combined equal about half the population of the EU.[1]

The Member States differ markedly in terms of population density, with the Netherlands and Belgium having by far the highest densities, and Ireland by far the lowest. In most cases these densities hide large differences in topography: for instance, France and Denmark have fairly low densities but Denmark, with its total absence of hills and mountains, has considerably more good-quality land per head of population. The Gross Domestic Product (GDP) per head in both

Table 3.1. Basic indicators for the European Community: mid-1980s and early 1990s

Indicator		EU-12	Belgium	Germany[c]	France	Italy	Luxembourg	Netherlands
Total area '000 km²	1993	**2,368.2**	30.5	357.0	549.1	301.3	2.6	41.5
	%	**100.0**	1.3	15.1	23.2	12.7	0.1	1.7
Total population m.	1984	**321.3**	9.8	61.2	54.9	57.0	0.4	14.4
	%	**100.0**	3.0	19.0	17.0	17.7	0.1	4.4
	1993	**346.8**	10.1	80.6	57.5	56.9	0.4	15.2
	%	**100.0**	2.9	23.3	16.6	16.4	0.1	4.4
Population density per km²	1984	**142**	322	245	100	189	141	386[d]
	1993	**146**	330	226	105	189	154	367[d]
GDP[a] per head ECU	1984	**10,845**	11,984	13,089	12,475	9,906	14,193	11,536
	1993	**15,832**	17,946	17,147	17,434	16,228	25,422	16,308

Indicator		Denmark	Ireland	UK	Greece	Spain	Portugal
Total area '000km²	1993	43.1	70.3	244.1	132.0	504.8	92.0
	%	1.8	2.9	10.4	5.6	21.4	3.8
Total population m.	1984	5.1	3.5	56.5	9.9	38.4	10.1
	%	1.5	1.0	17.5	3.0	11.9	3.1
	1993	5.2	3.6	58.0	10.3	39.1	9.8
	%	1.5	1.1	16.7	2.9	11.3	2.8
Population density per km²	1984	118	50	231	74	76	109
	1993	120	51	237	78	77	107
GDP[a] per head ECU	1984	13,240	7,702	10,920	6,210	8,181[b]	5,267[b]
	1993	17,815	12,833	15,690	9,999	12,330	10,934

[a] Gross Domestic Product—purchasing power standard (PPS)
[b] estimate
[c] 1993 includes eastern Länder
[d] the density statistics cannot be reconciled: the area of the Netherlands in 1984 is given as 37.3 km²; why it should have grown to 41.5 km² by 1993 is unexplained

Source: Agricultural Situation in the Community: 1986 and 1994 Reports.

1984 and 1993 indicates that Luxembourg is the richest Member State: in the latter year the gap between it and the next country—Belgium—was particularly wide. The level in Luxembourg is rather anomalous: it is by far the smallest Member State and the figure must be heavily influenced by the existence on its territory of a large number of highly paid EU officials. What is of greater interest is the changes in ranking of most Member States between the two years, most notably the decline of Germany from third to fifth position. This can be attributed very largely to the changed circumstances in Germany where the increase in GDP/head has been adversely affected by reunification. What is also of note, especially in 1993, is the cluster of Member States—Belgium, Denmark, France, and Germany—with very similar GDP levels per head: there is little to choose between them. This group of four is closely followed by the Netherlands and Italy, with the UK just behind them. Ireland and Spain come next with very similar GDPs per head; Portugal and Greece bring up the rear.

Table 3.2 comprises five indicators which link agriculture to the wider economy. The first such measure is the proportion of GDP which arises in the agricultural sector. For the original six Member States it is possible to make a comparison between the late 1950s and the early 1990s: the relative decline in the importance of the sector is very noticeable. Concentrating solely on the 1993 statistics, the interesting feature is the extent to which the original Six and most of the newer Member States are similar: the exceptions are Greece and, to a lesser extent, Ireland; in no other country is the agricultural share of GDP above 4 per cent. Statistics for Austria and Finland (not illustrated) would suggest a GDP share in agriculture and forestry of about 3 per cent, and in Sweden of about 1 per cent.

The situation is more confused where employment is concerned—the second indicator in Table 3.2. In the early 1990s, five Member States were above the average, Greece being about three times higher, and Ireland, Portugal, and Spain about twice the average.[2] The comparative statistics for EC-6 (1958/93) are a stark reminder of the extent of the change which has taken place in the agricultural labour force during the lifetime of the CAP. It is interesting to note that, in the original proposals on the CAP, the only measure of agricultural income was to be found in the comparison of GDP and employment in the sector: the larger the gap the less productive the sector, which suggests that only Belgium and the Netherlands were reasonably efficient. Judging by the statistics for the early 1990s, things have clearly improved.

The next three indicators in Table 3.2 all relate to trade. The really interesting comparison here is between imports in EC-6 in 1958 and 1993. The earlier statistics go a long way to explain the concern which policy-makers in the 1950s had with security of supply. Even in the Netherlands, which was a net exporter of food, agricultural imports represented over one-quarter of total imports. It is easy to forget that the sleeping giant of agriculture—France—was a very substantial importer of agricultural products until comparatively recently. The impact of membership of the Community can be seen in the UK where, over a twenty-year period, the proportion of agricultural imports in the total has more

Table 3.2. Agriculture and food in the context of the European Community economy, selected years 1958–1993

Indicator		EC	Belgium	Germany	France	Italy	Luxem-bourg	Netherlands
Gross Domestic Product: proportion in agriculture %	1958	**8.8**	7.4	7.1	10.7	18.5	0.7	11.2
	1993	**2.5**	1.8	1.2	2.9	3.6	1.8	3.6
Civilian employment: proportion in agriculture[a] %	1958	**22.7**	9.4	15.7	23.7	34.9	17.9	12.7
	1993	**5.5**	2.5[b]	3.0	5.0	7.4	3.0[b]	4.6
Total imports: proportion attributed to food and agricultural products %	1958	**37.9**	26.0[c]	43.6	44.3	38.7	c	26.2
	1993	**11.2**	13.0[c]	11.7	11.9	16.8	c	16.0
Total exports: proportion attributed to food and agricultural products %	1958	**13.8**	9.6[c]	3.3	17.6	22.6	c	33.6
	1993	**8.7**	11.9[c]	6.1	16.0	7.4	c	25.4
External trade balance in food and agricultural products (Mio ECU)	1993	**-12,569**	288[c]	-11,595	8,298	-10,621	c	11,595
Value added in industry: proportion arising in the food sector %	1991	**14.3**	16.2	24.7	14.4	10.7	9.0	16.7
Industrial employment: proportion arising in the food sector %	1991	**—**	14.0	n.a.	12.9	8.1	9.7	16.8

Indicator		EC-9	Denmark	Ireland	UK
Gross Domestic Product: proportion in agriculture	1973	**n.a.**	n.a.	n.a.	n.a.
	1993		3.0	8.9	1.4
Civilian employment: proportion in agriculture	1973	**9.0**	9.5	25.0	2.9
	1993	**n.a.**	5.4	12.7	2.1
Total imports: proportion attributed to food and agricultural products	1973	**28.9**	15.9	18.0	27.3
	1993	**n.a.**	16.7	11.4	11.6
Total exports: proportion attributed to food and agricultural products	1973	**9.2**	41.8	45.9	8.7
	1993	**n.a.**	29.4	22.9	7.8

Indicator	Year			
External trade balance in food and agricultural products (MIO ECU)	1993	4,728	3,623	−8,712
Value Added in industry: proportion arising in the food sector	1991	20.5	20.0	19.0
Employment in industry: proportion arising in the food sector	1991	19.3	18.3	11.3

Indicator	Year	EC-10[d]	Greece	EC-12[e]	Spain	Portugal
Gross Domestic Product: proportion in agriculture	1980s	**n.a.**	16.3[d]	**3.5[f]**	5.6[e]	n.a.
	1993		14.2		3.0	3.2
Civilian employment: proportion in agriculture	1980s	**7.9**	30.7[d]	**8.0**	15.1[e]	22.2[e]
	1993		21.3		10.1	11.6
Total imports: proportion attributed to food and agricultural products	1980s	**14.7**	14.6[d]	**15.7**	20.7[e]	33.8[e]
	1993		15.5		15.7	16.0
Total exports: proportion attributed to food and agricultural products	1980s	**9.7**	28.6[d]	**8.4**	15.1[e]	14.3[e]
	1993		33.1		16.6	8.2
External trade balance in food and agricultural products (MIO ECU)	1993		−554		−1,252	−2,222
Value Added in industry: proportion arising in the food sector	1991		n.a.		21.0	22.4
Employment in industry: proportion arising in the food sector	1991		n.a.		15.9	14.8

a agriculture, forestry and fishing except in 1993 which also includes hunting
b 1992
c Belgium and Luxembourg combined
d 1981
e 1986
f EC-11
n.a. = not available

Source: Agricultural Situation in the Community: 1976, 1984, and 1986 Reports.

than halved. In terms of agricultural performance an important factor is the rise in self-sufficiency in the UK (see Table 3.A1(*b*)), and in terms of sourcing of imports a switch to other Community countries (intra-EC trade being omitted from the table). Even in Spain and Portugal, already there has been a marked change in the proportion of agricultural imports.

The proportion of total imports in 1993 which were agricultural in nature was remarkably similar in the Member States, the variation being no more than 11–17 per cent. In contrast, the share of agricultural exports in the total was much more variable (6–33 per cent). In only four Member States was the proportion in excess of 20 per cent (Ireland, the Netherlands, Denmark, and Greece). The range was even wider in earlier years but, as with imports, the statistics hide a number of factors. For instance, in 1973 exports from Denmark and Ireland were very high (42 and 46 per cent respectively of total exports) but that was the year in which these countries joined the Community. The apparent decline in the proportion of agricultural exports is due in part to the exclusion of intra-EC trade from the statistics but also to the widening of their export base in terms of product range. Such explanations are also relevant to the sharp decline in the proportion of agricultural exports from Italy. However an added factor there must be the poor perfomance in terms of self-sufficiency levels over the lifetime of the CAP (see Table 3.A1(*a*)). The last trade measure is that of the external trade balance in food and agricultural products in 1993. This indicator points to the fact that only Belgium/Luxembourg, Ireland, Denmark, France, and the Netherlands are net exporters of agricultural and food products.

The final measures in Table 3.2 relate to the role of the food industry within total manufacturing. While the relative position of farming has diminished over time, the same is not true of the food industry. Both in terms of value added and of employment, food-processing is a significant part of manufacturing industry in practically all the Member States. Thus, in 1991, in Germany, Portugal, Spain, Denmark, Ireland, and the UK, about one-fifth to one-quarter of the value added in industry came from the food sector. It is also worth noting that the productivity record of the food sector is very creditable: the value added being higher in most cases than the employment. Indeed, in the UK, Portugal, Spain, and Italy the differential in 1991 was particularly high. This could be due to many factors: the scale of the enterprise, the degree of processing, the type of product being processed. . . . It is also important to remember that some of the raw materials used in the food sector do not originate in the Community but, even where this is the case, the CAP is involved as the import regimes for primary agricultural commodities used in processing are just as much part of the policy as the support mechanisms for the Community's own agricultural sector. In examining the CAP, it is all too easy to forget that the impact of the policy does not end at the farm gate.

Production, Yields, and Self-Sufficiency over Time

While soil, climate, altitude, and latitude have a fundamental influence on the type of farming undertaken in a particular region or country, the size and shape of the agricultural sector is also heavily influenced by the existence of the CAP. It is also affected by the changing dimensions of the Community itself. Each Enlargement has added not only new countries but also new features to the CAP—new commodities to be supported or new structural adjustments to be made.

In the original 1960 proposals on the CAP, the first Part of COM(60)105 was devoted to a review of agriculture and the agricultural policies in the individual Member States. One of the most striking features of the analysis then made is the scarcity of statistical data on which the policy-designers could build their new creation. Compared with the overwhelming amount of data available today, they really knew very little about the sector forty years ago. The most detailed information was on trade; information on production and consumption of the main products was reasonably good; there were few measures of the farming sector in terms of farm size, nothing on regional production patterns, and little on incomes. Many of the general statements made in the text were not accompanied by corroborating statistics: whether they even existed is not clear but one suspects not. Of course, such statistics as were available were of dubious comparability, as each country collected its own statistics, in its own way, according to its own definition and purpose.

However, such information as is available from those early days allows a few comparisons to be made between the situation prior to the introduction of the CAP and more recent times. If one concentrates on the original six Member States, it gives a small insight into the impact which the CAP has had. Some of the changes over time would probably have taken place anyway: it is impossible to know for sure. The limitations of the early statistics mean that the analysis has to be confined to the simplest of measures: production, yields, structural data. It is important not to read too much into the precise figures as there is no way of knowing how closely comparable they are; nevertheless interesting points emerge.

Table 3.3(*a*) compares the distribution of production by main commodity in the late 1950s and early 1990s for the original EC-6. One of the most fascinating of the inter-year comparisons is that of German crop production which in terms of total contribution to final production has hardly altered. In particular, the position regarding cereals should be noted: unlike every other country of the original Six, it is virtually unchanged—proof if proof were needed of the German negotiating success in terms of the prices originally set. The other countries which experienced a price decline on the introduction of the common cereals regime were Italy and Luxembourg and the value of their cereal production clearly declined as a result. The increase in the importance of cereals in France was predictable, given that it benefited from the largest increase in the support price.

Table 3.3(a). Percentage distribution of agricultural production in value terms, by major commodity, late 1950s and early 1990s, EC-6

Commodity	Belgium 1958/59	Belgium 1993	Germany 1958/59	Germany 1992	France 1958/59	France 1993	Italy 1958/59	Italy 1993	Luxembourg 1957/58	Luxembourg 1993	Netherlands 1958/59	Netherlands 1993
Wheat	7	3	4	5	6	8	17	5	10	2	2	1
Other cereals[a]	2	1	4	4	2	7	4	5	1	3	3	…
Total cereals	9	3	8	9	8	14	21	10	12	5	5	1
Sugar beet	4	5	4	4	2	3	2	2	0	0	4	2
Fruit[b]	4	4	6	7	}12[c]	3	11	5	0	1	3	1
Vegetables[b]	11	14	2	3		7	9	14	0	1	7	11
Wine	0	0	2	4	13	11	13	8	7	9	0	0
Potatoes	5	3	5	2	3	1	2	1	3	1	5	2
Other crops	5	1	1	2	2	5	8	9	0	…	9	2
Total crops	38	30	29	31	40	46	66	49	23[e]	18	34	19
Beef/veal	16	20	16	14	16	15	9	10	16[e]	27	14	11
Pigmeat	12	19	24	18	11	6	4	7	23	7	14	14
Poultry	3	4	1	2	6[d]	7	3[d]	6	0	…	3	4
Eggs	9	3	5	3	4	2	5	2	6	1	10	3
Milk	22	14	24	24	19	18	11	11	34	45	24	23
Other livestock	1	…	…	…	3	1	1	1	…	0	1	…
Total livestock	62	60	71	62	60	49	34	37	78[e]	81	66	55
Other unspecified	0	10	0	8	0	5	0	14	0	1	0	25

[a] including rice

[b] 1990s excludes dried pulses and citrus fruit

[c] includes dried leguminous vegetables

[d] includes rabbits

[e] includes products not specified

… = production of 0.5 or less

Note: Due to rounding, subtotals and totals do not always coincide

Sources: Commission 1960; Agricultural Situation in the European Union: 1994 Report.

Sugar beet maintained its relative position extremely well over time which is probably a reflection of the fact that sugar is subject to a quota system very largely based on historical levels of production and its price structure has kept in line with that of other arable crops. The universal decline in the share of the total value of production represented by potatoes is partly due to changes in consumption habits and livestock feeding practices but also, no doubt, to the fact that this crop is not supported under the CAP (except to the very limited extent of potatoes grown for the manufacture of industrial starch). One of the most notable changes over time is in the increased importance of vegetable production in Belgium, Italy, and the Netherlands. It is perhaps surprising that the same kind of expansion has not taken place in the fruit sector as both are subject to very similar market regimes, where most of the emphasis is on the control of the import price, rather than on internal support mechanisms.[3]

On the livestock side, the distribution of final production between types of livestock enterprises has changed quite markedly in some countries. For instance, although pigs, poultry, and eggs are all subject to similar types of market support concentrated at the frontier, with little (pigmeat) or no (poultrymeat and eggs) internal support, their relative situation has followed quite a different pattern, depending on the Member State concerned. Pigmeat has declined in relative importance in Germany, France, and Luxembourg but has risen substantially in Belgium; poultrymeat has increased significantly only in Italy; and eggs have declined in all EC-6 countries, notably in Belgium and the Netherlands. The decline in the proportionate value of eggs has much to do with the changes in production patterns away from land-based flocks to industrial-type production with lower unit costs, combined with a static consumption level.

The share of final agricultural production represented by beef and milk has changed remarkably little over time, probably due to their dependence on the right climatic and soil conditions in the countries and regions where these are important enterprises. The only two countries of the original EC-6 to show any marked change over time are Belgium, where beef has increased and milk has declined in importance, and Luxembourg where both have increased substantially. Luxembourg is mountainous and therefore more suited to pasture-based enterprises—borne out also by the decline in that country in cereals and cereals-based products (pigs, poultry, and eggs).

Tables 3.3(*b*) and (*c*) provide similar information for the remaining Member States from the time of their Accession to the Community to the early 1990s. For Denmark, Ireland, and the UK this gives a twenty-year span. With the exception of wine production, these three countries were not very different from the Member States which they joined and the distribution of the value of output between the different crops in EC-6 in 1973 was hardly altered with the Enlargement—which is why the table does not provide a comparison of EC-9 with EC-6 in 1973. In general, the changes which took place in Denmark, Ireland, and the UK over time were quite small—particularly for total crops. Within that category, the expansion in the value of wheat production at the expense of other cereals is very noticeable in Denmark and the UK. The increase in the value of vegetables in

Table 3.3(*b*). Percentage distribution of agricultural production in value terms, by major commodity, 1973 and 1993: EC-9

Commodity	EC-9 1973	Denmark 1973	Denmark 1993	Ireland 1973	Ireland 1993	UK 1973	UK 1993
Wheat	6	2	8	2	1	7	11
Other cereals	5[a]	11[a]	4	4[a]	2	7[a]	4
Total cereals	11	14	12	6	4	14	15
Sugar beet	2	2	2	2	2	2	2
Fruit[b]	} 7	} 1	...	} ...	...	} 3	2
Vegetables[b]			2		3		8
Wine	7[a]	0	0	0	0	0	0
Potatoes	2	1	1	2	2	3	3
Other crops	7[a]	2[a]	3	...[a]	2	7[a]	2
Total crops	36	21	22	10	10	29	32
Beef/veal	15	14	8	35	39	17	15
Pigmeat	14	35	31	11	6	12	7
Poultry	5	2	2	3	3	7	7
Eggs	5	2	1	2	1	9	3
Milk	17	23	25	27	33	18	24
Other livestock	2	0	...	4	5	4	5
Total livestock	57	77	68	82	87	67	62
Other unspecified[a]	7	2	10	7	3	4	6

[a] estimated
[b] 1993 excludes dried pulses, citrus fruit
... = production of 0.5 or less
Note: due to rounding, subtotals and totals do not always coincide
Sources: Commission 1974(*a*); Agricultural Stuation in the European Union: 1994 Report.

the UK is quite surprising. The changes which have taken place in livestock products have been more significant: in Denmark and the UK the value of these products has declined over time as a proportion of total production, whereas in Ireland it has increased. The concentration on beef and milk in Ireland, already very high, intensified over the twenty years. The importance of beef and pigmeat has diminished in Denmark and the UK, whereas milk—especially in the latter—has become more important in terms of relative value.

The two Enlargements of the 1980s brought into the Community three countries with some very distinctive production features although, in the case of Greece, as it is a small country, its particular features were too insignificant to have an impact on the Community 1981 average. Table 3.3(*c*) provides a twelve-year comparison for Greece.[4] The most notable feature of its production pattern is the importance of 'other crops'. This category includes tobacco, cotton, olive oil, citrus, grapes, and table olives—all typical Mediterranean products. To a lesser extent this is also true of the production pattern of Spain, where olive oil and citrus fruit are important commodities. Table 3.3 (*c*) includes a comparison

Table 3.3(c). Percentage distribution of agricultural production in value terms, by major commodity, 1980s and 1993: EC-10 and EC-12

Commodity	EC-10 1981	Greece 1981	Greece 1993	EC-10 1986	EC-12 1987	Spain 1986	Spain 1993	Portugal 1988	Portugal 1992	EC-12 1992
Wheat	7	8	4	7	6	4	4	4	2	6
Other cereals	5	4	4	5	5	6	5	6	4	4
Total cereals	12	11	8	12	10	10	8	10	5	11
Sugar beet	3	2	1	3	2	2	2	0	0	2
Fruit[a]	4	9	7	4	4	6[b]	7	5	5	5
Vegetables[a]	7	10	13	7	9	12[b]	16	11	10	9
Wine	4	2	2	6	5	2[b]	3	4	6	6
Potatoes	2	3	3	2	2	3	2	4	5	2
Other crops	5	27	28	4	7	15[b]	13	6	8	6
Total crops	37	64	63	39	39	52	50	41	38	41
Beef/veal	15	5	3	14	12	7	7	13	10	12
Pigmeat	12	5	3	11	9	12	11	11	14	12
Poultry	4	3	3	4	4	5	4	8	9	5
Eggs	3	3	2	3	3	3	3	3	3	2
Milk	19	8	11	19	18	8[b]	8	13	14	17
Other livestock	2	9	6	2	1	5	5	4	3	2
Total livestock	56	34	29	52	46	40	39	52	52	50
Other unspecified[b]	7	2	8	9	14	8	11	7	9	9

a 1990s excludes dried pulses and citrus fruit

b 1985

Note: due to rounding, subtotals and totals do not always coincide

Sources: Agricultural Situation in the Community: 1982, 1987, 1989, 1990, and 1994 Reports.

of the components of production in value terms for EC-10 and EC-12 at about the time Spain and Portugal joined the Community. The major new influence was, of course, Spain and the two sets of statistics illustrate the extent to which its Accession affected the total distribution of production. The importance of vegetables and 'other crops' is notable, as is the unimportance of beef/veal, and milk.

For all three Mediterranean countries, membership of the Community has meant a decline in the proportionate value of cereals in total production, and for Greece and Spain an enhancement of the value of fresh vegetables. For Greece in particular, there has been a decline in the relative value of most livestock products. In Portugal, although the proportion of livestock products in total production has remained very static, there has been a significant reorganization within the sector: a decline in beef but an increase in pigmeat and milk—products more suited to the small size of farms.

The creation of a customs union and the adoption of a common pricing system should in theory permit and indeed encourage greater specialization. While it is no doubt true that at the individual farm level production systems have become more specialized, at the Member State level it is not at all clear that specialization has increased. The only exceptions are Ireland and Luxembourg where milk and beef account for nearly three-quarters of final production in value terms and where this overwhelming specialization has increased over time.

At the other end of the spectrum, the southern Member States have extremely diverse production patterns. For instance, in all four countries the top three commodities only account for something in excess of one-third of final production. The other peculiarity of the southern Member States is that the commodities which fill the top three production slots are not always the same. For instance, although in 1980, 1985, and 1990 vegetables were the most important crop in value terms in Italy, the next two in importance were beef and cereals (1980); milk and cereals (1985); and milk and beef (1990), not illustrated.

In the northern Member States, not only is there greater specialization but also greater consistency over time: beef, milk, and pigmeat (Belgium and Germany); beef, cereals, and milk (France and UK); cereals, milk, and pigmeat (Denmark); and milk, pigmeat, and vegetables (Netherlands), not illustrated. The order may change but not the commodities. However, it should be stated that, excluding the special cases of Ireland and Luxembourg, there is some small indication that the degree of specialization in the northern Member States is declining slightly. The tendency is strongest in Germany, Denmark, and the Netherlands. Why this should be the case is not immediately obvious and may not persist throughout the 1990s with the changes in the price and market support brought about by the MacSharry reforms and the GATT agreement (to be discussed in later chapters).

Little information was given in the 1960 CAP proposals on yields, either in terms of crops or livestock. In fact, yield data were provided only for wheat, barley, potatoes, sugar beet, milk, and eggs per laying hen. From this group, the data for wheat and barley are reproduced in Table 3.4(a)[5] which follows the 1960 format, i.e. the average, maximum, and minimum. However, whereas in 1960 no

Table 3.4(*a*). Yields of wheat and barley, late 1950s–early 1990s: EC range and average

		Wheat tonnes/ha.	Barley tonnes/ha.
EC-6, 1954/59:	**Average**	**2.2**	**2.4**
	Maximum	3.8	3.7
	Minimum	1.8	1.2
EC-9, 1973:	**Average**	**4.2**	**3.9**
	Maximum	5.3 Netherlands	4.6 Belgium
	Minimum	3.0 Italy	2.2 Italy
EC-10, 1981:	**Average**	**4.7**	**4.1**
	Maximum	6.7 Netherlands	4.9 Belgium
	Minimum	2.8 Greece	2.5 Greece
EC-10, 1986:	**Average**	**5.7**	**4.8**
	Maximum	8.0 Netherlands	6.2 Netherlands
	Minimum	2.6 Greece	2.6 Greece
EC-12, 1986:	**Average**	**5.0**	**3.7**
	Maximum	8.0 Netherlands	6.2 Netherlands
	Minimum	1.7 Portugal	1.0 Portugal
EC-12, 1993:	**Average**	**6.0**	**4.2**
	Maximum	8.8 Netherlands	6.4 Belgium
	Minimum	1.7 Portugal	1.5 Portugal

Sources: Commission 1960, 1974(*a*); Agricultural Situation in the Community: 1984, 1987, and 1994 Reports.

indication was given as to which Member State held the top and bottom positions, this information is provided in later years. Despite their limitations, the statistics speak for themselves. Although there has been a very appreciable increase in cereal yield over time, there is still a wide range between the highest and the lowest.

Table 3.4(*a*) also includes in a similar format the average, maximum, and minimum yields for the Community at the time of each Enlargement. The minimum EC-10 yield in 1981 and 1986 for both wheat and barley was the Greek average. The average, maximum, and minimum are also given in the table for EC-12 in 1986 to illustrate the impact made on the Community of the inclusion of Spain and Portugal (the minimum EC-12 yield for both commodities is that of Portugal). The table ends with the 1993 statistics: the highest wheat yield was— as usual—in the Netherlands, and the highest barley yield in Belgium.[6] The lowest for both crops was in Portugal. One has to wonder at the economic sense of growing these crops in Portugal in the 1990s with yield levels which would have been regarded as low in EC-6 in the late 1950s!

The first part of Table 3.4(*b*) provides comparisons over time for the original six Member States of the average milk yield. While the Netherlands retained its dominant position as the country with the highest milk yield per cow, the increase in yield 1958–93 was one of the smallest. The most notable improvement

Table 3.4(*b*). Milk yield per cow, late 1950s to early 1990s, EC-6, 9, 10, and 12 as appropriate

	Belgium		Germany		France		Italy		Luxembourg		Netherlands	
	1958	1993	1958/59	1993[a]	1958/59	1993	1958/59	1993[b]	1958	1993[b]	1958/59	1993
kg./cow	3,760	4,493	3,293	5,237	2,273	5,396	2,074	4,489	3,200	5,255	4,106	6,014

	EC-9 1973	Denmark		Ireland		UK		EC-12 1993[a]
		1973	1993	1973	1993	1973	1993	
kg./cow	3,600[b]	4,100[b]	6,583	3,000[b]	4,208[b]	4,100[b]	5,383[b]	5,132[b]

	EC-10 1982	Greece		EC-10 1986	Spain		EC-12 1986	Portugal	
		1982	1993		1986	1993		1986	1993
kg./cow	**4,314**	2,913	3,668[b]	**4,509**	3,251	4,167	**4,405**	3,383	4,344[b]

[a] includes eastern Länder
[b] estimate

Sources: Commission 1960; Agricultural Situation in the Community: 1975, 1984, 1988, and 1994 Reports.

was in France, moving up from fourth to second position in EC-6. Belgium slipped back relatively—which is perhaps in keeping with the decline in importance of milk in the total value of production shown in Table 3.3(*a*). The improvement in yield in Luxembourg suggests that its greater concentration on milk has brought productivity gains. The remainder of Table 3.4(*b*) provides information on the milk yield around the time of Accession for each of the remaining Member States, and the increase to 1993. Denmark has overtaken the Netherlands as the country with the highest average yield. The relatively low yield in Ireland can be attributed to the widespread preference for spring rather than autumn calving, and the greater reliance on grass, hay, and silage than on concentrated feed.

As will become clear from Chapter 6, the history of the price and market policy within the CAP was overshadowed by the growing problem of the disequilibrium in supply and demand, and the financial burden of the accumulation and disposal of surpluses. In this context, it is of some considerable interest to see how the level of self-sufficiency has changed over time. High levels of self-sufficiency are not a new phenomenon, as an examination of Appendix Table 3.A1(*a*)–(*c*) at the end of this chapter will demonstrate. The commodities chosen are the ones for which market regimes were envisaged in the 1960 proposals on the CAP. Within this group, at that time, the only major commodity with a low level of self-sufficiency was coarse grain for animal feed. The change over time in the original Member States is, in some cases, quite spectacular: the expansion of cereals and sugar in France; the increases in most livestock products in Belgium; the confirmation of the Netherlands as a major livestock product producer (even if self-sufficiency in poultry has declined). The increase in the level of self-sufficiency in cereals and sugar in Germany is noteworthy, accompanied as it has been by a decline in self-sufficiency in some livestock products. The lack of expansion in self-sufficiency in Italy for many commodities is quite striking, and exceptional to the general trend.

When the Community was enlarged in 1973, two net agricultural exporting countries with high levels of self-sufficiency were added. However, as Denmark and Ireland are small countries, their high self-sufficiency was very largely counterbalanced by the UK which had quite low levels for most products. As a result, the overall self-sufficiency of EC-9 was little different from EC-6 at that time. While expansion continued for many major products in Denmark and even more strongly in Ireland, the real interest must surely lie in the changes in self-sufficiency levels in the UK. The very appreciable increase in arable crops and in some of the livestock products indicates a high degree of dynamism in the farming sector. There is something rather ironic that in the country with the most critical attitude to the CAP—and indeed to the whole concept and process of European integration—the farmers should respond so spectacularly to the opportunities offered!

The Enlargements in the 1980s added two countries—Greece and Portugal—which did not have high levels of self-sufficiency for the main commodities and that has remained the situation in the intervening years. Indeed, in both, there has been a tendency for the levels of self-sufficiency to decline. Given their poor farming structure and soil conditions, it is likely that their present circumstances will be maintained. Spain in contrast was very largely self-sufficient when it joined the Community and so far there has been little change in that situation. The final column of Table 3.A1(c) indicates that for EC-12 the level of self-sufficiency was below 100 for only one of the commodities shown—fresh fruit. Comparing that situation with the starting-point for EC-6 (1958/59 in Table 3.A1(a)), it can be concluded that there is a direct relationship between the type of support regime and the increase in self-sufficiency. The commodities with the most effective systems of frontier protection and internal support are arable crops and milk. The increase in self-sufficiency in wine is not the result of increased production but rather is due to the sharp decline in consumption of table wine combined with an overgenerous internal support system which has slowed the decline in production.[7]

Data for the late 1980s indicate that the three new Member States which joined in 1995 are not dissimilar from EC-12 and as they are relatively small producers they should, in general, have little impact on the overall level of self-sufficiency. All three are surplus wheat producers (the highest self-sufficiency level was 169 per cent in Austria in 1987/89); Austria and Sweden are more than self-sufficient in sugar but Finland is a deficit area (81 per cent self-sufficient in 1989/91). All are surplus butter producers (Finland substantially so with 184 per cent self-sufficiency); Austria and, to a lesser extent, Finland are surplus producers of beef and veal (Sweden was 95 per cent self-sufficient in 1988/90). Finland and Sweden are surplus producers of pigmeat and eggs (Finland especially so for eggs, with 133 per cent self-sufficiency). Of course, only Austria is a wine-producer, with a self-sufficiency level of 76 per cent.[8]

Despite occasional scarcities, the increase in production over the lifetime of the CAP has taken place against a background of oversupplied international markets. Internally, the population is expanding very slowly (at less than 1 per cent annually) which rules out one possible source of market increase. Worse still: an already well-fed and mostly sedentary population worried by possible links between diet and disease is likely to reduce daily calorie intake and to be more selective in the choice of foods. Increases in consumption of some foods are combined with decreases elsewhere. The underlying construction of the diet differs markedly from one part of the Community to another so that even where consumption per head has increased there remain tremendous differences in consumption levels which cannot be attributed to income.

Table 3.5 illustrates some of these points: it contrasts three-year average consumption levels at the end of the 1960s for EC-9 with three-year averages in the mid-1980s for EC-12 and, additionally, provides the maximum and minimum consumption levels among the Member States which are hidden in the Community averages. Over the roughly twenty-year period, average consumption per head of cereals, potatoes, sugar, fruit, and wine all declined. In addition, while there is no EC-12 average available for fresh milk products, due to the absence of statistics for Spain and Portugal, the data for the individual Member

Table 3.5. Human Consumption of main agricultural products, (kg./head), "1968/69" and "1985/86"

Year	EC	Maximum		Minimum		EC	Maximum		Minimum	
		Cereals excluding rice[a]					**Potatoes**			
"1968/69"	**85**	Italy	128	Netherlands	66	**90**	Ireland	127	Italy	45
"1985/86"	**83**	Italy	114	Netherlands	60	**80**	Ireland	140	Italy	37
		Sugar[b]					**Vegetables[c]**			
"1968/69"	**36**	Ireland	51	Germany	32	**99**	Italy	165	Denmark	41
"1985/86"	**33**	Denmark	41	Portugal	26	**116**	Greece	194	Germany	72
		Fruit excluding citrus					**Citrus**			
"1968/69"	**65**	Germany	93	UK	35	**n.a.**	Italy	30	Belgium/ Luxembourg France	16
"1985/86"	**60**	Germany	79	Ireland	30	**28**	Netherlands	82	Denmark	11
		Wine[d]					**Fresh milk products[e]**			
"1968/69"	**51**	France Italy	111	Ireland	2	**103**	Ireland	256	Italy	61
"1985/86"	**44**	France	81	Ireland	3	**n.a.**	Ireland	195	Germany	63

Table 3.5. (*cont.*)

Year	EC	Maximum		Minimum		EC	Maximum		Minimum	
		Eggs					**Meat**[f]			
"1968/69"	**13**	Germany	15	Italy	10	**68**	France	81	Italy	48
"1985/86"	**14**	Germany	17	Portugal	6	**83**	France	96	Portugal	51
		of which pigmeat					Poultrymeat			
"1968/69"	**28**	Germany	43	Italy	11	**9**	France Italy	11	Denmark	4
"1985/86"	**37**	Denmark	58	Greece Portugal	21	**16**	Spain	21	Denmark	11
		Oils and fats					of which vegetable oils			
"1968/69"	**n.a.**	Netherlands	31	France	18	**n.a.**	Italy	19	Germany Belgium/ Luxembourg	13
"1985/86"	**26**	Netherlands	36	Ireland	20	**14**	Greece	24	Belgium/ Luxembourg	5

a flour equivalent
b white sugar equivalent
c including preserved vegetables
d litres/head
e excluding cream
f excluding offal
n.a. = not available

Notes: "1968/69" and "1985/86" are three-year averages with the year in inverted commas being the middle year. For milk, eggs, meat, and oils and fats, calendar years are used with the second year shown being the middle year. "1968/69" statistics are EC-6. "1985/86" statistics are EC-12 except for citrus, and oils and fats which are EC-9 except for milk products which is EC-10.

Source: Agricultural Situation in the Community: 1979 and 1994 Reports.

States indicate a reduction. While total meat consumption per head expanded, the only changes of any great significance were for pigmeat and poultrymeat. The decline in the consumption of fruit is particularly surprising.

As to the differences in consumption levels between Member States, for some commodities the gap has narrowed over time: cereals, vegetables, wine, fresh milk products, pigmeat, poultrymeat. For others, the gap has remained the same: sugar and fruit; and for a third group the gap has actually expanded: potatoes,[9] citrus, eggs, total meat, oils and fats and, within this group, vegetable oils especially. There is no reason to believe that this very mixed picture will not continue for the foreseeable future.

The second measure of consumption used in this chapter is that of household expenditure on food. It is more usual to find statistics on food, beverages, and tobacco as a unit but it is much more useful to look at food expenditure alone, firstly because this is the main end-use of agricultural production, and secondly because expenditure on food tends to fall as income rises, whereas expenditure on beverages tends to do the opposite. An additional problem with the statistics for beverages and tobacco is that expenditure on these commodities is quite distorted because of the considerable variation in the level of excise duties applied in the Member States.

Table 3.6 provides data from 1975 to 1992 and, as might be expected over such a period, household expenditure on food declined as a proportion of total consumption expenditure. For EC-9 Member States, the 1992 level was somewhere

Table 3.6. Share of household consumption expenditure spent on food (%)

	1975	1981	1986	1992
EC	**n.a.**	**14**	**16**	**15**[a]
Belgium	20	17	18	15
Germany	17	14	13	11[b]
France	20	18	17	15
Italy	31	26	24	17
Luxembourg	n.a.	16	15	11[c]
Netherlands	20	15	15	11
Denmark	21	17	16	15
Ireland	26	24	24	18
UK	18	15	14	11
Greece		36	33	29
Spain			24	18[d]
Portugal			33	25[a]

a 1989
b excludes eastern Länder
c 1991
d 1990

Source: Agricultural Situation in the Community: 1977, 1983, 1984, 1989, 1990, 1991, and 1994 Reports.

between one-half and three-quarters of the 1975 level. The decline in Spain and Portugal over the short period since they joined the Community was one-quarter, and in Greece there was a decline of one-fifth between 1981 and 1992. In earlier times, when the proportion of income spent on food was much higher (as it was when the EC was established), the cost of food was a major preoccupation of governments. Today, this is not the case except, perhaps, in the two poorest Member States. This does not mean that there are no poor households in even the richest countries—far from it. But what it does imply is that such households should be helped to secure a good healthy diet, either by means of better employment prospects or by means of social security support, rather than through the manipulation of food prices in general.

There are two other policy implications: the first is that Table 3.6 indicates that the gap in the proportion of household expenditure devoted to food is widening between Member States. While many factors may be involved, relative income levels are clearly of importance and in a Union which is dedicated to the promotion of greater economic convergence more attention should be paid to the implications of these food expenditure data. The other policy implication is that, because the price which consumers pay is influenced more by the value added after the raw material has left the farm than by what the farmer is paid, changes in the producer price have little impact on the proportion of household expenditure spent on food. Marketing and processing costs are, in general, more important than the raw material cost.

EC Share of World Agricultural Trade

So far the statistics in this chapter have illustrated the increase in production, the rise in self-sufficiency, the mixed message from the per capita consumption data, and the decline in the level of household consumption expenditure being spent on food. What then is the position of the Community in the wider context of world trade? Table 3.7 provides an overview based on three-year averages from the late 1970s to the early 1990s for some of the major agricultural commodities to enter world markets.

The first and perhaps most surprising feature of this table is that, although world production has increased for practically all commodities shown, world trade is remarkably static. Not only that, but also for most of the commodities international trade represents a very small proportion of total production. Set against this background, the performance of the Community over time is most revealing. Not only have imports to the EC for most products declined as a percentage of world trade and exports increased but also in commodities such as cereals, feed grain, and meat a net trade deficit has been turned into a net trade surplus. For other commodities such as oilseeds (imports), wine, butter, cheese, and milk powder (exports), the Community is such a major player in the limited international market that what it does in trade policy has the power to make a major difference to the state of those markets.

Table 3.7. World production and trade in some agricultural commodities ('000 tonnes), and the EC share of that trade (%)

Year	World production	% traded[b]	EC share in trade		World production	% traded[b]	EC share in trade	
			% imports	% exports			% imports	% exports
	Cereals excluding rice[a]				Feed grain (excluding rice)[a]			
"1977"	1,204.4	12	16	5	762.9	11	24	3
"1986"	1,365.4	13	5	13	845.4	10	6	8
"1991"	1,407.0	14	3	16	839.4	11	4	11
	Oilseeds				Wine			
"1977"	194.4	14	46	…	28.6	9	22	27
"1986"	227.0	15	46	…	31.3	6	9	73
"1991"	260.7	13	43	…	27.6	5	18	75
	Sugar				Butter			
"1977"	105.2	23	8	10	7.0	8	23	37
"1986"	114.7	24	7	17	7.6	11	10	49
"1991"	125.8	23	7	18	7.3	10	9	32

Table 3.7. (cont.)

Year	World production	% traded[b]	EC share in trade	
			% imports	% exports
Cheese				
"1977"	10.5	5	15	36
"1986"	13.4	6	13	48
"1991"	14.5	6	12	52
Total meat[d]				
"1977"	133.4	3	18	8
"1986"	155.1	4	12	22
"1991"	179.6	4	10	22

Year	World production	% traded[b]	EC share in trade	
			% imports	% exports
Milk powder[c]				
"1977"	6.7	19	...	50
"1986"	6.5	30	1	42
"1991"	6.1	31	...	47

[a] grain only: processed products excluded
[b] calculated on the basis of exports (excluding intra-EC trade), and excluding processed products
[c] skimmed and whole
[d] excluding offal; salted meat included in world production but excluded in trade
Source: Agricultural Situation in the Community: 1980, 1989, and 1994 Reports.

Farm Size

Changes in production levels are not only influenced by factors such as price and yields but also by the availability of the means of production. Two such inputs were discussed in the 1960 proposals: land and labour. The measures which were used were simple ones: the number of hectares per holding and the number of persons working on the farm. These simple measures have been superseded by a range of more sophisticated ones, nevertheless they still have their uses—if for no other reason than that they are intuitively easier to understand. Measures related to the size and shape of the farm business will be discussed in Chapter 5.

Farm size changes very slowly over time, as the proportion of farmland coming on the market for sale or renting is small at any one time. Farms can only be increased in size by amalgamation and this requires either that farmers join forces (as sometimes happens within families or where neighbours combine in a joint venture) or that land is released by other farmers leaving the sector (through death, retirement, finding other employment, etc.). As the number of farmers declines more slowly than the decline in other sections of on-farm employment—family members and hired workers—the amount of land available for amalgamation is limited. Nevertheless, over a period as long as the lifetime of the CAP, changes can be observed.

A large farm is not necessarily more efficient in economic terms, although economies of scale are important for certain enterprises. The relationship between productivity and size of enterprise is a complex one and dependent on many factors. However, the physical size of the farm remains important if for no other reason than the fact that more land provides the farmer with more options in terms of production choices. Farmers may be unwilling to risk a new venture if its introduction would require the use of too high a proportion of the available resources, especially land. The change in the size distribution of farms shown in Table 3.8(*a*) and (*b*) is an indication of the awareness of farmers of the continued importance of the physical dimension of their farms.

The 1960 proposals on the CAP did not actually include a statistical table to illustrate the size distribution of holdings but the statistics used in Table 3.8(*a*) would have been available shortly after the proposals were drawn up. They are compared with 1989, which gives almost a thirty-year time-span. The most obvious change over time is the sharp decline in the proportion of holdings under 10 ha. or, in France, Luxembourg, and the Netherlands, under 20 ha. The Italian statistics are nothing short of amazing to the point that one must seriously question their accuracy. They indicate that there has been practically no change in structure in a generation![10] With the exception of Italy, the marked increase in the two largest size categories is very noticeable, particularly in France and Luxembourg where in 1989 50 per cent or more of farms were of 20 ha. and over. The dominance of large farms in France is consistent with the expansion of cereals, while the dominance of large farms in Luxembourg is consistent with its concentration on upland extensive grassland systems for beef and milk. The

Table 3.8(a). Distribution of holdings of >1 ha. by size group, about 1960 and 1989: EC-6

Size category	Belgium 1959	Belgium 1989	Germany 1960	Germany 1989	France 1960	France 1989	Italy 1961	Italy 1989	Luxembourg 1960	Luxembourg 1989	Netherlands 1959	Netherlands 1989
1–<5 ha.	48	27	44	29	27	20	65	67	32	19	38	25
5–<10	27	17	25	17	21	12	20	17	18	10	27	19
10–<20	18	23	21	22	26	18	10	9	26	12	23	23
20–<50	6	26	9	25	20	31	4	5	22	29	11	28
50+	1	7	1	7	6	19	1	2	2	30	1	5

Table 3.8(b). Distribution of holdings of >1 ha. by size group, early 1970s and 1989: EC-9, EC-10, and EC-12

Size	EC-6 1973[a]	EC-9 1973[a]	Denmark 1973	Denmark 1989	Ireland 1970	Ireland 1989	UK 1973	UK 1989	EC-10 1980	Greece 1980	Greece 1989	EC-10 1985	Spain 1989	Portugal 1989	EC-12 1989
1–<5 ha.	**46**	**42**	12	2	17	11	16	11	**46**	72	70	**45**	55	74	**49**
5–<10	**19**	**18**	20	15	20	14	13	13	**17**	20	19	**17**	18	13	**16**
10–<20	**17**	**18**	29	25	30	29	16	16	**15**	6	8	**15**	12	7	**13**
20–<50	**14**	**16**	32	39	25	35	26	26	**16**	2	3	**16**	9	3	**14**
50+	**4**	**6**	7	19	8	12	29	34	**6**	0	0	**7**	6	2	**8**

[a] Ireland and Italy 1970

Source: Commission 1968(*d*); Agricultural Situation in the Community: 1975, 1986, 1988, and 1994 Reports.

retention of a significant proportion of small-to-medium sized farms in Belgium is consistent with the increase in the importance of vegetable production indicated in Table 3.3(*a*).

Table 3.8(*b*) provides an interesting contrast to the original Member States. When Denmark, Ireland, and the UK joined the Community they already had a much higher proportion of medium and large farms than the EC-6. That difference still remains. Their size structure in 1973 was sufficiently different to show up in the statistics for EC-6 and EC-9, as indicated in Table 3.8(*b*). In Denmark and Ireland, only the holdings of 20 ha. and upward are expanding, while in the UK only the largest size group is increasing proportionately. In sharp contrast are the three Mediterranean countries which joined in the 1980s. In 1989, their farm structure remained more heavily skewed to the smallest size category (under 5 ha.) than the original Six nearly thirty years previously. Coupled with the Italian statistics referred to above, it is quite clear that, in terms of physical structure, farming in the European Union today is composed of two quite different subsectors: one with a preponderance of tiny farms, the other with a preponderance of medium to large farms. The final point of interest is that the Accession of Spain and Portugal, with their distinctive Mediterranean-type size distribution, was sufficient to alter the Community overall size distribution (see EC-10 in 1985 compared with EC-12 in 1989).

Labour Force in Agriculture[11]

While farm size has been rising slowly the farm workforce has been falling consistently and sharply over time, as is illustrated in Appendix Table 3.A2. In thirty years (1960–90), EC-10 has lost two-thirds of the workforce in the sector 'agriculture, hunting, forestry, and fishing' of which, of course, the bulk were in agriculture. By any standards, this has been a social revolution yet, by and large, it has been achieved peacefully. Much of the credit can be given to the CAP which has cushioned this change. It is, however, worth bearing in mind that if agriculture had not lost so much labour the income situation in the sector would have been far more serious. There is a fairly clear trend for the rate of decline in employment to slow down over time.[12] There could be a number of reasons for this: employment opportunities in other sectors have not been so freely available in recent years as they were in the 1960s; fewer young people are going into farming today so that the decline in the agricultural workforce is more likely to be attributable to retirement and death than to migration to other employment; and the proportion of farmers combining two occupations has increased slowly over time, thereby reducing the incentive—or perhaps even the necessity—to quit agriculture completely.

While the total workforce in agriculture has undergone a major contraction during the lifetime of the CAP, a much more ambiguous message can be found in the statistics on the distribution of the workforce by age. Appendix Table 3.A3 contrasts 1975 (EC-9) with 1992 (EC-12). This period is long enough to encompass an intergenerational handover of many farms in EC-9. One of the surprising features of this table is the increase in the proportion of younger people working on farms. Very few farmers inherit a farm before the age of 35 but the proportion of the workforce in that age-group has increased over time. For instance, in the Netherlands, which has tended for many decades to have a young workforce in farming, the proportion under 35 rose from 32 per cent in 1975 to 42 per cent in 1992. This cannot be attributed to a lowering of the retirement age as, even in 1975, the proportion of farmers aged 65 and over was low by EC-9 standards. The Netherlands is an extreme example of a wider phenomenon: Table 3.A3 indicates that the proportion of the farm workforce under 35 was higher in each Member State included in EC-9 in 1992 than it was in 1975. In four of these countries, the proportion had risen to over 30 per cent (Belgium, Luxembourg, Denmark, and the UK).

Is this indicative of a reconsideration of the advantages of entering or remaining in the farming sector? Is it an indication of the limited employment opportunities elsewhere in the economy? It is hard to know as, at the time of writing, statistics were not yet available for 1992 by type of labour force (i.e. farm heads, spouses, other family members, regularly employed non-family members). However, over the 1980s there was an increase in the number of farm heads in Denmark, Germany, France, Ireland, and the UK; an increase in the number of family members (excluding spouses) in Belgium, France, Italy, Luxembourg, and the Netherlands; and an increase in the number of regularly employed non-family members in Belgium, Denmark, Luxembourg, and the Netherlands.[13] As the 1980s were years of rising unemployment, it is very likely that people remained in the farming sector or sought employment there who otherwise might well have left.

One change which does seem to have taken place over the years represented in Table 3.A3 is that farmers are beginning to retire at the normal age of retirement. The decline in some Member States between 1975 and 1992 in the proportion of the farm workforce aged 65 and over is very striking. This is particularly true of Germany and France and, although the statistics are not available to demonstrate it, it must also be true by inference in Luxembourg. The proportion of elderly workers in Denmark, Ireland, and the UK in both years is striking and in 1992 anomalous in being so high. The general decline in the proportion of elderly persons in the agricultural workforce cannot be attributed to the attempts to persuade farmers to retire through early retirement schemes which have been something of a disappointment (see Chapter 8). It is probable that the social pressure for the self-employed to follow a work pattern more akin to that of the employed has reached farming, and that their financial ability to retire has increased also.

The third of the tables on labour force relates to the important issue of the extent to which farmers specifically have another gainful occupation (this is an issue which re-emerges in Chapter 4). Appendix Table 3.A4 provides data for 1989 only, which was the latest year available at the time of writing. No comparison with earlier years is made, as the way in which the information was expressed changed. However, even within Table 3.A4 doubts on interpretation arise: apparently all farmers in the Netherlands are full time in the sense that they have no other gainful employment. This stretches credulity!

There is considerable variation between the Member States not only in terms of the proportion of farmers with no other gainful employment (a range of 56 per cent (Germany) to 82 per cent (Luxembourg), excluding the Netherlands), but also in relation to the importance of other sources of employment; for instance, the high level of secondary employment in France, the UK, and especially in Denmark. While there may be definitional difficulties involved, what is clear is that a sizeable number of farmers are not wholly dependent on their farm for their income. Some farmers are probably also entitled to social welfare payments of various kinds and, of course, the household may also contain other members with gainful employment.

Budgetary Cost of the CAP

There is so much controversy on the cost of the CAP that this overview chapter could hardly end without some reference to this issue. More detailed information appears in Chapter 6 on the cost of support of the individual commodities under the price and market policy. Table 3.9 is limited to the total cost of FEOGA within the Community Budget, and to the place of the Guarantee Section (i.e. the price and market support) within that FEOGA total. The table starts with 1982 purely because from that date information on the net cost of FEOGA-Guarantee as a percentage of GDP was also provided.

It is important not to read too much into year-on-year changes in the proportion of the total Budget represented by FEOGA because many short-term factors intervene and, indeed, changes have taken place over time on the exact location within the Budget of certain items of expenditure. That said, however, there does seem to be a slight drift downwards in the proportion of the Budget attributable to FEOGA, although the optimistic estimates for 1993–5 should be treated with some caution.

This also applies to the decline in the share of the Guarantee Section in the total cost of FEOGA. When one considers what the original intention was—as outlined in Chapter 2—the overwhelming concentration of support on prices and markets and the resulting failure to tackle underlying structural defects comes sharply into focus. For all the discussion of the cost of the CAP, in truth in terms of GDP, it costs remarkably little. One is tempted to wonder what all the fuss is about! This heretical thought is reinforced by the final measure on Table 3.9: the cost of FEOGA per head of population. This measure is available only from 1987 onwards. It shows that the cost is spiralling upwards—but it is a pretty small spiral and does not appear—as yet—to be out of control.

If a group of the wealthiest countries in the world choose to spend considerably less than 1 per cent of their GDP on the agricultural sector, it hardly seems a wild extravagance. One might take issue with the distribution of the

Table 3.9. Budgetary cost of the CAP (m.ECU), 1982–1995

Year	Total budget	Total FEOGA[a]	FEOGA as % of budget	Total Guarantee	Guarantee as % of FEOGA	Net Guarantee as % of GDP[b]	CAP cost per head (ECU)
1982	20,705.8	13,055.6	63	12,405.6	95	0.4	
1983	24,807.6	16,539.6	67	15,811.6	95	0.5	
1984	27,208.8	19,022.7	70	18,346.5	96	0.6	
1985	28,085.1	20,463.8	73	19,744.2	96	0.6	
1986	35,174.1	22,910.9	65	22,137.4	97	0.6	
1987	35,469.2	23,875.1	67	22,967.7	96	0.6	64
1988	41,120.9	28,829.8	70	27,687.3	96	0.6	80
1989	40,917.8	27,225.2	66	25,872.9	95	0.6	75
1990	44,378.9	28,402.1	64	26,453.5	93	0.7	77
1991	53,823.1	34,541.7	64	32,385.9	94	0.6	92
1992	58,857.0	35,185.4	60	32,107.5	91	0.6	95
1993c	65,268.5	38,337.8	59	34,748.1	91	0.7	105
1994c	68,354.6	37,532.4	55	34,786.9	93	0.6	101
1995c	76,526.1	39,946.9	52	36,972.5	92	0.6	108

a total FEOGA from 1990 onwards contains a small amount of expenditure not attributable to either Guarantee or Guidance
b income from levy charges under the CAP is deducted from Total Guarantee to give net Guarantee
c provisional

Source: Agricultural Situation in the Community: 1986, 1990, 1993, and 1994 Reports.

available funds in terms of price support as opposed to structural aid; or in terms of the appropriateness of the particular groups of farmers who receive the greatest benefit; or in terms of the proportion of the funds which actually find their way to farms as opposed to other parts of the production chain; or in terms of the relative incidence of support as between commodities, regions, or Member States—but such discussion is little heard.

NOTES

1. These proportions were further altered in 1995 with the Accession of Austria, Finland, and Sweden. The total area of the Union increased by 37% but utilized agricultural area by only 7%. Population increased by 6%.
2. Of the three Member States which joined in 1995, Finland with about 9% of the working population in agriculture and Austria with 7% were above the EU-12 average; Sweden had 3% in agriculture.
3. One has to be a little careful about interpreting these statistics. Apart from the two categories of fresh fruit and fresh vegetables, the 1990s statistics include a third category 'other fruit and vegetables' which covers dried pulses and citrus fruit. This has been included in Table 3.3(*a*) under 'other crops'. However, its existence may go some way to explaining the apparent major decline in fruit in Italy. It is very likely that citrus was included with the rest of fruit in the 1950s statistics. There is no way of knowing.
4. Although Greece joined in 1981, value of production statistics were not available until 1983.
5. Potatoes are not included in the table as this crop is not supported under the CAP, although proposals have been made from time to time to introduce a potato regime. At the time of writing, such a proposal was once again being discussed. As for sugar beet, no comparison can be made over time as the basis of calculating yield has changed; for laying hens no comparable data are available.
6. An important reason why such unlikely countries are at the top of the performance league is that usually, in countries which are not major producers, cereals are only grown on the most suitable land. Ireland is another example of this phenomenon (for instance in 1993 wheat yield there was 7.8 tonnes/ha.).
7. Self-sufficiency statistics should always be treated with caution when based on the results of one year only, as production can vary quite markedly from one year to another, particularly for commodities such as wine or fruit and vegetables. It is better to use three-year averages but this was not always possible in the present context.
8. The data used in this paragraph were taken from the Commission's Opinions on the application for membership of Austria (Bull. EC Supp. 4/92); Sweden (Bull. EC Supp. 5/92); and Finland (Bull. EC Supp. 6/92).
9. Whether one can believe either of the Irish consumption figures for potatoes is open to question, as the three-year averages down the years varied and were revised on a regular basis in the most amazing manner.
10. Even more bizarre is the confirmation of the 1989 statistics in the national 1993 survey of farm size. There, holdings of 1–<5 ha. represented 66% of all holdings of 1

ha. and over. The only other differences from the 1989 results are: 5 ha.–<10 = 16%, and 20–<50 = 6% (INEA 1995).

11. Labour force statistics are very confusing. They are not all calculated on the same basis and therefore the total number employed in the sector varies somewhat depending on which source and definition are used. However, the differences are not sufficiently large to undermine the conclusions which can be drawn from the statistics.

12. There are a few exceptions to this general trend, e.g. Italy 1990/1980 compared with 1980/1970, and the Netherlands which actually recorded an increase in the decade of the 1980s. Whether this will be confirmed or is a statistical error remains to be seen.

13. These statistics are to be found in the Agricultural Situation in the European Union 1994 Report.

Table 3.A1(a). Level of self-sufficiency % in major commodities, late 1950s and early 1990s: EC-6

Commodity	EC-6 1958/59	Belg./Lux		Germany		France		Italy		Netherlands	
		1958/59	1992/93	1958/59	1989/90	1958/59	1992/93	1958/59	1992/93	1958/59	1992/93
Wheat	92	67	77	65	121[d]	109	273	107	84	29	46
Coarse grain[a]	75	37	65	67	105	99	270	85	79	31	21
Sugar	108	148	222	104	141	104	235	103	116	116	167[f]
Butter	101	98	101	98	96	101	92	76	76	180	510
Cheese	100	34	40	75	96	104	117	100	85	210	266
Beef and veal	92	101	179	90	120	100	122	72	69	105	179
Pigmeat	101	100	178	93	86	104	91	90	65	149	278
Poultrymeat	97	102	103	60	58	102	149	95	98	392	185
Eggs	90	109	124	56	76[d]	97	99	83	95	216	318[d]
Fresh fruit[b]	100	103	81	85	22	81	86[e]	128	117	117	63[f]
Wine	92	18	119[c]	63	88[d]	74	113	115	127	3	0

[a] in 1992/93, the self-sufficiency for barley is used
[b] in 1958/59 excludes citrus fruit and nuts; in 1992/93 excludes citrus fruit and covers only fruit subject to support regimes
[c] Luxembourg only
[d] 1990/91
[e] 1989/90
[f] 1991/92

Source: Commission 1960; Agricultural Situation in the European Union: 1994 Report.

Table 3.A1(*b*). Level of self-sufficiency % in major commodities, 1972/73 and
1992/93: EC-9

Commodity	EC-9	Denmark		Ireland		UK	
	1972/73	1972/73	1992/93	1972/73	1992/93	1972/73	1992/93
Wheat	97	120	152	56	83	52	131
Barley	107	101	88	96	124	98	147
Sugar	92	125	189	108	150	32	65
Butter	106	323	194	203	1,233	23	54
Cheese	102	246	365	522	404	61	74
Beef and veal	84	219	204	534	977	69	85
Pigmeat	100	458	414	172	126	63	75
Poultrymeat	102	315	229	111	110	97	90
Eggs	99	123	101	100	89[c]	98	95
Fresh fruit[a]	76	56	20[b]	25	14[d]	32	19[e]
Wine	89	0	0	0	0	0	0

[a] excludes citrus
[b] 1987/88
[c] 1990/91
[d] 1991/92
[e] 1988/89

Source: Agricultural Situation in the Community: 1975 and 1994 Reports.

Table 3.A1(c). Level of self-sufficiency % in major commodities, 1980s and 1992/93: EC-10 and EC-12

Commodity	EC-10 "1981/82"	Greece		EC-12 "1985/86"	Spain		Portugal		EC-12 1992/93
		"1981/82"	1992/93		"1985/86"	1992/93	"1985/86"	1992/93	
Wheat	127	158	132	124	94	98	38	21	133
Barley	116	96	82	119	104	115	49	25	123
Sugar	141[a]	110[a]	88[b]	123	109	79	2	1	128
Butter	122	61	29	n.a.	154[c]	180	100[c]	131	121
Cheese	107	89	80	n.a.	88[c]	89	94[c]	99	107
Beef and veal	103	49	28	107	95	100	87	79	108
Pigmeat	101	84	65	102	97	98	97	88	104
Poultrymeat	110	101	94	105	98	94	100	105	105
Eggs	102	99	99	n.a.	99[c]	97	101[c]	102	101
Fresh fruit[a]	85	141	122	87	116	94	95	78	85
Wine	102[a]	107[a]	120	104	118	117	113	117	115

[a] "1982/83"
[b] 1991/92
[c] 1988

n.a. = not available

Note: years in quotation marks are the average of three years

Source: Agricultural Situation in the Community: 1984, 1989, 1990, and 1994 Reports.

Table 3.A2. Persons employed[a] in agriculture, hunting, forestry, and fishing, 1960–1993: EC-12

Member States	'000s					Annual percentage change			1990 as % of 1960
	1960	1970	1980	1990	1993	1970/1960	1980/1970	1990/1980	
Belgium	300	176	116	100	n.a.	-5.3	-4.1	-1.5	33.3
Germany	3,581	2,262	1,403	990	849	-4.5	-4.7	-3.4	27.6
France	4,180	2,647	1,784	1,248	1,101	-4.1	-3.9	-3.5	29.8
Italy	6,611	3,878	2,899	1,863	1,504	-5.2	-2.9	-4.3	28.1
Luxembourg	22	12	7	6	6	-5.0	-5.2	-1.5	27.2
Netherlands	408	289	244	289	n.a.	-3.4	-1.7	+1.7	70.8
Denmark	362	303	199	150	140	-3.0	-4.1	-2.8	41.4
Ireland	390	283	209	169	144	-3.2	-3.0	-2.2	43.3
United Kingdom	1,134	806	669	603	547	-3.5	-1.8	-1.0	53.1
Greece	2,019	1,279	1,016	889	794	-4.5	-2.3	-1.3	44.0
Portugal	n.a.	984	1,052	805	n.a.	n.a.	+0.7	-2.6	81.8[c]
Spain	n.a.	3,310	2,228	1,486	1,198	n.a.	-3.9	-4.0	44.8[c]
EC-12	19,007[b]	16,230	11,830	8,599	7,198	-4.5	-3.1	-3.1	33.1[b]

[a] 'Persons employed' includes all persons working for remuneration or self-employed, plus unpaid family workers. Persons employed in more than one economic sector are counted only in the sector in which they mainly work.

[b] EC-10

[c] 1990 as % of 1970

n.a. = not available

Source: Agricultural Situation in the Community: 1990 and 1994 Reports.

Table 3.A3. Age structure in agricultural, selected years 1975–1992 (%)

Age-groups	EC-9 1975	EC-12 1992	Belgium 1975	Belgium 1992	Germany 1975	Germany 1992	France 1975	France 1992	Italy 1975	Italy 1992	Luxembourg 1975	Luxembourg 1992	Netherlands 1975	Netherlands 1992
>25 years	9.0	9.3	10.7	8.9	8.1	9.1	8.8	6.3	8.2	8.6	10.3	11.3	13.0	18.6
25–34	13.8	18.1	15.0	22.9	12.9	19.0	13.7	20.2	12.4	20.4	11.2	20.8	19.3	23.0
35–44	23.0	19.5	22.6	18.4	25.8	19.6	21.8	24.7	24.0	20.1	18.0	20.8	22.1	19.1
45–54	28.8	22.7	31.1	23.4	25.7	22.5	31.8	23.4	31.0	24.5	27.4	22.7	22.4	19.9
55–64	17.4	23.5	18.0	24.2	15.7	22.5	16.3	21.9	18.3	20.7	18.4	n.a.[b]	18.7	16.2
65+	7.9	6.9	2.7	2.2[a]	11.7	7.3	7.6	3.5	6.2	5.7	14.5	n.a.[b]	4.5	3.2

Age-groups	Denmark 1975	Denmark 1992	Ireland 1975	Ireland 1992	UK 1975	UK 1992	Greece 1986	Greece 1992	Spain 1986	Spain 1992	Portugal 1986	Portugal 1992
>25 years	7.6	14.3	10.8	10.3	13.5	14.3	9.2	7.8	14.1	10.5	18.7	8.1
25–34	14.8	17.8	14.3	16.5	19.2	22.6	12.0	11.3	14.7	15.8	12.0	11.5
35–44	19.1	15.6	17.0	19.7	19.6	18.3	17.5	16.2	16.4	18.5	15.2	14.2
45–54	25.6	20.5	21.6	19.5	23.2	19.0	26.7	24.1	24.9	22.6	21.9	20.3
55–64	23.8	20.0	22.0	19.7	17.6	15.9	24.9	31.0	25.5	28.9	21.5	28.0
65+	9.2	11.8	14.2	14.3	7.0	9.9	9.8	9.6	4.5	3.6	10.8	17.9

[a] estimate
[b] not available but 55 and over can be estimated at 24.4%

Source: Agricultural Situation in the Community: 1977, 1988, and 1994 Reports.

Table 3.A4. Proportion of farm heads who were full-time or part-time employed on the farm, 1989: EC-12

	No other gainful employment	With other main gainful employment	With other secondary gainful employment
EC-12	68.0	26.1	5.8
Belgium	65.8	32.0	2.2
Germany	56.5	34.7	8.8
France	72.7	15.6	11.8
Italy	69.7	27.9	2.5
Luxembourg	81.6	14.2	4.5
Netherlands	100.0	0.0	0.0
Denmark	66.4	11.8	21.8
Ireland	73.8	20.5	5.7
UK	70.4	17.3	12.3
Greece	67.6	26.4	6.1
Portugal	63.6	32.3	4.1
Spain	65.8	28.5	5.7

Source: Agricultural Situation in the European Union: 1994 Report.

4

Income Levels: *Perception of the Problem and Policy Responses*

The Definition of the Target Group

In the review of agricultural policy in the 1950s in Chapter 1, mention was made of the way in which concern with farmers' incomes came to dominate policy objectives and instruments. In general, the 'income problem' was perceived as the situation in which per capita incomes in farming lagged behind those earned in other sectors of the economy. Thus attention was concentrated very largely on the return to labour rather than to the other factors of production. The analyses of the problem tended to be vague and the remedies put in place were usually not well targeted.

Coppock (1961, 514) summed up the approach very accurately in describing the attempts to 'protect' farmers' incomes through price support:

In most countries, the governments undertake to assure for certain commodities specific prices which they deem will give most growers 'reasonable profits' on their farming operations. Given differing efficiency, sizes of holdings, quality of soil and various other factors entering into costs of production, it is clear that the maintenance of a price to provide a 'reasonable profit' to a politically sufficient number of agriculturalists is indeed a blunt tool. The price of a crop required to maintain a farm family on a small holding of poor land at or above subsistence level is bound to provide a wide margin of profit for a more efficient farmer working a large holding of good land.

Nearly four decades later, the issues raised in this passage remain valid and continue to bedevil agricultural policy, including the CAP. The fundamental question remains: what type of farm or farmer is policy aiming to protect? The Spaak report referred to 'the maintenance of an adequate level of income for normally productive farms' (Comité Intergouvernemental 1956, 48) as one of the objectives of the proposed common agricultural policy. This idea was expanded in the Rome Treaty where it was stated that those who work in agriculture are to achieve a 'fair standard of living' by means of increased productivity. The emphasis was placed very firmly on the need to raise 'the individual earnings' of the workforce (Art. 39.1(a) and (b)).

Given this background, it is not surprising that phrases such as 'reasonable income' or an income level 'comparable to that of workers in industry' were frequently heard at the Stresa Conference, but with no elaboration as to what exactly was meant. The use of product price support in the framework of a managed market was the most common way in which governments attempted to raise the level of incomes in farming. Krohn and van Lierde (1963, 246), both of whom were Commission officials, described the Commission's intention that: 'prices for products subject to intervention should offer a fair income reckoned over a period of years to persons working full time on farms which are economically viable and well managed, but not on all farms, or even on the average farm'.

However, it was in recognition of the limitations of price manipulation as a means of supporting the incomes of the weakest farmers that the Commission's proposals on the CAP were based not just on market policy but on four elements: market, commercial, structural, and social. Of course, as outlined in Chapter 2, the four pillars crumbled at the first hint of sustained opposition from traditionalists who preferred to continue to rely on price support within a managed market for the achievement of economic, structural, and social goals.

Krohn and van Lierde went on to state that social motives or the public interest required that even non-viable farms should be enabled to earn a fair income but that this should be done through structural, regional, and social policies: 'If neither structural nor regional measures prove sufficient, then measure in the field of social policy will have to be taken in the form of supplementary payments on income. These payments . . . should be regional, temporary and degressive' (Krohn and van Lierde 1963, 247).[1]

This quotation highlights the fact that agricultural policy has not been concerned solely with the economic concept of productivity and the exploitation of comparative advantage but that it has had a social dimension as well. Because of their organizational structure and the composition of their workforce, farms are not necessarily profit-maximizing enterprises. This does not mean that farmers are insensitive to price signals but it does mean that they need to balance the interests of the farm with those of the family unit which owns or rents it.[2]

The position of the 'family farm' as the basis of agriculture was acknowledged in the Spaak report and it was expected to continue in its dominant role. No definition was given of 'family farm' but the report did comment that 'some system would have to be found to reconcile this farm structure with the development of modern methods of production and trade' (Comité Intergouvernemental 1956, 47). The Rome Treaty made no direct reference to the family farm but did refer to the 'social structure of agriculture' and the need to bear it in mind when devising and implementing the CAP (Art. 39.2). The Stresa Conference was notable for the emphasis placed on the family farm, especially in the final declaration which referred to a unanimous wish to safeguard the existence of the family farm and that every effort should be made to raise its economic and competitive capacity (Communautés Européennes 1959).

Mansholt (1959, 203) used the term 'healthy family farm' which he defined as 'an enterprise which in its natural context and its social, technical and economic structure is able to ensure full time rational employment for two or three permanent workers who are also responsible for its management.' This definition found an echo in the Commission's draft proposals on the CAP: 'the family farm should be understood as an enterprise which permits . . . two or three full-time

workers to be occupied effectively . . . and which . . . , given rational management, allows a fair family income in relation to comparable groups of workers'
(Commission 1959, II/10).

This definition was immediately criticized in the European Parliament (Assemblée 1960) where the Lücker report recommended a minimum size structure
of one or two full-time workers as the basis for a fair income for a farm family.
This reduced size was reflected in the Commission's final proposals in COM(60)
105 where the family farm was defined as 'an enterprise which enables effective
employment to be given to at least one or two full-time workers (the lower limit)
whom a family may include in its varying composition as the generations develop, and which, if efficiently managed, can ensure for each worker an income
that is fair in relation to other comparable occupational groups' (Commission
1960, II/14).

Reading between the lines of the text, one senses a certain degree of irritation
by the Commission at the change in definition and the hint of ideological conflict. The text of the 1960 proposals puts the development of the family farm in
a wider context of:

an agricultural structure in which farms of various types and sizes complement each
other, and in which the farm operating with paid labour—a farm that is sound from the
socio-economic point of view—will have its place. This diversity will also permit a
division of labour between family farms and enterprises employing wage earners which
may well help to maintain the balance between supply and demand on agricultural
markets. In this respect, the family farm and the enterprise employing wage-earners
should both be considered as forms of the European agricultural structure which are
economically and socially justified. (Commission 1960, II/14).[3]

The concept of the family farm was further refined at the Rome Conference
(Commission 1962, 62) where it was described as:

an agricultural enterprise where the work required for rational production is provided
essentially by the family members and which—in the case of small farms—is adequate to
ensure full employment for at least one or preferably two work units. In addition, it ought
to be able to ensure for its workers an individual income sufficient for modern life and,
for as many as possible, equal to the average income of workers in other sectors. Finally,
it should provide to the farmer an income not only for his manual work but also for the
management and capital employed.

With every new attempt to define basic concepts new difficulties emerged. Was
the only distinguishing feature of the family farm the fact that it did not use hired
labour? But, if the farm was to ensure an *individual* income comparable to that
obtained by some other group of workers, it surely suggested the payment of a
wage to the family members which brought them much closer in concept to hired
workers. How was income comparability to be assessed? What group in society
performs tasks comparable to the work of farmers? Was the farm income to
remunerate all factors of production or only labour and, if capital and management were included, did comparability with non-agricultural occupations extend
to them also?

These issues—which were never resolved and which continued to cause difficulties in later years—are of some considerable importance first, because they provided a framework within which the market policy and the price support levels chosen were to function and secondly, because the ideal family farm was far removed from the actual circumstances which existed at that time.

Some of the speakers at the Stresa Conference had shown an awareness of the dangers of fixing support prices at socially acceptable levels. For instance, Forget—the Belgian Agricultural Minister—stated that 'the level of prices should be based on the average production costs obtained in rationally managed farms, using the most progressive techniques' (Communautés Européennes 1959, 91). Mansholt warned that if the future market policy was based 'on the level of production costs on insufficient or submarginal enterprises, all attempts to improve structure are virtually lost' (ibid. 106). Lübke, who presided over a high support price policy in Germany, queried the effectiveness of such a policy to improve the agricultural income situation because of the increase in surpluses. Price support measures 'contribute only in a limited way to a definite and, above all, lasting improvement in the situation in agriculture. Even more, to a considerable extent they prevent agricultural production from adapting to changes in market conditions' (ibid. 47).

At no stage during the late 1950s and early 1960s does there seem to have been any serious enquiry as to the viability of family farms, although a quotation from the 1960 price proposals (given in Chapter 2) certainly indicates that the Commission was concerned with the questionable viability of the two-thirds of all farms which were below 10 ha. In 1959, the European Parliament, in the Vredeling report, had discussed the income issue but were hampered by the absence of a suitable measure, partly because the statistics were out of date and partly because of the difficulties of making valid cross-border comparisons. They fell back on the statistics in the Stresa report, where agricultural production per head of the active agricultural population was taken as a percentage of non-agricultural income in 1956. The results ranged from 38 per cent in Italy to 76 per cent in the Netherlands, with the other four Member States between 54 and 58 per cent of non-agricultural incomes. The Vredeling report also pointed out that gross investment in agriculture as a percentage of total gross investment was below the percentage contribution of agriculture to national income (Assemblée 1959).

As the 1960s progressed, the debate shifted away from the family farm and concentrated instead on the efficient farm and income comparability. Apart from occasional passing references, the family farm did not resurface until the mid-1980s. A notable example of its revival appeared in the *Perspectives for the CAP*, where the Commission stated that 'an agriculture on the model of the USA, with vast spaces of land and few farmers, is neither possible nor desirable in European conditions, in which the basic concept remains the family farm' (Commission 1985(*b*), II). As most farms in the USA are family-owned, it is hard to understand what the Commission meant.

However defined, the family farm was back in fashion and renewed concern with its well-being proved to be useful in shifting the priorities in the CAP. Thus, later in 1985, a new policy guideline was announced which was: 'to deal more effectively and systematically with the income problems of small family farms' (Commission 1985(*d*), 5). In 1987, the Commission described itself as 'loyal to the pattern of farming approved at Stresa, it has opted for the maintenance of the family farm' (Commission 1987(*b*), 22). In the price proposals the same year, the Commission referred to the particular need to provide 'proper support for family farms, which are not only an irreplaceable aspect of the European identity but also have all the potential of sound and effective business units and thus deserve every assistance in their transition through the present period of adjustment' (Commission 1987(*a*), 2).

What is interesting about the rediscovery of the family farm is that the circumstances of the 1980s were totally different from those thirty years previously and yet the Commission thought it worth while to link its thinking on new directions for the CAP with the emotionally appealing—if vague—notion of the family farm.

The Efficient Farm and the Goal of Income Comparability

By the Commission's own admission, the farm on which it hoped to base market policy was a small production unit. Given the farm structure in EC-6, it was not a surprising choice; however, it did mean that the production costs—even on the best-managed farms—were inevitably high, as the farms were too small to benefit from economies of scale. This put the new Community at a disadvantage in comparison with many agricultural exporting countries elsewhere in the world. In addition, there was the immediate concern that the introduction and operation of the CAP would, in itself, adversely affect the incomes of some farmers. The Commission stated that in such cases 'special aid to maintain incomes in the areas or enterprises affected may be justified by social considerations or [be] required by the length of time it takes to convert farms or improve their structure' (Commission 1960, II/7). The original proposals on FEOGA were intended to meet the needs of this group of farmers (see Chapter 2).

Apart from any general disruption due to the introduction of a new price and market policy, there was the specific need to harmonize the price support levels operated by the individual Member States, starting with cereals. For some, this entailed a reduction in the level of support prices and therefore a fall in farmers' incomes. At that time (1963), the Commission stated that such an outcome would be contrary to the spirit of the Rome Treaty (as expressed in Article 2), and to the objectives of the CAP (in particular Art. 39.1(b)). Thus, accompanying the proposals on the establishment of a common price level for cereals, provision was made for farmers adversely affected.

Four types of compensation were proposed: (a) direct payments to farmers whose incomes were due to fall because of the lowering of cereal prices; (b) improvements in social welfare payments to farmers and their families; (c) aids for the improvement of productivity and the rationalization of agriculture; and (d) aids to producers of durum wheat (Commission 1963(f)).

The direct income payment would have been temporary and independent of the price of agricultural products and the factors of production. The payment could have been taken as a lump sum to assist in the rationalization of the farm, afforestation of marginal land, or transfer to the non-agricultural sector. In the event, the Community chose a different path to common prices and this package of measures was never implemented but it is an interesting speculation that if, in 1963, the concept of direct income aid as a substitute for high support prices had been accepted, the history of the CAP in the following thirty years might have been quite different.

Towards the end of the 1960s, the Commission acknowledged that, whatever had been the initial intention, the reality was that the price policy had been established largely on the basis of social considerations and that this was likely to remain the case so long as the existing production structure persisted. The smallest farms received little benefit from the market and price policy, while some of the most competitive farmers were receiving an unwarranted economic rent. This created important disparities within agriculture. The pace of structural change was so slow that, when new farms were created, they were already out of date economically and technologically. The real problem was that farms were continually being marginalized.

Despite all efforts, agricultural structure continued to be imperfect: most farms were physically very small, leading to even smaller individual enterprises. The sector was hampered by the preponderance of elderly farmers, many of whom did not have the basic education which would allow them to adapt easily to changing economic and social conditions. The limited potential of many farms and the absence of alternative or additional sources of income forced farmers to farm very intensively in order to achieve even a minimum income. This meant they could not adapt to changing market requirements.

Despite the improvements in productivity which had taken place, the gap between agricultural and non-agricultural incomes remained wide, with little chance of it being removed—even if commodity prices were raised. Similarly, agriculture itself contained many income differences, with a few well-placed farms able to generate an income comparable to those in other economic sectors but with many others on which the income was very low. By itself, market and price policy could not provide a solution to the fundamental difficulties of agriculture.

Indeed, the Commission was aware that, in some ways, the price policy was actually making the income situation worse. At that time, market intervention was open-ended—that is, there was no limit on the quantity of a product which could be withdrawn from an oversupplied market, provided it met the Community's minimum quality standards. In addition, market support was based on high prices and together these elements of the policy were an encouragement to the maintenance of marginal farms. As a result, the labour market in agriculture was distorted; price policy acted as a brake on the decline in the number of farmers. A reduction in their number was essential as one of the ways in which the incomes of the remainder could be improved.

The Commission decided that much more drastic action was required if it was ever going to be possible to ensure a fair income and better living conditions for those in farming and, at the same time, bring about the necessary balance between supply and demand. It was with these aims in mind that the Commission launched the Mansholt Plan (Commission 1968(*a*)) on a startled Community.[4]

The Commission suggested a two-pronged approach: immediate modifications to the price and market support mechanisms to achieve better market balance, and the adoption of long-term measures to improve the structure of production. The long-term measures can be grouped under three broad headings: changes in the organization of production, a reduction in the area devoted to farming, and the adaptation of marketing structures. The Commission regarded its proposals on production as the most important. They were divided into measures concerned with the people who wished to transfer to another occupation or to retire, and those concerned with the people who wished to remain in a reformed farming sector.

It was proposed that, to an ever-increasing extent, agricultural production should be located in efficiently managed farms, that is, those on which farm accounts were kept, where there was a development plan, and which were of such a size that those who worked on them would benefit from an income and a way of life comparable to that enjoyed by equivalent socio-economic groups. In order to achieve this goal, the Commission suggested the creation of new types of farms, namely 'production units' and 'modern farm enterprises'. The size of a production unit (PU) was dependent on the commodity involved but in all cases would have been large enough to allow the use of the most effective methods of production. It could have been formed out of a single farm or through a group of farmers coming together to carry out the particular activity in question. The Commission believed that this approach would have been particularly useful in non-specialized, small farm regions, where farmers could have combined to carry out part of their activities jointly. This would have helped to improve living conditions but have retained the individual characteristics of each farm unit.

The Commission gave examples of the minimum sizes of PUs which it envisaged. The range allowed for differentiation according to region:

arable crops (grain and root)	80–120 ha.
milk	40–60 cows
beef	150–200 cattle
poultry	100,000 birds per year
eggs	10,000 layers
pig fattening	450–600 pigs at a time

The modern farm enterprises (MFE) envisaged by the Commission would have been large enough to yield a standard and quality of living comparable to that enjoyed by other people. This meant not just an acceptable income but also that those who worked on these farms should have a reasonable number of

Table 4.1. Average herd sizes, 1973 and 1991 for selected Member States

Member States	Dairy herds		Cattle herds		Pig herds	
	1973	1991	1973	1991	1973	1991
EU-12	—	18.4	—	37.4	—	66.1
Belgium	11.7	27.6	27.9	58.2	68.1	393.5
Germany	—	17.3	—	40.9	—	76.4
France	11.0	25.0	26.2	51.1	21.0	81.5
Italy	5.0	12.9	9.2	23.6	7.1	23.5
Luxembourg	13.6	30.9	40.8	81.9	28.0[a]	75.7
Netherlands	23.7[a]	40.1	45.8	78.5[a]	132.3[a]	472.3
Denmark	15.0	35.8	33.9	62.6	81.6	345.2
Ireland	9.6	24.5	27.9	35.3	32.3	397.8
UK	38.2	65.6	69.3	85.6	141.7	453.4
Greece	—	4.5	—	10.4	—	20.1
Spain	—	8.2	—	17.7	—	40.1
Portugal	—	3.9	—	7.0	—	15.4

[a] 1975

Source: Commission 1974(*a*); Agricultural Situation in the European Community: 1976 and 1994 Reports.

working hours per day, have free time during the week, have holidays, and be able to cope with illness. The MFEs would have been formed from existing farms of suitable size or would have been created by a number of farmers coming together—ideally through the fusion of a number of PUs. The minimum size of the principal enterprises in the MFEs would have been similar to those suggested above for the production units, except for pigs, poultry, and eggs which would have been expected to be twice the size.

These proposals were not overambitious in terms of what was technically possible but they were stunning as medium-term policy objectives given the prevailing production systems of the vast majority of Community farmers. Even more than twenty years later some of the herd sizes would have been regarded as large. Table 4.1 illustrates this point for dairy cows, cattle, and pigs; (comparable data are not available for the other commodities—arable crops, poultry, and eggs). While the average dairy herd size in 1991 in the UK would have met the Mansholt 1968 target comfortably and the Dutch and Danish herd sizes would have been nearly large enough, no Member State in 1991 was anywhere near the cattle herd target of 1968. Mansholt must have based the proposed size on North American feed-lot production systems. The nearest that some Member States came in 1991 to meeting the target set in 1968 was for pigs. It is perhaps worth noting that the average herd sizes for dairy cows, cattle, and pigs in Greece, Portugal, and Spain in 1991 would have been small by the standards of most of the original Member States in the early 1970s. How these Southern countries can expect to compete with the more serious producers of northern Europe is difficult to comprehend.

Not surprisingly the Mansholt proposals ran into difficulties, to the extent that, in 1969, the Commission felt it necessary to provide an explanation and justification of its proposals.[5] Given that the intention was to raise individual incomes in agriculture in such a way that they would follow the income trend in other sectors, the Commission stated that the only solution was to raise labour productivity in farming. This could be done in four ways: raise production; lower production costs and improve farm organization; increase the real price of agricultural commodities; or reduce the agricultural workforce. The Commission ruled out the possibilities of increasing production or real prices. The Mansholt Plan was intended to reorganize production and help surplus labour to leave farming. The Commission gave examples of the economies of scale which could be achieved from increased enterprise size and stood firmly behind the proposals it had made on the need for farm enlargement and minimum enterprise size.

Not surprisingly the proposals were seen as an attack on the family farm. The point was made that a large enterprise was not necessarily economically viable: it depended on how it was managed. The proposals were regarded as too bureaucratic, in that they concentrated on a rigid view of the ideal minimum individual enterprise size and ignored the possibility of enterprise combination as a means of achieving viability.[6] In addition, there was no guarantee that the creation of these enterprises would eliminate the need for price support—the USA providing a good example. Most ominous among the criticisms from the Member States was the outspoken disapproval of both government and opposition in the Federal Republic of Germany.

Early in 1970 Mansholt indicated that the concepts of the production unit and the modern farm enterprise were to be dropped. When the Commission presented its legislative proposals on structural reform to the Council of Ministers in April 1970, farm modernization was defined in terms of gross output per labour unit. It was estimated that, over a five-year period, a total of 320,000 farmers would put forward development plans and achieve the desired income level (Commission 1970). In commenting on the proposals, the ESC (JO C60, 14–6–71) quoted a figure of 300,000 farms which were already viable. Together these two groups represented just below 15 per cent of the 4.4m. main-occupation farms in the EC-6 and, if part-time farms were included, 5 per cent of the total 6.4m. farms in the Community. Perhaps more than anything else, these statistics illustrate clearly the income problem as it was perceived at the time when the CAP price and market policy was coming into full operation.

The end of the 1960s and the early 1970s were years of turmoil for the new CAP.[7] The devaluation of the French franc and the revaluation of the German mark in 1969 threatened the newly agreed common price structure which, essentially, was based on fixed exchange rates. Inflation was rising; the biological and technological improvements in agriculture, which were a notable feature of the 1960s, were slowing down. The disposal of surplus production was becoming a major concern for the Commission but it failed to convince the Council of Ministers of the need to take urgent steps to tackle it. There was considerable farmer unrest, with demonstrations and riots protesting about their income levels. The situation was not helped by the inability of the Council of Ministers to agree on institutional price levels for the 1969/70 and 1970/71 farm-years. Thus, in effect, the 1968/69 price levels remained in place for three years. By the end of 1970, the CAP was in the throes of yet another of its periodic crises.

At a series of meetings with the Commission in December 1970, the Council of Ministers finally agreed in principle to link the forthcoming 1971/72 price proposals with socio-structural reform. As a result, early in 1971 in conjunction with the price proposals, the Commission presented the Council with a Communication and draft Resolution on the new orientation of the CAP, in COM(71)100 (Commission 1971(*a*)). In this document the Commission reiterated its concern with the state of the farming sector and, in particular, with the unfavourable economic and social situation of those in agriculture compared to other economic sectors. Many farmers were faced with growing income problems and the cost of support was constantly rising. Price policy by itself could not solve these difficulties: its most important drawback was that it applied indiscriminately to all farmers, irrespective of their economic circumstances. The result was that the gap between the already viable farms and those which were in need of restructuring did not narrow.

The Commission argued that, so long as the Community continued to use one policy instrument only, it would be impossible to lessen the income disparities within farming. Moreover, the absence of a Community structural policy was leading the Member States to apply national measures to assist those of their farmers who were in the greatest difficulties. This trend was threatening the existing achievements of the CAP. The Commission reminded the Council of the possible enlargement of the Community which was then in sight and pointed out that the existing Member States would be joined by a number of others with better-organized farming sectors than those in the Community.[8]

It is clear that discussion on the draft Resolution was detailed and far-reaching: many minor points as well as the broad principles were settled, as can be seen from the Resolution as finally passed by the Council (JO C52, 27–5–71). The general tone of the Resolution is restrictive and, compared with the 1970 reform proposals, left a greater number of activities in the hands of the Member States, without Community participation. With regard to modernization of farms, the Resolution differed from the draft in the method of calculating the results to be achieved by the end of the modernization plan, and in the number of labour units to be used in drawing up such plans. The first of these changes replaced the use of gross output per labour unit and substituted a straight comparison of the labour income in agriculture with that received in non-agricultural activities in the same region. The second change altered the basis of the modernization plans from at least two labour units to a theoretical basis of one or two labour units.

Both of these changes can be regarded as detrimental to the spirit of modernization. The first can be criticized because it replaced an output-based measure linked to the type of product and the conditions of production, with a simplistic comparison of agricultural and non-agricultural incomes, without any regard to the circumstances in which either was earned. The second change can be criticized on the grounds that it was a capitulation on a fundamental point. Two of the main reasons why the Mansholt Plan was so concerned with the size of farms were that larger units would yield a better income, and that they would ensure improved working conditions, by getting away from the idea of a farm unit being run in isolation by one person (or by an equivalent of one labour unit).

Further revisions to the proposal followed and it was not until April 1972 that the Directive *on the modernization of farms* was finally adopted by the Council of Ministers (Sp. OJ 1972 II). There, the comparable income was defined as the average gross wage for a non-agricultural worker in the same region, and Member States were free to adjust this to take account of differences in the social security arrangement between farmers and other workers. The size of the farm was defined in principle in terms of either one or two man-work units. Only farmers who received 50 per cent or more of their income from the farm and who worked on the farm for at least half their working time were eligible to be considered for development assistance.

As mentioned above, the years following the publication of the Mansholt Plan in late 1968 had seen a considerable deterioration in the economic circumstances of the Community and the wider world. It was not a very good time to ask farmers to invest in modernization and to expect them to achieve over a six-year period an income comparable to that earned in non-agricultural employment. Whatever the practical drawbacks, the fact remains that for the first time the Community had an income target for farmers, an agreement that price policy and structural policy were linked, a mechanism whereby farmers could be helped to achieve the income target and, if they were unable to reach the target set, a scheme to help them to leave farming. The logical outcome of these policy developments was that, in future, the price proposals each year needed to do no more than keep viable farms in that condition and assist in the balancing of supply and demand. As events were quickly to show, this was a wildly optimistic assessment of the future relationship between price and structural policy. However, starting with the price proposals for 1972/73, the Commission adopted a new approach to the calculation of price support levels. This was known as the 'objective method'.

The Objective Method

In COM(71)650, in proposing price changes for 1972/73, the Commission outlined its task as being to decide for which products would a price rise be possible, and what level of increase would be necessary and sufficient to stabilize the incomes of farms which had already achieved the comparable income standard (Commission 1971(*b*)). The basis of its calculations was an analysis of the results from a sample of farms which had obtained, during the farm year 1968/69, levels of labour income and a remuneration of capital which corresponded to those which had been obtained in non-agricultural sectors. In its comments on the price proposals, the European Parliament spelled out more fully exactly what this involved (JO C124, 17–12–71). The Commission took account of the trend in non-agricultural incomes; the trend in factor costs in agriculture and the return on invested capital; the rate of technical and biological progress in agriculture; and the situation on agricultural markets.

Early in 1972 the 1972/73 price proposals were revised and the Commission took the opportunity to make additional comments on the objective method. It stressed that this approach to the price proposals was intended as no more than a guide and that it was neither able to nor should it replace decisions of a political nature (Commission 1972). No doubt the Commission felt it necessary to reassure the Council of Ministers that it still had a role to play in setting prices. However, the political motivation of the Council was one of the factors which undermined the Commission's attempt to introduce some element of economic logic to the annual price-fixing exercise. The ESC, in 1974, recalled that it had 'repeatedly stressed the dangers of the method used by the Council to fix agricultural prices, a method based essentially on a search for a political compromise. Reference to *objective criteria* is provided for in the Treaty of Rome, but a political compromise cannot, by definition, take account of such criteria' (OJ C115, 28–9–74, 26). It remains true that in every proposal which the Commision makes, it must have regard to what it believes will be acceptable to the Council.

There were other reasons also why the objective method began to break down almost as soon as it was introduced. The market situation for individual commodities in surplus was such that the attempt to curb further expansion of production had to take precedence over the income situation of the farmers who produced that commodity. The price policy was based on the concept of fixed exchange rates and the institutional prices were expressed in units of account (a forerunner of the ECU). The exchange rates used to convert these prices to national currencies bore little resemblance to the market rates of exchange which, during the 1970s, were subject to severe fluctuations. Thus the farmers in any Member State gained or lost in an arbitrary way due to the fluctuation of their country's currency. These exchange rate distortions were directly linked with the wider economic problems of the time: severe inflationary pressures, rising unemployment, a slowing down of economic growth, and major disruptions to the international markets for agricultural commodities and raw materials in general.

In 1977, the Commission summarized the limitations of the objective method: it applied only in units of account and not in national currencies; it provided a quantitative guideline only on the development of common prices and not on their absolute level; it looked only at the average increase needed and not at the individual commodities; it was an approximation of the needs of the farming community and did not take into account the market situation for different commodities, the general economic climate, and the interests of consumers; and it did not reflect the actual development of agricultural incomes (Commission

1977(*b*)). Another drawback, although not one pointed out by the Commission, was that the calculations of income were based on a very small sample: in 1975/76, 2,000 farms out of 20,000 in the data accountancy network had achieved a comparable income. As the ESC stated: 'the 2000 farms are insufficiently representative, given the total number of farms in the Community (5,400,000)' (OJ C47, 27–2–75, 29).

The futility of the exercise can further be illustrated by the 1975/76 price proposals for which the objective method produced a result which meant that the modern farm needed a price rise of 12.4 per cent to maintain parity with non-agricultural incomes. The Commission argued that this figure was distorted by the high levels of inflation in Italy. An adjustment was made to take account of this factor, resulting in a proposed increase of 6.5 per cent. The Commission regarded this as too low and proposed an overall price rise of 9 per cent (Commission 1974(*b*)).

As the years passed, references to the objective method became fewer until, by 1982, it was being referred to as the 'so-called' objective method. The problem was that movements in exchange rates and in the green rates used to calculate agricultural support prices created significant distortions in the level of price adjustment needed to maintain the viability of the efficient farmer. Thus, the objective method produced different results depending on the rate of exchange chosen (Commission 1982(*a*)). Effectively, therefore, the concept was dead.

The Community still operates on the basis that a modern farm should yield an income comparable to the average non-agricultural wage in the same region. This may have some merit as a target but in other respects is quite meaningless and it does nothing to tackle the issue of the range of income levels between regions, types of farms, and Member States. Nor does it necessarily coincide with the way in which farmers perceive their income needs and goals. In 1981, in a review of the CAP, the ESC made the point that farmers have more than one perception and that the particular circumstances dictate how they define comparability:

'Comparable' is a difficult concept: many farmers, for instance, only have part-time occupation on their farms, and land is a very special form of capital, whose value is itself partly dependent upon the levels of intervention and aid under the CAP. Nevertheless, this is a fundamental objective, both for economic reasons—agriculture must be able to attract in the market the capital and skills it needs—and for social reasons—those who work in agriculture should not be an underprivileged section of the Community. (OJ C348, 31–12–81, 29)

This is a much more nuanced view of comparability.

The history of the objective method is a good illustration of the difficulties encountered in the use of price policy as the main means of supporting farmers' incomes. The objective method was intended to free price policy from the dual role of market clearance and income support. For it to have had any chance of success, it should have been accompanied by other measures of direct income support, which is the subject of the next Section.

Direct Income Aids Linked to Changes in Policy[9]

Earlier in this chapter, reference was made to the attempt to introduce direct income payments to compensate farmers for the change in support levels brought about by the creation of the common price level for cereals. The countries concerned were Germany, Italy, and Luxembourg. The package of measures proposed in 1963 was never implemented, although subsequently these three countries did receive Community funds with which to compensate their cereal farmers in 1967/68–1969/70. A special section was created in FEOGA for this purpose.

Another early example of a direct income aid was the suggestion (it never got as far as a formal proposal) that certain milk producers should receive a direct social payment independent of production. Even in the early 1960s, milk was already a problem commodity and the Commission was keen to put in place a series of measures which it hoped would prevent the creation of a long-term commitment to heavy expenditure for the disposal of surpluses. At the same time, it recognized that plans to curb production could result in income difficulties for producers heavily dependent on milk. The subsidy would have been limited to particular regions or types of farming (Commission 1963(*d*)).

These early examples were specific to difficulties being experienced in the production of a particular commodity. Much wider issues came to the fore in the Mansholt Plan. The reform of agriculture envisaged there was based on measures to remove surplus labour of all ages from farming, the creation of farm enterprises of an adequate economic size, the improvement of the operation of markets, and the adjustment of supply to demand. In order to achieve the desired results, the Plan envisaged that it might be necessary to provide a personal aid to farmers who would not be in a position to benefit from the modernization and retirement assistance being offered. These personal aids would have been independent of the volume of production and the inputs on the farm. They would have been granted within limits set by the regional situation, and the age of the farmer or farm worker involved.

Subsequent proposals by the Commission did not reflect these intentions, an omission criticized by both the ESC and the European Parliament.[10] The Commission tried to meet some of the objections by proposing the introduction of an income aid for those farmers with a low income, who were aged 45–55, who could neither modernize nor find alternative employment, and who would agree to leave farming when they reached 55 (i.e. the age at which the proposed early retirement scheme became operational) (Commission 1971(*a*)). This proposal was not endorsed by the Council of Ministers in its *Resolution on the new orientation of the CAP* (JO C52, 27–5–71).

Despite this, there was a genuine problem which came to the fore once more when the Commission, in its price proposals for 1972/73, based its calculations for the first time on the objective method. In COM(71) 650, the Commission divided farmers into three groups: those who already earned a labour income comparable to the non-agricultural level and whose capital earned a proper return; those who fell below this level but whose farms were capable of being developed with the assistance of an investment aid and a degressive income aid during the lifetime of a development plan; and a third category who were not in a position to use the modernization aid and whose income was so low that the price policy was not very relevant to their circumstances (Commission 1971(*b*)).

For this third group, who were mostly aged 45–55, the Commission proposed a temporary income aid under the condition that they would leave farming at 55 under the proposed early retirement scheme.[11] The Council of Ministers remained opposed to the idea of a temporary income aid of this kind and, when it finally agreed to the structural Directives in 1972, no scheme for middle-aged poor farmers was included, and the early retirement scheme which was enacted was limited to those aged 55–65 (Sp. OJ 1972 II). This scheme was so hedged around with qualifications as to make it virtually useless.

The logic of the need for a direct income aid in circumstances in which the price proposals were based on modern farms seems irrefutable. It will be recalled from the previous Section than an estimated 300,000 farmers were already earning a comparable income and that a further 320,000 were expected, over a five-year period, to benefit from the modernization scheme. To these 620,000 farmers can be added those who were expected to retire, approximately 1.2m.[12] Together these groups account for under 2m. farmers. This left about 4m. farmers (plus family members and hired workers) who either had to find employment in other sectors or who were to remain in agriculture with little prospect of earning an adequate income.

The existence of this group was widely recognized but, in the face of opposition from the Council of Ministers to make provision for it, even the Commission began to play down the problem. In 1973, it stated that it had 'reached the conclusion that additional measures in the form of . . . direct aid to farm incomes might well form an obstacle to the structural changes needed in agriculture, engender major administrative difficulties in most of the Member States, and entail unduly heavy expenditure for official budgets' (Commission 1973(*d*), 4).

Given the opposition of the Member States, commentators began to shift the emphasis away from compensating farmers who could not earn a comparable income to schemes intended to help farmers for some reason unconnected with price-fixing. For instance, it was suggested that farmers could receive aid in regions where incomes were low generally and agriculture was the dominant sector, or where farming was difficult due to natural conditions, or where it assisted in environmental protection, or where there were particularly high expenses at the time of intergenerational transfer. So widespread were these ideas that the farmers' organizations began to become concerned about the possible erosion of the dominant position of price policy.

While they accepted the role of income aids for certain categories of farmers, such as those in less-favoured areas, or those setting up in farming, or about to retire, they rejected 'any general policy of aids to income as a substitute for an effective price policy. Such a policy, which would bring farmers as a whole into the category of those socially assisted, is wrong in principle, is costly to apply and is difficult to manage. Farmers must in the main look to the market for their returns and not become too dependent on budgetary decisions' (COPA/ COGECA 1975, 10).

This, of course, is the heart of the matter: farmers and governments alike wish to believe that price policy can solve the income problem in agriculture, despite all the evidence to the contrary since the end of World War II. Farmers also like to maintain that economic principles and not social subsidies underpin the price level set. As Bergmann (1980, 13) commented: 'In national accounting terms, the concept of transfer is fairly well defined. There already are huge transfers accruing to the agricultural sector. Why should they be gladly accepted when they are hidden . . . and considered evil when they are in the form of direct payments?' Ministers for Agriculture and their departments collude with farmers in their preference for price support. The complexities of operating a managed market help to maintain their power base within government which, significantly, has not been eroded by the decline in the importance of agriculture in terms of gross domestic product and employment.[13]

Despite the reluctance to admit that price policy alone could not solve the problems of the farming sector, events forced the parties involved to rethink its role. The 1970s were difficult years for the economy as a whole. There was increasing unemployment, so that the possibility of farmers and members of their family finding work in other sectors became less of an option. Within agriculture, there was almost total saturation of the market, due to the rise in the level of self-sufficiency, and markets abroad were only available with the use of expensive export subsidies. The cost of the CAP was rising at a time when there was growing public resentment of farmers. It was clear that a more selective use of policy instruments was required, particularly because so many farmers were still perceived as having an income problem.

The Commission made a number of announcements in the course of the 1970s of its intention to examine further the use of direct income aids as a means of alleviating hardship. The obvious reluctance of the Commission to move in this direction was in sharp contrast to the enthusiasm of many agricultural economists, who saw direct support as a means whereby the Community could lower commodity support prices while offsetting the negative income effect on certain groups of producers.[14] Of course, the academic economists did not have to try to implement such a scheme nor did they have to persuade the Council of Ministers and the farmers to accept the implications of such a policy development. Williamson (1980, 9), the then deputy Director-General for Agriculture in the Commission, queried whether it would be possible 'to achieve the necessary rigour in the setting of prices because governments would not be prepared to abandon their medium or bigger farmers to the pressures which might be necessary'. He also drew attention to a real political difficulty for governments 'in terms of precedents for other groups such as small shopkeepers or small business who are under real financial pressure . . . because of the economic situation generally' (ibid.).

Whatever the misgivings, the circumstances of the time forced a policy re-think. In 1981, the Commission spelled out the reality facing the farming sector:

[F]arm income considerations, important though they may be, cannot be the sole point of reference for fixing guaranteed prices; it is neither economically sensible nor financially possible to give producers a full guarantee for products in structural surplus; given the Community's degree of self-sufficiency for most agricultural products and bearing consumers' interests in mind, prices must reflect market realities more than they have in the past. (Commission 1981(*b*), 11)

In this context, the Commission put forward guidelines for future decisions on the CAP which included 'the possibility of income support subsidies to certain producers in specific circumstances' (Commission 1981(*b*), 12). Because of cost, such subsidies would be confined to small producers and 'a Community con-tribution to their financing could be envisaged' (ibid. 13). The dangers in this approach were considerable, partly for the reasons cited by Williamson above and partly, as the ESC pointed out, because direct income payments, in order to be adequate, would be expensive, and difficult to administer. As the Committee commented: 'even if eligibility were confined to people with no income outside farming; putting a figure on a small farmer's income is notoriously hard' (OJ C348, 31–12–81, 35).

The ESC also stressed the importance 'that any scheme should lay down Community-wide criteria for the Member States to follow, and that it should be binding upon them' (OJ C348, 31–12–81). This was a timely warning: there was a growing tendency for the Member States to try to circumvent Community curbs on agricultural spending by the introduction of illegal or at best semi-legal support schemes of their own. The renationalization of the CAP by stealth was very much in the air in the late 1970s and early 1980s.

During the 1980s, the Commission moved with incredible caution on the ques-tion of direct income aids. Its first tentative steps were to propose, for 1982/83, a derogation for small producers from the co-responsibility levy for milk (which had been introduced some years previously). This was accepted by the Council and was followed some years later by a scheme for small cereal growers, when a co-responsibility levy was introduced in that sector.[15]

Probably the most detailed policy statement on direct income aids was made in *The Perspectives for the CAP* (Commission 1985(*b*))—one of the major policy reform documents in the history of the CAP. It reiterated the, by now, familiar cautionary words on the political, administrative, and financial aspects of the question, and acknowledged, once again, 'the resistance of the agricultural population to measures of the character of "assistance" ' (p. VII). It affirmed the need for the financial participation of the Community, commenting that in part this would be a reflection of the shift in the income support burden away from the market policy.[16]

The Commission stressed that 'great care would have to be taken to keep, as far as possible, [direct income aid] schemes neutral with respect to production and compatible with market policy' (Commission 1985(*b*), 56). This echoed a view of the Commission ten years earlier when it stated that income aid 'must not be linked with specific types of production: so long as the beneficiary continues to practise farming it is preferable that he should concentrate on those products in relation to which—at market prices—his productivity is highest' (Commission 1975(*a*), 35). In the light of these firmly stated views, it is surprising to find that so many other forms of aid in use under the CAP are anything but neutral and are directly linked to particular commodities and levels of production.

At the beginning of 1987, the Single European Act came into force under which the single internal market was to be completed by the end of 1992. Although, as a sector, agriculture was much more integrated internally than many other sectors of the Community economy, it had its own problems. By 1987, it was once again in the throes of a new attempt to curb production, this time through the use of commodity stabilizers (discussed in Chapter 6). In a discussion document: *Making a Success of the Single Act*, there is a section headed 'Preserving a European agricultural model where most farms are family farms'. Under this heading, the Commission describes one of the functions of the socio-structural policy as being 'to guarantee a fair standard of living for the poorest farmers, if necessary with the help of income support to supplement inadequate earnings from farming' (Commission 1987(*b*), 13).

This is a quite remarkable section! In a document plotting the course for the achievement of a common internal market, the Commission is reaffirming the existence of the managed market for agriculture and fidelity to the concept of the family farm. At the same time, it is reinterpreting Article 39 of the Rome Treaty. Readers are reminded that the fair standard of living was to be achieved by raising agricultural productivity (see the first Section of this chapter). This appears to have been quietly forgotten in an era in which the last thing that the Community needed was increased productivity—unless it could have been achieved by some means which did not include higher production levels. For over two decades this had proved to be impossible. Moreover, Article 39 does not limit the objective of a fair standard of living to the poorest farmers.

The Commission went on to state that additional machinery was needed at Community level to support agricultural incomes and that 'a Community framework should be provided for national aids to prevent the member governments from drifting into policies of their own' (Commission 1987(*b*), 16). The Commission continued to be concerned with the constant threat of renationalization of aspects of the price policy but it was also worried about the dilution of the common policy itself. Within the price policy, every scheme which gave concessions or exemptions from the general rules to farmers with particular problems rendered the resulting policy that much less universal. The whole idea behind a common price policy was that it allowed for an improvement in the allocation of resources to agriculture in general and to each commodity specifically. By this means, the natural or locational advantages of a country, a region, or an individual farmer should have been enhanced for the benefit of all taxpayers and consumers.

It was a very long time since price policy in agriculture had, in practice, functioned in this way but certainly in the European Community that theoretical basis had never been changed. Indeed, the whole exercise of attempting to base the price proposals on the objective method, which recognized the need to maintain the efficiency of the already efficient farms, was founded precisely on a concept of comparative advantage. Deviation from that concept was perfectly justifiable for political, social, regional, environmental—or even short-term economic—reasons. But clearly there were limits not only in budgetary terms but, more importantly, in the distortion of the internal market and, therefore, in the goal of an economic union.

The Community faced another problem, namely that the efficient farmers were themselves running into financial difficulties. The need to bring the market back into balance by curbing growth in production and, even in some cases, reducing production levels meant that by the early 1980s farmers found themselves in a cost–price squeeze. Added to this was the need to eliminate accumulated surpluses which in itself was a very costly exercise. As will be seen in Chapter 6, the 1980s saw a succession of efforts to balance the market, none of them particularly successful but the issue of compensating farmers in the short run for the financial difficulties in which they found themselves was never very far away.

In 1987, the Commission proposed the introduction of two schemes for farm income support, one Community funded and the other to be funded by the individual Member States. The Community scheme was intended to assist farmers in current financial difficulties as a result of the efforts to achieve market equilibrium but who were potentially viable and who, once the market was in balance, would be able to farm in an economically satisfactory way. The national scheme was intended to curb the activities of various Member States which were trying to circumvent the restrictions on State aids under Articles 92–4 of the Rome Treaty. The Commission believed that, by defining a framework within which certain national aids would be allowed, Member States would be prevented from taking unilateral actions which 'would entail distortion in production and in trade and would be bound to hamper efforts to remedy the situation on the markets' (Commission 1987(*d*), 2).

At the European Council meeting in February 1988, it was agreed that a scheme to withdraw agricultural land from production (set-aside) would be introduced and that farmers would be compensated for lost income through an area payment. The European Council also instructed the Council of Agricultural Ministers to decide on the introduction of income aids by mid-1988 (Bull. EC 2–1988). In the event the income aid Regulation was not adopted until March 1989 (Reg. 768/89, OJ L84, 29–3–89). Not all Member States took part in the scheme and the practical difficulties encountered in its implementation are instructive.

In 1992, the Commission produced a report on the operation of the scheme (Commission 1992(*d*)). By then, 180,000 farmers were benefiting, which fell well short of the 850,000 which had been budgeted for (Commission 1988(*c*)). The intention had been to create a link between the aid provided and the income lost due to CAP reform but, in the event, only the Netherlands operated the scheme by assessing the individual loss; the other participating Member States applied a flat rate aid. By adopting this approach 'it is possible for there to be over-compensation of some producers in relation to their individual CAP reform induced losses' and 'it is possible that some beneficiaries may . . . receive aid simply because of low family incomes even if they have experienced little or no income loss due to CAP reform' (Commission 1992(d), 6–7). In other words, the scheme was misconceived. Worse than that, the market stabilizers, which were introduced with the intention of restoring equilibrium to the market, had failed to achieve this objective. Therefore, the income aid linked to their introduction could not be justified either. It was time to think again.

The Commissioner for Agriculture—MacSharry—took up the challenge. His aim was twofold: to reduce support prices so as to make the EC more competitive with production overseas, and to recognize that, for many farmers, income support was a social necessity and therefore Community assistance should be much better targeted.

Income support, which depends almost exclusively on price guarantees, is largely proportionate to the volume of production and therefore concentrates the greater part of support on the largest and most intensive farms . . . The effect of this is that 80 per cent of the support provided by FEOGA is devoted to 20 per cent of farms . . . The existing system does not take adequate account of the incomes of the vast majority of small and medium size family farms.   (Commission 1991(b), 2)

MacSharry's view was that efficient farmers could produce with a reduced price support base and that, for them, the aim of policy should be to increase their competitiveness. For other farmers, however, reductions in price support or the application of quantitative restraints (production quotas, set-aside, etc.) should be compensated for by means of direct aid, adjusted for factors such as size of farm, income level, the regional situation. In order to break away from the system whereby the bulk of support went to a minority of farmers, MacSharry's idea was that aid would be modulated, so that above a certain level compensation (per hectare or per livestock unit) would taper off.

Needless to remark, such revolutionary ideas did not pass unscathed through the Council of Ministers! As Williamson (1980) had predicted, governments did not abandon the interests of the medium and large farmers: the mould was not broken but a crack did appear in it. What MacSharry succeeded in doing was to modify the support system to the extent that prices were allowed to fall over a period of years, that farmers were compensated for this decline by measures which were not related to the quantities produced, and that limitations on the level of output were extended to include limitations on inputs.[17] However, MacSharry's failure to persuade the Member States to cease the overcompensation of the better-off farmers left a major issue unresolved. It taints the CAP and obstructs the identification of the farmers with a genuine income problem and the enactment of a suitable policy response to their needs.

Non-Farming Sources of Income

In discussions on farm income levels and the financial support made available to the agricultural sector, there often seems to be an assumption—explicit or implicit—that reference is being made to the situation in which a farmer is employed full time on the farm or that the farm is capable of supporting full time the equivalent of at least one labour unit. From much of what has gone before in this chapter one must conclude that such an assumption is simplistic and therefore misleading. Yet in a real sense that is the model which underlay the proposals on modern farm enterprises in the Mansholt Plan and, in the 1970s, provided the basis for the pursuit of the objective method of calculating price support.

It is surprising that in the first two decades of the CAP so little attention was paid to the question of non-farming sources of income on farms. Down the centuries farming in Europe had been quite commonly combined with other activities and, in many regions and among small farms everywhere, it was the ability to combine a range of activities which ensured the survival of them all. In 1975, a passing reference was made in the *Stocktaking* to the fact that nearly a decade earlier (in 1966/67) about 27 per cent of farmers in the Community had non-agricultural incomes (Commission 1975(*a*)). This was not a negligible proportion and may well have understated the true situation.

Indeed, for many years, the only recognition given to non-farming income was a negative one: under the structural policy assistance was only made available to farmers whose main occupation was farming. This category was one in which at least half of the farmer's total income came from farming and less than half of the farmer's total working time was devoted to non-farming activities. While this might seem a reasonable requirement if limited to investment aid, such as the modernization of a farm, it is less justifiable when it is used, for instance, as a criterion for aid to encourage retirement. It meant that many low income farmers were trapped in farming with neither the means to invest in the farm nor the financial incentive to leave.

The concept of main occupation farming suggests that the farmer has a secondary gainful occupation but in practice that is not the only possibility. In some cases farmers may, on income grounds, be entitled to unemployment benefit or some other form of social welfare payment; in other cases, because of the farmer's age there may be an entitlement to a pension of some kind. In certain regions and on small farms—wherever located—such payments may be far more important as a source of income than paid employment.

A different type of confusion arises with the use of the term 'part-time farming'. This can include two quite separate concepts: the part-time farmer and the part-time farm. The difference between the two is important: the former suggests that the farmer has another occupation; the latter suggests that the farm is too small to provide full-time employment for at least one labour unit equivalent. The two concepts are clearly very different and, while the part-time farmer may be earning a very satisfactory total income, this is not necessarily true of the farmer on a part-time farm. He/she may be working full time on such a unit and due to disadvantages of location, skills, education, or age may have no opportunity to find paid employment.

The situation is made even more complex if farm family income or the income of the farmer's spouse is taken into account, rather than the income solely of the farmer. This is true irrespective of whether the farmer is full time or not. Income definition is universally a problem in farming and is not confined to the European Community. However, it is important in relation to the CAP which, whatever its origins and philosophical basis, is biased in practice towards rewarding the full-time and main occupation farmers. If other farming groups are growing in importance, for whatever reason, then the level of farm income as a measure of the success or failure of the CAP is bound to lead to distorted conclusions.

Prior to the 1980s there was little discussion of non-farming sources of income and of part-time farming. Since the time of the Mansholt Plan the policy emphasis had been on the creation of the modern farm capable of yielding an income comparable to the non-agricultural income in the same region. As already discussed in this chapter, the pursuit of that goal had sidelined large numbers of farmers whose income problem was never going to be solved solely through the price and market policy. The realization of that fact was a long time in coming and, even in the 1990s, one cannot state with any confidence that the limitations of the price and market policy as an income support are fully accepted.

However, by the early 1980s, disenchantment with the functioning of the CAP combined with wider concerns on rural depopulation (especially in regions heavily dependent on farming), and growing unemployment resulted in a change in the perception of the role of farming in the wider community. In a sense, the economic aspects of agriculture had been overemphasized to the detriment of its other roles and the balance needed to be redressed. The change in mood is well illustrated by a comment of the ESC:

The emphasis on agriculture's place in the economic and social structure, and on the importance of the family farm, means that policy must take into account the place of agriculture as the centre of a complex of supplying and processing industries, as the creator and preserver of the countryside, and as a storehouse of independence and entrepreneurial effort, which cannot be allowed to be reduced to a limited number of large industrial units without a new and deliberate political decision. (OJ C348, 31–12–81, 30)

If farming could be combined with another activity—on or off the farm—this would help to retain people in rural areas, reduce dependence on farming as the sole income source, and thereby reduce the pressure to increase agricultural production. Part-time farming, which had been largely ignored or perceived only as a stage on the transition from full-time farming to quitting agriculture permanently, was at last seen in its true guise as a permanent feature of farming organization.

Because so little attention had been paid to it, little was known about part-time farming. Williamson (1980) drew attention to the inadequacy of information on what he called 'the phenomenon of part-time farming'. This was despite the fact that, in 1975, only 36 per cent of the Community's farmers were farming full time; a further 20 per cent worked 50–<100 per cent of their time in farming; the remaining 44 per cent worked less than 50 per cent of their time in farming. The 64 per cent who were not full time controlled 32 per cent of the utilized agricultural area, indicating that they were clustered among the smaller size categories of farms. They also accounted for only 25 per cent of the livestock (in LU terms), which is not surprising as livestock is more labour- and time-intensive than arable production and therefore less suited to part-time work.

The extent of part-time farming varied widely from one Member State to another, with a particularly high concentration in Germany and Italy. As Williamson (1980, 6) stated: 'it is clear that a fall in real incomes from farming will have a very different social effect in the different member states. In terms of social justice we may need to take these structural elements more into account when fixing price rises and levels of aid'. In fact, many years were to elapse before part-time farming was extensively analysed, and total family income (as opposed to farm income) scrutinized in detail.[18]

In practice, very little has been done under the CAP to take account of either multiple income sources or, more importantly, of part-time farms which are too small to yield an adequate (let alone a comparable) income. The CAP has not, for instance, included a price support system which varies with the quantity produced, i.e. a two-tier or multi-tier price structure. A very few proposals to introduce such a system were made but were never pursued. The only occasions on which some differentiation has been made relate either to a simplified support system (e.g. for small olive oil producers) or to modifications to schemes intended to curb excess production (e.g. the operation of the milk levy in LFAs (less-favoured areas), and the compensation paid to small cereal growers on the introduction of the co-responsibility levy). These concessionary arrangements were broadly based and not specifically targeted at part-time farms but rather were intended to help small producers 'whose principal income is from agriculture, and whose opportunity for other economic activity is limited' (Commission 1983(*d*), 11).

On the structural side of the CAP, as has already been mentioned, the 'main occupation' requirement excluded many farmers from the schemes. However, an early and important exception came in Dir. 75/268 on less-favoured areas, (discussed in Chapter 9). A farm undergoing a development plan under Dir. 72/159, if situated in a designated LFA, was subject to less onerous rules than farms elsewhere. For instance, on completion of the plan the percentage of income from non-agricultural activities could be at a maximum of 50 per cent of the total, rather than 20 per cent, and the agricultural income level to be achieved was at least 70 per cent of the comparable earned income, rather than 100 per cent. Furthermore, a farm development plan in an LFA could include investment in on-farm touristic or craft activities.

In 1985, under Reg. 797/85 (discussed further in Chapter 8), while the 'main occupation' requirement was retained the eligibility requirements for investment aid were much relaxed. A development plan only had to bring about a lasting and substantial improvement in income, and the comparable income being aimed at was replaced by a reference income which had, as a maximum, the average gross wage of non-agricultural workers in the same region. The requirements were further relaxed in 1991 when Member States were empowered if they wished to extend investment aid to farmers who did not qualify as 'main occupation' farmers but who derived at least half of their total income from a combination of farming, forestry, tourism or craft activities, or activities related to maintaining the countryside. At least one-quarter of the income had to come directly from farming, and the off-farm activities had to account for not more than half the farmer's total work time.[19] The Community had come a very great distance in twenty years.

What is perhaps surprising is not that there was a shift away from the aim of creating a farming sector dominated by full-time or main occupation farms capable of yielding an income comparable to that in other sectors but rather that the belief that this was a feasible objective lingered for so long. The change in approach was an absolute necessity brought about by the rise in unemployment, which meant that the farming population could no longer look to other sectors for job opportunities, in the manner which had been possible in the 1950s and 1960s. If there was underemployment in farming, then a more localized solution had to be found which would involve the farmer or family member remaining part time in farming.

Another aspect of this shift in policy arose from the need to curb the cost of the price and market policy. As will be seen in Chapter 6, the 1980s were years in which the Community struggled unsuccessfully to bring surplus production under control and to limit the continual increase in price support in money terms. If farmers could become less dependent for their income on the maintenance of high levels of price support, it would make reductions in expenditure less contentious. One obvious way to achieve this would be through encouraging the combination of income sources: if the farmer or a family member had other gainful employment, it would cushion the impact of any curtailment of price support. In 1988, the Commission reported that only 32 per cent of farms in EC-10 provided work for one person on a full-time basis; a further 30 per cent supplemented their farm income with other activities (Commission 1988(f)).[20]

This looked quite encouraging but what of the remainder? They were clearly underemployed on the farm and, unless they were receiving pensions or other social welfare payments, their income situation was very precarious. However, the solution of their income problem most certainly did not lie in the price policy, as their output would be so small that the benefit of price support would be negligible. As the ESC had stated in 1981:

The marginal farmer is an extremely difficult problem. No acceptable set of prices will give the man with a farm that provides only part-time occupation, or on which yields are very small an adequate living from his farming.   (OJ C348, 31–12–81, 35)

The solution has not yet been found and, if anything, the rate at which farmers are being marginalized has increased.

NOTES

1. Krohn and van Lierde were writing at the time when the Commission was proposing a series of Community Plans to tackle the income problems of farmers in backward regions. This initiative is discussed in Ch. 9.
2. It is notable that economists have had very little influence on the development of agricultural policy, and that their criticisms of its shortcomings and failures are largely ignored. This can be attributed to their tendency to use the framework of the theory of the firm for their analysis and to ignore political and social factors. It is not that their analysis is wrong, rather that it is on a different wavelength.
3. This passage did not appear in the 1959 draft proposals.
4. The Mansholt Plan and its aftermath are the subject of Ch. 8. Only the proposals on a new farm structure are discussed here.
5. Quoted in Corti (1971), ch. 7.
6. Although not mentioned at the time, the proposals would have encouraged mono-culture which, today, is regarded as detrimental to the natural environment.
7. See Neville-Rolfe (1984) for a summary of the issues, and *Agence Europe* for a contemporary account.
8. Negotiations were taking place with Denmark, Ireland, Norway, and the United Kingdom and, on 1 Jan. 1973, all except Norway joined the Community.
9. The aids discussed here are held to be neutral in terms of current production (though they may be based on past production levels). Many of the aids outlined in later chapters most certainly are not production neutral. Indeed many actively encourage or discourage output.
10. See JO C19, 13-2-70 and JO C19, 1-3-71.
11. In its revised price proposals in COM(72)150, the Commission actually widened the age band to 40-55 (Commission 1972).
12. In COM(70)500, the cost estimates of the proposed retirement schemes were based on 400,000 farmers taking early retirement and 780,000, who were already of retire-ment age, actually leaving agriculture (Commission 1970).
13. It is often forgotten that the original negotiations on the introduction of the CAP were undertaken by the Foreign Ministers of EC-6. The concept of a Council of Min-isters which changes personnel with the subject under discussion came later. Faced with the complexity of the issues involved, the Foreign Ministers had sought the assistance of the Agricultural Ministers who, once invited in, effectively never left!
14. Bergmann (1980, 8) listed eight studies which, in the 1970s, had advocated direct income payments, and outlined a scheme of his own devising. He described such payments as: 'at least among economists, the most popular method for alleviating the income effects of lower support prices'.
15. These and other production curbs are discussed in Chs. 5, 6, and 10.
16. This was an oblique admission that the price policy based on the modern farm and the objective method, introduced in 1972/73, which had been intended to free price policy from its income support role, had not achieved this goal.
17. These issues are discussed more fully in Chs. 6 and 11.
18. The issue of farm family incomes is discussed in Ch. 5. A major study was undertaken on behalf of the Commission into pluriactivity on farms by the Arkleton Trust. The final report was J. M. Bryden *et al.* (1992).

19. Art 5.1(a) of Reg. 2328/91 *on improving the efficiency of agricultural structures* (OJ L218, 6–8–91).
20. There is an urgent need to improve statistics on pluriactivity. The data quoted here for 1988 for EC-10 are at variance with those shown in Table 3.A4 for EC-12. In addition, much more needs to be known about part-time farms particularly where they are farmed full time.

5

Statistical Evidence on Incomes

Measurement of Labour Income in the EAA

Chapter 4 outlined the various policy issues which have arisen down the years in relation to income. The point was made that the 'income problem' was perceived very largely in sectoral terms, i.e. that incomes in farming were not keeping pace with those in other activities. Far less attention was paid to differences within the agricultural sector itself. In the present chapter both the macro- and micro-aspects of income are considered. The measurement of income in farming is by its very nature complicated and the choice of a particular measure is dependent on what one is attempting to demonstrate. Three types of statistics are used here: the Economic Accounts for Agriculture (EAA) which provide macro-data on the sector; the Farm Accountancy Data Network (FADN);[1] and the Total Income of Agricultural Households (TIAH). Only a small selection of the available data is used and whenever possible reliance has been placed on material which permits examination of income trends over time. In some cases this has meant the use of rather dated statistics. This does not lessen their validity as illustrations of issues which have existed over the lifetime of the CAP.

The EAA are based on the calculation of the final production of the sector which, when disaggregated, provides three different levels of income indicator.[2] Indicator 1 has been available longest and is based on the net value added (NVA) at factor cost. NVA is the value of final agricultural output minus intermediate consumption, depreciation, and taxes linked to production, plus subsidies. The value which results from this calculation is then deflated to remove the influence of inflation. Real NVA is then divided by the total labour input to agriculture, expressed in Annual Work Units (AWU).[3] Thus, real NVA/ANU = Indicator 1.

In 1987, two further indicators were added: Indicator 2 is calculated in the same way as Indicator 1, except that rents and interest payments are subtracted from NVA at factor cost before the calculations are carried out. Indicator 2 therefore is an expression of net income from agricultural activity of total labour. Indicator 3 is even narrower, in that it is based on net income of agricultural activity minus wages and salaries paid to employees. This indicator, therefore, is an expression of net income from agricultural activity of family labour input; it represents the residual rewards to farmers and their (unpaid) family members for the land, labour, capital, and management which they contribute to the production of the agricultural sector.

The disadvantage of these aggregate indicators derived from the EAA is that they are concerned with the sector as a whole and cannot provide information

Table 5.1. Annual growth rates of labour productivity in agriculture and in the rest of the economy (%)

Member States	GVA/AWU[a] "1974"–"1986"	Agriculture, forestry, and fishing GVA/ person employed "1974"–"1986"	Rest of the economy GVA/person employed "1974"–"1986"
Germany	4.2	4.0	2.1
France	4.1[b]	5.6	1.8
Italy	3.9[b]	4.1	1.3
Netherlands	5.0	4.9	1.6
Belgium	4.0[b]	4.5	1.9
Luxembourg	5.0	–0.5	1.3
UK	4.6	4.4	1.4
Ireland	3.9[b]	3.4	2.9
Denmark	7.4	3.5	0.9
Greece	3.3[b]	n.a.	n.a.
Spain	7.0[b]	n.a.	n.a.
EC-9	4.3	4.6	1.7
EC-11	5.0	n.a.	n.a.

[a] ratio of gross value added in agriculture at factor cost to number of annual work units
[b] "1974"–"1987"
Source: derived from Terluin 1991.

on income by farm type, size of enterprise, or—at present—by region. FADN, which is based on an annual farm business survey, can provide such information for commercially orientated farms. Because it is based on surveys which take time to organize and analyse, it does not have the immediacy of the Economic Accounts Indicators which can be made available very quickly, at least in an estimated form, soon after the close of the year in question. Both sources are used to illuminate year-on-year changes; the EAA have the advantage that they can be readily used as a time series. This is much more problematical with FADN due to discontinuities in sampling. Because everything to do with agricultural production—whether in relation to final output or inputs—is subject to short-term fluctuations, changes from year to year may be quite misleading. Yet it is on short-term observations that much of agricultural policy is based.

In examining the question of incomes in agriculture, this chapter uses as its starting-point Art. 39.1(a) and (b) of the Rome Treaty where a clear link is made between increasing agricultural productivity (and especially labour productivity) and ensuring a fair standard of living (with particular emphasis on individual earnings of the agricultural workforce)—see Chapter 1. The level of labour productivity in agriculture is usually measured in terms of gross value added (GVA) at factor cost in constant prices per AWU. Two aspects of productivity are of interest: the rate of increase over time, and the relativities between Member States.

Table 5.1 provides the annual growth rate of labour productivity per AWU in each Member State in the period "1974" to "1986" or "1987". For most countries, the increase was around 4 per cent per year, with Denmark and Spain well above that level.[4] It is interesting in this regard to see how agriculture compares with other sectors of the economy. For this comparison GVA per person has to be used (i.e. there is no equivalent in the rest of the economy of Annual Work Units), and the sector includes forestry and fisheries. Terluin (1991) provides this comparison for the period "1974"–"1986" which is reproduced in Table 5.1 for EC-9. There are a number of unexplained anomalies, such as the negative figure for Luxembourg and the halving of the growth rate in Denmark when compared with the first measure (GVA/AWU). However, the important comparison is with the rest of the economy and the striking feature there is the strength of the growth rate in agriculture, forestry, and fisheries. Apart from the anomaly of Luxembourg, only in Ireland did the growth rate in the rest of the economy come anywhere near that in the primary sector. One explanation for the poor showing of the rest of the economy is that the very large service sector contains a high proportion of part-time workers and their output is usually lower than that of full-time workers.[5]

The interpretation of comparisons of this kind is fraught with difficulties. Allowance should be made for the fact that labour statistics in agriculture, forestry, and fishing may be less reliable than those in many other sectors of the economy. It should also be borne in mind that the growth of labour productivity is affected by changes not only in GVA but also by the size of the workforce. As the numbers employed in agriculture, forestry, and fishing have been subject to a sustained decline over a long period of time, GVA is being measured in relation to an ever-shrinking labour base. Thus the productivity gain may not be as encouraging as it at first appears in that much of it has been achieved by the replacement of labour by capital.

Turning to the question of the position of each Member State in relation to the Community as a whole, Figure 5.1 provides the information over the same period as Table 5.1, using four 3-year points of reference. In "1974" and "1979" the graph is based on EC-11=100 (i.e. Portugal is excluded), and in the remainder the base is EC-12=100. This should make no material difference, given the small size of Portugal. The most striking feature of the graph is the range of productivity levels. GVA/AWU was highest in the Netherlands, being up to 1.5 times the Community level, whereas Portugal was less than one-fifth the Community level. Belgium and Denmark were also noticeably above average; the middle range comprised Italy, Luxembourg, France, Germany, and the United Kingdom. Ireland, Greece, and Spain as well as Portugal were all below the EC average.[6] This wide range requires some explanation.

Terluin (1991) points out that the data are subject to certain inherent shortcomings. One very important factor is that labour productivity varies from one type of production to another and tends to be highest in capital-intensive activities. Therefore, the product mix in each Member State affects the results (see Table 3.3 as an illustration of the differences). This is also relevant to the fact that, with a few exceptions, the Member States showed little variation in their position over time, relative to the Community. What would be useful would be

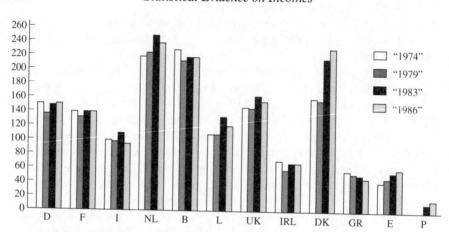

Fig. 5.1. Agricultural labour productivity[a] per AWU in the EC (EC-11 = 100 in "1974" and "1979"; EC-12 = 100 in "1983" and "1986")

[a] measured in terms of gross value added per annual work unit

Source: derived from Terluin (1991).

a comparison across Member States for the same production activity but the macro-data cannot provide that.

Despite the differences between Member States, some of which may be unavoidable, and any shortcomings in the data, it is clear that labour productivity has improved over time and in that respect the first objective of Art. 39.1 of the Rome Treaty is being fulfilled. The next issue is whether that increase in productivity has led to the achievement of a fair standard of living. As Chapter 4 indicated, the standard of living objective became confused with the achievement of an income comparable to that in other sectors. This raises the question, therefore, of the relative changes in income levels. Terluin (1991) devotes considerable attention to the various possibilities of measurement. The situation is by no means straightforward and there are limitations to any comparison.

Earlier in this chapter reference was made to the three indicators which can be derived from the Economic Accounts for Agriculture. The first of these is based on net value added at factor cost which is a concept used in national accounts for the economy as a whole and it is this measure which is used here. The agricultural labour force is expressed in AWU, whereas the labour force in the whole economy is given in persons employed without any distinction as to whether they are part-time or full-time.[7] Table 5.2 provides the outcome in terms of annual growth rate for the period "1975"–"1986". What this shows is that, for the Community as a whole, NVA in agriculture lost ground (–1.7 per cent annually) in relation to income in the whole economy. This was not true for all Member States: for instance, relative sector income improved in the Netherlands, Luxembourg, Denmark, Greece, and Spain—though in some cases by such a small amount as to be meaningless, given the crudeness of the comparison.

Whatever the limitations of the data, the outcome appears to suggest that

Table 5.2. Annual growth rate of agricultural income[a] in relation to growth rate in the whole economy, per person employed (%)

Member States	NVA agr./AWU: NVA whole economy/per worker "1975"–"1986" (current prices)
Germany	−3.3
France	−2.1
Italy	−2.7
Netherlands	0.1
Belgium	−1.2
Luxembourg	3.2
UK	−2.2
Ireland	−3.1
Denmark	3.3
Greece	1.4
Spain	0.9
EC-9	−1.7
EC-11	−1.0

[a] measured in terms of net value added in agriculture per annual work unit

Source: Terluin 1991.

changes in the level of NVA/AWU in agriculture did not keep pace with a roughly comparable measure in the economy as a whole over an extended period in the 1970s and 1980s. Given that labour productivity in agriculture was rising at the same time, why did the return to the factor labour not keep pace? The answer lies in the relationship of the value of final agricultural production to the costs of production.

These costs are composed of intermediate consumption (i.e. mostly the cost of feeding-stuffs for livestock, fertilizers, and energy), the cost of the non-labour factors of production (rents, interest, and depreciation), the balance of subsidies and taxes (which in the Community is in fact positive and therefore a benefit, as subsidies are greater than taxes), and finally the cost of labour itself. In a very real sense this is a residual as only a small part of the cost of labour is committed to the payment of wages and salaries. If the relationship of non-labour costs to the value of final production deteriorates, then labour income is squeezed. This is precisely what happened in the 1970s and 1980s: the share of net income from the agricultural activity of total labour input fell from 48 per cent of final agricultural output in "1974" to 38 per cent in "1987" (Terluin, 1991).

This meant that the increase in labour productivity (i.e. in the value of goods which each unit of labour produced), was not sufficient to ensure an increase in the reward to labour. This suggests that the goal of a comparable income was not attainable in this way. The only way in which it could have been achieved would have been through an even greater increase in capital intensity in farming, thereby pushing out more labour which would have raised the reward to the remaining labour. Such a development would have been in direct conflict with the desire to retain labour in farming, which was bound up with the advocacy of family farming referred to in Chapter 4.

The data being discussed here tell only a small part of the story as they are limited to a macro-view of agriculture. Art. 39.1(b) of the Rome Treaty makes it clear that the objective of a fair standard of living was concentrated particularly on the improvement of the individual earnings of all those who worked in agriculture. This requires analysis at a micro-level, and the source of the relevant data is FADN.

Measurement of Labour Income in FADN

As with the Economic Accounts for Agriculture, in general the FADN results are expressed in year-on-year changes and it is rare to find long-term series. Those that are available do not cover exactly the same topics in the same way, so continuity cannot be achieved. What is presented here is a series of illustrative snapshots. FADN is based on a sample of commercial farms across the European Union. Whether a farm is classified as commercial or not depends on the size of its Standard Gross Margin (SGM), which is an indicator of the volume of agricultural activity. The level of the SGM threshold differs from one Member State to another to reflect the different farm structures in each country, and SGMs are revised from time to time.

A series of studies is used here to deepen the discussion of incomes in this chapter. These studies use different ways of measuring income, thereby yielding a range of perspectives from which to view this complex issue. The first provides information on farm net value added (FNVA) per agricultural work unit by type of farm, for the period 1979/80–1985/86. This measure is the farm level equivalent of NVA/AWU used in the previous Section. The results are reproduced in Table 5.3. FNVA/AWU is taken to represent agricultural income and is shown in index form (1981/82=100) based on all types of farming. What the table illustrates, therefore, is the deviation by year and type of farm from the average for all farms. The categories used are the main groups into which farming can be classified and relate to EC-9.

The first thing to notice about this table is that there are certain farming activities which yield an agricultural income consistently above the average: these are cereals, general crops, horticulture, milk, pigs/poultry.[8] Of these, cereals, horticulture, and pigs/poultry (granivores) show the greatest deviation from the average for all farm types. These three farm categories illustrate very well the danger of assuming that large farms in area terms are necessarily correlated with high incomes when different activities are being compared. Horticultural holdings, in particular, are often very small in area but very intensive; pigs or poultry units—often referred to as factory farming because the animals are reared

Table 5.3. Agricultural income[a] per annual work unit by main type of farming in real terms

Type of farming	% of total commercial holdings	Average all types of farming, EC-9 (1981/82=100)[c]						
		1979/80	1980/81	1981/82	1982/83	1983/84	1984/85	1985/86
Cereals	6	140	136	135	155	139	173	131
General crops	14	117	112	119	122	132	137	116
Horticulture	2	128	127	128	116	134	148	147
Wine-growing	6	143	102	96	121	101	88	87
Fruit and permanent crops[b]	9	91	85	84	74	88	75	77
Milk	19	110	104	112	123	113	111	110
Beef/veal	4	65	70	96	93	88	88	77
Mixed cattle	4	94	86	86	98	87	87	81
Sheep and goats	5	81	79	93	84	82	88	75
Pigs and poultry	1	197	163	223	187	144	195	192
Mixed cropping	10	75	63	59	61	64	63	57
Mixed livestock	7	88	75	86	95	79	85	81
Mixed crops/livestock	13	90	85	90	99	92	99	86
All Types		102	94	100	106	102	105	97

a measured in terms of farm net value added (FNVA)
b including olives and other permanent crops
c FADN results 1979/80–1983/84, weighted on basis of current year
  FADN estimates for 1984/85 and 1985/86

Source: European Community 1986.

intensively and are infrequently free range—are also small in area (see Table 5.6). As with the data in Figure 5.1 referred to in the previous Section, the different levels of capital investment required in the various types of farms influence the relative levels of income. A low FNVA/AWU in Table 5.3 does not suggest that, in some sense, the farm or the labour is 'inefficient' but rather that the capital investment required in the particular type of enterprise is lower than in some others.

The second feature highlighted by Table 5.3 is that some types of farming may be particularly prone to wide variations in income due to the very nature of the product being produced. Wine production is an extreme example due to the major fluctuation in yield and quality from one year to another. Beef is subject to a cyclical pattern of production, as is pigmeat. Thirdly, all types of farms are subject to year-on-year income variations but the range of experience is very different depending on the type of farming. For instance, take 1981/82 itself which is the base for the index, the range in that year was from a low of 59 in mixed cropping to a high of 223 in pigs/poultry.

Incomes vary not only by type of production but also by location of the farm, which is the subject of the second FADN study discussed in this Section. It is surprising how little attention has been paid to this aspect of incomes—particularly as the income spread has increased as the Community has expanded. Any further expansion—for instance, eastward in the early twenty-first century—is going to add importance to this issue. Later chapters pick up various aspects of the regional impact of the CAP but more on the structural side than in relation to the price and market policy.

The only aspect of locational income differences to be highlighted here is the level of agricultural income per labour unit (FNVA/AWU) in 'normal' areas compared to that in areas designated as less-favoured or mountainous. Less-favoured areas (LFAs) are established according to certain criteria[9] and, within them, some areas qualify as mountainous because of their high altitude. Natural handicap clearly limits production possibilities and therefore income possibilities. Table 5.4 illustrates the range of FNVA/AWU by Member State for a 3-year average (1987–9), for LFAs and mountain areas (MAs) compared with the EC-12 'normal' average. Denmark has never designated any LFAs and the area in the Netherlands is too small to provide a sample for FADN. Only Germany, Greece, Spain, France, Italy, and Portugal have areas classified as mountainous.

The data are in the form of an index based on the FNVA/AWU for 'normal' farms = 100. Thus, the table provides information on the deviation of LFAs and MAs away from 'normal'. Taking EC-12 as a whole, the agricultural income per labour unit in LFAs was just over half that in normal areas but this low level was adversely affected by the inclusion in the EC 'normal' average of Denmark and the Netherlands where agricultural incomes were particularly high. If the comparison is made between LFAs and 'normal' areas within the same Member State the difference is not nearly so great. However, in one respect the comparison with EC-12 'normal' areas is justified and interesting: in Belgium, Luxembourg, and the UK the agricultural income in LFAs was appreciably above that of

Table 5.4. Productivity of the agricultural workforce[a] by area

Member States	Average 1987–9 (EC-12 NA=100)		
	NA[b]	LFA[c]	MA[d]
Belgium	188	183	—
Denmark[e]	191	—	—
Germany	114	95	71
Greece	40	36	34
Spain	61	51	48
France	136	85	78
Ireland	102	67	—
Italy	75	54	52
Luxembourg	—	138	—
Netherlands[f]	230	—	—
Portugal	20	17	18
UK	148	120	—
EC-12	100	53	42

a measured in terms of farm net value added (FNVA) per Annual Work Unit (AWU)
b NA = normal area
c LFA = less-favoured areas
d MA = mountain areas
e Denmark has no designated LFAs
f Netherlands has LFAs but too small to provide a FADN sample

Source: Commission 1993(*f*).

EC-12 'normal', and in Germany the level was very close to the average. The difference between LFAs and MAs is not very great in Greece, Spain, Italy, and Portugal.

Incomes vary not only by type of farming activity and location but also by the economic size of the holding—the third FADN measure examined here. The Commission has devised an economic measure—the European Size Unit (ESU) —as a means of classifying holdings which 'avoids the problems associated with land of different quality and intensity of use' (Hill 1993, 29). Economic size is obtained by dividing the SGM of the farm by a fixed number of ECUs, so that, say, 1 ESU = ECU 1000.[10] Farms can then be grouped by ESUs into size categories, as shown in Table 5.5.

This table illustrates very clearly how, in a period when incomes per AWU were effectively standing still in real terms, there was considerable variation by economic size. Only the largest economic units improved their labour income situation—and they were already well above the Community average. The very smallest units clearly faced considerable difficulties in a situation in which they were already very weak.

Table 5.5. Agricultural incomes per work unit,[a] by economic size category[b]

Economic size Category of holdings	EC-9 average of all farming types, 1981/82=100				
	1979/80	1980/81	1981/82	1982/83	1983/84
Very small (1–<4 ESU)	42	37	32	33	34
Small (4–<8 ESU)	65	58	58	57	56
Medium (8–<16 ESU)	100	90	95	99	91
Large (≥16 ESU)	174	166	174	182	170
All holdings	102	94	100	106	102

[a] Measured in terms of farm net value added (FNVA) per annual work unit (AWU)
[b] 1 ESU (European size unit) = 1000 EUA (European unit of account) standard gross margin (SGM) in 1972/74 prices
Source: European Community 1986.

Table 5.6 combines information on the economic size of farms in 1989 with information on work units, and utilized agricultural area (UAA). The number of ESUs in the small, medium, and large size categories in this table differ appreciably from those in Table 5.5, which reflects changes in the level of standard gross margins over time. The purpose of reproducing Table 5. 6 is to illustrate how difficult it is to achieve an equitable distribution of income support if the means chosen are the price and market policy. The range of economic size is very great and the output of a small unit is often spread over roughly the same number of AWU as are employed on medium-sized farms in ESU terms.

When it comes to the physical size of these units, small units in ESU terms are often appreciably smaller than medium-sized units for UAA (horticulture being the only exception). The importance of this is the limitation which physical size places on opportunities for diversification (a point made in Chapter 3). When it is borne in mind that the small units in ESU terms in 1989 represented 68 per cent of all farms and produced 24 per cent of total output in value terms, the problem of income support through the price mechanism comes sharply into focus. In the same year, the medium-sized units in ESU terms represented 21 per cent of the total and produced 31 per cent of output, while the largest 11 per cent produced 45 per cent of output (Hill 1993). The switch-over to compensatory payments in the early 1990s (discussed in Chapter 6) did not improve targeting, as they were based on historic production levels.

So far in this chapter reliance has been placed very largely on the measure of net value added—whether at the macro- or micro-level—as a proxy for agricultural income. However, strictly speaking NVA is the sum available to reward all factors of production, i.e. not only labour but land and capital as well and when it is divided by the volume of labour input—as it is in Indicator 1—it produces a measure which is, in a very real sense, illogical. Nevertheless, NVA/

Table 5.6. Economic size groups and corresponding measures of size, 1989

Type of farming group	Economic size of farm (ESU)	Average economic size (ESU)	Average annual work units (AWU)	Average family work units (FWU)	Average utilized agric. area (UAA) (ha.)
All	Small	7.3	1.4	1.2	10.1
	Medium	31.9	1.7	1.5	33.1
	Large	93.8	2.6	1.6	74.9
Cereals	Small	7.3	0.9	0.9	17.6
	Medium	31.5	1.3	1.1	60.9
	Large	104.6	2.1	1.3	141.0
General cropping	Small	7.0	1.5	1.3	8.3
	Medium	31.4	1.7	1.4	30.6
	Large	102.5	2.4	1.5	93.2
Horticulture	Small	8.0	2.7	1.5	3.5
	Medium	31.5	2.5	1.7	3.1
	Large	138.2	4.4	1.9	5.3
Vineyards	Small	7.2	1.1	1.0	4.2
	Medium	32.4	1.8	1.4	11.7
	Large	88.0	3.0	1.5	26.4

Table 5.6. (*cont.*)

Type of farming group	Economic size of farm (ESU)	Average economic size (ESU)	Average annual work units (AWU)	Average family work units (FWU)	Average utilized agric. area (UAA) (ha.)
Other permanent crops	Small	6.3	1.2	1.1	5.4
	Medium	30.3	1.9	1.4	13.9
	Large	85.0	4.0	1.6	26.7
Dairy	Small	10.1	1.4	1.4	12.9
	Medium	32.6	1.6	1.5	32.8
	Large	78.3	2.3	1.8	57.6
Drystock	Small	8.0	1.4	1.3	19.4
	Medium	30.8	1.7	1.5	56.8
	Large	79.5	2.5	2.0	189.7
Pigs and/ or poultry	Small	9.5	1.1	1.0	3.3
	Medium	32.3	1.5	1.2	6.8
	Large	101.1	2.1	1.5	18.8
Mixed	Small	7.2	1.6	1.5	10.2
	Medium	32.9	1.6	1.5	34.4
	Large	84.6	2.3	1.7	73.4

Source: Hill 1993.

AWU is frequently used in a policy context as a measure of the effectiveness of the CAP in supporting income. The situation is no better at the micro-FADN-level. While labour is undoubtedly the most important of the factors, the use of FNVA/AWU as a proxy for the return to labour does not accord with the way in which farmers perceive income. To them, income and profit are closely related and therefore a measure which reflects the amount remaining after all other charges have been paid is more in line with the farmer's concept of income. This measure is Family Farm Income (FFI), i.e. 'the reward to the farmer and his family from using their owned land, owned capital and personal labour in agricultural activity on the farm . . . it accords broadly with the notion of profit from farming which is available for spending on consumption goods and services, for saving and investment, and for meeting other calls on personal income' (Hill 1993, 7).

FFI is derived from FNVA by deducting interest payments, rent, and the cost of hired labour. It too can be expressed in terms of labour input but, in this case, it is Family Work Units (FWU), i.e. labour after deduction of hired labour units. Given all the emphasis on the importance of the family farm (see Chapter 4), the use of FFI/FWU might appear to be in sympathy with what the CAP exists to support. However, one should not lose sight of the fact that Art. 39.1(b) of the Rome Treaty does not refer to the farm family but to 'the individual earnings of persons engaged in agriculture'.[11]

While it is clear from Table 5.6 that Family Work Units make up by far the greater part of labour on the small and medium-sized economic units, this is not the case on the largest units—particularly in the highly specialized areas of horticulture, vineyards, and other permanent crops. However, when one looks at FFI in absolute terms and per FWU, by economic size, the largest units yield the greatest return to the family. Table 5.7 illustrates this point well: in 1989, FFI in total and per FWU rose steadily throughout the size groups to a point where FFI was nearly twenty-three times the level in the smallest ESU group, and FFI/FWU was fourteen times higher. This suggests that the organizational structure of farming in terms of labour type—which caused so much philosophical concern in the early days of the Community—is of little importance compared with the economic size of the unit.

The final measure of income differences to be discussed in this Section is that of the age of the farmer. There is a general perception—based on common sense and the experience of the wider population—that high age is linked to low income. In agriculture, the elderly are found in disproportionate numbers on small farms and suffer from all the difficulties of that situation. Having a small farm probably also means they are less likely to have a known successor to the farm which must affect their interest in innovation and investment. As later chapters will show, a considerable effort has been made down the decades to persuade farmers to retire and/or retire early; much of this effort has been unsuccessful.

It is clear from the FADN results for 1989 that there is a link between age of farmer and the economic performance of the farm. One must be a little cautious in interpreting the data in Table 5.8 because, while the titular head of the farm

Table 5.7. Income indicators by economic size of farm,[a] FADN 1989

Indicators	All sizes	Small			Medium 16–14 ESU	Large	
		0–4 ESU	4–8 ESU	8–16 ESU		40–100 ESU	100–999 ESU
Labour input (AWU)	1.6	1.3	1.4	1.5	1.7	2.2	4.7
Unpaid labour input (FWU)	1.3	1.2	1.2	1.3	1.5	1.6	1.8
Farm net value added (FNVA) (ECU)	17,218	4,144	6,846	10,965	24,365	55,467	147,243
FNVA/AWU (ECU)	10,946	3,232	4,922	7,286	14,383	25,167	31,116
Family farm income (FFI) (ECU)	12,422	3,677	5,907	8,742	18,515	37,681	74,113
FFI/FWU (ECU)	9,305	3,106	4,729	6,519	12,587	23,260	42,110

[a] measured in terms of European size units (ESU)

Source: derived from Hill 1993.

Table 5.8. Economic performance by age of holder, FADN 1989

Indicators	All ages	<35	35–45	45–55	55–65	>65
Economic size (no. ESU)	18	22	22	19	15	12
Utilized agricultural area (ha.)	22	26	25	22	18	16
Farm net value added/ annual work unit (ECU)	10,947	13,215	13,217	11,046	9,025	7,346
Family farm income/ family work unit (ECU)	9,306	11,203	11,274	9,297	7,862	6,425
Output/ha. (ECU)	1,932	1,901	2,082	2,036	1,814	1,452
Output/AWU (ECU)	26,772	33,221	33,205	27,385	21,129	16,003

Source: Hill 1993.

may be old, it does not necessarily mean that he/she is the most active person on the farm. However, even allowing for that fact, it is clear that the best economic performance was recorded in those units where the titular head was aged 35–45, and that economic performance in the age categories above that level declined as age increased.

Measurement of Total Income of Agricultural Households

So far in this chapter the data, whether macro or micro, have been concerned solely with the measurement of income arising from the production of goods within the agricultural sector. They have not even included on-farm enterprises such as tourism or a farm shop. However, as the final Section of Chapter 4 indicated, it is quite wrong to assume without further investigation that the farmer or other members of the farm household are solely dependent on the production of agricultural commodities for their income. Chapter 4 and earlier Sections of the present chapter have drawn attention to the practical impossibility in present circumstances of ensuring that those who work in agriculture receive from farming alone an income comparable to that in other sectors in the same region. The Treaty objective which calls on the CAP to ensure a fair standard of living was, in effect, highjacked and misdirected along the path of income comparability.

For a variety of reasons it has proved very difficult to rethink the income-generating role of the CAP; one of the obstacles has been the absence of reliable information on the non-farming activities and/or income of the farmer and other members of the farm household. As was mentioned in Chapter 4, greater interest was taken in this issue from the early 1980s onwards. Midway through that decade the Community's Statistical Office—Eurostat—proposed the establishment of a programme to collect and analyse information on the Total Income of Agricultural Households (TIAH). The objectives of this programme were refined and clarified in 1990; briefly the task of TIAH is to monitor year-on-year changes in total income, aggregated by Member State; to monitor the changing composition of income; to compare trends in total income with those in other socio-professional groups; and to compare absolute levels of total income of farmers with those of other socio-professional groups on a unit basis (Hill 1995).

This programme is still in its infancy and a tremendous amount of work remains to be done. There are considerable methodological problems involved in the establishment of this new income indicator in a consistent manner across all Member States. Thus, this Section is confined to the discussion of a few key factors which are already reasonably well established. The income which TIAH exists to ascertain is the net disposable income (NDI) of the household, which is calculated on the basis of all income sources of all household members combined, from which payments such as taxes, social contributions, and insurance have been deducted. The units used are the household in total, the household member, and the consumer unit (i.e. household members adjusted by coefficients to reflect the composition of the household in terms of adults and children). NDI is then expressed in terms of these various units, irrespective of whether they work on the farm.

This is, perhaps, the first controversial point in the TIAH exercise: while it is perfectly reasonable to include dependent children, it is quite another matter if NDI is distributed over a household which contains adult members who neither work on the farm nor contribute to the running expenses of the household. Although the entire household is typically taken as the unit over which income measurement is made in welfare studies, and this approach is adopted in the EU's Household Budget Survey, it is difficult to see why the income of such persons should be included as part of agricultural household income, especially if the assumption is being made that in some way the NDI is available to those who are partially or wholly dependent on the farming activity. There are many loose ends to tidy up in the TIAH approach including the way households share income and expenditure.

Agricultural households are divided by TIAH statistics into three categories to reflect the importance or otherwise of farming activity in the total income stream. There is the 'narrow' definition which signifies that the *main* income of the household reference person (typically the head of the household) is from farming; the 'broad' definition which signifies that *someone* in the household has *some* income from farming; and there is the 'marginal' definition which signifies that there is *some* income from farming but where it is *not* the main income source of the household head.[12] In itself, the need to have a three-way classification such as this points to the complexity of the income situation in agricultural households. The number which qualify under the 'narrow' definition in most Member States is less than half the total number of agricultural holdings as defined in the Farm Structure Survey.

The use of the holding as a proxy for the number of farmers has long been recognized as a dangerous simplification—though one frequently made—and has always led to overestimation.[13] It is clear that TIAH is turning up similar problems. If one assumes that the 'narrow' definition is representative of those

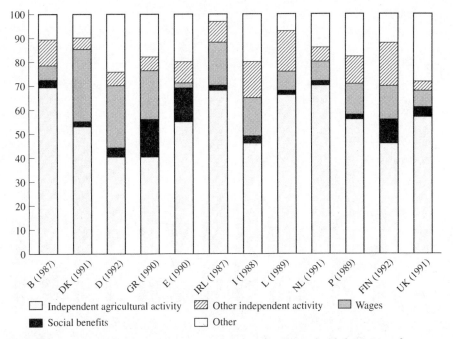

Fig. 5.2. Composition of the total income of agricultural households by source, for selected Member States, various years

Notes:
1. Results for the Netherlands and Greece are based on the household as the unit of classification (rather than the reference person).
2. In France problems of comparability arise because of the way in which social contributions are treated.
3. In the UK the current data source does not cover households with holdings arranged as corporate businesses, and there are other statistical problems that should preclude direct comparison with other Member States.
4. 'Other' includes income from property, imputed value of domestic dwelling, and other miscellaneous current transfers.
5. For Germany figures for 1992 are taken; although 1993 results are available, they are subject to substantial revision.

Source: Hill 1995.

households with the greatest dependence on agriculture, it appears that, even for them, non-agricultural sources of income are important. Figure 5.2 illustrates this point: in general, only about one-half to two-thirds of income comes from farming. Care should be taken not to read too much into the exact situation in the various Member States, as some of the difference between them may be due to lack of complete harmonization of definitions. What Figure 5.2 indicates is that the income indicators used in the EAA and in FADN which are based on net value added per annual work unit (at the macro- or micro-level) are not good sources of information on the income situation of agricultural households— even where the main income source for the reference person is farming.

The second TIAH measure to be illustrated here is that of the average

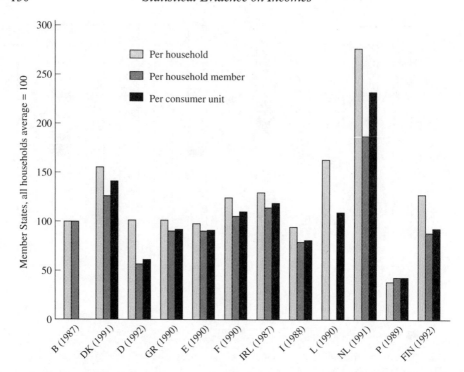

Fig. 5.3. Average disposable income of agricultural households relative to the all-household average, selected Member States, various years

Note: for Luxembourg, in the absence of a comparison being generated with the TIAH statistics, interim figures taken from a survey of living standards have been substituted

Source: derived from Hill 1995.

disposable income of agricultural households (narrowly defined) relative to the all-household average in a selection of Member States. The year used was the latest available in each Member State. Figure 5.3 indicates that average disposable income of agricultural households was roughly similar to or above the all-household average except (marginally) in Italy and very significantly in Portugal. The situation was not so favourable when household members or consumer units are compared, due to the fact that agricultural households contain more members on average than all-households.

These findings are important in the context of the perceived income problem in agriculture. As Hill (1995, 25) states: 'these results do not suggest that agricultural households are a particularly disadvantaged group in terms of their average disposable incomes, a major finding in the light of the objectives of agricultural policy in the European Union'. However, TIAH does not suggest that there is no income problem within farming as it does not throw any light on income distribution around the mean nor on income variation by type of farm business, type of production, region, age of farm operator, or educational level. It is very likely that one would find considerable differences in total income levels if these other factors could be researched as well, indicating the existence of localized problems or sets of personal factors which result in income deficiencies. Also, given the variability of agriculture from year to year, one would need to have a run of years to test to what extent one year's data are representative of the income situation.

The Commission publishes data on poverty based on information derived from the Household Budget Survey. As these statistics are based on expenditure rather than on income, they are not strictly comparable with the data discussed above. However, they do add another dimension to the discussion. Poverty is defined in terms of the deviation in expenditure of the household from the average equivalent expenditure. Using a 50 per cent cut-off point (i.e. the proportion of households whose expenditure was less than half that of the group being analysed), farmers and agricultural workers combined were, in most Member States, among the socio-economic groups with the highest risk of poverty (Hagenaars *et al.* 1994). As hired agricultural workers are not a significant category in most Member States, the findings of the poverty survey can be assumed to be representative of farmers.

These results do not contradict the TIAH results but rather indicate that there must be an enormous range of income levels (and therefore expenditure levels) hidden within the averages considered here. Certainly, the FADN results discussed earlier in this chapter would support that possibility, in those cases where agriculture is a major income source in the household. Despite the fact that income levels and income ratios have lain at the heart of agricultural policy in the developed world at least since the 1950s, the statistical data presented in this chapter suggest that, in policy terms, there is a lack of clarity about objectives and the impact of particular policy instruments. In income terms, the role of the CAP is to ensure the integration of agriculture and those who work in that sector into the economic and social life of the Union. That requires much more sensitive targeting of income support than has been the case to date.

NOTES

1. Also known as RICA from its French title: Reseau d'information comptable agricole.
2. It is important not to lose sight of the fact that the indicators are all at the sector level and do not provide information on the personal income of farmers, family members, or hired workers. Despite this, there is a tendency to use Indicators 1–3 as proxies for personal income. This is inappropriate and potentially misleading. (See Hill (1989) and (1991) for an analysis of the origin, merits, and shortcomings of the indicators and the equivalent measures in FADN.)
3. The number of persons working in agriculture is converted into Annual Work Units so as to avoid the problem that not everyone works full time in the sector. A full-time worker equals 1 AWU, and part-time and seasonal workers are converted to full-time equivalents.

4. The inclusion of Spain is questionable as it had only joined the Community in 1986. Therefore, its growth rate refers to a period which—for the most part—predated entry.

5. This assumption is confirmed in those Member States where labour productivity for industry alone could be measured. However, even there, the annual increase in labour productivity in agriculture, forestry, and fishing remained well above that of industry (see Terluin 1991).

6. Given the period in question, the results for Greece, Spain, and Portugal are taken from a period either prior to or contemporary with their Accession to the Community, and their situation may have changed subsequently. Their presence in the graph also influences the Community average.

7. This problem was met with before. Where agricultural income data are used by themselves (as opposed to being combined with forestry and fisheries), the labour unit used is the AWU and not persons employed. The comparison of NVA per worker for the economy as a whole with NVA/AWU in agriculture has the effect of enhancing the relative income per AWU.

8. It should not be thought that classification into a particular farm type means that the activity listed is the only one on the farm. Rather it is the dominant activity.

9. The introduction of the Less-Favoured Areas Directive is discussed in Ch. 9.

10. In fact the ratio of ESU:ECU is adjusted from time to time. By the early 1990s, the ratio was 1 ESU = 1,200 ECU.

11. The Commission's view on the appropriateness of omitting hired labour costs from the calculation of income seems to have undergone a change during the 1980s. In 1982, it argued against the removal of wage costs citing Art. 39.1(b) and commenting that the CAP was 'concerned with the incomes of all those engaged in agriculture, rather than the distribution of agricultural incomes between salaried and non-salaried workers' (Commission 1982(*b*), 10).

12. The 'marginal' group includes, for instance, part-time farmers whose main income is from an off-farm source—a job or a pension perhaps, and full-time farmers whose main income is from social security.

13. Thirty years ago in Ireland, the present author discovered a 25% discrepancy between the number of farmers as declared in the Census of Population and the number of holdings in the Agricultural Enumeration. Even the Census figure was an overstatement, as 8% of farmers declared a subsidiary occupation which was probably below the true percentage, and no account was taken of farmers above retirement age who were in receipt of a retirement pension (Fennell 1968).

6

Price and Market Support:
Contradictions and Dilemmas

The Choice of Market Support Mechanisms[1]

The dominance of price policy and market regulation as the main instruments of agricultural policy in the 1950s was described in Chapter 1. It was against such a background that, in 1956, the Spaak report was drawn up; naturally the authors gave some thought to the manner in which agricultural markets should be supported and managed in the proposed new Community. Their experts examined three systems: crop limitation, price intervention, and deficiency payments.

The crop limitation system used as a model was the US soil bank or set-aside, under which farmers agreed not to plant a proportion of their land for a stated number of years and in return were paid compensation for the income forgone. This system was accompanied by a public storage scheme. It is quite surprising that the Spaak team were so forward thinking in the mid-1950s, when surpluses were only just beginning to be discussed as a potential problem in Western Europe. Events were to prove how right they were. As Ries commented in relation to the Spaak experts: 'long experience . . . demonstrates that it is always financially less costly to pay a farmer to persuade him not to produce than to have unsaleable surpluses on your hands' (Ries 1978, 56).

The second system examined—price intervention—was already widely used; under it, when a harvest was bountiful and the market price consequently low, a public body intervened on the market to purchase part of the supply. This system was always combined with a stocks policy, which allowed for market stabilization through release of stocks when prices were high. This was to the benefit of both producers and consumers. This system was particularly appropriate for circumstances in which the level of self-sufficiency for key commodities was high, but usually below 100 per cent, and where the market needed fine-tuning at different seasons and in certain years.

The third system—deficiency payments—was a British speciality, which was particularly appropriate when the level of self-sufficiency was low. It allowed consumers to be supplied at prices which reflected the usually low import prices, while it guaranteed a higher price to domestic producers. The taxpayer made up the difference between the consumer price and the guaranteed price. This system was very effective where the number of farmers producing a given commodity was small and the number of taxpayers was large. It was also socially equitable where the taxes were levied more on income than on expenditure and where the tax rate was progressive. These features ensured that poor consumers were not contributing to the support of farmers.

All of these systems require public funds for their operation and critical to the cost is the level of self-sufficiency. In the context of the proposed Community this would have required a decision on the commercial relationships which were to be established with third countries. While in general favouring a liberal trade policy, the authors of the Spaak report decided not to become involved in detailed policy issues and confined their remarks to setting out the principles which were to guide the later designers of the agricultural policy.

As indicated in Chapter 1, the Rome Treaty was equally vague: it provided a list of objectives for the CAP, some of which were clearly related to market organization (security of supply, stable markets, reasonable consumer prices), and it made a very brief reference to the establishment of a common price policy. The Stresa Conference was of some help: its final Resolution referred to the need for a balance between production and potential outlets, given export and import possibilities, and specialization based on natural conditions and on economic structure within the Community. How the Commission transformed these general sentiments into concrete proposals was outlined in Chapter 2.

Until the reforms introduced in 1995 with the implementation of the GATT Agreement, the key mechanism of the managed market was the variable levy.[2] This was the classic frontier control instrument of the CAP. It represented the difference between the threshold price—an institutional price fixed annually at the Community frontier—and the lower import offer price. Its effect was to raise the offer price to the threshold level, thereby preventing imports from undercutting the internal market price. The variable levy was applied to the market for all major cereals (including rice), sugar, the main dairy products, beef, and olive oil. Because of the importance of cereals in the feeding of pigs, poultry, and laying hens, the frontier protection for pigmeat, poultrymeat, and eggs is dependent on the mechanism for grain. These products were protected by a sluice-gate price which acted as a minimum import price. To this sluice-gate price was added a levy made up of two parts, one of which represented the difference in cereal prices inside and outside the Community.

In the early days of the Community, Mansholt maintained that the market support mechanisms were in themselves neutral (see Chapter 2) and that the critical factor in determining whether the policy was protectionist or liberal was the price level at which these mechanisms were set. This was not a completely accurate portrayal of the situation. By their very nature, import levies were powerful market insulators in their ability to exclude produce from a third country, except on the Community's price terms. In this, they performed completely differently from an *ad valorem* customs tariff which can, in effect, be absorbed by an exporting country dropping its offer price.

The Community did use customs tariffs for certain agricultural commodities: beef (in conjunction with a levy), sheepmeat, fresh and processed fruit and vegetables, tobacco, seeds for sowing, hops, and wine. However, even with these products, the import regimes became more protectionist over time, as the tariff was combined with a reference price. This was a minimum import price based on average prices on representative markets over a period of years. It was used for fresh and processed fruit and vegetables, wine, and seeds for sowing and, if it was not observed, a countervailing charge might be made.

Until the conclusion of the Uruguay Round of GATT, one of the most characteristic features of the analysis of the CAP by the Institutions of the Community (whether Commission, Parliament, or the ESC) was the unquestioning acceptance of the frontier mechanisms. When they were discussed, it was usually in the context of Community Preference,[3] especially in relation to whether it was being observed or undermined. Attention, therefore, was focused much more on the internal mechanisms of price and market support. Just as the variable levy was regarded as the classic frontier mechanism, so internally the classic mechanism is market intervention.

In practice, the variable levy and intervention were often linked and, indeed originally, the linkage was intended to be very close, with each major commodity having a separate fund financed primarily from the import levy. However, this idea was soon dropped and over the years the intervention mechanism was introduced for a wide range of commodities, many of which did not have a frontier levy. Intervention prices are set annually for the main cereals, sugar, the main dairy products, olive oil, some oilseeds, tobacco, beef, pigmeat, sheepmeat, wine, certain fruits and vegetables. It is important to realize that the way in which the intervention mechanism is used, its effectiveness, and its frequency of use differ markedly from one commodity to another, and have also changed over time. The commodities for which intervention is most significant are those which represent a major proportion of gross agricultural product (GAP), which are regionally dispersed, and which are produced by large numbers of farmers.

In essence, the purpose of intervention is to support market prices and to assist in the management of the internal market.[4] Intervention prices are set each year and are intended to prevent prices on an oversupplied market from spiralling downwards. The intervention prices act as a trigger for the support mechanism. The agencies in each Member State which administer the intervention system either act as buyers of last resort when the market price is already weak or they anticipate a market fall and provide subsidies for private storage, so as to encourage traders not to market produce at periods of heavy supply.

As mentioned in Chapter 2, intervention works best when the level of self-sufficiency is high but not excessive. In such a case, the mechanism can operate to regulate supply either seasonally or from year to year, and thus can help to keep market prices stable. The system does not function well when the market is oversupplied on a regular basis. This latter has been the situation throughout most of the lifetime of the CAP. The level of oversupply and the range of commodities suffering from oversupply have increased over time. Much of the effort to control expenditure on the CAP, especially since the early 1980s, has hinged on the reduction of surpluses and on limitation of access to intervention, whether in terms of quantities eligible for intervention, the periods of the year, or quality standards.

The effectiveness of intervention and its cost are also influenced by the nature of the commodity in terms of its storability without loss of quality. Thus, although intervention is possible for a perishable commodity such as beef, it is not a particularly suitable tool for market regulation. The beef must be processed, usually by freezing, thereby losing much of its value and limiting the purposes for which it can be used subsequently.

The existence of the intervention mechanism influences farmers' decisions because it insulates them from the market by providing an outlet for a commodity for which there is no genuine demand. Extreme examples of this are the accumulation in store of unsaleable varieties of tobacco, and the compulsory distillation of surplus poor-quality wine into industrial alcohol. Intervention also distorts processors' decisions by providing an outlet for a product for which demand is limited in preference to alternative products where demand is more elastic. An example of this is to be found in the dairy sector. For practical reasons of storability, intervention is limited to butter, skimmed milk powder, and certain hard cheeses. The market for butter/skimmed milk powder[5] is grossly oversupplied not only in the Community but also internationally but processors find it easier to manufacture these products because of the sure 'market' provided by intervention, rather than to manufacture the more perishable dairy products for which no support of any kind is available.

It could be argued quite reasonably that these distortions are not inherent in the system but are the result of its misuse. This is undoubtedly true and efforts have been made to correct some of the worst features of certain support regimes. However, a more fundamental problem is that the intervention mechanism is inappropriate for certain commodities and unsuited to the market situation today. Having introduced the system thirty to forty years ago, it is extremely difficult to abandon it in favour of something else.[6] The Community does have other support mechanisms and, given the changed circumstances of agriculture today, perhaps more thought should be given to the wider use of alternatives to the intervention mechanism. As they operate currently, these include a variety of production aids paid either directly to the farmer or to the first-stage processor.

Some production aids are intended to reflect at the level of the farm the support given to the processor. In these cases, there is usually only one or at most a very limited number of outlets for the commodity and it is simpler and more cost-effective from the Community's point of view to inject the support at the processing stage. Examples are sugar beet, cotton, certain fodder crops, and potatoes grown for starch. Other production aids are paid directly to certain farmers based on the physical quantity produced or the area grown. These are specialty commodities produced in well-defined regions of the Community. Examples of area-based payments are durum wheat, fibre flax, hemp, and hops; examples of volume-based payments are olive oil, seeds for sowing, tobacco, and silkworms.

There remain two types of market support to be outlined here: export refunds, and aids to processors to compensate them for higher purchase prices in the Community. While these types of support differ fundamentally from each other, they are both in their own way a direct outcome of the particular types of commodity regimes set up. Export refunds are subsidies paid on a wide range of commodities (in raw and processed form) exported from the Community. So widespread is their appearance in the various support regimes, it is easier to list the regimes where they do *not* feature: soya beans, linseed, peas/field beans/lupins, dried fodder, fibre flax, hemp, cotton, seeds for sowing, hops, and silkworms.[7]

The purpose of an export refund is to lower the cost of a product so as to make it competitive with products from other sources in markets outside the Community. Where export refunds existed alongside import levies, it could be argued that the effect of the refund was to bring the export price down to the equivalent of the import price prior to the imposition of the import levy. In this sense, the granting of an export refund could be seen as a neutral exercise. This is not an argument which achieved wide acceptance internationally. It might have been more acceptable if it were not for the fact that the existence of export refunds has permitted the retention and even expansion of external markets for Community agricultural produce which otherwise would not have existed. In turn, this has encouraged production. In this, its impact has been similar to that of intervention. Indeed, the link is even closer, as export refunds have been used as an alternative to intervention storage. It is clearly much less costly for the Community to pay one export refund than to incur storage costs and ultimate disposal costs for the same product.

It is probably true to state that the existence and use of export refunds is the aspect of the CAP which has caused the most criticism outside the frontiers of the Community. Yet, within the Institutions of the Community, there has been remarkably little discussion of this aspect of policy. This uncritical attitude may well stem from the key role allocated to export refunds in the basic Regulation 25/62 (see Chapter 2), where it is clear that the intention was to use them as a market-clearing mechanism. As with the variable levy, export refunds were taken as given until the GATT agreement of 1994—an issue which re-emerges in Chapter 12.

The aids to processors arise directly either from the operation of certain commodity regimes or because of trade agreements entered into in the framework of GATT in the early years of the Community. Examples of the first type of aid arise under the cereals and sugar regimes where the raw material cost to manufacturers of starch is increased and, due to the operation of the frontier protection system, manufacturers are unable to substitute cheap imports for the high-priced Community cereals or sugar. The starch manufacturers pass on the cost to the end-user but the latter is able to claim a subsidy which negates the high cost of the raw material.

The second type of aid to processors arose from the agreement to freeze frontier protection of oilseeds at zero or very low levels. In the light of subsequent developments, this was a most important agreement. It had its origin in the acceptance by the USA of the introduction of the variable levy for cereals in return for concessions by the Community on oilseeds, for which at the time the Community had very low levels of self-sufficiency. The world price for oilseeds is usually well below the target price[8] set annually in the Community; because of this price differential the oil crusher in the Community has no incentive to purchase internally produced oilseeds. To counteract this, the crusher is paid a production subsidy in the form of a deficiency payment. It represents the difference between the target price and the world market price. Similar arrangements operate for soyabeans, dried fodder, and cotton.

Mention has been made in this Section of the annual fixing of certain key institutional prices. This usually takes place in the spring though sometimes, due to the inability of the Council of Ministers to reach agreement, the decision is delayed and the existing price regimes have to be temporarily extended. The Commission normally presents the Council with the price proposals for the following farm year in January or February. Originally the intention was that the proposals should be made much earlier but from the late 1960s onwards the timetable became compressed. One of the reasons for this was a desire on the part of the Commission to be able to take into account the most up-to-date statistics on production, income, and trade when making its proposals, so as to ensure their relevance to the marketing year for which they were made.

The negative side of this approach is that many production decisions have already been taken by farmers before the price proposals are announced and so changes in the form or level of support are not reflected in farmer response until a full farm year later. For instance, the farm year for cereals runs from July to June but winter cereals are planted in the previous autumn, usually three to four months before the Commission agrees its proposals and perhaps six to seven months before the Council of Ministers actually agrees the new price levels. Any important changes in the support system or the level of prices will, therefore, have to wait until the following autumn or spring before farmers have an opportunity to respond. By that time, of course, it is quite likely that the market situation will have undergone some further adjustment.[9]

This built-in response lag makes it very difficult to achieve a change in the production level of any particular commodity, even one with an annual production cycle. It is even more problematic when dealing with livestock products, especially milk and beef, and tree crops such as orchard fruit, olive oil, and wine. The interrelationship of commodities adds further complexity: to take the cereals example again—price or market support changes in this sector have a knock-on effect on farmers' decisions on other arable crops, milk, beef, pigs, poultry, and eggs. It can be appreciated that trying to change direction within the price and market elements of the CAP is not easy.[10]

In outlining the 'objective method' in Chapter 4, reference was made to the political nature of the annual price-fixing exercise. The Commission's proposals are almost always adjusted upwards by the Council of Ministers. Where modifications to the commodity regimes are proposed, in order to curb expenditure or to make the regimes more responsive to market trends, the Council is quite likely to reject the change or to accept it in some heavily emasculated version. The reasons for the Council's behaviour are firstly, that, as a Community Institution, it wishes to assert its authority as the decision-maker and not to appear as a cipher of the Commission, and secondly, because the Ministers represent national interests.

The collective interest of the Community on any issue is not necessarily in the individual interest of each Member State. Therefore, decision-making in the Council is heavily influenced by bargaining between groups of countries. Alliances may differ from one commodity to another and because, for practical purposes, each commodity has to be considered separately, although it forms part of a whole package, each Member State concentrates on the few issues of direct relevance to itself. Thus much of the price package is externalized by each Member State and an overview of the total impact of the annual price decisions is never achieved.

It is ironic that one of the most forceful of the bargainers—Germany—was able to comment in all seriousness in 1975 that 'Council decisions on the use of funds for the agricultural policy have often been politically motivated, while objective considerations have had to take second place' (Council 1975(*b*), 3). The outcome of the annual bargaining is often not even the second-best option but rather the minimum acceptable to all. This prompts the question as to what the Community is actually trying to achieve collectively in the price and market policy—which is the subject of the next Section.

Conflicting Policy Goals

The existence of a price support policy and of instruments of market regulation indicates that price is intended to do more than provide a means of achieving market equilibrium. It is in no way unusual to find that governments regard the provision of food as being too important an activity to be left to farmers, traders, manufacturers, and the vagaries of the market-place. Having decided that price must serve additional ends, it becomes important to identify these goals and the means by which they are to be achieved.

In all collective activities of the Community, the overriding consideration must be the achievement of the objectives laid down in Article 2 of the Rome Treaty, namely the promotion throughout the Community of harmonious development of economic activities, continuous and balanced expansion, increased stability, an accelerated raising of the standard of living, and closer relations between the Member States. The means of achieving these goals are the establishment of a common market and the approximation of the economic policies of the Member States. The common market includes agricultural production and trade in agricultural products, and the CAP exists because of the existence of that market.

In its 1960 proposals on the establishment of the CAP, the Commission spelled out the role of the market policy as being the integration of 'the agricultural markets of the Member States into a common market with the characteristics of an internal market' (Commission 1960, II/18). The main objective was a balance between production and potential outlets inside and outside the Community. Measures intended to promote this goal were to have due regard to production specialization 'appropriate to the economic structure and internal natural conditions of the Community' (ibid. II/19). Externally, the market policy was to allow for the development of production and demand in the associated countries and territories, and the role of trade with non-member countries (both imports and exports) was to be given due recognition.

The market policy was also given specific objectives in relation to income and price stabilization. On income, it was to ensure 'that the value attached to agricultural products is such that it helps to guarantee to farming activities a fair remuneration approaching that obtained in the other sectors of the economy'; and on prices, it was 'to stabilize agricultural markets in order to prevent excessive price swings with their unfavourable consequences for farmers' incomes. It should not, however, completely eliminate economic risks and retard possible adaptation to any changes in demand' (Commission, II/19).

These general principles were reflected in the proposals for the individual commodity regimes. For instance, for wheat, where there was a danger of surpluses, production was to be stabilized at the existing level, but with encouragement to shift to more saleable types of wheat. Regional specialization was to be encouraged and the income objective was to be linked to those farms which achieved the normal standard of productivity in the predominantly grain-growing regions. Similarly with sugar, the fair income was to be attained in specialized districts and for a quantity equivalent to domestic requirements, with surpluses being disposed of at world market prices. For milk, a fair income was to be assured on well-managed and well-equipped family farms.

In 1962, with the passing of the first set of commodity Regulations, the general principles of the 1960 proposals were put into a legal framework. Under Reg. 19/62 on cereals (JO 30, 20–4–62), the setting of the transitional target price became the responsibility of the Council and the Regulation stipulated that the price decisions were to be based on acquired experience and certain criteria which were yet to be determined. These were to take account of the opportunity to promote specialization, in accordance with the economic structure and natural conditions inside the Community. This in turn would lead to the determination of the future common target price as a function of rationally managed and economically viable farms in the Community, and the proper relationship between the prices of the various products (Art. 6.4).

The criteria were the subject of a separate draft Regulation; they were divided into three categories relating to the incomes of the people who worked in farming, the guidance of production in relation to demand, and the development of the wider economy. No indication was given as to whether any order of priority was intended, although it is true that the income criterion was the most fully worked out. Their merit lies in the fact that they were an attempt to link the price-fixing exercise firmly into the income objectives (Article 39) and the common market objectives (Article 2) of the Rome Treaty.[11] In the event, this draft Regulation was never put into effect; indeed, it was never even discussed by the Council of Ministers (De Veer 1979). Thus, the new market policy started out with no clear legal guidelines on which price decisions could be based.

This fundamental lack of direction in the price policy has handicapped its operation ever since: if a policy has no defined framework, how can its performance be judged, how can its success be measured? The barrage of criticism which has accompanied the policy throughout its lifetime has concentrated on five main accusations, namely that it is driven by political considerations; that it lacks production and trade targets; that it is expected to achieve contradictory goals; that it carries too much of the burden of fulfilling the objectives of the CAP; and that it costs too much. All of these accusations are interrelated.

The issue of political considerations was touched upon briefly in the previous Section in relation to the price-fixing exercise. For many years there were few constraints on the agricultural ministers where the price policy was concerned and it is not surprising, therefore, that they were unmindful of the implications of their actions. Individually, ministers are determined to achieve the best results for their clients in their own country. These clients include not only farmers but also the industries upstream and downstream of agriculture, which include many powerful interests. Ministers also wish to uphold the interests of their own department, and their own personal prestige and influence among their governmental colleagues. In a situation in which economic and political constraints are minimal, it is hardly likely that the politicians concerned are going to invent a set of constraints for themselves.

Two procedural factors have added to the political nature of price-fixing; the first was the unanimity rule which hampered decision-taking in the Council for so many years; the second is the existence of the price package. The unanimity rule, referred to briefly in Chapter 2, was totally at variance with the procedures laid down in the Rome Treaty. It gave to an individual minister an excessive amount of bargaining power. The price package is a sensible device in that it concentrates the negotiations to one time of year and it should, in theory, make it easier to view the effect of price and market support changes across the range of commodities, though in practice it is doubtful that it does so. However, it does mean an increase in the amount of political bargaining, as none of the elements of the price package comes into force until all are agreed.[12]

As the problem of market imbalance became more serious in the 1970s, so the calls for some guidance on the size and shape of the agricultural sector grew. Even the farmers were bewildered, calling for a clearer indication of the objectives of the production policy. They were not seeking firm quantitative objectives but rather a series of indicators: the level of internal consumption requirements which could be met by production within the Community; import requirements, especially those needed on grounds of quality; export opportunities; buffer stock levels to ensure security of supply and price stability; and the Community's contribution to food aid (COPA/COGECA 1973). 'Once the objectives have been determined, the problem of the balance and the orientation of production in the framework of a global strategy could be put forward' (ibid. 11).

In both 1974 and 1975, the ESC called for the introduction of production objectives,[13] making, on the first occasion, the tart comment that, if the Commission was intending to propose new regimes for commodities not yet included in the price policy, 'it would be advisable to try to fix overall production objectives first of all, before setting up types of market organizations liable to engender trends which may prove inappropriate' (OJ C115, 28–9–74, 29). The European Parliament also recommended long-term policy strategies which included production targets.[14] Even the Danish Government suggested that, in order to improve the annual price-fixing, the Community should decide what level of self-sufficiency it wished to achieve, product by product (Council 1975 (*a*)). At a meeting at Echternach organized by the Agricultural Committee of the European Parliament, attended by outside experts as well as parliamentarians, Priebe called for the setting up of basic criteria for the market policy and 'the maintenance of a predominantly home-based food production system' which would leave a certain market share for imports. He also recommended that there should be 'specific supply targets for individual products and consumer goods' (EP, rapp. Caillavet, 1979, 52).

As will be seen later in this chapter, when the Community eventually introduced some forms of production control to halt the growing problem of surpluses, it did so without addressing the fundamental issue of the most appropriate level of self-sufficiency for individual commodities. Rather, existing levels of production were used as the base without comment as to their desirability on economic grounds.

The complaint that the policy has contradictory goals stems from a failure to define the purpose of the price policy with sufficient precision:

[O]ne purpose of the common price policy is to guarantee the level of the incomes of those working in agriculture; another is to be an instrument for steering production and, in general, ensuring adaptation of supply and demand. It must be stated that the Community has never made a clear choice between what could be termed the 'economic' price concept and . . . the 'social' price concept. Perhaps it would have been premature to make such a choice. . . . At all events, the result was that the Community was reduced to putting the emphasis on political factors.   (ESC, rapp. Bourel, 1974, 71)

In 1975, using the relevant Articles of the Rome Treaty as its starting point, the Commission commented extensively on the contradictions which had emerged in the functioning of the price policy (Commission 1975(*a*)). When agriculture was included in the common market (in Article 38), it did not merely mean that obstacles to the free movement of agricultural products had to disappear but also that production had to be located in accordance with the optimum allocation of resources and the need for specialization.[15] Thus, there was a need for a division of labour geographically which reflected comparative advantage. This had not happened to the extent to which it should, either because the price relationships between commodities were incorrect or because the support prices were set at too high a level, thereby allowing production to be maintained in regions where it should have disappeared, or because the instruments of policy were in themselves an obstacle to the process of specialization.[16]

Indeed, a few years later, the Commission commented again on this shortcoming of the policy: 'the prices policy ought to take more account of a principle often overlooked, that of product specialization within the Community. Greater weight ought to be given to certain economic criteria when guaranteed price levels are fixed' (Commission 1980(*c*), 21). Whatever the cause of the failure, the suboptimal allocation of resources has worked against two of the objectives of Art. 39.1 of the Rome Treaty: increasing the incomes of those in agriculture, and ensuring reasonable prices for consumers.

At the meeting at Echternach, Priebe criticized the manner in which the price policy was geared excessively to income support. The dual function of price—to support incomes and to guide production—was causing conflict and he recommended that the functions be separated. There was also a fundamental problem in the way in which agricultural prices were set by political bodies. 'It is asking too much of political bodies to strike the right economic balance between the influences of prices on earnings, which is clearly perceivable, and their impact on market equilibrium, which is more difficult to assess' (EP, rapp. Caillavet, 1979, 49).

Closely linked to the criticism that the price policy is expected to achieve contradictory goals is the criticism that it is carrying too much of the burden of fulfilling all the objectives of the CAP. The uneven development of the various components of the CAP, with the dominance of the price policy, was alluded to in Chapter 2 and will be discussed further in later chapters. The introduction of the 'objective method' (outlined in Chapter 4) was an attempt to confine price policy to an economic role but it was doomed to failure because the measures necessary to support farmers with income problems were not put in place.

In reviewing the extent to which the policy had achieved the objectives of the Treaty, the Commission, in 1975, spelled out one of the dilemmas it faced:

[T]o seek to attain the objective of improved productivity solely by the operation of market and pricing policies is not only vain but, in the last analysis, involved a contradiction, for, in order to support incomes, it is necessary to fix prices at a high enough level to provide a living for the marginal farms. Productivity on these farms is low since they are too small to use an optimum combination of production factors. Thus, action is necessary in respect of the factors of production themselves. (Commission 1975(*a*), 15)

The clarity of this comment is in contrast with the much more confused statements made by the Commission from time to time. For instance, in 1973, in discussing problems in the sugar sector, the Commission identified the level of production quotas as the source of the deficiencies in the policy. They were set in 1967 at levels which maintained production in regions unsuited to sugar beet, while they allowed increased production in the best regions. The Commission speculated that, if quotas did not exist and price was lowered to a market-clearing level, many regions would drop out of production, causing difficulties in social and investment terms. It commented in a categorical way: 'there can be no question at the present time of a decision being taken at Community level which would mean that, within a short space of time, all or a substantial part of the sugar industry would disappear and that beet would cease to be grown in a number of regions' (Commission 1973(*b*), 5). Not only are sugar beet farmers a relatively prosperous group who do not normally excite much sympathy, but sugar was a crop which, in 1960, the Commission recommended should be subject to a very cautious market regime, because of its surplus potential.

A more genuine dilemma exists for a product such as olive oil. In 1977, the Commission pointed out that, if the Community were enlarged to include Greece, Portugal, and Spain, it would have a surplus of olive oil for which market outlets would be few. 'Since it is a perennial, traditional crop of undisputed socio-economic and ecological value (the olive tree often grows where nothing else will) and despite the efforts which the Commission intends to make at the structural level . . . there is no hope of a reduction in the areas under olives and consequently in production' (Commission 1977(*f*), 8).

Milk production poses another kind of dilemma. In 1962, Mansholt commented: 'we have whole regions in the mountains where the production of milk is marginal and should disappear' and he advocated the development of a regional structural policy (national and Community) 'to reduce the production of milk and to reserve it to the regions having the lowest production costs' (Mansholt 1962, 11–12). However, in 1978 when milk surpluses were an even bigger problem, the Commission stated that 'the disappearance of the least efficient farms ought to be encouraged on economic grounds, but the common agricultural policy must not neglect its social responsibility to these holdings' (Commission 1978(*d*), 7). In other words, the problem should not be devolved to some other policy but rather dealt with by the agricultural policy in some way or another.

The final major area of criticism of the price policy is its cost. Not surprisingly this is a criticism most frequently voiced by academic commentators and politicians not involved in the administration of agricultural policy. There is much less discussion of this issue within the Institutions of the Community. In the context of this chapter, it is not so much the total cost of price and market support which is of interest but rather the way in which the expenditure is distributed between commodities and between internal support measures and export subsidies. If the price policy has a dual role to support incomes and guide production, how well are these functions reflected in the disbursement of FEOGA-Guarantee funds?

Budgetary Cost of Price and Market Support

Appendix Tables 6.A1–6.A6 at the end of this chapter provide an analysis of FEOGA-Guarantee expenditure over the lifetime of the policy to 1993. The details of the statistics are of less importance than the general picture which they provide. Indeed, there are many inconsistencies in the data; for instance, prior to 1971 budgetary revenue and expenditure were on a different basis than later years. Total expenditure from FEOGA-Guarantee in some years included overseas food aid for certain commodities. Especially in the 1970s, payments attributable to currency fluctuations were an appreciable additional cost within FEOGA-Guarantee. The level of expenditure on a particular commodity in each Member State is derived for the year in question from the returns made by the Member States. They are based on a system of advance payments and may require later adjustment. As a result, the accounts for any year are not closed until some years later and subsequent Budgets include closing positive or negative balances for earlier years.

Table 6.A1 provides an overview of the distribution of expenditure by commodity group, by year. Excluded from the table are those commodities for which the annual level of support has been consistently below 1 per cent of FEOGA-Guarantee expenditure. This means the exclusion of rice, seeds for sowing, and hops (though these commodities are included in Table 6.A4). Other minor commodities have been included in Table 6.A1 only because they have been grouped together—for instance into textiles (flax and hemp, silkworms, cotton), protein crops (dried fodder, peas, and field beans). The inclusion of 'non-Annex II products' requires some explanation.

Annex II of the Rome Treaty lists the products covered by Article 38 under which the CAP was established. In Art. 38.1 agricultural products are defined as 'the products of the soil, of stock-farming and of fisheries and products of first-stage processing directly related to these products'. The Article makes no reference to manufacture at a later stage in the processing chain. Thus, for instance, while wheat and the products of milling are included in Annex II, bread and biscuits are not. This created an anomaly, as the industries which use agricultural raw materials are clearly affected by the support system applied to the primary product. Where exports were concerned, it was quickly realized that the manufactured product would become uncompetitive abroad if some form of compensation for higher input prices were not given. Therefore, from 1966 onwards, export refunds were made available to manufactured products which used inputs based on commodities for which a price support regime existed (such as products based on cereals, milk, or sugar).[17]

Table 6.A1 illustrates the manner in which the support system has been expanded over time to include a wider range of commodities. This, of course, is part of the reason why the proportion of expenditure on cereals and milk products has fallen over time. The addition of new Member States has also affected the distribution of expenditure—for instance, the increase in expenditure on olive oil since the late 1980s is due to the inclusion of Spain which is a major producer.

Relative levels of expenditure are also affected by the nature of some commodities and by outside events. For instance, expenditure on beef is highly cyclical due to the length of the reproductive cycle in cattle (see the noticeable decline in 1977–9 and in 1987–9).[18] The very sharp decline in the proportion of expenditure accounted for by cereals and sugar in the mid-1970s is a reflection of the international commodity crisis at that time, when prices were very high and there was little need for support. Expenditure on sugar is also affected by another factor, namely the production levy which is used to support the cost of exports. Given its importance among the arable crops and the unit level of support, sugar would be a much more expensive commodity in budgetary terms in the absence of the levy.

One of the most interesting features of this table is the way in which it illustrates the unimportance of so many commodities in terms of their relative cost to FEOGA-Guarantee. Apart from cereals and milk products, which have always been dominant in terms of support, of production, and of the number of farmers involved, only sugar, oilseeds, and beef have ever each represented 10 per cent or more of total price support. A great many farmers producing a wide range of commodities are being supported by the price and market policy at a relatively small cost to the Budget. It is very easy to forget this in the clamour for curbing expenditure on the CAP.

For instance, in many respects it makes sense to try to reduce the overproduction of table wine, for which consumption is falling and for which the cost of disposal through the production of industrial alcohol is high. But such a reform is going to make very little difference to the overall level of expenditure from FEOGA-Guarantee. The room for manœuvre and the opportunity to make a significant difference to the level of price and market support is far less than might be imagined.

Tables 6.A2–6.A5 examine expenditure according to the support mechanism used, i.e. whether export refund or domestic intervention. The latter covers a wide range of types of support and is not limited to the withdrawal of produce from an oversupplied market. Indeed, for some commodities, that is not an option and internal support is confined to production subsidies.[19] Table 6.A2 covers the small group of commodities for which both export refunds and domestic intervention are important. It provides the absolute level of expenditure by year and the proportion of that total spent on intervention of all kinds.

To some extent—and particularly for cereals which can be stored for a considerable length of time without deterioration—the support mechanisms are interchangeable depending on the state of the international market. It is a moot point whether sugar should be included in this table as, although intervention is used on a regular basis, the preferred option is to export surplus sugar. Unlike for cereals, milk products, and beef, the practice has been not to allow the accumulation of sugar stocks. Therefore, domestic intervention is very largely limited to the refund of storage costs for sugar which is either used internally or rapidly exported. Although part of the intervention cost of beef is attributable to various headage payments (for instance, for suckler cows to encourage specialist beef enterprises), the bulk of it is to cover storage costs. As mentioned earlier in this chapter, the use of storage for a perishable product can only be achieved by transformation into a more manageable product by freezing or canning. This reduces its ultimate sale value and limits the purposes to which it can be put.

Table 6.A3 provides the same kind of information as Table 6.A2 but for those commodities for which intervention is the dominant support mechanism. For oilseeds, olive oil, processed fruit and vegetables, tobacco, and sheepmeat, the dominant system of support is through some form of payment linked to output, either directly to the producer or through the first-stage processor. Fresh fruit and vegetables, and wine are supported by a withdrawal system. The market regimes for the other commodities in Table 6.A3 (with the exception of oilseeds) provide for a withdrawal system but it is little used.

Support for tobacco is very costly in terms of tonnage produced and the number of growers involved. In addition, the varieties produced are of limited market appeal and attempts have been made through the manipulation of the price support mechanism to persuade growers to switch to more marketable varieties. One might question why the Union continues to support such a costly product which has the added disadvantage of being a health risk. It is, however, a traditional crop in certain regions and its support fulfils a social role as it provides an income for small farmers who have few alternative production possibilities.

The same is true for many olive-oil- and wine-producing areas where the soil conditions are such that other crops would not grow without irrigation or where, due to the slope of the land, it would be hard to find an alternative crop which did not result in soil erosion. These considerations are particularly important in the southern parts of the Union and are given insufficient attention by policy commentators who tend to overlook the non-economic factors which underlie many of the support regimes.

Table 6.A4 provides information on the commodities for which no export subsidization is available. These are deficit commodities and ones which are specific to certain regions only. Cotton is almost exclusively a Greek product, with the remainder being grown in Spain; it is turning out to be a rather costly commodity. The regimes for dried fodder, and peas and field beans arose out of the protein crisis in animal feed in the mid-1970s. They were intended to broaden the range of protein feeds available in the Community as alternatives to imported soyabeans. Peas and field beans had the added advantage of being products which could be produced in the southern Member States, thereby broadening their production base.

Table 6.A5 completes this group and features those commodities for which export refunds are the dominant or sole support mechanism. Pigmeat is one of the oldest regimes and, like eggs and poultrymeat, is closely linked to cereals. While intervention in the form of withdrawal from an oversupplied market is possible under the pigmeat regime, it is little used. The cost of support has risen considerably as the level of self-sufficiency has gradually crept up. The subsidization of exports was the only means of stabilizing the market. The same has also been true of poultrymeat which was in a state of considerable overproduction in the early 1980s (see Table 3.5). As there is no form of domestic intervention for either poultrymeat or eggs surplus production must be disposed of through exports. Rice is, of course, a highly specialized crop traditional in certain regions, with Italy by far the largest producer followed by Spain. The tendency for expenditure to rise since the mid-1980s can be attributed to the Accession of Spain. Non-Annex II refunds have risen in line with the increases in the level of support for the basic raw materials included in their manufacture. As Table 6.A1 illustrated, in terms of FEOGA-Guarantee expenditure, there has been no change in the relative share of support going to these products.

Table 6.A6 provides a breakdown of expenditure from FEOGA-Guarantee by Member State over time. The earlier years are somewhat anomalous in that the range of commodities subject to support regimes was being expanded gradually and, as Table 6.A1 illustrated, it was not until the early 1970s that the majority of regimes came into force. The early years are also peculiar in that FEOGA-Guarantee took over the cost of support gradually during the 1960s and only reached 100 per cent in 1967/68. The unusually large payment to Italy in 1966/67 was compensation for the delay in the introduction of certain regimes of particular interest to that country. The 1970s saw not only the first Enlargement of the Community but also the impact of the serious currency fluctuations and the greatest excesses of the use of monetary compensatory amounts intended to maintain the fiction of a single market. There is a much more settled look to the table since the beginning of the 1980s. One interesting feature is the way in which expenditure in Spain increased as the transition to full integration into the CAP progressed.

The overall impression left by this table is its remarkable consistency over time. The percentage distribution between Member States has, of course, been affected by the addition of new Member States and the addition of new commodity regimes but far more important than that is the relative share of final production arising in each Member State. Table 6.A7 illustrates this point by putting side by side for selected years the proportion of total production of all commodities arising in each Member State and the FEOGA-Guarantee expenditure in the same Member State. This is a crude comparison, partly because the production statistics include some commodities not covered by market regimes (for instance, table potatoes), and partly because production can be influenced quite markedly in one particular year because of local conditions. Nevertheless, for most Member States the match is quite close. Some of the smaller countries, in particular the Netherlands, Ireland and, more recently, Greece gained a significantly higher level of expenditure than their share of production might suggest, although the decline in the Netherlands FEOGA-Guarantee share over time is hard to explain. It will be interesting to see whether, as the 1990s develop, the trend towards decoupled payments, i.e. ones not linked to current levels of production, makes a difference in terms of the relationship between FEOGA-Guarantee expenditure and total production in each Member State.

Underlying Causes of Surplus Production

The issue of surpluses has been with the Community from the very beginning and was recognized by the Commission as an existing, and potentially more widespread, problem. For many years, other interest groups—including the Council—chose to ignore surpluses or argue over their seriousness. In fact, over time, the problem has grown in terms of the range of commodities involved, the size of surpluses and their persistence, and the cost of disposal.

There have been disagreements over the definition of a 'surplus'. In 1977, in answer to a parliamentary question, the Commission defined a surplus as a situation in which 'under normal market conditions and taking account of international contractual commitments, the supply of a product is greater than the demand' (OJ C265, 7–11–77, 11). However, even this definition could be queried. How does the Commission define 'normal'? Does the definition include exports on which export refunds are paid? The inclusion of 'international commitments' is problematical—for instance, food aid comes under this heading but is that a normal part of production?

The Commission was on safer ground when it defined a 'structural surplus' as the situation in which 'supply is greater than demand for several consecutive years and this situation is not due to accidental causes (weather conditions, diseases, etc.) but to a heavy output compared with demand' (OJ C265, 7–11–77, 12). It is this long-term overhang on the market which is the real problem and is an issue of importance in the Community. It is the cost of disposal of structural surpluses and the incorrect signals given to producers that matters rather than the precision of the definition.

When the Commission made its initial proposals on the CAP, it was very conscious of the market situation and the need to aim for a balance between production and potential markets 'in view of the difficulties which would arise from a state of permanent overproduction' (Commission 1960, II/18). It also recognized the need to take international trade into account when working out the market policy. Its original analysis of the agricultural sector covered all the major commodity groups: cereals, sugar, milk, beef and veal, pigmeat, poultrymeat, eggs, fruit and vegetables, and wine.

As mentioned in the previous Section, production of wheat for human consumption was at a level which was a cause for concern; the same was true of sugar, which was already in surplus. Milk was a problem, particularly in relation to the production levels of butter and cheese. In contrast, beef was a deficit commodity, although with a high level of self-sufficiency. The Commission wished to encourage dairy farmers to switch to the fattening of cattle, and beef farmers to concentrate on beef breeds in order to raise quality. The emphasis on meat rather than milk would have reflected the market situation better and, in addition, would have encouraged the consumption of coarse grain for which the market was buoyant. This in turn would have relieved the pressure on the wheat market.

There was a slight surplus of pigmeat but consumption of quality products was expected to rise. The poultry sector had a small deficit and was in the early stages of the move to large-scale production units. Consumption was rising strongly and the rationalization of the sector was expected to lower costs and stimulate consumption further. Self-sufficiency in eggs was, if anything, falling and consumption was rising rapidly.

Fruit and vegetable trends were difficult to analyse because of the range of commodities, the volatility of supply and demand from year to year, the seasonal concentration of availability, and the remoteness of some of the production regions from the main markets. Certain products were already in difficulties, most notably apples, peaches, pears, cauliflowers, lettuce, and tomatoes. In some years it was not worth harvesting the whole crop, and part of what was harvested either went for animal feed or was wasted. Two separate policy issues were identified: the short-term balance between supply and demand at a given moment on the market; and the long-term balance which could only be achieved by a better pattern of production, based on greater regional specialization.

Wine, too, was already a problem. Although yields fluctuated widely from year to year, extensive use had had to be made of distillation in the 1950s to relieve the market pressure on wine:

[T]here is a danger that this state of affairs will become even worse in the future: improved methods of growing and of pest control are contributing to an all-round increase in yields and the present production potential, even without any extension of the area cultivated, is capable of supplying the market with ever-larger quantities of wine. (Commission 1960, III, wine p.1)

The Commission mistakenly assumed consumption would increase, whereas demand for table wine has fallen dramatically, thereby exacerbating the surplus problem.[20] Even in 1960, it was recognized that the long-run market balance might require structural changes such as vine-clearing, either without replanting, or with replanting with different varieties, and new planting where there was a specific demand. The Commission also envisaged extensive controls on every aspect of production, from the growing of the vine root-stock to the methods of vinification.

Given that the market situation for the main commodities was, in general, analysed correctly, why did it deteriorate as rapidly as it did? Partly the problem lay with the choice of policy instruments: the variable levy, which quickly insulated the internal market for key commodities from outside competition; the open-ended nature of intervention as originally conceived and for many years operated; and the high level of target price for cereals, which dictated the entire pricing structure of all commodities directly or indirectly related to cereals. However, these policy instruments were capable of being adjusted and eventually—after decades of delay—were adjusted. Underlying their misuse was the failure to define the desired size of the agricultural sector in terms of production, and the role of imports and exports.

This goes to the heart of the CAP: Art. 39.1(d) states the fourth objective of the policy—'to assure the availability of supplies'. It has often been suggested that this means full self-sufficiency but there is no evidence that such was intended. Indeed, this would have been contrary to the spirit of Article 110 of the Rome Treaty which states that the creation of the customs union was intended to contribute 'to the harmonious development of world trade, the progressive abolition of restrictions on international trade and the lowering of customs barriers'.

One could argue that in some sectors—most notably for the cereals and oilseeds used in livestock production—imports were essential because the Community had a major deficit in these commodities. But things are not that simple. There has always been an underlying fear of relying too heavily on imports of vital raw materials—a fear which is much older than the CAP and which transcends political systems and different cultures. In 1967 at a meeting of the ESC, Mansholt stated that he was ready to defend the proposition that European farmers had the right to increase production in step with the increase in consumption (CES 1967). The implications of this position are that imports are a residual (which is normally true) and that, in an expanding market, they are a declining element.

They are also a potentially unreliable element. In 1975, in discussing the 'security of supply' objective of the Treaty, the Commission pointed out the absence of any guidance as to how it was to be fulfilled. It put forward three possibilities: increased self-sufficiency; an intensive storage policy; and a stable short- or long-term import policy. This discussion took place in the wake of the international commodity crisis during which the USA had cut off its exports of soyabeans. The Commission raised fears of the non-honouring of contractual obligations and the danger of relying on a few sources of supply. It singled out, in particular, the dangers in the animal feed sector (Commission 1975(*a*)). It returned to this theme in 1980 when it stated: 'We need only think of the dependence of Europe as regards energy and of the vulnerability of supplies from overseas in order to understand that an entity such as Europe . . . cannot afford to rely on others for its food supplies and has the duty to exploit the richness of its soil' (Commission 1980(*c*), 5).

Following on from this line of argument, it is almost inevitable that, if the market is stagnant or shrinking, it is imports which will be squeezed out. Given this approach, it is not surprising that 'assuring the availability of supplies' becomes synonymous with supplying 100 per cent of normal internal market requirements. Added to this are the views of the Member States which are net agricultural exporters and for which a surplus is both natural and a necessity. Given this background, the slide into structural surpluses becomes more understandable. Such a philosophy was re-enforced by the objective of raising agricultural incomes. If this was the central goal of agricultural policy and, if its achievement was linked with higher production, then any problems which that caused had to be accepted as a common financial burden.

An example of this approach can be found in the price proposals for 1980/81 (Commission 1980(*a*)). In the explanatory memorandum, the Commission described 1979 as:

a record year for sugar and . . . milk, the wine harvest was the second largest this century; there were also very good results for cereals, beef and veal and pigmeat. These records may be bad for the balance of markets and for keeping budget spending down, but on the other hand they do boost producers' incomes. (p. 3)

This fatalistic approach to surpluses was accompanied by a continual under-estimation of productivity improvements, and of producer response to price and market signals. Changes in productivity can take many forms and be measured in different ways. In the EC, there is a tendency for change to be measured in quantitative rather than economic terms and, on that basis, productivity has risen strongly over time due to increased biological yields.

By the end of the 1970s, it was possible to look back over two decades since the Commission had made its initial proposals on the CAP. The relentless increase in production was there for all to see: annually sugar yields had risen by 2.5 per cent since the early 1960s, milk by 1.7 per cent, beef by 2 per cent, wine by 1 per cent; cereals by 0.7 per cent annually since 1968, with much higher rates for maize and durum wheat (4.6 per cent and 2.4 per cent annually respectively) (Commission 1979(*a*)). These increases in output were the result of changes in the pattern of production on a land base which was slowly declining (discounting the discrete increase due to the Enlargement in 1973).

Given the clear evidence of long-term expansion on the supply side, it is puzzling to find that there has been a certain ambivalence among commentators as to the role played by price and market support in this development. It is as if production increases can be explained away as being solely dependent on changes in farming techniques. In arguing for the existence of a direct link between price and supply response, Priebe cited the example of the cereals price decision of 1964, which resulted in a significant increase in output, especially in France which had had the largest price increase and the greatest reserves of production capacity. He commented that production capacity 'and farmers' powers of economic reasoning were persistently underestimated at every subsequent price increase' (EP rapp. Caillavet, 1979, 52).

Mansholt would have agreed with Priebe's views on producers' response to price signals for a commodity such as cereals but he was much less convinced of the role of price in the case of milk. While acknowledging that a relatively high price for beef and a relatively low price for milk would shift production towards beef to some extent, he believed there were serious limits to this. In certain regions, where there were few alternatives to milk production, Mansholt believed that lowering the price of milk could actually provoke an increase in production as farmers strove to maintain their income levels (Mansholt 1962). This view was supported by the farmers' organizations (COPA/COGECA 1973).

It is true that, because of the length of many of the production cycles in agriculture, there are significant lags between policy changes and producer response but that does not mean that no response occurs. The problem of time lags is made worse in the Community by the way in which the annual price-fixing exercise is conducted (outlined earlier in this chapter). It is also true that there are locational and structural factors which inhibit supply response to price signals, and these need to be tackled by other policy instruments, such as direct payments to compensate for a harsh farming environment or to encourage structural change.

By the late 1970s, however, attitudes seemed to be changing and the Commission was able to comment that:

[O]f all the instruments employed in the milk sector, the price policy is the most important. The price freeze applied between 1969 and 1971 showed clearly that producers react to such a policy, as they did also when prices caught up in subsequent years.
... an increase in production is set off by three phenomena ... (a) an attractive milk price level; (b) an unconditional guarantee system ...; (c) the limited possibilities for conversion to other types of production.
... farmers naturally tend to increase production as long as an incentive is provided by the relationship of the milk price to feeding costs and to the interest rates on the loans raised to cover investment expenditure. The price policy should therefore act as a brake on investments in this sector. (Commission 1978(*d*), 12–13)

Coupled with the underestimation of productivity improvements and producer response to price and market signals was an overestimation of the possibility of increasing consumption through various devices, including quality improvements. For most foods, consumption trends in the Community have, at best, shown modest increases per head of population over time and, for some products, there have been decreases. Due to the low birth rate, population is increasing very slowly and the average age is rising, therefore there is little opportunity for market expansion. The reality of the situation is that market equilibrium can only be achieved by a reduction in supply. Throughout the lifetime of the CAP, there has been a marked reluctance to accept this fact.

The final consideration in relation to surpluses is that, as self-sufficiency levels rose, certain distortions within the price and market policy and certain contradictions between the CAP and other policies became more evident. Some distortions were amenable to adjustment: for example, the pricing structure within the cereals regime discouraged the production of feed grain for which there was a good market. By altering the relationship between the support for bread grain and feed cereals, it was possible—although not without a struggle—to rectify this imbalance.

Much more difficult issues are involved, however, when the distortions are due to fundamental policy considerations. For instance, the high internal price of milk is supported by the effectiveness of the frontier protection, whereas there is little or no frontier protection for vegetable oils and the producer price is supported by a deficiency payment. The result of these differences is that the market for milk products for human consumption (especially butter) has been undermined by the competition from vegetable oils and related manufactured products; and the market for protein for animal feed (especially skimmed milk powder) has been undermined by the availability of the much cheaper vegetable alternatives. Very similar distortions have occurred in the cereals market for animal feed, with the importation of cheaper substitutes (e.g. manioc, citrus pulp). The effect in both the milk and the cereals markets has been to exacerbate the surplus problem. It has also undermined the concept of Community Preference in a particularly effective way.

What is puzzling is the reaction of the Commission which is almost one of resentment that traders and processors take advantage of these policy anomalies, and there is never any suggestion that the Community's own producers should accept the logic of the system and reduce production accordingly. For instance, in 1981, in an analysis of the market for cereals for animal feed, the Commission discussed the increase in use of imported cereal substitutes and stated that 'in the absence of any change in import conditions and relative prices, future additional demand for animal feed would be covered by imported substitutes rather than by Community cereals, and the increase in Community's cereal production would therefore have to be exported at a cost to the Community budget' (Commission 1981(*c*), 26).

A somewhat different problem—but one with much the same outcome—has arisen in the sugar sector where, under the Lomé Convention, the Community guarantees the importation of a certain quantity of sugar annually from a group of developing countries. When this agreement was first entered into, the Community did not lower its production level of sugar to accommodate the new supply. As a result, the Lomé Convention sugar competes with the Community's own sugar on an oversupplied market.

Some of these issues will be raised again in Chapter 12 in the context of commercial policy. So far as their contribution to the surplus situation is concerned, any improvement must come from changes to the price and market policy of the CAP and not from any expectation that the external situation is going to change.

The Failure to Come to Grips with Oversupply: 1960–1986

Attempts to control surpluses have taken many forms throughout the lifetime of the CAP, although there has been a marked reluctance until very recently to use the most obvious method: a reduction in the level of institutional support prices. Given this reluctance, the Community has indulged in a whole series of measures of market management intended to achieve the same objective by a more circuitous route. A considerable amount of space in this Section is devoted to charting the failure to make progress in curbing agricultural production. By the second half of the 1980s the position had become nothing short of a scandal, with expenditure roaring ahead, much of it ending up in parts of the economy far removed from the farmers in whose name the whole operation was being carried out. The purposes of the relevant Articles of the Rome Treaty had long since been forgotten.

It is important to understand that trying to change direction in a policy as complex as the CAP is extremely difficult. It is easy to look back on the extravagance of the 1970s and the feeble attempts in the 1980s to rectify a situation going steadily more out of control but it is not so easy to see what is happening when one is in the middle of such events. It is particularly difficult to change direction when there is no guidance as to the ultimate goal and in circumstances in which the instruments of policy are quite inadequate to the task. The underestimation of producer response to price signals, the failure to grasp the significance of the supply-side dynamism in contrast to the demand-side stagnation, and the polit-ical nature of price-fixing are all symptoms of an unwillingness to accept that there are too many resources in agriculture. Throughout the lifetime of the CAP radical change has only taken place as the result of a build-up of intense pressure from outside—for instance, a budgetary crisis, Community enlargement, or international agreements.

In the absence of major outside pressures, the pace of change is leisurely. This can be observed from an examination of the annual price negotiations. The Commission's proposals, which are always moderate, are never strengthened by the Council but rather are weakened, postponed, or rejected in the short-term interests of the Ministers' clients. This 'short-termism' is part of the normal political process but it is particularly damaging in a sector where long-term planning is essential, where change can only take place in accordance with the biological rhythm of production, and where year-on-year variations in output and price can be highly misleading.

While all the above factors are common to the functioning of agricultural policy throughout the developed world, the CAP is unique in that it requires the close co-operation of the Member States, and stability in their currencies. Common prices are set annually in an accounting unit[21] which is then converted into national currencies. With fixed exchange rates this is a totally neutral exercise but with the onset of unstable currencies came opportunities in the various Member States to manipulate the rate at which common prices were converted into national currencies.

This meant that one of the purposes of common pricing: to encourage special-ization on the basis of comparative advantage, was undermined. Producers, particularly during the 1970s when currency instability was at its worst, were receiving price support in their own currency on a basis which had little to do with comparative advantage but which had a great deal to do with the negotiat-ing skills of their agricultural ministers, and the value of currencies, which were strong or weak for reasons which had nothing to do with the agricultural sector.

The other purpose of common pricing: to allow products to flow freely within the Community under conditions of a common, or single market, was also frustrated. In the absence of currency stability, the fiction of a common market for agricultural products was maintained through the use of border taxes and levies (collectively known as monetary compensatory amounts) to negate the impact of the currency movements.

Of course, most products do not cross frontiers—at least in their unprocessed form—and therefore the price signals which the producers received were seriously at variance with market reality, and with the nominal price fixed by the Council of Ministers. The extent of the divergence is illustrated in Table 6.1, which shows the history of price fixing from 1967/68–1980/81, on the basis of an index with 1972/73 = 100. By the beginning of the 1980s, common prices in ua/ECU had risen since 1972/73 by 62 per cent, whereas converted to national currencies, the increase was 126 per cent. The situation was even more extreme in some individual Member States.

Table 6.1. Common agricultural prices[a] in money and real terms, 1967/68–1980/81

Index of prices 1972/73 = 100			Annual real price change %		
Year	ua or ECU	National currency[b]	Year	ua or ECU	National currency[b]
1967/68	92.5	90.9			
1968/69	91.3	90.3	1968/69 1967/68	−10.1	−4.3
1969/70	91.3	90.3	1969/70 1968/69	−6.7	−5.4
1970/71	91.8	91.7	1970/71 1969/70	−6.1	−5.1
1971/72	95.5	95.4	1971/72 1970/71	−2.9	−2.9
1972/73	100.0	100.0	1972/73 1971/72	−2.1	−2.0
1973/74	106.4	106.5	1973/74 1972/73	−2.2	−0.8
1974/75	121.2	127.8	1974/75 1973/74	1.7	8.0
1975/76	133.4	145.2	1975/76 1974/75	−1.8	2.4
1976/77	143.5	161.8	1976/77 1975/76	−1.9	3.0
1977/78	149.1	175.1	1977/78 1976/77	−4.9	0.0
1978/79	152.3	190.1	1978/79 1977/78	−6.1	1.0
1979/80	154.2	204.3	1979/80 1978/79	−8.3	−2.8
1980/81	161.6	225.8	1980/81 1979/80	−6.5	−1.4

a 21 product groups, weighted according to importance in final agricultural production
b national currencies converted at agricultural rate of exchange
Source: Commission 1980(*c*).

The second part of the table shows the change in support prices, expressed in real terms, i.e. corrected for inflation. The response to the commodity crisis of 1973–4 is clearly visible and it heralded a period in which many farmers were receiving price signals totally unrelated to the serious state of market imbalance. The table does not show the considerable variation in the experience of the individual Member States[22] but it does illustrate most starkly that, despite all the increases in support prices, there was little change in real income levels over time. If the main aim of agricultural policy is to improve the incomes of those who work in the sector, this table must raise serious doubts as to the effectiveness of price policy as a means of achieving that goal.

In 1980, the Community was in the middle of one of its periodic crises, with a major dispute over the budgetary contribution of the UK and the imminent exhaustion of the Community's own resources. At the meeting of the European Council in May 1980, the Commission was asked to carry out an examination of all the major policy areas, and to make recommendations for the development of the Community (Bull. EC 5–1980). In December 1980, the Commission issued one of its most important discussion documents on the CAP—the *Reflections*—which paved the way for a whole series of reform memoranda over the following few years, culminating in the price proposals of 1984/85.

The Commission listed the main criticisms of the price and market policy which were current at the time:

- the absence of effective regulatory mechanisms to help balance supply and demand;
- the lack of equity in the operation of the policy, with the largest producers and the most prosperous regions receiving the greatest benefits;
- the social inequality involved in singling out farmers for assistance at a time when the Community was facing a serious slow-down in economic growth;
- the cost of the policy in absolute terms and in relation to other Community policies, the distribution of costs and benefits between Member States, and the level of expenditure on surpluses without benefit to income (Commission 1980(*c*)).

In proposing adjustments to the market organizations to meet some of these criticisms, the Commission stated that they were based:

on the principle that in the present state of agricultural technology it is neither economically sound nor financially feasible to guarantee price or aid levels for unlimited quantities. . . .
It is necessary . . . to adopt the principle that any production above a certain volume . . . must be charged fully or partially to the producers.   (Commission 1980(*c*), 17–18).

This principle was called 'producer co-responsibility'. Effectively it meant that production was to be divided into two parts: one part would be supported entirely by the Community price policy as previously; the cost of the other part would be divided between the Community and the producers according to some formula, which could vary from one commodity to another.

When it is recalled that, in the following year, the Commission went even further and stated that 'farm income considerations . . . cannot be the sole point of reference for fixing guaranteed prices' (Commission 1981(*b*), quoted in Chapter 4 above), it can be appreciated that the basis of the policy was shifting. It had a very long way to go and progress was painfully slow. The irony of the situation is that this supposedly new concept of co-responsibility actually went right back to the original proposals on price policy.

As outlined in Chapter 2, the original intention was that each of the main commodities would have its own stabilization fund, financed in the first instance from revenue raised by import charges. It was foreseen that this source might not be adequate and that producers might have to contribute, in particular in the wheat, sugar, milk, and wine sectors. In the light of later events, it is interesting that in 1960 the Commission was hesitant in suggesting producer participation in milk sector funding. Milk was the only commodity for which a financial contribution by government was envisaged and it was only if all else failed that producers were to be called on to participate. The suggested form of co-responsibility in wine was a tax proportionate to the area of vineyards cultivated or the quantity of wine marketed (Commission 1960, pt. III, *passim*). The idea of separate stabilization funds for each of the main commodities was quickly abandoned and a single fund—FEOGA—came into existence instead (see Chapter 2). No mention was made in the relevant legislation (Regs. 25/62 and 17/64) of the concept of producer financial participation in funding operations.

The concept of co-responsibility re-emerged with the establishment of the support regime for sugar in 1967. Production is subject to quota and any additional sugar must be sold on the export market without the benefit of export refunds. As the quota exceeds internal consumption, part of the in-quota production must be exported also and the producers pay a levy which today is intended to finance these exports in their entirety.[23]

The Commission returned to the theme of producer participation in 1969 when it stated that, as part of the effort to reduce existing stocks of cereals, sugar, and dairy products and to prevent the formation of new surpluses, there should be a better alignment of prices with the market situation, a reduction in the price guarantee by adaptation of the intervention mechanism, and greater producer participation in the financial responsibility for surpluses (Commission 1969). Despite the breadth of these suggestions, nothing was done apart from making a proposal to increase the levy on sugar producers to help pay for the disposal of surpluses.

A more serious attempt to introduce co-responsibility was made in the *Improvement* memorandum (Commission 1973(*d*)), in which the Commission proposed the 'introduction of a temporary levy on production, on milk delivered to the dairy, chargeable to the farmer and not reflected in the consumer price. Every farm would be granted a levy-free quota for the first 10,000 litres delivered. Dairies selling a certain percentage . . . of their output to intervention agencies would pay a supplementary levy' (p. 12). This proposal was greeted without enthusiasm by both the European Parliament and the ESC,[24] although it is interesting that, as far back as 1970, the ESC had accepted the principle of co-responsibility, provided it functioned in a clearly defined framework: the existence of a structural surplus, an indicative output programme for the product concerned, and a farm income policy (OJ C119, 13–2–70).

The levy proposed in 1973 was not introduced and the situation on the milk market continued to deteriorate. In 1976, the Commission produced an Action Programme (1977–80) for milk. The situation was truly out of hand: supply was 10 per cent above requirements and rising. Even during the severe drought of 1976, milk production had increased by 1.7 per cent and was expected to rise by 2–3 per cent in 1977. Deliveries to dairies were rising even more rapidly: an increase of 2.5 per cent in 1976 and an expected increase of 3–4 per cent in 1977.

At the end of 1976, butter stocks had reached 260,000 tonnes and skimmed milk powder stocks were 1.1m. tonnes (Commission 1977(*b*)). The state of desperation which the situation induced can be guessed from the response of the European Parliament which invited the Commission to consider 'the possibility of offering special inducements to dairy farmers to convert to cereal production (such inducements may include ploughing-up grants)' (OJ C93, 18–4–77, 13). It is hard to believe that such a suggestion could have been made.

The Commission eventually got its way and a co-responsibility levy was brought into force under Reg. 1079/77 (OJ L131, 26–5–77). Farmers in less-favoured areas (LFAs) were excluded and the levy was only temporary: from September 1977 to the end of the 1979/80 milk-year. The proceeds of the levy were to be used to expand milk outlets both inside and outside the Community, to seek new uses for milk, and improved products. The introduction of the levy was an empty victory for the Commission. In 1978, it expressed its disappointment that the levy was not functioning as intended. It was set at a fixed rate rather than being variable in relation to levels of production, and what little effectiveness it had was undermined by the fact that the Council had increased the milk support price at the same time (Commission 1978(*d*)). In addition, the level at which the levy was set was inadequate. As a result, late in 1979, the Commission proposed a tightening-up of the arrangements for producer co-responsibility so as 'to ensure that the milk budget is not burdened by the cost of disposing of new surpluses' (Commission 1979(*e*), 2).

As described in the *Reflections*, the principle of producer co-responsibility was not intended to be limited to the payment of levies, as in the milk and sugar sectors, but could cover a variety of circumstances. For instance, it could involve the manipulation of the level of direct aids such as area payments, or the intervention price. The key element had to be the existence of some cut-off point in production: to exceed that level would result in the triggering of some form of financial penalty. The Commission was at pains to emphasize that this maximum volume (or quantum) was acceptable 'so long as this system does not become one of production quotas either by farm or by processor' (Commission 1980(*c*), 19). It was not long before the Commission's condition was broken.

The Commission used this co-responsibility concept in its price proposals for 1981/82 (Commission 1981(*a*)) in recommending changes to the market regimes for cereals, rapeseed (colza), olive oil, tobacco, processed fruit, milk, and beef. In all except beef, some form of production threshold was proposed, beyond which a financial penalty would be incurred.[25] The Council of Ministers was extremely wary of this new development and did not support the Commission's proposals. However, it did agree 'in principle to the application of co-responsibility measures in the cereals sector but decided that any adjustments of the . . . prices would not apply during the current marketing year but would be postponed until 1982/83' (quoted in Commission 1982(*a*), 33).

The European Parliament, in an important Resolution on the CAP, gave a cautious endorsement to the concept of co-responsibility based on production levels but stipulated that the penalty it preferred was a reduction in the support price for each additional tranche of output over the threshold. It therefore opposed the use of the levy which it stated had not controlled overproduction but had 'acted as an incentive to expand output and had increased the burden on the taxpayer' (OJ C172, 13–7–81, 36).[26]

In June 1981, the Commission responded formally to the Mandate it had been given a year previously by the Council to review the operation of the various policies. The Commission set out a series of guidelines on which future decisions in the CAP should be based. These included a narrowing of the gap between Community prices and those applied by its main competitors, and the modulation of guarantees in line with Community production targets. 'Producers must be made more aware of market realities than they have been in the past. To this end production targets in terms of volume must be set for every sector at Community level. Once these are reached producers would be required to contribute or the intervention guarantee could be reduced' (Commission 1981(*b*), 12).

Later the same year, the Commission spelled out in much greater detail what it had in mind for the agricultural sector. It considered that decision-making would be much improved if a longer-term view of production, consumption, and trade were used as the basis of price policy. Therefore, it took 1988 as the end-year of the period under review. This had the added advantage in the particular circumstances of the time that it allowed the Commission to take into account the possible entry of Portugal and Spain to the Community.[27] The Commission stressed that its proposals for production objectives for 1988 were not intended to set an artificial limit on agriculture. Producers were free to continue expanding output but there would be a financial cost to themselves. If nothing was done to change the price and market policy, production would continue to rise more rapidly than consumption.

The detailed objectives set out in COM(81)608 in fact allowed for an expansion of output for cereals, milk, beef, and rapeseed. For tobacco, processed tomatoes, and apples it proposed the same production level as in 1980. For wine, the Commission's courage failed and it stated that it hoped the gap between production (rising) and consumption (falling) would get no worse (Commission 1981(*c*)). Given that the majority of these commodities were in serious surplus, these guidelines cannot be regarded as anything other than the mildest response to a chronic and worsening problem.

The ESC which, for over twenty years, had called for the introduction of long-term objectives for production welcomed the Commission's initiative in principle. It recognized that this would not remove the CAP from politics:

[T]he annual fight over prices will doubtless continue. But the fundamental political decisions will become the more long-term ones, what the Community wishes to do with its great resource of land, what part it wishes to play in world trade and in the feeding of the hungry, to what extent, and for which products, it attaches importance to self-sufficiency, and how far it wishes to permit imports (or subsidize, or not subsidize exports) for reasons of political advantage or solidarity.   (OJ C348, 31–12–81, 31)

Sadly, the Commission initiative did not lead to this Promised Land.

The Commission chose the cereals sector as the one in which it would propose action to reduce the gap between Community prices and those of its main competitors. This would have the double advantage of reducing the input costs for the livestock sector and lessening the attractiveness of cereal substitutes. Imports of these products in 1980 amounted to the equivalent of 14m. tonnes of cereals and their presence on the market in such quantity was regarded as a major breach of Community Preference (referred to earlier in the chapter). The Commission stated that:

[I]t would be in the Community's interest to embark on a programme of progressive reduction of cereals prices in *real* terms and relative to the prices of other products. To avoid unacceptable consequences for production and income, such a programme must be gradual: one could not envisage a reduction in *nominal* terms.   (Commission 1981(*c*), 28, emphasis added)

As it had done in its price proposals for 1981/82 (but without success), the Commission based its proposals for 1982/83 on the principle of co-responsibility and the setting of production thresholds for the same commodities as in the previous year (Commission 1982(*a*)). On this occasion, the Council accepted the imposition of thresholds for cereals, milk, and rapeseed.[28] It is important to be clear about the consequences of the imposition of these guarantee thresholds. It did *not* mean that the support price in Year 2 would fall by a predetermined percentage if production in Year 1 exceeded the threshold. What it did mean was that, in Year 2, the price *increase* which the product received was reduced by the predetermined percentage. This was a highly unsatisfactory situation because it meant that exceeding the threshold might still result in a support price increase. This must have given an extremely confused signal to the producer. Another drawback to the guarantee threshold was that the percentage penalty was too small to be useful as a source of funds to help dispose of the surplus, and was only allowed to function when it was manifestly too small to act as a deterrent to production.

On the wider front, the Community was still finding it very difficult in the early 1980s to move forward with some major policy initiatives—Enlargement, the Budget, the next stage of European integration, and new policies on industry, research, and the environment. Part of the problem was that the Member States considered that any expansion of the Community's activities which involved additional expenditure required, as a quid pro quo, better control of agricultural expenditure. Unfortunately, it was not a good time to seek such control, as the Commission was anticipating a deterioration in the market situation in 1983 and a resultant increase in expenditure. For that reason, in its preparation for the European Council meeting in Stuttgart in June 1983, the Commission produced a new set of guidelines for the CAP which threatened the introduction of additional reform measures, aimed at the creation of a situation in which expenditure on agriculture would increase less rapidly than the Community's own resources (Commission 1983(*b*)).[29]

The Commission slipped two important statements into this slim document.

The first related to the manner in which market support was given: it stated that 'for a number of products the granting of an unlimited guarantee, irrespective of the quantities produced, must be abolished. This will be done by modulating guarantees once a production threshold is exceeded. The modulation must be large enough to discourage production and contain expenditure' (Commission 1983(*b*), 3). The second statement reminded the Council of its involvement in the cost of the CAP: 'the Commission will undertake a systematic examination of various items in the chapters of the budget devoted to agriculture to establish whether further management savings are possible. It would point out, however, that much of current agricultural expenditure is the result of political compromises in the Council' (ibid. 4).

In the event, progress was made on many of the wider policy issues at the Stuttgart meeting. On agriculture, the Council called for yet another review of the CAP to include virtually every facet of price, market, commercial, and structural policy (Bull. EC 6–1983). This review went much further than the Commission had envisaged before the meeting and its response to the European Council's request was an extremely gloomy assessment of the market situation.[30]

Much of what the Commission had to say was familiar but it did touch on a number of issues which had not featured significantly—if at all—previously, and which were to become much more widely discussed over the next decade. The stagnation of the food and feed market led the Commission to mention the possibility of developing other outlets for agriculture—organic chemicals, energy from biomass, wood products. The relation of agriculture to the natural environment and the need to preserve traditional landscapes, flora, and fauna were mentioned, as was the need for more agricultural research to identify new markets, especially for products in surplus (Commission 1983(*d*)). Some of these issues will be referred to again in later chapters.

Most of this document is, understandably, taken up with the price and market policy. The Commission warned once again of the need 'to accept the market disciplines to which other sectors of the Community's economy are subject' (Commission 1983(*d*), 7). It reviewed all the major sectors of production and suggested various changes in the support arrangements, including the extension of guarantee thresholds to durum wheat (until then excluded from the arrangements for cereals), and sunflower seeds. The Commission warned that it might be necessary to introduce a co-responsibility levy for cereals to cover part of the cost of exports.

However, the undoubted bombshell of COM(83)500 was the analysis of the milk situation, in which the Commission concluded that the guarantee threshold was not working. The increase in production year on year was actually accelerating, while milk consumption was stagnant. The overrun in production should have resulted in an abatement of the support price by 12 per cent in 1984/85—which might have had an effect. However, the Commission abandoned the whole system and proposed production quotas instead. Deliveries of milk in excess of those quantities were to be subject to a levy calculated to cover the full cost of disposal of the additional milk.[31]

Quotas were a controversial tool for production limitation, except in the sugar sector where they were already in use in most of the original six Member States prior to the formation of the Community. Curiously, in the 1960 CAP proposals, the Commission discussed the imposition of quotas for sugar only in the context of a fall-back position if the market system proved inadequate to the task of stemming the production of too large a surplus (Commission 1960). In 1963, quotas were referred to in a similar manner in a discussion of measures which might be needed in the event that a structural surplus of milk developed (Commission 1963(*d*)).

As previously mentioned, quotas were introduced in the sugar sector in 1967 and, right from the start, there was a problem: the level at which the quotas were set was too high. Already in the price proposals of 1970/71, the Commission was calling for a reduction to a level equal to domestic human consumption (Commission 1969). The 1967 quotas had been set quite deliberately at a level which allowed—at least during a transitional phase—for the maintenance of some sugar production in regions which were not best suited to the growing of this crop (Commission 1973(*b*)). Some passing references were made during the 1970s to the possible use of production quotas more widely and the Commission's views were predominantly negative on the grounds of the limitation on competition between producers, the retention of production in high-cost farms or regions, high prices for consumers, and windfall gains for producers with a comparative advantage in production (Commission 1975(*a*)).

In relation specifically to milk, in 1978, the Commission discussed quotas in the context of seeking a means to curtail the open-ended price guarantee. It conceded that they had the advantage of immediate effect but argued against their introduction because:

they would be difficult to reconcile with the Community's approach, based on free decision and internal trade; it would be almost impossible to construct such a policy without some inequity between different producers or regions of the Community; production quotas tend to fossilize the existing structure; quotas would be extremely difficult to negotiate and even more difficult to change; and consequently there is a risk that in due course there would be a return to surplus production. (Commission 1978(*d*), 26)

This was a very accurate assessment of the problems involved six years later in the introduction of the milk quotas, and in their management.

The introduction of milk quotas in 1984 did not solve the problem of over-supply, very largely because the whole purpose of the scheme was undermined by setting the quotas at too high a level and by modifications to the initial rules which meant that in practice the swingeing penalty for producing over-quota was severely undermined. In addition, the impact of the system was quite different, depending on whether the quota was applied at the farm level (marginal return) or at the processing stage (average return).

By the first quarter of 1986, it was clear that production was forging ahead: an increase of 2 per cent over the same quarter the previous year. The impact of this development manifested itself in the additions to intervention stocks of butter and skimmed milk powder. At the end of August 1986, there were 1.5m. tonnes of butter in store (equivalent to nearly one year's consumption in the Community), and 1m. tonnes of skimmed milk powder. It is not surprising that the Commission described the situation as 'explosive' and 'alarming' (Commission 1986(g)), and that it put forward an urgent programme of adjustments to the Council (Commission 1986(h)).

With surprising speed, the Council agreed in December 1986 to introduce additional measures aimed at achieving a reduction of 9.5 per cent in the milk supply over a period of two years—a target which was not fully achieved. In 1987, the intervention arrangements for butter and skimmed milk powder were changed, so as to discourage the use of the system, and in the following year the quotas were extended to 1992 (Commission 1989(f)).[32]

The other major example of the failure of the guarantee threshold system occurred in 1985. This was a much more damaging episode in the history of CAP reform because of its political implications and the manner in which it illustrated the fragility of the commitment of the Member States to the concept of reform and the control of surplus production. In the 1985/86 price proposals, the Commission proposed a reduction in the cereals intervention price of 3.6 per cent, as a response to the overrun of the guarantee threshold the previous year (Commission 1985(a)). This reduction was based on a proposed price increase of 1.5 per cent, abated by a 5 per cent penalty.

When the negotiations on the price package opened in March 1985, Germany categorically refused to accept a fall in the money level of the support price although, when the guarantee threshold system had been introduced, it was clear that its operation might well result in such a fall. Indeed, in 1983, specifically in relation to cereals, the Commission had warned that a restrictive price policy combined with a guarantee threshold could result in a decline in support prices, expressed in national currencies (Commission 1983(d)).

Ill-tempered negotiations continued until June, by which time the Germans were declaring that their vital national interests were at stake! They were prepared to accept a decline of 0.9 per cent in the intervention price, while the Commission's original proposed reduction shrank to 1.8 per cent—and still no agreement could be reached.[33] In fact, the price change was never voted on by the Council, and the Commission administered the policy as though the 1.8 per cent cut had been agreed.

Such an anarchic situation could not continue and an alternative means of curbing cereal production had to be found. Despite what Avery (1985) referred to as the 'trauma' of the introduction of quotas in milk, the Commission was prepared to threaten their introduction in cereals (Commission 1985(b)), although it recognized that it would be almost inevitable that the quota system would have to cover competing crops as well, in order to prevent farmers switching to other crops, thereby merely transferring the problem to another sector (Commission 1985(c)). The Commission was also aware that Germany had been one of the strongest advocates of milk quotas when they had been introduced in 1984, precisely because quotas were perceived as less damaging to farmers' interests than a straight reduction in the support price (Hendriks 1991).

However, late in 1985, the Commission proposed the introduction of a co-responsibility levy as the preferred control mechanism (Commission 1985(*c*)) and, starting with the 1986/87 farm-year, it was duly applied to cereals. Needless to remark, it did not achieve the necessary reduction in production and, as is indicated in the next Section, the Community had to return to the question of cereals overproduction in the remaining years of the 1980s.

Budgetary Stabilizers 1987–1991

The unedifying bickering in the Council of Ministers and the record of under-achievement in the control of production provided strong evidence of the unwillingness or inability of agricultural ministers to reform the price and market policy from within. However, towards the end of the 1980s, they became caught up in much wider Community issues which had important consequences for the future direction of agricultural policy.

Three major interrelated political and economic developments came together: the preparations for the establishment of the Single Market (to be in place not later than the end of 1992); the reform of the Community's financial resources and the administration of its Budget; and, externally, the negotiation of the Uruguay Round of GATT. Early in 1987, the Commission tackled the first two of these issues in two discussion documents: one which reviewed existing policies and how they should be reformed in the context of the Single Market (Commission 1987(*b*)), and the other which discussed the financial needs of the Community (Commission 1987(*c*)).

Fundamental to any review of policies, and to the size and shape of the Community's budget was the perennial problem of agricultural spending. Five objectives were set out for reform of the CAP: control of production; stabilization of FEOGA-Guarantee expenditure; stock reduction; preservation of the family farm (referred to already in Chapter 4); and international co-operation in controlling production and trade (Commission 1987(*b*)). The first three of these objectives are clearly different aspects of the same problem and were the continuation of existing objectives. What was of significance was the attempt to link them to the wider issue of budgetary discipline.

Even this was not new: in 1981, in the context of the proposed introduction of production targets, the Commission had stated that the growth in agricultural expenditure should be at a slower pace than the growth in the Community's budgetary resources (Commission 1981(*a*)). While this principle had not been converted into a legal requirement, it was accepted by the European Council and, in 1984, the Council had reiterated the principle (Bull. EC 12–1984)). How-ever, it had proved impossible to respect this guideline.

The budgetary crisis in the Community extended well beyond agriculture. By 1987, the Community was 'on the brink of bankruptcy' and it had 'sunk into a morass of budgetary malpractices' (Commission 1987(*c*), 2). Because the CAP represented such a major element in the Budget, control of agricultural expenditure was essential in any budgetary reform. The Commission's proposal was that, by 1992, FEOGA-Guarantee would represent just over 50 per cent of the total Budget, compared with 60 per cent as it then was. In order to achieve this reduction, the Commission proposed that each commodity sector should be subject to a budgetary stabilizer, intended either to save expenditure or to generate additional income. The budgetary limits 'would be unavoidable, coming into operation automatically' (ibid. 15).

Three important international meetings took place in the space of a few weeks in May–June 1987. The first was a meeting of OECD Ministers which recognized the state of serious imbalance in international agricultural markets and the need 'to refrain from actions which would worsen the present situation, in particular by avoiding measures that would tend to stimulate production in surplus agricultural commodities and by acting responsibly in disposing of the stocks built up' (Bull. EC 5–1987, 74).

A few weeks later, at the meeting of the seven major industrialized countries in Venice, a further commitment was made to rationalize agricultural policy internationally. The long-term objective was 'to allow market signals to influence the orientation of agricultural production, by way of a progressive and concerted reduction of agricultural support, as well as by all other appropriate means, giving consideration to social and other concerns, such as food security, environmental protection and overall employment' (Bull. EC 6–1987, 143).

The last of these three meetings was of the European Council which was devoted to a discussion of the preparations for the Single Market, and to reform of the Community Budget. The Council endorsed the views of both OECD and the Venice Summit—which is hardly surprising as many of the participants were common to two or three of these meetings. In addition, it agreed in principle to the introduction of measures to encourage set-aside and more extensive farming. The Council added that there could be 'direct, selective income support which should be subsidiary in relation to price policy, have no impact on the level of production and fall within a Community framework' (Bull. EC 6–1987, 10).

One might have expected that agreement at such a high political level would have ensured the smooth passage of these developments into the CAP but it was not to be. Shortly after these meetings the Commission—once again—reviewed the action taken to control agricultural markets and discussed the introduction of additional curbs on production. Its review of the existing attempts to bring production and expenditure under control makes sorry reading. The supposedly restrictive policy on prices had done no more than reduce average support levels by 0.5 per cent per year in real terms (expressed in national currencies). The Commission admitted—perhaps for the first time—that the intervention mechanism had been abused. Instead of providing a safety net as purchaser of last resort, it has become 'an outlet in its own right, particularly attractive because it spared the farmer all effort and risk involved in actual marketing, but particularly harmful since it constituted an artificial, open-ended incentive to production' (Commission 1987(*h*), 5).

While the Commission's comments about the misuse of intervention were well founded, it was quite wrong to lay the blame at the door of the farmers. It was not they who abused intervention but rather the first-stage handler or processor who bought their produce. It was also rather naïve to believe that an open-ended mechanism—as intervention then was—will not be used as such. The Commission listed all the production curbs then in place but without comment on their success or otherwise in achieving a better market balance. It highlighted budgetary savings but had to admit that, despite these, expenditure on FEOGA-Guarantee had increased by over 40 per cent between 1984 and 1987. Nearly half of this rise was attributable to external factors, in particular the shift in the ECU/$ rate.[34]

The Commission sought to minimize the implications for farmers' incomes of the curbs already in place in the price and market policy. It stated that earnings were not solely dependent on the institutional prices agreed annually in Brussels: earnings were 'determined by a wide range of factors, including the volume and cost of farmers' inputs, land prices and rents, taxation, and social security and welfare schemes' (Commission 1987(*h*), 3). While these factors are clearly of importance, it was disingenuous of the Commission to play down the role of price and market policy in this way. The level of support and the choice of mechanism used for support are basic to the price and market policy: if they were not, then the annual political wrangle over price-fixing would be totally illogical! The comment can, however, be seen as another attempt to break the link between price policy and income support, which had been such a feature of policy pronouncements in the 1970s. In another sense, the Commission was correct: with the rise in self-sufficiency and the resultant chronic problem of surplus storage and disposal, much of the expenditure on the price and market policy was devoted entirely to these functions.

The Commission also took the opportunity to distance itself from the obvious ineffectiveness of the attempts to control production. Some of the limitations were due to the nature of farming—climate, production cycles, fixed capital—which made it difficult for farmers to respond promptly to policy changes. Another limitation was the need to avoid policy measures which would merely result in farmers shifting from one enterprise to another, thereby moving the problem sideways—something which had happened frequently already. But most important of all, the Commission stated that the limits to rigorous production controls are 'mainly determined by political imperatives, and depend on what it is felt should be or can be imposed on Community farmers, given the present circumstances with regard to incomes and employment' (Commission 1987(*h*), 11).

The curbs on production, of whatever kind, were now collectively called 'stabilizers'. The concept of the 'maximum production quantity' was introduced. (This was later to be called the 'maximum guaranteed quantity'.) The difference between this and the discredited guarantee threshold lay in the immediacy of the response to a production overrun, and its automatic enforcement by the Commission, within guidelines laid down by the Council.[35] The package of reforms should have been agreed at the December meeting of the European Council but it was not until February 1988 that agreement was reached on a series of measures concerning the Community's future resources, budgetary discipline and management, reform of the structural funds, and the CAP.

It was agreed that the annual growth rate of FEOGA-Guarantee expenditure should be subject to a ceiling: a maximum of 74 per cent of the annual growth rate of the Community's GNP. It was not clear how this was to be achieved in practice nor what penalty (if any) might be incurred if the target was not met. Within that budgetary framework, the European Council also agreed the details of the stabilizer arrangements for cereals, oilseeds and protein products, olive oil, cotton, sugar, wine, fruit and vegetables, tobacco, milk, sheepmeat and goatmeat. In some cases, this was no more than a confirmation of what was already in place but in others—particularly cereals—the curbs on production were enhanced.

The really significant development for cereals was the setting of a maximum guarantee threshold for four marketing years (i.e. to 1991/92) at 160m. tonnes, and the arrangements in relation to the co-responsibility levy and the intervention price if the threshold was exceeded. Detailed arrangements for three years (i.e. to 1990/91) were also made for oilseeds and protein products. The European Council also agreed to the withdrawal of land from production under a set-aside programme for arable land, the details of which the Council actually laid down. It agreed to the introduction of an early retirement scheme and instructed the agricultural Council to take a decision on direct income aids by 1 July 1988 (Bull. EC 2–1988). This deadline was not observed.

Was the 1988 agreement a breakthrough in CAP reform? If it is seen as an exercise to curb budgetary expenditure and to restore (or at least improve) market equilibrium, the answer must be: No. Initially, in terms of budgetary expenditure, it looked as if the restrictions on production (and, in particular, the restrictions on recourse to intervention which had been strengthened as the 1980s progressed) were having an effect, but it was a false dawn. By 1991, the Commission was concerned once more by the growth in stocks, after a few years respite. For instance, at the end of January 1991, cereal stocks were over 16m. tonnes; butter and skimmed milk powder were 253,000 and 333,000 tonnes respectively; and beef stocks were over 700,000 tonnes (Commission 1991(*a*)). While stocks had been higher in some earlier years, it was a worrying trend, especially after the huge effort in the late 1980s to dispose of the 'stock overhang' which was believed to be distorting the market. The Commission anticipated that the budgetary ceiling for FEOGA-Guarantee would be breached.

If the 1988 agreement is viewed as an exercise in promoting market stability, then the stabilizers were a failure. For instance, if one examines the out-turn of each farm-year 1988/89–1991/92, the maximum guaranteed quantities were exceeded on a regular basis for most commodities. This was the case in each of these four years for oilseeds, protein crops, cotton, and sheepmeat; in addition, there were overruns, actual or anticipated, for many other commodities in one or more of these years. The extent of the overrun in some of the crops was so massive as to suggest that the price support was far too high in the first place and that the drop in the support level in response to the overrun was much too small.[36] The only stabilizers which functioned more or less effectively were the production quotas, although it must be said that these were set at too high a level in relation to consumption trends.

The effectiveness of the stabilizers was diminished because they were not applied cumulatively: that is, the penalty started afresh each year. For instance, the oilseed overrun in 1988/89 was 17.7 per cent for rapeseed, 44 per cent for sunflower, and 23.1 per cent for soya. This resulted, in 1989/90, in deductions of 7.6, 19.8, and 10.3 per cent respectively in support prices. However, all of these crops had been subject to a deduction of 10 per cent in 1988/89 (due to the overrun in 1987/88). Effectively, therefore, because each year started afresh, the changes in support prices 1989/90 on 1988/89 were +2.4 per cent for rapeseed, –9.8 per cent for sunflower, and virtually unchanged for soya (Commission 1989(*a*)).

Not only was the 1988 agreement no more than an exercise in containment, rather than a fundamental reform, but it was defective in a manner familiar down the years in the CAP. It was intended as a package to include not only price and market adjustments but also structural and social measures—income aids, early retirement, set-aside, extensification. These measures were introduced very slowly and in a limited way: at the beginning of 1991, income aids applied in three Member States only; early retirement in one Member State; only 2 per cent of cereals land was in set-aside; and extensification had hardly started (Commission 1991(*b*)).

The start of the 1990s saw the CAP—once again—in crisis: the market remained out of balance and in some respects it was deteriorating. The need to dispose of heavily subsidized surpluses abroad was a source of rising resentment and criticism. Internally, in a period of high unemployment, farmers were perceived as a favoured group by an increasingly alienated urban society, which also found much to criticize in the impact which agriculture was having on the environment. The price and market policy lay at the heart of these criticisms. Through it, price support was linked directly to the quantity produced. This provided 'a permanent incentive to greater production and further intensification' (Commission 1991(*b*), 8). What was needed was a fresh approach: it was time to rethink the policy objectives and mechanisms.

The MacSharry Reforms 1992–1996

Early in 1991, the Commission issued a discussion document (COM(91)100) '*The Development and Future of the CAP*' (Commission 1991(*b*)), commonly called the MacSharry Plan (referred to in Chapter 4 above). The purpose of this document was to open a debate; in many ways it follows a train of thought which originated in *The Perspectives* (Commission 1985(*b*))—discussed mainly in Chapters 8 and 11. Its basic objective was to retain a sufficient number of farmers to carry out on behalf of society the tasks of food and raw material producer and protector of the natural environment, in the framework provided by family farming.

To support this objective, the price and market policy had to continue its perennial tasks of controlling production and balancing the market but to do so more effectively. To that end, the support mechanisms had to be reviewed 'so as to adapt them to a situation different from that of the sixties' (Commission 1991(*b*), 9). While the three principles of a single market, Community Preference, and financial solidarity remained, they needed to be put into a 1990s context. In particular, 'financial solidarity implies the need . . . for a better distribution of support . . . taking into account the particularly difficult situation of certain categories of producers and certain regions' (ibid. 12). Greater emphasis needed to be placed on environmentally friendly farming, and extensification; competitiveness and efficiency had to be pursued, so as to assist the Community in its commercial activities,[37] and a strong rural development policy had to be put in place to work alongside the CAP to maintain the rural population and strengthen the rural economy.

In COM(91)100, the Commission did not go into detail on the types of price and market reform which it had in mind but rather outlined the main features only. As always, the cereals sector was critical: a reduction in support prices would make them more competitive with substitute products in the feeding of livestock. Producers would be compensated for the price fall by a direct area payment which would be the same for all producers up to a certain level, but beyond that would become degressive. Similarly, above a certain level, payment would be conditional on the withdrawal of arable land from production. Both the level of aid per hectare and the amount of set-aside would be dependent on the state of the market. Corresponding regimes were envisaged for oilseeds and protein crops. The implementation of these new systems would result in the abolition of the existing stabilizers for the crops concerned. The reduction in prices would, of course, have an effect on the input prices for livestock, where the payment of targeted premiums would reduce recourse to intervention and promote extensification, through the use of maximum allowable stocking rates per hectare as the basis for premium payments.

Having waited for a few months to test reaction to the MacSharry Plan, the Commission issued a follow-up document—COM(91)258—in which it outlined some of the reactions it had received. Two of these are of importance because they illustrate how difficult it is to rescue agricultural policy from a time-warp which still favours unit price subsidies, despite their proven inequity as between producers, and their inherent tendency to encourage intensification, monoculture, environmental damage, and the generation of unsaleable surpluses. Some Member States and farming organizations (which the Commission did not name) 'argued that maintaining existing institutional prices, coupled with more effective supply control on a voluntary basis, and the reduction of imports, would bring about a more stable situation for Community agriculture, without prejudicing other essential Community interests' (Commission 1991(*c*), 4). It is hard to credit that after two decades of turmoil in the price and market policy, such sentiments could be seriously expressed.

The second negative reaction related to the proposed differentiation of support on the basis of the circumstances of the farmer, or the region. As outlined in Chapter 4, this was crucial to what MacSharry was trying to achieve: the approach was 'designed to maintain economic and social cohesion to the benefit of the vast majority of farmers who are less well placed to fully avail of the benefits of the Policy' (Commission 1991(*c*), 5). The Commission had anticipated the criticism by meeting it head-on and answering it in COM(91)100. Because of the diversity of structures within agriculture, farmers were not on an equal footing and therefore public funds should be used to correct the inequalities. The Commission was committed to the efficient farm—just as it had been in the 1970s—but 'it is precisely because the larger farms are . . . in a position to produce with reduced support that it is possible to envisage the development of the policy as suggested' (Commission 1991(*b*), 16).

In COM(91)258, the Commission explained its proposed market reform adjustments for cereals, oilseeds and protein crops, tobacco, milk, beef, and sheepmeat in greater detail. Later in the same year, it produced draft legislation on these commodities and, after lengthy discussions, agreement was reached in the Council in May 1992. Some important features of the original MacSharry Plan were lost (in particular, the attempted shift in emphasis away from support for medium and large farm businesses to the socially and economically deprived farms on which there was an income problem). Other features were modified, so as to lessen their impact (the support levels were more generous than in the Commission's proposals).

The package of measures was for three farm-years: 1993/94–1995/96, for the list of commodities referred to above (with the addition of dried fodder).[38] The market regimes for the remaining commodities were to remain in place for the time being but it was expected that these would be reformed as time allowed. The target and intervention prices for cereals were laid down for the three years, as were the compensatory payments. The latter were on a per-hectare basis and regionalized on the basis of yields in the 1986/87–1990/91 period. The proportion of arable land to be set aside was decided each year on the basis of the market situation. The direct aid for small cereal producers was replaced and, instead, they were exempted from the set-aside requirements, and received a payment per hectare for all arable crops.[39]

Parallel arrangements were made for oilseeds, except that the area payment was in two instalments in the year, so as to allow for it to be varied in the light of price developments on international markets. The previous system of support for protein plants was replaced with an area payment. The support arrangements for tobacco were extensively modified, with the varieties being divided into eight groups, three of which were exclusive to Greece. Each group was subject to quotas allocated to each producing Member State. A single premium was payable for each group. Intervention and export refunds were abolished.

Minor adjustments were made to the milk quotas and to the support price for butter. The beef regime was considerably altered. The intervention price was reduced by 15 per cent over the three years 1993–5, and access to intervention was made subject to a declining annual ceiling to 1997. The various premiums payable on different kinds of cattle were made subject to a maximum density of livestock per hectare of forage area, declining over a four-year period (1993–6) to 2 LU/ha. forage area.[40] As the sheepmeat regime had been revised in 1989, the adjustments were minor (and more generous than the Commission proposals). The interest here lies in the regulation of the transfer of producers' rights to premiums, both between producers and between regions.

When the MacSharry Plan came into operation in the farm-year 1993/94, it was in the context of an agricultural sector in the throes of the usual state of oversupply. The outturn for 1992/93 was that stocks of cereals and beef had increased while those for butter and milk powder had declined. The maximum guaranteed quantity (where they still applied) had been exceeded for tobacco, cotton, certain fruits and vegetables, sheep, and wine. The outlook to 1997/98 was not encouraging: cereals stocks were expected to remain at an estimated level of 16–22m. tonnes, although with the anticipated increase in consumption, this would be a major improvement on the stock of 40m. tonnes in 1991/92. Wine was expected to be an even greater problem than in 1993/94: although production was falling, the surplus was expected to be equal to one-third of production.[41] Beef surpluses and stocks were expected to be higher, and the surplus of milk was expected to be stable at its existing level (Commission 1993(*a*)).

In other words, despite all the efforts, markets were not expected to be in balance at the end of the MacSharry reforms. The direct payments to farmers and the monitoring of set-aside land involved farmers and the Member States in a major administrative exercise. While the direct payments (for the arable crops at least) were 'politically correct' internationally, in that they were not linked to current production levels,[42] their introduction was an opportunity lost. They did little—if anything—to shift support in the direction of disadvantaged farmers. Thus, the contradictions and dilemmas of the price and market policy remained unresolved.

NOTES

1. The aim of this Section is to provide the reader with no more than an outline of the important features of market support mechanisms. Detailed information on individual commodities, if required, must be sought elsewhere.
2. The economic implications of the use of this policy instrument are outlined in Ch. 7, and the changes made to the frontier support mechanism by the implementation of the GATT Agreement are discussed briefly in Ch. 7 and also in Ch. 12.
3. Briefly referred to in Ch. 2 and discussed further in Ch. 12.
4. Although the agricultural market is referred to as 'managed', this only refers to the institutional framework within which it functions. Within that framework, market prices are free to fluctuate. They are, of course, influenced by the existence of the framework so that the extent of the daily/seasonal variation is less than it would be if markets were completely free and price were allowed to find its own level unhindered.

5. These products are reciprocal: the production of butter creates a residue of skimmed milk which is then turned into powder.

6. Despite the drastic attempts to limit its use in recent years, at no stage has the Commission ever proposed its complete replacement. The reason is probably more psychological than anything else.

7. As with intervention, just because a commodity regime permits the payment of export refunds does not mean that they are necessarily frequently used.

8. A target price (or its equivalent) is set annually for most products with a support system. It is an institutional price which can be seen as the internal equivalent of the threshold price at the frontier. Because of the high level of self-sufficiency in the Community, target prices are in practice rarely achieved, as the market price is normally lower. However, they are of importance because of the link with threshold prices and because intervention prices are fixed in relation to them.

9. The timing of Council decisions was brought into sharp focus with the introduction of set-aside under the MacSharry reforms (outlined later in the chapter). Arable farmers participating in the support scheme for cereals need to know before the planting season commences how much of their arable land they will be required to leave unplanted.

10. It is even worse when coping with currency instability which was a particular night-mare during the 1970s and 1980s. For a brief account of this added hazard see Fennell (1987), Ch. 6.

11. The source of this draft Regulation used here is not the original but rather the version as amended by the European Parliament: Débats, Session 1962–1963, Séances du 4 au 8 février 1963.

12. Thus, for instance, the price for milk might be agreed early in the negotiations but it would not come into force at the beginning of the milk-year (1 Apr.) unless the whole package had been agreed. Instead, the previous year's arrangements for milk would be extended and, when the whole package was accepted by the Council, the new Regulations on milk would be published and their application backdated to the beginning of April. In some years, the delay is quite considerable, with the Regulations for all commodities not appearing in the *Official Journal* until the summer.

13. See OJ C115, 28–9–74 and OJ C270, 26–11–75.

14. See OJ C157, 14–7–75 and OJ C140, 5–6–79.

15. It will be recalled that the promotion of specialization was one of the features of the Commission's proposals of 1960, referred to earlier in this chapter.

16. On this last point, the existence of production quotas for sugar based, as they are, on the historical production pattern of the individual Member States prior to 1967 (or the date at which the country joined the Community) has meant the perpetuation of that pattern throughout the lifetime of the sugar regime. There are therefore fourteen national markets masquerading as a single market (Belgium and Luxembourg are counted as one market) and, in addition, there are separate cane sugar quotas for the French overseas departments, and the Azores.

17. On the import side a parallel protective system was introduced to discourage im-porters from switching to the purchase of inputs for manufacturing from cheaper overseas sources. See Harris *et al.* (1983) for a more detailed explanation of the non-Annex II support system.

18. These declines are even more marked in Table 6.A2 where actual levels of expendi-ture are shown. There the downturn can be seen to have lasted four years in each case.

19. The use of the term 'intervention' is fraught with confusion. In the first Section of this

chapter it was used in its classical sense of the withdrawal of produce from an oversupplied market.

20. Even in the original EC-6, consumption fell from an *annual average* of 70 litres/head in 1956–60 to 65 litres/head in 1970–4 (Commission 1980(*c*)). Subsequent Enlargements of the Community have only served to bring the average down further.

21. The nature of these units has changed over time but the principle has remained the same. Since 1979 the unit has been the ECU.

22. This is shown in the original source: COM(80)800 (Commission 1980(*c*)). The most positive impact was felt in the three new Member States (Denmark, Ireland, and the UK) which were, over a five-year period, moving to the common price level.

23. This arrangement has changed over time and has not always worked as intended; the Community Budget has had to assist in the disposal of excess sugar. The producers have also had to pay additional levies from time to time to help get rid of accumulated surpluses.

24. See OJ C23, 8–3–74 and OJ C88, 26–7–74. One of the problems with both Institutions was that, while they were prepared to accept co-responsibility in principle, they were often opposed to the particular proposal of the Commission: see OJ C157, 14–7–75.

25. For beef, the Commission proposed that co-responsibility should take the form of restrictions on access to intervention.

26. This view was consistent with its view on the co-responsibility levy on milk, expressed in OJ C97, 21–4–80.

27. They joined at the beginning of 1986; Greece had joined at the beginning of 1981. The use of five-year forecasts became a feature of the annual price proposals from 1981 onwards.

28. There is some dreadful confusion of terminology in Commission documents: production targets, production objectives, production thresholds, and guarantee thresholds are all the same concept. They were used haphazardly in the early 1980s but by about 1984 'guarantee threshold' had become fairly firmly established as the preferred term. Another confusion was caused by the Commission in COM(83)500 where it defined guarantee thresholds so as to include production levies and quotas. This was not helpful!

29. At that time, the main sources of income for financing Community activities were import and production levies on certain agricultural commodities, the customs duties, mostly on industrial imports, and a contribution from the Member States calculated on a VAT base. Collectively these funds were known as 'own resources'.

30. The European Council gave the Commission six weeks in which to respond—a deadline which the Commission met. One can only assume that the discussion paper was virtually complete at the time of the Stuttgart meeting—and that the Council knew this!

31. This would have been consistent with the quota system for sugar, which had been revised in 1981, so that the levy covered the full cost of exports other than food aid and the sugar displaced by the imports under the Lomé Convention.

32. They are still in operation at the time of writing (1996).

33. See Hendriks (1991) for an account of this episode in the context of German attitudes to and influence over the CAP. It is ironic that, before the end of the 1980s, Member States had accepted reductions in support prices expressed in national currencies.

34. Because the price of agricultural raw materials is usually expressed in $US on international markets, any change in relative values of the ECU or the $ has an immediate impact on the cost of agricultural product support in the Community.

35. The details of budgetary stabilizers were discussed in COM(87)101 (Commission 1987(*c*)) and the principle had been accepted by the European Council in June 1987 (Bull. EC 6–1987).
36. The actual or anticipated production level compared to the maximum guaranteed quantity was given in tabular form each year in the price proposals, starting with 1988/89 (Commission 1988(*a*)).
37. It is not easy to achieve these goals simultaneously.
38. The most important Regulations of the reform package are to be found in OJ L181 (1–7–92) and OJ L215 (30–7–92).
39. A small producer is one who produces less than 92 tonnes of cereals per year.
40. Producers with fewer than 15 livestock units (LU) were exempt from these controls. The maximum densities proposed in COM(91)258 included a lower figure for less-favoured areas, where the soils are more fragile. No reference is made to this lower level in the legislation.
41. This applies to table wine only. Wines classified as quality wines are not a problem.
42. This issue is discussed in Ch. 12.

Table 6.A1. Distribution of expenditure from FEOGA-Guarantee by commodity group, by year (%)

Year	Cereals[a]	Pigmeat, eggs, poultry	Milk products	Sugar	Oilseeds[b]	Olive oil[b]	Fruit and Vegetables[c]
1962/63	98	2					
1963/64	97	3					
1964/65	79	6	14				
1965/66	49	6	43	2			
1966/67	37	5	36	1	} 20		...
1967/68	41	4	31	6	} 12		2
1968/69[h]	42	2	25	10	} 14		2
1970	34	2	38	7	} 11		2
1971	30	4	38	7	3	1	3
1972	40	3	25	7	4	7	3
1973	27	3	39	4	2	7	1
1974	10	3	39	3	...	4	2
1975	13	1	24	6	1	4	2
1976	12	1	41	4	2	3	3
1977	9	1	43	9	1	3	3
1978	13	1	46	10	2	2	1
1979	15	2	43	9	2	4	4
1980	15	2	42	5	3	3	6
1981	17	2	30	7	5	4	6
1982	15	2	27	10	6	4	7
1983	15	2	28	8	6	4	7
1984	9	1	30	9	3	6	7
1985	12	1	30	9	6	3	6
1986	15	1	24	8	9	3	4
1987	18	1	23	9	12	5	4
1988	16	1	22	7	10	3	3
1989	12	2	19	8	10	6	4
1990	15	2	19	5	13	4	5
1991	16	1	17	6	11	6	3
1992	17	1	12	6	13	5	4
1993	19	1	15	6	9	7	5

Table 6.A1. (*cont.*)

Year	Beef	Non-Annex II[d]	Textiles[e]	Tobacco	Wine	Protein products[f]	Sheepmeat and goat-meat[g]
1962/63							
1963/64							
1964/65							
1965/66							
1966/67							
1967/68	1	...					
1968/69[h]	1	...					
1970	1	1	...	...			
1971	1	1	...	4	2		
1972	...	1	...	5	2		
1973	...	1	...	3	...		
1974	10	...	...	6	1	...	
1975	21	1	...	5	3	...	
1976	11	1	...	3	2	...	
1977	7	2	...	3	1	...	
1978	7	2	...	2	1	...	
1979	7	2	...	2	1	...	
1980	12	2	...	3	3	...	...
1981	13	2	1	3	4	1	2
1982	9	3	1	5	5	1	2
1983	11	2	1	4	4	1	2
1984	14	2	1	4	7	1	2
1985	14	2	1	4	5	2	2
1986	16	2	2	3	3	2	3
1987	9	3	1	3	3	2	2
1988	9	2	2	3	6	2	5
1989	9	2	2	4	4	2	6
1990	11	2	2	5	3	3	5
1991	13	2	2	4	3	3	5
1992	14	2	2	4	3	2	5
1993	11	2	2	3	4	3	5

[a] excluding rice
[b] oilseeds and olive oil combined 1966/67–1970; 1970–9 expenditure understated as a small amount of aid could not be identified as relating to oilseeds or olive oil
[c] from 1976 onwards includes fresh and processed products
[d] export refunds for manufactured products based on raw materials subject to market support regimes
[e] includes flax and hemp, and silkworms until 1980; cotton included 1981 onwards
[f] 1974–9 dried folder only: 1980 onwards includes peas and beans
[g] prior to 1982, sheepmeat only
[h] 18 months
... = under 0.5%; 0.5–0.9% rounded to 1

Sources: Commission 1973(*e*), 1976(*c*), 1977(*h*), 1978(*e*); Agricultural Situation in the Community: various years.

Table 6.A2. Breakdown of expenditure for those commodities for which export refunds and domestic intervention are both significant (m. ua/ECU)

Year	Cereals (exc. rice)		Sugar		Milk products		Beef	
	Total expenditure	of which % intervention	Total expenditure	of which % intervention	Total expenditure	of which % intervention	Total expenditure	of which % intervention
1962/63	28.0	21						
1963/64	49.0	18						
1964/65	126.5	12			22.4	18		
1965/66	116.8	14	4.0[c]	0	103.6	31		
1966/67	146.3	19	3.2[c]	0	143.4	36		
1967/68	434.2	34	67.6	48	319.8	27	6.2	0
1968/69[a]	1,387.4[b]	42	339.1	54	845.7	[d]	32.4	19
1970	894.4	45	192.9	52	991.5	56	30.8	19
1971	472.2	39	113.1	43	564.2	49	17.6	5
1972	970.0	38	161.4	56	598.6	72	7.9	0
1973	1,029.5	48	136.5	59	1,497.0	49	16.6	76
1974	399.7	81	108.8	93	1,219.2	72	324.4	83
1975	620.8	45	272.1	88	1,149.8	71	980.0	85
1976	655.9	38	229.3	73	2,277.7	66	615.9	78
1977	629.9	42	598.4	32	2,924.1	51	467.7	72

1978	1,112.5	25	878.0	27	4,014.6	61	638.7	77
1979	1,563.7	24	939.8	27	4,527.5	54	748.2	64
1980	1,669.0	29	575.2	50	4,752.0	42	1,363.3	47
1981	1,921.4	37	767.5	47	3,342.7	43	1,436.9	42
1982	1,824.5	42	1,241.9	40	3,327.7	54	1,158.6	44
1983	2,441.2	37	1,316.2	42	4,396.1	70	1,736.5	52
1984	1,650.0	44	1,631.5	27	5,441.7	64	2,546.8	45
1985	2,310.2	55	1,804.5	25	5,933.2	66	2,745.8	51
1986	3,391.2	49	1,725.5	28	5,405.8	60	3,481.7	65
1987	4,223.8	25	2,035.6	25	5,182.3	53	2,148.7	59
1988	4,422.8	30	2,081.8	25	5,983.6	48	2,475.8	69
1989	3,213.5	17	1,979.8	27	5,040.7	42	2,428.5	45
1990	3,856.0	35	1,391.1	33	4,971.7	61	2,833.2	61
1991	5,077.4	29	1,814.9	31	5,636.6	60	4,295.0	70
1992	5,456.9	42	1,937.4	33	4,006.8	49	4,413.8	70
1993	6,560.3	57	2,188.6	30	5,211.3	56	3,986.3	57

[a] 18 months

[b] includes special expenditure attributable neither to refunds nor to intervention

[c] total expenditure was a special payment, see [b] above

[d] total expenditure 180m. ua lower than the sum of refunds and intervention, reason unspecified

Sources: as Table 6.A1.

Table 6.A3. Breakdown of expenditure for those commodities for which intervention is the dominant support mechanism (m. ua/ECU)

Year	Oilseeds[a]		Olive oil[a]		Fruit and vegetables[b]	
	Total expenditure	% inter-vention	Total expenditure	% inter-vention	Total expenditure	% inter-vention
1966/67	81.1[c]	93 }			1.7	6
1967/68	129.8	97 }			17.9	100
1968/69[d]	473.4[c]	98 }			67.0	63
1970	281.3	99 }			57.7	70
1971	50.9	96	20.4	100	52.7	88
1972	105.5	95	166.1	100	60.1	47
1973	87.1	97	281.4	100	34.9	25
1974	11.1	93	129.6	100	66.9	73
1975	26.1	97	203.7	100	90.3	61
1976	95.7	89	191.1	100	185.1	76
1977	78.1	99	205.1	100	178.2	72
1978	142.5	100[g]	182.2	100	100.7	52
1979	217.5	99	388.2	100	442.9	92
1980	369.4	99	317.9	100	687.3	94
1981	582.7	99	442.7	99	641.1	93
1982	720.7	99	493.1	98	914.3	93
1983	945.6	100[g]	675.3	98	1,196.1	95
1984	655.6	100[g]	1,096.4	99	1,454.6	96
1985	1,110.6	100[g]	692.2	97	1,230.7	94
1986	2,027.5	100[g]	604.3	95	986.0	92
1987	2,687.4	98	1,139.2	98	967.1	93
1988	2,971.8	99	945.0	93	708.2	91
1989	2,673.6	100[g]	1,464.7	94	1,018.6	92
1990	3,477.0	100[g]	1,169.6	88	1,253.0	93
1991	3,549.5	100[g]	1,874.2	94	1,106.5	91
1992	4,132.0	100[g]	1,754.3	97	1,261.7	91
1993	3,063.4	100	2,468.2	97	1,672.2	89

Table 6.A3. (*cont.*)

Year	Tobacco		Wine		Sheepmeat and goatmeat[e]	
	Total expenditure	% intervention	Total expenditure	% intervention	Total expenditure	% intervention
1966/67						
1967/68						
1968/69[d]						
1970	5.0	100				
1971	62.5	100	28.3	100		
1972	111.0	100	43.8	99		
1973	129.6	100	12.4	95		
1974	183.6	100	41.9	100[g]		
1975	228.5	99	139.1	100[g]		
1976	185.4	99	133.8	99		
1977	205.2	98	89.9	98		
1978	216.1	99	[f]	[f]		
1979	225.4	98	61.9	92		
1980	309.3	98	299.5	91	53.5	100
1981	361.8	98	459.4	94	191.5	100
1982	622.6	97	570.6	94	251.7	100
1983	671.3	96	659.2	97	305.6	100
1984	776.4	95	1,222.6	98	433.5	100
1985	862.9	96	921.4	98	502.4	100
1986	782.2	96	630.8	98	616.9	100
1987	803.6	95	800.3	97	573.8	100
1988	966.1	95	1,545.6	97	1,293.7	100
1989	1,138.8	94	1,147.7	96	1,452.8	100
1990	1,232.1	87	745.2	93	1,452.3	100
1991	1,329.6	95	1,047.8	95	1,790.4	100
1992	1,233.0	94	1,087.2	93	1,749.2	100
1993	1,165.1	97	1,509.6	93	1,800.4	100

a oilseeds and olive oil combined 1966/67–1970; 1970–9 intervention expenditure understated as a small amount of aid could not be identified as relating to oilseeds or olive oil
b from 1976 onwards includes fresh and processed products
c includes special payments
d 18 months
e sheepmeat only prior to 1982; a very small amount of export refunds were paid in 1983, 1984, 1991–3 which is not shown due to rounding
f the total expenditure, export refund, and intervention statistics are impossible to reconcile
g a very small amount of export refunds was paid but due to rounding does not show up in the percentage

Sources: as Table 6.A1.

Table 6.A4. Expenditure on those commodities for which intervention is the only support mechanism (m. ua/ECU)

Year	Flax and hemp	Seeds for sowing	Hops	Silk-worms	Dried fodder	Peas and beans	Cotton
1970	0.6						
1971	0.7						
1972	11.5	0.4					
1973	6.4	14.6	4.6	0.3			
1974	11.8	15.2	4.4	0.5	3.6		
1975	13.9	23.8	7.9	0.8	11.1		
1976	20.3	24.1	16.0	0.4	15.4		
1977	14.5	18.1	9.9	0.3	13.8		
1978	15.4	20.3	11.1	0.5	42.6		
1979	17.6	30.1	10.1	0.5	46.6		
1980	16.8	32.0	6.2	0.4	33.5	27.0	
1981	17.0	38.8	5.9	0.4	34.1	31.4	54.9
1982	19.5	43.5	5.4	0.7	41.7	41.1	96.2
1983	19.3	43.0	8.2	0.3	57.7	84.6	140.1
1984	19.2	42.4	9.1	0.6	76.1	139.4	88.2
1985	27.2	46.4	8.2	0.7	116.9	255.5	212.7
1986	32.3	46.5	8.6	0.5	154.1	305.4	532.2
1987	21.2	41.9	1.5	0.5	167.3	419.4	284.7
1988	25.5	50.4	8.5	0.5	217.5	471.1	428.2
1989	29.1	62.2	21.0	0.7	218.9	423.5	570.9
1990	40.3	73.5	10.6	0.2	298.0	536.4	539.8
1991	33.6	66.7	0.9	0.3	403.9	550.8	487.9
1992	29.0	81.5	9.9	0.2	380.2	480.3	742.1
1993	29.6	70.4	24.5	0.2	523.7	558.7	830.8

Sources: as Table 6.A1.

Table 6.A5. Expenditure on those commodities for which export refunds are the dominant or sole support mechanism (m. ua/ECU)

Year	Pigmeat		Rice		Eggs total expenditure	Poultrymeat total expenditure	Non-Annex II total expenditure
	Total expenditure	of which % refunds	Total expenditure	of which % refunds			
1962/63	0.0	100			0.5	0.2	
1963/64	—	—			1.0	0.7	
1964/65	7.8	100	0.6	100	1.0	1.6	
1965/66	10.7	100	0.0	100	1.3	2.3	
1966/67	15.4	100	1.3	100	0.2	2.8	
1967/68	40.5	100	6.5	98	0.9	3.4	1.1
1968/69[a]	73.7	100	45.0	97	3.3	8.5	3.5
1970	43.4	100	59.6	97	n.a.	n.a.	24.8
1971	51.1	94	49.8	97	n.a.	n.a.	18.2
1972	56.0	100c	50.3	95	n.a.	n.a.	25.0
1973	96.7	100	11.4	93	n.a.	n.a.	26.2
1974	66.5	83	1.2	42	n.a.	n.a.	12.8
1975	53.8	73	4.2	86	n.a.	n.a.	23.8
1976	29.0	85	18.4	99	6.2	8.9	67.0
1977	37.3	78	13.5	98	5.6	20.0	136.3
1978	45.0	71	17.9	94	6.9	31.2	208.5

Table 6.A5. (*cont.*)

Year	Pigmeat Total expenditure	of which % refunds	Rice Total expenditure	of which % refunds	Eggs total expenditure	Poultrymeat total expenditure	Non-Annex II total expenditure
1979	104.9	75	42.9	97	15.9	63.5	252.1
1980	115.6	79	58.7	76	17.5	68.0	221.3
1981	154.6	86	21.7	79	18.1	65.8	282.4
1982	111.6	86	50.3	81	24.2	79.7	414.4
1983	145.0	83	92.9	73	30.4	92.9	343.2
1984	195.9	80	47.8	56	20.4	49.4	382.4
1985	165.4	62	50.1	73	18.2	45.0	440.8
1986	151.8	50	93.7	98	27.3	70.5	502.9
1987	158.6	70	103.0	96	29.1	122.9	590.2
1988	215.6	80	88.7	87	33.3	160.8	602.4
1989	261.0	76	126.7	48	48.4	185.7	552.1
1990	246.9	70	94.2	40	33.1	145.4	511.5
1991	252.2	79	111.9	69	35.7	133.5	704.1
1992	141.6	92	87.3	105[b]	32.8	160.4	699.6
1993	200.9	96	69.5	85	40.7	250.2	743.5

[a] 18 months

[b] refunds are greater than total expenditure because intervention was a negative amount

[c] a small amount of intervention was paid but due to rounding it does not appear in the percentage

n.a. = not available

Sources: as Table 6.A1.

Table 6.A6. Breakdown of expenditure FEOGA-Guarantee by Member State (%)

Year	Total expenditure m. ua/ECU	Belgium	Germany	France	Italy	Netherlands	Denmark	Ireland	UK	Greece	Portugal	Spain
1962/63	28.7	1	6	85	4	3						
1963/64	50.7	1	5	90	1	3						
1964/65	159.9	1	4	78	1	16						
1965/66	238.6	6	8	58	2	26						
1966/67	395.5	5	7	39	27	20						
1967/68	1,039.1	9	12	39	19	21						
1968/69[a]	3,311.5	6	21	35	21	16						
1970	2,603.9	7	26	30	21	16						
1971	1,571.2	6	25	38	13	17						
1972	2,391.7	5	20	37	23	14						
1973	3,928.3	5	20	30	14	15	9	2	4			
1974	3,089.6	5	19	22	17	15	9	5	9			
1975	4,727.4	4	13	25	19	10	7	5	17			
1976	5,570.7	6	16	25	19	14	8	4	8			
1977	6,662.4	6	19	24	14	13	9	9	5			
1978	8,672.7	7	29	20	9	15	9	6	5			

Table 6.A6. (cont.)

Year	Total expenditure m. ua/ECU	Belgium	Germany	France	Italy	Netherlands	Denmark	Ireland	UK	Greece	Portugal	Spain
1979	10,440.7	7	24	24	13	14	7	5	5			
1980	11,314.9	5	22	25	15	14	6	5	7			
1981	11,141.2	4	18	28	18	10	5	4	10	1		
1982	12,405.6	4	16	23	20	11	4	4	10	5		
1983	15,919.7	4	19	23	18	11	4	4	11	6		
1984	18,371.9	4	18	19	22	11	5	5	10	5		
1985	19,744.2	5	18	23	17	10	4	6	10	6		
1986	22,137.4	4	20	25	14	10	5	5	9	6	...	1
1987	22,967.7	3	17	25	17	12	5	4	8	6	1	3
1988	27,687.3	3	18	22	16	14	4	4	7	5	1	7
1989	25,872.9	2	16	18	18	14	4	5	7	6	1	7
1990	26,453.5	3	16	19	16	11	4	6	7	7	1	8
1991	32,385.9	4	15	20	16	8	4	5	7	7	1	10
1992	32,107.5	4	15	21	16	7	4	4	8	7	1	11
1993	34,748.1	4	14	23	14	7	4	5	8	8	1	12

a 18 months

Notes: Luxembourg has been omitted as its share of FEOGA-Guarantee is always less than 0.5%. The basis on which the statistics prior to 1981 are calculated is not strictly comparable to the later years but it is unlikely that this materially alters the distribution between Member States. Total expenditure in some years cannot be reconciled with the total expenditure statistics (not provided) on which Tables 6.A1–6.A5 are based.

Sources: Financial Reports on the European Agricultural Guidance and Guarantee Fund: various years; Agricultural Situation in the Community: various years.

Table 6.A7. Individual Member States' share in final agricultural production, and FEOGA-Guarantee expenditure, % selected years

Year	Belgium	Germany	France	Italy	Nether-lands	Denmark	Ireland	UK	Greece	Portugal	Spain
1975	4 (4)	22 (13)	28 (25)	21 (19)	8 (15)	4 (9)	2 (5)	12 (9)			
1980	3 (5)	19 (22)	27 (25)	21 (15)	8 (14)	4 (6)	2 (5)	12 (7)			
1985	3 (5)	17 (18)	26 (23)	21 (17)	9 (10)	4 (4)	2 (6)	12 (10)	5 (6)		
1992	3 (4)	14 (15)	23 (21)	19 (16)	8 (7)	3 (4)	2 (4)	9 (8)	4 (7)	2 (1)	12 (11)

Notes: figures in brackets are FEOGA-Guarantee expenditure from Table 6.A6. Final agricultural production is taken from the Agricultural Situation in the Community, various years. Luxembourg has been excluded due to the small size of its share of production and FEOGA-Guarantee.

7

Implications of the Choice of Particular Market Policy Instruments

Introduction

The development of the market policy over the lifetime of the CAP was traced in Chapter 6; earlier chapters sought to establish the CAP in its policy context in post-World War II Europe. The purpose of the present chapter is to highlight some of the implications of the choice of particular policy instruments, especially for producers, consumers, and the Community Budget. The decision to support the farming sector—for whatever reason and to whatever purpose—is primarily a political one but with strong economic undertones, not least because the instruments chosen are usually economic in nature. The outcome of that choice can have far-reaching consequences. This chapter is not intended to provide a comprehensive account of all the instruments used in the market policy, rather it is a review of a few of the more important ones.

The choice of policy instruments was in no way unusual and the market policy within the CAP was part of a well-established continuum. Governments down the centuries have regarded the production and distribution of food, and the price at which it is sold, as matters of such fundamental importance that they have not been willing to run the risk of leaving the organization of these activities to farmers and traders alone. Such concerns have been as true of oligarchic and dictatorial governments as of democracies. The motivation may have been the desire to court popularity, to appeal to an electorate, to prevent civil unrest, or to pander to sectional interest groups. Failure to attend properly to such matters has sometimes had grave consequences for governments and people alike. The CAP grew out of a policy context which had long abandoned belief in the merits of free and open markets in agriculture, although the value of such markets was readily accepted for manufactured goods.

Over a wide range of essential commodities, most countries are deficit producers and because historic experience has been much more in the direction of food scarcity than abundance, governments have regarded it as prudent to promote production at home in the interests of improved supply availability. However, in order to ensure the necessary investment, governments have accepted the argument of producers who maintain that the short-term price oscillations which an open market would entail are inimical to the long-term planning which agriculture requires. Governments are therefore caught between the producers' demands for market stability and the consumers' preference for continuity of supply at reasonable prices.

Art. 39.1(c) of the Rome Treaty required the CAP to pursue the objective of market stabilization. As outlined in Chapter 6, this took the form of frontier protection to control supplies and thereby smooth out price fluctuations; internal market support to prevent prices falling to unacceptably low levels which might have damaged investment; and export subsidies to fine-tune market balance so that abundant supplies would not undermine the internal market price.

These market-stabilizing instruments were set at a level which encouraged producers inside the Community to respond to the opportunities provided by their preferential treatment within the managed market. These price incentives encouraged the fulfilment of another Article 39 objective: the assurance of the availability of supplies. Given the perceived need to establish institutional structures in the furtherance of market stability and supply availability, it is not surprising that Art. 39.1(e), to ensure that supplies reach consumers at reasonable prices, was somewhat overshadowed.

The Classic EC Support/Protection Model

As mentioned in Chapter 6, the variable import levy was regarded as the archetypal Community protective mechanism. Linked to it were the intervention support mechanism and the system of export refunds. Figure 7.1 illustrates in a rather simplified form the relationship of the three elements of the classic EC model. The detailed arrangements differed from commodity to commodity[1] but an understanding of the basic principles of the system is all that is required.

Each year the Council of Ministers agreed a series of institutional price levels.

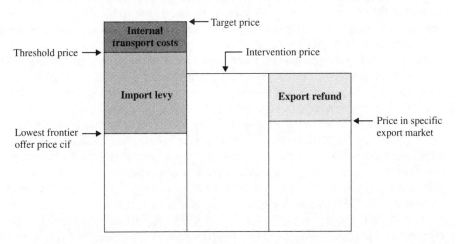

Fig. 7.1. Relationship of main CAP support mechanisms prior to 1995

The threshold price—shown on Figure 7.1—was a form of minimum import price. It was the at-frontier equivalent of the target price, the difference between the two being the cost of internal transport. The frontier price was the landed price for a representative cargo which met Community quality standards. This landed price is often referred to as the 'world price'—which is an acceptable description for a commodity such as wheat but meaningless for many less widely traded commodities. The import levy was the difference between the frontier price and the threshold price. It was variable because it rose and fell in step with changes in the frontier price. It was this variability which gave the levy its potency as a protective device because it was impossible to circumvent it: any lowering of the offer price would merely result in an increase in the levy.

The actual market price which would have applied inside the Community is not shown in Figure 7.1 but it usually fluctuated somewhere between the target price level and the intervention price (to be discussed below). The closer the target and intervention prices were to one another, the greater the degree of market stability. It will be recalled from Chapter 2 that one of the great criticisms of the original price structure was that the level at which the institutional prices for cereals were set was too high and that this filtered down to the remaining commodities. The prices most criticized were the target and threshold prices. However, the protectionism of which the Community was often accused lay not so much in the high level of these institutional prices but in the way in which they were reinforced by the existence of the variable levy.

Thus, even if the target and threshold prices had been set at a lower level, the existence of the variable levy would still have prevented imports from undercutting the internal market price. This watertight system at the frontier provided great internal price stability and prevented external price movements from being reflected internally. This ability to externalize price shocks applied even in those circumstances when the international prices were above the threshold level (as happened very occasionally). This was achieved by, in effect, inverting the levy system so that it became a variable export charge instead. This effectively maintained the supply of the commodity within the Community and prevented prices internally from rising above the target level.

The purposes of intervention through purchase and the provision of financial aid for storage were—and still are—to prevent market prices from tumbling in an uncontrolled way in times of oversupply, and to regulate the release of a commodity on to the market over the span of the year. Intervention agencies were established in each Member State and their function is to act as buyer of last resort, reselling the commodity when prices internally have strengthened or exporting the commodity with the aid of an export subsidy (= refund), if that seems more appropriate. The other function of intervention—orderly marketing—can be seen to greatest effect in the case of cereals where total annual supply becomes available over the few harvest months. It is in the interests of orderly marketing that traders should be encouraged to hold back supplies and to release them gradually over the year. In order to encourage this to happen, the price at which intervention agencies are willing to purchase grain is stepped month by month from October (when it is at its lowest) to May (when it is at its highest), just before the start of the harvest in southern Europe.

In Figure 7.1, the intervention price is illustrated in relation to the target price but this is something of a simplification: the two do not always go together. For instance, for pigmeat, although there is a basic price (= target price), buying in (= intervention) is not automatic and in fact is rarely used; for fruit and vegetables, although there is an intervention mechanism (= withdrawal), it too is seldom used as the price at which withdrawal is triggered is so low that it rarely comes into force. For both these product groups, other forms of market stabilizer are used instead.

As originally perceived, the support of an oversupplied market would have been intermittent and limited to a small volume. However, over time, as levels of self-sufficiency rose this situation changed. For those commodities where intervention was an important support mechanism, due to its excessive use, efforts were made, especially during the 1980s, to curtail access to it. This was done by a variety of means: seasonal or quantitative restrictions; tightening the rules on quality acceptable for intervention; setting more stringent conditions for the operation of intervention trigger mechanisms. Therefore, what is illustrated in Figure 7.1 and subsequently in Figure 7.2 is no more than a stylized representation of the functioning of the system.

The third and final element of the classic EC support and protection model is the export refund. The original argument put forward in favour of refunds was that, like the original purpose of intervention, they were a means of fine-tuning the internal market by assisting the export of commodities temporarily in over-supply. The point was made in Chapter 6 that for those commodities for which both intervention and export refunds exist, the two mechanisms can be used interchangeably to support the internal market. If an external market exists for a commodity in surplus in the Community, it is much less costly in budgetary terms to offer traders an incentive to export than to intervene on the market internally and to put the commodity in store where it may deteriorate or lose value through the need to transform it into a more storable product. The worst situation from a cost point of view is both to intervene and incur storage costs and subsequently to export with an export refund; this became a more frequent occurrence as the production of surpluses increased.

In Figure 7.1, the export refund is illustrated as being equal to the difference between the intervention price level and a price close to the frontier offer price. This is an oversimplified representation. For instance, supposing the internal market price was below the intervention level,[2] then the refund would be the difference between the internal market price and the price in the country to which the commodity is going. This latter price is likely to be above the frontier offer price in the Community which is a price at which a major exporter is willing to sell to the Community. The price in a deficit country is likely to be higher. If, on the other hand, the commodity has already been in store for some time with no prospect of a sale within the Community and beginning to deteriorate then it will be exported anywhere and almost at any price.

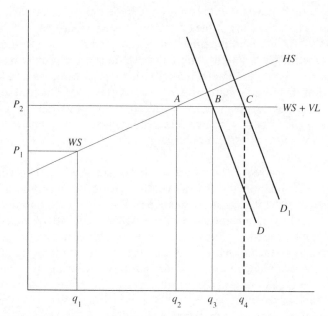

Fig. 7.2. Application of the variable levy and the functioning of the intervention mechanism

Having outlined the rough relationship between these mechanisms, the question arises as to the implications of this system for trade and production. In Figure 7.2, P_1 is the price at which supplies came into the Community from overseas (i.e. the lowest frontier offer price described in Figure 7.1).[3] Over most of the length of the internal supply curve (HS) the assumption is that Community farmers were only able to supply the commodity in question (say cereals) at a price above the frontier offer price (i.e. only a small section of the curve HS lies below the P_1WS line, which indicates that only a small amount of Community grain could have been made available at below the 'world price').

In the absence of any frontier protection, Community farmers would have supplied the market at q_1. However, because the internal support system set the target price at above the world market level, a variable import levy was applied which had the effect of raising the landed price to $P_2(WS + VL)$. At the level of P_2, the Community's farmers were able to raise their output to q_2, which presented no problem as total demand was q_3, leaving room for imports of q_2q_3. In this circumstance, no intervention would have been required. However, farming conditions vary from year to year and supplies are only predictable within a quite wide margin of error. Suppose, for example, that there was a bumper harvest and that actual supply from Community sources was not q_2 but rather q_4. This would mean that, at price P_2, the Community's farmers would supply total internal requirements (B on demand curve D), thereby pushing imports out of the market. The excess supply BC (over and above internal demand) had to be removed from the market if price P_2 was to be maintained. This was achieved through the purchase by the intervention agencies in the Member States of the excess. In Figure 7.2, this is represented as a shift in the demand curve to the right at D_1, indicating that there were in effect two markets: the commercial demand on D, and in addition the buyer-of-last-resort demand on D_1. From the Community farmers' point of view, the market had expanded from q_1 to q_2 through the operation of the variable levy, and from q_3 to q_4 through the operation of the intervention mechanism. In buying the amount BC, the intervention agencies would incur costs of q_3BCq_4.

Welfare Implications of Frontier Protection

In a general sense, one could conclude from the previous Section that the existence of frontier protection was beneficial to the Community's farmers because it limited overseas competition, ensured higher market prices, and improved market stability. However, the benefit was spread more widely than the farmers who grew the crops and reared the livestock because the market circumstances faced by the farmers encouraged them to expand production. This benefited the upstream and downstream activities which provided goods and services for the farming sector and processed and distributed its output. Overseas suppliers were clear losers.[4]

The Community Budget benefited in a partial sense but ultimately lost in a general sense. The gain was in the form of the levy and tariff revenue collected which was then available to fund various Community activities. The loss came about by the decline in these frontier revenues as internal self-sufficiency levels rose and the costs of supporting the higher levels of production necessitated the raising of budgetary revenue from alternative sources.

Increases in price which resulted from protection damaged consumers, although the extent of their loss depended in part on the existence of close substitutes for the product in question. It could be argued that there was some element of benefit in the achievement of greater price stability but, given the state of oversupply on international markets for most of the lifetime of the CAP, security of supply was not in doubt. However, any increase in price reduces consumer choice and therefore consumer welfare; when that increase is achieved by the manipulation of the market in favour of producers then the welfare of the latter is increased. Therefore the existence of frontier protection changes the relationship in economic terms between producers and consumers—which is the subject of this Section.

The concept of economic welfare is based on the idea of producer and consumer surplus. 'Producer surplus' is a term used to denote the net return obtained by the owner of productive assets—in this case in agriculture—after variable costs have been deducted. It is assumed that the supply curve (S in Figure 7.3) represents, at each point along its length, the level of production which it is profitable to produce at each corresponding price along the price axis. Thus, for

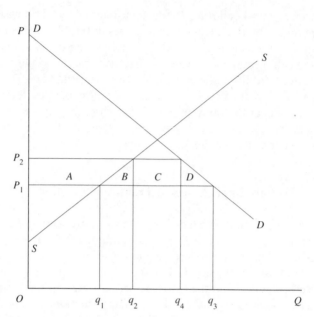

Fig. 7.3. Welfare gains and losses from frontier protection

example, at price P_1 the quantity produced is q_1.[5] To produce at that level, the owner of the assets has to incur variable costs which are represented by the area below the supply curve S. The area above the supply curve but below the price line P_1 depicts the producer surplus.

'Consumer surplus' is a somewhat different idea: it is used to denote the advantage gained by consumers from the difference between what they actually pay on the market and what they would be willing to pay. In other words, it is the net benefit which consumers collectively gain from their ability to purchase as much as they want at the price which prevails in the market rather than having to pay the highest price which they would be prepared to offer for each additional unit. Thus, in Figure 7.3, at price P_1 consumers purchase quantity q_3. If it is assumed that they would have been willing to pay (say) P_2, then the benefit to them of price P_1 is equal to the area $A + B + C + D$.

Suppose that Figure 7.3 is applied specifically to the issue of frontier protection and that at price P_1 the situation depicted is one in which there is no frontier protection. Total consumption is q_3, internal production is q_1, and the difference between q_1 and q_3 is represented by imports. Some form of frontier protection is now imposed which raises the price to P_2. This encourages domestic producers to expand output to q_2 but total demand has shrunk to q_4. Imports are now the difference between q_2 and q_4.

In terms of economic welfare, domestic producers gain area A (i.e. the area above the supply curve and below the price P_2); the Community Budget gains the revenue from the import tax which is represented by area C (i.e. the difference between q_2 and q_4 being imports). Consumers lose areas $A + B + C + D$. There is a net loss of areas $B + D$. Area B is an efficiency loss incurred by the economy as a whole: additional resources had to be brought into agriculture to raise output from q_1 to q_2 and the assumption is that there is a cost involved in the shift. If that is so, and if imports were available at the lower price P_1, then overall efficiency in resource use has declined. Area D represents a deadweight loss, i.e. a loss of consumer surplus not picked up as a gain by any other interest group in the economy.

Exceptions to the Classic Support/Protection Model

So far in this chapter only the classic model has been discussed but, from the beginning, other protection and support systems existed as well. They were used either because of the nature of the commodity in question or of the state of the market. This Section deals with the two main exceptions: customs tariffs (as an alternative to the variable levy), and deficiency payments (as an alternative form of support internally).

Customs tariffs. For over thirty years of the lifetime of the CAP, tariffs were not an important control mechanism, being used most prominently for highly seasonal products such as fruit and vegetables. From the point of view of a liberal trade policy, tariffs are regarded as the least damaging form of frontier protection, in that they are applied to the landed price in terms of a fixed percentage of that price or as a fixed monetary amount per unit imported, without any restriction as to quantity. The manner in which a tariff works is illustrated in Figure 7.4, ignoring, for the moment, the dotted lines.

The assumption is made that the 'world price' is given at P_1 and that world supply is totally elastic, i.e. that supply is available on the world market in any quantity needed by the Community at price P_1. This is known as the 'small nation' situation and is a simplifying assumption which, given the size of the EC/EU, might well not be true.[6] At price P_1, the Community's farmers are only willing to supply quantity q_1 (point B on the supply curve CS), whereas total demand is q_2 (point E on the demand curve D). The difference is provided by imports $(q_2 - q_1)$.

In order to encourage Community suppliers to expand production, a tariff is imposed which raises the price on the market to P_2. The immediate effect is to make imports more expensive which reduces demand for them. Buyers turn to the Community's suppliers whose response is to divert extra resources to the commodity and this involves higher costs of production and, in the longer-term, new investment. Therefore, they require the higher price P_2. But at that price total demand shrinks to q_3 (point K on the demand curve D); Community production expands to q_4 (point F on CS); and imports contract to $q_3 - q_4$. In terms of economic welfare, as illustrated in Figure 7.3, the changes brought about by the imposition of a customs tariff are the same as those for a variable import levy.

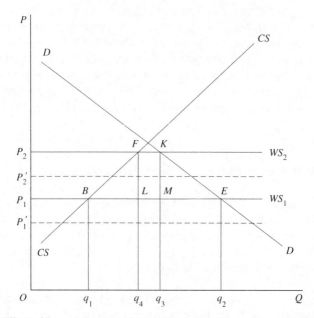

Fig. 7.4. Effect of the application of a tariff (small-nation case) contrasted with a variable levy

Supposing, however, the overseas suppliers do not wish to lose the market now subject to a tariff. Under such a regime they have the option, if their own cost structures allow it, to meet the imposition of the tariff by lowering their offer price. In this case, the tariff—being a fixed charge in percentage or value terms—is applied to the lower offer price. This might, for instance, mean that all or part of the difference between P_1 and P_2 was absorbed by the exporting country, thereby reducing the impact of the tariff as a protective device. It is this aspect of tariffs which makes them a somewhat ineffective means of excluding imports, unless applied at a swingeing level.

Contrast that situation with what would happen if a variable levy rather than a fixed tariff were applied. In the explanation above the 'world price' was given at P_1. Under the small nation assumption, it is the state of the world market at large which determines that price, and supply or demand fluctuations elsewhere in the world can influence the price level. Suppose, for instance, that the world price declines from P_1 to (say) P_1', under the variable levy system, the frontier charge imposed is increased (in this example to $P_2 - P_1'$) and there is no effect on the internal price P_2. However, when a fixed tariff is imposed the internal price falls to P_2'. In a similar manner, if the world price were to rise then the internal price would exceed P_2 if a tariff were applied but would remain unaltered if a variable levy were applied.

In order to improve their protective properties, and to prevent external suppliers from circumventing the tariff, the Community sometimes combined a customs tariff with a minimum import price (MIP). This was based on actual market prices in representative markets in the Community over a reference period. Provided the external suppliers observed the MIP, the normal tariff was applied. If, however, the offer price fell below the MIP, then a countervailing charge was applied to bring the offer price up to the desired level.

Deficiency payments. From an external perspective, frontier protection was the most visible element in the price and market policy under the CAP. In this context, deficiency payments are an anomaly as they provide internal support without frontier protection and in a situation where there is no overt intention to limit imports. The system works particularly well in situations in which imports form a large part of total supply with the result that the price at which they are offered establishes the price on the internal market. This is to the benefit of consumers but does not damage producers internally, as they are paid a price supplement over and above what they get on the market. This supplement (= deficiency payment) raises their total return to a guaranteed level which is funded entirely from government tax revenue.

The system as described above was used for many years in Britain and worked reasonably well although, even there, the very existence of the guaranteed price encouraged farmers to expand output to the extent that eventually the government had to introduce quantitative restrictions on the amount covered by the guarantee. The system was particularly suited to Britain where, even in the 1950s, the number of farmers was small. By way of contrast, in the Community the number of producers of the main commodities was large and the bureaucratic exercise of making payments directly to farmers would have been immense and very costly. However, from earliest times, the Community did use a modified version of the deficiency payments system. It was especially well suited to circumstances in which the Community had a considerable deficit and where processing outlets were few. The low level of self-sufficiency reduced both the number of farmers involved in production and the volume on which the subsidy had to be paid, while the limited number of processors meant that they could be used as the distributors of the support.

Thus, for instance, when the oilseeds regime was set up in 1966, oilseeds were supported in this way. Frontier controls were very limited: tariffs were either zero or at low levels; imports were large and their price set the overall market price. Oilseeds from Community sources were able to compete with imports because the crushers were paid a production subsidy which allowed them to pay the farmers a price above the market price. Figure 7.5 illustrates the way in which the system worked.

At price P_1, which represents a market situation without frontier protection, Community producers supplied q_1 and the remainder of demand was filled through imports of q_1q_2. A guaranteed price of P_2 was then made available to Community producers through the deficiency payment mechanism described above. The total size of the market remained unchanged at q_2 because the market price remained at P_1 but Community producers expanded production to q_3. The dotted line represents their new supply curve. Although imports were reduced by

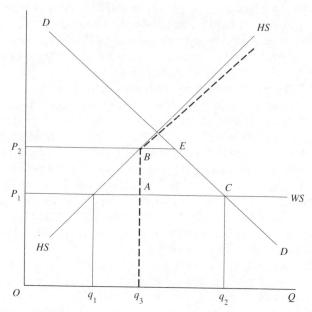

Fig. 7.5. Operation of a deficiency payments mechanism

q_1q_3, from the overseas suppliers' point of view, this was a better outcome than if a variable levy or even a tariff had been imposed when the total market would have contracted from point C on P_1WS to point E. The consumer benefited because the support arrangements left the market price unchanged. The Community Budget lost out as it had to bear the total cost of the deficiency payment represented by P_1P_2BA, with no offsetting revenue from a tariff or levy.

Production Controls

Chapter 6 explained how, faced with the relentless rise in production, the Community tried to find ways of controlling expansion—without actually reducing the value of the institutional support arrangements for farmers. Before examining some of these schemes, the point should be emphasized that the very existence of the support mechanisms changed the perception of the market for both producers and consumers. As was pointed out in Figure 7.2 when price went up to P_2, the Community's producers would plan to increase their output to q_2, which could, if conditions were favourable, turn into the production at q_4 and a surplus of BC which was removed from the market by the intervention agencies.[7] Producers, however, got used to the higher price and the security provided by the system; as a result the speed of application of new technology increased and the proportion of farmers adopting new technology rose. This involved investment in new capital equipment, a greater use of variable inputs

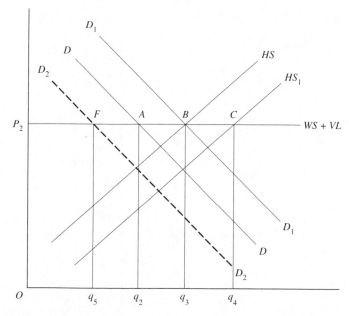

Fig. 7.6. Longer-term implications of a high price support system for producers and consumers

such as fertilizers, pesticides, better seed varieties, improved breeding stock, and so forth. The net result was that, for a given level of fixed assets, a higher output could be obtained. Thus, in the terms of Figure 7.6, there was a shift in the Community supply curve (HS) to the right (HS_1), so that output increased from q_3 to q_4. This can be regarded as a permanent change in producers' intentions.

However, on the demand side, the users of agricultural raw materials began to look around to see whether a substitute could be found for some at least of the commodities (for instance, corn gluten for cereals, oilseed cake for skimmed milk powder). Such substitutes were available on international markets and, as the relevant import regimes in the Community were very light in protective terms, imports soared. The net result was for a shift in the original demand curve D to D_2. This meant that the commercial market contracted from q_2 to q_5 and the intervention agencies were faced not only with the original surplus of AB but instead of one equal to FC. This situation could not be allowed to go on for ever and if (as was the case) the Community was not prepared to reduce price from P_2, then some form of production control became inevitable. Only the two most notable forms of control are discussed here.

Production quotas. As described in Chapter 6, quotas were applied to sugar production from the inception of the sugar regime in 1967 but the extension of this form of control to other commodities was resisted for the two decades which followed. Finally, in the first serious attempt to control production, quotas were introduced for milk in 1984. Figure 7.7 illustrates the situation. At price P prior to the imposition of the quota, the milk output was q_1 with an internal demand

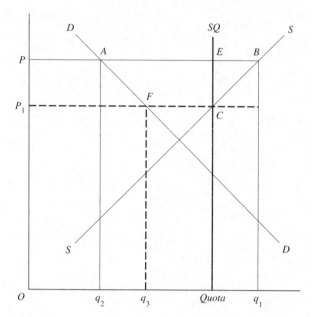

Fig. 7.7. The introduction of a production quota compared with a produce price decline

of q_2 and a surplus of AB which had to be disposed of in whatever way was possible: subsidized export, food aid, cheap sales to food manufacturers, subsidized milk for school children, etc. On the imposition of the quota, the supply curve S became vertical (SQ) which indicates that production beyond that level would not take place because the penalty for exceeding the quota would have made the additional output financially unattractive for the farmers. Production fell back, therefore, from point B to point E with price P unchanged but a welfare loss to producers of EBC. The position of the consumers remained unaltered, as the introduction of the quota made no difference to the price, but the Community Budget benefited by the reduction in surplus from AB to AE, resulting in lower expenditure on intervention purchases or export refunds.

As explained in Chapter 6, the milk quota was introduced as an alternative to a reduction in the support price. Supposing, however, that the Community had gone ahead with the reduction, lowering the support price to (say) P_1 on Figure 7.7 which would have resulted in an equivalent decline in production to that achieved by the quota. Production would have declined to point C on original supply curve S, but in welfare terms producers would have lost not only the area EBC (as with the quota) but also the area $PECP_1$. Part of that loss would have been offset in a wider economic sense by the gain to consumers. As a result of the fall in price, consumption would have expanded from q_2 to q_3 and the consumer surplus would have increased by $PAFP_1$. There would still have been overproduction of FC but, in terms of budgetary cost, this would have been a

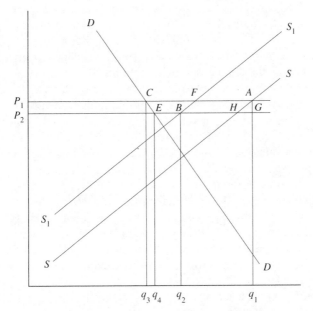

Fig. 7.8. Operation of support system which combines a price reduction with land set aside

considerable improvement on both *AE* and *AB*. Not only would the amount of overproduction have been less in volume terms but, because the level of price support was lower at price P_1, the cost of disposal of the reduced tonnage would also have been lower.

Set-aside. As will be shown in Chapter 11, set-aside for arable crops was originally introduced in 1987 on a voluntary basis but the scheme under consideration here is the one introduced in 1993/94 under the MacSharry reforms. It was designed for large-scale cereal producers who wished to receive compensation for the decline in support prices. Figure 7.8 illustrates the scheme.

P_1 is the original support price prior to the reform and at that level farmers produced at q_1 which is point *A* on the original supply curve *S*. The price was then reduced to P_2 and farmers were able to receive compensation for this decline, calculated on their historic production levels, provided they agreed to the temporary withdrawal of a predetermined percentage of their arable land from production (= set-aside). The land could be fallowed or used for specified permitted purposes and the reason why its withdrawal was required was to ensure that any decline in cereals output was not accompanied by an increase in the production of alternative arable crops.

The result was a reduction in the total supply of arable land and therefore in production potential. In relation to cereals, this is represented in Figure 7.8 as a shift in the supply curve from *S* to S_1, on the assumption that all eligible farmers joined the compensatory scheme. Thus, at price P_2 the quantity produced was

q_2, or point B on S_1. The consumers clearly benefited from this price reduction, expanding their purchases from q_3 to q_4 and, in welfare terms they also gained by the area P_1CEP_2. The situation for producers is not quite so clear-cut as, although the price fell from P_1 to P_2 and output declined from q_1 to q_2, the intention was that the compensation scheme based on historical output levels and the set-aside payments should have been enough to offset the price reduction, with a neutral effect in terms of economic welfare for producers. In other words, in the absence of the scheme, the producer welfare loss resulting from the price reduction from P_1 to P_2 would have been P_1AHP_2. The scheme was intended to neutralize that loss in welfare terms but to reorganize the way in which that position was achieved. Thus, the compensation for the price fall was intended to maintain the producer surplus of P_1FBP_2 and the set-aside payment was intended to maintain the producer surplus of $FAHB$.

However, theoretically it is possible that the payments package fell short of the intended effect. In such a situation the farmers would have misjudged the benefits of the scheme and would have been better to opt out rather than to opt in. In that circumstance, they would have continued to produce at some point along the original supply curve S taking their chance on the state of the market and the actual market price rather than on the institutional price P_2 plus the compensatory and set-aside payments.

So far as the Union Budget was concerned, the only positive element of the scheme was the decline in surpluses: in Figure 7.8 from CA to EB. This would have resulted in a saving on the cost of intervention or of export refunds, or of both. However, it should not be overlooked that the administrative costs of setting up and running this direct payments scheme was a new cost not a replacement of the existing costs of administering intervention and export refunds which still remained. Export countries outside the Union would not have benefited directly from the kind of price decline illustrated in Figure 7.8, as the Union is shown as remaining a surplus producer. However, they might have benefited indirectly from a reduction in competition from Union exports.

Voluntary Export Restraints

Over the lifetime of the price and market policy the initial situation in which the Community was a surplus producer of a limited number of commodities changed. Both the volume of surpluses and the range of commodities involved increased. In budgetary terms the result was a decline in the income from levies and tariffs as imports expanded more slowly or actually contracted, while on the expenditure side the cost of intervention and export refunds rose relentlessly. Attempts were made to dampen down production indirectly by reducing access to intervention and directly by the use of production quotas and, more recently, set-aside.

At the frontier, the Community tried to reduce the level of competition faced by its own producers on the internal market without interfering fundamentally with the frontier protective mechanisms. Reference was made earlier in the chapter to the introduction of minimum import prices alongside customs tariffs to improve the effectiveness of the latter. However, such measures were limited in nature and were most suited to commodities such as fruit and vegetables which are highly perishable and seasonal in nature. A more significant attempt to limit competition was the introduction of voluntary export restraints.

As is discussed further in Chapter 12, in the early years of the Community certain open-market agreements were entered into which, under GATT rules, could not be revoked unilaterally nor without the payment of compensation to injured exporting countries. Two of the commodities involved were manioc (cassava) and sheepmeat. As the level of self-sufficiency rose in the Community, the maintenance of these zero or low-tariff import agreements became more irksome, as they allowed overseas supplies to compete on favourable terms against higher priced Community-produced commodities. International markets were, in general, oversupplied and exporting countries which already had markets in the Community were extremely reluctant to see their foothold in these markets disappear. The markets were worth far more to the exporters than any compensation which they might have received from the Community in the event that it had sought to abandon the open-market arrangements.

In these circumstances it became possible in the 1980s for the Community to negotiate restraint agreements under which the exporting countries of manioc and sheepmeat 'voluntarily' limited their exports of the commodity in question to an agreed annual tonnage in exchange for the maintenance of the open-market concession. If exports exceeded this agreed level, the Community was free to apply the relevant levy or tariff. It was very much in the exporting country's interests to police its exports so as to ensure the agreed tonnage was not exceeded and indeed it was its responsibility to see the agreement was honoured.

Voluntary restraint agreements differed from tariffs and levies in a number of respects. Firstly, they took the form of an administrative control in the exporting country. Secondly, their existence was not a source of revenue for the Community Budget whereas tariffs and levies clearly were. Thirdly, because they limited the market share of the imported commodity and at the same time did not result in any additional internal market support, they were cost-free from the point of view of the Community Budget. At a time when expenditure on the CAP was coming under increasing pressure, this was a welcome relief. However, in terms of economic welfare a cost to the Community was involved. In Figure 7.3, the imposition of a customs tariff or a variable levy is shown as causing a producer gain of A and a consumer loss of $A + B + C + D$. However, part of that loss (C) accrues to the Community as revenue from the tariff or levy. In the case of a voluntary export restraint, the negative impact was greater because area C did not accrue to the Community Budget but rather it represented a gain to the exporting country. In this circumstance, the only gain to the Community from the loss of consumer surplus was that of the producers, i.e. area A.

Changes to the Protection Mechanisms: Uruguay Round of GATT

Despite the changes to the levels of self-sufficiency in the Community over time and the successive Enlargements from six to (at present) fifteen Member States, for the majority of that time the frontier protection mechanisms changed little. The system was still based very largely on mechanisms intended to fine-tune a market and the results of this fine-tuning were in theory unlikely to have any influence on markets or prices elsewhere. Figure 7.4 above is based on such a principle: that the application of a tariff (or variable levy) would not affect the international market. However, over time such a 'small nation' assumption in relation to the Community became increasingly untenable. Figure 7.9 illustrates a more likely situation.

WS is the supply available for trade in the rest of the world; unlike in Figure 7.4 it is shown as being responsive to price change. *CD* is the original Community import demand curve in the absence of frontier protection. At price P_1 there is an import of q_1 from the rest of the world. P_2 represents a situation in which frontier protection has been imposed (either by a customs tariff or a variable levy). At this level, Community demand for imports falls due to the expansion of internal production behind the protective barrier. *CD* therefore shifts to a new demand schedule CD_1. This reduces imports to q_2. The difference between q_1 and q_2 has to find alternative outlets and this can only be done by a reduction in the offer price which, in order to restore equilibrium on the international market, falls to P_3.

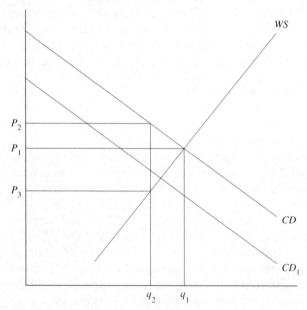

Fig. 7.9. Application of a tariff (large-nation case)

A similar situation can be said to exist in relation to the Community's own exports which, due to the need to find outlets for surplus products on a permanent basis, have influenced the relevant international markets. The sensitive nature of these markets was clearly illustrated in Table 3.7 which highlighted the importance of the Community as an importer and, increasingly, as an exporter.

It is hardly surprising, therefore, that the role of the Community in international trade negotiations has increased over time, and that it was one of the main players in the drama of the Uruguay Round of GATT, which is referred to in more detail in Chapter 12. The only point to be made here is to outline the changes to the frontier protection system which result from the Uruguay Round. The most fundamental change is the abolition of the variable import levy (see Figure 7.1) and its replacement by customs tariffs. From a situation in which tariffs were a rather unimportant protective mechanism under the CAP they have become of much greater significance. Where commodities were previously subject to variable levies (or other roughly comparable protective mechanisms), the incidence of protection has now to be expressed as a tariff equivalent.

Over the implementation period of the Uruguay Round, the level of tariffs (and tariff equivalents) is scheduled to fall. If that were to result in greater imports by the Union, then there could be a resulting increase in the international prices of some commodities. However, in practice, the impact may be muted. This is because the critical commodities were all subject to variable import levies for which the tariff equivalent was extremely high. That was the level which was applied at the beginning of the implementation period. Even at the end of that period, tariff rates for major agricultural commodities will remain well above the kinds of levels applied to manufactured goods.

As to the voluntary export restraints, when they were introduced in the 1980s, the exporting countries concerned accepted them most reluctantly. Ironically, in the long run the agreements worked to their advantage, as they gained the status of traditional suppliers *vis-à-vis* other potential suppliers. Thus, they held a valuable asset in the form of access to Community markets. This can be seen as the creation of an economic rent for the country/firm/government agency which administered the agreement. Under the Uruguay Round of GATT, the small improvement in market access for overseas suppliers which must be granted during the implementation period does little more, in the case of the Union, than confirm the advantages of the traditional suppliers. This came about by the conversion of the restraint agreements into privileged quotas with the right to supply over-quota at the full tariff rate (see Chapter 12).

NOTES

1. For instance, the three elements did not always coexist: export refunds were available for commodities not subject to a variable levy (or its equivalent), and were available for commodities supported internally by a system other than intervention.

8

The Mansholt Plan and Its Legacy

The Mansholt Plan

The origins of structural policy and the basic legislation relating to it were outlined in Chapter 2. The present chapter, and Chapters 9 and 10 examine aspects of the policy as it developed. The Mansholt Plan has already been referred to in Chapter 4, in the context of changes to the price and market policy, and the attempt to introduce the objective method in price-fixing. The document which became known as the Mansholt Plan was the work of a small group of officials who held a series of private meetings in the Luxembourg village of Gaichel, from which they became known as the 'Gaichel group' (Ries 1978). Their work expanded into a massive exercise within the Commission and, in December 1968, the Commission presented the outcome to the Council. It took the form of a series of documents under the collective call number COM(68)1000 (Commission 1968(*a–f*)).

There were six parts, all interrelated. Part A was entitled 'Memorandum on the reform of agriculture in the European Economic Community'—the Mansholt Plan itself. Part B was a statistical annexe which accompanied the Plan. Part C was a discussion document on the medium-term measures which should be taken in various problem agricultural markets (milk, sugar, fruit and vegetables, and oils and fats). Part D was, in effect, the first annual report on the situation in agriculture but was confined almost exclusively to an analysis of the market and trade situation. Part E contained the price proposals for the year 1969/70 for the commodities which were subject to common regimes. Finally, Part F was a report on the national structural policies in operation in the Community.

It is important to remember that the Mansholt Plan is a policy discussion document and the reforms suggested in it are expressed in fairly general terms. The Commission hoped that the Memorandum would lead to a wide discussion within the Council, the European Parliament, the ESC, and the farmers' organizations. Above all, the Commission was trying a new tactic with the Council; it was hoping to get a general policy agreement on reform from the Council before presenting it with detailed concrete draft legislation. In this the Commission failed utterly: the Council regarded the Mansholt Plan as political dynamite and neither discussed it nor gave the Commission any indication of whether the approach being suggested would be acceptable or not.

The early sections of the Memorandum outlined the rising level of self-sufficiency for all agricultural products, the growing problem of surpluses in certain commodities—particularly soft wheat, milk, and sugar—and the possibility of new surpluses arising in fruit and vegetables. They drew attention to the increasing cost of market support at Community level[1] and the rising expenditure on structural aids in the individual Member States. The Commission believed that the key to the success of 'Agriculture 1980', as it called the development proposals in the Mansholt Plan, lay in the successful reduction of the farm labour force by half over a ten-year period, i.e. by more than 5m. persons, about 4m. of whom would be persuaded to retire, either immediately or after a few years. The remaining 1m. would need to be found alternative employment in other sectors. The Commission estimated that, of the 4m. retirements, about two-thirds would be of farmers (as opposed to family members and hired workers), thus releasing about 20m. hectares to be used either for reorganized farming or for non-farming purposes. To put the labour reduction into perspective: a decline of 5m. persons between 1970 and 1980 was the same in absolute numbers as the decline which was expected to take place between 1960 and 1970 but, whereas the latter represented a fall of one-third on the 1960 base, the former was a fall of one-half on the 1970 base. In percentage terms, the reform would have meant a decline from 13 per cent of the workforce in 1970 to 6 per cent in 1980.

If the reform measures were not adopted, the expected decline in the farming population was of the order of 2.5m. persons or about one-quarter, i.e. to 9 per cent in 1980. Not only would the absolute decline be much smaller but its composition would be different, because the Commission's recommendations were aimed at raising the retirement rate of the elderly, thereby reducing the average age of farmers and, at the same time, dissuading a larger than normal number of young persons from entering farming in the first place.[2] In the event, in the absence of the implementation of 'Agriculture 1980', the Commission's expectations were almost exactly fulfilled. The decline in numbers by 1980 in EC-6 was 2.8m. or about 30 per cent, and the workforce in agriculture fell to 8.8 per cent of the total. It was not until 1990 that the absolute decline in the workforce in agriculture in EC-6 amounted to 5m. on the 1970 base.

The second long-term reform was the reduction of the amount of land devoted to agriculture. The reason why the Commission recommended its reduction was to prevent a worsening of the surplus situation. According to the Commission, surplus production in developed countries was the result of two factors: strong pressure to raise farm income through higher output, necessitated by the retention of excess labour in farming; and the expansion of the area devoted to certain crops accompanied by higher yields. Although the reduction in the labour force called for by the Mansholt Plan would reduce pressure on output as a generator of income, the creation of the production units (PUs) and modern farm enterprises (MFEs)—referred to in Chapter 4—would, in itself, make the application of better technology easier, with the likely outcome of an acceleration in the growth of production. This had to be prevented, as surpluses were already a heavy financial burden on the Community, requiring expenditure on their storage and disposal which could be better used for other purposes, and they were upsetting the harmonious development of world trade.

The Commission suggested a three-stage approach to the eventual reduction in agricultural land. Firstly, the prevention of any increase in farmland through such public works as coastal protection: land so reclaimed should be used for other purposes. Secondly, the cancelling of aid—other than in exceptional circumstances—which encouraged the use in farming of uncultivated forest or other land not currently farmed. Thirdly, the deliberate withdrawal of unprofitable land from agriculture over a ten-year period. Through these means it would be possible to reduce farmland by 5m. hectares by 1980. The Commission envisaged that at least 4m. hectares of this liberated land would be afforested, in order to combat the Community's growing deficit in forest products.[3] The Commission recommended the provision of aid to encourage afforestation to assist in this work. It also recommended aid for the creation of nature parks and recreational areas on some at least of the remaining 1m. liberated hectares.

The third long-term reform was the adaptation of marketing conditions to improve market balance.[4] The belief was that, if producers combined to sell their produce, supply would be more concentrated and therefore prices would be more stable, while quality could be more easily adapted to fit market requirements. The Commission also gave notice of its intention to submit a proposal to the Council which would regulate professional and interprofessional organizations set up at Community level to promote, on a common basis, the interests of individual commodities or groups of commodities. Such organizations would play a large part in the pursuit of market improvements.

In its suggestions on long-term reform measures, the Commission was concerned with the issue of regional differentiation of aid. The reasoning was that, as agriculture had achieved different levels of development in different regions, so structural policy should take account of this diversity—unlike market and price policy. The Member States were reluctant to agree to regional differentiation—presumably because their governments did not wish to be criticized at home on the grounds of favouring one region above another. But far more important than any hesitation on regional differentiation was the reluctance of Member States to accept a common structural policy at all. In order to meet this resistance, the Commission had stated in the Mansholt Plan that, while the policy concept would be a Community one, its actual operation would depend on the Member States. This meant that the objectives to be achieved and the methods to be used would be set by the Community but that the Member States would carry out the programmes through their normal legislative process. In technical terms, the Commission was suggesting that Programme 'Agriculture 1980' would find legal expression at Community level in Directives and not in Regulations.

The financing of the reform programme was to be undertaken jointly by the Member States and by the Community. The Commission recommended that the Community contribution should be at least 50 per cent of the cost of projects of a social nature, those relating to the reduction of the area devoted to farming, and those relating to the improvement of the structure of production. For improvements to market structure, the Commission recommended limiting the

Community contribution to 30 per cent. The successful launching of Programme 'Agriculture 1980' would have meant a steep rise in the cost of agricultural support, both nationally and at Community level up to 1975, with a decline thereafter. It would also have meant a significant shift in the weight of support away from the market and price regimes to structural expenditure.

Modifications to 'Agriculture 1980'

The Commission moved slowly in the preparation of concrete legislative proposals, based on the Mansholt Plan, allowing time for debate to develop as widely as possible. Debate there most certainly was, much of it hostile, but the one place where debate did not occur was in the Council of Ministers. In contrast, the farmers took the Plan seriously and discussed it extensively. In a very interesting contemporary article, Pignot (1969) summarized the reactions to the Plan of the farmers' organizations at national and Community level. It is clear that their views were well modulated and thoughtful, not shortsighted or reactionary. Of course, there were many facets of it with which they took issue: for instance, they were concerned with its internal balance, in particular criticizing its weakness on the marketing front. They worried about the implications for income of the proposed moderation in price levels. They were cautious about the suggested PUs and MFEs (although significantly the young farmers' groups were very positive in their response to the structural reforms).

The same willingness to discuss the issues seriously is evident in the Opinion of the ESC (in which farmers are well represented). In large part the Committee was in agreement with the Commission's ideas, although critical on a number of points (JO C19, 13–2–70). For instance, it questioned the ten-year time-scale of the Plan, believing that the reforms should be introduced more gradually. It was most anxious to ensure that the encouragement given to a reduction in the farm workforce should be matched by a Community regional policy, and questioned whether the expected growth in real GNP would be sufficient to generate the required extra employment in agricultural and semi-agricultural regions.

The greatest doubts expressed by the ESC were centred on the Commission's suggestions on the reform of production. It particularly stressed the need to have regional differentiation in the application of any production aids and disagreed with the ultimate limitation of all national aids to PUs and MFEs. The Committee agreed with the suggested limitation of agricultural land, regarding the alternative uses of the freed land as valuable. However, it doubted whether land retirement would have much impact on total output and the improvement of market equilibrium, because the land retired would be almost exclusively of marginal quality.

Late in 1969, the Commission complained about the attitude of the Council which, with one minor exception, had neither taken decisions nor given guidance on the policy (Commission 1969). The truth of the matter was that the Council did not want to discuss the Mansholt Plan. Apart from any considerations of the

Table 8.1. Estimates of expenditure from FEOGA (Guarantee and Guidance) under various assumptions, 1970-1975, m. ua

	1970	1971	1972	1973	1974	1975	Total
A. Cost of Guarantee Section, unreformed	2,615	2,775	2,935	3,095	3,255	3,415	18,090
B. Cost of expanded FEOGA[a]	2,950	3,095	3,250	3,410	3,580	3,750	20,035
C. Cost of Guarantee Section, reformed	2,510	2,475	2,465	2,265	2,315	2,365	14,395
D. Redistribution to Guidance (B–C)	440	620	785	1,145	1,265	1,385	5,640
E. Staggered introduction of 'Agriculture 1980'	150	550	850	1,300	1,350	1,500	5,700
F. Full implementation of 'Agriculture 1980'	900	1,000	1,200	1,500	1,450	1,400	7,450
G. Cost in COM(70)500[b]		107	420	615	732	897	2,771
H. Cost in COM(71)600[c]							923
I. Cost of 1972 Structural Directives[d]							830

[a] on the assumption that FEOGA was to grow in line with the rate of increase in GNP, estimated at 5% p.a.
[b] based on estimated cost of six draft proposals
[c] based on estimated cost of four draft proposals
[d] costs as set out in the Directives

Sources: Commission 1969, 1970; JO C75, 26–7–71; Directives 72/159, 160, and 161, (Sp. OJ 1972(II)).

Plan's political sensitivity, the Council had no intention of committing itself to new broad policy objectives in advance of seeing the Commission's concrete proposals. In practice, the Council dislikes discussing policy documents which are, of necessity, somewhat vague and concerned with principles rather than with details. Concrete proposals, on the other hand, define the parameters of the subject much more narrowly, which gives the opportunity for detailed and often petty argument in Council working parties, in the Special Committee on Agriculture (SCA), the Committee of Permanent Representatives (COREPER), and around the Council table itself. If a proposal is disliked it can be modified extensively, or even killed, with no opprobrium attaching to the Council.

The Commission followed up the Mansholt Plan in COM(69)1200, in which it reiterated its arguments on the need to stem the rising tide of surpluses and expenditure. This document provides a far more detailed analysis than did the Mansholt Plan of the estimated cost of the situation facing the Community— with and without reform. It also set out for 1970–5 the manner in which it was proposed that the funds available to FEOGA could be shifted from price guarantees to structural reform under various assumptions (Commission 1969). Table 8.1 illustrates the possibilities available, from the cost of an unreformed Guarantee Section (Line A) to the full implementation of 'Agriculture 1980' (Line F). The basis of the Commission's reform proposal was an expansion of total expenditure on FEOGA (Guarantee and Guidance) annually at a rate equivalent to the expected rate of increase in GNP (about 5 per cent p.a.). The Guidance Section would have received the difference between this permitted ceiling and the actual expenditure on the reformed Guarantee Section (Line D).

The Commission estimated that the structural reform measures suggested in the Mansholt Plan would require—over the period 1970–5—a cumulative total of 7,450m. ua for the Guidance Section (Line F). This compared with an estimated availability of 5,640m. ua, on the assumption that the realignment of the Guidance and Guarantee Sections was pursued. As Table 8.1 illustrates, the difference between the two estimates was particularly acute in the earlier years and, in order to overcome this shortfall, the Commission proposed that the reform measures be introduced in a staggered fashion. With this in mind it suggested that those measures which would have the most rapid impact on reducing expenditure on market and price support should be introduced first (Line E). A considerable psychological spin-off from this suggestion (not shown in the table) was that it reduced the Member States' matching contributions to the reform measures from an estimated 8,050m. ua over the six years 1970–5 to 6,100m. ua.

In COM(69)1200, the Commission promised to submit concrete proposals, based on the Mansholt Plan, to the Council as soon as possible. This it did at the end of April 1970 in COM(70)500 (Commission 1970). There were six proposals in all: five were draft Directives and the sixth was a revised proposal for a Regulation on producer groups.[5] The five proposed Directives were on modernization of farms; retirement from farming and the release of land for structural improvement; the provision of socio-economic information and the professional training of those working in farming; the limitation of agricultural area; and the provision of certain aids complementary to the modernization proposal.

In outline, the 1970 proposals envisaged the provision of the following Community assistance:

Modernization
1. an interest rebate to help farmers with a development plan to achieve its goal;
2. aid to help the keeping of farm accounts in the first three years of a development plan;
3. launching aid for producers with a development plan who come together to form a producer group;
4. aid to help farmers utilize agricultural equipment more rationally.

Retirement
5. annual supplementary income aid to retiring farmers, family members, and hired workers aged at least 55;
6. a structural premium equal to at least eight times the rental value of the freed land, to farmers aged at least 55;
7. aid to encourage the creation of long leases for land freed by farmers benefiting from (5) or (6) above;

8. annual aid to farmers not benefiting from (5) or (6) above who rent their land on a long lease to farmers developing their farms under the modernization scheme.

Socio-economic information
9. aid to help train counsellors and to place them in post;
10. aid to create, develop, and operate educational and retraining establishments, and to provide attendance grants for farmers at such establishments.

Reduction of agricultural land
11. forestry premium equal to 80–90 per cent of the cost of afforestation on freed agricultural land;
12. aid to retiring farmers benefiting under (5) or (6) above to plant their freed land with trees;
13. for at least nine years, the granting of an annual income aid to owners of land whose tenants benefited under (5) or (6) above;
14. for owners releasing land for recreational and similar uses, aid of equivalent effect to that at (12) and (13) above.

Supplementary measures
15. a guidance premium over three years to encourage beef and sheepmeat production on modernizing farms;
16. up to the end of 1973, the provision on modernizing farms of a cow slaughter premium to encourage the abandonment of milk production.

Producer groups
17. a launching aid in the first three years after official recognition of a group;
18. investment aid in the first five years after official recognition to assist in improving production and marketing conditions;
19. a lump sum aid paid during the first five years after official recognition.

In the provision of all types of aid, except those relating to producer groups, FEOGA was to reimburse 50 per cent of Member States' eligible expenditure. In the case of producer groups, the FEOGA contribution was to be 30 per cent.

Estimates of the financial implications of the six proposals over the five-year period 1971–5 were provided in COM(70)500, as illustrated in Table 8.1 (Line G). In total, the Community cost was put at 2,775m. ua,[6] and, even allowing for the fact that this estimate covered five years rather than six (as were covered in COM(69)1200), it shows a substantial reduction on the earlier estimate. Given that the two documents appeared within five months of each other, this revision in the estimated Community cost is astonishing. It indicates that the Commission was already in full retreat from the ambitious programme of reform outlined in the Mansholt Plan. This retreat was to continue once discussions in the Council of Ministers got underway.

Little happened in 1970, with no agreement in the Council on the reform proposals. As already mentioned in Chapter 4, early in 1971 the Commission tried to move things forward by requesting the Council to pass a Resolution indicating its commitment to the broad principles of structural reform

(Commission 1971(*a*)). The Council adopted a Resolution the terms of which represented a further retreat from the reform proposals (JO C52, 27–5–71).[7] Examples of the restrictive changes made to the 1970 proposals in the Resolution are:

(a) a less generous approach to retirement pensions, both in terms of age group and level of aid;

(b) a less generous interest rate subsidy to help modernization, both in terms of the percentage of the subsidy and the amount to be found by the recipient (which had to be higher);

(c) most important of all: a reduction in the level of Community participation. This had been proposed at a rate of 50 per cent (except in the case of producer groups); in the Resolution it was lowered to 25 per cent of Member States' eligible expenditure. The only exception was in the case of the retirement scheme in disadvantaged regions where no national retirement scheme was then in operation. In such cases, the Community commitment was to be 65 per cent.

A further change detrimental to the spirit of reform was the weakening of the commitment to reduce the area devoted to agriculture. This commitment had already been lost in the Commission's draft Resolution and the rewording in the Resolution as adopted weakened the resolve still further. Instead of actively trying to reduce the agricultural area, all that the Member States agreed to do was to take 'all preventative measures likely to hinder an extension of the area used for agricultural purposes' (Commission 1971(*a*), 6). This feeble expression of intent was consistent with the weakening of the commitment to assist farmers to transfer their land to other purposes which also emerges from the Resolution.

The Commission had taken the opportunity presented by the draft Resolution to add certain items to the 1970 proposals. One such addition was the revival of the idea put forward in the Mansholt Plan that there should be study grants for the children of farmers who wished to leave agriculture. This was altered in the Resolution as passed and down-graded to a recommendation (which is not legally binding) that Member States should set up such a scheme for the children of farmers of modest means. Another addition to the 1970 proposals inserted into the draft Resolution was the provision of aid for farmers aged 45–55 who could neither modernize their farms nor retrain for other employment, but who agreed to leave farming and to make their land available for other farmers. The Resolution as passed omitted any reference to this proposal.

Armed with the Council Resolution, the Commission went to work on the revision of its 1970 proposals and later in 1971 presented a revised version to the Council in COM(71)600 (JO C75, 26–7–71). The draft Directive on the limitation of the agricultural area was (not surprisingly) dropped, as was the draft Directive on supplementary aids. However, one of these aids—the guidance premium for beef and sheepmeat production—was included in the revised draft Directive on modernization. All the retained drafts, i.e. on modernization, retirement, socio-economic advice, and producer groups, were modified to a greater or lesser extent in line with the Resolution, and the Commission also made a number of additional alterations. For instance, the modernization proposal now specifically stated that aid was to be limited to farmers whose main occupation was farming.

Certain features of the revised drafts indicate that the Commission was moving further away from the original Mansholt Plan. Reference has already been made in Chapter 4 to the modifications made in relation to the modernization of farms in the calculation of income and the number of labour units on the farm. An even clearer indication of the continuing retreat from the Mansholt Plan is provided in the revised draft retirement Directive, the success of which was vital to the rejuvenation of the farming population, and to the availability of adequate supplies of land for modernization. In essence, the revision emasculated this proposal. The retirement indemnity was reduced in amount and limited to those aged 55–65, in accordance with the terms of the Resolution. The structural premium was excluded from Community financing and was made optional if a Member State so wished. Furthermore, the aid to encourage long leases was withdrawn, the reason given being that the Commission intended to present the Council at a later date with a draft recommendation for the Member State to take legislative action in favour of long leases. As recommendations are not a form of Community legislation, they carry no weight and, in effect, the Commission was acknowledging the existence of insurmountable opposition to this measure.

The effect of the revisions to the proposals on reform can be illustrated most tellingly from a consideration of the changes in the estimated cost of the package. It will be recalled that the 1970 proposals were expected to cost 2,775m. ua over a five-year period—itself a reduction on the 1969 estimate (see Table 8.1). The 1971 revision brought the five-year estimate down to 923m. ua (Line H). This very substantial drop was caused by a combination of the reduction to 25 per cent of the FEOGA contribution to Member States' expenditure, the omission of certain proposals, and the weakening of others. Of the drafts which remained, the one to suffer the worst cuts (not illustrated) was that on retirement, which fell from 1,040m. ua in the 1970 proposal to 288m. ua in 1971. The modernization draft estimate fell from 960m. ua to 400m. ua. These figures also emphasize the change in direction of the structural reform package, away from a reduction in the labour supply as the critical element, towards a concentration of effort, albeit on a smaller scale, on the modernization of existing farms within the structural and organizational framework of the time.

In November 1971 the European Parliament adopted a Resolution on the revised reform proposals (JO C124, 17–12–71), which was on the whole favourable, although it did emphasize the need to proceed as a matter of urgency to the enactment of other measures not covered in the structural proposals. It specifically listed the need to improve the marketing and processing of agricultural products, the encouragement of long-term leases, the lightening of the burden of work of women in farming, the adoption of special measures for mountain farmers, the promotion of reafforestation, and the creation of leisure areas within the framework of regional programmes.

The proposals were further revised both by the Commission and the Council. The draft Regulation on producer groups was put back for additional consideration, so that the structural package finally comprised the Directives on modernization (72/159), on retirement (72/160), and on the provision of socio-economic advice (72/161) (Sp. OJ 1972 (II)). As Table 8.1 indicates, the total estimated cost of the package had once again been cut, this time to 830m. ua over a five-year period (Line I): the Community had indeed come a long way from the heady days of 1969 and the six-year estimate of 7,450m. ua. The adoption of the three Directives required matching, enabling national legislation. The Member States were given one year in which to comply but the deadline was not met. It was many years before all three Directives were applied in some form in all Member States and indeed certain aspects of the Directives were never applied in a few Member States.

What Went Wrong?

The main event in the early 1970s, as far as structural policy was concerned, was undoubtedly the Mansholt Plan which took the Community by storm, promising peaceful revolution. From the perspective of a quarter of a century later it is difficult to appreciate the circumstances in which it was proposed and the passions which it aroused. There is a danger that the Mansholt Plan may be viewed purely as the first major exercise to reduce the cost of the CAP—particularly because in more recent times the European Community has been obsessed with the cost of the Budget in general, and the CAP in particular. Although control of expenditure on price and market support was an important aspect of the Plan—and the one which the Commission hoped would persuade the Council of Ministers to accept the package—it would be quite wrong to see cost reduction as its only purpose.

The economic circumstances of the 1968–72 period were entirely different from those of the 1990s. The earlier period represents the closing phase of an era of unprecedented economic growth and full employment. Agriculture was one of the few major sectors which was not participating in this prosperity and, indeed, the working and living conditions of many farming families were a scandal. The affluence of society at large meant that a major reorganization of agriculture could be financed without difficulty. The employment situation meant that excess farm labour—where it still existed—could be absorbed into other sectors. The growth of leisure meant that rural areas were in increasing demand as sources of recreation for an urbanized population with ready access to cheap private transport.

Concern with the plight of agriculture was not confined to the European Community. In the USA, for instance, President Johnson had already commenced his war on poverty, an important aspect of which was concern with the rural poor. These efforts were linked to a much wider questioning in the developed world of economic and social inequalities in the midst of plenty. There was an increasing awareness that certain regions were experiencing much faster growth than others and that backward regions could not make up lost ground without outside assistance. While some of these regions could point to the decline of certain extractive or manufacturing industries as the cause of their difficulties, a far greater number could point to their excessive dependence on agriculture as the source of their problems. Nowhere was this more true than in the European Community.

The various suggestions made by the Commission within the context of Programme 'Agriculture 1980' were not exclusively agricultural in nature but were a combination of ideas encompassing agricultural, social, and regional policy. The Mansholt Plan is a curious mixture of the old and the new. Many of the suggested remedies followed the traditional patterns already well established within West European policy; nor does it represent a break with previous Commission thinking. For instance, much of the discussion of the problems facing agriculture and many of the solutions proposed had already appeared in the Commission's proposals on the CAP in 1959 and 1960, in the Community Plans of 1963, and in the Community Programmes of 1967.[8] What made the Mansholt Plan unusual was the way in which the suggested remedies—old and new—were combined to make a coherent whole. Individually the proposals were not particularly revolutionary, with the exception of the attempt to speed up farm modernization by the adoption of new production structures.

Where the Mansholt Plan was a radical break with previous West European agricultural policy was that it represented a deliberate and openly admitted attempt to reduce the workforce in farming and to remove land from agricultural production. Pursuit of these aims necessitated close links with regional and social policies and such links were provided in the Plan. This recognition of the interdependence of agriculture and other sectors was a considerable improvement on much of the pre-existing agricultural policy.

What went wrong with this grand design? Why was it that the Mansholt Plan, which had roared on to the Community stage like a mighty lion should, by the time of the 1972 structural Directives, have become a rather tame and timid mouse? There is no single or simple explanation but much of the blame must rest with the Council of Ministers and the Member States' governments. It is true that many farmers were opposed to the Mansholt Plan as originally outlined and would have required considerable persuasion to participate wholeheartedly in its implementation but this could probably have been achieved.

As was indicated in Chapter 1, the Member States 'discovered' the benefits of structural policy in the late 1950s and early 1960s as an adjunct to market support and, by the end of the 1960s, they were promoting it vigorously at home. They preferred their own schemes to ones emanating from the Community. For one thing, they were loath to surrender another aspect of policy to the Community so soon after agreeing to the introduction of the common price and market policy. Under that policy, once a commodity regime was agreed, the manner of its administration was laid down in Regulations and the Member States were required to cease all national support and apply only the measures allowed under the regime. This clearly limited their freedom of manoeuvre. The continuation of their national structural schemes gave the Member States an indirect means to circumvent the common market and price policy, and to maintain or gain illicit advantages. The Commission, although having the power to monitor and control national aids which conflict with the price and market policy, and with competition policy, has always moved too slowly to combat the actions of the Member States intent on pursuing their own private ends.

When the Commission put forward its concrete legislative proposals on structure in 1970, it went to great lengths to make them palatable to the Member States, by presenting them in the form of draft Directives rather than draft Regulations (all except the revised proposal on producer groups). This meant that the Member States had considerable scope for legislative flexibility at the national level. Apart from any opportunities which this afforded individual Member States to take local conditions into account, it should also have removed any lingering fears about the role of the Community in the structural field.

Whatever the fears of the Member States, the fact is that they did not respond to the Commission's gesture concerning the use of Directives. The proposals were whittled down bit by bit and, once enacted, the Member States failed to make imaginative use of what remained. For instance, the scope given in the Directives for regional differentiation in the application of specific measures was very largely ignored. The unimaginative approach was probably inevitable, because the Member States were now implementing their own national schemes within a loose Community framework and any criticisms by farmers of the schemes or of the way in which they were being implemented would have been laid at the door of the individual Ministries of Agriculture and not passed on to Brussels. Such a situation did not lend itself to originality or bold initiatives.

The resistance of the Member States to a balanced CAP was very great. The disappearance of the social policy was referred to in Chapter 2, as was the hesitant start to structural policy. Mansholt himself attacked the Member States for having kept structural policy in the national sphere of influence 'thus depriving the common agricultural policy of an element which was essential to its success'. The Council had never discussed the structural chapter of the original 1960 proposals; the price policy had always been based on political consensus rather than on economic principles and it could never be reformed unless the structure of farming was reformed. If nothing was done, expenditure on agriculture 'would soon be sufficient to finance a programme for landing on Mars' (*Agence Europe*, 8–12–1969, 8–9).

The most powerful resistance of all came from Germany, as can be illustrated by comments quoted in two European parliamentary questions asked around this time. Both were put forward by Vredeling—the most tireless questioner the Parliament has ever seen. The first related to a comment by Ertl (created Minister for Agriculture in Federal Germany in 1969) made before the Bundestag in 1968 to the effect that the Commission should never be given competence in matters of structural policy (JO C34, 24–3–70). The second related to a comment reported to have been made by the Federal German Chancellor during the discussions at the Hague Summit in 1969 to the effect that the financing of structural policy should remain a national matter (JO C122, 7–10–70).

As to 'Agriculture 1980' specifically, the German Ministry of Agriculture produced a lengthy rebuttal to it. Their preferred solution to the problems facing the CAP was the limitation of 'the price guarantee to maximum quantities (for instance by means of a production quota system').[9] They opposed the creation of large farm units and the reduction of the agricultural labour force. As if that were not enough, they maintained the Member States could not afford it (*Agence Europe*, 7–7–1969, 6–7). (At that stage, the Commission had not yet published its detail costing of the Plan!)

In retrospect, the most astonishing thing about the whole episode of the Mansholt Plan is that the Commission ever thought that it would succeed in persuading the Member States to agree to the Plan. They had clearly shown their reluctance to accept the earlier, milder approaches to a Community structural policy, yet the Commission hoped that they would accept a much more radical package than anything yet seen. Possibly it believed that shock tactics were the only chance of success. Whether the Commission was intellectually arrogant or politically naïve is hard to judge but it certainly miscalculated the mood of the Member States.

It is true that the cost of the CAP was already the object of much criticism and that surpluses were unpopular, and a source of embarrassment. But the Council of Ministers was being asked to take decisions of momentous importance which required it to accept that earlier policies had been a failure, to pin its faith on a plan which meant a switch of resources away from price support into structural reform on a massive scale, and to accept that this would result over a ten-year period in a fundamental restructuring of the farming sector. To have done these things would have required courage, daring, and vision—not the qualities one normally associates with Ministers for Agriculture.

An almost contemporary critique of the shortcomings of structural policy generally and of the Mansholt Plan specifically came from the ESC. It stated that the Member States were unwilling to yield political responsibility for structural change to the Community while, at the same time, they were prepared to bow to pressure from certain agricultural interests who favoured price policy over structural policy. The Member States were reluctant to allocate resources to structural policy, as it would have required a long-term and costly commitment. Some Member States which had already carried out extensive structural reform were unwilling to help finance similar efforts in other Member States which had not previously made such investments. The ESC also believed that a major problem lay in the difficulty which had been encountered in the establishment of common policies in other related fields (it probably had regional policy particularly in mind), and that it was precisely in the area of structural policy that agricultural policy came closest to them (ESC, rapp. Bourel, 1974). More than twenty years later it is depressing to note how much of this analysis remains valid.

Perhaps the Mansholt Plan would have failed. It would certainly have been less successful than its promoters predicted. This is both because response to policy instruments is usually smaller than anticipated and, more importantly, because the reform package would have been caught up in the adverse economic circumstances of the 1970s. However, if the reform package had been started in 1970 (as was originally intended), it would have made some impact on the performance of agriculture by the time the economic difficulties really began to bite in the mid-1970s. Agriculture might well have been in better shape to meet the crisis when it came: no one will ever know. The fate of the Mansholt Plan is a good illustration of the absence of political will among the Member States to take bold decisions to reform the CAP. They prefer to seek innocuous solutions which will perpetuate the existing mould and protect national interests. The Commission has responded to this mood and has never proposed a bold initiative in the structural field since.

The remaining Sections of this chapter examine three aspects of the legacy of the Mansholt Plan: the 1972 structural Directives and their replacements, which are its best-known outcome; the attempt to promote forestry; and the withdrawal of land from production. Regional differentiation of structural aid, and assistance to processing and marketing are discussed in Chapters 9 and 10 respectively.

The 1972 Structural Directives

The intention was that the three Directives on modernization, retirement, and advice and training should be interrelated. Farmers needed advice on the long-term viability of their farms, and training to help them achieve higher incomes through better management of their farms and improved levels of skills. Viable or potentially viable farms needed investment which, in some cases, included an expansion of the area of agricultural land. One source of such land was to be found in the farms of elderly farmers who, given suitable financial inducements, might be willing to retire. This was the theory but it was not how things worked out in practice.

The modernization Directive (72/159) was limited to 'main occupation farms', i.e. those on which 'the proportion of income from farming be not less than 50% of the farmer's total income and that the working time devoted to non-farming activities be less than half of the farmer's total working time', Art. 3.1 (Sp. OJ 1972 (II)). In order to qualify for aid, the farmers had to have adequate farming skills, implement an approved development plan over not more than six years, and agree to keep financial accounts. At the completion of the plan, the farm was to be 'capable of attaining as a minimum, in principle for either one or two man-work units, a level of earned income comparable to that received for non-agricultural work in the region in question' (Art. 4.1, ibid.). The comparable income was defined as the average gross wage for a non-agricultural worker.

Five types of aid were available:

(a) an interest rate subsidy for investment (excluding expenditure on the purchase of land, or pigs, poultry, or calves intended for slaughter), Article 8;

(b) where the plan provided for specialization in the production of beef, veal, mutton or lamb, a guidance premium[10] to assist in the adaptation of production, Article 10;

(c) a financial incentive for the keeping of farm accounts, Article 11;

(d) assistance to groups of farmers coming together to utilize their resources in a more rational way, the aid being a contribution to the management costs of the group during its initial phase, Article 12; and

(e) aid for reparcelling land and for irrigation, where the modernization process required it, Article 13.

According to the Commission's own data, only a small minority of farms had the potential to yield the comparable income,[11] and so, under Article 14, the Member States were given the freedom to assist farmers who could not achieve the required level and who were not eligible for the retirement aid. Originally the intention was that such aid would be temporary but in fact it became a permanent feature of the scheme. The result was that farmers received very mixed signals on the desirability of modernization.[12]

This aid to farmers who could not achieve the comparable income level also ran counter to the spirit of the Directive which, in Art. 1.1, referred to 'selective incentives'. This selectivity was intended to apply regionally as well: the Member States were free to vary the financial aids under Articles 8, 10, 11, 12, and 13, or to withhold any of these aids from certain regions, presumably so as to concentrate effort on the regions with the greatest need.[13]

Farmers undertaking a development plan under Article 8 had priority access to land released by farmers retiring under the terms of Directive 72/160. This Directive was very restrictive. In theory, it applied to farmers whose main occupation was farming and who were aged 55–65. However, in the first five years, Community aid was limited to those aged 60–65 (except in certain very restricted circumstances). At least 85 per cent of the utilized agricultural area which the farmer was giving up had to be leased or conveyed to a farmer benefiting from the interest rate subsidy (Art. 8, Dir. 72/159), or the land had to be withdrawn permanently from farming and put into some other approved use (such as forestry or recreation). If no modernizing farmer could be found, then the land could be allocated to other farmers under rules laid down by the Member States. The form of retirement aid was an annuity or a lump-sum payment.[14]

The third Directive (72/161) had two functions: the first was the creation and development of services to provide socio-economic advice to farmers and their families on whether to continue farming or to move out of agriculture, either into alternative employment, or to retire. The type of Community aid available was for the training of counsellors. The second function was to provide those who were to remain in farming, and who were 18 years or over, with new or improved skills. The Member States were to set up training schemes for this purpose but they had to be outside of the normal agricultural courses available as part of the second and third level of education. These were key functions, and the Directive was fundamental to the development of the farming sector as it was designed to improve the standard of the human capital in farming. Yet, as things turned out, it was one of the least successful elements in the 1972 structural package.[15]

Because these structural programmes were established in the form of Directives, the Member States had to enact (or adapt) their own legislation to bring them into force. This proved to be the first serious obstacle to the success of the whole project. Some Member States were extremely slow to enact the relevant national legislation. For instance, France only began to apply the modernization Directive in 1976, and Italy in 1977 (and then only partially). The training of counsellors to provide socio-economic advice took longest to establish: in 1978 only Germany, Denmark, and the UK had counsellors in post and, in the same year, Italy, Luxembourg, and the Netherlands still had not applied for funding for courses of training for farmers.

Throughout the lifetime of these three Directives, the Commission put forward a series of proposed amendments, based on its experience of their operation, and on the need to adjust the value of the aids available in line with inflation. As with the attempts to adjust the price policy referred to in Chapter 6, the Council never displayed any sense of urgency in improving the performance of these measures. It was normal for proposals to be delayed for years and, if eventually passed by the Council, to be seriously modified, so that the original intention was virtually lost. Probably the best example of the seriousness of the delays can be found in the measures to reform the Directives which were enacted in 1981[16] but which had started as Commission proposals in 1976 and 1977, and were subsequently superseded by further proposals in 1979![17]

The original estimates of the cost of the reform proposals in COM(70)500 were based on a take-up of the interest rate subsidy for investment by 256,000 farmers over a five-year period; the retirement over the same period of 780,000 farmers aged over 65, and of 400,000 farmers aged 55–65; the provision of 3,000 counsellors by the end of four years, and the provision of training for 120,000 farmers over a five-year period (Commission 1970). The three Directives were expected to be in use for ten years but their operation was to be reviewed after five years. This review was contained in COM(79)438 (Commission 1979(*d*)).[18] Given that these measures were intended to relieve the price and market policy of much of its role as an income support, allowing it to fulfil its role in balancing the market and maintaining the viability of the efficient farm, the results show that they were totally inadequate for the task. Table 8.2 summarizes the impact of the Directives in the period 1972–7, distinguishing between the original Member States and the three countries which joined in 1973, and which were not taken into account in the original estimates. Italy and Luxembourg are omitted as they did not enact the necessary legislation until 1978 and 1979 respectively.

The extremely low figure for retirement needs some explanation. In fact nearly 37,000 farmers in seven Member States retired in the three years 1975–7, and received an annuity or a lump-sum payment. However, in order to qualify under Dir. 72/160, the retirement aid had to satisfy simultaneously the three requirements of age, complete cessation of farming activity, and the transfer of land to a developing farm (or other sanctioned purpose). Of the 80,000 farms enlarged

Table 8.2. Uptake of the three structural Directives, 1972–1977

Member State	Dir. 72/159[a] Development plans	Dir. 72/160[b] Number of retirements	Dir. 72/161	
			Counsellors appointed[c]	Farmers trained[d]
Germany	27,083	939	484	4,376
France	3,338	98	32	33,543
Netherlands	11,153	82	219	—
Belgium	4,211	12	—	13,469
Original Member States[e]	45,785	1,131	735	51,388
UK	9,721	34	13	334
Ireland	11,360	64	—	2,322
Denmark	10,795	—	4	769
All Member States	77,661	1,229	752	54,813

a cumulative 5 years
b cumulative 3 years
c cumulative 2 years
d cumulative 3 years, except France (5 years). These figures on farmers trained may include double counting, as a farmer could have attended more than one course.
e no data were available for Italy and Luxembourg

Source: Commission 1979(*d*).

by land released by retiring farmers, fewer than 12,000 had a development plan under Dir. 72/159.

The three Directives were due to expire at the end of 1983 and, in October, the Commission put forward proposals for their replacement (Commission 1983(*f*)). The eventual outcome was Reg. 797/85 which is discussed below. While no new aid is now available under the 1972 Directives, they will remain in the Community accounts for some years to come. The most recent detailed information on these schemes was published in the last annual FEOGA-Guidance report before the reform of the structural funds (discussed in Chapter 11). Table 8.3 gives the cumulative number of beneficiaries over the lifetime of the Directives, the payments made to each Member State from FEOGA-Guidance up to the end of 1988, and the percentage share of those payments received by each Member State. A few general comments are called for.

While eventually every Member State applied Dir. 72/159, the same is not true of the other two Directives. Denmark, Greece, and Luxembourg did not apply the retirement Directive; Greece, Ireland, and Luxembourg did not appoint socio-economic advisers; and Greece and Luxembourg did not operate farmer-training schemes under Dir. 72/161. All three Directives were dominated by a small group of countries: the UK and Germany received over half of the funds for modernization; Germany received 70 per cent of the retirement funds, and France received 77 per cent of the funds under Dir. 72/161.

There is no correlation between the countries with the greatest structural

Table 8.3. Uptake of the three Structural Directives, 1972–1988

Member State	Directive 72/159: farm modernization						
	(1) Art. 8	(2) Art. 10	(3) Art. 11	(4) Art. 12	(5) Art. 13	Reimbursement by FEOGA-Guidance	
						m.ECU	%
Belgium	16,383	158	22,042	1,066	—	35.1	3.3
Denmark	16,230	31	11,351	62	—	67.1	6.3
Germany	44,145	228	27,214	116	523	267.5	24.9
Greece	1,009	—	8,759	1	—	4.4	0.4
France	48,800	8,490	88,625	19,129	30	186.8	17.4
Ireland	34,030	1,461	24,683	29	—	61.5	5.7
Italy	8,446	850	104,767	353	—	36.2	3.4
Luxembourg	254	9	—	3	—	2.8	0.3
Netherlands	21,942	103	—	961	66	102.0	9.5
UK	37,775	16,847	32,224	3	—	308.9	28.8
Total	229,014	28,117	319,665	21,723	619	1,072.4	100.0

(1) number of development plans approved
(2) number of farmers qualifying for the premium for changing over to beef and veal, or sheepmeat production
(3) number of farmers qualifying for aid as an incentive to keeping accounts
(4) number of groups qualifying for launching aid for mutual assistance between farms
(5) number of land reparcelling and irrigation projects

Member State	Directive 72/160: retirement	
	No. of beneficiaries	Reimbursement by FEOGA-Guidance
		m.ECU %
Belgium	188	0.2 2.3
Germany	3,998	6.3 70.4
France	2,517	1.8 19.9
Ireland	113	0.3 3.3
Netherlands	253	0.2 2.1
UK	244	0.2 2.0
Total	7,313	9.0 100.0

problems and the number of recipients of aid. For instance, Italy with a much poorer farming structure than Denmark, Ireland, and the Netherlands received a smaller proportion of the modernization funds than each of these three small countries. Much of the explanation must lie in the relative efficiency of the public administration in the various Member States, rather than in the needs of their farmers.

Table 8.3 (*cont.*)

Member States	Directive 72/161: advice and training			
	(6) Counsellors	(7) Trainees	Reimbursement by FEOGA-Guidance	
			m.ECU	%
Belgium	189	13,769	1.5	2.8
Denmark	12	4,194	0.9	1.7
Germany	847	23,816	4.5	8.3
France	63	517,014	41.8	77.1
Ireland	—	11,944	1.6	3.0
Italy	101	25,501	2.5	4.5
Netherlands	26	1,348	0.6	1.2
UK	331	1,246	0.8	1.4
Total	1,569	598,832	54.2	100.0

(6) number of socio-economic counsellors planned and appointed
(7) number of farmer-trainees who have followed a complete course to
obtain a new professional qualification

Source: Commission 1989(*h*).

One thing which Table 8.3 cannot illustrate is the distribution of the funds within Member States by region, and by size and type of farm. These three Directives were not targeted but applied right across the Community. In theory, therefore, there was no clear indication of the likely pattern of response, although it could be assumed that the farmers with the greatest income potential would try to modernize and those who had the lowest potential would opt for retirement. Such an outcome would indeed have been rational but it also presupposes a clear acceptance that structural policy in agriculture serves economic and not social ends.

This issue was first raised in a somewhat unlikely quarter: an interdepartmental group within the Commission which was set up to investigate the co-ordination of the Community's financial instruments, and which reported in 1976. In the case of FEOGA-Guidance, the group was given two tasks: to examine its activities in the light of its performance in relation (a) to the objectives of agricultural policy and (b) to its coherence with the objectives of regional policy, both mainstream and arising out of Article 39 of the Rome Treaty. The group limited itself to an examination of those aspects of the Guidance Section which related directly to agricultural structure in a narrow sense, i.e. to those measures which promoted structural change or which provided income maintenance, where such change was neither feasible nor desirable.

The bulk of this lengthy report is concerned with the regional aspects of structural policy. The realization that certain regions require a disproportionate amount of aid to alter their structure was not new—its origins can be traced back through the 1968 Mansholt Plan to the Community Programmes of 1967. The group paid particular attention to the modernization Directive, into which certain regional options had been built, but which did not necessarily relate directly to the severity of local problems. The group's unease was based on the fact that this Directive was fairly demanding in terms of the input by the farmer applying for aid (the development plan, the income level currently received and to be attained at the end of the plan, the account-keeping). Some of the group felt that the personal qualities needed were more likely to be found among middle-ranking farmers, whatever their location, and that a disproportionate number would be located in the relatively prosperous farming regions.

The only Member State which, at that time, could provide any concrete evidence on which to test the group's fears was Germany. Two facts emerged from an examination of the German data: the first was that 'the main beneficiaries, in terms of Länder securing a share of the grants much in excess of the shares of agricultural production, labour force or surface area, were Schleswig-Holstein and Niedersachsen, both of which contain relatively large expanses of extensive, well-structured agriculture by West German standards' (Commission 1976(*d*), 20).

The group thought that special circumstances might have produced this outcome and so it examined the returns at a lower level of aggregation (the Regierungsbezirke), from which it excluded the aid granted for field reorganization which was held to have distorted the other data. This exercise yielded the second fact which was that, when Land Bayern was examined in detail, its two most favourably placed Regierungsbezirke (Oberbayern and Schwaben) received nearly two-thirds of the funds allocated and that this was disproportionately large in relation to production, labour, and agricultural area.

Considerable thought was given by the group to the validity of the use of the comparable income concept (as for example in Directive 72/159). While recognizing that such a criterion for eligibility helped to avoid the subsidization of investment which might not be viable in the long term, there was the risk that it also resulted in concentrating investment in reasonably well-developed regions, because it was in precisely such regions that a high proportion of farmers would be near to the comparable income threshold and therefore qualify for aid. Equally, the group was not convinced that the comparable income concept was relevant in judging the economic efficiency of investment and similar grants. For instance, it was possible that the return on an investment might be much greater if raising a farmer's income from a point 'far below' to 'just below' the comparable income level than from 'just below' to 'just above'. Yet the farmer in the former circumstance would be ineligible for Community aid.

The group pointed out that the original intention was that Directive 72/159 would become the dominant means of providing investment aid on farms but that this had not occurred in practice. The reason was that the Member States were continuing to provide national aids on a large scale and, for these, the comparable income concept was not applied. Such differences in approach to individual farmers were clearly unsatisfactory.

A further drawback to the use of the comparable income concept was that the income comparison was based on the non-agricultural wage rates in the same region. This was an unsatisfactory basis in poor regions with intractable unemployment problems. There, it was possible that the basic wage rates were too high in terms of economic efficiency and that this in itself was causing the chronic unemployment. In such circumstances the group questioned the advisability of basing investment on comparability and wondered if it would not make more sense to aid investment at below the comparable income level. This would lessen the risk of creating even further unemployment which, if it occurred, might require other and perhaps more expensive forms of aid to correct.

Despite their doubts and fears, the group was conscious that there were problems involved in the abandonment of the comparable income concept. For example, there would be repercussions on the annual price negotiations as these could no longer be based on the proposition that increases were to do no more than maintain modern farms in that state (i.e. yielding a comparable income to those who worked on them). Thus, the Commission would have to take into account the requirements of the less viable farms when making its price proposals. Such a change would result in increased Guarantee expenditure from FEOGA.

Although the group had misgivings about measuring economic efficiency in terms of comparable income, it did recognize the need to ensure the effectiveness of the investment of limited public funds, and also acknowledged the existence of certain economies in making large investments rather than a series of smaller investments over time. It was also sensitive to the likely reaction of the farming community to the dropping of the comparability concept, as parity of income with other socio-economic groups had been a long-standing claim of the farmers. The group felt that the weight of these various arguments for retaining the comparable income concept was very great and concluded that on balance it should be retained.

Later evidence on the impact of the Directives is unsatisfactorily sketchy. For instance, as mentioned above, in 1979 the Commission published its third report on these Directives with data relating to 1976 and 1977. The regional trends were unclear but there was a pronounced concentration of development plans on the medium size farms (20–<50; and 50–<100 ha.), except where horticulture was important (Commission 1979(*d*)). It was estimated that by the end of 1978, just over 100,000 farms had development plans—which was less than 2 per cent of all farms. They were distributed very unevenly, with more than 10 per cent of farms in Denmark and the Netherlands having a plan, about 5–6 per cent in Belgium, Ireland, and the UK, less than 4 per cent in Germany, and less than 1 per cent in France. Statistics for Luxembourg and Italy were not available (OJ C53, 3–3–80).

There were also anomalies within Member States due to the link between development plans and the comparable income. The ESC made the point:

[F]armers located in economically developed zones are able to submit a development plan even though their income is often already higher than that of farmers who are located in under-developed areas and cannot submit development plans. Regional disparities are therefore perpetuated and can even be exacerbated. Whilst it is reasonable that the aim of the first stage of development should be to catch up with average non-agricultural incomes in the same area, subsequent efforts should be concentrated on finding ways and means in less-developed areas of achieving average Community incomes. (OJ C53, 3–3–80, 29)

By the late 1970s, there was a realization that the Directives were not functioning properly: 'the existing measures have not been such as to bring about improvement in the structural situation of a substantial number of farms, particularly those which are small and especially those in difficult areas' (Commission 1979(*a*), 48). The Commission announced its intention to propose changes so that the measures could be applied 'more selectively by concentrating them on farms which are in real need, while at the same time steering such farms towards economically sounder types of farming' (ibid. 49). A major package of structural measures was proposed in March 1979; most of these proposals were regional in nature and are outlined in Chapter 9, but the package also included modifications to the 1972 structural Directives.

The most important modifications were in the modernization Directive, where the intention was to exclude farms above a certain income level from receiving development aid; to lower the target income which had to be achieved by the end of the development plan; to make it easier to achieve the target income; and to concentrate aid on those products with the best demand prospects. In commenting on these proposals, the ESC made the point that there were drawbacks to the whole concept of a development plan to be implemented over a relatively short period of time—a concept which would be even less appropriate when applied to a wider range of farmers. As the Committee stated, this approach to development:

calls for a high level of technical competence, a capacity for controlling large investments, an ability to adjust to the problems posed by bigger farms and more equipment, and considerable strength of character—and all these at the same time. Farmers cannot really be expected to show all these qualities when so far they have had to tackle problems on a scale commensurate with their modest holdings. (OJ C53, 3–3–80, 26)

The Committee believed that a gradual approach would be more satisfactory and regretted that this had been rejected.

On the retirement Directive, the Commission proposed improving the level of pension and the contribution from FEOGA-Guidance; relaxing the conditions for farmers over 50 to receive a pre-pension; and facilitating the intergenerational transfer of farms. This last proposal was a significant development: one of the main deficiencies in the retirement scheme was the requirement to cede the farm to a farmer operating a development plan. This excluded the many farmers who had a successor already working on the home farm. The proposal sought to ease the requirements in certain less-favoured areas (LFAs), so that farmers of 60 and over, with a direct successor working on the farm, would receive an allowance for a maximum of ten years. A requirement was that the farmer 'formally and permanently transfers responsibility for the management of the farm to that successor' (Commission 1979(*b*), 7).

When the 1979 package was finally enacted in 1981, changes to the moderniza-tion Directive were included (but not the reforms to the retirement Directive and it was not until 1985 that discussion of this issue re-emerged). Apart from easing the requirement on comparable income and widening the range of income sources which qualified as 'agricultural income' (e.g. to include income from forestry), restrictions were placed on investment in pig production and milk (OJ L197, 20–7–81). The legislation also included aid to young farmers under the age of 40. This was not in the original proposals but had been recommended by the European Parliament in its Resolution on the 1979 package (OJ C85, 8–4–80). Aid to young farmers was a long-standing issue in the Community, which will be referred to again in Chapter 9.

Sequel to the Structural Directives

As mentioned in the previous Section, the 1972 structural Directives were scheduled to expire at the end of 1983 and, in October of that year, the Com-mission put forward proposals on their replacement (Commission 1983(*f*)). Surprisingly, it did not take the opportunity to provide an extensive analysis of the impact of the legislation being replaced. The ESC was clearly puzzled by this omission, commenting that if information had been available it 'would undoubtedly have made it easier to assess more adequately the need for changes' (OJ C103, 16–4–84, 30). The limited comments made by the Commission were quite depressing and perhaps it felt it would be counter-productive to reveal too much.

One of the few useful pieces of information which it did provide was confirma-tion of the increase in farm productivity in the good farming regions through intensification and specialization. Land mobility had been minimal—on de-velopment farms the increase in size had been, on average, less than 5 ha. 'In this sense the policy has contributed to an increase in the output of surplus farm products' (Commission 1983(*f*), 3). This, of course, was precisely the opposite of the original intention. In addition, the Commission acknowledged the failure of structural measures to solve regional income disparities but, as will be clear from Chapter 9, given the small size of the measures specifically aimed at problem regions, this failure was inevitable. The modernization Directive had been a disappointment because the increase in the level of interest rate subsidies had risen more slowly than the cost of borrowing and, because of the cost–price squeeze in the price and market policy, the number of farmers with the financial resources to modernize had been reduced. The result was that development plans averaged only about 20,000–30,000 per year, of which 20 per cent were in LFAs. The link between modernizing farms and retirement of elderly farmers had never worked properly and, as a result, only 15 per cent of the land released through retirement had gone to developing farms.

In the wider context, the socio-economic situation in the Community was very different in the early 1980s from what it had been ten years previously. The economy was stagnant, unemployment was high and rising, the economic disparities between regions had increased. The Commission proposed replacing the 1972 Directives and the LFA Directive (discussed in Chapter 9) with one multi-purpose Regulation, which would cater for most aspects of on-farm structural policy.[19] The scale of the proposal was very large indeed and, although the analogy was not drawn, what the Commission was attempting to do was reminiscent in scope—but not in content—of the approach last used in the Mansholt Plan. It would probably have been fatal to the success of the 1983 proposal if such an analogy had been drawn but echoes of the past there certainly were.

The package of proposals on improving the efficiency of agricultural structures included:

(a) the improvement of agricultural incomes and other conditions on the farm by the provision of aid to:
   (i) improve quality and convert production to commodities required by the market,
   (ii) reduce production costs, save energy, improve living and working conditions,
   (iii) protect and improve the environment;
(b) assistance to young farmers under 40;
(c) encouragement for the keeping of accounts;
(d) provision of launching aids to groups:
   (i) formed to use agricultural equipment more rationally, or to operate a holding jointly,
   (ii) providing farm relief services,
   (iii) providing farm management services;
(e) special assistance in less-favoured areas through
   (i) compensatory allowances based on the type of permanent handicap of the area, as set out in Article 3 of Dir. 75/268,
   (ii) investment aid for tourist or craft industry purposes, as part of the investment on the farm,
   (iii) investment aid for joint schemes for fodder production,
   (iv) aid for the removal of serious structural/infrastructural handicaps to improve farming in the region as a whole, undertaken in conjunction with work in non-agricultural sectors, and with the needs of environmental protection;
(f) the extension, in certain circumstances of the aid at (e) (iv) to non-LFA regions;
(g) afforestation of agricultural land and improvement of woodland;
(h) in regions where it was necessary, the provision of:
   (i) vocational instruction and training for farmers, family helpers, and agricultural workers past the age for compulsory education,
   (ii) courses for leaders/managers of producer groups and cooperatives, where this was necessary to improve production, processing, and marketing,

    (iii) courses for young farmers and their spouses to meet the occupational skills required under (b) above;

(i) financing pilot schemes to:
    (i) demonstrate to farmers the possibilities of production systems, methods, and techniques,
    (ii) disseminate the results of schemes to improve structure,
    (iii) assess the economic efficiency of the measures provided under the Regulation.

While most of these measures were ones which had existed in some form already, some were new, in particular the aid for forestry and the aids for environmental improvement. The range of measures is deceptive because the only one which was compulsory for Member States was that at (a) above: all the remainder were optional for the Member States. This was an interesting strategy: it reduced potential opposition from certain Member States which were not interested in particular measures, and left to the farmers of those countries the task of persuading the national administrations to adopt optional measures. It also avoided the delays which had taken place in the enforcement of the 1972 Directives because, by using the legal form of a Regulation, the legislation took effect almost immediately after its adoption by the Council of Ministers, and its publication in the *Official Journal.*

As in Dir. 72/159, various restrictions were proposed for investment aid in dairying and pigs; and aid for eggs and poultry was prohibited.[20] The requirements on the target income to be achieved on completion of a development plan were further relaxed, so that the plan had to do no more than materially improve the income in a lasting manner. The estimated cost of this package to FEOGA-Guidance was 4,432m. ECU for the first five years. By the time the proposal was adopted as Reg. 797/85 *on improving the efficiency of agricultural structures* (OJ L93, 30–3–85), the estimated cost had been drastically reduced to 1,988 m. ECU. Once again, just as with the Mansholt Plan and, as will be seen in Chapter 9, the LFA proposals, the reality was far less ambitious than the original intention. Once again, the Council of Ministers demonstrated its reluctance to tackle the underlying causes of low incomes among some farmers.

As was indicated in Chapter 6, in the mid-1980s the Community was, for the first time, beginning to make some serious efforts to curb the production of surpluses and to limit the growth of expenditure on FEOGA-Guarantee. However, the reliance on price and market support as the main instrument of policy was undiminished: it was much easier—and more acceptable to agricultural interests—to cut back proposed expenditure on structural improvements. The mould had still not been broken.

While many aspects of Reg. 797/85 are discussed elsewhere, the remainder of this Section concentrates on those aspects which were the direct descendants of Dirs. 72/159 and 161, namely farm improvement plans, account-keeping, and training.[21] Table 8.4 provides a cumulative total, up to the end of 1988, of the number of beneficiaries and of the aid granted to Member States by FEOGA-

Table 8.4. Reg. 797/85: On-farm investment and training cumulatively to the end of 1988

Member States	No. of beneficiaries			Reimbursement by FEOGA-Guidance	
	Art. 4[a]	Art. 7.1[b]	Art. 7.2[c]	'000 ECU	%
Belgium	1,604	119	221	3,651.5	2.4
Denmark	116	865	45	1,873.5	1.2
Germany	3,115	2,659	448	11,769.4	7.6
Greece	5,065	172	20	8,906.2	5.7
Spain	d	d	d	25,799.7	16.6
France	—	22,755	—	72,177.8	46.5
Ireland	3,317	69	121	3,599.3	2.3
Italy	313	7	—	581.1	0.4
Luxembourg	67	80	22	732.7	0.5
Portugal	2,487	1,054	918	17,910.3	11.5
UK	7,144	—	153	8,181.0	5.3
Total	23,228	27,780	1,948	155,182.5	100.0

a improvement plans approved
b young farmers receiving installation aid
c young farmers receiving additional aid when operating a development plan
d transitional scheme applied in Spain, not shown here

Member States	No. of beneficiaries			Reimbursement by FEOGA-Guidance	
	Art. 9[e]	Art. 10[f]	Art. 12[g]	'000 ECU	%
Belgium	1,735	1	—	87.7	4.4
Denmark	140	1	—	9.7	0.5
Germany	—	2	—	5.8	0.3
Greece	2,101	—	—	53.7	2.7
Spain	983	122	8	1,523.2	76.5
Italy	7	—	5	310.0	15.6
Luxembourg	—	1	—	0.6	...
Total	4,966	127	13	1,990.7	100.0

e aid to encourage the keeping of accounts
f launching aid for recognized mutual aid groups
g launching aid for associations providing farm management services

Guidance. The number of improvement plans is low, partly because many farmers were operating development plans entered into under the earlier legislation (see Table 8.3), and partly because young farmers with development plans are shown separately (under Art. 7.2). Aid to encourage the keeping of accounts is very low (under Art. 9), partly because not all Member States were applying this measure but, most probably, also because so many farmers would have received such an aid already. Training courses for farmers, family helpers, and

Table 8.4. (*cont.*)

Member States	No. of beneficiaries			Reimbursement by FEOGA-Guidance	
	Art. 21[h]	Art. 21[i]	Art. 21[j]	'000 ECU	%
Belgium	614	—	—	110.4	1.7
Denmark	3,658	3,784	—	2,989.3	46.2
Germany	94,747	—	—	1,152.4	17.8
Greece	4,296	598	—	376.1	5.8
Spain	11,089	—	6	967.4	14.9
Ireland	4,783	—	—	733.6	11.3
Italy	1,331	—	—	147.5	2.3
Total	120,518	4,382	6	6,476.7	100.0

[h] farmers, family helpers, and agricultural workers attending courses
[i] farmers attending courses to qualify for young farmer aid
[j] training centres which have received aid in LFAs
Note: no aids were paid for the provision of farm relief services, nor for training courses for leaders/managers of producer groups and cooperatives.

Source: Commission 1989(*h*).

agricultural workers continued to be popular[22] but the remaining categories of aid were of little importance.

As with the 1972 Directives, the distribution of aid between Member States was very skewed, with the majority of countries receiving only a small proportion of the total aid, and an absence of any clear relationship between the needs of the farming sector for structural improvements and the level of aid. Also, as previously, some Member States were much quicker to benefit from the schemes than others. The statistics relate to a few years only and it is impossible to know whether a different pattern emerged subsequently.

It must always be borne in mind that, unlike the price and market policy where the total cost of support is charged to FEOGA-Guarantee, under the structural policy FEOGA-Guidance reimburses the Member States for part of the cost only. The level of reimbursement can differ both in relation to the particular scheme in question and the Member State. The ability and willingness of the Member States to make the necessary parallel investment is an important determinant of the success or failure of any structural measure.

The proposals in COM(83)559 which formed the basis of Reg. 797/85 made no provision for the continuation of the pension scheme under Dir. 72/160 and it was not until the publication of the important discussion document *The Perspectives for the CAP* in 1985 that the question of retirement aid was raised again (Commission 1985(*b*)). The context was the provision of direct income aids, particularly in circumstances where alternative employment opportunities are limited or could only be created at considerable expense. The idea under discussion was a revival of the pre-pension scheme which had formed part of Dir. 72/160, i.e. the provision of a pension to farmers aged 55 and over who agreed to give up farming. Given the failure of the whole retirement Directive, the Commission stated that any new scheme would need to be more generous and should not be burdened with restrictive conditions. However, it still recommended the limitation of the pre-pension scheme to main occupation farmers. No reason was given as to why part-time farmers were excluded. If the intention was to reduce the area in farming and/or reduce production, there is no logic in excluding part-time farmers. Perhaps it was on the purely practical grounds of trying to limit the number of possible recipients to manageable levels in financial terms.

The thinking behind the pre-pension scheme was set out more fully in a follow-up document later the same year (Commission 1985(*d*)). The farm investment aspects of Reg. 797/85 were intended to refocus 'investment aids on targets such as conversion of production, improvement of quality, improvement of living and working conditions, protection of the environment, and, in general, an effort to enhance productivity by cutting costs rather than by increasing production (ibid. 16). The Commission believed that elderly farmers would find it difficult to adapt their farming practice to this new approach to production, nor would it be easy for them to find alternative employment.

The proposal was that, if a farmer took a pre-pension, he/she would receive not only an annuity but also a lump-sum payment per hectare when the farmer ceased farming and the land was either withdrawn from cultivation, used for a non-agricultural purpose (e.g. afforestation, sport, recreation), or transferred to a young farmer. In this last case, the incoming farmer would have to convert the farm to the production of non-surplus commodities, quality products, or farm in an environmentally friendly way. The draft legislation was submitted to the Council in 1986 (Commission 1986(*c*)). The assumption was that, over a five-year period, 125,000 farmers would take a pre-pension; of these, 55,000 would cease farming and the remaining 70,000 would transfer their land to their successor. The scheme was expected to appeal to smallholders in particular and the costings were based on an average farm of 8 ha. One must wonder at the wisdom of encouraging the continuation of such very small farms into a new generation.

The proposal was not accepted by the Council, and the Commission submitted a new proposal in 1987 which was accepted and became Reg. 1096/88 *establishing a Community scheme to encourage the cessation of farming* (OJ L110, 29–4–88). The link with young farmers had disappeared and, where the farm was used to enlarge an existing holding, the farmer had to undertake not to increase production of surplus products. With the gradual extension of surpluses to more and more commodities over time, this kind of restriction—logical though it is— must make it extremely difficult to find such a product. Indeed, in most cases the only way in which this requirement could be met would be if the farmer used the additional land to assist in a programme of extensification.

Brief reference was made in the MacSharry Plan (Commission 1991(*b*)) to the possibility of improving the pre-pension scheme, as part of the wider reform of agriculture. Indeed, by 1991, the scheme was operating in one Member State only. Detailed proposals were made later the same year (Commission 1991(*c*) and (*d*)). The Commission stated that about 4.6m. farmers were aged over 55, 2m. of whom were already over 65. Elderly farmers are concentrated on the smallest farms and a large proportion of them have no obvious successor: 'the economic viability of many small farms is under continual threat, and the scope for availing of extra aids, e.g. through extensifying production and for other environmentally friendly practices is limited' (Commission 1991(*c*), 36). The Commission clearly wanted to try to remove many of the elderly farmers and to ensure either that the land released was used to increase the size of other farms or to remove it from farming to be used for some purpose compatible with preserving the countryside.

The legislation was passed in 1992 (Reg. 2079/92 *instituting a Community aid scheme for early retirement from farming*, OJ L215, 30–7–92) and, while in most respects the provisions followed the original proposals, some subtle changes were made which weakened the impact. Most importantly, the scheme was not compulsory, contrary to the original intention. Also, whereas in the proposal, the transferee had to be already working on a farm for at least the two previous years, and for at least half of his/her working time, no such requirement was laid down in the Regulation. The 1988 retirement scheme was repealed and the new scheme was part-funded by the Community from FEOGA-Guarantee rather than Guidance, thereby indicating that it was intended to be a contribution to better market balance. Whether or not this scheme proves to be any more attractive to farmers than its predecessors remains to be seen.

On-Farm Forestry

The Mansholt Plan was based on three interrelated reforms: a major reorganization of the structure of production, the withdrawal of land from farming, and the improvement of marketing conditions. As mentioned in the first Section of this chapter, the Commission estimated that it would have been possible to reduce farmland by 5m. ha. by 1980, that at least 4m. ha. of that land should have been transferred to forestry, and that this development should have been encouraged through the provision of financial aid (Commission 1968(*a*)).

In 1970, when the Commission presented its draft Directives to implement 'Agriculture 1980', one of the proposals was devoted to the limitation of agricultural land. This was intended as part of the solution to agricultural surpluses and had the added advantage of facilitating the production of wood products in which the Community had a large and growing deficit. The proposal was to encourage farmers to plant all or some of their land with trees by the provision of a premium to cover 80–90 per cent of the afforestation costs in the early years. An additional incentive to plant trees was to be given to farmers who were retiring under the provisions of the retirement Directive (Commission 1970).

As has been mentioned already, there was considerable opposition to the whole idea of reducing the amount of land in farming and, as a result, the proposal was omitted from the Commission's views on the new orientation of the CAP set out early in 1971 (Commission 1971(*a*)). In the Council Resolution which followed, the Member States went no further than agreeing to try to prevent an extension of agricultural land. However, the Council undertook to enact measures to encourage afforestation within the framework of regional programmes for forestry and recreation (JO C52, 27–5–71). The Commission followed up this undertaking by announcing in the *Improvement* memorandum that it would propose a Directive on afforestation to improve agricultural structures. The intention was to encourage new tree planting and to upgrade existing woodland, 'not only to increase the incomes of farmers . . . but also to contribute to safeguarding the natural environment, especially in problem areas' (Commission 1973(*d*), 30).[23]

The Commission forwarded its proposals to the Council early in 1974 (OJ C44, 19–4–74). It saw on-farm forestry very much in the context of the 1972 socio-structural Directives: i.e. as a means to assist in the improvement of marginal land so as to raise the viability of farms. There were other advantages as well: the eventual reduction in the Community's dependence on timber imports; the enhancement of the landscape; the conservation of soil, flora, and fauna; and the improvement in the productivity of the adjacent agricultural land through the provision of windbreaks and shelter belts. Four types of activity were to be encouraged: (a) afforestation of areas under agriculture, and of uncultivated land; (b) improvement of unproductive or low productivity woodland; (c) establishment and improvement of shelterbelts; and (d) creation of recreational facilities, such as picnic sites and paths.

Both the ESC and the European Parliament were favourably disposed to the initiative (indeed, if anything, they thought the Commission had not been sufficiently ambitious).[24] This positive response was in sharp contrast to the attitude of the Council which was hopelessly divided on the proposal. The main opposition came from Germany and the UK on grounds of cost. During the remainder of the 1970s, various members of the European Parliament repeatedly asked for an explanation of the delays in the Council and, in 1979, the European Parliament adopted a Resolution in which it asked the Commission to resubmit its 1974 proposals (OJ C140, 5–6–79).

Apart from the fact that the question of the removal of land from farming was still an emotive issue, the forestry proposal became caught up in wider issues of forestry policy, and the suitability of including forestry measures within the CAP. As far back as 1959 the Commission's legal service had expressed an opinion that there was no reason why forestry measures should not be included in agricultural policy, because the protection of forests and reafforestation were necessary in the context of raising land productivity. Furthermore, the establishment of a balance between the various uses of land was one of the objectives of structural policy (Fennell 1982). This interpretation was confirmed by the Council in 1965, yet as late as 1984, the British Ministry of Agriculture was objecting to a Commission proposal for encouraging on-farm forestry (House of Lords 1984). The proposal in question was part of the great package of measures put forward in 1983 to replace the 1972 socio-structural Directives and the less-favoured areas Directive of 1975, to which reference was made in the previous Section (Commission 1983(*f*)).

In the explanatory memorandum to the proposed package, the Commission acknowledged that farm modernization had favoured the farmers with the greatest potential to develop, thereby making the surplus situation worse. The new approach was intended to shift the balance in favour of farmers with a lower income who had the greatest need for investment aid:

The aim is to help them to improve their income, living and working conditions without, however, inducing them to increase the production of products which are already in surplus. In this latter context the afforestation of farmland which has a particular aptitude for it and the improvement of woodland within the farm are seen as additional measures which are particularly relevant. (Commission 1983(*f*), 9)

The proposal was that Member States should have the option of introducing, as part of the investment aid on a farm, a scheme to improve the management of woodland and the revitalization of neglected woodland. The scheme would be part-funded by FEOGA-Guidance. The Commission believed that such a measure would be particularly attractive to farmers in LFAs and it estimated that up to 0.5 per cent of such land would be planted with trees each year. The proposed level of aid per hectare was very generous: up to a maximum of 2,300 ECU/ha. for afforestation, and up to 2,000 ECU/ha. for woodland improvements and shelter belts. However, when enacted, Reg. 797/85 was far less generous, offering a maximum of 1,400 ECU/ha. for afforestation and only 300 ECU/ha. for woodland improvements and shelter belts (OJ L93, 30–3–85). There were three circumstances in which forestry aid was available: within farm modernization plans; in schemes to help regions suffering from structural handicaps; and, in LFAs, for farmers who qualified for the livestock headage payments (see Chapter 9). 'After many years of being excluded, the incorporation of forestry into the structural policy for agriculture is a step forward even if the scope and attraction of the relevant provisions do not go as far as the Commission originally intended' (Commission 1986(*b*), 44).

While this was, no doubt, a disappointment, it was a small triumph that a measure first proposed in 1974 should have been finally accepted by the Council of Ministers. It was indicative of the fact that the relentless pursuit of production of agricultural commodities was undergoing a subtle modification. This was also true of the acceptance at the same time of the idea of providing aid for investment in tourist or craft activities as part of a farm improvement plan in the LFAs, and the authorization of national schemes of aid in environmentally sensitive areas.[25] The acceptance of the validity of such activities within farming can be seen as a belated admission that it is the people on the farm and their livelihood which is of importance and that agricultural production is a means to improve their living conditions rather than an end in itself. Table 8.5 provides the cumulative results of the forestry measure to the end of 1988. By then, only one Member State—Spain—was a significant recipient of FEOGA aid. In the

Table 8.5. Reg. 797/85: On-farm forestry aids, cumulatively to the end of 1988

Member States	No. of beneficiaries	Reimbursement by FEOGA-Guidance	
		'000 ECU	%
Denmark	3,289	240.0	7.6
Germany	1,147	223.0	7.1
Spain	22,272	2,677.4	85.1
Portugal	6	7.0	0.2
Total	26,714	3,147.4	100.0

Source: Commission 1989(*h*).

follow-up document to the MacSharry Plan, the Commission commented that the existing woodland aids were too low (Commission 1991(*c*)). A new forestry measure was passed by the Council in 1992, and is discussed further in Chapter 11.

NOTES

1. It should be pointed out that much of this increase was due not so much to increased production as to the extension of the price and market policy to a wider group of commodities and the assumption of the full cost of support for the commodities subject to common market regimes.
2. These labour force statistics are taken from Zeller (1970) who is a better source of detailed statistics on the implications of the Mansholt Plan than the Plan itself.
3. It was not until the mid-1980s that, in practice, the amount of utilized agricultural land in EC-6 declined by 5m. ha. At the same time, the increase in afforested land amounted to only 600,000 ha.
4. Improvements in market organization are discussed in Ch. 10.
5. The whole topic of producer groups is discussed in Ch. 10.
6. Table 8.1 shows the cost as 2,771m. ua which is the sum of the individual components, as they appeared in COM(70)500.
7. There is confusion in the literature as to whether this Resolution was passed on 25 March or 25 May 1971. In fact, in a sense both dates are correct. The Resolution was passed in March at the end of one of the most difficult negotiations in the history of the CAP. When the Resolution came before the Council for formal approval in May, some Member States reopened the discussions on certain accompanying texts. It was only with some difficulty that the Resolution was formally adopted and therefore 25 May is correct (see *Agence Europe*, 25–5–1971, 4, and 1–6–1971, 9).
8. The 1963 Plans and 1967 Programmes are discussed in Ch. 9.
9. The consistency of the Germans is quite remarkable. Readers are reminded that the Germans were in favour of milk quotas in 1984 and, later in the 1980s, preferred the

quantitative limitation of price guarantees to a drop in support prices in money terms. (See Ch. 6.)

10. The detailed arrangements for this guidance premium were set out in Dir. 73/131 (OJ L253, 9–6–73). It provided for a payment per hectare over a three-year period. The development plan had to stipulate that, on its completion, the earnings from cattle and sheep sales would represent at least 50% of farm sales.

11. The 1970 proposals were based on a take-up by 256,000 farmers in the first five years of the programme (Commission 1970). There were at that time 7.3m. farmers in the Community.

12. From the farmer's point of view, the only difference was that the scheme wholly funded by the Member State carried a lower rate of subsidy.

13. The circumstances under which these regional variations could be applied were laid down in Dir. 73/440 (OJ L356, 27–12–73), and were very restrictive, especially where a region was to be excluded.

14. The normal rate of reimbursement from FEOGA-Guidance was 25% of eligible expenditure but provision was made for a 65% reimbursement in problem regions of Member States which were not operating retirement schemes at the time the Directive took effect. Only two countries (Ireland and Italy) qualified and, in 1974, two Decisions were enacted in their favour to provide for the higher rate of reimbursement: Decisions 74/157 and 74/158 (OJ L290, 29–10–74).

15. One of the few studies undertaken on the provision of socio-economic advice under Dir. 72/161 was that of Woods (1980).

16. Regs. 1945/81 and 1946/81, and Dirs. 81/528 and 81/529 of 30 June 1981 (OJ L197, 20–7–81).

17. Commission 1976(a), 1977(g), and 1979(b).

18. This review seems to be the last occasion on which the Commission published information on the detailed operation of the three Directives. It is much to be regretted that more analysis has not been made available.

19. This also required adjustments to a whole series of much less important regionally targeted structural measures, which had been dependent on Dir. 72/159 as the basis of their aids to modernization. These are discussed in Ch. 9.

20. Subsequently, in an amendment to Reg. 797/85, restrictions were also placed on investment aid in the beef sector to avoid encouraging intensive production (Reg. 3808/89, OJ L371, 20–12–89).

21. It also covers the later history of the retirement Directive, which was actually terminated under Reg. 797/85—temporarily as it turned out.

22. Training aid was later extended to include courses to help farmers reorientate production to quality products, to learn about environmentally friendly farming practices, and to improve their skills in managing on-farm woodland (Reg. 1760/87, OJ L167, 26–6–87).

23. The Community's first environmental action programme had been adopted three months previously. The *Improvement* memorandum is one of the very first Commission documents on agricultural policy to mention the environment.

24. See OJ C125, 12–10–74 and OJ C127, 10–10–74.

25. Environmental issues are discussed in Ch. 11.

9

Disadvantaged Farmers and Problem Regions

Identifying Disadvantaged Groups

The Mansholt Plan and the attempt to define and promote the efficient farm were based on an interpretation of Art. 39.1(b) of the Rome Treaty which equated a 'fair standard of living' with the achievement of a labour income comparable to that in other sectors. However, the problems of the farming sector were considerably more complex than this equation would suggest. Running through the agricultural Articles of the Rome Treaty, there is an awareness of the need to pay particular attention to the diversity of circumstances in which farming takes place. There was a requirement to bear in mind, when devising and implementing the CAP, 'the structural and natural disparities between the various agricultural regions' (Art. 39.2(a)). In addition, under Article 42, provision was made for a derogation from the rules on competition so as to allow the granting of aid 'for the protection of enterprises handicapped by structural and natural conditions'.

Chapters 4 and 8 have shown that few farmers in the 1960s and 1970s enjoyed an income level comparable to that in other sectors. Even with a programme of modernization (and particularly one as limited as that provided under Dir. 72/159), there were many farmers whose income would remain below the relevant level unless some specific action were taken to remedy this. Such farmers need to be distinguished from those who might be adversely affected by some change in policy, for instance, the cereals farmers in the 1960s or the arable farmers in the early 1990s, referred to in Chapter 4; or the middle-aged farmers who were too young to retire but who could not adapt to the original proposals under the Mansholt Plan (see Chapter 8). Given the transient cause of their difficulties, farmers in such circumstances should not expect to receive assistance indefinitely, although experience has shown that it is extremely difficult in practice to terminate a temporary aid.

Putting these to one side, there are some quite different categories of disadvantaged farmers whose income problem is not so easily dealt with. In these cases, the cause of their difficulties is to be found in some attribute of the agricultural workforce, the farm, natural phenomena, or institutional defects—or any combination of two or more of these. Before examining how the CAP has, in practice, attempted to cope with these types of deficiency, it is useful to look back at the early years of the CAP and examine how the policy-makers perceived the problem and how they proposed to deal with it.

The 1960 proposals on the CAP recognized in a somewhat rambling and disorganized fashion the structural and social shortcomings which had led to low incomes, and the types of action required to remedy them.[1] Infrastructural deficiencies in certain regions and on certain farms were said to lie at the root of many of the sector's problems. The Commission also recognized that even agriculturally efficient regions manifested a range of shortcomings.

But it was not just the infrastructure on and off the farm which needed improvement. The farmers themselves required a better level of technical knowledge and, therefore, there was a need for more scientific research, training of farmers, and better advisory services.[2] Young people coming into the sector were singled out for special attention in this context. Farmers also needed better advice as to their future prospects in agriculture and, if necessary, training to help them leave. This in turn meant that off-farm employment opportunities had to be improved. For the farmers who were to remain in farming, better access to credit, and the development of the co-operative movement were vital. The area devoted to farming required careful consideration: marginal land should be transferred to other uses, especially forestry. An assessment was needed of the desirability of the cultivation of fallow land and of additional reclamation in the light of efforts being made to achieve market equilibrium.

The Attempt to Introduce Community Plans and Programmes

It was against this background that the early proposals on structural policy were made, which were outlined in Chapter 2. During 1963, at the time of the debate on the future of FEOGA, and when FEASA was abandoned, the Commission made its first proposal on the establishment of a common price level for cereals. Accompanying this proposal was a group of measures of a structural nature intended to facilitate the adjustment to the new system. These were discussed in Chapter 4 in the context of direct income aids. The interest in these measures here lies in the fact that the Commission seized the opportunity to propose a range of measures to assist other farmers who suffered from structural disadvantages. The proposal was that, starting in 1966, there should be a series of Community Plans for the improvement of the living-standards of the agricultural population.

Community Plans were to be of four different kinds: (a) to improve farm incomes in regions which suffered from unfavourable structural circumstances; (b) to aid certain categories of farms in which the economic or social situation was particularly unfavourable; (c) to improve the social policy regime within agriculture; and (d) to provide an income aid which was independent of production (Commission 1963(*f*)).

The Commission envisaged that the aid under (a) would be very wide indeed. It covered the improvement of production and marketing; intensification of agricultural education and farm advice; the enlargement of smallholdings; the provision of a supplementary old-age pension for those farmers who abandoned their farm and who were too old to change their occupation; the transfer of agricultural land to non-agricultural uses; aids to education and retraining for young farmers wishing to take up employment outside agriculture; the creation of employment opportunities outside agriculture; and the improvement of infrastructure, including schools.[3]

The categories of farms to be aided under (b) above were not worked out in detail, but the examples given by the Commission were those situated in mountain or hill areas, those which were too small in size, and those which were situated at a distance from markets. Little information was provided on (c) above, but this was understandable because the Commission had only recently put forward its ill-fated action programme on social policy in agriculture (Commission 1963(*e*)), and it did little more than urge the Council to adopt it quickly and energetically. The fourth element—the income aid—was intended to supplement the other measures and was to be used only if they were inadequate to ensure a lasting improvement in the standard of living in all regions of the Community.

The first plan was to run from 1966 to 1969 and the Community was to contribute to the total cost through FEOGA, the Social Fund, and by the creation of a special Title within the Community Budget. In the event, the Community did not move to common cereal prices in 1964/65, although the Council agreed to introduce common prices in 1967. It also agreed to the creation of a special Title in the Community Budget—the FEOGA-Special Section—from which for a number of years compensation was paid to cereal farmers in Federal Germany, Italy, and Luxembourg (the three countries in which cereal prices fell). The rest of the proposal disappeared, although not totally without trace, as many of the ideas contained in it were to find echoes in later proposals by the Commission.

Once Reg. 17/64—outlined in Chapter 2—was enacted, the funding arrangements for the price policy and the structural policy were assured. Under that Regulation, structural projects qualifying for aid had to come within the framework of a Community Programme (Sp.OJ 1963–1964). The Commission immediately set about drawing up these Programmes and, right from the start, there appear to have been difficulties of a serious nature. The preparation of the Programmes was an ambitious exercise and the Commission did not submit its proposals to the Council until June 1967 in COM(67)194 (Commission 1967(*b*)).

Ten Community Programmes were put forward: four were concerned with infrastructural improvements—land reorganization, irrigation, drainage, and forestry intended to improve farm structure; five were concerned with the quality, marketing, and processing of specific products—fruit and vegetables, milk, meat, wine, and olives; and the tenth Programme was intended to develop agricultural regions which were backward or in difficulty. This last Programme was particularly far-reaching: not only did it cover all the activities permissible under the other nine Programmes but it envisaged a more varied Community role in investment. For instance, it included the extension of electricity and of water supply to farm buildings and farmhouses; and the construction, enlargement, improvement, and equipping of facilities intended for the education, re-education, or further education of those who worked in farming. It also envisaged Community financing of schemes smaller than those allowed under the other Programmes.

Within each Programme, zones or regions of principal effort were designated. The idea was that the Guidance Section funds should be concentrated as a matter of priority—but not exclusively—on these zones. In drawing up the zones the Commission had been guided by consideration of the urgency in a particular region of improving structure, the existence of real investment need, and the profitability which might be expected. Certain regions from within the designated list were singled out for special help in the form of a higher percentage reimbursement from Community funds. While agreeing with the Commission's regional approach, the European Parliament was strongly critical of the Commission on the grounds that it had designated too many regions of principal effort. It also feared that some of the Programmes—particularly those for irrigation and drainage—might lead to an undesirable increase in output (JO C27, 28–3–68).

The Community Programmes met with opposition in the Council of Ministers: the general suspicion of Community structural policy, which had appeared in the discussions on FEASA, re-emerged. This was reinforced when the Member States realized that they were being faced by a detailed integrated structural policy which would have limited their scope for action. The Programmes were drawn up in the form of draft Regulations which meant that, once passed, they would have been automatically applicable and that, where Community financing was concerned, there would have been no room for national flexibility or variation. However, the Programmes came very close to being accepted when the Commission revised them into four more flexible groups which provided the Member States with greater freedom of choice (*Agence Europe*, 24–1–68).

There was also opposition to the Programmes from within the Commission itself: the services responsible for the development of regional and social policies did not like the idea of Mansholt and the agriculturalists having an indirect say in their areas of policy. The final blow came, ironically, from within the Agricultural Directorate-General itself, when Mansholt announced that radical proposals on structure were to be made at a later date, in the context of solving the Community's growing surplus problem. A preliminary discussion was held with the Council as early as October 1967 and it was expected that the Commission would present a discussion document to the Council in spring 1968 (*Agence Europe*, 17–10–67). This timetable was not observed and it was not until December 1968 that the document was ready: what has become known as the Mansholt Plan. The promise of this alternative and more radical document gave the Council the opportunity to shelve the Community Programmes for the time being—which meant forever.

Despite their demise, the Community Programmes are both interesting and important. Not only do they indicate how Reg. 17/64 was intended to operate but they were linked also with the 1962 Decision on the co-ordination of national structural policies. In putting them forward, the Commission was taking the opportunity to reinforce the co-ordination of national policies, by the application of more effective means of stimulating and guiding them in a *communautaire* spirit. In essence, they were an attempt to fulfil the Commission's own understanding of the co-ordination exercise: to define the objectives and guidelines of structural policy, to make the objectives obligatory, and to ensure that the action taken by Member States conformed with the objectives. Good ideas never die and it is fascinating to see how various structural measures of much more recent date have had an affinity with many of the ideas set out in the Community Programmes.

The Programmes are also instructive because they highlighted for the first time in the Community's history the contradictions inherent in the CAP. The logic of the single market, based on a common price structure, was to favour those areas which had a production advantage—whether locational, structural, or in terms of natural endowment. The Programmes, by contrast, were clearly intended to help the areas lagging behind. The interest groups in the more privileged production areas lobbied hard to retain their position. Their success was evident—particularly in the 1970s, as chronicled in Chapter 8—in the extent to which structural funds were spent in the better-off farming regions. This is especially true of measures which are available throughout the Community. In addition, as will be clear from later Sections of this chapter, the funds allocated to deprived farming regions have (with the exception of the LFA funds) been quite inadequate.

The failure to enact the Community Programmes left Reg. 17/64 in a curious position: under it, structural aids were being provided to individual projects on a temporary basis and this arrangement had to be continued throughout the lifetime of the Regulation, i.e. until the end of the 1970s.[4] Both the Community Plans and the Community Programmes acknowledged the existence of groups of farmers who, for a variety of reasons, faced wide-ranging handicaps; Reg. 17/64 made no such distinction and the failure to enact legislation to help them left these farmers in an anomalous situation. It was not until the mid-1980s that the Community tried to tackle their circumstances in a multifaceted programme. The 1970s and early 1980s witnessed the enactment of an array of piecemeal measures on structure. The remainder of this chapter examines these measures to see how the Community attempted to remedy some of the basic defects in the farming sector.

The Development of the Farm Workforce

With a few notable exceptions, agricultural policy has very largely ignored the question of the need to improve human capital and has concentrated either on the support of prices and the management of markets, or on the adaptation of the land farmed and the capital invested in buildings and equipment. Yet investment in people is of fundamental importance if they are going to be able to benefit from improvements in the other factors of production. One of the most critical areas is that of education and training.

From the earliest days of the Community there was an awareness of the deficiencies in the standard and availability of general education and of the technical training required for modern farming. The Consultative Conference on the social aspects of the CAP (Commission 1962) discussed this subject extensively and also called for the creation of an information service and career guidance for young people in rural areas. The Mansholt Plan repeated the call for career guidance, maintaining that it would contribute to a decline in 'the number of young people who come into agriculture only because they have not been prepared for another occupation' (Commission 1968(a), 45).

Agriculture is very much under the control of the middle-aged and the elderly: Mansholt stated that half of the farmers were over 57 and that often they did not have the education which would allow them 'to adapt easily to changing social and economic conditions' (Commission 1968(a), 6). While educational levels have improved appreciably in rural areas in the intervening years, farming is still largely in the hands of the middle-aged and elderly. In 1991, MacSharry stated that over half the farmers were over 55 (Commission 1991(b)), so in that respect little had changed.[5]

Underlying the proposals to reduce the farm workforce and to modernize farms, set out in the Mansholt Plan, was the need for a well-educated rural population, which would be able either to seek employment outside agriculture or to remain in farming, and if the latter to possess the knowledge necessary to maintain the profitability of a modernized sector. To help in this reformation, farm families needed advice on their individual circumstances and on the long-term viability of their farms. This meant the creation of a specialist counselling service, which was one of the purposes of Dir. 72/161, as outlined in Chapter 8. Financial assistance was also provided under this Directive for short training-courses for those who had already chosen a career in farming. The outcome of these schemes and the ones which replaced them are illustrated in Tables 8.2–8.4 in Chapter 8; all that needs to be stated here is that the data convey the impression that comparatively little has been spent by the Community on this aspect of policy and that the main beneficiaries are not necessarily the Member States with the greatest deficiencies in farming skills.

If, therefore, the Community has not been very active in providing farmers and farm workers with advice and training, has it assisted in the development of the workforce in any other way? The best-known measure is the retirement scheme (Dir. 72/160, and its successor Regulations), to which reference was made in Chapter 8. Older farmers were perceived as being trapped on farms which were often too small to be viable, where there was no obvious successor, and therefore where there was little incentive to innovate. The thinking was that, if elderly farmers could be persuaded to take early retirement, the modernization of farming could be speeded up or land could be removed from farming. It is very clear that the main purpose of the early retirement measures was to compensate elderly farmers for giving up their land—for whatever purpose—and only incidentally was it intended to help them improve their income situation.

In the early 1970s when the Commission was trying to get the Council to accept its package of reform proposals, it identified farmers willing to undertake modernization as a group in need of special short-term assistance. To carry out a development plan required a commitment over a period of years to a scheme of investment which might include a change of enterprise, the learning and application of new techniques, the erection of new buildings, and the purchase of new equipment. While the end-result was expected to be a higher income, there was the distinct possibility of cash flow problems while the investments were being made.

For this reason the Commission put forward a proposal in the draft Resolution of 1971 for the payment of a degressive income aid during the years in which the farmer was carrying out a development plan (Commission 1971(a)). However, in the Resolution as adopted by the Council, this proposal was reduced to an exceptional aid for certain regions only, and was to be funded by the Member States without a Community contribution (JO C52, 27–5–71). In other words, the Council had given the idea the kiss of death. Undeterred, the Commission used the 1972/73 price proposals to revive the idea in its original form and repeated it in the revised price proposals for the same farm-year (Commission 1971(b) and 1972). It was not accepted by the Council.

Although the Commission abandoned this particular idea, in 1973 in the context of its proposals on aid in mountain areas and in certain other poorer farming areas, it proposed an income aid for young farmers of less than 38. The idea was that the aid should be paid in three annual instalments on the establishment of the farm—including where the transfer was intergenerational (Commission 1973(a)). Nothing came of this proposal either, but still the Commission persisted and, in 1974, it proposed an income aid for young farmers, which bore a distinct resemblance to the income aid for developing farmers proposed in 1971.

The context was the rapid deterioration in the cost–price relationship within agriculture in the summer of 1974. The causes were twofold: firstly, the onset of the energy crisis which resulted in sharp and unprecedented increases in input prices (particularly of fertilizers, pesticides, fuels, and feeding-stuffs); and secondly, the effects of general inflation which raised the cost of capital and labour. Alarmed by this turn of events, the Commission sent a memorandum to the Council on the 'Special Measures to Deal with the Present Economic Situation in Agriculture' (Commission 1974(d)). Among the suggestions it put forward to help farmers overcome these unexpected difficulties was aid to young farmers who, the Commission felt, faced particularly serious problems. 'Young farmers' is something of a misnomer, as the critical factor was not merely age but age combined with recent acquisition of the farm. In a follow-up to this memorandum and in conjunction with the price proposals for 1975/76, the Commission proposed an aid to young farmers (Commission 1974(b)). The rationale was that the very great increases in production costs and the price of capital experienced over the previous two years had hit hardest at young farmers. They were the ones who had to invest, either to increase productivity or sometimes merely to keep at the existing level, and they had insufficient funds of their own. The first few years after setting up a farm were especially difficult when they were building up stock and equipment—and possibly having to compensate co-heirs at the same time.

The basis of the proposal was the provision of an income subsidy for farmers aged 40 and under who were modernizing their farms under Directive 72/159 and whose development plans were approved after January 1975. The aid was to be for a period of not more than five years and degressive in nature. Despite the apparent urgency of this measure when proposed it was withdrawn from the price package in January 1975. The main difficulty seems to have lain in the very different laws governing the taxation of intergenerational transfers of land in the various Member States. In some countries the young farmer has an easy passage, in others this is not so. Some Member States felt that the real solution lay in the reform of the tax laws in certain countries rather than in legislation under the CAP.

In 1980, the European Parliament criticized the Commission for paying inadequate attention 'to the problems of young people working in farming, as their presence should be seen as an essential precondition for the profound transformation which is needed in European agriculture' and it called on the Commission 'to consider the possibility of setting up an organized system of aids to encourage young people to take up farming' (OJ C85, 8–4–80, 59).[6] Persistence was rewarded when, in 1981, the Council finally accepted the idea of special aid for young farmers (Dir. 81/528, OJ L197, 20–7–81). Member States were empowered to grant special aid to farmers below the age of 40, who undertook a development plan under Dir. 72/159 within five years of their installation on the farm.

In 1983, when the Commission put forward its proposals to replace the 1972 structural Directives, it took the opportunity to assemble a whole package of structural measures, some of which were new, but most of which were old ideas resurrected. It was in this context that aid to young farmers appeared again. Apart from the widespread difficulties created for all farmers by high interest rates and high input costs, young farmers faced their own particular difficulties: high land prices (if purchasing a farm);[7] high starting-up costs where inheriting a farm run down by the retiring farmer, or where compensating the co-heirs whose shares in the farm are being bought out. Young farmers were needed if the sector was going to adapt to new economic circumstances where a spirit of innovation was required. This could only be assured by a rejuvenated farm population (Commission 1983(*f*)).

The proposal, which was optional for the Member States, was for an installation aid and enhanced investment aid if carrying out a development plan within five years of starting up. The legislation as enacted was not as generous as the Commission's proposals but nevertheless the results were roughly in line with the Commission's original assumptions of an uptake (in a Community of 10) by about 13,000 farmers annually. Table 8.4 (see previous chapter) provides cumulative statistics on the number of young farmers who received installation aid or the additional investment aid if carrying out a development plan (Art. 7.1 and 7.2). As with other aspects of Reg. 797/85, the striking feature of this table is the difference in response in the various Member States: France dominates the installation aids, the UK does not operate this scheme, and the response in Italy is worryingly small. The number of development plans is disappointing and calls into question the Commission's expectation of the role of young farmers in reforming the approach to farming.

In fact, there are a number of contradictions surrounding the encouragement of young farmers. While it is quite true that innovation in farming is more likely to be carried out by younger rather than older farmers, it is also the time when, because of family and economic circumstances, a young farmer is under the greatest pressure to farm intensively. This is not helpful when surpluses are a problem and technology encourages the expansion of supply. The situation is made even worse due to the limitations of the land market and the difficulty of acquiring an adequate amount of land to allow farming in any way other than either very intensively or only part time. The Commission reasoned that, if elderly farmers could be persuaded to give up farming in favour of a young farmer, this would help the latter to be viable without being overintensive. There would be benefits from an environmental standpoint and it would also help to contain the problem of market imbalance. It was against this background that, in 1986, the Commission proposed an aid for young farmers to help them to switch to the production of non-surplus commodities, to the production of high quality products, or to farm less intensively.

While there was logic in this approach, the reality is that elderly farmers tend to farm very small holdings and the suitability of many of them to sustain another generation must be called into question. This is confirmed by the Commission's own statistics: it based its calculation of the cost of such an aid scheme on the assumption that 80,000 young farmers start farming each year and that 10 per cent of them would opt for reorientation or extensification of production. The average size of such farms was estimated to be 20 ha., and that one-third of the area would be involved in the programme (Commission 1986(*c*)). Unless these were specialist enterprises, it would be surprising that such small farms would be viable if providing the farmer's main occupation and indeed that the farmer would be willing to risk such a large proportion of the land to reorientation or extensification.

This proposal was not accepted by the Council although, of course, young farmers are free to apply for any of the general aids to reorientation or extensification open to all farmers who meet the requirements. The only change to take place in the young farmer scheme under Reg. 797/85 in the late 1980s was an easing of the requirement that farming should be the main occupation (Reg. 3808/89, OJ L371, 20–12–89). However, at the same time, the requirement to be the farmer in the fullest legal sense was strengthened. There may have been a suggestion that elderly farmers were not really abandoning farming in favour of a new generation. There is a genuine problem in family businesses in that the titular head of the firm is not always the most active worker, and that the legal niceties of transfer of title are not always followed, for cultural or social reasons. The ESC was alive to the dilemma of young people who could not buy a new farm because of the cost and who, therefore, either had to make an investment of their own in the family farm or turn to another occupation (OJ C56, 7–3–90). The ownership of the farm might well not be an issue within the family at the time the young person makes the decision but the question of title might be important in the context of access to investment funds.

Regional Implications of Policy

The comment has been made already that it was surprising that no explicit reference was made in the Treaty of Rome to the need for a regional policy, although the need to reduce the economic and social differences between regions was recognized. In the preamble to the Treaty reference is made to the need to ensure harmonious development 'by reducing the differences existing between the various regions and the backwardness of the less favoured regions'. The danger in any integration process is that the existing differences may become magnified: when internal barriers to the movement of goods, people, services, and capital are removed, the more prosperous regions may forge ahead, drawing resources from the poorer regions, thereby making their situation even worse.

The creation of a common market is, therefore, a balancing act between maximizing the undoubted advantages of integration in terms of economies of scale and specialization in production, which the larger market should bring, and minimizing the disadvantages of the people and regions left behind by helping them to adjust. While the centripetal tendencies of integration were well understood in the late 1950s, the new Community was hampered by the inadequacy of statistical measures of the regional economy and interregional transfers. Nevertheless, even in the absence of a formal regional policy, the Commission lost no time in the 1960s in acquiring a better understanding of regional issues, culminating in its proposal for the establishment of a Regional Fund (Bull. EC 12–1969, Supp.).

However, long before that, the regional implications of agricultural policy were acknowledged. Throughout the history of the CAP there has been an awareness of the regional dimension of policy and of the impact which a common price policy was capable of having on the regional income differentials. During the Stresa Conference, Mansholt warned of the negative effect of raising prices which, quite apart from its impact on production, would widen the income gap between the farmers in the Netherlands and northern France, and the mountain farmers of southern Germany, France, and Italy (Comité inter-gouvernemental 1958). In its policy proposals of 1960, the Commission warned that price and market policy alone could not achieve the objectives of Art. 39.1

of the Rome Treaty because it could not eliminate the causes of the inadequate incomes and would accentuate the existing disparities between regions (Commission 1960).

As events were to show, this was not just a theoretical possibility but it became a reality in a manner which the Commission had not anticipated. The piecemeal introduction of the common commodity regimes over the 1960s brought about distortions between the products of southern regions (fruit and vegetables, olive oil, tobacco, and wine) and those of the northern regions (cereals, livestock, and milk) which latter were established first. Even within the southern regions, there were distortions, as some producers do produce northern-type commodities and of course these benefited from the early introduction of the regimes. In addition, the various regimes are not all the same: the manner in which commodities are supported and the level of support differ. This adds another dimension to the main north–south divide. More generally, however, as outlined in Chapter 4, the operation of a common pricing structure should result in benefits to the most economically efficient farmers and regions, accentuating differences which exist for other reasons.

Regional income differences have many causes: the natural conditions of soil, climate, and altitude clearly affect the range of products which can be produced successfully. Many regions suffer from the negative long-term impact of poor land management techniques in former times, which have seriously undermined a fragile ecosystem. On-farm and off-farm infrastructure varies considerably from one region to another, thereby helping or hindering profitable production in an arbitrary manner. In many cases, conditions conspire to re-enforce each other: thus the mountainous regions, where natural conditions are at their most severe, may well be regions of poor infrastructure. Most of the poorest regions are also geographically peripheral within their own country and within the European Union itself. This affects not only agriculture but also the level of economic development generally and the degree of social viability.

Regional differences were well described by the Commission in 1975:

[D]ifferences in income are observed between Member States, between regions of the Community (the difference can vary in the ratio of 1 to 5 among the 55 regions considered in the original Community), between farms of the same size within the same Member State (a difference of more than 50% was recorded between farms engaging in general agriculture and those engaging in stock rearing) and between farms of the same type but of a different size. . . .

[T]he beneficial effects on farm incomes of the common agricultural policy have been felt to a different degree in each region, to the detriment of those with weak farming structures. This trend raises particular problems, since the regions concerned are generally those already experiencing difficulties in relation to their overall economic structures, and consequently offering few alternative occupations.   (Commission 1975(*a*), 16–17)

In 1978, the Commission asked the European Council to endorse a new guideline for structural policy which 'should be strengthened and adapted to take better account of regional needs, specific market difficulties, and the changing economic environment' (Commission 1978(*f*), 4). This new orientation was subsequently re-enforced when the Commission advocated the development of a long-term structural policy which would give priority to the weakest regions. It acknowledged that:

the existing measures have not been such as to bring about improvement in the structural situation of a substantial number of farms, particularly those which are small and especially those in difficult areas.

To exclude these categories of farm from the 'benefits of the common structures policy' is also extremely unsatisfactory for the overall economic development of those regions. (Commission 1979(*a*), 48)

The following year, the Commission stated that, when the 1972 Directives were enacted as the basis of structural reform, the Community had failed to appreciate that a multiplicity of obstacles to reform could coexist in certain regions (Commission 1980(*d*)). This was an extraordinary—and frankly un-believable—assessment of the situation in the early 1970s. Collective *naïveté* on such a scale is hard to imagine against the background of a Community which had discussed the introduction of Community Plans and Programmes during the 1960s. These, by their very essence, assumed the existence of multidimensional problems in certain regions.[8] Whatever the truth of the situation, the fact was that the regional income differential had widened during the 1970s, due to the fact that the richer regions received more support than the less-favoured regions because of their respective product mixes, and because the proportion of rich producers was higher in rich regions (Commission 1980(*c*)).

While the reorientation of structural policy towards problem regions and farmers would help to redress the balance, the Commission warned that it was 'an illusion to believe that socio-structural policy on its own can bring about the requisite economic development of the less-favoured agricultural areas' (Commission 1981(*c*), 20). What was required was an integrated approach to regional development. It would have been helpful if the Commission had also underlined the need to ensure that the price and market policy was not making the regional income differentials worse. By 1985, in the *Perspectives*, the Commission was not only reiterating the kinds of comments it had made ten years previously and which were quoted above, but was adding the observation that the structural change in agriculture which it believed to be essential would have to take place in an economy suffering from high levels of unemployment (Commission 1985(*b*)). This was a very different situation from the one in which the Mansholt Plan had been put forward, although on both occasions the Commission was calling for the creation of new employment in agricultural regions.

The persistence of regional differences in income throughout the lifetime of the CAP raises the question as to whether anything has been done to limit these differences? The shaky start to structural policy and the virtual abandonment of social policy within the CAP did not help, and some of the structural policy put in place served other purposes. In these circumstances, it was difficult to provide a counterweight to the price and market policy which, by its very nature, was intended to create a common support structure which would inevitably favour the economically stronger producers. The Community could have introduced differentiated price support to favour smaller volume producers but in general this has been resisted. Certain commodity regimes have been established for minor products which are of special significance in particular regions but these are not always disadvantaged.[9] Also it should never be forgotten that the CAP does not cover the whole range of policies applied to the farming sector. Credit, taxation, and social security, for instance, remain in the hands of the Member States and variations in these 'are capable of aggravating regional disparities in agricultural incomes' (Commission 1981(*d*), 86).

The Regional Dimension in Structural Policy before 1975

Earlier in this chapter reference was made to the attempts to introduce Community Plans and Programmes which had a regional element built into their provisions. Nothing came of these initiatives but shortly afterwards the regional dimension of agricultural policy re-emerged in the Mansholt Plan. There, the differences between regions was acknowledged and the need to differentiate structural policy by region was recognized. Mansholt envisaged a partnership between the Member States and the Community, with the latter defining the objectives to be achieved and the principal methods to be used but leaving to the Member States the responsibility of incorporating the general guidelines in their national legislative and administrative arrangements, including the matter of regional differentiation. Clearly the Commission was trying to avoid the negative responses of the Member States which it had encountered with the Community Programmes.

The regional differences within the Community were important in relation to the stated intention of the Mansholt Plan to reduce the farm workforce. It will be recalled that the Plan envisaged a decline in the workforce, over a ten-year period, of 5m. persons, mostly through retirement but a substantial number (one million) needing to find alternative employment. In a wider context, the Commission was already differentiating regions according to their degree of industrialization and the Mansholt Plan adopted a similar approach.

Predominantly agricultural regions were defined as those in which more than 20 per cent of the workforce was directly employed in farming and where (with a few exceptions) the population density was very low (less than 100 inhabitants/km^2). Some of these regions had a thriving agricultural sector with good farm structure, whereas others were areas of low agricultural productivity. There was the danger that a reduction in the farming population would result in outmigration in search of work, thereby contributing to a damaging depopulation. The Commission believed that it was important to try to prevent this outcome and therefore it proposed that assistance should be given to employment creation in agricultural and semi-agricultural regions.[10] As a working hypothesis, it assumed the need to create annually an additional 80,000 jobs with public assistance.

The fate of the main aspects of the Mansholt Plan has already been outlined in Chapters 4 and 8; the regional aspects of that Plan were very largely put to one side in the wider debate on the main structural proposals. However, regional issues were raised in the Resolution on the new orientation of the CAP of May 1971. It was agreed that the Member States could, if they wished, differentiate by region the level of aid granted and exclude certain regions from some or all of the structural measures. This latter freedom may sound negative but it could have been used positively in order to concentrate effort on those regions in greatest need. It was also agreed that the FEOGA-Guidance reimbursement (which was fixed at 25 per cent of eligible Member State expenditure) would be 65 per cent in the retirement proposal in disfavoured agricultural regions or where a national retirement scheme was not already in place.[11]

The Council agreed that Member States would institute a system of aids for those in farming who wished to retrain for a non-agricultural job, and that the Social Fund would assist with the costs. Finally, at the very end of the Resolution a direct link was made between the need for rapid progress in the development of other Community policies (notably economic, monetary, regional, and social) and the achievement of agricultural reform. The Council agreed that the Member States and the Community would promote regional development, by encouraging employment creation, particularly in the regions with a significant surplus of people in farming (JO C52, 27–5–71).

It must be said that for a Community which, in principle, was aware of the major economic and social differences between its regions, the practical response to the needs of the backward regions was completely inadequate. The gap between theory and practice is a recurring feature of the Community, of which this happens to be a particularly good—but not unusual—example. However, the Commission followed up the Resolution by presenting the Council with a programme for Community action in the priority agricultural regions (JO C90, 11–9–71). There were three related documents: a Communication, and two proposed Regulations. These latter were on the financing by FEOGA-Guidance of projects of a developmental nature within these regions, and on the creation of a Fund for interest rebates. The whole programme should be read in the context of the belief of the time that the agricultural reform package would be swiftly passed by the Council. This did not happen and when the three reform Directives were passed in 1972 they were a pale reflection of the original intention.

The Commission suggested in the Communication that, with the radical changes expected in the farming sector between 1972 and 1976, about 2m. persons could be released from agriculture. Many would be aged 55 and over and would be eligible for a retirement pension but many younger farmers would leave the sector only on condition of finding new employment—preferably in their own region—which would give them an income higher than that which they had earned in farming.

It was estimated that around 600,000 new jobs over the period 1972 to 1976 would have to be created in the industrial or tertiary sectors for those leaving agriculture. Of this total, half should be created in basically agricultural regions where industry and services were little developed and offered little new employment. If the jobs were not created the substantial fall in the active agricultural population could result in a massive migration to other regions which already suffered from overconcentration. Such an eventuality, leading to the denuding of certain regions of an essential element in their population and seriously handicapping their economic development, was regarded as unacceptable from a social and an economic point of view.

For these and other reasons the creation of new employment in agricultural regions was regarded by the Commission as a matter of urgency. Priority agricultural regions were defined as those which had a percentage of the population engaged in agriculture above the Community average, a GDP per head at factor cost below the Community average, and a below-Community-average percentage of the population engaged in industry. The necessary development of such regions would require the co-ordinated intervention of the Member States and the Community, which in turn would require the intervention of the Guidance Section of FEOGA, the creation of a European Fund for interest rebates,[12] the participation of the Social Fund, and the European Investment Bank.

The particular task to be assigned to the Guidance Section was that of assisting in the creation of a sufficient number of non-agricultural jobs for persons leaving farming, and for their direct descendants. This was to be done by giving financial assistance to projects coming within the framework of development programmes in the priority agricultural regions. Projects involving the marketing and processing of agricultural products were to have prior claim on the funds available. The aid was to take the form of a lump-sum grant paid per new job created, which was capable of being filled by someone leaving farming or by his/her direct descendants.

In the context of the proposed reduction of the agricultural workforce, the link between job creation and membership of a farm family is understandable but in practice it could have been inequitable and divisive. The ESC, in a lengthy and often critical Opinion, pointed out that these regions had high rates of unemployment, underemployment, and bad employment generally, and that this should be reflected in the measures proposed (JO C21, 3–3–72). However, the Commission persisted with its proposal and drew up a list of priority agricultural regions which it submitted to the Council at the end of 1972. This list was replaced in October 1973 by a new list which took account of the Enlargement of the Community at the beginning of that year (Commission 1973(c)). Nothing further happened to this proposal: progress was delayed at first due to the delays in implementing the European Regional Development Fund. In the event, when this Fund came into existence, the draft Directive on priority agricultural regions and the proposed creation of the European Fund for interest rebates were dropped.

The Less-Favoured Areas

From the previous Sections of this chapter, it is obvious that little was done in the early days of the CAP to provide for the special needs of the backward regions—a policy gap which was part of the wider neglect of structural policy. It was not for the want of trying: the Commission had put forward a series of structural proposals with a regional element but the Council of Ministers was resistant to the implementation of this aspect of policy. So far as the regional dimension of structural policy was concerned, matters came to a head in the early 1970s in the context of the Enlargement negotiations. This was true both in the wider context of the introduction of a common regional policy with its own source of finance, and in the context of accommodating the new Member States within the framework of the CAP. During the Enlargement negotiations the UK delegation laid stress on the particular problems faced by hill farmers—a group which had received special aid in the UK for over twenty years previously. The purpose of the aid in the UK was to assist hill farmers to maintain a reasonable income, and it took the form of livestock headage payments, and more favourable terms for farm investment grants.

The issue was a controversial one in the context of the negotiations and not all the existing Member States were convinced of the need to make special Community provision for problem farming areas. From the UK point of view the provision of such assistance was a matter of some importance: firstly, because the existing hill aids were a significant element in UK agricultural policy and, secondly, because the extension of FEOGA aid to disadvantaged areas would have provided the UK with one of its few important sources of revenue from Community funds. Because the matter was politically sensitive it was handled very carefully in the negotiations and skirted round rather than discussed in any detail.

At one point in the negotiations Rippon, who was leading the UK side, made a curiously worded statement in which he outlined the situation concerning hill farming in the UK and added that he recognized that many of the existing members of the Community had areas with similar problems. He sought confirmation 'that it is necessary for all members of the enlarged Community who face situations of this kind to deal with the problem of maintaining reasonable incomes of farmers in such areas' (HMSO 1972, 127). The Community spokesman—Schumann—responded to this rather obscure statement with an equally curious one, in the course of which he acknowledged that 'the special conditions obtaining in certain areas of the enlarged Community may indeed require action with a view to attempting to resolve the problems raised by these special conditions and, in particular, to preserve reasonable incomes for farmers in such areas. Such action must . . . be in conformity with the provisions of the Treaty and the common agricultural policy' (ibid.).

The practical outcome of these vague statements was that in February 1973 the Commission presented the Council with a draft Directive on agriculture in mountain areas and in certain other poorer farming areas (Commission 1973(*a*)). In doing so, the Commission broadened the scope of the measure from the need to preserve reasonable incomes for farmers, which was the issue dealt with in the Treaty of Accession Declaration on hill farming (see above), to include the need for continued conservation of the countryside, and to offset the dangers inherent in depopulation of mountain and poor land areas. The handicaps faced by farmers in disadvantaged areas are permanent—poor soil quality, slope of the land, short growing season—and these lead to high production costs. This situation prevents farmers from achieving a level of income similar to that enjoyed by comparable farmers in other regions. The Commission felt that, given these circumstances, farmers in poorer areas were not adequately catered for under the modernization Directive and many could well be ineligible for the investment aids provided. As a result, one of the proposals was that disadvantaged farmers should receive more favourable treatment under Directive 72/159.

The main form of assistance proposed, however, was an annual compensatory grant, based on the number of livestock units kept, to be made to farmers with at least three hectares of utilized agricultural land who undertook to remain in farming for five years or more. The Member States were to decide at what level the actual payments would be made (within a predetermined band) based on the severity of the handicap faced by the farmer. The original proposals also contained the provision referred to earlier in the chapter that, in order to counteract the poor age structure in these areas, 'steps should be taken to encourage younger farmers to establish themselves . . . by granting them a premium on first establishment' (Commission 1973(*a*), 3). The Commission also proposed the provision of aid to joint investment schemes for such things as fodder production and land improvement. It proposed that the launching aid for mutual aid groups, available under Directive 72/159, should be replaced in disadvantaged areas by a permanent annual aid.

The Council moved with unaccustomed speed on the draft Directive and in May 1973 issued a Resolution on the subject (OJ C33, 23–5–73). However, even that early in the deliberations, the draft Directive was substantially weakened, in particular by the removal of the compulsory element in the aids proposed: Member States were to be free to implement the Directive or not as they wished, and in designated areas to implement only some of the measures proposed. The Council undertook to implement the Resolution by means of a Directive before 1 October 1973. This deadline was not kept and it was not until January 1974 that the Council adopted the Directive but with two issues still outstanding: the list of areas eligible for assistance, and the percentage of the Community contribution to the cost of the compensatory payments.[13]

Despite the apparent urgency of getting this Directive launched, it was not until December 1974 that, on the basis of information supplied by the Member States, the Commission submitted a proposal to the Council setting out the list of disadvantaged areas for each Member State, excluding Denmark—which had decided not to apply the Directive (Commission 1974(*c*)). The whole package, i.e. the basic Directive and the lists of eligible areas, was finally agreed by the Council in April 1975. It comprised Directive 75/268 *on mountain and hill farming and farming in certain less-favoured areas*, together with eight further Directives (75/269–276), one for each Member State except Denmark (OJ L128, 19–5–75). The final agreement on the percentage refund of eligible expenditure was a disappointment as it was fixed at 25 per cent compared with the original proposal of 50 per cent reimbursement.

The less-favoured areas (LFAs) are divided into three categories: mountain areas 'in which farming is necessary to protect the countryside, particularly for reasons of protection against erosion or in order to meet leisure needs'; areas in danger of depopulation 'and where the conservation of the countryside is necessary'; and other smaller areas which are affected by specific handicaps 'and in which farming must be continued in order to conserve the countryside and to preserve the tourist potential of the area or in order to protect the coastline' (Dir. 75/268, Article 3). In some cases the various aids available under the Directive differ according to the specific designation of the area into one of the above categories.

Although Dir. 75/268 was a policy innovation in that it was the first time that the Community had enacted a major piece of agricultural legislation specifically targeted at farmers working in difficult natural conditions, yet it was not a new idea. Provision was made under Article 42 of the Rome Treaty for such legislation and the description earlier in this chapter of the Community Plans and Programmes provides evidence of earlier thinking on the issue of disadvantage. The enactment of the Directive owed much to the circumstances of the 1973 Enlargement, as can be inferred from an answer given by the Commission to a European parliamentary question submitted in late 1973. Part of the question was concerned with ascertaining whether similar national schemes were already in force in the Community. The Commission's reply (OJ C39, 6–4–74) indicated that, apart from the UK, the only countries with disadvantaged areas schemes of any kind were Italy, Germany, and France. Where these schemes related to direct income subsidies (as opposed to schemes to give more favourable investment aids), the scale of the operations in the latter countries was far smaller than in the UK. Yet it was this direct income subsidy (or compensatory payment) which was to form by far the largest single element in the Directive. It is not surprising, therefore, that the UK has been a leading beneficiary from this Directive despite the relatively small size of its farming sector (see Table 9.1(*a*) and (*b*)).

Dir. 75/268 recognized that farmers in difficult natural conditions need assistance to compensate them for their location and that the aid provided should be quite separate from aid intended to raise efficiency. Unfortunately, as time was to demonstrate, the compensatory payments provided a production incentive which led to environmental damage to a fragile ecosystem. This is a topic which will be discussed further in Chapter 11.

Over the lifetime of this legislation, the area classified as less-favoured has expanded—not merely because of successive enlargements of the Community but also because the Member States have sought to expand these areas in order to allow more of their farmers to benefit from the special programmes of aid and to receive more favourable treatment under legislation intended to control output. In 1988, the ESC commented critically on this trend, stating that it opposed 'the tendency to over-extend the geographical areas of the disadvantaged regions in

Table 9.1(a). Dir. 75/268: Aid to farmers in LFAs, cumulatively to 1988

Member State	No. of farmers qualifying for the compensatory allowance	%	No. of joint investment schemes	Reimbursement by FEOGA cumulatively to end 1988	
				'000 ECU	%
Belgium	11,696	1.8	1,180	22,216	1.8
Germany	153,244	19.9	554	110,547	9.1
Greece	182,516	23.7	353	126,199	10.4
France	140,394	18.3	1,661	269,982	22.3
Ireland	91,557	11.9	15,146	206,425	17.1
Italy	130,275	16.9	1,454	144,900	12.0
Luxembourg	3,810	0.5	—	8,060	0.7
Netherlands	286	...	—	167	...
United Kingdom	53,996	7.0	220	321,971	26.6
Total	767,774	100.0	20,568	1,210,468	100.0

Source: Commission 1989(*h*).

Table 9.1(*b*). Reg. 797/85: Aid to farmers in LFAs, cumulatively to 1988

Member State	No. of farmers having received an annual compensatory allowance	%	No. of joint investments for fodder production	No. of investments for improving and equipping pasture farmed jointly	No. of small-scale irrigation projects	Reimbursement by FEOGA cumulatively to end 1988 '000 ECU	%
Belgium	8,928	0.7	40	—	—	4,880	0.9
Germany	225,733	18.5	—	64	—	176,006	34.4
Greece	287,081	23.5	—	488	—	36,170	7.1
Spain	286,164	23.5	4	439	96	42,384	8.3
France	130,322	10.9	340	606	26	77,871	15.3
Ireland	77,752	6.3	3	—	—	68,935	13.5
Italy	11,417	0.9	—	7	—	2,402	0.5
Luxembourg	2,676	0.2	—	—	—	4,421	0.9
Netherlands	318	...	—	—	—	58	...
Portugal	130,576	10.9	—	—	—	19,440	3.8
UK	56,066	4.6	186	—	—	78,521	15.4
Total	1,217,033	100.0	573	1,604	122	511,091	100.0

Source: Commission 1989(*h*).

some Member States as a way of offsetting the effects of milk quotas and market policy' (OJ C175, 4–7–88, 50).

The criteria of eligibility have been relaxed from time to time with the result that, by the early 1990s, about 55 per cent of the utilized agricultural area of the Community was classified as less favoured. This is a staggeringly high percentage which has implications for the management of the farming sector and the costs of operating the CAP. The LFAs are regarded as having a permanent handicap which means in effect that funds allocated to them are also permanent. This ties up a significant proportion of the funds available for structural assistance within the CAP. It also distorts the attempts to curb surplus production. No doubt the argument is that LFAs should be treated more leniently because these areas have natural restrictions on the range of products which can be produced and the levels of yields obtained. However, intensification of production has undoubtedly occurred in LFAs—particularly in cattle and sheep—encouraged by the link between production and compensatory payments.

These payments, and the derogations from the curbs on surplus production, have also inhibited the logic of the price and market policy, which should result in the shift of production to the areas most suited to the particular commodity. Income assistance to LFAs could have been provided in a manner which was not linked directly to production and which, therefore, would not have interfered with the process of rationalization. There is no evidence that any serious discussion of these issues has ever taken place.

As with the 1972 structural Directives, the legislation on LFAs was incorporated into the new Regulation 797/85, subsequently replaced by the consolidated Reg. 2328/91. Table 9.1(*a*) and (*b*) provides details of the number of farmers who benefited from LFA legislation under Dir. 75/268 and Reg. 797/85 to the end of 1988. The figures exclude the number of farmers who had development plans for which they received more favourable financial assistance. The two parts of the table are not strictly comparable. However, the overall picture is clear: the main aid provided to farmers in LFAs is the compensatory payment which is mostly paid on livestock numbers. The size of the payments to the UK is notable, particularly in relation to the small number of farmers involved. Ireland—a large livestock producer in relation to its size—also received a disproportionately large payment. The nature of this legislation clearly favours certain types of farmers in certain types of regions within the general LFA designation.[14]

Targeted Structural Aid: The Mediterranean

Earlier in this chapter reference was made to the fact that the operation of the CAP has been distorted not only because of the concentration of effort on prices and markets to the detriment of the socio-structural aspects of policy but also because of the way in which the commodity regimes themselves provide widely differing levels of internal support and frontier protection. By and large, the commodities which are typical of northern production (such as milk, cereals, and sugar beet) receive more favourable treatment than the products which are typical of the south (most notable in this group are fruit and vegetables). In a study undertaken for the Commission to examine the regional impact of the CAP, the situation was summarized as follows:

Without being able to attribute a decisive role to the CAP in aggravating growth imbalances in regional agricultural incomes, it can be confirmed:

- that the supports for agricultural production proportional to volume produced and the higher support given to milk, cereals and sugar have favoured the large and medium size farms of Northern Europe;
- on the other hand, the weakness of socio-structural policy to develop supports for production in regions of southern Europe and the lower support given to fruit and vegetable type products have been unable to remove the relative poverty of these regions. (Commission 1981(*d*), 81)

Although considerable efforts have been made to limit the impact of basic differences in the support mechanisms, this process only started in the 1980s. Almost as important, historically speaking, is the fact that the Community completed its move to a unified support system earlier for many of the northern-type commodities (i.e. 1966–8) than for some important southern products. In many cases, it was not until 1970–2 that a similar degree of integration was achieved for the latter. Given that the southern parts of the Community also suffered from the greatest natural handicaps and the highest population densities on the land, the absence of an effective structural policy combined with the limited support of the price and market policy did nothing to alleviate the low income problem in these areas.

The apparent neglect of the south can be linked to Italy's lack of political influence in the Council of Ministers. It will be recalled from Chapter 2 how FEASA—the original structural fund—died at the hands of the Council of Ministers, largely at the instigation of Germany which was unwilling (as it saw it) to pay for structural improvements in the south of Italy, while at the same time paying for financing the market and price policy for the benefit of France. The subsequent limitation of FEOGA-Guidance funds to the ceiling imposed under Reg. 130/66 (also referred to in Chapter 2) was a further blow to Italy's hopes on the structural front. The slow introduction of commodity regimes for southern products illustrates another facet of Italy's limited negotiating strength: the special payments made to her under Reg. 130/66 were but a small recognition that her treatment in the early days of the Community was unfavourable.

The change in Italy's bargaining fortunes came in the latter half of the 1970s, when the prospect of Enlargement to include Greece, Portugal, and Spain brought France on to Italy's side. The French increasingly played their southern card with as much skill and adroitness as they had previously displayed in pursuing the interests of their northern farmers. Another important development was the attention which the Community was giving to its policy towards countries in the Mediterranean outside the Community, in particular to those of the North African littoral.

The international economic crisis of the early 1970s hit peripheral areas of the Community hard: the downturn in economic activity, the rise in inflation and unemployment focused the Commission's attention on the Mediterranean, and it began a detailed study of the area in 1975. The following year, the Council requested the Commission to draw up a report on the Mediterranean and to submit it, with any proposals for legislation which it thought necessary, to the Council without delay. The Commission communicated its findings to the Council in a series of documents in 1977. This flurry of activity had not come a moment too soon, as Greece had applied for membership of the Community in 1975, and Portugal and Spain had applied in 1977.

The basic document (COM(77)140) is disappointing and sketchy—a point taken up by the ESC in its Opinion on the package of Commission documents. It remarked that it was 'deplorable that no comprehensive analysis of the economic and social situation of the Community's Mediterranean area has been made in support of the policy the Commission is proposing' (OJ C114, 7–5–79, 28). The definition of 'Mediterranean' in COM(77)140 is rather *ad hoc*: based on climatic conditions alone it included most of Italy and south-eastern France, but to this climatic criterion was added a second, based on the share of certain products in the total agricultural production of the area. These products were durum wheat, vegetables, flowers, tobacco, wine, olive oil, fruit (excluding apples), citrus, and sheepmeat. Where these equalled at least 40 per cent of total agricultural production, the area was classified as 'Mediterranean'. In 1977, the regions so defined in total contained 15.6m. ha. of utilizable agricultural land, with 1.8m. holdings, and 2.6m. people engaged in farm work. This area represented 17 per cent of the land, and 30 per cent of the holdings and farm population of the Community (Commission 1977(*c*)).

The definition of 'Mediterranean' is unsatisfactory in that it suggests that any region could lose its status if it merely diversified away from Mediterranean-type products, thereby lowering the percentage below 40 (in itself a strange and no doubt arbitrary figure), while at the same time its level of underemployment, unemployment, income, and dependence on agriculture as a whole remained unchanged! Presumably, equally illogically, any region which met the climatic criterion could have itself reclassified as Mediterranean merely by raising its dependence on the group of commodities listed above.

The Commission stated that the problem of the Mediterranean was a combination of factors, some in agriculture (socio-structural, marketing, and production) but also in manufacturing and services. Yet, despite this, all the measures discussed in COM(77)140 related solely to the agricultural sector. This partial approach has been one of the long-standing inadequacies in policy as it relates to rural areas and, despite the recognition by the Commission of the extent of the social and economic problems in the Mediterranean area, it did not take any steps at that time to promote a more broadly based solution. The structural measures suggested related to irrigation, producer groups, restructuring of vineyards, the provision of agricultural advisory services where they were lacking, and raising the level of FEOGA reimbursement for existing schemes. The Commission also suggested a number of market measures for olive oil, wine, protein-rich beans, sheepmeat, and fruit and vegetables.

COM(77)140 was followed by the 'Guidelines concerning the development of the Mediterranean regions of the Community' in two volumes (Commission 1977(*e*) and (*f*)). Volume 1 consists largely in a further attempt to set out the difficulties facing the Mediterranean regions of the Community, while volume 2 contained the actual text of most of the proposed Mediterranean legislation referred to above. Why the document is called 'Guidelines' is hard to see, as it consists very largely of a sequence of inadequately substantiated statements about the conditions prevailing in the Community's Mediterranean regions. There is little indication that the Commission had developed some coherent overview of the contemporary situation on the basis of which it was proposing an integrated and logically consistent programme of measures to solve the problems confronting these regions.

The Commission drew attention to the need to avoid a conflict with measures intended to reduce structural surpluses, and the need to avoid the creation of new surpluses or greater levels of protection. It is very debatable whether the measures proposed to improve the market organization for fruit and vegetables, wine, and olive oil exactly matched these intentions. Equally, on the structural side, it could be argued that encouragement of irrigation and the provision of an agricultural advisory service where such was lacking were more likely to increase production than to reduce it, and there was no guarantee that such an increase would be limited to products in deficit.

The ESC Opinion (referred to above) was very critical of the Commission. It drew attention to the slow progress made in presenting the proposals, pointing out that the Commission itself maintained it had been working on Mediterranean policy since 1975: 'the Committee cannot understand why it has taken 18 months to work out a blueprint which is confined to the agricultural sector and consequently inadequate'. It deplored[15] the absence of any consideration of the possible Enlargement of the Community to include Greece, Portugal, and Spain. The ESC wished the Community to implement comprehensive programmes and warned that action needed to 'concentrate on causes rather than symptoms, so as to give the Mediterranean areas the chance of balanced development in line with the rest of the Community' (OJ C114, 7–5–79, 29).

The outcome of the Mediterranean initiative was a package of structural measures, enacted in 1978 and 1979, together with the adaptation of some existing legislation to provide better investment incentives in Mediterranean regions, and the strengthening of some of the market regimes to provide greater internal support and frontier protection for the producers of typically Mediterranean commodities. The infrastructural measures in this package are outlined below and in Appendix Table 9.A1 at the end of the chapter, while the schemes to encourage the formation of producer groups are outlined in Chapter 10.

As with the structural schemes in general, analysis of the impact of the Mediterranean package is hampered by the limited information available from Commission sources. The data collected together in Table 9.A1 suggest that, in relation to the problems identified, the schemes were of little impact. The level of aid granted from FEOGA was not great and some of the schemes were subject to administrative shortcomings. For instance, the training and installation of agricultural advisers in Italy (Reg. 270/79, OJ L38, 14–2–79) ran into major organizational difficulties and delays which necessitated its extensive modification in 1987. Training the trainers only started in 1983 and the actual training of advisers only began in 1985 (Commission 1989(*d*)). The irrigation scheme on Corsica was intended to provide improved irrigation for up to 15,000 ha. over a five-year period (Commission 1978(*c*)) but by the end of 1987—as indicated in Table 9.A1(*a*)—only 3,146 ha. had been completed, with a further 215 ha. in progress. This poor performance was attributed by the Commission to organizational difficulties and a lack of national funds. On its expiry the scheme was continued within the Integrated Mediterranean Programme (IMP) for Corsica, but implementation remained a problem (Commission 1988(*e*)).

The size of the response to the Mediterranean problem was clearly inadequate, as the plethora of small-scale schemes summarized in Table 9.A1 amply illustrates. Greece joined the Community in 1981, thereby adding to the southern axis and, although a small economy, was one with many structural, social, and production-based difficulties. The further Enlargement to include Portugal and Spain still had to be faced. In its Report on the Mandate of 30 May 1980, the Commission singled out the Mediterranean region for particular mention, and announced that it intended to propose 'a number of medium-term Community programmes covering an integrated policy for incomes, markets, production and structures' (Bull.EC Supp. 1–81, 13).

The Commission followed up this announcement when, in March 1983, it issued a discussion document which outlined a series of programmes to improve the agricultural sector (both on-farm and in the processing of agricultural products), and to stimulate economic activity in other sectors, with a view to providing employment for people leaving farming, or to provide an additional source of income for those remaining in agriculture (Commission 1983(*a*)). The areas in which these programmes were to operate differed somewhat from the areas defined as 'Mediterranean' in 1977 and, of course, Greece was included.

The Commission put forward individual programmes for the whole of the designated areas in each country (France, Greece, and Italy). These were very detailed in nature, something which was reflected a few months later in the draft legislation sent to the Council (Commission 1983(*c*)). By the time—two years later—that the legislation was enacted, the approach had changed significantly: the Commission was no longer the designer of the programmes, that task had been transferred to the Member States. Reg. 2088/85 (OJ L197, 27–7–85) provided a financial and organizational framework within which the Member States were to draw up programmes for submission to the Commission. These could include projects to assist agriculture, fisheries, manufacturing, services, and training in accordance with guidelines set out in an annexe to the Regulation. Funding was drawn from all the structural funds (Regional, Social, and

FEOGA-Guidance), the European Investment Bank (EIB), and the New Community Instrument (NCI).

The Community was committed to a financial contribution of 2,500m. ECU from the Structural Funds over a seven-year period, an additional 1,600m. ECU from the general Budget under a special allocation, and access to 2,500m. ECU in loans from the EIB and the NCI. Interestingly—and unusually—the total (6,600m. ECU) was almost exactly what the Commission had estimated the cost would be when it made the original proposals in 1983—although expressed in terms of five years, and there was no mention of loans. The proposal had been based on a 40 : 60 split between agriculture and other activities. The Regulation made no mention of the sectoral breakdown. Given the sums of money allocated under the Regulation, it is clear that the intention was to make a significant investment in the Mediterranean region.

The management structure set up to agree the Integrated Mediterranean Programmes (IMPs) and monitor their implementation was a complex one, involving not only the Commission and the national and regional authorities in the Member States, but also an Advisory Committee, and a Monitoring Committee.16 Implementation of the IMPs was regulated by a contract concluded between the relevant parties (Commission, Member States, regional or other authorities). It was inevitable that this cumbersome structure would lead to delays and would expose most cruelly the administrative inadequacies in some of the poorest parts of the Community.

The Commission was required to make an annual report on the operation of the Regulation, the first of which was issued in 1988. This provides a detailed explanation of the procedures adopted in the drawing up and implementation of the IMPs, and an outline of the IMPs which had already been established. By the end of 1987, all French and Greek IMPs had been approved (seven in each country) but only one in Italy (Commission 1988(*h*)). The remaining fourteen IMPs in Italy were sanctioned in 1988. As with so many structural measures, while it is possible to find some statistical information concerning the amount of funds committed or paid in each year (see Table 9.A1(*b*), (*d*), and (*e*)), it is much more difficult to find information on the impact which the IMPs made.

The first report to provide some evaluation of the Programmes was that relating to 1989, which outlined the operation of the French IMPs (Commission 1991(*g*)). Less informative summaries were provided in the 1990 report for Greece and Italy (Commission 1992(*c*)). However, as no indication was given of the size of the problem to be alleviated, it is impossible to evaluate the relative impact which the various schemes had on the local economy. As is so often the case, considerable difficulties were experienced with the implementation of the IMPs in Italy. While the central and northern regions were reasonably well organized, implementation in the south (the Mezzogiorno) was very disappointing, to the extent that the Commission threatened to withdraw some of the funds (Commission 1991(*g*)). Table 9.2 provides a summary of the financial commitments and payments for the IMPs cumulatively to the end of 1992. This indicates that implementation had made the greatest progress in Greece (which had

Table 9.2. Integrated Mediterranean Programmes: Financial situation at the end of 1992

	Programmed m. ECU (1)	Commitments m. ECU (2)	Payments m. ECU (3)	%		
				2/1	3/1	3/2
French IMPs	843.5	752.8	644.4	89	76	86
Italian IMPs	1,256.5	759.5	425.5	60	34	56
Greek IMPs	2,000.0	1,941.6	1,783.2	97	89	92
Total	4,100.0	3,453.9	2,853.1	84	70	83

Source: Commission 1993(*c*).

received the largest allocation of funds). The poor performance of Italy under all headings is very obvious.

Deficiencies in national and regional administration is an important issue in the context of narrowing the income gap between rich and poor regions. Attempts to promote the philosophy of subsidiarity, i.e. that action should take place at the lowest appropriate level of administrative aggregation, is a dangerous philosophy if the institutional structures do not function effectively.[17] The likelihood of poor performance is enhanced in the poorer Member States and, within them, in the poorer regions. Italy is not alone in experiencing this problem. Evolution of power back to the Member States could actually prolong the time needed to achieve economic integration.

As new southern Member States joined the Community, structural measures intended to help reform their farming sector were introduced. Some took the form of an extension of existing measures to the new Member State, while others were specially designed for the country or region concerned. Where possible, these measures have been included in Table 9.A1(*a*, *c*, *e*, and *f*). Within the bewildering array of targeted structural measures introduced from the late 1970s onwards, undoubtedly the IMPs were one of the more interesting. In their organization they were a foretaste of the changed approach to structural assistance following the reorganization of the structural funds in 1988 (outlined in Chapter 11). The development of framework programmes and the participation of more than one fund in their financing is now an established practice but, in 1985, it was a considerable innovation.

Targeted Structural Aid: Non-Mediterranean Areas

At the same time as the Commission was issuing its first discussion documents on the Mediterranean in 1977, it was also undertaking a review of the operation of the 1972 structural Directives and the 1975 LFA Directive. It was already aware that the effect of much of the structural policy then in operation was to favour the better regions and the more prosperous farmers—even in LFAs. In addition, the poorer Member States were experiencing difficulty in finding the national element of the financial cost of the various measures. This was not a situation in which the regional disparities in income in farming were likely to be reduced. The narrowing of the regional income gap was a goal of particular importance in the late 1970s, when the Community was trying to restore normality to the exchange rates after years of turmoil.

Currency stability was a necessary first step if the Community was ever to achieve its long-postponed objective of economic and monetary union. In that context, it was essential to begin to narrow the gap between rich and poor regions. Some poor regions were, of course, urban—in particular those which had been heavily dependent on a declining industry, or the depressed inner city areas suffering from serious economic and social dysfunction. Many poor regions were, however, rural and dominated by farming. It is often difficult for people who have spent their lives in urban areas to appreciate that deprivation can exist in areas which appear superficially visually attractive, but such is the case.

Apart from the Mediterranean region, the Commission identified Ireland as an area requiring targeted assistance. As a result, in the late 1970s and early 1980s, a series of measures was introduced which concentrated on the west of Ireland, the border areas of both Ireland and Northern Ireland, the LFA in Northern Ireland, and improvements to cattle production in both areas. Appendix Table 9.A2 summarizes these various schemes. However, it must be said that, as a response to the regional income differences within the Community, targeted assistance to the Mediterranean and the island of Ireland was hardly adequate. It is not surprising, therefore, that in 1979 the Commission put forward a package of measures which was clearly intended to cater for the needs of a greater number of Member States, all of which had structural projects they wished to see part-financed by the Community. It was quite a mixture, some of the programmes were for improvements in the production of a particular commodity, some were adjustments to existing legislation. However, in concept, the most interesting group of measures was the Integrated Development Programmes (IDPs) for the Western Isles of Scotland, the department of Lozère in France, and the province of Luxembourg in Belgium[18] (Commission 1979(*b*)).

In practice, the IDPs were a strange idea. They were intended to improve not only agriculture but also other sectors (e.g. fisheries, tourism, crafts, and small-scale industry) but the only funding proposed was from FEOGA-Guidance and the purposes for which these funds could be used were all related to agriculture. There was a strong hint in the preamble to the legislation that the European Social Fund and the European Regional Development Fund were expected to contribute in their own way to the development of the regions in question—but nothing more. This funding vagueness was avoided when the IMPs (outlined in the previous Section) were set up some years later.

The ESC was extremely sceptical about many aspects of the 1979 package and highly critical of some of the projects proposed. While it approved of the concept of the IDPs, it was dubious about the choice of region and the criteria used. The regions were very different one from another and, while it acknowledged that useful lessons might be learned from the establishment and operation of such a programme, the Committee stressed 'that a regionalized structural policy should not lead to a state of affairs where areas of intervention are determined by political factors' (OJ C53, 3–3–80, 37).

This is an important point: there is a danger in structural policy that each Member State tries to ensure that it derives a benefit from the limited funds available, even though the needs of others may be greater in an absolute sense. The result is that resources may be too thinly spread, financing schemes that are too small to make any discernible difference to the economic viability of the region or the sector. Apart from the clear political motivation of the individual Member States, there is a genuine economic point: people live within their own society, and poverty, whether personal or regional, is measured in that context. Thus the need to narrow the income gap between regions of the Union is matched by the need to narrow the gap within the Member States, and the latter is often more immediately important than the former.

At the European Council meeting in November 1979, it was agreed that steps should be taken to strengthen the less prosperous Member States, and to reduce the economic disparities between the countries of the Community. It was also agreed that Community action in relation to agricultural structural policy needed to be strengthened, particularly in view of the anticipated Enlargement (Bull. EC 11–1979). This extremely vague agreement was open to all sorts of interpretation —as was very quickly demonstrated.

A classic example of a politically motivated aid to a rich Member State was the introduction of a measure to improve public amenities (i.e. water control and rural roads) in some of the LFAs in the Federal Republic of Germany (Reg. 1938/81, OJ L197, 20–7–81), as part of the structural package first proposed in 1979, although this German measure was not in the original package. The estimated cost to FEOGA-Guidance of this aid to Germany was 45m. ECU, which contrasted with the 85m. ECU for the development of agriculture in the French overseas departments (DOM) in the same package. These islands are among the poorest regions of the Community and yet they did not appear either in the original proposal! No doubt the Germans would have argued that, as a major contributor to the Budget, they should have benefited from the new package and they were able to demonstrate that, within the context of their economy, the LFAs concerned had deficiencies in their infrastructure. But this example does raise interesting questions as to the proper use of structural funds. The IDPs came into operation as part of the same package (OJ L197, 20–7–81), and Appendix Table 9.A3 summarizes the FEOGA contribution to them (Table 9.A3(*a*)–(*c*)) and to the other targeted regions in the 1981 package.

Later in 1981, in the *Guidelines* for European agriculture, the Commission repeated the need to concentrate structural funds on deficient farms and LFAs, with expenditure on such measures rising to two-thirds of FEOGA-Guidance (Commission 1981(*c*)). In the following few years, discussions got under way on the reform of the structural funds generally. In agriculture, there was an enormous range of schemes in operation. Apart from the major schemes—Dirs.

72/159 and 75/268 (on farm modernization and LFAs) which were replaced by Reg. 797/85—there were the targeted schemes outlined above and in the previous Section, and a series of schemes intended to improve and reorganize production and marketing (see Chapter 10).[19]

In 1983, the Commission drew attention to the fact that:

the funds available have not kept pace with the diversification of tasks, and this has forced the authorities to insert into the regulations a considerable number of technical limits which are not necessarily compatible with the objectives pursued; the result has been that the money has had to be spread out too thinly over too wide an area. (Commission 1983(*e*), 9)

One of the major difficulties was that a handful of measures absorbed a very high proportion of the total funds. The Commission cited the example of the LFAs Directive which, in 1983, accounted for 47 per cent of commitments for measures in disadvantaged regions. The remaining funds were 'spread over 24 regional programmes ranging from forestry or irrigation work to the integrated development programme for particular rural regions, and including the programmes to encourage farmers to convert out of surplus products' (Commission 1983(*e*), 9).

This piecemeal approach continued due, in large part, to the successive Enlargements of the Community in the 1980s and the need to extend to the new Member States certain structural measures already in force or to provide them with specially designed measures to fit their particular needs. In addition, certain LFAs in France, northern Italy, and Scotland were granted aid for infrastructural and commodity improvements analogous to many already in place in some other Member States.[20] This type of 'copycat' legislation has been a feature of structural policy down the years. Member States have found that such schemes provide them with a political advantage at home without arousing opposition from other Member States. The Community cost is low and Member States are careful not to oppose these schemes lest they themselves may wish to benefit from something similar at a later date. In 1988, the Community agreed to a new approach for all the structural funds but the legacy of the previous system lingers on, until such time as all the payments for the earlier targeted schemes have been made, or the schemes are integrated into the post-1988 framework, outlined in Chapter 11.

NOTES

1. The remainder of this Section is a distillation of the issues raised in Part II of COM(60)105 (Commission 1960).
2. These are issues which are specifically referred to in Art. 41(a) of the Rome Treaty.
3. The link between these proposals and the deficiencies of the farming sector set out in COM(60)105 (Commission 1960) is unmistakable.

4. These schemes are discussed in Ch. 10.

5. The age profile of farmers is more biased towards the upper age-groups than that of the sector as a whole (see Table 3.A3, Ch. 3). There are proportionately more family members and hired workers in the younger age-groups, as farmers usually do not take over a farm until they are in their thirties or forties.

6. The Parliament actually went much further and recommended that there should be a special policy for young people to include—among other things—study grants. The Commission must have derived some wry amusement from this suggestion, as it had been made as long ago as the 1960 proposals on the CAP, and had been repeated in the Mansholt Plan in 1968!

7. The price of land was, of course, inflated by the operation of the price and market policy itself.

8. Even if the membership of the Council of Ministers may have changed, there were members of the Commission staff who had been involved with the 1960s proposals!

9. Contrast e.g. the support for the textile fibres flax and hemp—traditional northern European arable crops—with support for oriental tobacco—a traditional southern European crop grown in regions with very limited production options.

10. A semi-agricultural region was defined as one in which 10–20% of the workforce was directly employed in agriculture.

11. In the event, this meant Ireland and Italy, see Ch. 8 n. 14.

12. *Fonds européen de bonifications d'intérêts pour le developpement régional.* In spirit, this proposed Fund owed much to the concept of the ill-fated FEASA of 1963.

13. There seems to be some confusion over the date on which the Council adopted this Directive. In OJ C39, 6–4–74 it is given by the Commission as 20 Nov. 1973 yet elsewhere (as, for instance, in COM(74)2222 final) the date is given as 21 Jan. 1974. This latter seems the more likely.

14. The extremely low figure for compensatory payments in Italy under Reg. 797/85 is due to the fact that payments were made under that Regulation for the first time only in 1988. This suggests that, once again, the Italian administration was slow in organizing the implementation of the new legislation.

15. The irritation of the ESC with the Commission documents is very evident from the frequency of the use of the verb 'to deplore' and the noun 'deplorable' in its Opinion.

16. The Advisory Committee consisted of representatives of all the Member States and the European Investment Bank, under the chairmanship of the Commission and its function was similar to that of a commodity Management Committee under the price and market policy. The Monitoring Committees were set up for each IMP and were intended to ensure the proper integration of all the activities across sectoral boundaries.

17. Under the Maastricht Treaty of 1992, an addition was made to the Treaty of Rome which stated that: 'In areas which do not fall within its exclusive competence, the Community shall take action, in accordance with the principle of subsidiarity, only if and in so far as the objectives of the proposed action cannot be sufficiently achieved by the Member States and can therefore, by reason of the scale or effects of the proposed action, be better achieved by the Community' (Art. 3(b) of the Rome Treaty). There has been a tendency, most notably in Britain, to extend this principle to areas where it is not appropriate.

18. Not to be confused with the independent country of Luxembourg. Later the IDP was changed to the less-favoured areas of Belgium.

19. That was not all: there was a whole series of measures of an emergency nature to help

groups of farmers severely affected by natural disasters, measures to eradicate livestock diseases, and to assist with the cost of statistical surveys. None of these measures is discussed here.
20. Regs. 1400/86–1402/86 (OJ L128, 14–5–86).

Table 9.A1. Structural aid specific to the Mediterranean cumulatively for the years stated

(a) Hydraulic works

(i) Reg. 1362/78: On . . . collective irrigation works in the Mezzogiorno

No. of projects 1980–4	Aid granted to end 1988 '000 ECU	Total investment '000 ECU
5	265,435	755,982

(ii) Reg. 2968/83: On . . . collective irrigation works in Greece

No. of projects 1984–5	Aid granted to end 1985 '000 ECU	Total investment '000 ECU
4	16,083	46,164

(iii) Dir. 79/173: On . . . irrigation works in Corsica[a]

No. of beneficiaries	Irrigated area (ha.)		Reimbursement to end 1987 '000 ECU
	completed	in progress	
662	3,146	215	2,689

[a] subsumed into Reg. 2088/85 concerning the IMPs: no detailed statistics available

(iv) Dir. 79/174: Concerning the flood protection programme in the Hèrault valley

	Reimbursement to end 1988 '000 ECU
Dams and additional works	3,168

Sources: Commission 1988(*e*), 1989(*h*).

(b) Public amenities

(i) Reg. 1760/78: To improve public amenities in certain rural areas

Member State	No. of projects 1980–5	Aid granted to end 1985 '000 ECU	Total investment '000 ECU
France	461	47,487	124,360
Italy	679	163,576	359,470
Total	1,140[a]	184,063	483,830

[a] 831 projects were completed by end 1988 (377 in France, 454 in Italy); 35 projects were not carried out, leaving 274 projects still in progress (71 in France, 203 in Italy)

(ii) Reg. 1760/78 subsumed into Reg. 2088/85 concerning the IMPs, results cumulatively to end 1988

Member State	No. of projects 1986–8	Aid granted to end 1988 '000 ECU	Total investment '000 ECU
France	127	17,932	46,412
Italy	13	12,072	30,518
Total	140	30,004	76,930

Source: SEC(89)1984 Commission 1989(*h*).

(c) Agricultural advisory services

(i) Reg. 270/79: On the development of agricultural advisory services in Italy

	No. of beneficiaries	Reimbursement to end 1988 '000 ECU
Training	22	164.7
Interregional bodies incl. centres	5	463.9
Course attendance allowance	164	362.9
Total		991.5

(ii) Reg. 2966/83: Development of agricultural advisory services in Greece

	Reimbursement to end 1987 '000 ECU
Training of advisors	194
Employment of advisors	2,340
Total	2,534

Sources: Commission 1988(*e*), 1989(*h*).

(d) Forestry

(i) Reg. 269/79: Forestry in certain Mediterranean zones of the Community

Member State	No. of projects 1980–5	Aid granted '000 ECU	Total investment '000 ECU
France	24	89,538	181,928
Italy	61	197,088	426,413
Total	85[a]	286,626	608,341

[a] 12 projects in France and 44 projects in Italy were completed by end 1988

(ii) Reg. 269/79 subsumed into Reg. 2088/85 concerning the IMPs, results cumulatively to end 1988

	No. of projects 1986–8	Aid granted to end 1988	Total investment '000 ECU
France	9	23,887	55,622
Italy	5	19,837	39,673
Total	14	43,724	95,295

Source: Commission 1989(*h*).

(e) Special development programmes in Greece

(i) Reg. 1975/82: Agricultural development in certain regions of Greece

Measures	Reimbursement to end 1988 '000 ECU
Rural infrastructure	36,971
Irrigation	17,080
Land improvements	9,141
Cattle, sheep, and goat farming	2,884
Equipment related to agr. training	539
Forestry improvement	39,853
Total	106,468

(ii) Reg 2088/85: Integrated Mediterranean Programmes in Greece

Measure	Reimbursement to end 1988 '000 ECU					
	Crete[a]	Western Greece/ Peloponnese	Northern Greece	Aegean	Central/ Eastern Greece	Other areas of Greece
Electrification	389.9	772.6	1,556.1	231.7	1,579.1	173.5
Roads	1,081.2	84.5	932.2	481.9	429.8	—
Irrigation	5,050.0	1,346.6	5,543.9	78.5	1,110.5	29.6
Forestry	560.7	248.9	10,229.4	517.3	562.5	547.3
Advisory work	437.3	1,860.8	1,623.8	460.1	1,038.4	154.8
Water	—	696.2	518.7	—	—	
Total	7,518.9	5,009.5	20,418.1	1,769.5	4,720.4	905.3

[a] old Reg. 619/84 and Reg. 2966/83

Source: Commission 1989(*h*).

(f) Special development programme in Portugal

(i) Reg. 3828/85: Special programme for the development of agriculture in Portugal

Measures	Reimbursement 1988 '000 ECU
Advisory services, training, agr. research	3,626
Improving efficiency of agricultural structures	1,323
Improving the structure of land ownership	—
Physical improvement	17,828
Land improvement	1,160
Forestry measures	8,337
Total	32,274

Source: Commission 1989(*h*).

Table 9.A2. Structural schemes in Ireland and Northern Ireland

(a) Dir. 78/628 and Reg. 2195/81: Drainage operations in . . . the West of Ireland

No. of beneficiaries	Area (ha.)	Reimbursement to end 1988 '000 ECU
31,945	221,614	57,700.4

(b) Reg. 1820/80: For the stimulation of
agricultural development in . . . the West
of Ireland

No. beneficiaries/projects	Reimbursement to end 1988 '000 ECU
94,936	70,072.2

(c) Dir. 79/197: On a programme to
promote drainage . . . on both sides of the
border between Ireland and Northern
Ireland

	Reimbursement to end 1988 '000 ECU
Ireland	3,268.8
UK	5,599.4
Total	8,868.2

(d) Reg. 1942/81: Agricultural development
in the LFAs of Northern Ireland

No. beneficiaries/projects	Reimbursement to end 1988 '000 ECU
9,600	38,666.7

(e) Reg. 1054/81: Development of beef cattle production in
Ireland and Northern Ireland

Member State	No. beneficiaries/projects	Reimbursement to end 1988 '000 ECU
Ireland	600,744	26,134.5
UK	92,473	4,850.8
Total	693,417	30,985.3

Source: Commission 1989(*h*).

Table 9.A3. Integrated Development Programmes and other structural measures enacted in 1981, excluding measures to improve production and marketing and those already covered in Table 9.A2

(a) Reg. 1939/81: IDP for the Western Isles of Scotland

No. beneficiaries/projects	Reimbursement to the end of 1988 '000 ECU
11,384	12,112.1

(b) Reg. 1940/81: IDP, Lozère, France

Measures	Reimbursement to the end of 1988 '000 ECU
Land/pasture improvement	2,079.4
Land consolidation	806.1
Cattle and sheep farming	1,389.5
Renewal of chestnut production	9.2
Winter isolation	3.6
Forest clearings	69.5
Cost of development work	132.3
Total	4,489.6

(c) Reg. 1941/81: IDP for the LFAs in Belgium cumulatively 1985–8

No. of projects	Aid granted '000 ECU	Total investment '000 ECU
23[a]	1,223.0	3,888.0

[a] of which 10 projects were completed and 13 in progress

(d) Reg. 1938/81: To improve public amenities in certain LFAs of the Federal Republic of Germany cumulatively 1982–7

No. of projects	Aid granted '000 ECU	Total investment '000 ECU
157[a]	44,885.0	157,437.0

[a] of which 113 completed, 1 not carried out, 43 in progress

(e) Dir. 81/527: On the development of agriculture in the French overseas departments (DOM)

Measures	Reimbursement to the end of 1988 '000 ECU
Irrigation	10,767.9
Infrastructure	33,830.1
Soil improvement	13,308.3
Forestry	3,310.3
Guidance/diversification of production	6,077.4
Total	67,294.0

(f) Reg. 1944/81: Adaptation and modernization of the structure of production of beef and veal, sheepmeat and goatmeat in Italy

Measures	Reimbursment to the end of 1988 '000 ECU
Modernization, rationalization and construction of cattle accommodation	8,374.9
Purchase of production machinery	9,486.1
Improvement of meadows, grassland, pastures and fencing	3,946.5
Premiums for beef calves	551.4
Premiums for the retention of cows	743.5
Total	23,102.4

Source: Commission 1989(*h*).

10

Improvements in the Organization of Production and Marketing

Structural Aid under Regulation 17/64

Reference has been made in earlier chapters to Reg. 17/64 *on the conditions for granting aid from the European Agricultural Guidance and Guarantee Fund* (Sp. OJ 1963–1964): in particular in Chapter 2 in setting out the requirements which a project had to meet before it qualified for structural aid, and in Chapter 9 where the Community Programmes were outlined. These Programmes should have provided the sectoral and regional framework for aid but, as already indicated, they were never put in place and the derogation in Reg. 17/64, which allowed individual projects to be grant-aided for the first two years, continued throughout the lifetime of this Regulation, i.e. to the end of the 1970s.

Article 11 of Reg. 17/64 set out the broad purposes for which FEOGA-Guidance funds would be available. They were:

(a) the adaptation and improvement of conditions of production in agriculture;
(b) the adaptation and guidance of agricultural production;
(c) the adaptation and improvement of the marketing of agricultural products;
(d) the development of outlets for agricultural products.

Marketing projects were limited to products which were subject to common price and market regimes but, as the range of commodities within the price policy expanded, this was no obstacle. Article 12 provided an interpretation of the four categories listed in Article 11 and it is interesting, even at such an early stage in the history of the CAP, that 'the adaptation and guidance of production' meant 'the quantitative adaptation of production to outlets' and 'improvements in the quality of the products' (ibid. Art. 12.2).

During the 1960s—and indeed for a large part of the 1970s—Reg. 17/64 provided the main source of funds for structural reform. The range of activities covered by the Regulation was very wide, encompassing production and marketing projects, and those which were a mixture of the two. Over the lifetime of the Regulation, projects to improve production structures received 53 per cent of the funding, marketing structures 41 per cent, and mixed projects 6 per cent (Commission 1980(*b*)). The Community contribution to the investment was initially very low at 25 per cent for all projects but, in 1973, this was raised to 45 per cent of eligible expenditure in projects related to production, with the beneficiary only having to provide a minimum of 20 per cent of the cost (originally a

Table 10.1. Reg. 17/64: Breakdown of aid granted by sector, cumulatively 1964–1979

Sector	No. of projects	Total 1964–79 ('000 ua/EUA)	
		Aid granted	%
Land improvement and hydraulic works	2,417	683,602	32.3
Milk	709	241,227	11.4
Wine	727	245,461	11.6
Fruit and vegetables	685	137,456	6.5
Meat	775	226,176	10.7
Olives	214	45,139	2.1
Cereals	203	55,061	2.6
Forestry	227	59,790	2.8
Fisheries	475	86,210	4.1
Animal feed	124	40,174	1.9
Flowers and plants	56	15,884	0.8
Eggs and poultrymeat	110	20,362	1.0
Seeds and nurseries	87	16,009	0.8
Research and advisory services	98	24,264	1.1
Sugar	3	4,188	0.2
Miscellaneous	546	214,143	10.1
	7,456	2,115,146	100.0

Source: Commission 1980(*b*).

minimum of 30 per cent).[1] Thus, right from the beginning, the Community element in structural legislation was low, unlike the price and market policy where, by the end of the 1960s, FEOGA-Guarantee was providing 100 per cent of the support. However, it should be noted that, for structural measures generally, the tendency over time has been for the Community contribution to rise, particularly in the poorer regions or in the poorer Member States.

During its lifetime, Reg. 17/64 was extremely popular and far more projects were submitted for funding each year than were ultimately aided. Table 10.1 provides a summary of the sectoral distribution of aid, 1964–1979. Three sectors —milk, wine, and meat—accounted for one-third of the aid; land improvement and hydraulic works accounted for about another third; and all other purposes the remainder.

Reference was made in Chapter 8 to concerns expressed in the 1970s that structural policy was not acting as a counterweight to the price and market policy but was in fact re-enforcing the latter. The result was that the better-off farmers and the more prosperous farming regions were benefiting disproportionately from all aspects of the CAP. An interdepartmental group within the Commission reported *inter alia* on this issue (Commission 1976(*d*)), and its findings in relation to the regional impact of Dir. 72/159 have already been discussed. As to the regional impact of Reg. 17/64, if it had been operating as originally intended, each Community Programme would have had specified zones of principal action within which investment aid would have been concentrated. The Commission had estimated that, as a general rule, these zones would have represented about one-third of the designated area or other appropriate measure, such as volume of production (Commission 1967(*b*)).

In reality, in Reg. 17/64, there was no provision for regional differentiation of aid, rather the funds available were allocated to the Member States according to a prearranged system of quotas. Thus, prior to Enlargement, Italy received annually an allocation of just under 34 per cent of available credits, Germany 28 per cent, France 22 per cent, and so forth. These percentages were adjusted downwards to accommodate the three new Member States after 1972. The interdepartmental group was interested to examine how these national quotas had operated in practice and to compare them with the percentage distribution among the Member States of: (a) the agricultural labour force; (b) final agricultural production; (c) the simple average of (a) and (b), which in effect gave production weighted by the inverse of agricultural labour productivity; and (d) agricultural area. In no case did the quota exactly match any of these measures, although it came reasonably close to (c). For some countries the divergence was considerable—which was hardly surprising, as the quotas had been devised more on a basis of horse-trading than on any economic or social indicator.

Within some of the Member States, the group discovered that the quotas were apparently being divided by region, according to the size of the agricultural area. This meant that 'some of the relatively extensive and well-structured agricultural regions of the community (such as Schleswig-Holstein, Niedersachsen, Scotland, Emilia Romagna, Toscana and Lazio) receive much higher expenditure than agricultural employment or structural criteria would suggest' (Commission 1976(*d*), 14). The group also commented on the considerable difference between expenditure commitments for Italy and actual payments: in 1964–72 it received about one-third of total commitments but only half that amount had been paid by 1974. Thus, even at this early stage, administrative difficulties were preventing Italy from gaining access to structural funds—a pattern that was to become familiar as the years went by.

It is of some interest to examine whether or not the perceived lack of balance between the need for structural improvement in poorer regions and the distribution of total payments from Reg. 17/64 persisted over the lifetime of the scheme. In 1989, the Commission published a cumulative regional breakdown of the aid granted—see Table 10.2.[2] While Italy received the largest payments, and while the South and the islands received a considerable share of the total, Emilia-Romagna remained a main beneficiary, and Lazio received more than Sicily.

Germany, which received the second highest payments, still had Niedersachsen as its second highest recipient, although Schleswig-Holstein did not maintain its earlier position. In the UK, Scotland remained by far the largest recipient. In Belgium, the south is poorer than the north but received less aid, while in Ireland

Table 10.2. Reg. 17/64: Regional breakdown by Member State of projects financed cumulatively 1964-79, ('000 ua/EUA)

Belgium		Denmark		Germany		France		Ireland	
Community region	Aid granted	Community region	Aid granted	Community region	Aid granted	Community region	Aid granted	Community region	Aid granted
Nord	68,146	Øst for Storebaelt	10,521	Schleswig-Holstein	52,560	Region parisienne	3,106	Donegal	5,523
Sud	43,910	Vest for Storebaelt	28,371	Hamburg	2,487	Bassin parisien	58,954	North-West	2,939
Brabant	11,600	Grønland	1,554	Bremen	8,383	Nord	20,646	North-East	6,947
Multi-regional	12,156	Multi-regional	5,831	Niedersachsen	101,595	Est	21,553	West	2,491
				Nordrhein-Westfalen	52,291	Ouest	93,646	Midlands	1,745
				Hessen	44,023	Sud-ouest	48,594	East	5,485
				Rheinland-Pfalz	44,170	Centre Est	55,850	Midwest	4,814
				Baden-Württemberg	71,881	Méditerranée	72,096	South-East	11,890
				Bayern	109,728	D.O.M.	8,329	South-West	12,716
				Saarland	815	Multi-regional	22,468	Multi-regional	18,770
				Berlin (West)	401				
				Multi-regional	15,039				
Total	135,812		46,277		503,373		405,242		73,320

Table 10.2. (*cont.*)

Italy		Luxembourg		Netherlands		UK	
Community region	Aid granted	Community region	Aid granted	Community region	Aid granted	Community region	Aid granted
Nord Ouest	31,798	Grand Duché	8,852	Noord	46,624	Scotland	35,469
Lombardia	31,351			Oost	23,188	North	5,963
Nord Est	111,818			West	45,600	Northern Ireland	28,225
Emilia-Romagna	91,156			Zuid-West	4,222	North-West	7,325
Centre	106,994			Zuid	18,952	Yorkshire-Humberside	14,698
Lazio	49,630			Multi-regional	808	Wales	4,331
Campania	20,024					West Midlands	6,070
Abruzzi-Molise	34,508					East Midlands	5,725
Sud	120,901					East Anglia	8,906
Sicilia	44,995					South-West	5,514
Sardegna	7,327					South-East	2,667
Multi-regional	17,649					Multi-regional	9,749
Total	668,151		8,852		139,394		134,642

Source: Commission 1989(*h*).

Table 10.3. Reg. 17/64: Projects financed, aid granted, and payments made, cumulatively to end 1992

	Belgium	Denmark	Germany	France	Ireland	Italy	Luxem- bourg	Nether- lands	UK	Total
Projects financed	788	145	1,645	1,049	313	2,414	39	513	550	7,456
completed	766	143	1,609	992	287	1,753	38	485	519	6,592
abandoned	22	2	36	54	25	661		28	30	859
under way				3	1		1		1	5
Aid granted by FEOGA ('000 ua/EUA)	135,812	46,277	503,373	405,242	73,320	668,161	8,852	139,394	134,642	2,115,073
Payments made ('000 ua/EUA)	126,811	42,808	513,411[a]	311,758	38,695	296,411	8,572	134,845	98,874	1,592,285

[a] why payments made to Germany are greater than aid granted is not clear

Sources: Commission 1989(*h*), 1993(*e*).

two regions—South-East and South-West—dominated, although the West and North-West were much poorer.

Table 10.3 provides a summary by Member State of the total number of projects financed. Most were already completed by the end of 1992. About 11.5 per cent had been abandoned, for whatever reason, by far the greatest number of these were in Italy. Despite its late arrival, the UK made very good use of Reg. 17/64. Table 10.3 also provides a summary by Member State of the aid granted, cumulatively to the end of 1992. This should be compared with the payments made, which forms the third part of the table. While the sources are not the same, which may have resulted in some discrepancies, in broad terms one can conclude that the account is nearly closed on this scheme. In Italy there is a considerable difference between aid granted and payments received, which presumably is a reflection of the large number of projects which were abandoned.

So the life of this extraordinary piece of legislation draws to a close. For so many years, it provided a link with the earliest days of the CAP and, in the distortions which so quickly developed in its operation, was a reminder of how soon in the life of the policy the politics of the CAP usurped the ideals of the original designers. However, some aspects of Reg. 17/64 have remained. In 1976, the interdepartmental group referred to earlier recommended that, when Reg. 17/64 ceased, its infrastructural aspects should be restricted geographically in any replacement legislation. In a sense, this did occur with the measures which came into force in the late 1970s and early 1980s (as discussed in Chapter 9). However, it was not until the reorganization of the Structural Funds in the late 1980s that a more systematic approach to regional concentration of effort was introduced into the CAP. The aid to processing and marketing was carried forward with the enactment of Reg. 355/77, which is discussed later in this chapter.

Aid to Encourage the Establishment of Producer Groups

One of the most obvious features of agricultural production in Western Europe (and in many other parts of the world) is its organizational structure, dominated by small and medium-size independent farms. Production in such a framework comes very close to the economist's definition of a perfect market. Farmers are price-takers: they are very rarely in a position to dominate the market, even if they are organized into a commodity or special interest group. In general, they produce a homogeneous product and therefore cannot benefit from higher prices achieved through product differentiation. They are in a weak bargaining position, whether selling a product for direct consumption or for processing, and this is particularly true when the product is perishable (as with milk) or perishable and seasonal (as with fruit and vegetables).

The poor structural organization of agriculture was even more pronounced in the 1960s in the new Community than it is in the 1990s. Farming was characterized by a very large number of exceedingly small producers, each with an extensive range of products. This situation was not conducive to orderly marketing, particularly at a time when consumer demand was changing rapidly due to the marked increase in living standards. What was required was regular supply, known and constant quality, and stable prices. It was essential that producers respond and that they took greater responsibility for the marketing of their own products. Vague references were made by the Commission as far back as the 1959 and 1960 proposals on the CAP to its intention to encourage initiatives by farmers' organizations, which would lead to better information on markets, to improve their stability, and their response to consumer demand.

The Commission reasoned that, if producers of the same commodity came together in an alliance, it would enable them collectively to improve the quality of their product by enforcing grading standards, and the continuity of supply, by having centralized storage and processing facilities. The group would market the output of its members, thereby improving their bargaining power and, as a result, obtaining a higher unit price. This in turn would help to further the aims of Art. 39.1 of the Rome Treaty, in particular as regards incomes, market stability, and supply availability. These thoughts were carried a stage further in Reg. 26/62 *on the application of certain rules of competition to production of and trade in agricultural products* (Sp. OJ 1959–1962). Under this Regulation, farmers and their organizations were, in general, excluded from the ordinary Community rules on competition, in so far as their activities were concerned with the production and sale of agricultural products, and the use of common facilities for the storage and processing of such products.

Although, theoretically, the case for collective action is strong, in practice a recurring difficulty with any sector dominated by small-scale independent producers is to persuade them to join a group which will have power to impose standards, control prices, and even production, and once they have joined to prevent them from breaking their contractual obligations to the group, thereby undermining its collective bargaining power.[3]

One way in which the advantages of membership of a producer group can be enhanced is to give to such groups certain formal market intervention responsibilities. Prior to the establishment of the European Community, the Netherlands provided good examples of how such a system functioned, especially in the fruit and vegetable sector. The characteristics of the Dutch system were outlined in the 1960 proposals on the CAP (Commission 1960), and certain features of that system found an echo in some of the commodity regimes. The first example came in Reg. 159/66 *concerning additional arrangements for the common organization of the market in the fruit and vegetable sector* (JO 192, 27–10–66). This Regulation completed the arrangements for fruit and vegetables which had been hanging fire since 1962. A novel feature of this regime is the important role played by producer groups which act as the agency for internal market support.

For many commodities, provision is made in the relevant market regime for the withdrawal of produce from an oversupplied market, its storage, and disposal. These tasks are normally undertaken by an official agency or agencies established in each Member State. However, for a small number of products, market management is in the hands of the producers themselves, through producer groups which receive official recognition.[4] Given the characteristics of fruit and vegetable production—a highly perishable product, many small-scale producers, local markets, seasonal production, volatility in supply and price—flexibility and speed of response are required if any form of market management is to be effective. Apart from market support for certain commodities, more generally producer groups provide their members with facilities for handling and marketing the output of the relevant commodity. In their turn, the members are expected to market this total supply through the group (unless the group allows otherwise), and they must abide by the rules adopted by the group for the improvement of quality and the adaptation of supply to demand.

The involvement of FEOGA-Guidance lies in the financial encouragement it provides for the establishment of producer groups. The first example of such aid appeared in Reg. 159/66 under which Member States were given the possibility of helping producer groups to get started, by providing them with a degressive aid during the three years following their establishment. This annual aid was not allowed to exceed 3, 2, and 1 per cent respectively of the value of the production marketed by the group. The Guidance Section reimbursed 50 per cent of the Member States' eligible expenditure under this scheme. Tentative references were made in Reg. 122/67 *on the common organization of the market in eggs* and in Reg. 123/67 *on the common organization of the market in poultrymeat* (both in Sp. OJ 1967) to the need to encourage efforts to improve the organization of production, processing, marketing, and quality through trade groups. However, in these commodity regimes, no financial support was offered to help launch such groups.

In the light of all this piecemeal and unco-ordinated interest in producer organizations in various commodities, it is not surprising that the Commission eventually proposed the establishment of a Community framework within which Member States could encourage the formation of producer groups in any commodity. The Commission was also prompted to do so because certain Member States were already promoting these groups and there was a danger that problems would arise at Community level through the use of different criteria and objectives in the various countries concerned (Ries 1967).

Thus, in 1967, the Commission proposed a Regulation on producer groups and their unions in COM(67)68 final (Commission 1967(*a*)), which set out common rules on the type of aid which could be given by the Member States to encourage the formation and development of these groups, and on the conditions under which they could be officially recognized. Despite the Commission's evident interest in the creation of producer groups and despite the existing Community launching aids in the fruit and vegetable sector, the 1967 proposal did not make provision for Community aid. This was somewhat surprising and indeed was criticized by the European Parliament in its Resolution on the draft (JO C10, 14–2–68).

Although Mansholt always regarded producer groups as an extension of market organization rather than as a part of structural policy, his 1968 Plan did contain a discussion of the need to improve marketing, and one of the measures suggested to aid that process was the immediate adoption by the Council of the proposed Regulation on producer groups. The Council clearly did not heed this exhortation because, in its 1970 structural reform proposals, the Commission made a pointed reference to the thorough discussions which had taken place in the European Parliament and in the ESC on the 1967 producer group draft and stated that the Council had not even begun a discussion on it (Commission 1970).

The 1970 reform proposals included a considerably revised draft Regulation on producer groups—the most important change being the provision of Community aid to help launch the groups. In the explanatory note to the proposals, the Commission made it clear that it regarded the improvement of market structure as primarily the responsibility of the Member States. For that reason, it proposed that the Community should refund only 30 per cent of eligible national expenditure. The logic of this position is unclear, as it will be recalled that the Community was already refunding 50 per cent of eligible expenditure on producer groups in the fruit and vegetable sector.

In 1971, when the revised structural reform package was presented to the Council, the draft Regulation on producer groups appeared again—now in a third version (JO C75, 26–7–71). The changes made were generally of a technical nature but, importantly, the Community contribution to eligible expenditure by the Member States had been reduced to 25 per cent. It was all to no avail, as the draft Regulation was not passed by the Council.

In the *Resolution* on the new orientation of the Common Agricultural Policy in 1971, the Council finally agreed in principle to the introduction of a regime to encourage the formation of producer groups but, once again, it appeared that Community aid would not be offered and that the funding would be by the Member States (JO C52, 27–5–71). Despite this, however, the Council remained unable to agree to the proposal, although discussions dragged on into 1972. The only progress which was made was under Reg. 1696/71 *on the common organization of the market in hops* (Sp. OJ 1971(II)). The hops producer groups are not involved in price support operations but are intended in a more general way to assist in the centralization of supply and in the adaptation of the product to market requirements. Member States were free to grant a launching aid and FEOGA-Guidance reimbursement was limited to 25 per cent of eligible expenditure. An extra feature of this regime was the option given to Member States to aid producer groups on a temporary basis (i.e. to the end of 1975) to reorganize hop gardens and to switch to more suitable varieties. The form of aid was a payment per hectare replanted or reorganized, and FEOGA-Guidance refunded 50 per cent of the eligible expenditure of participating Member States.

Discussions resumed in 1976 on the introduction of a general producer group regime and, in the following year, the Commission put forward yet another revised proposal. This was so radically different from previous drafts as to be, in effect, a completely new proposal (Commission 1977(*d*)). In the explanatory memorandum, the Commission tried to explain why such a harmless piece of legislation was causing such difficulties. Basically the problem was that certain Member States with well-developed production and marketing structures could not see the necessity for this legislation. If anything, the differences between the Member States had grown since the original 1967 proposal. The Commission, therefore, proposed that instead of a Regulation of universal application, there should be a measure which would apply only in those areas where the supply of agricultural produce was structurally very inadequate. Primarily this meant Italy and indeed the proposal referred solely to that country, with the provision that the Regulation could be extended to other Member States.

The Council had agreed in February 1977 that it would adopt the proposal by the end of June. It was in fact a full year later that Reg. 1360/78 *on producer groups and associations thereof* (OJ L166, 23–6–78) was enacted. It was almost totally unrecognizable from the draft and covered not just Italy but also Belgium, Southern France, and DOM (the French overseas departments). The commodity coverage differed by country, and in France by region. It was intended to be of assistance to farmers in regions and sectors where there were severe structural deficiencies, due to the small size of farms and poor organization. For a measure which was to last initially for five years only, at a total FEOGA cost of 24m. ua, an incredible amount of bureaucratic effort was involved. When Greece, Portugal, and Spain joined the Community, Reg. 1360/78 was extended to them, and to Ireland and the remainder of France in 1988, all for specified lists of commodities.

The only other commodity for which producer group launching aids are available is cotton under Reg. 389/82 (OJ L51, 23–2–82). Under the terms of Accession, when Greece joined the European Community, market support was extended to cotton and producer groups were seen as an important mechanism for the rationalization of production and the centralization of handling and marketing. For this reason, the Regulation covers not only launching aids but also investment aid to assist with structural improvements in harvesting, ginning, storage, and packaging. Producer groups in Italy and Spain are also eligible for aid under this regime.

Having sketched the rather confused history of the development of legislation on producer groups, the remainder of this Section reports on the statistical evidence of the success or failure of the various structural measures to persuade farmers to come together to improve the organization of particular commodities. Data on structural aids are available for producer groups in fruit and vegetables, hops, cotton, and miscellaneous products under Reg. 1360/78. Table 10.4(a)–(d) summarizes the results and the message seems to be that if the producer groups have a serious role in the organization of the market or in the restructuring of the sector, producers will respond and join, but otherwise not.

The first part of Table 10.4 relates to fruit and vegetables. In 1972, Reg. 159/66 was replaced by Reg. 1035/72 (Sp. OJ 1972(II)), which consolidated all the existing Community legislation on fruit and vegetables. Arrangements for launching aids for producer groups were retained unchanged. The pattern which is so familiar from other structural aids is present here also: aid is concentrated in a

Table 10.4. Structural aid for producer groups: Fruit and vegetables, hops, cotton, and miscellaneous, by Member States

(a) Reg. 1035/72: Fruit and vegetables

Member States	No. of groups	Member State Expenditure '000 ECU	Reimbursement by FEOGA cumulatively to end 1988	
			'000 ECU	%
Belgium	4	2,142	1,071	4.0
Denmark	21	1,730	865	3.2
Germany	78	6,534	3,267	12.1
Greece	158	2,453	1,226	4.5
France	239	7,419	3,710	13.7
Ireland	5	212	106	0.4
Italy	73	24,297	12,149	45.0
Netherlands	6	2,416	1,208	4.5
UK	44	6,774	3,387	12.6
Total	628	53,976	26,988	100.0

(b) Regs. 1696/71 and 2253/77: Hops

Member States	Launching aid		Conversion/ Restructuring aid		Reimbursement by FEOGA cumulatively to end 1985	
	No.	'000 ECU	Hectares	'000 ECU	'000 ECU	%
Belgium			230	426.9	213.5	2.9
Germany	4	93.4	8,397	10,701.6	5,397.5	75.2
France			642	907.3	453.6	6.3
Ireland			8	2.8	1.4	0.0
UK			1,881	2,100.0	1,109.2	15.4
Total	4	93.4	11,159	14,138.7	7,175.2	100.0

(c) Reg. 389/82: Cotton

Member State	No. of groups	Member State expenditure '000 ECU		Reimbursement by FEOGA cumulatively to end 1988 '000 ECU
		Launching aid	Investment aid	
Greece	687	110.3	23,182.6	9,317.2

(d) Reg. 1360/78: Miscellaneous products, various Member States[a]

Member States	No. of groups	Member State expenditure '000 ECU	Reimbursement by FEOGA cumulatively to end 1990 '000 ECU
Greece	8	248.7	62.2
Italy	100	9,114.1	2,353.5
Total	108	9,362.9	2,415.7

[a] eligible Member States were Belgium, Greece, Italy, Portugal, Spain, and regions of France, and its overseas departments. The Regulation was extended to the rest of France, and Ireland during 1988. Data were available for Greece and Italy only.

Sources: Commission 1986(*e*), 1989(*h*), 1991(*e*).

very small group of countries and it is not necessarily related to the size of the sector. For instance, the very small number of producer groups set up under this legislation in Belgium and the Netherlands is indicative of the strength of the previously long-established marketing structures based largely on the co-operative movement.[5] Therefore, there was little incentive or need to seek launching aids. In contrast, the relatively large number of launching aids in the UK is an indication of the previous absence of joint ventures by farmers rather than an indication of the size of the horticultural sector. The size of producer groups varies considerably from one Member State to another, as evidenced by the absence of any relationship between the number of groups and the level of investment.

Hops (Table 10.4(*b*)) provide a real contrast to fruit and vegetables. This is a very small sector, highly localized in traditional areas of production where, of course, it can be quite a significant crop. Much of the output is grown on contract. The schemes of aid came to an end some years ago and 1985 was the last year for which data were available. The situation with regard to cotton is quite different (Table 10.4(*c*)). Greece is the largest producer and so far (at the time of writing) was the only Member State to have made use of the launching and investment aids, although the Commission anticipated that Spain, which is the only other significant producer, might well begin to show an interest in this measure (Commission 1987(*f*)).[6]

In 1991, the Commission reported to the Council on the operation of Reg. 1360/78 (Commission 1991(*e*)). By the end of 1990, the Member States had granted recognition to 560 groups.[7] This contrasts sharply with the figure of 108 in Table 10.4(*d*). The discrepancy is explained by 'the slowness of the Member States' administrations in drawing up implementing rules and requesting refunds' (ibid. 8). Despite the fact that Belgium was included in the scheme right from the start, no groups in the relevant production sectors (cereals, cattle, pigs, and lucerne) had applied for recognition, even though the requirements had been made easier. Indeed, the Commission stated that the Belgian authorities had reported 'that those concerned are uninterested in the very idea of producer groups and that, in the present circumstances, this is unlikely to change in the future' (ibid. 9). For that reason, the Commission proposed that, when the life of the Regulation was prolonged, Belgium should be excluded. This was rejected!

Structural Adjustment in Certain Commodity Sectors

Throughout the lifetime of the CAP, there have been certain commodities which have been the source of constant concern, not only because of the level of production in relation to demand but also because of the organizational structure of the sector, the quality of the product, and the location of production. This Section is devoted to a discussion of structural schemes which have been put in place to try to change some of these features. The commodities are milk, citrus, orchard fruit, and wine. The last three of these commodities all have characteristics in common: they are produced in locationally well-defined areas, often where there are few alternatives; being permanent crops, there is a long commitment to their production. Thus, changes within the same sector or shifts out of the sector to another crop are difficult to achieve and carry with them considerable income risks. They are often the product of small or medium-size farms. Milk, too, has many of these characteristics although its production is much more widespread.

Structural legislation aimed to facilitate adjustment in specific commodities has three distinct (though often related) purposes. It is intended to enable farmers: (a) to switch to another product; (b) to upgrade the quality of the existing product; and (c) to improve marketing and processing by the producers. The first of these aims has been associated most notably with milk and wine; the second with citrus and wine; and the third with the promotion of producer groups for fruit and vegetables, as discussed in the previous Section.

Schemes to improve quality, and marketing and processing run the risk that modernization not only improves productivity and, hopefully, income but also increases production. If a citrus grove or a vineyard is grubbed up and replanted with new varieties, almost inevitably they will be of higher yield. If an obsolete processing plant is modernized, it is very likely that the new machinery has a greater capacity, necessitating a higher throughput if the plant is to be commercially viable. The potential for conflict between the farmers' welfare and macro-policy objectives is very real. Sometimes they can be reconciled: the demand for citrus and quality wine is more buoyant than for most food products, but for milk and table wine there is a fundamental clash, as total demand is falling over time.

Milk. In Chapter 6, in the discussion of the original proposals on the CAP, reference was made to the fact that milk was already a problem commodity. This basic situation was made considerably worse by the introduction of a common target price in 1968 which was well above the level which would have achieved market clearance.[8] The error of this initial position was then compounded by the reluctance of any of the main institutional forces—Commission, Council of Ministers, European Parliament—to accept that market support prices needed to be controlled far more rigorously than they were. On the supply side, reliance was placed on mechanisms such as production levies and quotas to curb output, while on the demand side, schemes were devised to stimulate consumption and to subsidize sales to unlikely groups, such as the military.[9] Apart from quotas, which have at least kept production from getting completely out of hand, none of these schemes was of any lasting use. The unpalatable truth still is that there are too many dairy cows, yielding too much milk, and too many farmers dependent on dairying for their livelihood.

The structural schemes outlined here were intended to tackle that unpalatable truth. Farmers should be persuaded to give up milk production and turn to another enterprise, or to utilize the milk on the farm and not to market it, or to retire. The first structural scheme was adopted as long ago as 1969: Reg. 1975/69 *instituting a system of premiums for the slaughter of cows and for the non-marketing of milk and milk products* (JO L252, 8–10–69). This legislation arose out of the Mansholt Plan where the situation in the milk sector was described as 'alarming'. The Commission suggested various measures on the price and market front to control the immediate situation and it also recommended the slaughter of 250,000 cows each year in 1969 and 1970 (additional to normal culling), and the granting of aid in the same two years for the production of beef. The Commission further suggested that dairy farmers who were willing to retire should receive additional aid over and above that being offered under the normal retirement scheme. Dairy farmers setting up one of the new Production Units (PUs) should receive additional aid if they switched from milk to beef fattening (Commission 1968(*a*)).

The draft Regulation on cow slaughter and beef promotion appeared in COM(68)1000(c). By the time Reg. 1975/69 was passed in October 1969, the beef promotion aspect had been dropped and had been replaced with the non-marketing of milk premium—which indirectly could achieve the same results, by encouraging farmers to feed whole milk to calves reared for beef. The cow slaughter premium was less generous than in the original proposal and a ceiling had been placed on the amount of aid which any one beneficiary could receive, which effectively limited compensation to 10 cows. FEOGA-Guidance reimbursed 50 per cent of the cost of the premiums. The scheme ran until 1974, during which time nearly 234,000 cows were slaughtered on 54,000 farms (see Table 10.5(*a*)). Considering that the original intention was to cull over twice that number of cows, and in no more than two years, it must be assumed that this scheme would have had very little impact in a Community with a dairy herd at that time of about 22m.

The second measure intended to curb milk production was Reg. 1353/73 (OJ L141, 28–5–73).[10] Under this scheme a premium was paid on condition that the producer gave up, for four years, all sales of milk and milk products from the holding in question and simultaneously kept a specified number of adult cattle on the same holding. The level of the premium was based on the quantity of milk

Table 10.5. Measures intended to reduce the number of cows and milk marketed, cumulative results by Member States

(a) Reg. 1975/69: Premium for cow slaughter and non-marketing of milk, cumulatively to 1977

Member States	Slaughter premium			Non-marketing of milk premium			FEOGA reimbursement	
	Holdings	Cows	Cows/ holding	Holdings	Cows	Cows/ holding	'000 ua	%
Germany	36,501	149,875	4.1	5,872	115,278	19.6	25,467.4	53.6
Belgium	4,415	19,760	4.4	826	15,463	18.7	3,408.1	7.2
France	9,349	42,494	4.5	5,880	115,350	19.6	15,359.7	32.4
Italy	1,911	8,187	4.2	—	—	—	818.4	1.7
Luxembourg	196	777	3.9	48	795	16.5	153.8	0.4
Netherlands	2,097	12,672	6.0	596	10,650	17.8	2,267.4	4.7
Total	54,469	233,765	4.2	13,222	257,536	19.4	47,474.9	100.0

Sources: Commission 1975(*b*), 1977(*h*).

Table 10.5. (*cont.*)

(b) Reg. 1353/73: Premiums to encourage a switch from dairying to beef production, cumulatively to 1983

Member States	Beneficiaries	Hl. qualifying for premium		Premium paid by Member States	FEOGA reimbursement	
		Total	per farm	'000 ECU	'000 ECU	%
Belgium	685	359,627	525.0	2,613.9	1,309.7	1.7
Denmark	621	568,289	915.1	4,059.0	2,029.4	2.6
Germany	7,243	4,133,393	570.6	37,711.8	18,855.9	24.0
France	5,719[a]	3,702,344	647.3	25,879.9	12,947.6	16.5
Ireland	537	321,730	599.1	2,509.1	1,254.6	1.6
Luxembourg	47	35,491	755.1	282.3	141.1	0.2
Netherlands	5,672	504,766	882.4	3,822.7	1,911.3	2.4
UK	6,643	9,720,679	1,463.2	79,836.5	39,922.6	51.0
Total	22,067	19,346,319	876.7	156,715.1	78,372.3	100.0

[a] plus 84 farmers in Corsica who received premiums for the development of specialized cattle farming

Source: Commission 1984.

supplied by the producer in the twelve-month period preceding the reference date. As an alternative to this scheme, Member States could in certain circumstances grant a development premium for the specialized raising of cattle for meat production. The whole scheme was scheduled to cost 60m. ua and to be completed by the end of 1974, although in fact it was extended. FEOGA-Guidance contributed 50 per cent of the eligible expenditure.

In 1974, the Commission published a very detailed report on the operation of the scheme (Commission 1974(e)), in which it indicated that the cows for which the premium was granted represented just over 1 per cent of the dairy herd and milk yield. The report provided a regional breakdown of the impact of the scheme and, not surprisingly, in many Member States, it was in the regions with larger farms that the scheme was most popular. For small producers, to abandon dairying, with its regular income, in favour of rearing cattle, for which the return is lower and paid once only, is a considerable risk. In some of the Member States, the recipients tended to be in the 50–60 year age-group, which suggests that the shift to beef production was the first step to retirement.

Practically all the farmers who participated in this scheme had done so by 1976 but the reimbursements by FEOGA to the Member States were only completed in 1983. This slow pace of reimbursement is a feature of structural schemes and is partly due to the slow pace at which the Member States complete their own accounts and requests for payment. It does not necessarily mean that the individual beneficiary does not get paid promptly (though this may happen) but it does mean that Member States may be less than enthusiastic in publicizing the existence of schemes, because for some years they have to finance the total cost.

The results of Reg. 1353/73 are given in Table 10.5(b) and one noticeable feature is that the size of dairy herd participating in the scheme differed considerably from one Member State to another. Thus, Germany had the largest number of beneficiaries (as was also true in the 1969 scheme) but the quantity of milk which qualified for the premium only averaged 571 hl. per farm, whereas in the UK, with the second highest number of beneficiaries, the average quantity was 1,464 hl. This is a good illustration of the difference in the structure of the industry in the two countries and explains why over half the total reimbursements from FEOGA went to the UK.

In its 1974 report on the scheme, the Commission concluded that it had been a success in slowing down the expansion of milk production. However, its optimism was misplaced and, in 1976, the Commission issued its Action Programme (1977–1980) for the progressive achievement of balance in the milk market (Bull. EC Supp. 10–76). By the mid-1970s, the dairy sector was very different from what it had been in the early 1960s. Although the number of dairy cows had remained fairly static over time and, if anything, was tending downwards, milk production had risen by about 1.7 per cent per year from 1960 to 1975. The average milk yield per cow in 1960 was 3,083 kg. and 3,637 kg. in 1975, with the best regions having an average of more than 4,600 kg.

Another change was that far fewer farmers were feeding fresh milk to calves on the farm but instead were sending all the milk for processing. A major cause of these organizational changes was undoubtedly the price incentive. As the Commission described it: 'The behaviour of producers and dairies has been influenced mainly by the substantial increase in milk prices and the high level of the guarantee which together ensure them an unlimited market' (Bull. EC Supp. 10–76, 7). However, there was no suggestion in the Action Programme that the market imbalance was to be tackled head-on by a decline in the money support price. Instead, the Commission announced a package of measures which included a new scheme for the non-marketing of milk and the conversion to beef cattle or sheep.[11] It also proposed the suspension of national and Community-supported aid to the dairy sector, and the introduction of a co-responsibility levy (see Chapter 6).

At first glance it may seem irrational that, at a time when there were schemes to reduce the number of dairy cows and to lower the amount of milk going for processing, there should still have been investment aid for the modernization of milk production and processing. However, it could be argued that a slimmed-down dairy sector would still need to be modern and efficient and, if the provision of cheap capital would help to achieve that goal, it was a good long-term investment. The real problem was much more profound: the various elements of the milk policy were sending confused and contradictory signals to the farmers, and the weight given to each element of policy did not correspond to the stated objective of restoring market balance. Thus, the imposition of a co-responsibility levy (rather than a cut in the money support level) did not represent a serious attempt to dampen down supply. Investment aid far outweighed the structural schemes being discussed here. Thus the farmers who were likely to leave dairying were often the elderly and those with very small herds. But these were not the categories of dairy farmers who were responsible for the surplus in the first place.

The Commission tried to inject a sense of urgency into the discussions on milk production controls but the Council of Ministers did not respond with matching speed on any aspect of the Commission's recommendations—in Chapter 6, reference was made to the length of time it took to get the principle of co-responsibility accepted, and its inadequacy when finally put in place. Things were no better with the structural scheme. Two draft proposals in succession on the introduction of a scheme for the non-marketing of milk, and conversion of dairy cow herds to other livestock enterprises were put forward in 1976. The second was radically different from the first and, by the time the Council finally accepted the scheme in 1977, major changes had once more taken place.

Reg. 1078/77 (OJ L131, 26–5–77) provided farmers with a choice: either a premium to compensate for agreeing to cease dairying or a premium to convert to the production of beef cattle or sheep. Unusually, this scheme was funded in part from FEOGA-Guarantee as well as from the Guidance Section. In its comments on the proposed scheme, the European Parliament drew attention to the danger that such a measure might well solve one problem by creating another: 'a conversion policy is likely to have favourable results . . . only if the beef and veal market, which in many ways is just as sensitive as the milk market, is not to be disrupted as a result' (OJ C259, 4–11–76, 32). This was a very real issue at the time, as the beef sector had been displaying increasing signs of instability since the early 1970s.

Applications for aid under Reg. 1078/77 were made from mid-1977 to mid-1981. During that time, the Commission issued five reports on the progress of the scheme. In total, about 123,000 applications for premiums were approved by the end of 1981, representing over 6 per cent of dairy farmers and 6.7 per cent of the Community dairy herd. This was equivalent to the whole dairy herd of Belgium and Denmark. Table 10.6 summarizes the results. Germany was by far the largest recipient of the non-marketing premiums in terms of total applicants but the average size of herd was by far the smallest. As with the 1973 scheme, the large herd size in the UK is very much in evidence: only 5 per cent of the applicants but 16 per cent of the cows. As to the conversion scheme, applications were dominated by France and Germany, although in terms of the number of cows kept, France and the UK accounted for about two-thirds of the total. The significant differences between the size of herd in the two premiums is quite striking: converting to beef or sheep production is unrealistic for a small dairy farmer.

In the final report on the scheme, the Commission expressed its disappointment at the results. Although the withdrawal of nearly 1.7m. cows from milk production exceeded the original target of 1.3m., the net impact was very modest. Between 1977 and 1981, milk deliveries to dairies rose by about 10m. tonnes, while the scheme only removed 6m. tonnes. It was an expensive scheme, with eligible expenditure being fully funded by the two sections of FEOGA. The average cost per cow was about 700 ECU and the scheme was expected to cost 1,200m. ECU (Commission 1982(*d*)). It was confirmed by the Commission in 1987 that the scheme had caused problems on the beef market and it recommended that the scheme should not be reintroduced (Commission 1987(*i*)).

In 1987, the Commission issued a discussion document on the implementation of stabilizers in the milk sector, which was mostly concerned with the operation of the quota system. Although the sector had changed appreciably since the early 1970s, it was clear it had not changed sufficiently. In 1973, 43 per cent of all farms produced milk; by 1983 this had fallen to 31 per cent. However, as a proportion of Gross Agricultural Product (GAP), milk had become more important, rising from 17.3 per cent in 1973 to 19.2 per cent in 1985. Not surprisingly, milk was one of the most costly sectors in the Community's Budget: 38 per cent of FEOGA-Guarantee expenditure in 1973 and nearly 30 per cent in 1985, and the latter figure was expected to rise. Full self-sufficiency had been reached in 1974, and between then and 1983 milk deliveries had increased by an annual average of 2.6 per cent, while consumption rose by about 0.5 per cent each year (Commission 1987(*i*)).

When the milk quotas were introduced in 1984, all Member States except Denmark and Greece established national schemes to facilitate producers who wished to discontinue milk production. In return for the surrender of their quota, they received compensation. Approximately 100,000 producers took part in this scheme. In 1986, the Council agreed to a reduction in the quotas by 2 per

Table 10.6. Reg. 1078/77: Non-marketing of milk and conversion of dairy herds, cumulative results by Member State

Member States	Non-marketing premiums					Conversion premiums					FEOGA-Guidance Reimbursement to end 1988	
	Applicants		Cows kept		No. of cows/applicant	Applicants		Cows kept		No. of cows/applicant		
	No.	%	'000	%		No.	%	'000	%		'000 ECU	%
Belgium	2,122	1.9	26.6	2.0	12.5	338	3.0	9.5	2.9	28.1	7,390.1	1.5
Denmark	7,577	6.8	153.3	11.3	20.2	93	0.8	2.6	0.8	27.9	49,046.1	9.9
Germany	73,831	66.2	609.0	44.8	8.2	2,659	23.6	61.7	18.8	23.2	234,688.4	47.8
France	15,777	14.1	213.4	15.7	13.4	4,489	40.0	114.3	34.7	25.5	73,647.9	15.0
Ireland	2,280	2.0	58.7	4.3	25.7	950	8.7	33.3	10.1	35.0	16,239.3	3.4
Luxembourg	389	0.4	4.8	0.4	12.3	11	0.1	0.3	0.1	32.6	1,363.7	0.3
Netherlands	3,895	3.5	69.0	5.1	17.7	172	1.5	4.6	1.4	26.7	25,851.0	5.3
UK	5,694	5.1	223.5	16.4	39.2	2,510	22.3	102.8	31.2	41.0	82,544.9	16.8
Total[a]	111,565	100.0	1,358.3	100.0	12.2	111,222	100.0	329.1	100.0	29.3	490,771.4	100.0

[a] this scheme did not apply to Italy

Sources: Commission 1982(*d*), 1989(*h*).

cent in 1987, and a further 1 per cent in 1988. In order to facilitate these reductions, a Community cessation scheme was introduced under which producers who gave up milk production permanently received annual compensation for a period of seven years.[12] The initial response to this scheme by producers varied considerably from one Member State to another, with some countries being well below expectations. The Commission suggested that this was due to three factors: the earlier national schemes had removed many of the potential outgoers; in some regions, the absence of adequate alternatives to milk production; and the level of the premium was too low to persuade farmers to abandon dairying (Commission 1987(*i*)).

There can be no doubt that the size and shape of the dairy sector has changed significantly over the lifetime of the CAP, and yet problems remain. The tendency towards overproduction has been curbed but not eliminated. The various structural schemes must have eased many producers out of the sector relatively painlessly but, having removed many marginal producers, it may actually be more difficult to achieve change in the future. Neville-Rolfe (1984, 364) commented:

It is sometimes said that the disappearance of tens, or even hundreds, of thousands of . . . small operators would *ipso facto* solve the problem of the milk surplus. It would be unlikely to do so. The larger the herd, the greater the probability . . . that its operator will be adopting the feeding and breeding practices needed to increase milk yields per cow. In this respect structural reform, unless accompanied by measures to restrict output, is liable to increase total output.

It was precisely for these reasons that quotas became inevitable. However, ominously, in 1987 the Commission pointed out:

The introduction of the quota system has not prevented but rather encouraged rationalization and improved management at farm and dairy level to the present and future advantage of producers and consumers. Technical and biological development has continued since 1983 with the result that an important production potential is still remaining untapped within the sector.   (Commission 1987(*i*), 26)

The Commission made the above statement in the context of the expected termination of the quota system in 1989 and it added that if the quotas were abolished without any other action being taken it would result 'in an unparalleled explosion in milk deliveries. History would then record that the five-year experiment of the quota system had failed to resolve any of the fundamental problems of market imbalance but had only postponed the collapse of the common market organisation under the financial burden of ever-increasing stock levels' (Commission 1987(*i*), 35). In fact, the quota system was retained but the comments quoted remain valid. The underlying tendency to overproduction is being kept in check—but that is all. The removal of the quota system would present the Union with a very tricky situation, which would have to be managed with great care. Otherwise, all the efforts made to change the structure of the sector, carried out at considerable expense, could well be negated.

Citrus and orchard fruit. Two of the oldest schemes to improve the structure of production were concerned with citrus fruit, and apples, pears, and peaches. The reasons for the measures were not the same. In the case of citrus, there was a low level of self-sufficiency in the Community and a rising demand but the producers found they could not exploit this situation, as their competitive position on the internal market was poor. The deficiencies were at every stage of the market: production of varieties with little consumer appeal, and poor handling and processing of the fruit. For apples, pears, and peaches there were also problems with the varieties being grown but this was in an already oversupplied market, so that the solution lay in encouraging growers to leave the sector rather than attempting some improvement in production and marketing.

Reg. 2511/69 *laying down special measures for improving the production and marketing of Community citrus fruit* (Sp. OJ 1969(II))[13] provided aid to assist growers of oranges and mandarins to replace existing varieties of trees with others more suited to consumer demand, and to encourage better handling, storage, and processing of citrus. Growers who replanted were eligible for an additional income aid to help tide them over the reorganization period. This aid was payable in five annual instalments and was based on the extent of the area replanted. FEOGA-Guidance reimbursed 50 per cent of the expenditure incurred by the Member States on the grubbing and marketing aids, and the whole of the additional income aid. The Member States were required to draw up improvement plans and these were approved by the Commission in 1973. Thus, even with a highly targeted scheme such as this, the administrative delays were considerable.

Table 10.7 provides cumulative information on the operation of this scheme up to the end of 1988. The table is unusual in that the Commission has provided data on the extent to which the various aspects of the scheme have been carried out. Some have been reasonably successful—market reorganization in Italy, replanting in France, and restructuring in Greece but otherwise, given the length of time the scheme has been in operation, its results are very disappointing. In 1989, the Commission published a report on the implementation of this scheme (Commission 1989(c)). It is quite impossible to reconcile some of the statistics in the report with those in Table 10.7 but the message is still the same: very little progress had been made. One of the problems of the scheme is that growers are unwilling to grub up and replant their groves with better varieties, because of the expense involved and the loss of income while the new trees are reaching maturity. This, of course, is what the income aid was intended to provide for, but obviously it has failed in its purpose.

Reference was made in Chapter 6 to the analysis of supply of all the main commodity sectors in the proposals on the CAP in 1960. Fruit and vegetables were identified as presenting particular problems of data interpretation but, even allowing for the uncertainties, a number of products were identified as being in surplus. Among these were apples, pears, and peaches. The original aid scheme was Reg. 2517/69 *laying down certain measures for reorganising Community fruit production* (Sp. OJ 1969(II)). The aid provided was for the grubbing up of apple,

Table 10.7. Regs. 2511/69 and 1204/82: On the improvement of the production and marketing of citrus fruit

Italy

Measure	Expenditure provided for in the plan m. ECU	Expenditure incurred by Italy '000 ECU	Extent of completion (%)	Reimbursement by FEOGA cumulatively to end 1988 '000 ECU
Replanting and nurseries	154.0	29,868.5	19.4	14,934.2
Restructuring	190.5	24,032.7	12.6	12,016.3
Marketing	74.9	55,409.4	73.9	27,704.7
Additional aid	99.3	10,835.7	10.9	5,417.9
Total	518.7	120,146.3	23.2	60,073.1

France

Measure	Expenditure provided for in the plan m. ECU	Expenditure incurred by France '000 ECU	Extent of completion (%)	Reimbursement by FEOGA cumulatively to end 1988 '000 ECU
Replanting	6.5	2,928.9	45.3	1,464.5
Restructuring	5.5	1,022.3	18.5	511.1
Marketing	2.4	688.0	28.2	334.0
Additional aid	5.9	2,045.2	34.4	1,022.6
Total	20.3	6,664.4	32.8	3,332.2

Greece

Measure	Expenditure provided for in the plan m. ECU	Expenditure incurred by Greece '000 ECU	Extent of completion (%)	Reimbursement by FEOGA cumulatively to end 1988 '000 ECU
Reconversion	76.4	3,016.1	3.9	1,508.0
Restructuring	9.0	7,849.9	87.6	3,925.0
Marketing	30.0	5,740.9	19.1	2,870.5
Nurseries	2.8	171.5	6.2	85.7
Additional aid	53.9	1,562.2	2.9	781.1
Total	172.0	18,340.6	10.7	9,170.3

Source: Commission 1989(*h*).

pear, and peach trees. The recipient had to undertake not to replant with similar fruit for five years. The aid was in the form of a payment per hectare grubbed, payable in two instalments. The Guidance Section refunded 50 per cent of the grubbing premiums, and the Member States were forbidden to encourage in any

Table 10.8(a). Reg.2517/69: Aid for grubbing fruit trees, cumulatively to 1980

Member States	No. of beneficiaries	Area grubbed		Expenditure by Member State	Reimbursement by FEOGA	
		ha.	ha./ farm	'000 ua/EUA	'000 ua/EUA	%
Belgium	11,828	9,007	0.76	7,203.3	3,601.6	10.2
Germany	34,827	26,095	0.75	20,872.7	10,436.3	29.4
France	12,600	22,459	1.78	17,966.9	8,983.5	25.3
Italy	10,069	19,389	1.92	15,516.4	7,763.6	22.0
Luxembourg	409	228	0.56	182.2	91.1	0.3
Netherlands	9,970	11,404	1.14	9,122.9	4,561.4	12.8
Total	79,703	88,582	1.11	70,864.4	35,437.5	100.0

Source: Commission 1980(*b*).

Table 10.8(b). Reg. 794/76: On the reorganization of fruit production, cumulatively to 1982

Member States	No. of beneficiaries	Area grubbed		Expenditure by Member State	Reimbursement by FEOGA	
		ha.	ha./ farm	'000 ECU	'000 ECU	%
Belgium	215	379.9	1.77	517.2	258.6	4.3
Denmark	32	42.3	1.31	52.5	26.2	0.4
Germany	553	431.3	0.78	656.0	328.0	5.4
France	4,130	5,655.6	1.37	6,082.9	3,041.5	50.2
Italy	3,054	4,441.1	1.45	3,577.2	1,788.6	29.6
Luxembourg	15	10.9	0.73	14.7	7.4	0.1
Netherlands	538	938.9	1.74	1,209.5	604.7	10.0
Total	8,537	11,900.0	1.39	12,110.0	6,055.0	100.0

Source: Commission 1982(*c*).

way, directly or indirectly, the planting or replanting of fruit trees of the types concerned.

In 1972, when the Commission proposed certain amendments to Reg. 2517/69 (which, in the event, were not accepted by the Council), the ESC took the opportunity to make some wide-ranging comments about this scheme. Among a number of critical observations was one to the effect that the measure was not sufficiently well targeted. Varieties of fruit which were in demand were being grubbed up, along with the less desirable varieties (JO C131, 13–12–72). This particular point was addressed in Reg. 794/76 *laying down further measures for reorganizing Community fruit production* (OJ L93, 8–4–76). It re-enforced Reg. 2517/69 and made provision for the granting of a premium for grubbing named varieties of apple and pear trees, the actual level of the premium to be fixed in relation to the state of growth of the trees, with a maximum amount of aid per hectare grubbed. The estimated total cost of the measure was put at 8.55m. ua and the Guidance Section of FEOGA reimbursed 50 per cent of Member State eligible expenditure.

Table 10.8 summarizes the out turn of these two schemes. The first part of the table, relating to Reg. 2517/69, indicates that almost 80,000 growers participated, grubbing up nearly 89,000 ha. of trees. The major beneficiary was Germany, although the area grubbed per grower was much smaller than the average in France and Italy. The second part of the table relates to Reg. 794/76, which was a much smaller scheme with only 8,500 participants and less than 12,000 ha. grubbed. It was very largely confined to France and Italy, although the actual area grubbed per grower was very similar right across the Community.

In 1979, the Commission issued a report on the operation of the 1976 scheme which stated that the original target had been the removal of 15,500 ha. of orchards. On the basis of the removal of about 12,000 ha., the Commission estimated that the scheme would reduce the production of apples by about 186,000 tonnes and pears by 48,000 tonnes. Given that the area represented about 4–5 per cent of the total area of apple and pear orchards, the impact of this scheme in improving market equilibrium must have been negligible. Over the same winter that this scheme was operating, an additional 7,000 ha. were grubbed without receipt of the premium. The Commission suggested that these were varieties which did not qualify for aid, or were on plots below the minimum accepted for the payment of the premium, 'or possibly because the producers did not wish to commit themselves to not replanting apple trees, pear trees or peach trees on the plots grubbed' (Commission 1979(c), 4). This is another example of a scheme which may well be helpful to the individual producer who is thinking of leaving the sector to do so in a less painful manner, by the provision of an income cushion, but it achieves little else.

The problem of overproduction of apples, pears, and peaches still remains: in 1994, in its review of the future of the fruit and vegetable sector, the Commission provided estimates of production and use in 2000 compared with 1990–2. All three fruits were expected to remain in surplus. It was clear that the deterrents to overproduction in the fruit and vegetable sector generally, applied since the late 1980s, were not functioning as intended. The growers were content to produce not for the market but for withdrawal. The Commission was contemplating the need for considerable changes to the system of market support and to the role of producer groups, as well as to the system of grubbing up. The Commission stated that it was 'not convinced that large-scale subsidized grubbing up is sufficient in itself to solve the problems of structural surpluses. At all events, to be effective, a grubbing-up scheme must be accompanied by rules on planting rights, with appropriate monitoring measures' (Commission 1994(c), 20). At the time of writing, the reform of the fruit and vegetable sector was still under discussion.

Wine. As mentioned in Chapter 6, wine was already identified as a problem commodity at the time of the 1960 price and market proposals, when the Commission recognized that long-term market equilibrium might require structural changes to involve the grubbing-up of vines, and changes in the varieties of grapes. However, despite this early identification as a problem sector, it was not until 1976 that a scheme was adopted to facilitate the grubbing-up of vineyards. This measure was introduced at a time of considerable crisis in the wine sector, involving very heavy expenditure for market withdrawals and the compulsory distillation of unsaleable surpluses.

Wine must be the least homogeneous of all agricultural commodities but, in the broadest terms, its production is divided into table wine and quality wine psr (produced in specified regions). The market is dominated by table wine and it is this part of the sector which causes the problems on the supply side. Production of table wine is declining slowly but not at a sufficient pace to match the decline in consumption. In the early 1970s, when new plantings of quality vines began to exceed new plantings of table wine varieties, replantings were still heavily dominated by the latter. By the second half of the 1970s, replantings were also dominated by quality vines.

Over the lifetime of the CAP, the disequilibrium in the wine sector has proved to be more intractable than even that of milk, although the latter has received much more publicity. Milk has been a high-profile commodity firstly, because of the very high expenditure on its market support and secondly, because it is a Community-wide commodity, dominated by northern producers. Wine is a regional commodity, mostly in the south—Italy mainly and southern France, until the Enlargements of the 1980s. The addition of Greece, Portugal, and above all Spain, has made the production and marketing difficulties very much worse but, because of the tendency of commentators to ignore southern-type commodities, the scale of the problem is not appreciated outside the Institutions of the Union.

There are, however, many similarities between the wine and the milk sectors: the existence of many small producers, often with few viable alternatives, and production in both LFAs and in lowland areas with lower costs. There are also similar experiences with modernization: the elimination of the small producers with low yields and their replacement with higher yielding, more intensive, and specialized units. One major difference between wine and milk is the unpredictability of output of wine from one year to another, which makes the kind of control mechanisms used for milk totally inappropriate for the control of the supply of wine.

As mentioned above, the chronic imbalance in the wine sector was first seriously addressed in the mid-1970s. In 1977, the Commission warned that, if anything, the situation was going to deteriorate further:

[T]here is an ever-increasing tendency to plant vines on more fertile land which permits higher yields; furthermore there is a spread in modern know-how concerning fertilizers, irrigation and plant health, and this will inevitably bring yields closer to the maximum levels which are theoretically possible. . . . It is possible that the average yield throughout the Community within a few years may be the same as those at present found only in certain wine-growing regions, and this would mean, if the area under vines remained stable, that supply would be much higher than the present level of consumption. (Commission 1977(a), 13)

It was in the light of considerations such as these that, in 1976, a temporary ban on new plantings was imposed but the Commission was clear that such a step could not provide a solution to overproduction. Indeed, there was a danger that the ban might itself prompt growers to try to raise the yields of their existing vines through better management techniques. The Community faced a real dilemma: in hill areas yields tend to be lower than in the plains, so from a narrow point of view, economic logic might suggest that production should move to the more fertile sites on the plain. However, lowland areas have many more options in terms of possible crops than hill areas. In addition, the cultivation of vines and the making of wine are labour-intensive, unless carried out in very large undertakings. In hill areas, where employment opportunities are not good, wine is an important user of labour. Finally, because wine is not homogeneous the varieties suited to high-yielding mechanized production on the plains are more likely to be the ones for table wine rather than quality wine. These thoughts were very much in the minds of policy-makers in the late 1970s, in the context of the recent introduction of Dir. 75/268 on LFAs (referred to in Chapter 9).

In 1978, the Commission put forward an Action Programme (1979–1985) for wine. Production of table wine was increasing by 1 per cent annually over the long term, while consumption was virtually static. The area planted was practically constant but yields were rising due to replanting with high-yielding varieties, and new plantings on the plain. The Commission proposed a programme which included market management and structural measures. An important aim was to reduce the area under vines by progressively removing from cultivation regions which had no natural advantages for vine growing. In addition, naturally suitable areas should be replanted with quality varieties (Commission 1978(*b*)). Despite the seriousness and urgency of the situation on the wine market, the Council displayed its usual tardiness in strengthening the structural reform measures. It was not until 1980 that a new package of structural schemes came into force. Prior to that, in the 1970s, three measures had been introduced, two of which applied only in France. Table 10.9(*a*)–(*c*) provides the cumulative out turn of these schemes.

The first structural measure was Reg. 1163/76 *on the granting of a conversion premium in the wine sector* (OJ L135, 24–5–76). It covered the three years 1976/77–1978/79 and consisted of a payment per hectare of vines grubbed, the actual level of payment depending on the type and condition of the vine. FEOGA-Guidance reimbursed 50 per cent of Member States' eligible expenditure. The total FEOGA cost of the measure was estimated to be 78m. ua. One interesting comment on this measure is to be found in the Resolution of the European Parliament on the proposal. While agreeing in principle with the proposal, the Parliament was clearly sceptical about its effectiveness. In particular it recalled 'that previous Community measures for the grubbing-up of fruit trees and the voluntary slaughter of cattle did not produce satisfactory results and made very little impact' (OJ C79, 5–4–76, 35). It regarded as 'purely theoretical' the Commission's estimate that the grubbing aid would affect as much as 120,000 ha. of vines. In this it was to be proved absolutely correct. Table 10.9(*a*) indicates that the area grubbed amounted to 78,000 ha. belonging to 61,000 producers. Not

Table 10.9(*a*). Reg. 1163/76: Measure to encourage conversion in wine-growing

Member States	No. of beneficiaries	Area grubbed (ha.)	Eligible expenditure by Member State '000 ECU	Reimbursement by FEOGA cumulatively to end 1986 '000 ECU
Belgium	262	17	39.8	19.9
France	35,805	43,757	61,643.6	30,821.8
Italy	24,991	34,268	34,020.9	17,010.4
Total	61,058	78,042	95,704.3	47,852.2

Source: Commission 1987(*e*).

Table 10.9(*b*). Dir. 78/627: Restructuring and conversion of vineyards in the Mediterranean regions of France

Member State	Measure	No. of beneficiaries	Area concerned (ha.)	Reimbursement by FEOGA cumulatively to end 1986 '000 ECU
France	Restructuring	37,931	31,192	32,658.5
	Conversion	10,659	19,169	21,448.5
	Irrigation	232	1,518	880.6
				54,987.6

Source: Commission 1989(*h*).

Table 10.9(*c*). Dir. 79/359: Conversion of vineyards in the Charentes

Member State	Beneficiaries	Area grubbed (ha.)	Reimbursement by FEOGA cumulatively to end 1985 '000 ECU
France	4,307	6,190	13,575.7

Source: Commission 1986(*e*).

surprisingly, the final FEOGA cost was also much lower than the original estimate.[14]

The second measure—Dir. 78/627 *on the programme to accelerate the restructuring and conversion of vineyards in certain Mediterranean regions of France* (OJ L206, 29–7–78)—was part of the Mediterranean package referred to in Chapter 9. The intention was twofold: to improve those areas where quality wine could be produced, and to encourage growers in other areas to change to other products. Effort was concentrated mainly on Languedoc-Roussillon, with lesser amounts available in the departments of Ardèche, Bouches-du-Rhône, Var, and Vaucluse. The results of this scheme are given in Table 10.9(*b*): 31,000 ha. were restructured and 19,000 ha. converted. Based on statistics published in 1986, this out-turn was considerably less than originally intended namely, 66,000 ha. restructured and 33,000 ha. converted (Commission 1986(f)).

The third reorganization scheme set up in the 1970s was for the conversion of vineyards in the Charentes departments in France, (Dir. 79/359, OJ L85, 5–4–79). This was quite a different measure from the other vineyard schemes, as it was intended to reduce the area devoted to the production of cognac, demand for which had fallen due to the recession of the early 1970s. As there was a surplus of white table wine, the French wished to discourage the diversion of wine from cognac production to the general white wine market. The plan was to grub up 5,000 ha. and, as Table 10.9(c) indicates, this was overachieved.

By the time these three schemes had come to an end, something in excess of 100,000 ha. had been removed from wine production.[15] However, in a sector which, at that time, had about 2m. ha. in production, of which almost two-thirds were for table wine, these measures would have had an insignificant effect. Clearly more needed to be done. In 1978, at the same time as the Commission made its proposals on the Charentes and the Mediterranean areas of France (outlined above), it presented a major package of wine measures to the Council.[16] It was not until 1980 that the structural elements of the package were accepted by the Council.

There were three linked measures; the first—Reg. 456/80 *on the granting of temporary and permanent abandonment premiums in respect of certain area under vines and of premiums for the renunciation of replanting* (OJ L57, 29–2–80)— followed on from Reg. 1163/76. However, it was broader in scope, in that it provided not only for temporary abandonment of wine production as previously but also an incentive to those who had received the temporary abandonment premium under the earlier legislation to make that permanent.

The second measure—Reg. 457/80 *establishing a system of premiums for the cessation of wine-growing in France and Italy* (OJ L57, 29–2–80)—was intended to encourage elderly wine-growers to leave the sector. It provided an enhanced payment to growers who were receiving the permanent abandonment premium under Reg. 456/80, or the conversion aid under Dir. 78/627 in the Mediterranean regions of France (see above). This incentive was in addition to any retirement pension which they might be receiving under Dir. 72/160. As far as can be ascertained, no payments were ever made, for which over 11m. EUA had been allocated.

The third measure was Reg. 458/80 *on collective projects for the restructuring of vineyards* (OJ L57, 29–2–80). This was intended to apply in any wine-growing region, naturally suited to wine production, which was not included in any other structural adjustment scheme for wine. It was designed to assist groups of growers to undertake restructuring of vineyards collectively and included not only aid to improve the vineyards but also to assist with related works such as road improvement.

Table 10.10(a) and (b) provides the information available on the first and third of these schemes to the end of 1988. Under Reg. 456/80, about the same number of producers participated in the temporary and permanent abandonment

Table 10.10(*a*). Reg. 456/80: On the abandonment of vineyards and renunciation of planting, cumulatively to end 1988

Member States	Temporary abandonment		Permanent abandonment		Planting renunciation		FEOGA reimbursement '000 ECU
	Bene-ficiaries	Area (ha.)	Bene-ficiaries	Area (ha.)	Bene-ficiaries	Area (ha.)	
France	33,297	54,006	36,354	54,626	5,236	7,135	105,502
Greece	184	520	1,760	680	—	—	607
Italy	18,165	21,019	12,235	13,981	—	—	27,789
Total	51,646	75,545	50,349	69,287	5,236	7,135	133,598

Table 10.10(*b*). Reg. 458/80: On restructuring of vineyards, cumulatively to end 1988

Member States	Beneficiaries	Area restructured (ha.)	FEOGA reimbursement '000 ECU
Germany	8	3,709	3,273.7
France	218	20,241	15,737.7
Italy	23	4,311	3,324.1
Total	249	28,261	22,355.5

Table 10.10(*c*). Reg. 777/85: Premium for permanent abandonment of vineyards, cumulatively to end 1988

Member States	Beneficiaries	Area abandoned (ha.)	FEOGA reimbursement '000 ECU
Greece	2,815	1,168	4,538.8
France	14,473	26,465	81,391.3
Total	17,288	27,633	85,930.1

Source: Commission 1989(*h*).

schemes, a little over 50,000 in each category with 70,000–76,000 ha.[17] Reg. 458/80 attracted 249 growers with 28,000 ha. of vines. A ceiling had been placed in this latter Regulation on the total area eligible for FEOGA reimbursement of 223,800 ha., which was actually subsequently increased. Based on the 1988 data, there seemed little likelihood it would be reached—let alone exceeded.

Table 10.10(*c*) contains information to the end of 1988 on the successor Regulation to Reg. 456/80. The oversupply in the wine sector had continued to deteriorate: in the words of the Commission—'the measures relating to structures adopted by the Council since 1976 . . . had not really succeeded, by 1984, in prompting a qualitative and quantitative reform of Community wine production' (Commission 1986(*f*), 27). It was in this context that Reg. 777/85 was enacted.[18]

It was targeted predominantly at the producers of table wine but included also table grapes, grapes for drying, and wine for cognac in the Charentes because, to some extent, these categories are interchangeable with table wine. It also included aid for the cultivators of vine root-stock. The aim was to reduce the total area devoted to table wine production by about 180,000 ha. (about 8 per cent of the wine growing area in the Community at that time).

By the end of 1988, 28,000 ha. had been abandoned but only in two Member States—France and Greece. The life of this Regulation was cut short at the end of the 1987/88 wine year by the introduction of a new scheme covering all areas under vines—table wine and quality wine.[19] This new measure was prompted by the introduction for wine of production stabilizers, i.e. the budgetary controls on expenditure from FEOGA-Guarantee, outlined in Chapter 6.

The series of structural schemes enacted in the 1970s and 1980s to reorganize and reduce the area devoted to wine production give the impression of frenetic and increasingly desperate activity in a sector which was out of control. In 1986, the Commission commented that 'the future must be viewed with great concern'. No end to overproduction was in sight and, as if the situation was not bad enough, Enlargement of the Community in 1986 increased the area under vines by 80 per cent! Although yields are low in Spain, it is a major producer (the area under vines is greater than in France or Italy), and it is in structural surplus. As a result, the overproduction of EC-12 was bound to get worse (Commission 1986(*f*)).

Little had changed by the early 1990s: the area under vines continued to decline but not at the same rate as the decline in consumption. The structural surplus remained; the market support mechanism had become too complex and was still allowing growers to realize an adequate return on wine destined for industrial distillation, thereby encouraging producers to regard this as a normal outlet. The response to the grubbing up schemes had resulted in environmental damage in hill areas and had created patches of waste ground in the countryside (Commission 1993(*b*)).

The structural schemes reduced area by about 50,000 ha. per year but 'the premiums granted seem more to accompany than to foster a natural decline in areas under vines' (Commission 1993(*b*), 1). This is a situation already observed for other problem commodities. Put bluntly, if nothing was done, the surplus by the end of the century would be twice its 1986/87–1990/91 level. The removal of surplus wine through distillation is no solution as it merely transfers the problem, at considerable budgetary cost, to the industrial alcohol sector—a parallel disruption to that experienced in the beef sector by the encouragement given to dairy farmers to reduce milk deliveries and move to beef production.

The 1993 discussion document put forward a bewildering range of ideas to try to achieve the Commission's stated objective of market balance by the end of the century, without increasing overall budgetary expenditure. This document is no different from earlier discussion documents on wine in its failure to emphasize that the real problem in the wine sector has been that distillation of surpluses has been carried out at too high a price, i.e. the price received by the producer is sufficiently attractive so that it does not act as a deterrent. Unless this fundamental aspect of pricing is adequately addressed, no structural programme and no reorganization of the market regime can succeed in achieving market equilibrium. At the time of writing, the new arrangements for wine were still being discussed and it is not possible to be confident that equilibrium can be achieved in the few wine years remaining before the turn of the century.

A footnote to the structural measures for wine: as from the beginning of 1990, funding for the measures still in place—Regs. 458/80; 777/85; 2239/86;[20] and 1442/88—was transferred from FEOGA-Guidance to Guarantee. This recognition of the link between structural measures intended to improve the performance of the market, and the market support regime itself goes right back to the original proposals on FEOGA in Reg. 26/62, before the Fund was divided into two sections. Originally, FEOGA had three tasks: to provide refunds on exports, to intervene on the internal market, and to support 'structural changes necessitated by the development of the common market' (Art. 3.1(d), Sp. OJ 1959–1962). The achievement of a common market in a particular commodity, through the operation of a market regime and structural measures directly linked to that regime, was an idea which very quickly disappeared in the early struggle to launch the CAP. Nothing more was heard of it after 1963. Yet it is ironic that, nearly thirty years later, such a link was recreated by putting market support and market reorganization under the same heading in the Fund.[21]

Improvements in Processing and Marketing

In the first Section of this chapter, reference was made to the fact that the processing and marketing support activities of Reg. 17/64 were continued in Reg. 355/77 *on common measures to improve the conditions under which agricultural products are processed and marketed* (OJ L51, 23–2–77). This Regulation was a long time in coming. The life of Reg. 17/64 was limited following the introduction of the financial Regulation 729/70, which laid down the basis for future assistance of a structural nature. If for no other reason than that of legal necessity, consideration had to be given to the replacement of Reg. 17/64 by some other measure in the sphere of marketing and processing. More than that, however, there has always been a tendency to concentrate aid to agriculture in that sector of the industry which lies on the farm and to neglect the need to improve the handling of the products once they leave the farm. For many years, Reg. 17/64 was the only Community measure of any importance providing such post-farm aid, despite the fact that it was recognized that the agricultural sector was weak in the handling of produce.

In setting the new guidelines for the CAP in 1971, the Council had invited the Commission to continue to study the problems of marketing and processing, and to submit a proposal on their alleviation. In 1973, in the *Improvement* memorandum, the Commission announced its intention to make such a proposal but it was not until mid-1975 that it finally managed to submit this proposal to the

Council in COM(75)431 (Commission 1975(c)). The Commission reasoned that a more efficient processing and marketing sector would be in a position to pay better prices to producers, to diversify output, thereby stimulating demand, to concentrate more on exports, and (rather obscurely) to 'better handle products from remote areas of the Common Market' (ibid. 4). The proposal was for the establishment of multi-annual programmes, each of which would cover one or more agricultural products. Within these programmes the Community would provide aid for suitable projects intended to promote the rationalization and expansion of processing and marketing. Assistance was to take the form of a capital subvention of not more than 25 per cent of the value of the investment, with the beneficiary providing at least 50 per cent and the Member State participating in the funding as well. The estimated cost of the scheme was 400m. ua over a five-year period.

While largely in agreement with the intentions of the Commission, the ESC had a number of reservations (OJ C45, 27–2–76). For one, the Committee was of the opinion that the proposed Regulation was 'of direct concern to consumers, farmworkers, and workers in the food industry and the distributive trade' (p. 12) but that insufficient regard was being paid to the interests of these parties. The ESC also believed that the effectiveness of the measure could be improved by the formation of producer groups and urged the Council to adopt the long-outstanding draft Regulation on such groups. This point was echoed by the European Parliament (OJ C178, 2–8–76).

Another point on which the two bodies agreed was their scepticism concerning the Community's ability to control the new measure in a manner which would avoid exacerbating the surplus problem. Both Parliament and ESC considered the proposed scheme as financially inadequate. The Parliament stated that 'the Commission's proposal represents a limited step which will result in a decrease in the total real amount of Community aid to be granted for the improvement of marketing and mixed production/marketing structures, and which will make no substantial contribution to reducing agricultural surpluses and limiting the need for intervention' (OJ C178, 2–8–76, 37). The ESC commented that '80 million units of account per year is not enough to solve all the problems of improvement of agricultural product marketing and processing facilities, especially as costs will continue to be pushed up by inflation' (OJ C45, 27–2–76, 13). It was not until 1977 that a modified version of this proposal was passed by the Council and it is hard to believe that either the Parliament or the ESC would have regarded the changes as beneficial.

The programmes 'to develop or rationalize the treatment, processing or marketing of one or more agricultural products' (Article 2) had to be drawn up by each Member State and agreed by the Commission before applications for the funding of individual projects could be considered. These projects could be for a wide range of activities: the development of new outlets for agricultural products; lightening the burden on intervention by improvements to the structure of a market; assistance to regions having difficulty adjusting to some aspect of the CAP; improvement of marketing channels or rationalization of the processing of an agricultural product; improvement of quality or presentation . . . (Article 11). While the contribution from FEOGA-Guidance to eligible expenditure was fixed at 25 per cent, in later years this was modified in various countries and regions, e.g. in the Mediterranean, and the West of Ireland. Strange little schemes were added on from time to time as, for instance, a special measure to rationalize and improve slaughterhouses in Belgium.[22]

The support arrangements for processing and marketing were overhauled in 1990, so as to bring them into line with the new arrangements for the Structural Funds. Basically, the format remained the same but the rates of reimbursement from FEOGA were revised and simplified.[23] As with Reg. 17/64, information is available (1978–88) on the regional distribution of the aid under Reg. 355/77. Appendix Table 10.A1 provides the details; while it is not completely compatible with Table 10.2 and provides more detailed information, Table 10.A1 does indicate that some of the regional inequalities which appeared in the earlier measure are repeated here; for instance, the importance of Scotland in the UK, and of Emilia-Romagna and Lazio in Italy. However, in some Member States there have been shifts, with new regions coming to the fore, such as the North-East in Ireland. There still was evidence that the poorest regions were not achieving the enhanced level of investment necessary for them to narrow the income gap.

Table 10.A2 provides the breakdown by Member State of the total number of projects according to the sector of investment. There were great differences by country, with one or two sectors in each dominating: meat in Belgium; fish in Denmark;[24] cereals and wine in Germany; fruit and vegetables, and tobacco in Greece; fruit and vegetables, and meat in Spain; wine, and fruit and vegetables in France; meat in Ireland; fruit and vegetables, and wine in Italy; fruit and vegetables in Portugal; and fish and meat in the UK. Taking the Community as a whole, fruit and vegetables, meat, and wine projects dominated in terms of number, and together they also accounted for over 57 per cent of the funds.

Table 10.A3 provides a summary of the number of projects financed and their state of completion. As with Reg. 17/64 (Table 10.3), the outstanding feature of the table is the relatively large number of projects abandoned in Italy—over 38 per cent of the total. The figure for the UK—although much lower—is also rather high. The second part of the table gives the cumulative figures (1978–88) for funds committed and actually paid. The rate of reimbursement is an indication of the efficiency of the programme in the Member States, both in terms of the take-up of the investment opportunities and of the national bureaucracies. Five Member States had achieved a payment/commitment level in excess of 70 per cent; France and the UK achieved levels in excess of 60 per cent; Ireland and Italy in excess of 50 per cent. Greece, Portugal, and Spain were well below these levels. While the last two countries had only recently joined the Community and therefore could be expected to be somewhat slow the same cannot be said for Greece.

In terms of total funds, aid to marketing and processing is one of the biggest sources of structural investment in agriculture—just as Reg. 17/64 had been before it. Together with funds spent on improving the efficiency of farms, and LFAs, these three are the most significant programmes. While aid to LFAs has a large social element in it, in that it is intended to compensate for inherent locational handicap, the other major aids are intended to make lasting improvements to the economic framework within which farming takes place and agricultural produce reaches the market. Despite their popularity, one must question to what extent they have been successful in raising levels of efficiency, so that one could see a time when the need for palliative measures under the price and market policy would be reduced or even eliminated. If such a time is not yet in sight, then one needs to question whether the commitment to and content of structural policy within the CAP are adequate.

NOTES

1. Reg. 2809/73 (OJ L290, 17–10–73). Initially the changed level of funding was for one year only but this was subsequently extended.
2. Nine Member States only, as the countries which joined the Community in the 1980s were not eligible for aid under Reg. 17/64.
3. Not very different from the issues which confront the European Union and the Member States which comprise it!
4. Other commodities organized in the same way as fruit and vegetables are olive oil and hops. Fish, which used to come under the CAP, is similarly organized. For an explanation of the role of intervention agencies generally see Fennell (1987).
5. Legislation on co-operatives differs from one Member State to another and, in promoting the advantages of producer groups, the Commission has always been careful to frame its proposals in sufficiently broad terms that the formation of producer groups is not dependent on their compliance with national legislation on co-operatives. Thus, it would be fair to state that all producer co-operatives would qualify as producer groups, but not vice versa.
6. The number of cotton-producer groups given in Table 10.4(*c*) is impossible to reconcile with the statistics quoted in COM(87)362 (Commission 1987(*f*)), where only about 350 groups were stated to exist in 1985. The statistics for investment aid are, however, very similar in the two sources.
7. Greece (23), Spain (30), France (99), Ireland (2), Italy (406). No groups had been recognized in Belgium or Portugal.
8. See Neville-Rolfe (1984) for an account of the milk regime from the early 1960s to the early 1980s.
9. See Fennell (1979) for a list of these schemes, 1972–7.
10. Reg. 1353/73 *introducing a premium system for the conversion of dairy cow herds to meat production and a development premium for the specialized raising of cattle for meat production.*
11. It is surprising that the Action Programme makes no reference to the earlier schemes to reduce milk production.
12. Reg. 1336/86 *fixing compensation for the definitive discontinuation of milk production* (OJ L119, 8–5–86).

13. This Regulation was extensively amended in 1982 (Reg. 1204/82, OJ L140, 20–5–82).

14. At some stage, the Commission must have drastically reduced its forecast of the area to be grubbed because, in 1986, it stated that the objective had been 50,000 ha. which meant that the target had been exceeded by a healthy 56%! (Commission 1986(*f*)).

15. It is hard to be accurate about this, as the terminology is not precise and the same words are sometimes used to mean different things. Thus 'conversion' under Reg. 1163/76 meant temporary abandonment for a period of six years. 'Replanting' can mean planting with better-quality vines or planting with another crop.

16. Something very strange was going on in the Commission in 1978, as two sets of proposals on wine were submitted to the Council, one in August, the other in September. Although they cover much the same subject, two of the measures had been substantially altered in the course of one month (see OJ C209, 2–9–78 and OJ C232, 30–9–78).

17. The very small third element in Reg. 456/80—renunciation of replanting rights—was intended to persuade growers whose rights to replant had been suspended under Reg. 348/79 to renounce them permanently.

18. Reg. 777/85 *on the granting, for the 1985/86 to 1989/90 wine years, of permanent abandonment premiums in respect of certain areas under vines* (OJ L88, 28–3–85).

19. Reg. 1442/88 *on the granting, for the 1988/89 to 1995/96 wine years, of permanent abandonment premiums in respect of wine-growing areas* (OJ L132, 28–5–88).

20. Reg. 2239/86 *on a specific common measure to improve vine-growing structures in Portugal* (OJ L196, 18–7–86). As none of the existing structural measures suited the situation in Portugal, a special scheme was set up for it. A similar situation had occurred in Greece under Reg. 895/85 (OJ L97, 4–4–85).

21. Previously, some structural measures were part-funded by the two Sections of FEOGA.

22. Reg. 3974/86 (OJ L370, 30–12–86). An even more peculiar scheme was introduced under Reg. 1943/81 (OJ L197, 20–7–81) on processing and marketing in the cattle feed sector in Northern Ireland which specifically catered for projects which were *not* eligible under Reg. 355/77.

23. Reg. 866/90 *on improving the processing and marketing conditions for agricultural products* (OJ L91, 6–4–90).

24. From 1984 until 1989 fishery and aqua projects were included under the Regulation.

Table 10.A1. Reg. 355/77: Regional breakdown by Member State of projects financed, cumulatively 1978–1988 ('000 ECU)

Belgium			Denmark			Germany		
Region	Projects	Aid	Region	Projects	Aid	Region	Projects	Aid
Oost Vlaanderen	52	9,326	Storkøbenhavn	13	3,798	Schleswig-Holstein	94	19,486
West Vlaanderen	91	20,064	Øst for Storebaelt[a]	55	7,753	Hamburg	5	3,623
Antwerpen	39	8,931	Vest for Storebaelt	254	47,115	Niedersachsen	115	38,584
Limburg	23	5,974	Multi-regional	1	102	Bremen	18	1,797
Brabant	35	8,424				Nordrhein-Westfalen	93	23,291
Hainaut	35	5,899				Hessen	107	23,400
Namur	10	4,681				Rheinland-Pfalz	87	26,389
Liège	36	6,333				Baden-Württemberg	442	54,620
Luxembourg	7	1,295				Bayern	94	43,385
Multi-regional	3	841				Saarland	4	2,312
						Berlin (West)	—	
Total	331	71,768		323	56,768[b]		1,059	236,887

a excluding Storkøbenhavn
b total does not tally with the regional details

Table 10.A1. *(cont.)*

France			Greece			Spain		
Region	Projects	Aid	Region	Projects	Aid	Region	Projects	Aid
Île-de-France	10	2,520	Nisoi	16	8,255	Galicia	59	19,647
Champagne-Ardenne	32	12,926	Anatoliki Sterea	40	34,279	Asturias	11	2,245
Picardie	21	5,030	Ditiki Sterea	58	18,377	Cantabria	5	952
Haute-Normandie	35	9,210	Peloponissos	70	52,365	País Vasco	20	3,943
Centre	20	7,453	Thraki	11	11,670	Navarra	27	4,630
Basse-Normandie	37	13,059	Anatoliki Makedonia	21	19,789	Rioja	14	2,679
Bourgogne	19	6,832	Kentaiki Makedonia	52	69,774	Aragon	30	8,294
Nord-Pas-de-Calais	34	14,376	Ditiki Makedonia	9	2,645	Madrid	25	6,846
Lorraine	9	4,134	Ipiros	24	20,220	Castilla-Leon	56	14,856
Alsace	17	6,896	Kentriki Sterea	21	4,493	Castilla-La Mancha	74	9,771
Franche-Comté	3	1,795	Thessalia	32	31,307	Extramadura	21	5,613
Pays-de-la-Loire	54	24,274	Kriti	25	21,421	Cataluña	77	20,854
Bretagne	60	30,061	Multiregional	8	48,927	Comunidad Valenciana	72	16,706
Poitou-Charentes	13	5,414				Baleares	5	1,002
Aquitaine	135	31,397				Andalucia	197	34,344
Midi-Pyrénées	54	15,277				Murcia	23	7,750
Limousin	16	7,770				Canarias	6	944
Rhône-Alpes	62	24,444						
Auvergne	7	4,605						
Languedoc-Rousillon	438	104,050						
Provence-Côte d'Azur	194	32,479						
Corse	10	883						
DOM	24	12,161						
Multi-regional	15	9,284						
Total	1,319	386,330		387	343,522		722	161,076

Table 10.A1. (*cont.*)

Ireland			Luxembourg			Italy		
Region	Projects	Aid	Region	Projects	Aid	Region	Projects	Aid
Donegal	41	17,556				Piemonte	34	18,961
North-West	11	4,813				Valle d'Aosta	6	1,842
North-East	74	35,520				Liguria	5	4,472
West	42	22,898				Lombardia	45	40,568
Midlands	28	16,782				Trentino-Alto Adige	82	37,156
East	63	23,812				Veneto	85	39,851
Midwest	34	11,586				Friuli-Venezia Giulia	4	8,102
South-East	73	31,283				Emilia-Romagna	239	76,676
South-West	63	24,491				Toscana	81	20,739
Multi-regional	4	2,401				Umbria	46	18,709
						Marche	65	42,175
						Lazio	111	66,468
						Campania	32	58,487
						Abruzzi	34	36,210
						Molise	8	7,133
						Puglia	49	52,342
						Basilicata	32	36,676
						Calabria	44	51,522
						Sicilia	63	58,181
						Sardegna	50	38,422
						Multi-regional	18	19,252
Total	433	191,142		17	3,020		1,133	733,944

Table 10.A1. (*cont.*)

Netherlands			Portugal			UK		
Region	Projects	Aid	Region	Projects	Aid	Region	Projects	Aid
Groningen	4	932	Entre Douro e Minho	32	10,999	North	41	7,652
Friesland	7	3,834	Trás-os-Montes	27	5,883	Yorkshire-Humberside	60	11,257
Drenthe	2	231	Beira Litoral	45	13,915	East Midlands	72	16,332
Overijssel	16	3,304	Beira-Interior	16	7,193	East Anglia	83	18,651
Gelderland	57	9,107	Ribatejo e Oeste	84	35,668	South-East	80	16,871
Utrecht	8	1,887	Alentejo	32	8,486	South-West	61	12,132
Noord-Holland	32	10,657	Algarve	16	4,737	West Midlands	41	9,954
Zuid Holland	71	25,116	Açores	13	6,585	North-West	36	7,548
Zeeland	34	4,172	Madeira	3	858	Wales	41	7,785
Nord Brabant	50	11,090				Scotland	235	37,888
Limburg	18	3,790				Northern Ireland	125	32,125
Z.I.J.—polders	3	600				Multi-regional	2	391
Multi-regional	2	230						
Total	304	74,950	Total	268	94,324	Total	877	178,586

Source: Commission 1989(*h*).

Table 10.A2. Reg. 355/77: Projects aided by sector, by Member State, cumulatively 1978–1988, ('000 ECU)

Sector	Belgium		Denmark		Germany		Greece		Spain	
	No. of projects	Aid granted	No. of projects	Aid granted	No. of projects	Aid granted	No. of projects	Aid granted	No. of projects	Aid granted
I Milk products	25	5,586	17	3,597	67	30,674	24	32,941	60	12,897
II Meat	110	30,087	83	21,890	60	28,186	19	48,502	103	37,726
III Wine	—	—	—	—	282	44,734	36	27,639	79	12,539
IV Fruit and vegetables	70	17,029	22	3,475	181	46,142	98	96,343	212	44,220
V Flowers and plants	3	255	15	2,971	35	9,037	3	5,258	9	2,080
VI Fishery products	22	3,625	131	12,499	58	7,677	22	8,029	46	15,646
VII Cereals	47	5,714	7	378	230	30,125	29	53,059	81	11,451
VIII Animal feed	2	961	11	4,254	—	—	3	2,996	5	1,257
IX Seeds	13	1,553	13	2,281	73	14,072	4	8,199	5	1,017
X Eggs and poultry	17	2,997	11	1,203	6	2,743	14	13,025	31	9,290
XI Olive oil	—	—	—	—	—	—	48	26,457	63	4,920
XII Tobacco	—	—	—	—	1	169	84	19,381	—	—
XIII Other	22	3,960	13	4,220	66	23,329	3	1,694	18	8,033
Total aid granted	331	71,767	323	56,768	1,059	236,888	387	343,523	722	161,076
Total investment		372,877		435,119		1,231,064		798,266		780,922

Table 10.A2. (*cont.*)

Sector	France No. of projects	France Aid granted	Ireland No. of projects	Ireland Aid granted	Italy No. of projects	Italy Aid granted	Luxembourg No. of projects	Luxembourg Aid granted	Netherlands No. of projects	Netherlands Aid granted
I Milk products	17	9,681	62	19,227	73	40,405	—	—	41	12,665
II Meat	165	92,258	146	104,476	64	55,484	—	—	85	17,397
III Wine	517	102,990	—	—	193	104,945	12	2,402	—	—
IV Fruit and vegetables	365	97,030	15	7,029	381	258,522	—	—	67	22,979
V Flowers and plants	10	2,929	2	356	1	2,169	—	—	16	12,049
VI Fishery products	56	13,840	61	21,131	103	56,563	—	—	43	4,468
VII Cereals	36	14,452	38	7,002	167	80,995	3	385	—	—
VIII Animal feed	1	92	25	11,598	11	10,358	1	23	—	—
IX Seeds	62	23,666	1	70	6	2,175	1	211	16	1,609
X Eggs and poultry	3	902	45	11,224	3	2,913	—	—	30	3,525
XI Olive oil	10	1,632	—	—	43	30,735	—	—	—	—
XII Tobacco	—	—	—	—	55	61,503	—	—	—	—
XIII Other	77	26,856	38	9,027	33	27,175	—	—	6	255
Total aid granted	1,319	386,328	433	191,140	1,133	733,942	17	3,021	304	74,947
Total investment		1,641,689		625,316		2,250,865		13,479		602,345

Table 10.A2. (*cont.*)

Sector	Portugal		UK		Total		% of sectors
	No. of projects	Aid granted	No. of projects	Aid granted	No. of projects	Aid granted	
I Milk products	33	10,907	58	14,375	477	192,955	7.6
II Meat	25	20,294	180	58,903	1,040	515,203	20.3
III Wine	42	10,719	—	—	1,161	305,968	12.1
IV Fruit and vegetables	68	26,088	106	16,369	1,585	635,226	25.1
V Flowers and plants	2	150	5	631	101	37,885	1.5
VI Fishery products	43	11,609	189	20,990	784	176,077	7.0
VII Cereals	24	6,771	126	27,954	788	238,286	9.4
XIII Animal feed	—	—	28	4,500	87	36,039	1.4
IX Seeds	—	—	23	2,040	217	56,893	2.2
X Eggs and poultry	4	980	66	13,977	229	62,779	2.5
XI Olive oil	16	2,093	—	—	181	66,360	2.6
XII Tobacco	1	1,983	—	—	141	83,036	3.3
XIII Other	10	2,730	97	18,849	382	125,605	5.0
Total aid granted	268	94,324	877	178,588	7,173	2,532,312	100.0
Total investment		215,068		871,899		9,838,899	

Note: small discrepancies exist between the Total and the individual Member States' statistics for some commodities. Also, some of the 'total aid granted' does not tally exactly with the equivalent in Table 10.A1.

Source: Commission 1989(*h*).

Table 10.A3. Reg.355/77: Summary of projects financed, aid granted, and payments made, cumulatively to end 1988

Member States	Projects financed	Projects completed	Projects not carried out	Projects in progress
Belgium	331	226	1	104
Denmark	323	263	10	50
Germany	1,059	878	30	151
Greece	396	126	22	248
Spain	722	31	3	688
France	1,319	816	34	469
Ireland	433	244	35	154
Italy	1,133	636	130	367
Luxembourg	17	11	1	5
Netherlands	304	184	10	110
Portugal	268	17	—	251
UK	877	567	58	252
Total	7,182	3,999	334	2,849

	Belgium	Denmark	Germany	Greece	Spain	France
Aid granted '000UA/EUA/ECU	71,767	56,768	236,888	343,523	161,076	386,328
Aid paid '000UA/EUA/ECU	52,663	45,208	188,019	72,828	21,378	257,037
% paid	73.3	79.6	79.3	21.2	13.2	66.5

	Ireland	Italy	Luxembourg	Netherlands	Portugal	UK	Total
Aid granted '000UA/EUA/ECU	191,140	733,942	3,021	74,947	94,324	178,588	2,532,312
Aid paid '000UA/EUA/ECU	105,169	389,610	2,546	61,862	14,351	111,106	1,321,777
% paid	55.0	53.0	84.2	82.5	15.2	62.2	52.1

Source: Commission 1989(*h*).

11

Broadening the Policy Horizon

Introduction

Earlier chapters have recorded the attempts made over the lifetime of the CAP to reshape it. To a large extent, these efforts concentrated on weakening the level of price and market support so as to discourage surplus production, periodic attempts to dispose of surpluses already accumulated, and the promotion of improvements to the structural framework within which farming takes place. An overriding conclusion must be that these efforts were always too little, too late, and that the dominance of price and market policy was never challenged once the Mansholt Plan of 1968 failed in its objective to reverse the importance of market and structural support. A further conclusion must be that the continued dominance of price support made it inevitable that the inequity of the distribution of the benefits of the policy by farm size, farm type, and region would remain.

Although many of the efforts made in the 1980s to curb the excesses of the price and market policy, and to target structural funds more effectively were to prove to be inadequate to the task, there is no doubt that there was a change of pace. A sense of urgency, which had been absent in the 1970s, began to appear. This was largely due to factors external to the CAP—the budgetary crisis in the Community being one major source of pressure which necessitated the imposition of a ceiling on total expenditure on agricultural support. In order that cuts in the level of price and market support could be introduced and sustained without resulting in a dramatic decline in income, ways had be found of raising the level of productivity in farming by lowering costs rather than by increasing production which had been the approach in earlier years. It was in this context that the proposals on improving the efficiency of agricultural structures were made in 1983, which resulted in Reg. 797/85, referred to in earlier chapters.

However, it is well known that structural change takes place slowly and the market situation in the early 1980s was critical. Not only was the Community market heavily oversupplied but the international market was also saturated so that, even with the use of heavy subsidization of exports, the surpluses could not be cleared. Therefore, there was a pressing need to bring about greater equilibrium in the market which could not wait for the outcome of the efforts to improve production efficiency. To achieve the necessary adjustment in the market through a systematic lowering of support prices was extremely difficult and the efforts to carry through such a policy met with strong political resistance. Therefore, other means had to be found and these were sought through the promotion of alternative systems of farming and alternative uses of farmland.

The need to lower input costs and production levels coincided with a growing concern for the impact which agriculture was having on the natural environment. Because of the slow increase in the size of farms and the scarcity of land for renting, the single most effective way in which farmers could achieve a higher income was through intensification of production. Because of the emphasis on unit price support, the more one produced, the more one benefited from the system. This encouraged farmers to use more fertilizers, herbicides, and pesticides on their crops; to feed their livestock on bought-in concentrates; and to raise the productivity of grassland by reseeding pasture and increasing the use of nitrogen. Against this background, the promotion of alternative systems of farming which encouraged farmers to lower the intensity of production without a loss of income had a double attraction: it could reduce surpluses and environmental damage simultaneously.

The Community's budgetary crisis had its origin in the deep economic recession of the early 1980s, which produced a sharp rise in inflation and a relentless increase in the numbers unemployed. At its peak, unemployment in the Community was in excess of 11 per cent and the labour market only began to recover in the late 1980s. Traditionally, much of the income shortfall in farming has been dealt with by the farming population either through combining farming with other activities or by migration to other occupations, often in other regions or countries. The poor employment prospects in other sectors made it essential that farming should become a more attractive employment option for young members of farm households. In turn, the existence of a well-trained younger generation of farmers was essential if the sector was to adapt to a new, harsher economic environment.[1]

Thus, as the 1980s progressed, the task facing agricultural policy-makers in the Community began to crystallize around an interrelated group of objectives: to maintain a viable farming population, enjoying an acceptable standard of living, in a production system which achieved a better market balance and preserved the natural environment.

On the population front, the emphasis was on the creation of circumstances in which the elderly could be persuaded to retire, and the young persuaded to take over the management of the farms. On the income front, the emphasis was on widening the range of options available to farmers to enhance their incomes, either through the provision of direct income aids, or through compensation when they changed their production patterns, or through encouragement to broaden the range of on-farm activities. As for market balance, the emphasis was on a restrictive price policy and on curbs on production, coupled with encouragement to diversify. On the natural environment, the emphasis was on raising the awareness of farmers of the issues involved, coupled with encouragement of ecologically sound farming practices, and discouragement of damaging practices. Many of these strategies have been outlined already in other contexts.[2] Many of them proved to be of little significance, or took so long to get under way that their impact was still unknown at the time of writing. The next two Sections of this chapter examine the efforts made to encourage alternative systems of farming and alternative uses of farmland.

Alternative Systems of Farming

With the growing acceptance of the pace of technological and biological change came a realization that the open-ended commitment to support unlimited quantities of products had to cease. Over the 1980s, the concept of producer co-responsibility was extended in various guises to a wider and wider range of commodities. However, this development did little to curb production which constantly outran the almost stagnant level of consumption internally, thereby requiring the continued export at high cost to an oversupplied international market. Anything which reduced the pressure on the market was to be welcomed and, in this context, three alternative systems of farming were proposed: extensification, set-aside, and organic farming. Of these, by far the most important was set-aside but, in origin, extensification predated it and, in a sense, set-aside could be regarded as a form of extensification.

Under Reg. 1760/87 (OJ L167, 26–6–87), amendments were made to Reg. 797/85 to include an aid scheme to encourage farmers to reduce their output of surplus commodities. These were defined as 'products for which, consistently at Community level, there are no normal unsubsidized outlets' (Article 1). Until the end of 1989, Member States were free to limit the aid to cereals, beef and veal, and wine; in each sector the scheme was to result in the reduction of output by at least 20 per cent. It was not a very attractive scheme, as it was based on a compensatory premium paid to participating farmers by the Member State, with FEOGA-Guidance reimbursing 25 per cent of the cost. The scheme ran into operational difficulties and did not, in fact, start in 1989, even though the Member States had been given the opportunity to introduce it on an experimental basis. However, the Community persisted with the scheme and it was incorporated in Reg. 2328/91 which replaced Reg. 797/85. In 1992, as part of the MacSharry Plan, it became part of the wider programme to encourage environmentally friendly farming: this policy development is discussed later in this chapter.

Extensification was completely overshadowed by the background to and introduction of set-aside. Apart from the perennial difficulties with milk, the other major commodity sector which gave serious cause for concern in the mid-1980s was cereals. Yields had risen relentlessly since the 1950s and by the mid-1980s were more than double the level of thirty years previously. This was due to the introduction of high-yielding varieties, (especially of common wheat which replaced the less productive coarse grains), improved farming practices, and greater specialization. The frightening situation was that, under the controlled conditions prevailing in research stations, yields of 20 tonnes/ha. were

being produced—nearly four times the average yield actually recorded at farm
level (Commission 1987(*a*)). Fortunately farmers never achieve the kinds of
yields theoretically possible but production techniques do improve all the time
and a further doubling of the average yield was not an unrealistic possibility.

Demand was stagnant: changes in the human diet meant that the consumption of wheat-based products had fallen, and cereals as a livestock feed had
declined, due to the competition from cheaper imported substitutes. This latter
situation was the direct result of the high support price for cereals which made
their use in feed rations expensive. The high support price also undermined the
non-food use of cereals in the chemical and other industries. The need to make
cereals more competitive with substitute products was extremely urgent. The
USA was forging ahead with its industrial uses of cereals: in 1984, it was
estimated that:

by 1990, 35 million tonnes of maize, equivalent to 21 million tonnes of starch, will be used
in the US to produce chemicals. If this does happen substantial additional amounts of
corn gluten products will be co-produced and add further pressure on world animal feed
markets, which have already had to absorb the corn gluten products associated with US
isoglucose production.   (Commission 1986(*d*), 5)

For some years the Commission had been advocating that the gap between
cereal prices in the Community and in its main competitor countries should be
narrowed, and that the unlimited support guarantee should be curbed by the
imposition of price penalties if certain production levels were exceeded. As mentioned in Chapter 6, the guarantee threshold was introduced in 1982 but the
system fell apart in the 1985/86 price negotiations when the Germans refused to
accept the proposal to reduce the money support price.

It is hardly surprising that when, a few months later, the *Perspectives* was
published more attention was paid to the problems facing the cereals sector than
to any other commodity. It was in the context of a discussion on the policy options for cereals that the possibility of directing land to other crops, or to use it
for non-agricultural purposes, or to leave it fallow was raised. These were not
seen as mutually exclusive options but rather ones which could be used in
combination. It was recognized, however, that the provision of subsidies to
encourage the diversion of cereal land would be expensive and would require a
level of monitoring which did not exist in all Member States. The Commission
also regarded such schemes as very much a second-best option to a rigorous
price policy (Commission 1985(*b*)).

The Commission continued to paint a gloomy picture of the state of the cereals
market when, later in 1985, it returned to the issue of oversupply, pointing out
that carry-over stocks were expected to be 25m. tonnes or double the average of
previous years. If supply and demand continued on their existing trends, by
1991/92, stocks would be 80m. tonnes or nearly half of total output. There was
no way that such a quantity could be disposed of on international markets.[3] The
Commission advocated a restrictive price policy, the participation of farmers in
funding the cost of surplus disposal, the pursuit of quality rather than quantity,

and the reorganization of the intervention mechanism to discourage its excessive use by traders (Commission 1985(*c*)).

While the possibility of set-aside had been raised, it was not seriously discussed in the context of the reform of the cereals regime at that time and indeed there was opposition to set-aside within the Commission. In March 1987, the Commissioner for Agriculture—Andriessen—replied to a question in the European Parliament with some very negative comments about set-aside:

[T]he Commission takes the view that the systematic withdrawal of farmland from the productive system cannot enable better equilibrium to be achieved on the agricultural markets on a lasting basis: the rapid development of agricultural productivity . . . would quickly cancel out any effort to reduce land potential and thus would force further set-aside of land. There are many other considerations supporting a very sceptical attitude towards this system of land withdrawal. (OJ C171, 29–6–87, 4).[4]

Despite these misgivings, in mid-1987 the European Council, in confirming the need for a more market-orientated approach to policy, referred to the possible role which set-aside and extensification might play in support of market reform (Bull. EC 6–1987). The broader issue of the non-agricultural use of farmland was very much in the air at that time, particularly in the context of the proposals made in September 1987 on production stabilizers. As already outlined in Chapter 6, a few months later at a further European Council meeting, it was agreed that cuts in budgetary expenditure on agriculture would be introduced, and that the concept of producer co-responsibility would be strengthened if the guarantee thresholds for the major commodities were breached.

As part of that programme, the Council agreed to the introduction of set-aside for arable land. The scheme was to be compulsory for Member States but optional for farmers, and was to run for five years. Certain regions were to be exempt if natural conditions or the danger of depopulation suggested it would be an unwise policy. The scheme was outlined in considerable detail by the European Council, almost as if the heads of government did not trust the Agricultural Council to make the necessary decisions! (Bull. EC 2–1988). Set-aside was introduced under Reg. 1094/88,[5] and, in order to qualify, at least 20 per cent of the arable land on a farm had to be withdrawn from cultivation. It could be left fallow as part of a crop rotation system, wooded, or used for non-agricultural purposes. Member States were authorized for a period of three years to permit set-aside land to be grazed in an extensive livestock system, or to be used for growing lentils, chick-peas, and vetches.[6]

Farmers were compensated for the loss of income within a range laid down in the Regulation and, if the producer set aside at least 30 per cent of the arable land, an additional incentive was provided by way of relief from liability for part of the co-responsibility levy. As the Commission's report on the first year of operation made clear, the scheme got off to a slow start. In 1988/89, over 38,000 farmers participated and over 434,000 ha. were set aside. At the time cereals were grown on nearly 4m. farms so the response by farmers to the scheme can be seen as minuscule.

The area set aside represented less than 1 per cent of total arable land, and the Commission estimated that about 1–2m. tonnes of cereals were not produced as a result of set-aside. This should be seen against an annual cereals output level of about 160m. tonnes at that time. The annual increase in cereals production due to yield improvements alone was estimated at 3–4m. tonnes (Commission 1989(*g*)). As a contribution to the control of surplus production, the first year's experience of set-aside suggests it was something of a disappointment. The Commission blamed the poor results on the late launch of the scheme, inadequate publicity by the Member States, and, in some cases, the low levels of aid set by the Member States. What the Commission did not say was that many Member States were dubious about the whole idea of set-aside and that the only one of them with any real enthusiasm for the scheme was Germany. As has been mentioned previously, the Germans have consistently favoured market controls over price support reductions, and the introduction of voluntary set-aside must be seen in that context.

Table 11.1 provides an analysis of the results of the set-aside scheme for 1988/89, including the use to which the land was put. Not surprisingly at such an early stage in the scheme, over 80 per cent of the land was fallowed, and less than 4 per cent was taken out of agriculture and into forestry, or some other use. By early 1991 (i.e. into the third season of operation), the scheme had still not made much of an impact: only 800,000 ha. or about 2 per cent of the cereals area had been set aside, and most of the land was of low yield (Commission 1991(*b*)).

German reunification took place in 1990 and, as a consequence, there was an increase in the cereals surplus. The Commission anticipated that the poor marketing conditions would persist internationally, and that stocks would remain high (Commission 1991(*a*)). Because of the limited response to set-aside, the Commission proposed an increase in the co-responsibility levy in the 1991/92 farm year as an added deterrent to production. By way of compensation, farmers were offered various financial inducements if they agreed to withdraw 15 per cent of their arable land from the production of crops subject to price support. Thus, although set-aside was still voluntary, it was beginning to take on the appearance of a much more significant element in the organization of the cereals sector.

This role was further enhanced under the MacSharry reforms: his original proposal was that all existing production incentives should be abandoned and that the price support for cereals would, over a period of years, fall to a level which would make production competitive with cereal substitutes. The fall in the support price would be compensated for on a sliding scale of aid per hectare. Full compensation would be paid up to a certain level and beyond that on a degressive scale. Above a certain area, the payment of aid would be conditional on the withdrawal of some arable land, the exact amount of which would be determined by the state of the market (Commission 1991(*b*)). A parallel scheme was proposed for oilseed and protein crops so as to prevent distortions arising between different parts of the arable sector.

A secondary aim of the MacSharry Plan was to try to lessen the stranglehold which the large producers had on the financial benefits of the policy; nowhere

Table 11.1. Area of land set aside, number of holdings participating and use of land, by Member State, 1988/89

| Member States | No. of applications | Area to be set aside ha. | of which % | | | | | | Proportion of the area set aside as a percentage of | | Average area set aside per applicant (ha.) |
			rotational fallow	permanent fallow	afforest- ation	extensive grazing	non- agricultural use	chick peas, etc.	arable land[a]	area in cereals[b]	
Belgium	32	329	18.1	42.5	10.1	7.4	21.6	—	d	d	10.2
Germany	25,289	169,729	46.3	52.8	0.5	1.1	0.3	—	2.4	3.6	6.7
Greece	n.a.	n.a.	n.a.	n.a.	n.a.	n.a.	n.a.	n.a.	n.a.	n.a.	n.a.
Spain	518	34,229	29.0	41.3	4.1	5.1	0.9	19.8	0.3*	0.4	66.1
France	1,002	15,707	28.8	62.6	4.9	—	3.6	—	d*	0.1	15.6
Ireland	77	1,310	2.5	23.5	3.1	64.5	6.2	—	0.1	0.3	17.0
Italy	9,301c	155,606c	25.4	44.4	3.4	23.7	0.7	2.2	1.8	3.1	16.7
Netherlands	195	2,621	63.5	31.7	4.0	—	0.4	—	0.3	1.3	13.4
UK	1,750	54,779	11.0	79.6	1.4	—	7.7	2.2	1.8	3.1	16.7
Total	38,164	434,310	32.4	52.0	2.1	9.4	1.6	2.3	0.9	1.3	11.3

a in the case of returns marked with an asterisk, the calculations are on the basis of data supplied by the Member States. For the other countries, the calculations are on the basis of the most recent Eurostat data for arable land (1987 or 1988)

b calculations are on the basis of 1985 Eurostat data for land under cereals

c applications provisionally considered eligible

d lower than 0.1%

n.a. = not available

Note: information communicated by Member States, 16 June 1989. The scheme was not applied in Denmark or Luxembourg in the 1988–9 agricultural season. Portugal was exempt.

Source: Commission 1989(g).

was this more obvious than in the cereals sector. Six per cent of cereals farms accounted for half the cereal area, and 60 per cent of production. Put another way: 94 per cent of cereals farms produced 40 per cent of the output and, given the nature of price support, which was based solely on the principle that the more you produce the more you benefit from the system,[7] by definition the vast majority of cereals farmers were receiving very little of the support provided by the policy. For a policy which was supposed to be mindful of income levels and income differentials, the existing arrangements were incapable of assisting the poorer farmers and were overcompensating the richer ones.

In the course of the negotiations on the reform package, the proposals were extensively modified and they lost much of their social equity element. Under Reg.1766/92 (OJ L181, 1–7–92), which reformed the common organization of the market in cereals, the levels of target, threshold, and intervention prices were fixed for the three marketing years 1993/94–1995/96. These prices declined each year and, under Reg. 1765/92 (OJ L181, 1–7–92), schemes were established through which farmers received a rising payment per tonne to compensate for these price declines. The compensation was based not on current production but on the average of the three years 1989–91.[8]

There were two schemes: one general and open to all producers, the other a simplified arrangement for small producers only.[9] Under the general scheme, producers are obliged to set aside part of their arable land. Initially, the set-aside requirement was fixed at 15 per cent of the average area in the three years 1989–91 and a compensation payment was made on that basis. The land set aside is subject to rotation so as to guard against farmers setting aside only their least productive land. While set aside, it can be used to produce non-food crops.[10] In 1994, this policy resulted in about 4.7m. ha. being withdrawn from production, of which 264,000 ha. were diverted to non-food crops (see Table 11.2). To the total area withdrawn as part of the new arable policy should be added a further 1.5m. ha. withdrawn for other purposes. As the Commission commented: 'such a reduction seems considerable but in relative terms it amounts to only 4.9% of the agricultural land in use and 2½ per cent of the Union's surface area' (Commission 1994(*e*), 113). Small though the total impact was, there was evidence of considerable regional variation, with a greater concentration of set-aside in the south and in the poorer cereal-producing areas. While this makes economic sense, it could result in the creation of new social problems in areas with limited alternative production possibilities.

As for the third alternative system of farming—organic production—in 1985 in the discussion document: *A future for Community agriculture*, the Commission announced that it was going to take action to promote organic farming. As it stated: 'this is a demand that Community farmers would find it in their interests to satisfy before farmers outside the Community do so' (Commission 1985(*d*), 13). The following year, the European Parliament advocated an action programme on organic farming which would have included not only the setting of standards of production but also provision for the training of farmers and their advisers, and financial support to help the transition from conventional

Table 11.2. Estimated set-aside in 1994
resulting from new system of price support
for arable crops

Member States	Set-aside '000 ha.	of which non-food production	
		'000 ha.	%
Belgium	19	3	16
Denmark	205	19	9
Germany	1,063	68	6
Greece	17	—	—
Spain	909	6	1
France	1,589	73	5
Ireland	24	—	—
Italy	207	43	21
Luxembourg	2	—	—
Netherlands	8	1	13
Portugal	78	—	—
UK	556	51	9
Total	4,677	264	6

Source: Commission 1994(*e*).

farming to organic farming (OJ C68, 24–3–86). The Commission did not have anything quite so grandiose in mind and the steps which it took were very small. For instance, in 1987, producer groups were given the power to decide on the rules of production to be followed by their members when supplying organic produce.[11] In addition, farmers producing organic commodities and the processors of these products were free to avail themselves of various types of assistance under Regs. 797/85 and 355/77.

In fact, the main issue was not one of financial support, except in the transitional phase which indeed can deter farmers from switching to organic production. The need at Community level was for a system of regulation and control which would ensure the observance of minimum standards and consumer protection. This latter was particularly important as it was generally agreed that consumers were prepared to pay a premium for products subject to strict production specification. In the event, the necessary legislation was not passed until 1991.[12] It covers labelling standards, rules of production, and inspection.

Alternative Uses for Farmland

Apart from the introduction of measures intended to lower the level of production of commodities in surplus (as outlined in the previous Section), attempts were made in the late 1980s–early 1990s to encourage the diversion of land to new uses. Among the ideas put forward were the introduction of new food crops, non-food uses, and forestry. Much attention was given to the question of alternative production in the *Perspectives*: the marketing difficulties for the major commodities, combined with a cautious price policy would—it was believed—prompt farmers to consider shifting to other lines of production. However, this process was being inhibited by inadequate research and advice on alternatives, the small size of the market, the need to adapt to different product specifications, and the absence of market support for many of the alternative products.

The Commission went into considerable detail in the *Perspectives* to outline the types of reorientation which could take place. Cereals could be replaced by certain oilseeds and protein crops, or by wood crops for a variety of uses—pulping, biomass for energy production, quality timber. Fruit trees could be replaced by other trees, in particular nut-bearing trees. Some of the Commission's suggestions were positively bizarre and the entire discussion took place in the absence of data on the size of the alternative markets. The Commission did recognize that some of the alternatives would be difficult to introduce in the absence of a system of income compensation for farmers to help them in the years of transition from one crop to another (of particular importance in relation to tree crops). It also stated that the alternatives 'would have to be considered with a rigorous economic approach, taking account of the possible markets, and whether production could be continued on a long-term basis after some initial financial encouragement, or would entail continuing budgetary cost' (Commission 1985(*b*), 30).

However, this sensible approach was undermined a few paragraphs later when, in promoting the possibilities of oilseed and protein crops, the Commission stated that in order to 'make such crops more attractive to farmers, and to speed up their development, only a very slight increase in support (in relative or absolute terms) would be necessary' (Commission 1985(*b*), 30). The illogicality of this statement is breathtaking: alternative crops were being promoted in the context of curbing support for products in surplus. If, therefore, cereals were to be made less attractive due to changes in their support levels, why would additional incentives be required for oilseeds and proteins, as their attractiveness would have risen automatically?

The Commission ended its discussion on alternative food products by summarizing the areas of policy which might need to be altered in order to accommodate new crops. They included the adaptation of the relevant support regimes, aid to assist farmers to make the switch in production, incentives to ensure the existence of appropriate processing and marketing facilities, creation of the legal framework to harmonize quality standards and consumer information, and the provision of aid for research, and for technical and economic advice. Clearly this would not be a costless exercise nor would it be achievable in the short term.

Even more problematical was the other main area of development explored in the *Perspectives*, namely the use of agricultural products as raw materials for industrial processes, far removed from the traditional outlets of food and fibre. The two examples used by the Commission to illustrate the possibilities of this development were bio-ethanol as a source of energy, and sugar and starch for industrial uses. The advantage of bio-ethanol is that, because of its agricultural origin, it is a renewable resource, unlike fossil fuel. It is obtained by fermentation, either directly from plant sugars or indirectly from raw materials which contain starch. It can be used in small quantities as an additive in petrol without the need to change engine design and can contribute to the reduction of the use of lead in petrol, thereby achieving an environmental gain as well.

The real problem with bio-ethanol is its price: fossil fuels are cheaper and, under present pricing structures, bio-ethanol would require a subsidy. Despite this price obstacle, the Commission listed the advantages for agriculture of its production. In particular, it would provide a new outlet for products in surplus, sugar beet being the best candidate and, to a lesser extent, cereals and potatoes. Once again, logic seemed to desert the Commission: if the aim was to bring supply and demand into equilibrium, by definition over time the surplus which would be used to produce bio-ethanol would disappear. Therefore, the only way in which its production would be possible would be to abandon the attempt to reduce surpluses. The other drawback was that suitable processing facilities were not available and these would need to be provided at considerable cost. Such facilities would require long-term guarantees as to the availability and continuity of the supply of the raw material. Despite the negative features, the Commission returned to the topic of bio-ethanol later in 1985 and suggested that a marketing subsidy equal to the export refund for cereals might be considered for this product. The finance to support such a venture could come from the income generated by the cereals co-responsibility levy which was applied at that time (Commission 1985(*c*)). It is unlikely that the last has been heard of bio-ethanol.

A less problematic possibility was the provision of sugar and starch for industry. Already about half the production of starch went to this end-use; the most important outlets were paper and cardboard, chemicals and pharmaceuticals, textiles, glues, and pastes. The discussion of the non-food uses of agricultural output coincided with the increased interest in biotechnology generally as part of the Community's research programme. As the Commission stated:

[D]iversification of production and the capture of new industrial markets through advances in plant and animal sciences or in the processing of agricultural outputs, are aims which will (at least in the medium to long term) both contribute to agricultural policy objectives, and strengthen the foundations of Europe's biotechnology industry. (Commission 1986(*d*), 3)

The development of the industrial uses of agricultural products was enticing: the Commission estimated that about 80m. tonnes of oil equivalent were used annually as chemical feedstock, and most of that was imported (Commission 1986(*d*), 3). To divert even part of that outlet to agricultural sources was a prize worth having. The issues raised in the *Perspectives* were discussed further in a follow-up document: *A future for Community agriculture* (Commission 1985(*d*)). While much of this document was little more than a rerun of the

Perspectives, the Commission did identify in a succinct way certain priorities for the CAP. These were: the gradual reduction of surplus production to the benefit of the taxpayer; the increase in the diversity of production and the improvement of its quality; the more effective and systematic tackling of the income problem of small family farms; the provision of support for farming in areas where it is essential for environmental and landscape purposes, and for the maintenance of a viable rural population; the promotion of environmental awareness among farmers; and the development of industries which process agricultural raw materials, so as to keep farming in the forefront of technological change.

The first positive response to the ideas raised in the *Perspectives* came with the changes made in 1986 to the aid for starch for industrial purposes. Under an earlier scheme, a subsidy had been paid to the manufacturer of starch but under the new system the subsidy was paid instead to the end user of the starch.[13] The purpose of this new system was to neutralize the benefits to third-country manufacturers of industrial products from their ability to purchase raw materials from international markets without payment of a levy. Manufacturers in the Community either had to pay the import levy or had to purchase internally produced raw materials at enhanced prices, due to the operation of the common price support mechanism. Considerable expansion in the non-food use of starch was anticipated and, without the change in the subsidy arrangements, there was a real danger that this expansion would bypass the Community's own farmers and processors.

In 1989, the Commission produced a report on the operation of the starch subsidy scheme which concluded that, overall, the scheme was working reasonably well. The impact varied from one industry to another and its benefits were dependent (not surprisingly) on the importance of starch as an input to the manufacture of the particular product, and the tightness of the profit margin on the finished product. Therefore, for some, the subsidy was a critical element, while for others it was no more than a welcome source of extra income (Commission 1989(*e*)).

At the European Council meeting in February 1988, when so many issues within agricultural policy were on the agenda—budgetary control, stabilizers, set-aside, early retirement, income aids—a request was made to the Commission 'to investigate all possibilities of increasing the utilization of agricultural commodities in the non-food sector and to submit proposals to that effect' (Bull. EC 2–1988, 18). The Commission's response to this request appeared in early 1990. What is interesting about the report is that, despite strenuous efforts to paint as positive a picture as possible, it was clear that the scope for non-food uses of agricultural products was very limited (Commission 1990(*a*)).

At that time, less than 1 per cent of the land area of the Community was used for non-food production (excluding forestry of course). The range of uses was very small—flax, cotton, tobacco, alcohol, sugar, and starches providing the bulk of the output, and many of these being the result of unsaleable surpluses rather than a genuine demand. The Commission reviewed what the Community was already doing to promote non-food uses—research and development, demonstration projects, structural aids of various sorts, and certain provisions in the relevant market regimes. The list was not very impressive.

Additional options open to the Community were to encourage the non-food use of agricultural products either by action at the farm level or by the provision of incentives to processors, and the assistance could be either temporary or long-term. Whichever approach was adopted, the Commission made it clear that it was vital that additional production of surplus commodities should not occur, and that the raw material made available to industry should be at a price comparable to the international price. Little of any practical value came out of this report: apart from recommendations that the research and demonstration efforts should be strengthened, the only concrete proposal was that the rules on set-aside should be altered so as to encourage farmers to use this land for the production of crops for industrial purposes in collaboration with a processor (Commission 1990(*a*)). This proposal was accepted by the Council but its adoption was optional for the Member States.[14]

The other attempt to encourage alternative uses for farmland came in 1987 in an amendment to Reg. 797/85. Reference was made in the previous Section to the introduction of aid for extensification; under the same Regulation (Reg. 1760/87, OJ L167, 26–6–87), provision was also made to encourage conversion to the production of non-surplus commodities, a list of which was to be approved before the end of 1987. This deadline was not observed and it is clear that there were major difficulties in the implementation of this scheme. For a start, there were few commodities of any importance which were not already in surplus or had very high levels of self-sufficiency. There was a grave danger that encouragement to switch to a less important product with a lower level of self-sufficiency would very quickly lead to the saturation of that market, thereby creating a new surplus problem.

In 1988, the Commission published a discussion document and a proposal for a Regulation in which it tried to identify products suitable for conversion, but it had little success. In part, this was due to the fact that it appeared more appropriate to adjust the provisions of the particular commodity support regime than to set up a separate scheme. This was true where the incentive was to convert to a variety with greater market demand, or to a 'quality' product. Similarly, promotion of organic farming could best be accommodated within the extensification scheme; and on-farm forestry was also best dealt with separately (Commission 1988(*g*)).[15] The extent of the difficulties can be judged from the fact that when, in 1991, Reg. 797/85 which had been heavily amended was replaced by a consolidated Regulation,[16] although conversion of production was included as a compulsory scheme for Member States, the list of products to be grant-aided had still not been agreed.

The third alternative use for farmland was forestry. The mid-1980s were years in which there was considerable interest in the whole question of forest development and frustration at the inability of the Council of Ministers to reach agreement on forestry measures, whether on or off the farm.[17] One of the few successes was the inclusion of aid to on-farm forestry under Article 20 of Reg.

797/85, outlined in Chapter 8. The situation in the forestry sector was very different from that in agriculture; despite the fact that about one-fifth of the Community's land area was planted to trees, there was a major deficit in forest products of all kinds. Existing forests were often underutilized and badly managed, and there were serious losses due to fire and atmospheric pollution. The wider debate on forestry cannot be considered here but part of that debate concerned the role which forestry could play in alleviating the problems associated with surplus production in agriculture and this issue is relevant to the alternative uses of farmland.

Reference has been made already in this chapter to the suggestion in the *Perspectives* that one of the possible uses for cereal land could be the production of wood crops. This idea was restated and developed in a discussion paper on forestry which was published a few months later (Commission 1986(*a*)). The cost of supporting forestry production needed to be weighed against the cost of surplus agricultural products, and against the cost of other measures designed to take land out of farming. 'The objective of agri-forestry action must be to develop an activity which is self-sustaining and does not require substantial subsidies (it is not envisaged that a regime of price supports or further external protection would be extended to forestry)' (ibid. 5).[18] In addition to this role as an alternative to surplus agricultural production, the Commission also saw forestry as providing a suitable crop for the less productive areas of a farm—as was already the case in many agri-forestry holdings. This possibility was regarded as having potential for short-term cropping for processed wood products, and for long-term timber production. However, the Commission was not unaware of the existence of some major problems related to on-farm forestry: the small size of forest plots, their scattered nature, the absence of suitable infrastructure for access and processing, the lack of a guaranteed supply of raw materials. Thus, unless farmers were to plant trees solely for their amenity value, the possibility of receiving an income from such a venture was fairly slim.

Accompanying this discussion document was a much more extensive memorandum in which the Commission commented on two major drawbacks to the schemes of aid for woodland under Reg. 797/85. Firstly, as with so many of the measures in that Regulation, the aid was optional for Member States and therefore they needed to be persuaded of the value of implementing them. In turn, farmers had to be encouraged to plant trees and for that they needed adequate information. Secondly, the aid available under Reg. 797/85 applied to certain types of farmers only—those with modernization plans, and in LFAs. There was a clear need to broaden the scope of the support to include other categories of farmers who wished to plant trees (Commission 1986(*b*)).

Later in 1986, the Commission put forward a series of proposals to amend Reg. 797/85, which included changes to the woodland incentives to extend the aid to farmers taking early retirement; to increase the level of aid for the costs of planting; and to raise the financial participation of the Community in the encouragement given to the establishment of forestry associations and co-operatives. The Commission assumed (rather optimistically) that, where a farmer took early retirement, in 80 per cent of the cases, the farm would be afforested (Commission 1986(*c*)). In the event, the early retirement (or pre-pension scheme) was not proceeded with at that time and the only changes made to the woodland element of Reg. 797/85 were to extend afforestation aid to farmers undertaking an extensification programme, and to raise the maximum level of afforestation aid per hectare.[19]

In 1988, early retirement became the subject of a separate Regulation on the cessation of farming in which additional aid was granted to the farmer if the farm was afforested.[20] At the same time, the provision of voluntary set-aside was introduced (referred to earlier in this Chapter), under which the land withdrawn from cultivation could be left fallow, planted with trees, or used for non-agricultural purposes.[21] Neither of these schemes was a success and therefore neither contributed in any meaningful way to the reduction of land in agriculture.

Later in 1988, the Commission returned once again to the broad issue of the future of the forestry sector. On this occasion, it proposed an Action Programme for forestry to cover the years 1989–92. Among its priority activities were the afforestation of agricultural land, the development and optimal use of woodland, and the encouragement of the production of cork (Commission 1988(*b*)). The Commission drew attention to the fact that, over the previous five years, the Community had made available nearly 500m. ECU for forestry development under a variety of schemes but that the funds had not been fully taken up by the Member States 'because the operations for which funds have been available have often been subsidiary to general agricultural schemes' (ibid. 4). It went on to state that what was needed were independent forestry measures in their own right.

Herein lay the dilemma: because of the continued opposition of some Member States to the development of a forestry policy, the Commission was trying to create such a policy by another name. It was using the needs of agriculture, rural employment creation, tourism, the environment, etc. as the means to circumvent the opposition. So often in the Community, policies introduced for one purpose are inappropriately used to serve some other purpose, and forestry was no exception. A good example of such a conflict was highlighted by the ESC in its Opinion on the Action Programme. It will be recalled that afforestation was one of the uses to which set-aside land could be put and, in commenting on the implications of this possibility, the ESC stated:

The amount of former agricultural land available for forestry differs greatly from one region of the Community to another. The use of set-aside mechanisms seems greatest in regions with larger farms and more efficient agricultural structures.

Should this trend be confirmed in the implementation of the relevant Community Regulations, holdings in disadvantaged areas—where farms tend to be smaller and the need to develop forestry activities is greater—would be doubly disadvantaged. (OJ C139, 5–6–89, 21)

In the event, the voluntary set-aside scheme of 1988 was a considerable disappointment as few farmers participated in it, and therefore the fears of the ESC were unfounded. However, it remains true that a policy established for purely forestry reasons would be very different from one which was seen as a means of alleviating difficulties created by, or exacerbated by, the CAP. Despite the poor uptake by the Member States of the existing forestry aids, the Commission put forward a package of proposals which included strengthening the financial incentives for on-farm forestry under Reg. 797/85; a new measure to develop woodlands for environmental, silviculture, touristic, and recreational purposes; and the inclusion of forestry within the terms of Reg. 355/77 on processing and marketing (Commission 1988(*b*)). These measures were accepted by the Council in a series of Regulations in May 1989.[22]

In the follow-up document which accompanied the MacSharry Plan, the Commission returned to a familiar theme, namely that farmers were not responding to the incentives on offer for afforestation (Commission 1991(*d*)). It proposed, therefore, that the existing investment aids available under Reg. 2328/91 (the successor to Reg. 797/85) should be replaced by a new scheme to promote afforestation as an alternative use for agricultural land, and to encourage the development of forest activities on farms. Once again, an important purpose was the improvement of production control in agriculture. For that reason the measure was to be part funded by FEOGA-Guarantee.

It is of some interest to note in passing that, in the Regulation as enacted (Reg. 2080/92, OJ L215, 30–7–92), the purpose of the scheme is stated as being to:

- accompany the changes to be introduced under the market organization rules,
- contribute towards an eventual improvement in forest resources,
- contribute towards forms of countryside management more compatible with environmental balance,
- combat the greenhouse effect and absorb carbon dioxide (Article 1).

This is a small illustration of the extent to which the CAP had shifted away from an earlier and more rigid position: that FEOGA-Guarantee was to support prices and markets, and FEOGA-Guidance was concerned with structural and organizational aid. Of course, in practice the bulk of FEOGA-Guarantee expenditure was still concerned with production and exports, but the previous sharp divisions were being eroded and wider considerations were intruding on the closed world of agricultural policy.

Reorganization of Structural Aid in Agriculture

In the early 1980s a number of factors came together which ultimately resulted in significant changes to the Community's Structural Funds—regional, social, and agricultural. Already, at that time, more emphasis was being placed on the design of structural aids to cater for the needs of individual agricultural regions and farmers with specific difficulties. Much of Chapter 9 was devoted to a description of the schemes proposed or introduced with these needs in mind. Greater targeting was also required in the distribution of aid from the Regional and Social Funds, in order to reduce economic and social imbalances and, as their activities were due for review, it seemed a good moment to rethink the role of Structural Funds.

At the request of the European Council, the Commission undertook a review of the operation of the funds: in the case of FEOGA-Guidance the Commission identified the slowness of implementation by the Member States as one of the shortcomings. In addition, some countries experienced difficulty in finding their share of the costs, and the effectiveness of FEOGA activities was sometimes hampered by the absence of appropriate regional policies to underpin its operations. The Commission also drew attention to the tremendous difference in expenditure on the price and market policy, and on structural reform. For many years, the ratio had been 95 : 5 in terms of total expenditure by the Community on the CAP (Commission 1983(e)). Of course, it should not be forgotten that the contribution of FEOGA-Guidance to Member State eligible expenditure was often as low as 25 per cent, rising to more significant levels only for certain schemes and in certain regions, whereas FEOGA-Guarantee covered all eligible expenditure on market support.

The question of improvements to the Funds became caught up in wider issues relating to the size of the Community's Budget, the introduction of new policies, and the resolution of a dispute with the UK on the size of its budgetary contribution. This last issue had soured relationships between the Member States since 1979 and the first real attempt to resolve it came in June 1984 at the European Council meeting at Fontainbleau. Also at that meeting, a statement was made by the Council as to the future of the Structural Funds:

The European Council considers that the structural Funds should become effective Community policy instruments aimed at reducing regional development lags and converting regions in industrial decline; promoting dynamic and competitive agriculture by maintaining and developing effective agricultural structures, in particular in the less-favoured regions; combating unemployment, in particular youth unemployment. (Bull. EC 6–1984, 9).

Improvements in the management of the Funds were also promised, as was the provision of additional financial resources. The question of resources was a major issue and the previous year the Commission had expressed the view that, in order to make a worth-while impact, the Funds needed to be doubled in size in real terms (Commission 1983(e)). There was also a need to improve the level of co-ordination in the activities of the Funds and, it was in that context, that the launching of Integrated Mediterranean Programmes (discussed in Chapter 9) was announced at the same Council meeting.

Despite this encouraging endorsement of reform of the Structural Funds at the highest level, little of a practical nature was done for some years. However, a new—and ultimately powerful—impetus was given to reform by the signing of the Single European Act in 1986. Under this Treaty (which amended the Treaty of Rome in various ways), the Community was committed to the establishment of a single internal market by the end of 1992. Within such a market, goods, persons, services, and capital should be free to move unhindered. As part of the process to bring this aim to fruition, a new Title was added to the Rome Treaty: Title V on economic and social cohesion. Under Article 130A, the Community was committed to the reduction of 'disparities between the various regions and the backwardness of the least-favoured regions'.

Economic integration carries with it the danger that existing backward regions are unable to compete on equal terms with more developed regions, unless steps are taken to counteract the centripetal forces. Already, as earlier chapters have indicated, there was plenty of evidence that, under the CAP, the richer regions and farmers had benefited disproportionately from market integration. The Single Market was a much larger version of the same integration process but with the added element of free movement of the factors of production, as well as of goods. To assist the integration process and prevent its undoubted benefits from being marred by economic and social distress in certain regions and for some groups of people, the Structural Funds needed to be made more effective as instruments of development. How this might be achieved was spelled out in detail in a discussion document issued in 1987 (Commission 1987(*b*)).

For the future, the Structural Funds were to concentrate on five objectives: aid to backward areas, declining industrial regions, the long-term unemployed, young people entering the labour market, and agricultural reform and rural development.[23] Within this group, the greatest emphasis was to be placed on assistance to backward regions. There was a real sense of urgency to do something constructive to aid these regions: since the Enlargement in 1986 to include Portugal and Spain, the income spread had widened appreciably. Before Enlargement, one person in eight had an annual income 30 per cent below the Community average, after Enlargement it was one in five (Commission 1987(*b*)). Once again, the Commission reiterated its view that the Structural Funds needed to be doubled in real terms by 1992. Along with the other requirements of reform to prepare for the Single Market, this meant new high-level discussion on the size of the Community's Budget. Reference was made in Chapter 6 to the budgetary difficulties of the late 1980s in the context of the introduction of a ceiling on agricultural expenditure, but the financial problems were much wider than that and there was a need to have a period of budgetary stability in order to allow the Community to carry out the policy adjustments necessary to the successful achievement of the Single Market. As the Commission stated: 'the Community cannot progress by lurching from financial crisis to financial crisis' (ibid. 25).

The Commission put forward formal proposals for the reform of the Structural Funds in 1987 (Commission 1987(*g*)) but the real impetus to the reform came in 1988 at a meeting of the European Council in February. The main features of the new Structural Funds were agreed, as was the doubling in real terms of the finance available over the period 1987–93. The Council also agreed on the level of Community reimbursement (Bull. EC 2–1988). The actual legislation was adopted by the Council of Ministers later the same year under Reg. 2052/88 (OJ L185, 15–7–88). The objectives of the renewed Structural Funds were set out in Article 1 as:

1. Promoting the development and structural adjustment of the regions whose development is lagging behind . . .
2. converting the regions, frontier regions or parts of regions . . . seriously affected by industrial decline . . .
3. combating long-term unemployment . . .
4. facilitating the occupational integration of young people . . .
5. with a view to the reform of the common agricultural policy:
   (a) speeding up the adjustment of agricultural structures, and
   (b) promoting the development of rural areas.

In 1993, these objectives were changed somewhat and Objective 5 was re-worded as:

promoting rural development by:
   (a) speeding up the adjustment of agricultural structures in the framework of the reform of the common agricultural policy;
   (b) facilitating the development and structural adjustment of rural areas. (Reg. 2081/93, OJ L193, 31–7–93)

This is an important shift of emphasis: no longer is the reform of the CAP seen as an end in itself but rather as a means of achieving a wider good for the rural sector as a whole.

Objective 5(a) corresponds most closely with the 'horizontal' structural aids previously available, i.e. the aids which applied across the territory of the Community rather than being region-specific. The enactment of Reg. 2052/88 necessitated a review of the existing Community-wide structural measures to see whether they complied with the new approach to structural aid. This review was contained in COM (89) 91. As most of the measures concerned had been introduced or amended within the previous few years, relatively little needed to be done to adapt them to the requirements of Objective 5(a): it was more in the nature of subtle changes to the philosophy which underlay the socio-structural aspects of the CAP. As the Commission stated: 'the measures to be adopted in future must be increasingly integrated into a broader vision of maintaining economic activity and the social fabric of rural regions' (Commission 1989(*b*), 10).

The necessary amendments to existing Community-wide schemes on improving the efficiency of agriculture, early retirement, and the setting-up of producer groups were contained in Reg. 3808/89 (OJ L371, 20–12–89).[24] Certain innovations in this Regulation should be highlighted: the encouragement of diversification of enterprises on the farm through tourism, craft activities, manufacture and sale of farm produce; the aid to improvement of hygiene in livestock enterprises, and animal welfare standards; and the easing of the requirement that farming must be the main occupation of the farmer before he/she can qualify for Community investment aid.

This last in particular was a real break with the past. Its introduction was surrounded by conditions: at least half of the farmer's total income must come from farming, forestry, tourism, or craft activities, or from activities connected with maintaining the countryside; at least one-quarter of the total income must come from farming; and the non-farming activities must not take up more than half of the farmer's work time. With so many obstacles to overcome, this innovation looks extremely grudging and reluctant—all the more so because its introduction is not compulsory but is optional for the Member States. However, it is an acknowledgement that it is the total income situation which matters: for many farm families the farm is not an end in itself but an integral part of an income-generating package.

Where agricultural structural policy is concerned, the most important innovation brought about by the 1988 Structural Fund reorganization was undoubtedly the creation of Objective 1: the development of areas lagging behind. All three Structural Funds participate in aiding these areas, with the Regional Fund playing the leading role. The requirement for inclusion under Objective 1 is that the per caput GDP over a three-year period is less than 75 per cent of the Community average. Provision was made to include other regions close to the 75 per cent cut-off point, if there were special reasons for their inclusion.

In the initial phase, 1989–93, the whole of Greece, Ireland, and Portugal, plus certain areas in other Member States were included.[25] They represented over 40 per cent of the land area of the Community and 21 per cent of the population. The list was revised for the 1994–9 period: while Greece, Ireland, and Portugal remained, changes were made in the areas which qualified in other Member States. Only one of these changes is of significance: the inclusion of the eastern Länder in Germany. The population involved rose to over 26 per cent of the Community total.

By far the greater part of the Structural Funds is spent in Objective 1 areas. This is partly because it was decided that effort should be concentrated in these areas, and partly because the rate of Community assistance is higher. Thus the involvement of the Funds is subject to a maximum of 75 per cent of the total cost and, as a general rule, at least 50 per cent of public expenditure costs in Objective 1 areas, compared with 50 and 25 per cent respectively elsewhere. In the period 1994–9, the Structural Funds have been allocated 141,471m. ECU, of which 96,346m. ECU (all at 1992 prices) are available for investment in Objective 1 areas.

The task of FEOGA-Guidance in Objective 1 areas is firstly to support the adjustment of agricultural structures in the context of CAP reform by implementing the Community-wide schemes available under Objective 5(a) but at a higher rate of reimbursement. Secondly, it supports development within plans put forward by the Member States. These are incorporated in Community support frameworks (CSFs) for which funding can come from a variety of Community sources, depending on their coverage.

The kinds of measures which can be funded by FEOGA-Guidance were set out originally in Reg. 4256/88[26] but were amended by Reg. 2085/93 (OJ L193, 31-7-93). Some interesting additions were introduced under the latter Regulation, including encouragement for the production of non-food agricultural commodities, the promotion of quality local or regional agricultural and forest products, the renovation and development of villages, and the protection and conservation of the rural heritage.

Objective 5(b) can be seen as a vehicle for assisting rural areas which do not qualify under the income criteria necessary for Objective 1 designation but which, nevertheless, suffer from some major economic or social handicap. The criteria for inclusion were revised slightly in Reg. 2081/93, so as to make a low level of GDP/inhabitant the critical factor. In addition, an area must have at least two of the following: a high percentage of the workforce in farming, a low level of agricultural income, low population density and/or significant depopulation. A special case can be made by a Member State for the inclusion of other areas on grounds such as peripherality, age, structure of the farm labour force, pressure on the environment, etc. The aid is provided within Community support frameworks and, so far as FEOGA-Guidance is concerned, any measure eligible in an Objective 1 area is also eligible in areas designated under Objective 5(b). While FEOGA-Guidance takes the lead in funding in these areas, the Regional and Social Funds are also involved.

The actual areas designated in the initial phase were listed in Commission Decision 89/426 (OJ L198, 12–7–89), and included parts of all Member States other than Greece, Ireland, and Portugal. The areas selected covered over 17 per cent of the area of the Community but only 5 per cent of the population. During 1990, CSFs were adopted for all the Objective 5(b) areas and, as with the Objective 1 areas, some of these CSFs were an adaptation of previously existing regionally targeted measures.

In 1992, in the context of the review of the progress towards the achievement of the Single Market, the Commission undertook an assessment of the structural policies and the manner in which the reformed Funds had functioned. Problems had certainly arisen: many good projects had had to be rejected because of inadequate Community funding; the weakness of the administrative system in some of the backward areas had made the task of developing programmes for investment difficult; progress had not been uniform and some of the weakest regions continued to lag behind and, worse still, even diverge further from the Community average (Commission 1992(*a*)).

It will be recalled that the 1992 price and market reforms were accompanied by new schemes on the promotion of environmentally friendly farming, early retirement, and on-farm forestry.[27] The Commission recommended that these measures and the new set-aside scheme which was also part of the MacSharry reforms should in future be fully funded by FEOGA-Guarantee. This would allow the concentration of the funds under Objective 5(a) on fewer measures, thereby increasing their impact, in particular on improvements to farm efficiency, aids to young farmers, compensatory payments for natural handicaps in LFAs, and aids to marketing and processing. This change was introduced from the beginning of 1993.[28] However, as part of the effort to concentrate structural funds on the most vulnerable areas and population, it was agreed that in the period 1994–9 the funding for Objective 5(a) measures in areas not covered by Objectives 1 and 5(b) would not be increased in real terms (Bull. EC 12–1992).

In the review undertaken by the Commission in 1992 of the progress being made towards the realization of the Single Market, reference was made to the inadequacy of the assistance being given to areas which qualified under Objective 5(b). Their plight was described in alarming terms:

[O]minous trends are threatening the future in a large part of the Community: the steady decline in agricultural employment, the widening gap between town and country in terms of the availability of services for individuals and firms, the flight of the young people from the land, the absence of factors to attract business, the damage caused to the environment by intensive cultivation and desertification. This situation could endanger the survival of the rural world, one of the pillars of the European development model. It calls for a political response and the marshalling of increased funds to obtain clearly defined objectives. (Commission 1992(*b*), 22)

It is not clear why such doom-laden warnings were being given at quite that juncture: it was certainly true that Objective 5(b) had received the smallest funding allocation in the 1988–93 period, and that it was the slowest to get started. It was mentioned above that its Community support frameworks were not approved until 1990. If the dire warnings of the Commission were a strategy to ensure that any budgetary savings which might result from the MacSharry reforms would remain pledged to rural interventions through FEOGA-Guidance in particular rather than being used for other purposes, then it did not succeed. Funding for Objective 5(b) areas was increased for the 1994–9 period only in line with the general increase for the Structural Funds.[29]

While the reform of the Structural Funds in 1988 was a welcome development, not only in terms of the considerable increase in their financing but also in terms of their greater use of targeting, there is a danger, so far as agriculture is concerned, that this may result in a belief that the income problem has been adequately addressed. Concentration on particular geographical areas where incomes are undoubtedly below average ignores the fact that poor farmers are not solely to be found there. Nor does it do anything to redress the inequality inherent in the price and market policy—which remains the greatest source of funding within the CAP. There is also some evidence that the Member States are beginning to indulge in their well-established practice of 'me-too-ism': the extension of the areas which qualify under Objectives 1 and 5(b) is reminiscent of the way in which over time more and more areas have been classified as LFAs. This dilutes the effectiveness of the targeting of support.

The Environmental Dimension of Agricultural Production

Environment policy was only added to the Rome Treaty in 1986 through the medium of the Single European Act. The environment first became an issue in the early 1970s and, after the meeting of the European Council in Paris in October 1972, the way was clear for the adoption at the end of 1973 of the first Action Programme for the Environment (OJ C112, 20–12–73). The absence of a Treaty commitment to the environment meant that the early Action Programmes were weak, though each was stronger than the one which preceded it. By the third (1982–6), the shape of the policy was well established and its goals clearly stated:

The ultimate objectives of environment policy are the protection of human health, the long-term availability of all the resources which determine the quality of life, of adequate quality and in sufficient quantity, namely water, air, space—from both the land-use and landscape points of view—climate, raw materials, the built environment, and the natural and cultural heritage, as well as the maintenance and, where possible, the restoration of the natural environment with suitable habitats for flora and fauna. (OJ C46, 17–2–83, 5)

So far as the CAP was concerned, no mention of the environment was made during the 1960s and, ironically, the earliest references to the protection of the environment seem to have been made in the context of the benefits which could accrue from land withdrawn from farming, as proposed under the Mansholt Plan.[30] What few references were made to the role of agriculture in relation to the environment were generally positive—at least until the late 1970s and early 1980s—and rarely went further than a declaration that agriculture protected the environment. An elaboration of this theme was that agriculture provided positive externalities for the benefit of the urban population who could find recreation and enjoyment in the landscape. A late example of this kind of statement was made by the Commission in 1983:

Agriculture, as the inheritor and guardian of the rural environment, contributes to the well-being of the vast majority of the population who live in urban conditions but wish to enjoy and preserve Europe's traditional landscape, flora and fauna. For these reasons the development of agriculture must continue to be made in a way which reconciles the interests of human recreation, and the protection of habitats and species, with the economic interests of those who live and work in the country. (Commission 1983(*d*), 7)

It is surprising how infrequently in the early years the link was made between the provision of positive externalities and the claim for a financial reward for this service. This was particularly true where the farm was too small to provide a comparable income or where it suffered from some natural or locational handicap. An early example where the link was made is to be found in the Bourel report in which the ESC advocated the introduction of aids unconnected with price policy, 'for example aids taking into account the role played by producers in the protection of the environment' (ESC (1974), 74). The Committee added that 'there is still a place for small farms in modern agriculture, particularly where they help to preserve a type of countryside which the general public finds attractive' (ibid. 79). The ESC saw the provision of such direct aids as no more than an extension of the concept, already accepted at the time, of measures to help farmers in less-favoured areas.

Indeed, the first piece of agricultural legislation under the CAP to make any reference to the environmental role of farming was precisely Dir. 75/268 on the LFAs (discussed in Chapter 9). However, the environmental aspects of this legislation were largely incidental. The main purpose of the Directive was to fulfil a commitment made to the UK during the Accession negotiations. A secondary purpose was to provide a means whereby farmers in disadvantaged areas could benefit from modernization aids under Dir. 72/159, as in normal circumstances they were not able to meet the eligibility criteria.

The three types of LFA are mountain areas, those suffering depopulation, and conservation areas. Although Article 3 of Dir. 75/268 refers to the protection and conservation of the environment in relation to the first two types of LFA, the emphasis is squarely placed on the production limitations of the land—altitude, slope, infertility. The only LFAs in which, conceivably, the environment might provide the main motivating force were those referred to in Art. 3.5: 'small areas affected by specific handicaps and in which farming must be continued in order to conserve the countryside and to preserve the tourist potential of the area or in order to protect the coastline. The total extent of such areas may not in any Member State exceed 2.5% of the area of the State concerned.'[31]

It is significant that no instruments of aid were provided under this legislation to help achieve environmental objectives. All the measures provided—livestock headage payments, the more favourable treatment of farms undergoing modernization—were made available without any requirement that the farming activities concerned were indeed likely to protect and conserve the countryside. The first small admission that farming was not, *ipso facto*, environmentally friendly, came in the *Stocktaking* where the Commission, having made a number of positive statements about the environmental benefits of farming, then added:

[A]griculture can also have certain unfavourable effects on the natural environment. In particular efforts should be made to mitigate the dangerous consequences of certain modern production techniques, for example cultivation methods which impoverish the soil or alter its properties, the intensive use of certain fertilizers, the excessive use of pesticides or intensive animal production. (Commission 1975(*a*), 27)

This statement was not coupled with any indication of how the CAP could be adapted to prevent or limit such unwelcome developments. The potential for conflict between agricultural and environmental interests was undoubtedly present. It arose initially in relation to certain peripheral farming areas where, in the late 1970s and early 1980s, regional structural measures were introduced to supplement the activities possible under Dir. 75/268.[32]

Two examples can illustrate the uneasy relationship between agriculture and the environment. In 1981, a Member of the European Parliament queried the use of Community funds to assist in land drainage operations in the West of Ireland under Dir. 78/628 and Reg. 2195/81. In its reply, the Commission outlined the benefits of on-farm drainage:

In areas of wet land . . . field drainage is economically advantageous to farmers in that production from the drained area can be increased allowing an increase in the farmers' income. Machinery may be used on drained land, allowing the conservation of fodder crops for winter feeding and thus reducing the need for purchased feed for winter fodder. Wet farmland is a source of various animal parasites . . . and drainage will improve the health status of the animals using the land. (OJ C129, 19–5–82, 1–2)

This positive statement was not accompanied by a balancing summary of the likely environmental damage of field drainage to a fragile eco-system. Rather, the Commission stated that the work had to be economically justified, and that the Irish Government was required to provide the necessary assurances that the environment would be protected. The Commission concluded its response by stating that it was confident that provided the necessary precautions were taken 'the environment will not be significantly damaged' (OJ C129, 19–5–82, 2).

In the second example—also from the European Parliament—the Commission was asked whether there was any intention to create 'environmental protection areas' within the LFAs where these were justified on the grounds of outstanding environmental value. As the MEP put it:

In order to protect these areas from change, it is vital not only to prevent rural depopulation . . . but also to allow farmers to earn their living without having to adapt their farming methods to technological change. Intensification of land use by means of drainage, removal of hedgerows, increased use of fertilizers etc. will eventually do irreversible damage to the most valuable areas of our environmental heritage. (OJ C222, 2–8–81, 12)

The MEP's solution was to restrict farmers in terms of farming methods but to compensate them fully for the loss of income resulting from the renunciation of certain production techniques. In his reply, the Agricultural Commissioner—Dalsager—was less than enthusiastic about the suggestion. He reminded the MEP of the possibility of designating areas under Art. 3.5 of Dir. 75/268, although he conceded the small size of this measure. The situation was quite different elsewhere: if existing technology was not applied, because of environmental considerations, and a loss of productivity resulted, then in Dalsager's view this was not a matter solely for the CAP. As he stated: 'unless absolutely necessary for reasons above the ordinary, the common agricultural policy should not encourage farmers to refrain from adapting to technological change' (OJ C222, 2–8–81, 12).

The second Action Programme on the Environment (1977–81) included a substantial section devoted to the 'non-damaging use and rational management of land', in which, not surprisingly, rural areas featured prominently. The issues discussed included the need to understand better the positive and negative effects of farming, so as to find ways of encouraging the former and minimizing the latter. The use of pesticides and fertilizers, the nuisance caused by intensive stockrearing, and the ecological consequences of changes in land use (such as drainage of wetlands), were all highlighted as topics which needed greater study. Worthy though these intentions were, they were made in the complete absence of any references to the price and market policy of the CAP. If one did not know otherwise, one might have been forgiven for assuming either that the CAP did not exist or that it was ecologically neutral and could therefore be ignored.

The only reference made in the Action Programme to the CAP was to Dir. 75/268 when it declared, with masterly understatement, that it was possible that the Directive would not 'directly solve the problem involved in conserving the natural environment of mountain regions' (OJ C139, 13–6–77, 25). It went on to state that more analysis was required of certain features of such areas:

- physical fragility (soil and climate) which makes these regions particularly subject to erosion and various natural disasters . . . such erosion can be caused by careless use of these regions;
- ecological complexity and fragility of the eco-systems, which ought to receive general protection as a matter of principle;
- need to preserve the countryside and the natural, semi-natural and cultivated environments;
- the balance to be sought between the natural uses of these regions and their use for tourism. (ibid.)

The positive effect conveyed by this list was undermined by the feeble conclusion that the Commission would 'consider the numerous aspects of the problems connected with mountain regions and will if necessary submit proposals to the Council' (ibid.).

It is quite clear that there was a strict policy hierarchy and that an Action Programme not rooted in a Treaty obligation was in no position to threaten a policy such as the CAP. If the designers of the CAP chose to ignore or marginalize environmental issues, there was little that could be done about this at Community level. Whatever their disagreements on detail, all Member States were in favour of an agricultural policy; this was not necessarily the case when it came to the environment and, in particular, the rural environment. The tensions were confirmed some years later when the Commission referred to the sensitive nature of Community environment policy as it related to land and natural resources: 'Member States are understandably hesitant about relinquishing direct control over . . . their basic natural—and non-renewable—resource' (Commission 1983(g), 37).

The relative strength of the CAP and the weakness of the environment policy might have remained unchanged had it not been for the rising tide of dissatisfaction with agricultural policy: its budgetary cost and the growing volume of surpluses. Concern with the ecological damage brought about by intensification and specialization added a further—and related—dimension to the criticism. This public perception began to be reflected in the statements made by the Community Institutions. For instance, in 1980, the European Parliament called upon the Commission 'to attach greater importance than hitherto to the consequences of further intensification, rationalization and industrialization of agriculture for the biological equilibrium in nature and the environment' (OJ C97, 21–4–80, 43). This point was put ever more strongly the following year when, in considering the role of the CAP, the European Parliament stated that one of its aims must be 'to safeguard and improve the ecological environment by maintaining the agricultural landscape' (OJ C172, 13–7–81, 35). The Parliament also revived the idea of direct payments to farmers 'for services which are necessary for regional policy, social policy and ecological reasons, and are not generally carried over into the market price' (ibid. 36).

Despite the growing awareness of environmental issues, the link was not made with the part played by the price and market policy in promoting intensification and monoculture. Indeed, there was a more ready acceptance—in the Commission at least—of the role which structural policy could play in promoting ecologically sound farming practices. In outlining the role of the structural policy, the Commission had stated in 1979 that the policy 'must serve to resolve or prevent clashes between the demands of agriculture and of environmental protection and improvement' (Commission 1979(*a*), 47). It is hardly surprising, therefore, that when in the early 1980s attention turned to the question of the replacement of the 1972 structural Directives and the 1975 LFA Directive, the opportunity was taken to include some environmental dimensions in the proposal.

The approach was cautious: in the explanatory memorandum to the draft Regulation the Commission stated that greater emphasis would need to be placed in future on the improvement in the living and working conditions in farming, energy conservation, and the protection and improvement of the environment. However, the draft Regulation itself did not contain any comparable statement of intent (Commission 1983(*f*)).[33] So blatant was this omission that the ESC, in its Opinion on the draft, stated:

The Committee welcomes the Commission's proposal that the Community's agricultural structures policy place greater emphasis on protection of the environment and nature conservation. . . . The Committee nevertheless cannot find any actual statements to this effect and Article 17(2) for example, which provides for aid in the case of drainage work, makes no reference to protection of the environment. . . . The Committee believes that it would be helpful for Member States if the Commission were to provide a general picture of how its policy on agricultural structures would be reconciled with environmental protection needs. (OJ C103, 16–4–84, 32)

The most important reference to the environment in the draft Regulation came in the revision of the modernization aid which had been the main feature of Dir. 72/159. Under Art. 3.1 the new investment aid was to apply to:

(a) the qualitative improvement and conversion of production in the light of market requirements;
(b) the adaptation of the holding with a view to:
 • reducing production costs,
 • improving living and working conditions,
 • saving energy;
(c) measures for the protection and improvement of the environment. (Commission 1983(*f*), 8–9)

When the Regulation was finally passed by the Council, the above requirement had been watered down so as to allow the Member States to choose which of the purposes to support.[34] This suggests that not all Member States were yet ready to embrace environmental concepts in farming. On the positive side, Article 19 had been completely rewritten to make provision for national aids (not supported at Community level) in environmentally sensitive areas, i.e. those which were 'of recognized importance from an ecological and landscape point of view' (Art. 19.2 of Reg. 797/85). The farmer had to undertake as a minimum requirement not to intensify agricultural production any further and that 'stock density and the level of intensity of agricultural production will be compatible with the specific environmental needs of the area concerned' (Art. 19.3).

While the environmental features of Reg. 797/85 appear minimalist, in fact the Regulation was an important break with the past and it provided a base from which a more adventurous approach could be launched. Indeed, the mid-1980s proved to be a watershed in this as in so many other aspects of agricultural policy. The interest in environmental issues grew appreciably over the remainder of the decade, which is evident from the upsurge in the number of questions in the European Parliament relating to environmental issues in agriculture.

The *Perspectives* was the first Commission discussion document to comment extensively on environmental issues in agriculture. It included a review of the negative environmental effects of intensive farming and the need to institute control measures to limit these effects. It articulated the principle of 'polluter pays' and the need to apply it to farming. It advocated the use of environmental impact assessments for major land-reorganizing activities, especially where public funds were involved.[35] It reversed its previously complacent view of land drainage, stating that there was growing evidence that:

the intensification and extension of drainage particularly in the wetlands has led to the degradation or loss of important habitats for wildlife. The destruction of such valuable ecosystems is generally irreversible, and the question is therefore posed whether public aids for this activity are any longer justified, particularly since the Community has passed self-sufficiency for many agricultural products. It would be desirable to conduct a review of agricultural drainage, with a view to limiting, or even in some cases or regions prohibiting the use of public aids for this purpose.   (Commission 1985(*b*), 51)[36]

Apart from measures to curb the negative effects of farming, the Commission also discussed the possibility of introducing policy measures which would actively promote farming practices with a positive impact on conservation and protection. 'Generally speaking such practices would be less intensive (and thereby less productive) and could have—to some limited extent—an effect on the growth of agricultural production' (Commission 1985(*b*), 51). The Commission put forward some tentative ideas on the types of farming practices, which farmers might be encouraged to adopt or maintain, which would be environmentally friendly. Such practices would produce a public good and 'society should recognize the resulting external benefits by providing the financial resources to permit farmers to fulfil this task. Corresponding payments would at the same time support and diversify farmers' incomes and contribute to the control of production' (ibid. 52). Another idea floated by the Commission was that public authorities might consider buying or renting land from farmers for environmental use, in particular the creation of large protected zones linked by ecological refuges and corridors to allow for the circulation of species of flora and fauna. Additionally, this would benefit the incomes of the farmers concerned, and might even help to promote rural tourism.[37]

Some of these ideas were discussed further in the follow-up document: *A Future for Community Agriculture* issued later the same year. In concluding a section on the protection of the environment and maintenance of the country-side, the Commission stated: 'on the whole . . . the concern for the environment is a positive factor where the agricultural sector is concerned. It may mean additional income for the farmer under specific aid schemes and it may help to remove certain marketing imbalances attributable to overintensive farming of the land' (Commission 1985(*d*), 21). It is clear from this statement and from many of the earlier pronouncements on the environmental dimension of farming that promotion of environmental considerations at Community level was little more than a means to an end—an alternative income source for farmers, and another weapon to use in the battle to curb production. In addition, there was some urgency in the setting of standards to be observed throughout the Community. Because some Member States were more advanced than others in their actions to protect the environment, there was a risk that the rules on competition might be breached and distortion created as a result of the observance of different environmental standards in different countries. Thus, there is no evidence that the environment was consistently valued for itself and, therefore, something to be respected as a matter of course in good resource management.

This was in contrast to the view held at the same time on forestry where equally there is a danger of environmental damage through exploitative commercial practices. The Commission suggested the establishment of an environmental code of conduct which would 'safeguard the fertility and long-term productivity of the soil and [the forests'] role in regulating the water cycle; ensure the conservation of wildlife; take account of characteristic landscapes; maintain an adequate diversity of species and wide genetic diversity within large woodland areas' (Commission 1986(*b*), 67).

Early in 1986 the European Parliament adopted a wide-ranging Resolution on agriculture and the environment in which it called for changes to the CAP to include a greater environmental dimension. The Parliament's view was very much that farmers should be rewarded for their positive contribution to the environment but with no mention of a balancing requirement that farmers who pollute should be penalized (OJ C68, 24–3–86). This omission was contrary to the position adopted in the Single European Act at almost exactly the same time in which it was stated that 'environmental damage should as a priority be rectified at source, and that the polluter should pay' (Bull. EC Supp. 2–86, 16).

Despite the length and breadth of the parliamentary Resolution, nowhere did it make the link between damage to the environment and the way in which the CAP supported prices. A rare occasion on which such a link was made by a Community Institution came in the Opinion of the ESC on the draft of the fourth Action Programme on the environment. There it highlighted the conflict between nature conservation and agriculture, stating that 'the Community's agricultural policy leads to the intensive use of available farmland; an effective nature conservation policy . . . often demands that ecologically important areas be left unfarmed' (OJ C180, 8–7–87, 33).

Reference was made earlier in this Section to the weakness of the commitment to the environment while its protection was not a Treaty obligation. That situation changed in 1986 under the Single European Act, one effect of which was to include in the Treaty of Rome a requirement that environmental protection must be a component of the Community's other policies. An early reflection of this change of status can be found in the discussion on biotechnology—referred to already in this chapter. This is an area in which there are dangers of environmental damage as well as the possibility of benefits. Both aspects of the promotion of biotechnology in agriculture were outlined and the Commission stated that protection of the environment had to be fully integrated from the outset in any action taken (Commission 1986(*d*)).

The first positive steps towards Community commitment to environmental protection in agriculture —as opposed to expressions of good intentions—came in 1987 in a revision to Reg. 797/85. Under Reg. 1760/87, the provision in the earlier Regulation, which had allowed Member States to carry out their own programme in environmentally sensitive areas (ESAs), was extensively amended so as to incorporate the support of ESAs among the measures funded by FEOGA-Guidance. However, the wording of the revised Article 19 made it very clear that the environmentally friendly farming practices were expected 'to contribute to the adaptation and the guidance of agricultural production according to market needs'.

The Member States (for which the scheme was optional) had to define the ESAs and the participating farmers had to undertake for a minimum of five years farming practices 'compatible with the requirements of the protection of the environment and of natural resources or with the requirements of the maintenance of the landscape and of the countryside' (Art. 19(a)). A feature of this scheme was that it was not confined to main occupation farmers but could also be availed of by part-time farmers. By 1994, all Member States other than Belgium, Greece, Spain, and Portugal had established ESAs, although in neither Ireland nor Luxembourg had there been any need for FEOGA reimbursement in the previous year (Commission 1994(*f*)), which suggests a possible lack of enthusiasm among farmers.

In 1988, the Commission returned to the question of the environment and agriculture when it issued a discussion document solely concerned with this topic. It listed the specific forms of damage arising from farming: deterioration of habitats, extinction of wildlife species, deterioration of water quality due to intensive farming, soil degradation and erosion, ammonia evaporation from intensive livestock rearing, the accumulation of heavy metals and acidification of soils, and landscape change (Commission 1988(*d*)).

By way of response to this depressing catalogue, the Commission listed the measures which had already been taken which are 'directly or indirectly aimed at promoting environmental objectives and reducing the impact of modern farming on the environment' (Commission 1988(*d*), 7). This list included the limitations and prohibitions under Reg. 797/85 (and its predecessor Dir. 72/159) of aid for intensive livestock production, the provision of compensatory payments in LFAs, the introduction of aids to encourage extensification, set-aside, and early retirement. It is almost beyond belief that the Commission could claim an environmental dimension to some of these measures; others had functioned in a manner which had produced negative environmental effects. This is an extreme example of the phenomenon referred to already namely, that so often in the life of the CAP measures introduced for one purpose end up pressed into service to fulfil some completely different goal.

One interesting aspect of this use of policy measures for lateral purposes was the Commission's claim in the same document that 'the rigorous market and price policy' which had just been introduced (the 'stabilizers' discussed in Chapter 6) which were 'indispensable for economic and financial reasons, will at the same time discourage unjustified intensification, which is harmful to the environment' (Commission 1988(*d*), 16). In a roundabout way, this must be an admission that the previous price and market policy had encouraged intensification and, thereby, environmental damage. Of course, as events were to prove, the stabilizers did not have the desired effect on output and presumably, therefore, intensification and environmental damage continued unchecked.

As mentioned in the previous Section, the Structural Funds were reformed in 1988 and, under Reg. 2052/88, FEOGA-Guidance was given four main tasks:

(a) strengthening and re-organizing agricultural structures, including those for . . . marketing and processing . . . especially with a view to reform of the common agricultural policy;
(b) ensuring the conversion of agricultural production and fostering the development of supplementary activities for farmers;
(c) ensuring a fair standard of living for farmers;
(d) helping to develop the social fabric of rural areas, to safeguard the environment, to preserve the countryside . . . and to offset the effects of natural handicaps on agriculture. (OJ L185, 15–7–88, 12)[38]

It is amazing how, in the course of a few short years, the preservation of the environment had changed from being an optional extra to a position of equality with the more traditional purposes of agricultural structural policy. This new status meant that some adjustments had to be made to existing structural legislation. The necessary alterations were made through the enactment of Reg. 3808/89. In relation to the environment, the most significant change was probably in relation to the compensatory payments in LFAs, under Reg. 797/85. Member States were now given the freedom to lay down additional conditions including those 'which encourage the use of practices compatible with the need to safeguard the environment and preserve the countryside' (Art. 14.3). The actual headage payment was also made subject to a limit of not more than 1.4 livestock units/ha. of the total forage area of the holding. Previously, the legislation had not included any restrictions on stocking density, which had long been a source of complaint by environmentalists, although many Member States had introduced their own upper limit. However, as the Commission had proposed a limit of 1LU/ha., the limit actually agreed was hardly a victory for conservation.[39]

Despite the greater awareness of environmental considerations by the end of the 1980s, the fact remained that the promotion of environmentally friendly farming was patchy: limited to certain locations (LFAs, ESAs) and to certain farming practices (extensification, afforestation). The implication was that elsewhere and in other circumstances farmers could farm if they so wished without any regard to the natural environment. This was hardly compatible with the often repeated dogma that farmers were not only food producers but also guardians of the natural heritage and managers of the countryside.

Other major influences in the situation were that the financial resources available for structural measures were limited, that the schemes themselves were optional for the Member States, and that, where they were applicable, the individual farmer was free to participate or not. In the case of headage payments in the LFAs, there was a major financial incentive to participate (and these payments were suspect in environmental terms), but in relation to other schemes a real commitment to environmental protection was required—which was not so readily forthcoming. Indeed, there was an added problem: some structural schemes introduced to help improve market balance were, in themselves, environmentally damaging. For instance, the grubbing-up of vineyards introduced to curb over-production of table wine (see Chapter 10) was described by the Commission as having had 'a negative impact on the environment' (Commission 1993(b), 6). In 1994, in its proposals on the reform of the wine regime, the Commission also proposed that, where vineyards were permanently abandoned, the aid for grubbing up should be accompanied by measures to preserve the environment 'such as reparcelling and soil protection by means of appropriate plant cover' (Commission 1994(a), 3).

In 1990, the Commission undertook a review of the operation of three schemes: ESAs, extensification, and set-aside (Commission 1990(b)). At the time, ESAs existed only in Denmark, Germany, the Netherlands, and the UK. Extensification had been adopted also in only four Member States—Belgium, France, Germany, and Italy. Set-aside operated in all but Denmark, Luxembourg, and Portugal (see Table 11.1). Although none of these schemes had been in operation for more than a few years, their limitations were already obvious.

The main problem with ESAs was precisely the need to designate certain areas, often on the basis of some very localized feature while, at the same time, some other more significant and more widespread landscape feature or farming practice was being completely bypassed. Also, the scheme was inappropriate for the management of areas subject to problems such as erosion, flooding, or fire. Extensification faced the considerable obstacle of verification: the need to be sure that a change in production technique actually led to a reduction of production of 20 per cent. Set-aside was inappropriate for environmental purposes, partly because of the limited duration of the measure (five years being too short a time for many environmental activities), and partly because the rules associated with set-aside were actually potentially environmentally damaging (for instance, disturbance to ground-nesting birds).

The Commission proposed a reorganization of these three measures so as to broaden their scope and to make them relevant to all farmers in order to persuade them of the need to farm in a manner which respected the environment and the countryside. The original proposals were extensively revised in 1991

(Commission 1991(*d*)), as part of the MacSharry reform package and were adopted by the Council in 1992 as Reg. 2078/92.[40] This Regulation encompasses many of the environmentally friendly measures which had existed previously but gives them wider application. The Community funding is through FEOGA-Guarantee, indicating the link between the desire to achieve market equilibrium and the desire to change farming practices.

The scheme is intended to promote:

(a) the use of farming practices which reduce the polluting effects of agriculture . . .

(b) an environmentally favourable extensification of crop farming, and sheep and cattle farming . . .

(c) ways of using agricultural land which are compatible with protection and improvement of the environment, the countryside, the landscape, natural resources, the soil and genetic diversity;

(d) the upkeep of abandoned farmland and woodlands where this is necessary for environmental reasons or because of natural hazards and fire risks, and thereby avert the dangers associated with the depopulation of agricultural areas;

(e) long-term set-aside of agricultural land for reasons connected with the environment;

(f) land management for public access and leisure activities;

(g) education and training for farmers in types of farming compatible with the requirements of environmental protection and upkeep of the countryside. (Article 1)

The scheme is implemented through zonal programmes in each Member State, each programme covering an area which is homogeneous in terms of the environment and countryside. Participating farmers undertake for a minimum of five years (twenty years in the case of set-aside) to farm in accordance with the requirements of their local programme. In return, they receive an annual premium which varies according to the nature of the activity undertaken. Part or all of the farm can be involved.[41]

This Section has chronicled the growing awareness of environmental issues and their inclusion as basic considerations in structural policy but there remains the much larger question of the role of the price and market policy and the influence of environmental constraints on it. It must not be forgotten that, despite the increase in the allocation of funds to structural purposes, as part of the 1988 reforms, the price and market policy still accounts for the great bulk of agricultural support. The transfer of certain measures from FEOGA-Guidance to Guarantee is a minor matter and should not be regarded as evidence of the 'greening' of price and market support.

The environmental record of this policy began to be questioned in the European Parliament. For instance, in 1990 the Commission was asked how Article 130R of the Rome Treaty (i.e. the requirement to make environmental protection a component of the Community's other policies) was applied to FEOGA-Guarantee. The answer was weak in the extreme and consisted mostly of a reminder that 'Community policy on markets and prices . . . is designed to gear agricultural production to market requirements and hence aims to reduce the intensity of farming, in the process making an important contribution towards adjusting agriculture to the needs of environmental protection' (OJ C94,

11–4–91, 45). In 1991, the Commission was asked about the environmental damage being caused by overgrazing by sheep in the West of Ireland, the stimulus being the ewe premium under the sheepmeat regime. The Commission's reply was highly unsatisfactory from an environmental point of view: sheep numbers had gone up, overgrazing was a problem, there were few alternative enterprises, the main one being beef production, which was experiencing marketing difficulties (OJ C214, 16–8–91).[42]

One of the lesser provisions of the 1992 MacSharry package can be seen as an initial step towards the creation of greater awareness of the environmental implications of price support. Under Reg. 2066/92 (OJ L215, 30–7–92), the premiums available in the beef regime were made subject to maximum stocking densities which declined from 3.5 LU/ha. (forage area) in 1993 to 2 LU/ha. in 1996. Unfortunately, there is nothing in the Regulation to restrict the farmer to that level, only that no premium will be paid above the relevant level. This point was raised by the Commission itself in 1994 in discussing the integration of environmental considerations into the price and market policy (Commission 1994(*d*)).

Two developments took place in 1992 which added some urgency to the question of the relationship of the environment to the price and market policy. Firstly, there was the signing of the Maastricht Treaty under which Article 130R of the Rome Treaty was strengthened. One effect of this was to replace the phrase: 'environmental protection requirements shall be a component of the Community's other policies' with 'environmental protection requirements must be integrated into the definition and implementation of other Community policies.'

Secondly, there was the adoption of the fifth Action Programme on the environment (1993–2000). It contained a depressing review of the environmental impact of agricultural activities in general and the role of the CAP in particular, especially the price support mechanisms. These, the Commission acknowledged, had led to intensification and thereby to 'overexploitation and degradation of the natural resources on which agriculture itself ultimately depends: soil, water and air' (OJ C138, 17–5–93, 35). There then follows a list of the various types of environmental problem which had occurred. In addition, there were the surpluses, the high budgetary cost, and the absence of improvement in the income situation of farmers. In the light of these circumstances, the Commission concluded that: 'it is not only environmentally desirable, but it also makes sound agricultural and economic sense to seek to strike a more sustainable balance between agricultural activity and the natural resources of the environment' (ibid. 37).

So far so good. However, later in the Action Programme where future activities are discussed, the Commission announces a review of the Structural Funds (referred to earlier in this chapter). In this context, it commented on the improvements which could be made to the management of land, forest, and ecosystems in the wake of the reform of the CAP (which was just then beginning to be implemented under the MacSharry Plan). It concluded that:

As a general principle to be applied in the long-term re-structuring of the CAP, entitlement to Community support will progressively become conditional on exploitation of agricultural and other rural resources in an environmentally acceptable way, and eventually in a way which enhances and improves the quality of the rural environment and the countryside in general.   (OJ C138, 17–5–93, 74)

This was a strange place and a strange context in which to announce a major shift within the price and market policy. Clearly much more is yet to happen to fulfil this requirement. The price and market policy remains dominant but no longer is the volume of output the only consideration; how that output is produced has now become important. Another crack has appeared in the policy mould but at the time of writing there is no evidence that, in practice, the policy has moved any distance along this path. Many farmers—and many Member States—are quite content to ignore long-term environmental degradation in the interests of short-term income support linked to historical production levels.

NOTES

1. It will be recalled from Ch. 9 that the Commission started actively to seek an improvement in the situation of young farmers in the 1970s. A decade later, when the off-farm employment situation was much worse, the need to persuade young people to stay in farming was much more acute.
2. Direct income aids, part-time farming, and alternative on-farm sources of income in Ch. 4; production curbs in Ch. 6; retirement in Ch. 8; and young farmers in Ch. 9.
3. In fact, nothing of the kind happened and stocks in the early 1990s were not very different from the 1985 level (about 30m. tonnes in 1990/91).
4. Similar negative views were expressed later in the same year by Andriessen in answer to yet another parliamentary question on set-aside (OJ C292, 2–11–87).
5. Council Regulation (EEC) No 1094/88 of 25 April 1988 *amending Regulations (EEC) No 795/85 and (EEC) No 1760/87 as regards the set-aside of arable land and the extensification and conversion of production* (OJ L106, 27–4–88).
6. In 1992, the Commission produced a report on this scheme. Like the voluntary set-aside on which it was based, it was not particularly successful (Commission 1992(e)).
7. The only exception was the exemption for small producers from the co-responsibility levy.
8. This is an example of a 'decoupled' payment. While initially it may appear quite reasonable as a compensation for a change in policy, the further away one gets from the base period the more anomalous the payment is likely to appear.
9. Small producers do not have to set aside any land. They are defined as producers who can claim compensation payments for an area capable of producing 92 tonnes of cereals, if they achieve the average yield relevant to their region or farm. For the Union as a whole, 92 tonnes are regarded as the average yield of an area of 20 ha.
10. The Regulation also made provision for non-rotational set-aside under which a farmer can opt to withdraw a fixed amount of land for a minimum period of years. As the land withdrawn is likely to be of inferior quality, the percentage withdrawn needs to be higher to achieve the same control of production. This option can be useful from an environmental point of view in regions where there is a danger of

nitrate leaching. In such areas it is better to have a permanent grass cover than to leave the land temporarily bare in rotation.

11. Under Reg. 1760/87, amending Reg. 1360/78 (OJ L167, 26–6–87).

12. Reg. 2092/91 *on organic production of agricultural products and indications referring thereto on agricultural products and foodstuffs* (OJ L198, 22–7–91). This legislation ran into operational difficulties and was extensively modified in 1995 under Reg. 1935/95 (OJ L186, 5–8–95).

13. Reg. 1009/86 *establishing general rules applying to production refunds in the cereals and rice sector* (OJ L94, 9–4–86). A parallel system was introduced at the same time for sugar.

14. Reg. 2176/90 (OJ L198, 28–7–90), later subsumed into Reg. 2328/91 (see fn. 16).

15. The list of products suggested included such exotics as medicinal and aromatic plants, and those intended for the production of spices; animals for their fur and fibre; berries, ornamental plants and flowers, etc. Such products are unlikely to absorb vast amounts of land.

16. Council Regulation (EEC) No 2328/91 of 15 July 1991 *on improving the efficiency of agricultural structures* (OJ L218, 6–8–91).

17. There is a good summary of the delays at that time in the discussion on forestry in Commission 1986(*b*), 50–2.

18. It should be noted that the ESC was very sceptical of the appropriateness of using forestry as a means of relieving agriculture from some of its production problems (see OJ C263, 20–10–86).

19. Under Reg. 1760/87 (OJ L167, 26–6–87).

20. Reg. 1096/88 (OJ L110, 29–4–88), discussed in Ch. 8.

21. Reg. 1094/88 (OJ L106, 27–4–88), referred to in the previous Section.

22. Regs. 1609/89–1615/89 (OJ L165, 15–6–89).

23. These categories were subsequently altered somewhat, see below.

24. Subsequently subsumed into Reg. 2328/91, see fn. 16.

25. Parts of Italy and Spain, the French overseas departments, Corsica, and Northern Ireland. The complete list is to be found in the Annex to Reg. 2052/88 (OJ L185, 15–7–88). The revised list for the 1994–9 period is to be found in Annex 1 of Reg. 2081/93 (OJ L193, 31–7–93).

26. In many cases this meant no more than taking over regionally targeted measures already in force, where they corresponded to the newly designated Objective 1 areas. Many of these measures were outlined in their previous form in Ch. 9.

27. Regs. 2078/92–2080/92 (OJ L215, 30–7–92).

28. Council Regulation (EEC) No 1992/93 of 19 July 1993 *transferring the financing of certain aids provided for in Regulations (EEC) No 1096/88 and (EEC) No 2328/91 from the EAGGF Guidance Section to the EAGGF Guarantee Section and amending Regulation (EEC) No 2328/91 as regards part-financing of the system to encourage the set-aside of arable land* (OJ L182, 24–7–93).

29. The areas designated under Objective 5(b) for the 1994–9 period are listed in Commission Decision 94/197 (OJ L96, 14–4–94).

30. Both the European Parliament and the ESC made comments of this kind, although the latter did also refer to the positive role of agriculture in safeguarding the environment (see OJ C19, 1–3–71 and OJ C60, 14–6–71).

31. In 1985, under Reg. 797/85, the wording of this clause was strengthened so as to read: 'small areas affected by specific handicaps and in which farming must be continued, *if necessary subject to certain conditions, in order to ensure the conservation of the*

environment, to maintain the countryside' (italics added). The eligible area was raised to a maximum of 4%.

32. Some of the legislation at that time included a requirement that an assurance was given that the activity receiving aid was compatible with protection of the environment. The puzzling thing is that this was not required in other circumstances which, on the facts available, appeared to be just as likely to raise environmental issues.

33. It is usual for the purposes of the Regulation to be stated in the Preamble to the Regulation. In this case, environment conservation was only referred to in relation to nature and national parks, and aids for joint investment activities in LFAs.

34. This was achieved by the simple device of changing the tense of the verb from the imperative ('shall apply to') to the conditional ('may be applicable to').

35. The Directive *on the assessment of the effects of certain public and private projects on the environment* (Dir. 85/337, OJ L175, 5–7–85) included within its compass major agricultural projects likely to have a significant effect on the environment.

36. One should not get too excited about this change of heart: three years later, in 1988, the Commission was still only announcing that it would undertake an early review of large scale arterial drainage projects (Commission 1988(*d*)), and was silent on the question of the appropriateness of field drainage.

37. This was an audacious idea: the Commission stated that some estimates had suggested that up to 10% of the Community's agricultural land could be used in this way.

38. These purposes were amended slightly in Reg. 2081/93, referred to in the previous Section.

39. An interesting proposal was made by the ESC to the effect that the link with area and livestock units should be completely rethought, and replaced by an income payment related, among other things, to the labour units on the farm (OJ C56, 7–3–90). This would have two advantages: it would emphasize the purpose of the payment which is income support, and would greatly lessen the temptation to overstock the land.

40. Council Regulation (EEC) No 2078/92 of 30 June 1992 *on agricultural production methods compatible with the requirements of the protection of the environment and the maintenance of the countryside* (OJ L215, 30–7–92).

41. The provisions on extensification and ESAs remained in place until the zonal programmes had been implemented.

42. Overgrazing and the resultant erosion of the peat soil remains a serious problem in the West of Ireland: see Holden (1995).

12

Commercial Policy: *An Uneasy Relationship with Market Policy*

The Origins of Commercial Policy in the CAP

Earlier chapters have chronicled the fate of three of the four pillars of the CAP—the structural, market, and social elements of the policy as it was proposed in 1960. It is time to return to the fourth pillar—commercial policy[1]—last referred to specifically in Chapter 2. On a world scale, international trade in agricultural commodities is a residual trade: the bulk of agricultural production never crosses a frontier and that is even more true of raw materials than of the goods manufactured from them. The vast majority of countries rely on their own production for a significant part of their requirements of food and feed. Imports are used to top-up their needs, sometimes seasonally, sometimes year-round, or as the inputs of other agricultural enterprises, such as feed for livestock production. Many countries use export outlets in exactly the same way: as a means of disposing of production which is excess to internal demand. Very few countries are net exporters of agricultural commodities, and even fewer are major players in the international market place.

This semi-autarkic system is not new but it was reinforced by the devastating effect on agriculture of the Depression in the 1920s and 1930s, and the shortages and dislocation engendered by World War II. The context within which the CAP was developed was outlined in Chapter 1. Even if West European countries had wished to import a higher proportion of their food supply from overseas, the possibilities of such trade were very limited in the immediate post-war period. The wartime destruction and scarcity of raw materials severely hampered exports of manufactured goods. Even where production was physically possible, countries faced import restrictions in potential markets. As a result foreign currency was scarce. In such a situation, it was hardly surprising that West European countries continued to favour reliance on the greater certainty of their own natural resources.

However, they did realize the urgent need to improve the efficiency of agriculture. Politically, the achievement of such an improvement was not easy and the difficulties faced by governments are well summarized by a contemporary comment:

The rigidity of the pattern of production and in the structure of costs in Western European agriculture, with its many small and poor producers, is one of the main hindrances to free trade in agricultural products. Most governments fear that to remove quantitative restrictions and to reduce tariffs on imports would depress farmers' incomes without inducing an increase in their productivity. Obviously, therefore any major steps towards free trade need to go hand-in-hand with internal measures in the importing (and in some cases also in the exporting) countries, aiming at facilitating the necessary adaptations in the production and cost structures. (ECE/FAO 1954, 69)

The existence of a highly structured agricultural policy which, as the 1950s passed, focused more and more on the issue of the welfare of farmers permitted a situation to arise in which restrictive trade policies could be explained away as attempts to aid a disadvantaged group internally, whereas liberalization of trade could be cast in the role of favouring foreign agricultural interests over those of domestic producers. The issue was not seen as one in which domestic agricultural interests were being favoured over other sections of the domestic economy.[2]

Thus, the question of agricultural trade liberalization in the 1950s was not purely an economic issue but also had a strong political dimension. Economists all too often forget this. At that time, the political dimension was in itself complex. The fear of shortages pointed to the need to have policy instruments which would allow the government to be confident that the major part of food requirements was secure, but that objective was balanced by a recognition that access by third-country suppliers of agricultural commodities was often necessary in order to facilitate the export of industrial goods into other markets. This was well understood and as a result the approach to trade liberalization was pragmatic not dogmatic.

A surprising aspect of trade policy in the 1950s was that many West European countries anticipated the need to find markets for agricultural exports at a time when, in general, they were not very significant. Agricultural production had recovered more rapidly after the War than manufacturing industry and it appeared likely that countries would need to build on their farm sector for some time to come. The industrial expansion (explosion in some countries, such as Italy) associated with the 1960s was not obvious to policy-makers in the 1950s.

Chapter 1 outlined the conclusions of the Spaak Committee on the future organization of agriculture in the proposed new Community and the declared intention that the managed market to be established for agricultural production would not be protectionist, in that price support would not be aligned to the needs of the marginal producers. However, it is interesting to note that the price comparison which the Committee favoured was between the internal prices of importing countries and the internal prices of exporting countries rather than with the prices which exporting countries were willing to accept on international markets—which were often much lower. There is no doubt that international prices can be misleading and may bear little relation to the costs of production in the exporting country. Many years after the Spaak Committee recommendations, the European Commission commented on the misleading nature of such prices:

World market prices are notoriously volatile because the quantities involved in international trade are often marginal in relation to total production (e.g. sugar, cereals, dairy products) and may reflect short-term fluctuations in production. For several products (e.g. beef, wine, tobacco) there is no real world market and prices vary according to the destination of exports.   (Commission 1981(*c*), 12)

While these comments are true, it should also be said that much of the unsatisfactory pricing which both the Spaak Committee and the Commission observed was due to the influence on the international market of the internal agricultural policies in exporting and importing countries alike.

In the light of later developments, it is significant that the objectives set out in Art. 39.1 of the Rome Treaty make no overt reference to trade. It could be argued that such a reference would have been inappropriate because commercial policy generally is set out in Articles 110–16. Within these Articles, there is no indication of a commitment in principle to trade liberalization with countries outside the customs union but rather that any liberalization which does take place should be achieved by the Member States acting together, with the Commission negotiating on behalf of the Community under the authorization of the Council.

Recognition is given in the Final Resolution of the Stresa Conference to the need to maintain commercial links with third countries but, as with other aspects of that Conference, the actual Working Party discussion was far less clear-cut. In answer to the question: What share of internal consumption should be covered by Community production?, one delegation argued that the long-term position was impossible to determine and would only become clear as the CAP was implemented, adding 'there can be no question . . . of limiting output, except if it is impossible to find markets outside the Community' (Communautés Européenes 1959, 211). In contrast, another delegation stated that the question could not be answered in isolation: 'this point . . . cannot be dissociated from the evolution outside the Community and the development of relations with third countries. Trade with third countries must be as developed as possible (ibid.).[3]

Although commercial policy was one of the pillars of the CAP, as outlined in the 1960 proposals, little was actually said as to its role but what there was suggests that it was regarded as subsidiary to the overriding requirement to ensure a fair income level for producers. It was to provide the link between the market policy (which was to support incomes, and balance supply and demand) and trade with the external world which came under the provisions of Articles 110–16 of the Rome Treaty.

The point was made in Chapter 2 that the market and commercial policies were from the start and by their very nature intertwined: the development of the one meant the development of the other. The market policy was founded on an integrated mechanism for the regulation of the internal market through price support and market manipulation, backed up by frontier measures to regulate the import price in sympathy with the institutional price levels set internally, and by export subsidies which facilitated the disposal of surpluses at internationally competitive prices. In the 1960 proposals, the Commission stated that the prices set for the various commodities had to fulfil two functions: the achievement of market equilibrium and the maintenance of the level of agricultural incomes, and in order to realize these goals it was essential 'not to expose the agricultural production of the Community to the full blast of competition from the world market' (Commission 1960, II/26). This is a significant statement of intent and underlines the subsidiary or residual nature of imports, and explains many of the later attitudes to trade as the CAP developed.

The Saga of the Oils Tax 1963–1987

One of the themes of this chapter is that, throughout much of the lifetime of the CAP, whenever there has been a conflict between price policy and trade policy it has been the former which has prevailed. It is possible that, as a result of the Uruguay Round of GATT, the balance between the two policies may be changing: this episode is outlined later in this chapter. However, prior to that, the only occasion on which trade policy seems to have held its own against price policy was in relation to the proposal to introduce a tax on oils—one of the longest running sagas in the history of the CAP.

In 1963, the Council agreed that, before 1 November 1964, it would adopt a support system for vegetable oils to be financed not only by FEOGA but also by means of a tax on vegetable oils used for human consumption. The Council even agreed on the level of the tax; it also made provision that, for one year after the entry into force of the new regime, Member States could if they wished be exempt from this tax, provided they contributed an equivalent amount through the Budget or by similar means (Council *Press Notice*, 23–12–63).

Three important issues were involved in this agreement. The first was that the recently introduced milk regime used butter and its residue skimmed milk powder as the main commodities of support. The Council perceived—quite correctly as it turned out—that their use as the basis of intervention would change the price relationship of animal and vegetable fats to the detriment of the former. This was of concern because vegetable oils compete directly with dairy products in many food uses. As indicated in Chapters 6 and 10, the level of butter production was already a cause for concern and anything which undermined its market was to be avoided if at all possible.

The second issue was that the milk regime was of little interest to Italy, where production and consumption were low but where olive oil was an important crop. This was particularly true in the depressed South where the range of viable crops was far less than in the North. Therefore, a support regime for olive oil and, by extension, for other vegetable oils produced in modest quantities in the Community was a political, economic, and social necessity.

Olive oil did not at that time compete to any extent with animal fats as it was consumed overwhelmingly in its areas of production. The main competitor for butter was undoubtedly margarine, manufactured very largely from imported vegetable oils, for which the USA was the dominant supplier. Therefore, the proposed oils tax would have fallen mainly on those imports: herein lay the third issue. The Community had just conceded, in the context of the Dillon Round of GATT (outlined in the next Section), low or zero tariffs on vegetable oils and their residues. As the revenue from frontier protection was one of the means of funding the agricultural support regimes (and a far more important means then than subsequently), the funding gap brought about by the oils agreement was a serious matter. No doubt the Council saw the proposed tax as a way to plug the gap and restore Community Preference. Because the intention was to charge the tax on imports and internal production alike, it could hardly be regarded as discriminatory. Others did not see it in quite the same light.

In the event, the timetable for the oils regime was not observed and it was not until 1966 that the regime was established under Reg. 160/66 (Sp. OJ 1965–1966)—but without the proposed tax. Two years later, in the Mansholt Plan, the proposal re-emerged. The international market for dairy products was in crisis and a major part of the problem lay in the intense competition from vegetable oils, prices for which were in sharp decline. These oils were competing in the market for human consumption (against butter and butter oil) and for animal feed (against skimmed milk powder). The state of the international market was reflected on the markets of the Community. In the Mansholt Plan, the Commission blamed the absence of frontier protection for oils for a great part of the milk crisis then being experienced in the Community.

The Commission proposed the conclusion of an international agreement on oils in order to stabilize the market. Recognizing that this would take some time to negotiate and that something needed to be done quickly, the Commission gave notice of its intention to propose a tax on vegetable and fish oils and their by-products. Where such a tax might harm the developing countries associated with the Community, compensation would be offered to them so as to ensure a satisfactory level of income (Commission 1968(*a*) and (*c*)).

Nothing came of the proposal at the time but, in 1976, in the face of continuing and worsening imbalances in the milk sector, the Commission conceived the idea of linking the milk and oilseeds regimes in its Action Programme (1977–80) for milk (see Chapters 6 and 10). In proposing a co-responsibility levy to be paid by milk producers, the Commission once again floated the idea of an oils tax which would correspond to the levy. In turn, the milk levy should be calculated taking into account the movement of import prices for vegetable protein. The Commission also suggested that the Member States should 'allocate a sum equivalent to that produced by the tax for improving development cooperation and aid, including food aid' (Bull. EC, Supp. 10/76, 15).

In the price proposals for 1977/78, the Commission acknowledged that objections had been raised to its proposed tax on oils. It countered by stating that, if the Council could not agree to the introduction of the tax, then it would be necessary to raise Community expenditure by an equivalent amount in order to finance the promotion of the consumption of dairy products, especially butter (Commission 1977(*b*)). The co-responsibility levy was introduced in 1977 but without the link to the price of vegetable protein and without the oils tax. Two years later, the European Parliament called for the introduction of a tax on margarine production in order 'to create equal competition between butter and this substitute product' (OJ C93, 9–4–79, 52).

Once again nothing happened but the issue would not go away and, in 1983, in the context of the proposal to introduce guarantee thresholds the question of an oils tax was raised again. The free entry for oils to the Community markets was helping to lower consumption of butter and olive oil and therefore pushing up the costs of these regimes. If the Community's producers were going to be subject to the imposition of guarantee thresholds for milk and oils, and if the co-responsibility levy on milk was to be strengthened, then such measures should be accompanied by the introduction of a 'non-discriminatory internal tax on the consumption of oils and fats other than butter, irrespective of their origin. Such a tax would be in conformity with the international commitments of the Community' (Commission 1983(*d*), 34).

Nothing came of this tax proposal, although the guarantee thresholds and a supplementary milk levy were introduced. The Commission then changed its tactics; in the *Perspectives* of 1985, having rehearsed the usual arguments on market distortion attributed to low import protection for one commodity and high internal market support for a competing or substitute product, the Commission floated the idea of a trade-off. If the level of protection on a high-protection commodity (such as cereals) was lowered, the level of protection on a low-protection commodity (such as vegetable oils) could be raised without changing the overall average level of protection. The Commission recognized that this was something which would have to be negotiated multilaterally in GATT (a new round of which was in the offing). It saw considerable possibilities in this idea in terms of the better management of the price and market policy and in its budgetary cost (Commission 1985(*b*)).

Later the same year, in the proposals to reform the cereals regime, the Commission suggested a co-responsibility levy for cereals the level of which would be based on the cost of disposal of the balance between production and unsubsidized consumption, the latter to include imported grain substitutes. The reason for their inclusion was, of course, the existence of low frontier protection which had encouraged their import and the displacement of cereals from traditional markets (Commission 1985(*c*)).

Attached to the price proposals for 1987/88 was a lengthy report on the oils and fats sector. This included an updated version of the oils tax, now called a price stabilization mechanism. The idea was that a reference price should be established based on the ex-refinery price of soya oil in the period 1981–5. Each year, the average price of soya oil would be compared with the reference price and, if the annual price was higher, a levy equal to the difference between the two prices would be charged on all vegetable and marine oils for human consumption. The revenue so raised would be used to help finance the oils regime (Commission 1987(*a*)).

When, early in 1987, rumours began to circulate of the Commission's renewed interest in an oils tax, there was widespread uproar. The arguments raged back and forth from February to June and, apart from COPA, it was hard to find any institution in favour of it. Trade organizations whose members used vegetable oils in manufacturing protested, making common cause with consumer organizations—two lobby interests not often on the same side. Not surprisingly, producing countries outside the Community were opposed to it, led by the USA. The Member States were seriously divided with Denmark, Germany, the Netherlands, Portugal, and the UK being on the whole against the proposal—some countries implacably so. The Foreign Ministers became involved as they were concerned about the international implications, as the Uruguay Round of GATT was just getting underway.[4] Within the Council of Agricultural Ministers, it appeared early on in the debate that it was likely a blocking minority could be formed and that, once again, the oils tax would be shelved.

There were a number of very difficult issues in the price proposals that year and the Council was deadlocked. As a result the entire package of measures was referred to the meeting of the European Council in June. The start of the farm-year had long since passed for many commodities and there was an urgent need to reach agreement. The European Council did not reject the oils tax but called for more work to be done on it and the Commission withdrew the proposal at that time in the interests of a speedy agreement on the remainder of the package—a typical example of a Euro-compromise!

In commenting on this outcome, the President of the Commission—Delors—stated that: 'An unjustified passionate climate was created around this project; those who were against, *will regret bitterly their decision in about two or three years*. What has happened *confirms that whenever the United States or the multinationals frown, we are no longer twelve, but four or five*' (*Agence Europe*, 2–7–87, 11, emphasis in original).

The Commission handed the review of the oils tax proposal over to outside consultants to report in time for the next European Council meeting in December 1987. Their conclusions were that the passionate opposition had not died down. Effectively, the proposed tax was dead nearly a quarter century after it was first discussed. Delors was right—in part at least—in his assessment: the opposition of the USA and powerful manufacturing interests were enough to see its burial. But there was more to it than that: the timing was all wrong and attitudes had changed. Disenchantment with the cost of the CAP was an important factor. The tax was perceived by many as a means of avoiding some of the painful adjustments which had to be made in the organization and administration of the price and market policy, and in its overall cost. The importance of the Uruguay Round and the inclusion of agriculture as a major element in those negotiations made it virtually inconceivable that the oils tax would have been successfully introduced. As later events were to show, the demise of the oils tax was not the end of controversy for vegetable oils.

Contradictory Attitudes to External Trade

The confused origins of commercial policy are reminiscent of the similarly confused origins of structural and social policy. There was a difference, however, in that the development of the market policy necessitated the development of the commercial policy whereas the structural policy could be sidelined and the social policy abandoned. Nevertheless, the relationship between the market and the commercial policies was an uneasy one. Of course, the creation internally of a single market for agricultural products was hailed as a great achievement[5] and the expansion of trade between the Member States was the visible sign of the success of this venture but the response to developments in external trade was much more mixed. There were four areas in which the contradictions were most marked: on imports from, and on exports to countries outside the Community, on trade with developing countries, and on issues of trade liberalization. The first three of these areas are discussed in this Section.

Right from the earliest days of the CAP, there was an anxiety to demonstrate that the policy was not intended to be protectionist nor was it going to be based on high internal prices. This position was adopted, in part at least, to assuage the fears of third countries that the establishment of the CAP would damage their exports to the Community. The original proposals on the CAP coincided with the preparations for the Dillon Round of negotiations in GATT. Under Article XXIV of the GATT Agreement, where a customs union was formed and a common external tariff replaced the individual tariff regimes of the participating countries, there was a requirement that the new common tariff level should not be higher or more restrictive in general terms than the previous level applied by the countries forming the union. It appeared that the introduction of the CAP might well breach this requirement, not only because certain *ad valorem* tariffs were going to be higher but also, and more importantly, because of the proposed use of the variable import levy.

The main protagonist was the USA and its main concern was with its exports of cereals.[6] The Community entered into negotiations with the USA and other exporting countries, in the context of the GATT Agreement, to find acceptable forms of compensation. While in certain respects the Dillon Round was inconclusive, the Community did agree to the binding of tariff rates at low or zero levels for various commodities including manioc, oilseeds, and oilseed products and, of a tariff rate for sheepmeat of 20 per cent. This binding meant that the rate of tariff could not be raised by the Community without negotiation with and compensation of countries affected adversely. From the Community's point of view at the time, these trade concessions were unimportant; however, they were to prove very troublesome as the years passed.

Because the USA had received no concession on cereals directly, the commodity remained a sensitive one. Therefore, when the Commission made its proposals in 1963 on setting a common price level for cereals, it continued its policy of reassurance to trading partners. It wished to demonstrate that the Community was not intent on a high price level which might result in full self-sufficiency, but rather that the level would be such as to ensure the retention of reasonable possibilities for imports from third countries (Commission 1963(*f*)). What was to be regarded as 'reasonable' was not made clear but, as reported in Chapter 6, a few years later Mansholt defended the proposition that Community farmers should have the right to increase production in line with consumption

(CES 1967).[7] As outlined in Chapter 2, the common price finally agreed was indeed set at a high level and it did result in an increase in self-sufficiency.

In one of the documents which accompanied the Mansholt Plan, the Commission announced that 1967 had been the first year since the establishment of the CAP that the total value of agricultural imports had not increased: in fact they fell by $700m., of which $300m. were for products subject to market regimes (Commissions 1968(*e*)). This coincided with the time when the common price level came into force for all the major commodities, when FEOGA-Guarantee became fully operative, and when the remaining frontier restrictions on trade in agricultural products between Member States disappeared.[8] All of this seems to have induced a certain sensitivity on the question of trade diversion due to the operation of the CAP.[9] For instance, in 1975, the Commission reported that intra-Community trade in products subject to market regimes had risen from index 1963 = 100 to 435 in 1972; imports from non-member countries had risen from 100 to 150; while exports to non-member countries had risen from 100 to 200 (Commission 1975(*a*)), all of which suggests a strong trade diversion effect which should surprise no one.

Such introspection is fairly rare in Community institutional circles and a comment by the ESC in 1974 acknowledging the success of the Community in fulfilling the objective laid down in Art.39.1(d) to ensure the availability of supplies is more typical:

[I]t must not be forgotten that excessive dependence on non-member countries or international markets for supplies of agricultural commodities can have serious consequences in certain cases—as for instance when the products needed are not available in sufficient quantity or when they are so expensive that the resultant outflow of currency upsets the Community's overall balance of payments.   (ESC, rapp. Bourel (1974), 36)

Even allowing for the fact that this comment was made during a particularly difficult time in international agricultural markets, it could easily—and more appropriately—have been written in the 1950s. Indeed, the same international crisis produced an even more bizarre comment from the Commission in the context of a discussion on the future sugar policy to be pursued in relation to developing countries. The Commission defended the increase in Community self-sufficiency on the grounds that it limited the need to purchase so much sugar on the world market, which meant that the Community 'did not help to accentuate the increase in world prices, a development which would have been very prejudicial . . . to importing developing countries' (Commission 1973(*b*), 15)!

An equally suspect concern with the needs of importing developing countries reappeared in 1994 in a discussion on food security. The Commission commented favourably on the success of the CAP in turning a long-standing food deficit into a surplus,[10] adding that 'many people say that these surpluses are highly useful and appreciated' (Commission 1994(*b*), 10). The reasons for these positive reactions were that the absence of a food deficit in the Community was helpful to others; emergencies and shortages elsewhere could be alleviated; and because it facilitated 'lower world market and consumer prices in importing countries' (ibid.). Admittedly there was a downside: 'it should be recognized that in certain countries these low import prices affected internal competition, discouraged national production (of cereals, meat, dairy production), have reinforced trends to abandon consumption of traditionally produced cereals and tubers' (ibid.). Quite!

Over the lifetime of the CAP, with very few exceptions, consumption of food per head of population has fallen. Combined with the low population growth, this has meant that food requirements have increased very slowly. Therefore, as the level of self-sufficiency rose, so the level of imports fell. One of the few growth areas in consumption was meat, most notably pigmeat and poultry meat, but this did not result in increased purchases of cereals and skimmed milk powder as major sources of energy and protein for livestock feeding. The reason for this absence of demand was the cost of these commodities: because of the high level of price support internally and the operation of the variable levy at the frontier, the manufacturers of animal feed sought cheaper ingredients outside the Community. These were to be found in the cereal substitutes—manioc, maize gluten, citrus pulp—and the skimmed milk powder substitutes—oilseeds and their derivatives.

By the early 1980s, the Commission was actively advocating a policy of co-responsibility (see Chapter 6) under which production thresholds would be imposed which, if exceeded, would result in a support price penalty in the following year. Right from the start this concept was given an external dimension: if Community farmers were to be asked to make a sacrifice, then there had to be some corresponding adjustment in the field of trade. For instance, in 1981 the Commission suggested that by 1988 the production threshold for cereals should be 130m. tonnes, a slight reduction on the projected level, given the existing trends. The production threshold was based on two assumptions: the retention of exports at their 1981 volume, and 'that additional demand for cereals in animal feed will be met from the Community's own production rather than from imports of cereal substitutes, whose volume should be stabilised or reduced' (Commission 1981(c), 29).

The Commission expected that the support price for cereals would decline in real terms over time, in such a way as to reduce the attraction of cereal substitutes in animal feed. In the meanwhile, however:

the Community should . . . open discussions with the principal third country suppliers of cereals substitutes for the introduction of arrangements to ensure that during the period of alignment of prices the volume of imports does not exceed present levels. These discussions should cover all the principal substitutes (and, if necessary, new substitutes) so as to ensure coherence and avoid displacement of demand from one product to another. (Commission 1981(c), 31)

The low cost of the substitute products was in large part due to the compensation agreement entered into by the Community in the early 1960s, when the levels of import tariffs on the relevant products were bound in GATT. The levels could not be raised unilaterally, hence the need for negotiations. The aim was to achieve a 'voluntary' export restraint which would limit supplies at an agreed tonnage. If the exporting country exceeded this level, the EC would impose heavy penalties. The best known of the agreements was that on manioc, the main supplier being Thailand. The USA did not prove to be so compliant and refused outright to limit its export volumes of maize gluten, soyabeans, and soyabean products, nor would it consider giving up the GATT-bound tariff level of zero.[11]

The expectation of the Community that its efforts to control the expansion of output should be matched by the actions of others continued as a policy guideline in later years. For example, in 1987 in the run-up to the start of the Uruguay Round, the Commission reiterated as a general principle that there had to be a correlation between what Community farmers were being asked to do and what other countries were prepared to do. If international price stability was to be achieved, then producing countries would have to control production and bring supply into line with demand: 'this must mean reduced support for agriculture. The Community can agree to this, and has acted accordingly. It expects its partners to follow suit' (Commission 1987(*h*), 29).

Before moving on to examine the attitudes to exports, one further point needs to be made in relation to imports, which is relevant also in the context of trade with developing countries, and trade liberalization. While lip-service was paid to the need to reserve a space on the Community's markets for imports, it was never exactly clear why this was being done. For instance, the admission of imports was never stated to be beneficial on grounds of quality or price. Once self-sufficiency became a reality for all major and many minor commodities, the reason could not even have been one of need. Moreover, the principle of Community Preference (see Chapter 2) was intended to ensure that producers inside the Community should always be more favourably treated than suppliers from third countries. Indeed it was the undermining of this principle by the concessions on frontier protection which permitted the growth in the import trade for cereal and dairy substitutes.

If, therefore, one gets the impression that imports were resented rather than welcomed, why import at all? Fear of retaliation and the existence of international obligations were certainly two reasons. From the earliest days it was recognized that the general situation in the new Community necessitated the vigorous growth of industrial exports and, if that required reciprocal imports of agricultural products, the CAP would have to accommodate them. Within a few years, with the growth in self-sufficiency in agricultural products, the need for reciprocity extended to agricultural trade itself: much of the growing volume of agricultural exports was destined for countries from which the Community also imported agricultural goods. In the late 1980s the Commission warned of 'the lure of protectionism', stating that the general growth rate in the economy was largely dependent on trends in international markets. Little good would come from ignoring this basic fact—even from the point of view of the farming sector alone. 'There would inevitably be a reaction which would be harmful to our agriculture, whose future depends not only on European policy decisions but also on developments in the world at large' (Commission 1987(*b*), 14).

There was also a tendency to see external trade links in political rather than economic terms. For instance, in 1974, the ESC criticized the Commission for neglecting the fruit and vegetable sector in its *Improvement* memorandum, despite the importance of this sector, commenting that the Committee wondered:

whether the Commission's silence . . . has something to do with the preferential agreements currently being negotiated with a number of non-member countries. . . . In this connection, the Committee points to the importance of these products for certain Community regions and calls the attention of the Commission to the need to ensure that the common policy in this field is not dictated by general political negotiations with certain States. (OJ C115, 28–9–74, 29)

Some years later the Commission itself remarked that it was 'unjustifiable to criticise the operation of the CAP while leaving the door completely open to competing products for political or other reasons' (Commission 1980(c), 23). At that time there was considerable sensitivity to the high cost of the price and market policy and the Commission was keen to apportion blame to the granting of trade concessions as well as to the production of surpluses. In 1981, it drew attention to two aspects of these concessions: certain imports of beef, butter, and sugar were admitted to the Community on special terms which, because of over-supplied markets, necessitated the subsidized export of comparable volumes; and the import of cheap inputs for animal feed under the GATT bindings which were largely to blame for the growing expenditure on cereals and livestock products (Commission 1981(c)). Clearly international obligations were seen as a burden. It is almost as if the price and market policy should be able to function in a vacuum free from consideration of the impact of imports on the internal market. There is no evidence that the Community has ever given serious consideration to the reduction of internal production, on either economic or political grounds, to accommodate imports. Indeed, one could go further: it is almost as if the price and market policy should be able to operate independently of the Community's external relations in total.

Viewed from the outside, probably the most contentious aspect of the price and market policy is the use of export refunds to enable products to be exported from the EC to third countries. There has been a suspicion that the existence of this mechanism has had much to do with the transformation of the Community from a net importer of agricultural commodities to a substantial exporter of certain products. It will be recalled from Chapter 2 that the export subsidy was originally intended as an instrument to fine-tune the market and ensure its balance. It was to do no more than permit the export of occasional surpluses by enabling their price to be lowered from the higher internal level to the level prevailing in the country to which the commodity was to go. Just as the withdrawal of produce from an oversupplied market was originally thought of as an exceptional practice but subsequently became commonplace, so the role of export refunds changed. Indeed, domestic intervention and export refunds have often been used interchangeably, depending on the state of the market and the amount of surpluses already in store (see Chapter 7).

Paradoxically, in view of later criticism of the EC by the Americans and other exporting countries, it was action predominantly by the USA which allowed the newly formed Community to include export refunds as one of its basic policy instruments. In 1958, the USA and other countries refused to accept an absolute ban on the use of export subsidies for primary products. Under GATT rules, therefore, such subsidies were permitted provided they did not allow a country to gain 'more than an equitable share of world trade' (Article XVI). The concept of an 'equitable share' was of course a source of much argument and, as markets became more difficult, it attained greater significance. For instance, in 1979, the Commission reported on a complaint by Australia on the EC's sugar export policy. In that instance, the GATT panel nominated to examine the complaint did not find that the Community had obtained an unfair share of the market but it did note that the export refunds had depressed world sugar prices (Commission 1979(e)). One has to wonder at the value of such a judgement.

Although other exporting countries were suspicious of the use of export refunds, the Community was equally suspicious of other countries. The Commission complained about their ability to take over markets which the EC believed belonged to it. The contention was that this was feasible not because of greater competitiveness but rather because they had a wider range of policy instruments at their disposal—cheap credit arrangements for instance—which the Community did not have. Williamson (1980, 4) raised this point when he enquired:

Is it right to operate with the single instrument, the export refund? Why should we not try to keep up with the increasing sophistication and varied mechanisms—particularly credit arrangements and pluri annual supply agreements—used by our competitors such as the United States, Canada and Australia? We ought to be thinking now whether some of these arrangements might not be cheaper or more effective.

Thus, from being a safety-valve which helped to regulate internal market equilibrium, exports had become over time an essential part of the management of the agricultural sector. The loss of market share would have been a serious matter as it would have made the surplus problem worse and have brought closer the day when a tighter grip would have needed to be taken on the level of production, either through volume controls or ultimately through price. In this context, the possibility of increasing exports to developing countries was an important consideration in the search for markets. It had a number of advantages: there were existing trade links based on the earlier colonial period, and some of the countries—particularly in Asia—with high population density, rapid urbanization, and limited availability of good quality agricultural land were of great long-term potential.

There was an added virtue in seeking to expand exports to developing countries in that some of them—especially in Africa—were facing a population explosion and, in the short term, an inability to maintain the per caput level of food production. The Community could assist either by providing food aid or by sales on favourable terms, thereby legitimizing the subsidization of exports on humanitarian grounds. As the European Parliament stated: 'the existing and potential capacity for food production . . . must be exploited to the full in order to remedy as far as possible the serious food problems facing the world' (OJ C140, 5–6–79, 103). The Commission extended this thought even further by linking the maintenance of a place for imports in the Community with the expansion of exports:

If [the EC] is to import agricultural produce it must also have the means to conduct an export policy. It must also contribute to the world food strategy, since one of the major challenges of the years to come will be the worsening food deficit in developing countries and *the need to ensure their rural development.* (Commission 1980(c), 23, italics added)

The final phrase in this quotation raises a most important point: rural development could, of course, be helped by aid programmes but a more lasting means would be by providing developing countries with the possibility of growth through trade. This means either access to the Community's market or, at the very least, not damaging their prospects on other markets. The contradictions in the Community's position are well illustrated in the European Parliament's Resolution of 1979, a sentence of which was quoted in the previous paragraph. Having stated that food production in the Community must be expanded to help the world food problem, in the very next sentence it states:

[T]he Community must show an increasing awareness of the need to promote the export of agricultural products from the developing countries since improved utilization of the potential for agricultural production in these countries, necessarily accompanied by an increase in agricultural exports to the industrialized countries, can alone enable the developing countries to attain a certain level of purchasing power and initiate the process of economic development in them. (OJ C140, 5–6–79, 103).

As long ago as 1973, the Community faced a major dilemma in trying to balance equitable treatment of cane-sugar producers in developing countries with the needs of its own producers who of course expected the observance of the principle of Community Preference. Prior to its Accession to the Community, the UK had for many years operated a preferential import regime in favour of the sugar-exporting Commonwealth countries. On Accession, this arrangement became a Community responsibility (under Protocol No. 22 to the Act of Accession), in so far as it related to developing countries. A new agreement needed to be negotiated with the relevant Commonwealth countries and various other developing countries with which the Community had close ties. That was finally achieved under the first Lomé Convention, signed in 1975.

That agreement was reached against a background in which the Community was already in surplus on the basis of the quotas set in 1967. This imbalance could have been removed either by manipulating the quota system or by dropping the producer price sufficiently. The Commission estimated that to do the latter would have meant a reduction of the price by at least 25 per cent. This would have had the advantage of shifting sugar production to the regions best suited to it but the disadvantage of causing considerable dislocation in some marginal production areas including, ironically, the French Antilles and

Réunion (whose cane production was included in France's quota). As if matters were not complicated enough, the Community also wished to accede to the International Sugar Agreement as a net importer! (Commission 1973(*b*)).

This is not the place to detail the outcome of this incredibly complicated situation; suffice to record that, under the Lomé Convention, agreement was reached on the admission, on an indefinite basis, of 1.3m. tonnes of cane sugar annually at a price linked to the support price which the Community's own farmers received for beet sugar. At the same time the unreformed production quota system was retained and, worse still, the world sugar shortage of 1973 and 1974 prompted the Council to raise the support price for sugar substantially in 1975/76. Combined, these decisions produced the worst of all possible outcomes with the Community exporting massive quantities of surplus sugar on to a highly unstable international market which, not surprisingly, had a detrimental effect on price. The cane producers had difficulty competing with the exports of beet sugar: the benefits gained under the Lomé Convention had to be set against the losses on other markets, and the worst affected of all were the developing countries which produced sugar but which had not signed the Lomé Convention.

This attempt to provide a guaranteed place on the Community's market for a product from a group of developing countries was flawed from the start because of the absence of a matching reduction in internal production of the competing product. Yet there has been down the years a recognition that, in a moral sense, the Community should act with fairness and indeed generosity towards developing countries. Such a sentiment runs through many of the Institutional pronouncements on the CAP. For instance, in 1974 when the episode on sugar was unfolding, the ESC commented that 'as regards agricultural products, the Community . . . will have to try, under conditions which are bound to be difficult, to give the developing countries access to its markets' (ESC, rapp. Bourel 1974, 67).

Similar sentiments were expressed in 1981 by the European Parliament which, in recommending an active contribution to the fight against world hunger, stated that Community agricultural policy should be regularly adapted 'whenever necessary to take account of the interests of the developing countries' and 'that if the Community is to encourage the building of a diversified economic base in the developing countries it must be willing to provide access to Community markets for their agricultural products' (OJ C172, 13–7–81, 40). Contrary to the generous spirit which prompted these words, the following year the Community concluded the 'voluntary' export restraint agreement on manioc with Thailand and other developing countries.

One might argue that the manioc example is exceptional, as it was merely an attempt to control a difficult situation which had existed for some considerable time and which was going to get worse unless action was taken. A different set of circumstances arose in the case of cotton for which, on the Accession of Greece, a support regime was established intended to apply in Member States which were traditional producers. In the *Perspectives*, in a discussion of possible alternative crops which could divert production away from commodities in surplus, the Commission singled out cotton as a likely candidate. It commented that if cotton were 'to be promoted in regions other than the traditional areas to replace surplus crops, a processing and marketing infrastructure at present entirely lacking must be built up' (Commission 1985(*b*), 32).

Two years later, in a report on producer groups in the cotton sector, the Commission returned to the question of promoting cotton production: 'cotton is not in surplus and an increase in its cultivation could replace other crops grown in southern areas of the Community which in many cases impose a heavy burden on the Community budget' (Commission 1987(*f*), 12). It went on to point out, however, that there was a 'general drop in cotton prices internationally' and that as a result, only a modern, efficient structure . . . can guarantee the competitiveness of the industry (in particular by reducing the production costs of Community cotton)' (ibid.). Not once in this discussion was any consideration given to the external implications of promoting this crop, in particular to the fact that it is extensively produced in developing countries and that an increase in the level of Community production would have implications for the level of imports from such countries.

New Pressures: Agricultural Commercial Policy in the 1980s

As recorded in Chapter 6, the Council instructed the Commission in 1980 to carry out a review of Community policies; a year later the Commission submitted its report. Concerning the CAP, the Commission concluded that farm incomes could not be the only consideration in setting prices; that it was unrealistic to give a full guarantee to producers for products in structural surplus; and that prices had to reflect market realities more than they had in the past (Commission 1981(*b*)). Based on these conclusions the Commission put forward a set of guidelines for future development of the CAP. Two of them specifically linked the internal market policy with external factors:

- a price based on a narrowing of the gap between Community prices and prices applied by its main competitors in the interests of competitiveness and a hierarchy of prices designed to improve the balance of production;
- an active export policy which would honour the Community's international commitments (ibid. 12).

The Commission recognized that there were dangers in taking international prices into account more than previously because of the volatility of these markets. Nevertheless, the goal should be 'the gradual alignment of guaranteed prices on prices ruling on a better organized world market' (Commission 1981(*b*), 12). The Community's contribution to this better organized market was to be achieved through 'a more active export policy designed to stabilize world prices by means of cooperation agreements with other major exporters. These could be supplemented by long-term export contracts' (ibid.).

These bold statements seem to have caused a certain nervousness in the

Commission because, a few months later, in the detailed *Guidelines* intended to complement the Report on the Mandate, there was a distinctly more cautious view of international price comparisons and their relevance to internal price-setting. Indeed, on this occasion, the Commission went so far as to state that it was 'convinced that a generalized and systematic alignment to world market prices would not be a practical policy guideline' (Commission 1981(*c*), 12). Instead, international price levels were seen only in the context of their influence on the level of export refunds. The cost of disposal of surpluses was high, which raised the question of financial responsibility: should it remain a Community charge alone, or should producers be required to participate?

Two years later, in 1983, the Commission returned to the question of commercial policy and made a point which had not featured before. If the Community wished to expand its exports and maintain its share of world markets, then agriculture 'must increasingly accept the market disciplines to which other sectors of the Community's economy are subject' (Commission 1983(*d*), 7). The implication was that greater emphasis had to be placed on production at competitive prices. However, these revolutionary thoughts were tempered by a more traditional view of the international market which the Commission clearly saw as managed rather than free. In particular, it advocated three developments:

- international cooperation with the principal exporting countries, to prevent the deterioration of world prices;
- the development of a policy at a Community level for promoting exports on a sound economic basis;
- the exercise of the Community's international rights, particularly in GATT, for the revision of the external protection system in those cases where the Community is taking measures to limit its own production.   (ibid. 13)

The first of these developments suggests the formation of international cartels to control price (an agricultural parallel to what OPEC tried to do for petroleum products);[12] the second was concerned with the often mentioned but rarely achieved conclusion of long-term contracts for the supply of agricultural products, particularly to developing countries; the third (which was referred to in the previous Section) was intended to open the door to a re-examination of all the trade concessions which the Community had given—for whatever reason—to suppliers of certain agricultural commodities.

These early 1980s musings on trade policy did not lead to much action but there can be no doubt that, for the first time, the whole question of the external dimension of the CAP was beginning to be taken much more seriously. It was the prelude to an extensive analysis of trade in the *Perspectives* where the Commission stated: 'If it was at one time possible to view the Common Agricultural Policy as insulated from the influence of world markets, that is no longer the case, as the forces of international competition more and more determine the framework in which European agriculture must operate' (Commission 1985(*b*), 2).

The Commission warned that the international market was changing: competition was intensifying, former importing countries were now exporting. As a result, the Community had to examine its own trade policy, and the trade policy instruments. The Commission conducted the analysis on the basis of three assumptions: maintenance of the existing share of international trade; the retention of the variable import levy and export refunds as mechanisms for stabilizing the internal market; and the retention of Community Preference as a fundamental principle. These are interesting assumptions in the light of the GATT negotiations which were shortly to become such a major preoccupation.

The Commission pointed out that the Community was still operating on the basis that it was a net importer—as it had been twenty-five years previously—but that in fact it was 'the major exporter of dairy produce and the second exporter of cereals and sugar and is a leading exporter of wine, spirituous beverages and processed products' (Commission 1985(b), 39). It reviewed the ways in which co-responsibility could be introduced to the export trade and how 'perhaps in the longer term, support prices could be fixed at a level close to those of other exporting countries, especially wherever, for a given product, the world market accounted for a significant share of Community production' (ibid. 41). Given that these ideas had been enunciated in 1981, it is indicative of the reluctance of the Member States to make progress in this direction that, four years later, they were still regarded as no more than long-term possibilities.

On imports, the Commission rehearsed the argument on the difficulties encountered with the low level of protection on certain commodities because of the GATT bindings. The consequence was the need to provide price support internally so that producers could compete with cheap imports, and subsidies on certain products to dispose of them either internally or externally. As mentioned above in the Section on the oils tax, the Commission suggested that a solution might be found in establishing 'some kind of trade-off between high protection and low protection without increasing the general average level of protection of European agriculture' (Commission 1985(b), 43). What is interesting about this suggestion is that the Commission was not advocating the lowering of support prices over all but rather a realignment with some producers gaining and some losing. The Commission recognized that this would not be easy to negotiate with those third countries which would lose their privileged position but it clearly had in mind the possibility of some deal being struck in the context of wider multilateral negotiations.

It was in September 1986 that agreement was reached by the member countries of GATT to open the Uruguay Round. Agricultural issues had been included in the two immediately preceding rounds—the Kennedy Round (1964–7) and the Tokyo Round (1973–9)—but little was achieved in terms of the liberalization of trade in agricultural products. This time, there was considerable pressure internationally to achieve more, particularly because surplus production had got worse on a worldwide scale and disputes between rival exporters—most notably the EC and the USA—had become more frequent and more acrimonious.

The Declaration adopted at Punte del Este outlining the topics to be covered in the negotiations stated in relation to agriculture that there was:

an urgent need to bring more discipline and predictability to world agricultural trade by correcting and preventing restrictions and distortions including those related to structural surpluses so as to reduce the uncertainty, imbalances and instability in world agricultural markets.   (Bull. EC 9–1986, 19)

Three specific goals were set for the negotiations: to improve market access; to increase the discipline on the use of direct and indirect subsidies which affected agricultural trade; and to minimize the adverse effects of sanitary and phytosanitary regulation and barriers on trade in agriculture (ibid.).

Nine months later, the members of the Organization for Economic Co-operation and Development (OECD) agreed that their countries would 'refrain from actions which would worsen the present situation, in particular by avoiding measures that would tend to stimulate production in surplus agricultural commodities and by acting responsibly in disposing of the stocks built up' (Bull. EC 5–1987, 74). This statement was followed within the month by a lengthy declaration of support from the meeting of the seven major industrialized countries at Venice. Among the statements on agriculture was the following:

The long term objective is to allow market signals to influence the orientation of agricultural pioduction, by way of a progressive and concerted reduction of agricultural support, as well as by all other appropriate means, giving consideration to social and other concerns, such as food security, environmental protection and overall employment. (Bull. EC 6–1987, 143)

The stage was set for the Uruguay Round of GATT.

Agricultural Negotiations in GATT: 1987–1992

The Uruguay Round was the most extensive since the system of GATT Rounds of international trade negotiations came into existence in the 1950s. It covered a wider range of issues and included more participating countries than ever before: when the Round started there were about ninety Member States, by the time the Final Agreement was being ratified there were 125 Members, with at least a further twenty applicants wishing to join the World Trade Organization (WTO) which replaced GATT at the beginning of 1995. Originally, the Round was due to last from 1987 to 1990 with a mid-term review of progress at the end of 1988. However, due to the difficulties experienced in the negotiations, the Round continued until the end of 1993, with the Final Agreement being signed in Marrakesh in April 1994.

Three broad topics were covered by the negotiations: (a) the opening-up of markets more effectively than previously, both through the reduction of tariffs and the elimination of non-tariff barriers to trade; (b) the re-enforcement of international control mechanisms so as to ensure that safeguards provided for the protection of a threatened market were not abused, and to improve the procedures established to settle disputes; and (c) the extension of GATT rules and disciplines to new subject areas such as trade in intellectual property rights (TRIPS), and services such as banking and finance.

The manner in which the Community conducts negotiations with third countries on commercial policy is laid down in Article 113 of the Rome Treaty: the Commission conducts the negotiations on behalf of the Community on the basis of a brief agreed by the Council of Ministers. While responsibility for the brief lies with the Foreign Ministers acting as the Council, clearly the views of many other ministerial interests need to be taken into account depending on the issue involved—trade, finance, agriculture. For instance, in the case of the agricultural brief for the GATT negotiations, the Council of Agricultural Ministers drew up their agreed position at various stages of the negotiations and forwarded it to the General Affairs Council in the form of a recommendation. While great attention must always be paid to the views of a specialist Council, it is by no means certain that its recommendation will be adopted unchanged and in its entirety, as wider issues may need to be considered. This shared system of responsibility has its parallel within the Commission where it is DGI—the external relations directorate-general—which has the ultimate responsibility for conducting international negotiations.

The Uruguay Round negotiations were particularly complex as so many topics were involved. The agricultural brief had to take account not only of the usual difficulties of achieving consensus between the Member States (twelve at that time), with the different preoccupations of importers and exporters, Mediterranean and northern countries, but also with the interests of non-agricultural sectors anxious to see the success of the agricultural negotiations, because failure in such an important area might have seriously jeopardized the conclusion of an agreement on other topics.

As will become clear later in this chapter, an additional complicating factor was the intrusion into the agricultural negotiations of disputes which were not strictly part of the Uruguay Round. Examples of these sideline issues were the disputes between the USA and the EC on oilseeds, corn gluten, and maize exports to Spain. These became very important hindrances to the GATT negotiations and, once resolved, became facilitators of the conclusion of the Final Agreement. The role of these disputes will be outlined further below.

The original Community agricultural negotiating brief divided future action into short term and long term, the former having as its objective the achievement of a better market equilibrium, through a reduction of support internally and at the frontier, so as to prevent a deterioration of the market situation. Effort should be concentrated on those sectors with the worst problems, and measures already taken since 1984/85 with a view to curbing production should be counted as part of any subsequent agreement on support reduction. At the same time, special efforts should be made to stabilize the international markets for cereals, sugar, and dairy products.

In the longer term, there should be a significant and concerted reduction in support linked to a realignment of frontier protection. Farmers should be compensated for the decline in the level of support through the provision of social payments which would not distort production. Agreement on support levels would require the development of a standard measure and the Community suggested a modified version of the producer subsidy equivalent (PSE) developed by OECD. In its original form the PSE was defined as 'the payment that would be required to compensate farmers for the loss of income resulting from the removal of a given policy measure. Expressed as a percentage, it represents that part of the value of output accounted for by assistance of various kinds' (OECD 1987, 25). The Community wished to see this measure modified so as to include only those forms of support which had a significant effect on trade, to quantify measures intended to limit production, and to take into account fluctuations in world prices and exchange rates (Commission 1987(*j*)).

Progress in the negotiations was extremely slow and, by the time of the mid-term review, which started in Montreal in December 1988, the agricultural negotiating brief had advanced very little. Indeed, the Agricultural Ministers were much more interested in using the Community's position-statement for Montreal as a means of emphasizing the progress already made in reforming the CAP than in developing concrete proposals to move the negotiations forward. It is a measure of the importance of agriculture in the Uruguay Round that almost half of the Community's position-statement for Montreal was devoted to setting out the totally anodyne agricultural brief (*Agence Europe*, 7–12–88). It should be remembered that these negotiations were taking place shortly after the introduction of the commodity stabilizers, the agreement on curbing budgetary expenditure on the CAP, and the introduction of set-aside and extensification (see Chapter 6). The Community was determined to reap maximum benefit in the GATT negotiations from the introduction of these measures.

The attention being paid to agriculture was viewed with some alarm by other parties with an interest in the outcome of the Uruguay Round. For instance, the Union of European Industrial and Employers' Confederation (UNICE) expressed its unease, declaring that European industry could not:

accept that persistent friction on agricultural issues should put the whole round of negotiations into jeopardy. The result of the Uruguay Round must be to enable European firms to gain better access to the markets of third countries, and to induce as many countries as possible to integrate into the GATT system, especially the newly-industrialised countries. (*Agence Europe*, 5/6–12–88, 11)

In sharp contrast, COPA and COGECA were issuing a very different message which included the dogmatic statement that the 'European agricultural model' should not be questioned. This model had to be respected because it was the 'essential basis to ensure the future of the rural world in the Community'. The mechanisms of import levies and export refunds were not to be questioned— indeed the levy system should be extended to include commodities at that time excluded. Where Community Preference was weak—as with some Mediter-ranean products—the existing aid system should be maintained and external protection should not be reduced (*Agence Europe*, 5/6–12–88, 11).

In the event, the mid-term review was a considerable disappointment in a number of very important areas including not only agriculture but also textiles, safeguards against the misuse of protective measures in times of market disruption, and trade in intellectual property rights. Where agriculture was concerned, the Director-General of GATT—Dunkel—tried to push the negotiations along by defining three principles on which all discussion should be based: that agricultural policies should be more sensitive to signals from international markets; that support and protection should be gradually reduced and harmonized in order to lessen trade distortion; and that developing countries should benefit from special and differentiated treatment.

In calling for a reduction in support and protection, Dunkel was signalling a rejection of the extreme US position which had been based on a proposal for the complete abandonment of these aspects of policy. Dunkel appeased the Community by proposing that, in the calculation of support reduction, any measures of policy reform undertaken since the 1987 Punte del Este Declaration would be credited to the countries taking them, provided they made a positive contribution to the reforms sought in GATT. However, the Community was less happy with Dunkel's proposal that all non-tariff barriers to trade should be transformed into tariff equivalents, reduced, and consolidated. At a stroke, this would mean the demise of the variable import levy which more than any other single mechanism was the symbol of protection under the CAP. Dunkel also proposed that export subsidies and internal support measures should be brought under control and in the longer term be shorn of their trade-distorting effects. In the meantime, there should be a commitment not to increase existing support levels and to maintain market access for imports at existing levels. In April 1989, the Community formally accepted the negotiated compromise which arose from the Dunkel initiative (*Agence Europe*, 28–4–89).

Tariffication of non-tariff barriers to trade was particularly favoured by the Americans who had been pressing for its introduction since October 1988. A system of protection based on tariffs or tariff equivalents is much less trade-distorting than any other protective device. Transparency is improved in that a multitude of forms of protection are reduced to a single mechanism expressed either as a percentage of the landed price or as a fixed amount per unit imported. It does not ensure greater market access as the rate of tariff may be high but it does make the task of the subsequent reduction of that rate very much easier, as it can be achieved by the application of annual percentage decreases.

The Community was extremely cautious in its approach to tariffication not only on the grounds that its introduction would permit a greater element of price instability to the internal market than was possible with the Community's existing forms of frontier protection but also because it was based solely on the calculation of the degree of frontier protection and ignored internal measures with trade-distorting implications. However, it was willing to consider some degree of tariffication provided certain conditions were met. These included compensation at the frontier for reductions in internal price support;[13] the inclusion of deficiency payments converted to tariff equivalents on the grounds that they distorted the relationship of internal and external prices; and an agreement that export subsidization would not exceed the level of import protection for the same or a similar commodity (*Agence Europe*, 29–12–89).

On the question of the reduction of internal support, the USA and the Community differed fundamentally. The USA sought to have all such measures eliminated if they distorted trade, and to have the remaining support measures divided into two groups: those which were marginally trade-distorting to be controlled, and those which were trade-neutral to be outside the GATT agreement and retained if the country in question so wished (*Agence Europe*, 21–10–89).[14] The Community favoured an approach which was not concerned with categorizing types of support but rather with the impact of support. To this end, it promoted the aggregate measure of support (AMS) which it defined as covering:

all measures which have a real impact on the production decisions of farmers. This includes mainly measures to support market prices, direct payments linked to production or to factors of production and measures aiming to reduce input costs which are commodity specific or where a distribution according to main commodities is feasible. (*Agence Europe*, Document No. 1590, 29–12–89, 3)

The Americans were opposed to the use of AMS because of its implications for US internal agricultural policy which relied heavily on a deficiency payment system which would be caught by the Community's definition of AMS.

There were two other very important areas of agricultural policy where the Community and the USA held strongly opposing views: the 'rebalancing' of frontier protection and the subsidization of exports. Rebalancing was particularly related to the question of the relationships between cereals, cereal substitutes, and oilseeds and the desire of the Community to seek compensation for any reduction in frontier protection of cereals through a parallel increase in protection for cereal substitutes and oilseeds. On export subsidies, the Community view was that they were an integral part of the support system which was based on dual pricing which permitted a high internal support price matched by an ability to lower that price to the external price in order to facilitate exports. Both rebalancing and the Community system of export refunds were anathema to the Americans who did not wish to lose their zero or low tariff rating for such products as oilseeds and cereal substitutes, and who believed that export subsidies would be irrelevant in a liberalized international market.

The American position was no more logical than the Community's: it was based on an unwillingness to surrender a privileged position which had been obtained nearly thirty years previously (oilseeds in the Dillon Round), and on a new-found desire to abolish a form of subsidy which only came into the Community's portfolio because of the USA's own GATT negotiating stance in the 1950s! It was advocating the application of free market principles which it would itself have rejected in earlier years. The fear in European Commission circles was that, through their radical proposals, the Americans were trying to eliminate the CAP—not liberalize it (*Agence Europe*, 21–10–89).

Negotiations dragged on during 1990 with very little to show for them. The Uruguay Round was scheduled to be completed in early December and 15 October had been agreed as the date by which proposals for the final phase of the agricultural negotiations would be submitted to GATT. The approach of this deadline heralded an intense period of discussion within the Community which revealed the anxieties in agricultural circles, the divisions between the Member States, and the fears of other parties, keen to ensure the successful conclusion of the Round, that disagreement on agriculture might still prove to be an insuperable obstacle. So much was at stake that the discussions within the Institutions of the Community were particularly difficult. Indeed, MacSharry's original proposals for the final agricultural negotiating brief were rejected by his fellow Commissioners on the grounds that they were too unyielding—particularly in relation to concessions on export refunds.[15] MacSharry's initial response was to withdraw his proposals but subsequently the Commissioners adopted them with some amendments.

The proposals then went to the Council of Agricultural Ministers for its views although, as explained above, it was not their function to endorse the negotiating brief which was the prerogative of the General Affairs Council. The Agricultural Ministers failed to agree to the proposals; joint Councils of Agricultural and Trade Ministers then tried to agree on the negotiating position but still no solution could be found. It was only after their seventh meeting in the space of one month that the Councils finally reached an agreement. The text which was forwarded to GATT—about three weeks after the October deadline—was little changed from MacSharry's original proposal. The two issues which had caused so much trouble in the lengthy debate were the guarantees to be given to Community farmers for the changes to the support system and the assurances needed on the maintenance of Community Preference.

Two aspects of this protracted period of discussion are worth noting. The first is the alliance between Germany and France which were the countries most firmly opposed to the Commission's formulation of the Community's negotiating position. However, as *Agence Europe* commented it would be 'erroneous to conclude that the two countries hold a similar view. In fact, their support of each other seems to be tactical in nature since their objectives are fundamentally different' (*Agence Europe*, 3–11–90, 6). The Germans were concerned to have a guarantee that their farmers could achieve or maintain a standard of living comparable to that of the rest of the population. To this end, they stressed the need for farmers to be allowed to fulfil their role of guardians of the land and the natural environment. Their main interest, therefore, lay in the changes which were needed in the internal support mechanisms to accommodate an agreement in GATT and had little interest in the changes required at the frontier.

France, by contrast, was deeply concerned with market liberalization in the Community and, even more than that, with the question of export opportunities and the continuation of export subsidization. The extent of the difference between the two countries can be gauged from a statement made by the German Agricultural Minister—Kiechle—that 'Community farmers should not produce beyond what is necessary to meet European "needs". Only marginal amounts of specialized products and surplus goods resulting from exceptional harvests should be exported from the Community' (*Agence Europe*, 3–11–90, 6). Thus, even after thirty years of the CAP, the aims and ambitions of these two powerful

Member States had not changed; divergent though they were, they were still able to find a means of making common cause.

The second noteworthy aspect of the protracted discussion was that Andriessen remained sceptical about the agricultural negotiating position. He pointed out that the Uruguay Round consisted of more than agriculture and, in particular, that the Community was vitally concerned with achieving an agreement on trade in services, and in intellectual property rights. He was worried that certain features of the Community position on agriculture would 'not facilitate the negotiations in Geneva', mentioning specifically the rebalancing of protection and the maintenance of export refunds (*Agence Europe*, 8–11–90, 5). His fears were justified.

The December 1990 negotiations, which were intended to conclude the Uruguay Round, were a failure and a further three years were to elapse before a Final Agreement was reached. Within that period, 1992 was a particularly important year for agriculture. In late December 1991, Dunkel presented the parties to GATT with a set of proposals on the liberalization of the sector. These were later to form the basis of the eventual agreement on agriculture. The proposals included:

On market access

(a) Tariffication of non-tariff barriers but without the adjustments for price fluctuations and currency movements sought by the Community;

(b) a reduction in tariffs and tariff equivalents, over a seven-year period, of 36 per cent on average, with a minimum of 15 per cent for any single item;

(c) guaranteed minimum access to markets, which would rise to 5 per cent of internal consumption.

On internal support

(a) A reduction of 20 per cent on all government subsidies, over a seven-year period, calculated on base 1986–8 and using the AMS or an equivalent where the AMS was inappropriate;

(b) an exemption for small scale subsidies (i.e. those not exceeding 5 per cent of the product's total value);

(c) an exemption from the subsidy reduction requirement for various forms of government intervention such as funds devoted to research, disease control, training and advisory services, infrastructure expenditure, direct income support not linked to production, pensions, set-aside.

On export subsidies

(a) A reduction of 36 per cent in expenditure and of 24 per cent in volume, over a seven-year period;

(b) the application of these reductions to payments in kind, stocks sold at a loss, internal subsidies on products for which there were at that time export subsidies, subsidies for processing, transport of goods, and where there were export quotas (*Agence Europe*, 11–1–92).

Negotiation dragged on during 1992 and the Community became troubled by the continued insistence of the Americans to concentrate on agriculture to the virtual exclusion of other outstanding issues, in particular market access in non-agricultural sectors, and the inclusion of trade in services within the GATT orbit. These subjects were just as important to the Community as agriculture. In October 1992, the Commission listed the outstanding issues which it regarded as vital if a well-balanced agreement was to be reached. Agriculture was one such area and four points still had to be settled: direct income aid, export subsidies, rebalancing of protection, and the 'peace clause'.

Direct income aid had become a major issue because of the agreement the previous May to implement the MacSharry reforms. These were heavily dependent on the use of direct payments to compensate farmers for the decline in support prices and the introduction of set-aside for all but the smallest arable producers. The Community insisted that these payments had to be excluded from any agreement on the reduction of internal support. Discussions were still taking place on the percentage reduction in export subsidies and the pace at which this might take place. The Community continued to hang grimly on to the need to balance the reduction in protection in one sector with an increase elsewhere. The introduction of a so-called 'peace clause' was intended to restrain parties to the Final Agreement from complaints on issues settled in the Uruguay Round, provided the terms of the Agreement were being complied with (*Agence Europe*, 8–10–92).

Another factor which interposed itself increasingly in the closing months of 1992 was a hardening of attitudes in France. The French Government had been rattled by the results of the referendum on the Maastricht Treaty and the slimness of the majority in favour of its ratification. Farmers, in particular, were perceived as having used the opportunity of the vote to protest about other issues, especially the changes which had so recently been agreed in the CAP and those which were anticipated as the result of the Uruguay Round. The French Government focused on the proposed reduction in export refunds—something which it had never liked and which it had resisted unsuccessfully in 1990 (see above). Its renewed opposition came at a critical juncture as, in November 1992, after eleven months of negotiation in the margins of the GATT Round, the Community and the USA had finally reached an agreement on a range of issues which had soured relations between them. This became known as the Blair House Agreement and, despite the apoplexy which it generated in Paris and the controversy over its compatibility with the MacSharry reforms, eventually it was the means whereby the agricultural chapter of the Uruguay Round was brought to a successful conclusion.

The Blair House Agreement and Its Aftermath

While nominally the Uruguay Round negotiations were conducted multilaterally, certain parties dominated the proceedings and without their co-operation the negotiations were doomed to failure. The USA, Japan, and the European

Community were by far the most influential players overall and, where agriculture was concerned, no agreement was possible unless the USA and the
Community were willing to accept it. The Dunkel proposals of late 1991 were an
attempt to find common ground between these protagonists and they contained
elements borrowed from the negotiating position of both sides. Their willingness
to negotiate seriously was undermined by disagreements on various trade issues
which, in themselves, were of far less importance than the issues at stake in the
Uruguay Round and yet which at times took on a significance which threatened
to overshadow all else. The most complex of these trade issues concerned oilseeds.

In 1989, the USA complained that various aspects of the EC oilseed regime
were damaging to American trading interests and, under the dispute settlement
procedure of GATT, a panel was established to investigate the claim. This panel
reported in December 1989 and found that in two respects the Community oilseeds regime violated GATT rules. Firstly, it was held that the payment of the
subsidy to the oilseed crusher put domestically produced oilseeds in a more
advantageous position than imported oilseeds used by the same crusher and,
secondly, that by extension this situation negated the benefit which should have
accrued to the USA by virtue of the agreement in 1962 that the Community
would charge a zero tariff on imported oilseeds.

A crucial element in the GATT panel deliberations was its investigation of the
support mechanism which compensated the crushers by way of a deficiency payment based on the difference between an external price and the higher internal
target price. The external price was a 'constructed' price as there was no genuine
international market price on which to base the calculation. This led to the possibility that the crushers were being overcompensated. Moreover, as the crushers
did not have to prove that they had actually paid the farmers an on-farm
equivalent of the target price, there was a clear incentive for them to try to bid
the price down and therefore there was a commercial advantage in buying
domestically produced oilseeds in preference to imports.

The Community accepted the findings of the panel but, because at that time it
was anticipated that the Uruguay Round would be completed at the end of 1990,
it was decided that the reform of the oilseeds regime would be carried out in the
context of the conclusion of the Round. This was of some significance in the
context of the Community's continued insistence on rebalancing the levels of
protection which would, of course, have directly affected oilseeds. Another
reason for combining the two events was that in its report the GATT panel had
established an important point of principle: that a deficiency payment was
capable of distorting trade. This gave increased impetus to the Community's
strongly held belief that deficiency payments should be included in the support
mechanisms to be subject to reduction. As deficiency payments were a far more
significant element in the farm support system in the USA than in the Community, much more hung on this oilseeds dispute than met the eye.

As indicated above, the Uruguay Round was not completed at the end of 1990
and so the opportunity to link the oilseed regime reform with the end of the

Round fell apart. In 1991, the Community embarked on the discussions of the MacSharry reforms (outlined in Chapter 6), a major component of which was the reduction in market support prices and a switch to direct payments to farmers. This provided an opportunity to amend the oilseeds regime so as to replace the payments to crushers with standardized area payments to farmers independent of actual oilseed output in any given year. The necessary legislation was adopted under Reg. 3766/91 (OJ L356, 24–12–91). The compensatory payment was linked to the level of payments for cereals in such a way as to prevent producers having an incentive to move between crops.

That, however, was not the end of the oilseeds dispute with the USA. While the Americans acknowledged that the new regime met the requirements under GATT so far as the oilseed crushers were concerned, they still maintained that their 1962 tariff concession was being adversely affected and requested the re-convening of the GATT panel. It upheld their claim. Two options were open to the Community: either to amend the oilseeds regime once again or to renegotiate the original tariff concession. The Community chose the latter option—much to the annoyance of the USA which threatened to impose various trade sanctions against products of Community origin.

Part of the GATT disputes procedure involved ascertaining whether the USA (and nine other producing countries which were joined in the action) had been adversely affected and, if so, to what extent and what compensation should be paid. Not surprisingly, the views of the main protagonists were far apart and, as the negotiations dragged on into the second half of 1992, the atmosphere became more poisonous. In truth, the USA did not actually want compensation but rather wanted a further change in the EC oilseeds regime. It demanded that production be reduced in the Community by 6m. tonnes p.a. from the then level of 13m. tonnes and that the compensatory payments to farmers should also be reduced (*Agence Europe*, 28/29–9–92).

The Community was concerned that, if such an approach were adopted, it would have a detrimental impact on the MacSharry reforms. Oilseed producers would be tempted to switch to cereals which were already in serious surplus. The Community also was aware that the loss of market share by the USA to countries such as Brazil and Argentina was as much due to the strength of the dollar as to the build-up of oilseeds production in the EC.

Early in November 1992, the USA laid the groundwork for unilateral retaliation against the Community for its failure to resolve the oilseeds issue, starting with penal tariffs of 100 per cent on imports of selected agricultural products. These measures were to take effect in early December but in late November the Community and the USA were able to announce that they had reached agreement on an oilseeds compromise and on other outstanding trade issues. This became known as the Blair House Agreement (BHA).

The agreement on oilseeds took the form of a Memorandum of Understanding (Commission 1993(*d*)), the main features of which were that the Community would introduce a separate base area (SBA) for oilseeds production of 5.1m. ha. from 1995/96 onwards. Crop payments would be made on this base area which could be reduced in line with set-aside requirements. The payments to producers would be subject to deductions if the base area was exceeded and such deductions would apply in the same marketing year and in the following year. On set-aside land, where industrial oil crops were permitted, if the by-products of such production exceeded 1m. tonnes annually (expressed in soyabean meal equivalent), corrective action would be taken. In exchange for these changes to the regime, the USA agreed that it would forgo any further compensation claims for impairment of the 1962 tariff concession.

On issues which arose specifically from the Uruguay Round, the Community and the USA agreed to support a reduction of 20 per cent in the level of internal subsidies, as determined by the AMS and using 1986–8 as base. Payments linked to production-limiting programmes would be excluded within certain limits. On export subsidies, they agreed to support a reduction of 21 per cent by volume[16] and 36 per cent by value on base 1986–90. They also agreed to support a 'peace clause' which, during the implementation of the Uruguay Round, would ensure that measures which were fully in accord with the commitments entered into would not be subject to challenge under GATT rules. They agreed to Dunkel's proposal on minimum access to markets.

The BHA also tidied away other bilateral sources of irritation. There was an agreement to end the dispute on imports of corn-gluten feed, an extension for 1993 of the arrangements under which maize and sorghum entered Spain from the USA at a reduced import charge, and an agreement to permit certain maize imports to Portugal from the USA, also at a reduced charge (*Agence Europe*, 26–11–92).

And what of the issue of rebalancing of frontier protection by which the Community had set such store? This was reduced to an agreement that, if Community imports of cereal substitutes reached a level which appeared to threaten the implementation of the CAP reform, the Americans would consult with the Community on ways of finding a solution to the problem.

The BHA was, of course, only a bilateral agreement and it was necessary to put its terms to the other parties in the GATT Round; they could—if foolish enough to do so—have rejected it. However, before that could happen, the BHA had to be accepted by the Community as its negotiating position. It was almost a year before that came about. Not only was the immediate reaction of the French Government wholly negative but the BHA was described by the farmers' organizations as 'irresponsible' and 'catastrophic'. The Commission was accused of giving in 'to the hegemonic determination of the United States, which plans to dominate world agricultural markets using any means possible' (*Agence Europe*, 25–11–92, 16). Worse was to follow when the Commission published an explanatory note addressed to the Member States on the compatibility of the BHA with CAP reform (Commission 1992 (*f*)).

The Commission foresaw no problems with the reduction in internal support levels and, on tariffication, it was confident that Community Preference would be maintained: the only possible difficulties might arise on sugar and skimmed milk powder if certain pessimistic hypotheses were realized. Matters were more problematical where export refunds were involved: it was here that the BHA became suspect. The assumptions made on future production, consumption, and imports were critical in assessing whether the reductions in volume and value of export subsidies were compatible with the quantities likely to be available. Provided the Commission's assumptions were correct, then there would be no problem in meeting the requirements for cereals, dairy products, pork, and poultry. However, the Commission acknowledged that there would be a problem with beef where the export volume at the end of implementation period would exceed the permitted level by 300,000–400,000 tonnes. In addition, stocks of many commodities were already very high—despite the efforts made in the late 1980s at considerable budgetary cost to eliminate them. Overhanging stocks had not been included in the BHA.

Although France was in the vanguard of opposition to the BHA, it was quickly joined by all Member States except Britain in finding fault with the agreement. Indeed, at a meeting of the Agricultural Ministers just before Christmas 1992, it almost looked as if the whole agreement was about to unravel (*Agence Europe*, 17–12–92). Right from the announcement of the BHA, the French began to mutter darkly about 'using their veto'. This was an allusion to the so-called Luxembourg compromise (referred to in Chapter 2). *Agra Europe* summed up the political situation raised by this threat by explaining that:

The Luxembourg compromise has no legal basis. It continues because most of the Council of ministers want it. British and Danish ministers, for example, despite being strongly in favour of a GATT deal, would feel constrained to vote with France if the French wanted to invoke the compromise. The alternative (outvoting the French and then saying that they had no right to use a veto) would destroy the compromise and enshrine the principle of majority voting, once and for all, in the running of the Community. (*Agra Europe*, 27–11–92, P/4)

However, this explanation was misleading as indeed was the French threat to use a veto—something which they must have known. The question of a veto was completely irrelevant in the context of the BHA, firstly because, although the Council of Ministers was discussing the agreement, no proposal had been put to the Council by the Commission and, in the absence of a proposal, no vote can take place—let alone a veto! Secondly, the only vote that actually mattered was the one which would take place at the very end of the GATT negotiations when the proposition would be to accept or reject the Final Agreement. Thirdly, and most fundamentally, a veto was a constitutional impossibility because trade issues fall under Article 113 of the Rome Treaty and are, therefore, decided by qualified majority. The real issue, therefore, was whether the French would have been able to muster a sufficient number of votes to provide a blocking minority. Even that looked highly unlikely as Member States—for all their posturing— would have thought long and hard about the rejection of such an important measure.

What the French were trying to do was to undermine confidence in the BHA. Two objectives for this strategy were suggested at the time: to delay the debate on GATT until after the French election in March 1993 by which time a change in government might have taken place and it would have become someone else's problem (*Agra Europe*, 4–12–92), or to provide an opportunity for the French to wring concessions out of their colleagues. As *Agence Europe* commented: 'one might . . . wonder whether France's objective is really to have the arrangement with the United States changed or to obtain further advantages for farmers in the framework of the reform of the CAP' (*Agence Europe*, 14–1–93, 7). Both views were correct.

Discussions within the Council of Ministers on the oilseeds part of the BHA dragged on during the first half of 1993, with France becoming more isolated and the USA reviving its threats of trade sanctions focused very pointedly on products of particular interest to France. Various face-saving devices were found to allow the French to back down in a dignified manner. The BHA held and the oilseeds part of it was finally approved by the General Affairs Council on 8 June (OJ L147, 18–6–93).

This still left the other aspects of the BHA unresolved; the French remained unhappy about a range of issues, although they indicated that they were not going to question the substance of the agreement. However, their shopping list of 'adjustments' was extensive and, in particular, they remained concerned about limitations to the Community's ability to export. Of course, in fact the BHA did not limit exports: it was concerned solely with curbing the availability of subsidies on exports. A country such as France with its good farm structure is much more likely to be able to export without subsidy than say Germany or Italy. Another French preoccupation was the 'peace clause' which it wished to see made permanent and not limited to the period during which the Uruguay Round was being implemented.

In September 1993, the Commission acknowledged that there was some truth in the French concerns: stocks had risen and it was going to be difficult to get rid of them; changes in the value of some currencies had already negated the impact of the CAP reforms; compatibility between the BHA and those reforms was dependent on the assumptions made; and the Commission admitted that it had overstepped its 1990 negotiating mandate in the BHA, although it maintained its actions were in accord with the December 1991 mandate (*Agence Europe*, 17–9–93).

This was not a good backdrop to the joint session of the Council of Ministers (Foreign Affairs and Agriculture) held in late September 1993; once again the Uruguay Round appeared to be threatened by the exaggerated positions adopted by various Member States, pressure groups, and, from the sidelines, the President of the USA (*Agence Europe*, 20/21–9–93). It became clear during the course of the meeting that agriculture was by no means the only cause for concern— financial services, shipping, textiles, the audio-visual sector, intellectual property rights, and so on. Despite this, agriculture dominated the meeting and the Commission was instructed to reopen discussions with the Americans with the intention of seeking 'interpretations, amplifications and additions' of the BHA.

The Council confirmed its view that:

the outcome of the agricultural chapter of the Uruguay Round could not, either directly or indirectly, be allowed to jeopardise the durability of the Common Agricultural Policy, nor stand in the way of compliance with its basic principles, particularly Community preference. In the same spirit, the Council emphasized that the Community's role as an exporter had to be maintained and that its rightful place on the international agricultural market had to be assured.   (*Agence Europe*, 22–9–93, 6)

This statement of principle sums up very well the uneasy relationship of the price and market policy, and the commercial policy under the CAP. It also comes perilously close to suggesting that the principles which underlie the price and market policy—market unity, financial solidarity, and Community Preference—were sufficiently important that they could threaten the conclusion of a major multilateral commercial agreement. There is no doubt that agriculture had become such a key issue in the Uruguay Round that failure to conclude that chapter would have caused the collapse of the Round. However, the brave and apparently uncompromising words of the Council were little more than window-dressing as the Council also reiterated the importance of concluding the Round by the end of the year. Therefore, practical politics dictated that a solution had to be found to the outstanding issues in the agricultural chapter.

Although the Americans had made it very clear that they would not reopen the BHA nor would they allow themselves be tricked into an indirect renegotiation, they too wanted to reach a settlement. Discussions took place between the Community and the USA between late September and early December 1993 which led to certain changes to the BHA—sometimes referred to as Blair House II. Among the items agreed was a limitation on the levels of frontier protection for the main cereals entering the Community so that the tariff-paid price was linked to the intervention price as well as to the landed price. On exports, the volume limits on subsidies were adjusted upwards where the volume exported in the early 1990s was higher than in the base period. Although the volume at the end of the implementation period remained the same, the modified arrangement gave greater flexibility in stock management. The 'peace clause' was extended for three years beyond the implementation period of the Round (*Agence Europe*, 9–12–93). On 15 December, the General Affairs Council unanimously approved the whole Uruguay Round package bringing to an end seven years of negotiations.

The Implementation of the Agricultural Chapter of the GATT Agreement

So far as the European Union was concerned, implementation started with the endorsement of the Final Agreement reached in the Uruguay Round by the Council (Decision 94/800, OJ L336, 23–12–94), within which the Agreement on Agriculture and the Agreement on the application of sanitary and phytosanitary measures formed two chapters. Shortly afterwards, the Council adopted Reg. 3290/94 (OJ L349, 31–12–94) which made provision for adaptations to the various commodity regimes to accommodate the changes to frontier protection, internal support, and export refunds. This was a general Regulation which, over the following months, was supplemented by a series of Commission Regulations which established the necessary details of administration for each commodity regime.

In administrative terms, the part of the Agreement on Agriculture which required the least immediate effort was that concerned with internal support. The agreement required a 20 per cent reduction in the level of support from the 1986–8 level, over a six-year implementation period (mid-1995 to mid-2001), with credit given for reductions in support made unilaterally prior to the Agreement. Support is calculated according to the aggregate measure of support (AMS) which is defined as the internal price minus the external price, multiplied by the quantity produced plus certain direct payments. Although the AMS is calculated commodity by commodity, the requirement to reduce support by 20 per cent is global. This allows for variation between commodities.

The internal price is (where relevant) taken to mean the intervention price; the external price is the average (1986–8) unit value for the basic commodity, adjusted where necessary for quality. Direct payments exclude the compensatory payments for crop production and headage payments, made under the CAP reform, subject to upper limits.[17] Also excluded are a whole series of payments which are deemed to have no, or at most a minimal, trade distorting effect, or effect on production. The Agreement on Agriculture is accompanied by an Annex which lists the types of payments excluded from the calculation of the AMS. From the point of view of the CAP, the most interesting are those of a structural nature (retirement of persons from farming or their movement to other occupations; retirement of resources such as land or herd reductions; restructuring to assist farmers' response to structural disadvantages); environmental or conservation programmes provided they include conditions relating to production methods or inputs; payments in designated disadvantaged regions.

The AMS base (1986–8) was calculated at 73,531m. ECU and the AMS target in 2000 was calculated at 60,378m. ECU. Because of the price cuts since 1986 and in particular since 1992 under the MacSharry reforms, it is not expected that the Union will experience any difficulty in meeting its commitment under this part of the Agreement. The situation is more problematic where trade is concerned. Four issues are involved here: tariffication of non-tariff barriers and the reduction of trade barriers; the use of safeguard procedures to limit the impact of sharp variations in price or volume of imports; the enhancement of import opportunities; and the control of the level of export refunds.

As already outlined in Chapter 7, from the Union's point of view, the most important non-tariff barriers to be abolished were the variable import levy, minimum import prices, import quotas, and voluntary export restraints. These instruments had to be converted to tariffs whether expressed *ad valorem* (i.e. as a percentage of the landed price) or as a specific amount (i.e. as so many ECU per unit landed). Where possible, the calculation of the tariff equivalent was to be based on the difference between an external price (i.e. an actual average c.i.f. value in the importing country) and a representative wholesale price internally in the base years 1986–8. However, in the EU, where intervention prices existed these were used instead of wholesale prices. Where no actual external price was available, a price was constructed according to guidelines provided in the Agricultural Agreement.

The resulting tariff equivalents, together with any pre-existing tariffs had to be reduced from the base of 1986–8 by a global average of 36 per cent (with a minimum reduction of 15 per cent for any one tariff) over the implementation period 1995–2000. At the end of the period the tariffs are to be bound at the level then reached. Although, as a result of tariffication, all protection at the frontier is now expressed either as specific or *ad valorem* tariffs, the outcome is not quite as simple as this statement would suggest.

Paradoxically, because the level of protection for many commodities was actually higher in 1986–8 than in 1995 when implementation began, the base from which the 36 per cent cut took place was correspondingly higher and it is most unlikely that tariffication of itself improves market access in any meaningful way.

Because of the structure of the previous protective measures, some commodities have a combined tariff system, i.e. a specific and an *ad valorem* tariff (beef, sheepmeat, and pigmeat are cases in point). Previously, protection for fruit and vegetables was based on a minimum import price (MIP) combined with a range of *ad valorem* tariffs. This was replaced by an entry price (a tariffied MIP): produce imported at or above the entry price is charged an *ad valorem* tariff. If, however, the entry price is not met, a tariff equivalent must be paid to bring the price up to the entry price. A further anomaly is that dried grapes (currants, sultanas, raisins) and certain types of processed cherries still retain an MIP; if this is not observed, a countervailing charge is applied in addition to the tariff. This latter system was retained by the Union by way of derogation from the Agricultural Agreement but is to be removed by 2000.

Because of the amendments made to the BHA in December 1993 (see above), the major cereals are treated differently from all other commodities. They are (with a few exceptions) subject to a specific tariff expressed in ECU/tonne. For wheat, rye, barley, maize, and sorghum the tariff is calculated as the difference between the intervention price raised by 55 per cent minus the average c.i.f. price.[18] In order to operate this system, the EU established a series of frontier reference prices, based on average import costs of the quality in question, from which the relevant tariff is then derived. The ink was hardly dry on this system before the Americans and Canadians were protesting about its operation.

One of the great fears which the Community had during the GATT negotiations was that the abandonment of the system of frontier protection, based on devices such as the variable import levy and the sluice-gate price, would result in the introduction to the internal market of the kinds of strong price and volume fluctuations to which international markets are subject. Such a development would undermine Art. 39.1(c) of the Rome Treaty which lists market stability as an objective of the CAP. In an attempt to take care of this fear, provision is made under the Agricultural Agreement for the application of special safeguards to accompany tariffication.

Under the safeguard system, additional tariffs can be imposed where falling import prices or rising import volumes threaten the stability of the internal market. On price, the trigger is based on the c.i.f. unit import value in the period 1986–8, modified if necessary for quality or stage of processing. If the actual import price falls by more than 10 per cent below the trigger price a safeguard tariff may be charged in addition to the normal tariff payable. There is a sliding scale of such tariffs. At maximum, the safeguard and normal tariff combined can be equal to 52 per cent of the trigger price.

On volume, the safeguard is based on a comparison of the quantity in question and the level of imports measured as a percentage of internal consumption in the three preceding years. In this case, the safeguard tariff is on a sliding scale with a maximum of one-third of the normal tariff payable. The safeguards on volume and value cannot be combined.

As mentioned above, tariffication of itself does not necessarily improve access and therefore many imports continue to enter the EU market on the basis of concessionary arrangements carried forward into the new system but in an amended form. Where access to the Community's markets in 1986–8 was governed by special import arrangements (quotas, voluntary restraint, etc.), the access must be maintained at the level then pertaining and at the concessionary tariff rate then prevailing.[19] The difference which the GATT agreement has made is that the volume permitted under these concessions can now be exceeded if the exporting country so wishes but the quantity outside the concession is charged the full tariff rate.

Provision was made in the Agricultural Agreement for the creation of supplementary import opportunities so as to ensure that imports represent 5 per cent of internal consumption by 2000. This access is provided by reduced-tariff quotas. In some cases, the existing concessionary access is sufficient to fulfil this requirement in the EU. In other cases—most notably certain types of pigmeat, eggs, butter, skimmed milk powder, and cheese—new tariff quotas have been required.

From the outline given above, it can be deduced that market access is still quite limited when combined with a high degree of self-sufficiency. Indeed, during the Uruguay Round negotiations, main exporting countries—in particular the Cairns group[20]—were not so concerned with gaining access to markets such as that of the USA or the Community as with achieving a situation in which these two giants were forced to reduce the level of their export subsidies (hidden or overt), as such subsidies were regarded as the main obstacle to export expansion by other countries. Tariffication, therefore, was mainly perceived as beneficial in aiding the transparency of the frontier protection system. Any reduction of market insulation was a bonus but not the main purpose of the exercise.

Under the Agricultural Agreement, countries are required during the implementation period 1995–2000 to reduce the volume of subsidized exports by 21 per cent and value of export subsidies by 36 per cent on base 1986–90, except in those cases where another base was agreed. For beef, for instance, the base is 1986–92; for wheat, certain dairy products, poultrymeat, and eggs the base is

1991/92. Unlike the decline in internal support where the requirement is global, the decrease in export subsidies is commodity specific.

The problem facing the Union is whether it will be able to get production levels sufficiently under control so as to meet the volume requirements. The main difficulty at the time of writing lies with beef where production is set to continue to outstrip internal consumption. This may require greater recourse to intervention purchasing than has been the case since the late 1980s.[21] If this is not to happen, production may need to be dampened down by adjustments to the beef premium scheme or the suckler cow premium, although initially that in itself might make matters worse by raising the rate of culling.

Beef is not the only possible area of difficulty: already provision has been made under the sugar regime to reduce production quotas if required in order to fulfil the commitment on exports (see Reg. 1101/95, OJ L110, 17–5–95). At the time of writing, the wine regime had still not been reformed, although proposals had been put before the Council of Ministers as far back as June 1994. If the problem of structural surplus is not resolved, there will be a continuing need to distil that surplus into industrial alcohol, much of which is exported with the use of subsidies.

Expenditure on export refunds is, of course, dependent not only on production but also on market prices in potential outlets. If prices are high, the unit level of refund is lower and the possibility of unsubsidized exports is enhanced. Clearly, there is an incentive for the exporting Member States to improve their cost–price structure. Another interesting thought is that the GATT agreement may actually favour those Member States with substantial and efficient export-oriented processing industries. The reason is that the requirement to reduce export subsidization on manufactured food products (i.e. the non-Annex II products referred to in Chapter 6) concerns expenditure only. Therefore, if there is scope to expand downstream industries, there could be advantages in terms of value added and employment, and the unit cost of subsidy on such products is much lower than on the raw material or on a product exported at the first stage of processing.

NOTES

1. Although the term 'commercial policy' is the one used in the Treaty of Rome and in many EC documents, 'trade policy' might be a more usual term and the two are used interchangeably in this chapter.
2. This may go some way to explain how the many exercises which show that the total cost of the CAP is greater than the total gain in the majority of Member States are largely ignored except by a handful of economists. It is intuitively hard to accept that a policy which has such good social motivation at its base could possibly yield such a result. (See European Commission (1994) for recent calculations illustrating this point.)

3. The rapporteurs did not indicate which delegations were responsible for the views stated but they have all the flavour of the French and the Dutch views on policy.

4. The interest in this issue can be gauged from the fact that between 9/10 February and 2 July, *Agence Europe* carried at least 26 reports on some aspect of the oils tax.

5. While it was not perfect, the internal market in agricultural commodities was, in effect, a single market from the time that the market regimes came fully into force, i.e. by 1970 for all major and many minor products. This was more than two decades ahead of the creation of the Single Market generally throughout the Union. The major shortcoming to the single agricultural market was the currency instability which started in 1969 and which reached a peak in the late 1970s. It necessitated the use of monetary compensatory amounts to try to maintain the semblance of the single market. It provides a salutary lesson in the need not just for currency stability but, preferably, for a single currency if the Union is to maintain the Single Market.

6. It was also concerned with its exports of poultry (a cereal-based product) to the FRG. See Harris *et al.* (1983) for a brief account of the subsequent 'chicken war'.

7. There is no evidence that consideration was ever given to the reciprocal proposition that a decline in consumption should mean an obligation on Community farmers to reduce production!

8. This refers to tariff and quota restrictions: other non-tariff barriers to trade were much more difficult to eliminate.

9. It also followed on from the very unsatisfactory Kennedy Round of GATT negotiations which produced very little in terms of trade liberalization in agriculture (see Harris *et al.* (1983) and Tracy (1989)).

10. It is actually very hard to take seriously some of the statements made. The transformation from deficit to surplus is described as having been an 'objective' of the policy. If so, why all the complaints down the decades of the costs of disposal?!

11. Another 'voluntary' restraint agreement had been reached in 1980 when the sheep-meat regime was introduced. The tariff was bound in GATT at 20%, so the variable import levy which would have been imposed could not be applied. The EC concluded restraint agreements with the suppliers (mainly Australia and New Zealand) in return for a reduced tariff of 10%. See Ch. 7 for a discussion of the economic implications of voluntary export restraints.

12. It was in fact an attempt to continue the efforts made in the Kennedy and Tokyo Rounds of GATT to introduce agreements to regulate international trade on the basis of minimum prices. Agreements had been set up for wheat, dairy products, and beef. However, at best these agreements were only partly successful.

13. The decline in the level of internal support would be matched at the frontier by a fixed charge on the equivalent import or its substitute which would be reduced at the same rate as the internal support. This fixed amount would be accompanied by a variable element to compensate for exchange rate movements and world price fluctuations which exceeded a given threshold.

14. This division of support measures is often referred to as Red, Amber, and Green Box respectively.

15. This rebellion was led by the former Agricultural Commissioner—Andriessen—who was by that time External Relations Commissioner in overall charge of the GATT negotiations on behalf of the Community. No doubt the irony of this event was not lost on the Commissioners!

16. This was a reduction of 3% on the Dunkel proposal of December 1991.

17. In the USA, direct payments exclude deficiency payments. These concessions were part of the Blair House Agreement.
18. The intervention price itself varies monthly so as to encourage orderly marketing over the farm-year.
19. A complete list of import quotas and the tariffs to which they are subject is contained in Annex 7 of Reg. 1359/95 (OJ L142, 26–6–95) which sets out the Common Customs Tariff of the Union.
20. Australia, Argentina, Brazil, Canada, Chile, Colombia, Fiji, Hungary, Indonesia, Malaysia, Philippines, New Zealand, Thailand, and Uruguay—all agricultural exporting countries which formed a loose negotiating group during the Uruguay Round.
21. Early in 1996, the beef market was thrown into turmoil by the knock-on effect of the BSE scare in beef production in Britain. Consumer confidence in beef was adversely affected right across the Union and export markets were seriously disrupted. This necessitated greater recourse to intervention and, at the time of writing, the future development of the beef market was most uncertain.

13

Unresolved Issues

Introduction

The CAP has come a long way since the early heady days when it seemed to herald a new era in agricultural policy. As was remarked in the Preface, a generation of farmers, who have known no other policy, has grown old with it. What was once innovative and exciting is now familiar and dull. This last chapter provides an opportunity to review some of the major themes to have emerged from earlier chapters and to draw attention to areas of conflict and contradiction which are unresolved. These are relevant to the future of the policy—if indeed it has a future as a separate sectoral policy.

In Chapter 11, reference was made to a discussion document issued in 1985 in which the Commission identified priorities for the CAP. They are worth repeating here: the reduction of surpluses; increased diversity of production combined with quality improvements; a more effective and systematic approach to the income problem of small family farms; support for farming for environmental and landscape purposes, and assistance in the maintenance of a viable rural population; promotion of environmental awareness among farmers; and the development of industries which process agricultural raw materials (Commission 1985(*d*)). Apart from the reduction of surpluses which has taken place, little of any significance has been achieved in the pursuit of other priorities listed. It is hard to believe that they are not all still valid: When are they going to be addressed?

Price and Market Policy

In reviewing the origins and early goals of the CAP, the point was made in Chapter 2 that one of the most imaginative aspects of the policy was that its designers visualized it as an integrated policy combining market and commercial policies with structural and social policies. It was a bold idea which was never given any real chance to succeed. One of the great weaknesses in the evolution of the CAP is that too much emphasis was placed on price support and market manipulation. It is no exaggeration to state that, in one way or another, this aspect of policy was expected to fulfil the diverse objectives laid down for the CAP in Art. 39.1(*a–e*). Not surprisingly, it proved incapable of achieving all the aims simultaneously. The overwhelming dependence on this one approach to sectoral support led to a belief that the multifarious problems which farmers faced could be adequately addressed through economic means which, in some unspecified way, would solve the social and structural problems as well.

While the limitations of price and market policy were well understood by policy-makers in the 1970s—if not before—little effort was made to redress the situation. The failure to introduce Community Programmes in the 1960s (despite the requirement under Reg. 17/64 to do so) and the saga of the Mansholt Plan (see Chapters 8–10) highlighted how isolated the market policy was. This isolation was surely indicative of the desire of the Member States to limit Community action in agricultural policy to the minimum required for the implementation of the common internal market. It was not until the 1990s that some fundamental changes were made and these were forced upon the policy-makers by the build-up of surpluses, the restrictions on the budgetary cost of the CAP, and the inclusion of agricultural support mechanisms within the negotiating agenda of the Uruguay Round of GATT.

The changes made in the price and market policy as a result of these pressures cannot be continued indefinitely in their present form without some consideration being given to the basis on which they were made, as this is becoming increasingly unacceptable. Two aspects of the present situation are untenable in the medium term: one is the historical base on which changes were made, the other is the issue of compensation for policy change. On the first of these, the MacSharry reforms were accepted and implemented on the basis of shifting market and price support away from current production levels to a historical level. The further away one gets in time from the base years, the more unrealistic and arbitrary the system becomes. The second aspect is that the decoupling of support from current production levels was made by way of compensation to farmers for this radical change of policy. While it may be reasonable to compensate farmers in such circumstances for a limited period of time, it is not reasonable to make what amounts to an open-ended commitment. It would be preferable that any such compensation should be limited in time and that the limitation is known from the start.[1]

A solution needs to be found to both these aspects of the price and market policy and added point is given to this need by the expected Enlargement of the Union to the East. On the assumption that some at least of the Central and East European Countries (CEECs) are in a position to assume the obligations and responsibilities of membership by, say, 2005, the extension to their farmers of compensatory payments based on production levels in the past, achieved in totally different circumstances, would be patently absurd. The Commission has argued the problem out of existence by maintaining that the gap between the internal price and the world market price for some key products is likely to be reduced further, and that the prices in the acceding countries will rise towards the Union level. 'If this is the case, there will be no economic reason for compensation, at least not in the logic of the 1992 reforms' (Commission 1995(*c*), 25).

Yet how could one justify a totally different support basis for the new Member States when they themselves are required to accept the *acquis communautaire* in all its aspects? Although no one does so, one could argue with good reason that the form of support now being given to EU farmers is inappropriate for the type of farming structure likely to be in place in the applicant countries early in the next century. The system of compensatory payments is inequitable as it is, because it perpetuates the overcompensation of a small minority of very large farm businesses and does little to assist farmers with a genuine income problem. How much more inequitable would this be in countries with more polarized farm structures composed of very small and very large units carved out of the old private plot/state farm/co-operative structure.

One aspect of the price and market policy which has not been discussed since the early days of the Community is whether the provision of support for such a wide range of commodities actually accords with the objective stated in Art. 39.1(d): to assure the availability of supplies, and at what level of self-sufficiency should such availability be deemed to be secure. When the CAP proposals were made in 1960, the range of commodities included under the market policy was limited. It covered the key elements in the basic nutritional requirements of the human population in terms of energy, protein, vitamins, and trace elements; this overlapped to a considerable extent with the feed requirements for animals as well. It also covered (with the inclusion of wine) the most widely produced farm-based commodities in the original EC-6.

If one were to make the choice again, it is possible that the range of basic commodities selected would differ somewhat; it might, for instance, place greater emphasis on those commodities which have a significant and potentially ex-panding use in the non-food sector.[2] What makes little sense is to continue with a range of commodities which has grown from the original core group in a haphazard manner because of the whim of a particular Member State in some negotiating bargain.[3] In fulfilment of Art. 39.1(d), it would seem reasonable to concentrate on the assurance of strategic supplies of major commodities (how-ever defined). From an international point of view, this would be a defendable position. Security of supply appears an acceptable goal of policy, provided it is limited to key commodities. Obviously there is a cost involved which the Union should recognize and be willing to pay, either through prices or taxes. The commitment to security of supply should not necessarily be the same for each strategic commodity, as the length of time required to replenish stocks is not the same in each instance, nor is storability.

The second aspect of supply security is the level of self-sufficiency which should be regarded as 'normal' or 'adequate'. This issue was raised originally in the Spaak Report (see Chapter 1). While it is unlikely that agriculture will feature quite so prominently in the first WTO Round of international negotiations (which should start in the late 1990s) as it did in the Uruguay Round of GATT, certain issues relating to market support will undoubtedly be raised. Production-based support may well feature and, in particular, the issue of the remaining export subsidies. More emphasis may, however, focus on the question of market access. This was of little significance in the Uruguay Round, overshadowed as it was by much bigger and more contentious matters. So far as the EU is concerned, as indicated in Chapter 12, the market access requirement has already been achieved in the majority of commodities. It is likely that some exporting countries may push for greater access. Indeed, that might well be true of some Member States of the Union which have large agricultural export interests which they would wish to exploit further by improving their access to markets outside the Union. In the context of market access, it is important to have some view of the level of internal production which would meet the requirements of Art. 39.1(d).

In addition to these points, however, the question of market access has another significance in the EU context. While it is true that production has shifted somewhat between Member States and that a greater element of specialization has come about, comparative advantage—whether in locational or production terms—has not functioned as well as it might. There has been a sense in which each Member State has tried to maintain production of a full range of major commodities (and indeed some minor ones) within its own territory. Undoubtedly the most extreme example of this is sugar, based as it is on production quotas, but the pricing structure generally has allowed the continuation of local production of many commodities which would have disappeared in a more rationally organized system.

Member States need to confront the issue of whether they are individually prepared to see a lowering of self-sufficiency levels in their own country to the benefit of another Member State. This is quite a separate matter from acceptance of the need to open the Union market as a whole to increased imports. In many respects, the former issue is actually of greater practical importance than the latter—which may be why Member States never seem to discuss it. Either the Single Market functions or it does not: in agriculture, where the whole concept of a unified market was pioneered, it appears that it does not function as intended.

The final issue to be raised in this Section is that of market stabilization. Over the years, the price and market policy lost its focus in relation to stabilization. The original aim was to promote orderly marketing, which is a legitimate objective in a policy area in which various forms of instability are inherent. However, orderly marketing gave way to rigidity which in turn resulted in the build-up of unsaleable surpluses carried forward from year to year. At the time of writing, it is not at all clear that the combination of MacSharry- and GATT-based reforms has returned the stabilizer mechanisms to their original purpose. Equally unclear is whether there is any coherent view of the extent to which market stability should be sought or the commodities for which a stabilization mechanism is essential. For instance, market stability is of far greater importance for staple food and feed products than for many lesser commodities.

Structural Policy

Earlier chapters have shown that the close relationship which, at Stresa and in the 1960 proposals on the CAP, was seen to exist between structural policy and the market policy never materialized. Structural policy remained underdeveloped and isolated. It was never fully funded by the Community and remained very largely in the hands and under the control of the Member States. One effect of this has been that structural measures have been regarded as an optional extra, even when their introduction has been directly linked to some change in market policy. The usual pattern has been for the market measure to be adopted relatively quickly and for the structural measure/s to be delayed, sometimes for years; for the proposals to be modified so as to be made less effective; and for the budgeted expenditure to be reduced. Where Member States are left free to introduce the structural measure or not as they wish, the majority often choose the latter course or, if it is adopted, it is at the lowest permissible level of expenditure and with minimal publicity, thereby lessening the potential benefit.

The original intention was to devise a structural policy targeted on those regions and commodities identified as requiring the greatest assistance. In practice, as Chapters 8–11 have illustrated, many years were to pass before such an approach finally came about. Equally, the original intention was to link structural and market policies but this never worked properly and indeed, in some instances, the two policies were pulling in opposite directions. While structural policy is now much more focused, its role has changed in that, since the late 1980s, it is now more closely linked to the regional and social policies than to the agricultural market policy. The result has been that the original integrated approach to policy not only failed to materialize but to all intents and purposes has been abandoned. In many ways, this can be seen as an indictment of the unimaginative and highly traditional approach of the Member States to agricultural policy.

Despite the abandonment of an integrated approach, links with the price and market policy remain. One such link is the overrepresentation of the larger and better-organized farm businesses in the receipt of structural funds. This is inevitable unless some satisfactory method is found to place a meaningful ceiling on the amount of structural aid any farm business can receive or, where appropriate, any unit of land can receive. In the establishment of such a ceiling, the total receipts of public funds for the unit in question should be taken into account. In addition to the overrepresentation of certain types of farm business, there has also been a concentration of structural support on a very small number of measures: farm modernization, compensatory payments in LFAs, and processing and marketing. This has meant inadequate funding for the many other forms of structural aid. The statistics provided in Chapters 8, 9, and 10 testify to this imbalance and one can only wonder what purpose was served by the proliferation of inadequately funded schemes scattered over wide areas of the Community.

Under the Agricultural Agreement arising out of the Uruguay Round of GATT, certain forms of support were excluded from the calculation of domestic support which had to be reduced over the lifetime of the Round; one such exempt measure was payments in disadvantaged areas (OJ L336, 23–12–94). Whether the exemptions will remain after the next Round is unclear but, even if they do, there is something absurd about the situation in the Union in which over half the

UAA is classified as less-favoured (see Chapter 9). Having once designated an area as an LFA, it is extremely difficult to reclassify it using stricter criteria.

There has always been an apparent contradiction between the objective of increasing agricultural productivity (Art. 39.1(a) of the Rome Treaty) and the support of production in areas and on farms where, by definition, unit costs are higher than in more-favoured regions. The only way in which one can reconcile LFA payments with Art. 39.1(a) is by interpreting the objective as applying regionally rather than Union-wide. This would accord with the requirement in Art. 39.2(a) to take regional disparities into account in working out the CAP. This point is relevant to the issue of surplus creation, which has been such a problem over the lifetime of the CAP.

From one point of view, it could be argued that surpluses are created by the small minority of farmers who produce the bulk of the output, aided and abetted by a policy which overcompensates such farmers through the support mechanisms. This might be called the physical or quantitative point of view. But from an economic point of view, surpluses are produced by the farmers with the highest costs, irrespective of location. Many such farmers are found in poor land areas—even if the farmers themselves are excellent in terms of technical skills. Indeed, one might argue that to be a successful farmer in an LFA requires the possession of greater skill levels, even if production costs remain higher than in more-favoured areas. With the continued downward pressure on production and price support, the anomalous position of LFA farmers is going to be highlighted and Member States may be tempted to press for further relaxation of the qualifying criteria for LFAs as a means of avoiding some of these controls.

The existence of contradictions and anomalies in the LFA policy is not an argument in favour of the view that the Union should cease its special help to such regions but it is an argument in favour of greater clarity as to the purpose of such support and the level of output regarded as appropriate. This ties in with a point made in the previous Section: that the geographic shift of production has not been as great as might have been expected, given common pricing and the unified market. The production possibilities are more restricted in LFAs and one could argue that support policies should be used to allow them to benefit from the few advantages which they may have (e.g. natural grassland for the production of milk, cattle, and sheep), or to use them to achieve a qualitative improvement in a product (e.g. quality wine in hill areas). However, such an approach requires either that the commodity in question is in deficit and is suited to the conditions in an LFA or that there is a matching contraction of output elsewhere in the Union. Member States have never given any indication of a willingness to recognize that certain aspects of the CAP are social in nature and nowhere is this more true than in relation to LFAs.

Since the redesigning of the Structural Funds in the late 1980s and their closer integration, one should raise the question as to whether the link in FEOGA-Guidance between production and aid is possibly detrimental to the wider and longer-term interests of the areas concerned. The importance of the compensatory payments in LFAs in relation to total FEOGA-Guidance expenditure stifles the development of new forms of investment. The justification for special assistance for any depressed region must lie in its structural defects, whether human or natural in origin, and that such defects are a contributory factor to low gross regional product and thus to lower personal incomes. The Union is dedicated to 'a harmonious development of economic activities, a high degree of convergence of economic performance, the raising of the standard of living and quality of life; and economic and social cohesion and solidarity among Member States' (Art. 2.2 of the Rome Treaty, as amended by the Maastricht Treaty). While compensatory payments may raise the standard of living and quality of life of the recipients, they do not meet any of the other objectives of the Union as stated in Art. 2.2. As currently designed, they encourage farmers to continue patterns of farming which may well never be viable. The assistance given to any backward region ought to make a lasting contribution to the stated objectives. This is not only on grounds of social equity and the better use of available resources but also in order to make the introduction of a common currency, and a single monetary and exchange rate policy, a feasible proposition. To have certain regions lagging permanently behind makes such goals extremely difficult to achieve.

Over the lifetime of the CAP, there has been a reliance on that policy to take care very largely of the needs of the regions which were predominantly agricultural in nature. The bulk of the remedial investment was, not surprisingly, linked to farming or to processing and marketing of agriculture-based products. This may not necessarily be the best approach for the future. If aid to designated rural areas was less clearly identified with agricultural production, it would leave greater scope for the utilization of the same level of resources in, possibly, more imaginative ways. For instance, it is perfectly reasonable to support activities of an environmental, scenic, or touristic nature, or to support processing and manufacturing. If such activities happen to take place on a farm, is the cost of such support correctly charged to the CAP or should it devolve on to some other part of the Union Budget? All expenditure must find its ultimate justification in the furtherance of the objectives of Article 2 of the Rome Treaty. The original concept of an integrated agricultural policy comprising market, structural, social, and commercial elements was intended to assist agriculture to play its part in the achievement of the objectives of Article 2. In the event, the CAP has evolved in a manner quite different from the original intention. Just as with the market policy where, in recent years, there has been much rethinking of its role, so too it is time to rethink the role of structural policy within the CAP.

Commercial Policy

The need for the Community to establish trade links with third countries meant that, from the beginning, commercial policy had to exist. However, as outlined in Chapter 12, in agriculture the role of commercial policy was secondary to that of market policy. This only changed—and then not completely—with the inclusion of the agricultural sector in the Uruguay Round negotiations to an extent unknown in any previous GATT Round. Certain safeguards were built into the agreement reached, so as to limit disruption on internal markets caused by fluctuations of world market prices or quantities traded internationally. Only time will tell how well such safeguards work and whether the members of the WTO will wish to continue them and in what form. A good case could be made for their continuance on the grounds that they are in every trading country's interests, both exporters and importers.

The situation on export subsidies is quite another matter and it is likely that an attempt will be made in the first WTO Round of trade negotiations to reduce them further or to abolish them entirely. While export subsidies have been part of the CAP since its inception, their impact on farming is only indirect and their reduction or removal needs to be considered in the context of the activities downstream of the farm. The form of price and market support under the CAP undoubtedly encouraged Member States to build up exports with a heavy reliance on export refunds. While this may have been unwise, it was completely logical in the circumstances of the time. However, the decline and possible removal of such subsidies could have a considerable impact.

The loss of an export market has a different impact from a price reduction for which compensation has been paid. The immediate impact is felt further down the production-to-consumption chain and the primary producer is only affected in so far as market prices weaken or demand for a particular product falls. If that were to happen, the initial reaction might be to place greater reliance on intervention purchasing. This could, of course, cause its own problems as access to intervention has been curtailed quite considerably in recent years. Such a series of events would add further pressure for price support reductions in an attempt to lower self-sufficiency levels.

Many processing industries were expanded to their present size in order to cater for the rising level of production induced by the price and market policy. The transformation of milk into butter and skimmed milk powder, the freezing and canning of beef, the canning of certain fruits and vegetables—all were expanded because of the existence of intervention and the possibility of subsidized export. The curtailment of export subsidies could have a negative impact on the profitability of many processing plants, their long-term viability, and the employment opportunities which they provide. These processing plants are often situated in rural areas where there are few alternative sources of employment. The long-run solution may well be to encourage diversification away from agriculture and activities dependent on farming rather than in attempting to prop up processing facilities whose long-term viability is not secure. In the medium-run, however, there may well be some painful adjustments to be made.

The other side of commercial policy is, of course, imports. Chapter 12 touched on the somewhat ambivalent attitude to imports which developed in the Community down the years. This was in complete contradiction to the original thinking in the Spaak Report (see Chapter 1). The point was also made in Chapter 12 that access to Union markets was not much enhanced by the

Uruguay Round agreement. This is likely to be a policy area for which there will be more pressure for greater liberalization in the next Round.

However, even before that happens, there is one area of import policy which could prove very difficult to deal with, namely the exclusion of agricultural products on sanitary or phytosanitary grounds.[4] For decades, countries have used frontier regulations to control imports on grounds of human, animal, or plant health. Many of these regulations were well intentioned and exporters recognized the need to adhere to standards laid down not in their own country but in the countries to which they exported. However, it is also true that import regulations were used from time to time for protectionist purposes rather than for genuine health reasons.

The control of sanitary and phytosanitary regulations was included in the Uruguay Round of GATT as a separate issue for negotiation. Perhaps because of the attention paid to the agricultural negotiations, less thought was given to the question of sanitary and phytosanitary controls than they deserved and otherwise might have had. The Final Agreement affirms the right of a country to protect human, animal, or plant life or health provided the measures taken are not applied in an arbitrary or discriminatory manner, and provided they are not a disguised restriction on international trade. Where such measures are imposed, they should be the minimum necessary to achieve their purpose and be based on scientific principles (unless such evidence is insufficient) (OJ L336, 23–12–94).

This sounds innocuous enough but in fact it contains within it the potential for considerable conflict. Under the Agreement, the imposition of controls must be based on a risk assessment and the types of considerations to be taken into account are listed. Among these are economic factors: 'the potential damage in terms of loss of production or sales in the event of the entry, establishment or spread of a pest or disease; the costs of control or eradication in the territory of the importing member; and the relative cost-effectiveness of alternative approaches to limiting risks' (OJ L336, 23–12–94, 42).

The emphasis placed on economic factors is, no doubt, in keeping with the mercantilist nature of the whole GATT system but it seems an inadequate basis for assessment. For one thing, it does not ensure the rights of consumers or the welfare of animals; for another, it is unclear over what time-period the potential damage is to be assessed. One of the problems with health risks is that they may not be immediately apparent either in animals, plants, or humans.

Many of the issues involved in these controls are highly emotive, many more are issues in which the scientific evidence is not conclusive, or where it is subject to revision in the light of more detailed research. Down the years there have been some major conflicts internationally concerning these controls—in particular between the EC/EU and the USA, usually because certain practices are allowed in the latter which are prohibited in the former. The result is a ban on imports followed by an international dispute and complaint. While one can appreciate the need to try to bring some order into the vexed area of sanitary/phytosanitary regulations, reliance on economic risk assessment and scientific evidence elevates both disciplines to positions of eminence and certainty which they do not deserve. It is not hard to envisage that these regulations will continue to be as contentious in the future as they have been in the past.[5]

Environmental Issues in Agriculture

When the CAP was being devised and in its first decade of implementation, no consideration was given to environmental issues related to it. That is not to say there were no environmental problems in agriculture in the individual Member States but rather to indicate that, where they existed, they were seen as localized and that the links between them and the CAP were not made. Even in the Mansholt Plan, the desire to reduce the intensity of production through the creation of larger farm units was linked to income levels and the control of surpluses, and not to environmental damage. Indeed, some of the proposals in that Plan, if they had been implemented, would probably have led to major environmental problems: for instance, the creation of large-scale livestock enterprises, especially for poultry, eggs, and pigs (see Chapter 4).

However, by the mid-1970s after the introduction of the First Action Plan on the environment, token gestures began to be made to include environmental considerations in the structural aspects of the CAP. This started with the LFA Directive in 1975 (see Chapter 11), but aspects of that Directive and other structural measures have themselves been environmentally damaging, whatever the fine words inserted in the legislation. However, the main problem lay not with the deficiencies of the structural policy but with the fact that the price and market policy was encouraging intensification and monoculture, both of which are detrimental to biological diversity, and both of which are capable of resulting in environmental pollution.

The CAP was not alone in its indifference to environmental concerns; the Treaty of Rome did not mention the environment and the very fact that the Community introduced Action Programmes rather than an environmental policy was indicative of a less than fulsome interest by the Member States in the environment as an issue in its own right requiring concerted Community-wide effort. Amendments were made to the Rome Treaty through the Single European Act and the Maastricht Treaty which improved the situation and, in a broader context, the environment has become an issue in OECD and in the United Nations. In agriculture, the interest lies specifically in the area of sustainability and the systems which encourage or maintain it, and which repair previous damage. More recently, and more specifically in relation to the CAP, the Swedes have expressed an interest in the inclusion in Article 39 of the Rome Treaty of an environment objective for the policy (*Agence Europe*, 11/12–12–95). It is inevitable that clashes will continue to occur between production systems, structural change, and good environmental practice.

Under the Agricultural Agreement of the Uruguay Round, payments made for environmental purposes are excluded from the calculation of internal support subject to reduction over the implementation period (see Chapter 12). Environmental payments must be made in the context of a specific programme and must comply with conditions laid down, including those on production methods or inputs. The level of payment is limited to the extra costs associated with the implementation of the programme or the loss of income incurred (OJ L336, 23–12–94). At first glance, this looks very positive but, in so far as the Union is concerned, there are some doubts about its relevance to the CAP as currently constituted. For instance, the amount of FEOGA funds devoted to specifically environmental purposes is small and very largely concentrated on structural measures. Within the price and market policy, environmental payments have been made more in the context of production reduction than as an aid to good environmental practice. As Mahé *et al.* (1994) have pointed out, the MacSharry reforms were based too much on compensation for acquired advantages and too little on rewarding the positive externalities of agricultural activities: the shift to a policy more compatible with the environment has still not been made.

There is also a very real danger that the efforts being made to diversify production away from food crops to those with an industrial end-use (see Chapter 11) may be potentially environmentally damaging and that the Union may merely exchange one confused policy full of internal contradictions for another. For instance, if the production of bio-fuels becomes an attractive proposition or if the industrial demand for farm-based chemical or biological products expands, the most economical way to produce the raw material would be intensively and under contract with a locally established processing plant. The kinds of restrictions which are currently imposed on pesticide and fertilizer use because of health fears from residues in food products would be unnecessary in products intended for industrial use. This could actually make existing pollution problems worse. There is nothing environmentally friendly or aesthetically pleasing about such a proposition.

One of the great criticisms of the market policy has been that it was expected to fulfil a multiplicity of tasks through the manipulation of price: to support agricultural incomes, stabilize markets, protect the producer from external competition, etc. It became very clear that it could not achieve all its imposed goals simultaneously. There is a danger that something similar may happen to environmental measures. They too may be seen as some kind of panacea capable of achieving a multiplicity of goals: extensification, improved biodiversity, water and soil quality, a pleasing landscape, protection of fragile sites, and many more, all within the context of agricultural production and the maintenance of satisfactory incomes for farmers.

This may not be the best approach to the creation of an environmental dimension to the CAP—apart altogether from the dubious legality of using Articles 39, 40, and 42 of the Rome Treaty for such purposes. Environmental objectives are probably best achieved through an environment policy created for that purpose and with its own dedicated funds. Such an approach could tackle more effectively the problem that certain Member States are reluctant and late converts to environmentalism, something which is not dealt with effectively in the context of the CAP as currently constituted.

The scale of the need for an environment policy is very great and encompasses not only the CAP but also other uses of rural land in the Union. It even transcends the borders of the Union and probably requires an international forum for its resolution. The Commission itself raised this point in the context of territorial development in the twenty-first century. It referred to the possibility of agricultural production being relocated to third countries:

Such a development . . . is likely to be less the result of the CAP-reform than of environmental constraints or a search for external markets. Some battery farms have already been moved from Brittany to the Middle East, for example, while some Dutch farmers are planning to move intensive breeding of pigs to Hungary and from a technical and financial standpoint there is nothing to prevent a massive relocation of egg production over a period of 5 to 20 years. (Commission 1994(*e*), 115)

There are important issues at stake here which were certainly not covered by the Uruguay Round. If a process is moved to another country in order to circumvent controls in the first country, then the creation or maintenance of sanitary or phytosanitary regulations, environmental controls, and animal welfare requirements of a high standard is undermined. This is not just a matter of trade liberalization: it should surely be morally unacceptable that concern for the environment or for animal welfare within the Union should stop at its frontiers and not also extend to environments and animals outside the Union. This is not something which the Union can deal with unilaterally and it remains to be seen whether multilateral negotiations under the auspices of the WTO would be a suitable forum for such a discussion.

The Income Issue in Agriculture

Earlier chapters—in particular Chapters 1 and 4—highlighted the central importance of income levels in agricultural policy. This has been a feature of policy across the developed world, at least since the mid-1950s and in some countries much earlier than that. Whatever else agricultural policy may have achieved, it has been deficient in fulfilling its income goals. Within the EC/EU, a small number of farmers has benefited significantly from the CAP—even excessively, while the majority has not. As a result, income differences between regions and types of farm have actually widened during the lifetime of the policy. This is a complete negation of the objectives of Article 2 of the Rome Treaty, which the CAP is ultimately intended to promote.

The explanation for the failure lies in the approach adopted: despite their known and obvious deficiencies as a means of improving income levels, price support and market manipulation have been the chosen mechanisms. Within price support, the emphasis has been on the use of an undifferentiated unit level of support for selected end-products. The natural outcome of this approach has been to ensure that the greater the number of units of output a farmer produces, the greater the benefit from the policy. By definition, therefore, the policy supports the larger business unit to a greater extent than the smaller. Yet it is among the smaller units that the chronic income problem occurs. The only possible excuses for the prolonged continuation of this illogical approach are its simplicity of administration, the fact that Ministries of Agriculture and big farmers like it, and that those who do not benefit have either solved their income problem in some other way, or are too poor to have a voice anyway. Whatever the explanation, the mechanism has shown remarkable resilience and Member States a high degree of resistance to change. As pointed out already, the MacSharry reforms—as adopted—perpetuated the system by using historical levels of production as the basis for compensatory payments.

The use of a differentiated price support structure in which payments were based on an inverse relationship to the number of units produced could have been a means to raise the income levels of the majority. This was suggested from time to time but nothing came of it. Numerous objections could be raised to such a scheme: it would be hideously difficult to administer, except for products such as milk or sugar beet where there is only one outlet; it would distort the market; and it would inhibit structural change towards larger more viable farm businesses.

Another approach might be to give certain farmers, chosen on the basis of criteria which include long-term difficulties, a special payment over and above what they can gain on the open market to compensate them for their disadvantaged circumstances. This, of course, is the basis for the special payments in LFAs. These too can be criticized on the grounds that they maintain production in high-cost areas and do not prevent the inequity of the greatest benefit going to the largest producers. As mentioned in an earlier Section, that situation could be improved by fixing a ceiling on total payments. However, if this were done, it might result in a slowing down of structural change, as farmers would have little incentive to expand beyond a certain limit. It might also inhibit farm amalgamation and force farmers to maintain separate units to maximize their compensation receipts.

A further approach would be to abandon completely the link between production and income support. This would allow prices to find their natural level within a framework provided by the frontier level of protection and the intervention system as purchaser of last resort. Income support would then be personal to the farmer.[6] At the moment the CAP has moved part of the way to this system but payments are still linked to production in one way or another.

Suppose, however, the Union were to move to a truly 'decoupled' payment system, on what basis should farmers be compensated for deficiencies in their incomes? If one goes back to the Rome Treaty, Art. 39.1(b) refers to the need to strive to achieve 'a fair standard of living for the agricultural community, in particular by increasing the individual earnings of persons engaged in agriculture'. As was recounted in Chapter 4, the fair standard of living became confused with quite a different concept, namely an income comparable with other activities in the same region. This proved impossible to achieve through price and market support and was dropped as a stated goal in the early 1980s.

However, even if this had not happened, income comparability was an inappropriate concept for an income policy within the CAP. It set the objective of a fair standard of living at far too high a level: the integration of agriculture into the social and economic life of the Community was achievable at a much lower level. Remember that, when the CAP was being devised, many farms were being worked at subsistence level or only a little above; there are not very many which fall into that classification today.[7] In the context of forty years later, what should the income objective be?

One approach might be to adopt in agricultural policy a concept which is widely accepted and used in the economy as a whole, namely the minimum wage. As for other workers, this would be related to the cost of living. In agriculture a decision would have to be taken as to whether labour income alone would be the basis for compensation or whether, in the case of farmers, the other factors of production would need to be taken into account. It would also be necessary to take other income sources into account, but income from schemes to encourage environmentally friendly farming, set-aside, and other on-farm activities deemed to be in the public interest would need to be exempt. However the base was defined, if actual income fell below that level, then a direct payment could be made to bridge the difference. In order to reduce administrative costs, the actual income would not need to be calculated for small farms, as standardized income levels could be used. If an individual believed the standard to be incorrect in his/her specific case, an appeal could be lodged, in which case the actual income level would need to be proved. Such an approach would fulfil quite adequately the objective of ensuring a fair standard of living. What such a system would achieve would be the provision for income of the kind of safety net which the intervention system is intended to provide for commodities.

An important issue in any direct payment scheme (including those in operation at the time of writing) is for how long should the payment be made. If the payments are, as suggested here, specific to the individual, then they could quite easily be linked to the date of retirement, death, or quitting farming for another occupation. If a pre-pension plan were in operation, say at the age of 55, then that could be the cut-off point. Given the age profile in farming, this is not a critical factor. A related issue is whether, in the case of farmers, the income top-up aid should be available to the person taking over the farm on its sale or on intergenerational transfer. If it was decided that the aid should cease with the present generation, then the scheme would be a means of bringing into sharp focus for the next generation the changed circumstances in which they would be farming and the income top-up would not become part of their policy expectation.[8]

One question which arises is whether such an income top-up scheme can be seen to make the link between the call in Art. 39.1 of the Rome Treaty for an increase in agricultural productivity and the assurance of a fair standard of living. The advantage of the top-up scheme is that it would free farmers from the need to interpret 'increased productivity' as meaning 'intensification of production' which all too often is what it has meant in the past. It would allow them to use their resources in imaginative ways in accordance with the needs of society. For instance, if environmentally friendly farming is to be fostered, farmers need to be encouraged to undertake the relevant activities. The receipt of an income top-up would not preclude receipt of aid for the provision of an environmental good and its existence as an income safety net might well make the farmer more willing to experiment. The 'rational development of production' does not and never did mean the creation of unsaleable surpluses; today it might mean the development of quality products or catering for the needs of a particular market which might not be the production of food crops. The income top-up would assist farmers to be more flexible in production decisions by lessening the risk factor.

The real difficulty of moving to such a system lies not in its compatibility with the Rome Treaty nor in its feasibility but rather with its acceptability by Member States and their farming interests. It would fundamentally alter the distribution of support as between Member States and types of farmers. In broad terms, it would shift support to the Mediterranean, and to small and medium-size farms everywhere, but particularly in the extensive livestock sector. It would require a degree of solidarity not usually seen among Member States, in actually trying at long last to tackle the income problem in farming. It would require breaking the mould.

Institutional Issues

The quality of institutional decision-making is and always has been a critical factor in the CAP. Earlier chapters provide many examples of the shortcomings in this area: the delays—particularly in agreeing to structural measures; the dilution of proposals in order to achieve agreement; the inability of some Member States to implement measures in a satisfactory manner—if at all. One of the reasons for such deficiencies lies in the minimalist approach adopted by each Member State. There is a tremendous gulf between broad policy statements and the detailed deliberations on any individual policy measure. This gulf exists in the Commission, the Council of Ministers, the European Parliament, and of course within each Member State. Faced with a concrete proposal requiring a decision, defensive postures are adopted and the greater good is quickly forgotten.

The reluctance to take bold decisions in the absence of overwhelming outside pressure can be attributed to an assessment of what is politically realistic at a particular time. For instance, in 1987 in the context of measures intended to curb spending on market support and to bring surpluses under control, the Commission referred to the political imperatives of decision-making: 'what it is felt should be or can be imposed on Community farmers, given the present circumstances with regard to incomes and employment' (Commission 1987(*h*), 11).

Two points should be made in this context: firstly, what is feasible in one country may not be in another (which is one of the reasons for the acceptance of the lowest common point of agreement), and secondly, the larger the number of countries the greater the divergence is likely to be in relation to the feasibility of any measure. Frustration with this situation sometimes provokes the advocacy of a multi-tier policy in which some Member States are permitted to move farther and faster than others. Such short-term political expediency is likely in the long term to create additional problems: the cohesion of the policy is lost and the Member States lagging behind have done no more than postpone inevitable change. The structural policy in the CAP is full of examples of the unsatisfactory nature of such an approach: for instance, the delays in implementing the structural Directives of 1972, and the poor response to the options available under Reg. 797/85 (see especially Chapter 8). Integration has a price and part of that price is delay because the institutional structure is not coping adequately with that process.

The answer is to improve decision-making because there are benefits to be gained from operating collectively. Indeed, in political terms, it is sometimes easier to act together than separately. This is particularly true in the context of a reform which may be unpopular but necessary when the ability to shift responsibility from the individual Member State to the collective may be advantageous. In this context, it is somewhat surprising to find that in the early 1990s there was a spate of suggestions on the repatriation of certain aspects of the CAP. These included income support (European Commission, 1994); and, in the context of Enlargement to the East, the compensatory payments under the price policy (Tangermann and Josling, 1994); and payments for certain environmental benefits (Buckwell *et al.*, 1994).

While it is quite true that there has always been joint funding of structural measures and that, in recent years, a certain amount of Member State funding has crept into the market policy (e.g. compensation for currency fluctuations), the above authors were suggesting major upheavals in the philosophy of the CAP. The suggestions were almost casual and made in the absence of any consideration of the nature and purpose of the CAP within the context of the Rome Treaty. They also seemed to be based on an apparent mistaken interpretation of the concept of 'subsidiarity'. If it is difficult at the present time to achieve uniformity of action within the institutional structure of the Union, how much more difficult would this be in a context in which the administative inadequacies of some would be in even sharper focus and to greater detrimental effect.

This issue is relevant to some of the ideas put forward by the Commission in the context of Enlargement to the East. In suggesting a need to simplify the functioning of the CAP, the Commission put forward the idea of giving the Member States greater freedom in the implementation of legislation agreed at Union level, particularly in non-market legislation. It commented that 'Member States would have to respect common rules rigorously, and would have to act to a large extent within predetermined budgetary limits' (Commission 1995(*c*), 24). It did not explain how this would be achieved and it was disingenuous of the

Commission to put forward such a proposal when already Member States are regularly in breach of existing legislation; when most fraud takes place in Member States due to their inadequate procedures in supervising the use of funds; when certain Member States have proved incapable, for whatever reason, of implementing specific structural programmes and of utilizing the funds allocated to them; and when the Commission's own ability to monitor activities and enforce common rules is inadequate to the existing task, let alone an expanded one.

Renationalization of parts of the CAP has surfaced from time to time but, as a principle, it runs the risk of exacerbating the centre–periphery stresses and strains which are always present. What is more important than abandoning the present system is a concerted effort to try to improve it—something which requires urgent attention in the light of possible Enlargement of the Union in the first decade of the twenty-first century. Improvement in the decision-making process is one of the tasks to be considered by the Intergovernmental Conference (IGC) of 1996. Part of its remit is to suggest ways in which the relationships between the Commission, Council, and Parliament can be improved, and how the internal functioning of each of these Institutions could also be improved. At the time of writing, the IGC was only beginning its work but it was not at all clear whether enough attention was going to be paid to these issues and whether any reforms agreed would be sufficiently radical. Without significant improvements in the institutional structures, many of the objectives of the Union are difficult to achieve. This might well suit the nationalistic interests of some Member States which fear the power and influence of a well-organized and smoothly functioning decision-making process at Union level. Failure to achieve significant improvements can only damage a major policy such as the CAP.

Enlargement to the East and the CAP

At the meeting in Copenhagen of the European Council in June 1993, it was agreed that:

the associated countries in Central and Eastern Europe that so desire shall become members of the European Union. Accession will take place as soon as an associated country is able to assume the obligations of membership by satisfying the economic and political conditions required.

Membership requires that the candidate country has achieved stability of institutions guaranteeing democracy, the rule of law, human rights and respect for and protection of minorities, the existence of a functioning market economy as well as the capacity to cope with competitive pressure and market force within the Union. Membership presupposes the candidate's ability to take on the obligations of membership including adherence to the aims of political, economic and monetary union. (Bull. EC 6–1993, 13)

The above declaration has been quoted in full because of its importance in terms of its breadth and depth. The Member States which have been the strongest advocates of Enlargement—most notably Germany and the UK—seem to pay inadequate attention to these requirements and the difficulty of their achievement in the short or even medium term. In 1995, the Commission published a major study on the preparation of these countries for integration into the internal market of the Union which indicated, in that one area alone, how much needed to be done (Commission 1995(*a*) and (*b*)).

By 1995, association agreements had been concluded with ten countries, subdivided into somewhat confusing groups. There were the four Visegrad countries (Poland, Hungary, the Czech Republic, and the Slovak Republic), sometimes augmented by Bulgaria and Romania (the Balkans) to make the CEEC-6,[9] and in turn this group is sometimes augmented by Slovenia. Finally, there are the three Baltic States: Estonia, Latvia, and Lithuania. Just as the EU-15 differ markedly one from another, which makes generalizations about them difficult and potentially very misleading, so the CEEC-10 have widely differing characteristics. The one feature which unites these countries is their interest in joining the European Union. Whether this is purely because it is seen as some all-embracing solution to their current problems or has a more philosophical basis will only become clear as negotiations progress, but the Union itself is facing some very serious policy decisions in the late 1990s, which may well shape attitudes on both sides of the negotiating table.

The first of these issues is the success or failure of the Intergovernmental Conference referred to in the previous Section. The IGC is due to be completed in 1997, and Cyprus and Malta have been promised that negotiations on their Accession to the Union will commence within six months of the conclusion of the Conference. At roughly the same time, decisions have to be taken about the future size and shape of the Structural Funds and, more generally, about the size of the EU Budget for the early years of the twenty-first century. The budgetary commitment is dependent on the ability and willingness of the Member States to fund the activities of the Union. Many of them may well be concerned with their own economic and financial circumstances in the run-up to the introduction of the single currency, scheduled for 1999 and, as a result, may exhibit a degree of caution about undertaking additional financial commitments, whether for existing policy areas and Member States or for an expanded Union whose new members would have even greater economic difficulties.

As if that were not enough, the implementation of the Uruguay Round of GATT will be drawing to a close and the members of the WTO will be taking part in the preliminary discussions leading up to the negotiation of the next Round of international trade arrangements. Somewhere time has got to be found for the opening of negotiations on the Accession of some or all of the Central and East European countries. Various commentators have written about the next Enlargement as though it were imminent and certainly due to occur by 2000. Writing in 1996, that timetable seems not only overambitious but also not particularly wise given the amount of work which the applicants need to do. A transition period lasting five to ten years in some policy areas can be envisaged, so that for some applicant countries at least full membership may not be achieved until well into the new century.

Not surprisingly, in view of the existence of the CAP, agriculture has been perceived as a policy area which might prove troublesome in any negotiations. This is because, in some applicant countries, agriculture has remained an important sector in terms of GDP and employment, and because the proportion of household income spent on food is high. An added factor has been the apprehension that the CAP itself might run into difficulties in the absorption of so many new countries, some of which are substantial producers. These various strands came together in the early 1990s in a rather muddled way: the CEECs were experiencing considerable difficulties throughout their economies and in agriculture there were disruptions in production and in the institutional structures; in the Community, the MacSharry reforms had only just been agreed, while the Uruguay Round had yet to be implemented. It was hardly an appropriate time to try to predict what agriculture might be like in the CEECs in ten years time nor was it a good time to begin agitating for further changes to the CAP when it was completely unclear what the impact of MacSharry and GATT combined was likely to be.

However, despite the difficulty in timing, 1994 in particular saw a whole series of studies on the possible impact of Enlargement on the CAP and the likely size and shape of the agricultural sector in various members of the CEEC group— usually the four Visegrad countries plus Bulgaria and Romania. Within the Commission, DGVI (Agriculture) had a study carried out by Nallet and Van Stolk (1994), while DGI (External Relations) had four studies undertaken by various sets of economists.[10] In many respects, these studies reflected the interests of the directorates-general which had commissioned them;[11] as a result their impact may actually have been counter-productive. DGVI reacted angrily to the intrusion into its policy area and an opportunity was lost to explore some important policy issues. It was also most unfortunate that the authors were drawn from the ranks of former administrators and academic economists. The CAP is not and never has been a policy solely concerned with economic issues and it would have been a good moment to widen the debate.

This is not the place to analyse in detail the studies referred to above, particularly because they have been overtaken by events. However, some general points can be made. All these studies concentrated on CEEC-6 but, even within this group, there are considerable differences in terms of the importance of the agricultural sector. Given that fact, it is perhaps surprising that none of these studies referred to the distinct possibility that by, say, 2005–10, agriculture may not be perceived as a particularly important sector in some at least of these countries. There has been a widespread presumption that there is great latent potential for expansion of agricultural production in the CEECs but it is not at all clear that this will materialize. All the studies were agreed that the structural shortcomings of CEEC-6 (and the same is true of the remaining countries) were a major obstacle to the expansion of on-farm production and the viability of upstream and downstream activities.

In 1995, the Commission published a series of studies on CEEC-10 which included production projections to 2000. These suggest that, by that date, production of most commodities in most countries will not have returned to its 1989 level (European Commission 1995). The obstacles are many and formidable. Individually, none would be insurmountable but collectively they are a considerable hindrance. In reviewing their available resources and the competing investment demands, some countries may wonder whether agriculture is the best sector in which to invest.

Buckwell *et al.* (1994) made an important point relevant to this issue. Much of the fear of competition from CEEC-6 is based on grounds of relative production costs, but lower costs are only a threat if the countries concerned can capitalize on the advantage by delivering the required quality on a consistent basis. Moreover, much of the argument has been based on the difference in wage rates; this however ignores the very considerable advantage which Western producers have in terms of labour productivity as measured by gross output per worker. The supposed Eastern advantage may be more apparent than real.

One aspect of Enlargement to the East which was not covered by the 1994 studies was the impact which any increased competition might have on particular areas of the Union or Member States. Given the location of CEEC-6, their climatic conditions and the range of commodities which they produce, it may be the case that any negative impact might be felt disproportionately in the Southern Member States whose agricultural structure and level of productivity is the weakest in the Union. Already the issue of the Cohesion Fund has come to the fore under which Greece, Portugal, Spain, and Ireland are in receipt of special funds to improve their infrastructure. Cohesion policy is in need of revision and will eventually cover any CEECs which join the Union. This, however, is bound to have an adverse effect on the existing recipients of the funds.[12]

While many commentators in the early 1990s were much exercised by the possible cost of the CAP in the event of Enlargement to the East, remarkably little attention was paid to the appropriateness of extending to the East the system of direct payments introduced under the MacSharry reform. This issue was raised in the second Section of this chapter and there is no need to rehearse that argument again. The Commission itself has drawn attention to the possibility that, at least during a transition phase, the provision of funds for structural improvement in agriculture and for rural development in general might be much more useful than a system of direct payments to farmers (Commission 1995(*c*)).

The final issue to be raised in this Section is that of the acceptance of Enlargement within the Union. At the Copenhagen meeting of the European Council in 1993, it was agreed that an important consideration was 'the Union's capacity to absorb new members, while maintaining the momentum of European integration' (Bull. EC 6–1993, 13). It has long been established by custom that any Enlargement should not place too large a financial burden on the existing Member States. While it is to be hoped that the economic circumstances of the CEECs will be much improved over what they were in 1993, their Accession would be the greatest Enlargement challenge to date. The willingness to accept any financial burden is not just dependent on a sense of political obligation but also on the economic vigour of the Union at the time. This applies also within particular policy areas. If surpluses reappear; if farmers feel under income pressure; if the implementation of the post-MacSharry policy and the Uruguay Round restrictions on support falters for any reason; if the burden of Enlargement appears to be distributed in an inequitable manner by region, commodity, or Member State, then the Union might find the willingness to accommodate the CEECs in the CAP beginning to fade. It is not at all clear, at the time of writing, that thought is being actively given to such a possibility.

The Role of a Sectoral Policy

At the Conference of Stresa so long ago, the participants were intent that agriculture should be considered as an integral part of the economy and as an essential factor of social life (Communautés Européennes, 1959). Despite this the CAP was organized along very traditional lines and, as a result, wider interests played little part in its development. The result has been the continued isolation of the agricultural sector from the rest of the economy. Integration has hardly begun. Throughout the lifetime of the CAP, commentators have expressed their unease at this isolation.

The situation was not helped by the fact that the CAP was the first common policy to be established and that for so many years it remained the only one. Within the CAP, there was the added unease that the price and market policy was being expected to do too much, and that greater integration with the structural policy was required. These deficiencies were seen very much in terms of the reluctance of the Member States to agree to the establishment of other common policies. A particularly good example of the expression of these thoughts is to be found in the Opinion of the ESC on the *Stocktaking* of 1975. Two quotations sum up the Committee's views.

Why have a European agriculture and what are its foundations to be? What will be the future of Europe's rural society and how will its structures evolve? How can agriculture in the EEC make an effective contribution towards the internal and external development of the Community? What means must it be given in order to fulfil this rôle under the most favourable conditions?

No policy on common prices is possible unless marked progress is made towards the attainment of monetary union. . . . No effective structural policy is possible without a social policy, a regional policy and an industrial policy . . . not forgetting an environmental policy. The common management of the markets is out of the question without a common commercial policy. . . . the common agricultural policy—being a sectoral policy —cannot by itself settle all the economic and social problems facing agriculture.   (OJ C270, 26–11–75, 24 and 27)

Three years later this last point reappeared in a throwaway comment made by the Commission in relation to the crisis in milk production. In a discussion of the need to define more precisely what the policy in the milk sector should be, the Commission listed a number of restraints which inhibited its actions. Among these was 'the socio-economic situation of many small milk producers farming in regions which offer hardly any alternative possibilities' (Commission 1978(*d*), 22). This social welfare role of the CAP has always existed but it has never been properly defined or recognized. One must wonder to what extent the very vagueness of the social role has affected the search, through other policy instruments, for a solution to such regional problems.

In 1980, the ESC returned to the issues it had highlighted in 1975: the isolation of the CAP, and the erroneous expectation that the development of agriculture could by itself solve wider difficulties which derived 'from overall economic underdevelopment or inadequate economic, social or cultural infrastructures' (OJ C53, 3–3–80, 35). These views were taken even further by the European Parliament in a Resolution in which it set out two principles:

- there can be no rurality without the maintenance of a certain level of agricultural activity,
- rural life and the rural economy cannot be confined to agriculture alone (OJ C66, 15–3–82, 22).

The Parliament called on the Community to concentrate its activities on improvements in the most backward regions by developing an integrated approach to the use of the various funds available, and better co-ordination of the activities of the Community, the Member States, and the regional and local authorities. In this regard, the Parliament called for greater consideration to be given to land development as a whole (ibid. *passim*).

A few years later, the Parliament returned to the need for a more integrated approach when it discussed the particular problems facing mountain regions. While it affirmed that viable agriculture and forestry were essential in these regions, they also needed balanced economic development. This involved the creation of secondary job opportunities for small farmers who could 'earn a reasonable income for a family only if, in addition to farming, they have employment outside the farm' (OJ C305, 16–11–87, 38). Around the same time, the ESC drew up a report on upland areas in which it called for a refocusing of the CAP so that it ceased to be 'a source of handouts' and became 'a force for the development and re-equilibrium of upland agriculture' (OJ C175, 4–7–88, 49). In this context, the ESC called for the establishment of guidelines for a Community land policy, stating that 'the Community cannot defer any longer from adopting a fully fledged land policy' (ibid. 50).

These undercurrents of discontent with the functioning of the CAP in the wider rural context came to a head in a report drawn up by the Commission entitled *The Future of Rural Society* (Commission 1988(*f*)). It pointed out that the importance of agriculture in terms of employment and regional product had declined to such an extent that there were only ten regions in the Community (in Greece, Italy, and Spain) in which agriculture provided employment for as much as 30 per cent of the workforce, while in 118 regions (71 per cent of the total) fewer than 10 per cent of the workforce were in agriculture. Its significance in terms of regional product was even less, with only seventeen regions (about 10 per cent of the total) in which agriculture represented more than 10 per cent of regional product.

The prospects for agriculture were not good: it will be recalled from Chapter 6 that many (and unsuccessful) attempts were made in the mid- and late 1980s to control production. Worse still, the Commission expected that inward investment in rural areas would slow down, and that rural regions would need to rely increasingly on their own ability to expand local indigenous economic activity. The Commission identified three types of problem facing rural society: all had land at the core.

The first was the difficulty common to all developed countries of rural land in close proximity to major conurbations or in coastal zones. The specific problems were competition for land, negative environmental impacts, inadequate regional planning to prevent ribbon urban development, excessive numbers of tourists, and holiday homes. The second type of problem was that which regions in decline had to face, particularly in the remoter Mediterranean areas where there was inadequate diversification in the rural economy. The third was akin to the second but more intense: mountain areas and islands which face depopulation and the abandonment of land. There, the challenge was to maintain 'a minimum population and minimum business and social activity to protect the fragile environment (the threat of erosion and desertification) and of maintaining the countryside' (Commission 1988(*f*), 4).

The Commission put forward a range of ideas as to how existing Community policies might be adapted to respond to the difficulties identified. As regards the CAP, its suggestions were limited to a continuance of the attempts then being made to shift some support away from price policy; to strengthen the integration of agriculture in the economy through alterations to the structural aids, so as to improve management and marketing; and to promote the production of quality products. It raised the possibility of providing incentives or compensation in both agricultural and forestry policies for the provision of environmental public goods.

These ideas do not constitute a radical response to the circumstances of the time but even this lack-lustre approach was criticized by the farmers' representatives (COPA/COGECA) for concentrating too much on non-agricultural activities! They stated that nothing had been put forward on the development of alternative products, nor on the non-food uses of agriculture (*Agence Europe*, 16/17–1–89). However, one could argue that the Commission was right to downplay agriculture. Rural areas covered 80 per cent of the land area of the Community and 50 per cent of the Community's population lived there, the majority of whom were in rural towns. Given the decline in the importance of farming in terms of employment and regional product, a review of the non-agricultural aspects of rural areas was long overdue.

The debate widened in the early 1990s with the publication of a report *Europe 2000* on regional planning across the Community. The fundamental question was whether, in the 1990s, 'the pressures arising from economic and geographical imbalances between the prosperous centres and the rest of the Community will encourage the mobility of economic activity and jobs or, the mobility of labour' (Commission 1991(*f*), 15). With regard to rural regions specifically, the Commission stated that 'estimates suggest that around half of the people working in agriculture will be employed in, or seeking, a second job by the year 2000. The solution to the problems of rural areas will therefore have to be found largely outside agriculture' (ibid. 20).

While the Commission's analysis may well prove to be correct, its solution is not easily achievable because of the skewed nature of employment in agriculture in the various regions. The Commission pointed out that over half of those currently in agriculture were employed in a mere forty-four regions, most of which were peripheral and many of which were in the Mediterranean: 'on present trends, by the year 2000, an estimated 75% of the Community's agricultural population will be in Mediterranean regions' (Commission 1991(*f*), 152). Thus agriculture—and therefore the CAP—will play a very different role as a generator of economic activity and as a means of redistributing income in different regions across the Union.

It is surprising that these predictions have produced so little comment but in the circumstances as outlined one must really ask whether a narrow sectoral policy based so largely on price and market manipulation is the best way to channel resources into rural areas. In the case of those regions heavily dependent on farming, it is that dependence which, to a very large extent, holds back their development. In those areas which have already diversified, the small size of the farming sector means that agricultural support is not a particularly effective method of injecting funds into such areas. The redistributive effect must be very small—particularly as there is no guarantee that the recipients of the support will spend the funds locally or that local industries and services will benefit directly or indirectly from the funds committed to price and market support.

If the role of farming within the rural sector is changing, what is the current and future purpose of the CAP? The policy only exists to help achieve the objectives of the Union as set out in Article 2 of the Rome Treaty (referred to earlier in this chapter). If some—or all—rural areas are still perceived as economically or socially deprived, if those who work in farming still do not have an adequate standard of living and quality of life, if the economic performance of farming in whole or in part is falling behind other activities, then there is a continuing purpose for the CAP but not necessarily in its present form.

Not only is there unease that the CAP has not adequately addressed the question of income differentials within farming but the very isolation of the policy with no other comparable rural policy has meant distortions in land use and land values. What is needed is a more widely focused perception of rural development and the creation of policies to sustain it. One approach might be the creation of a network of interlocking policies to care for rural land as a resource, through the management of its use. The CAP would then be perceived as providing the framework within which farming takes place but it would not hold the singular position which it has held over nearly four decades past. It would be accompanied by other policies covering other rural land-based activities—

forestry, tourism and recreation, water storage and extraction, and so forth. Farming might still remain the single largest user of rural land but a policy network would ensure that this was not equated with dominance in economic terms among land-based enterprises (Fennell 1988).

The difficulties inherent in changing an entrenched policy should not be underestimated: earlier chapters are a testament to the slow pace of change within the CAP, and a more radical change would not be easy to achieve. There is no suggestion here of replacing the CAP or abolishing it but rather that the half-hearted attempts to create a forest policy, to cater for rural tourism, and to introduce an environmental dimension into rural land use should cease and be replaced by a network of land-based policies with a meaningful agenda and proper funding.[13]

But what of the Member States? Individually and collectively they have prevented the development of coherent rural policies, and have ensured that the CAP did not evolve along new policy lines but remained very largely based on price and market manipulation. However, it may well be the case that they are more receptive to a change of emphasis now than they were even a decade ago. Within the agricultural sector broadly defined, farming has declined in importance while other on-farm activities have expanded, as has the downstream processing of agricultural raw materials. Of themselves, these developments call for a different policy approach.[14] Earlier Sections of this chapter have suggested the need for greater targeting within the market policy and in relation to incomes. Issues of product quality, animal welfare, and environmental externalities (positive and negative) can only increase in importance. Rural land is a precious resource; its management has been distorted by the overemphasis of one activity and one sectoral policy. A new balance in land use needs to be established. It is time to break the policy mould.

NOTES

1. The principle of compensation for policy change is an extremely dangerous one if it becomes accepted in practice. It is significant that the Court of Justice ruled against such a principle in relation to the definitive reduction in milk quotas without compensation in a case brought by a group of Irish producers. The Court stated that: 'no economic operator may entertain a legitimate expectation that the Council will not, in its administration of the common agricultural policy, reduce the guaranteed total quantities, and thus individual producers' reference quantities for the future.' It added that even if the applicants had suffered a loss of income because of the absence of compensation: 'a loss of earnings likely to cause a temporary lowering of the standard of living of farmers must be accepted in the context of measures adopted by the Council to limit production, in a market situation characterised for a long period by serious structural surpluses' (*Agence Europe*, 24/25-7-95, 12).
2. This would accord with the 1985 priority (referred to in the first Section) of developing industries which process agricultural raw materials.

3. Some commodities were added due to the various Enlargements of the EC/EU but even in these cases, which have some logical merit, the argument for their inclusion is not universally a strong one.

4. While the question of sanitary/phytosanitary controls is not strictly part of the CAP but of the wider commercial policy of the Union, it is included here because it formed part of the GATT Agreement and is closely related to the functioning of agricultural policy.

5. At the time of writing, this had already happened with the USA requesting consultations with the Union in the framework of the WTO on the continued Union ban on the use of growth hormones in cattle (see, for instance, *Agence Europe*, 27-1-96 and 28-2-96).

6. It is a great pity that, at the time of the MacSharry reforms, the Commission did not examine a direct income compensation scheme put forward twenty years previously by Van Riemsdijk (1973), to see whether it might have been incorporated in some way in the proposals.

7. Enlargement of the Union to the East would, however, introduce large numbers of subsistence or near-subsistence farms into the sector unless the structures created in the 1990s in these countries undergo rapid and radical improvement.

8. An analogous concept was put into practice in France in the 1950s as part of the government's anti-alcoholism drive. The home-distillation of spirits for sale was curtailed by the refusal to issue any new licences. Existing licence-holders were, however, permitted to continue the production and sale of home-made spirits until the death of the licence-holder. This secured their policy expectation unimpaired but created no new expectations. (I am indebted to Marie-Hélène Baneth for drawing my attention to this scheme.)

9. Also known by the French acronym PECO (Pays d'Europe Centrale et Orientale).

10. Buckwell *et al.* (1994); Mahé *et al.* (1994); Tangermann and Josling (1994); and Tarditi *et al.* (1995).

11. There was one further study sponsored by DG II (Finance) but this concentrated on issues of CAP reform with minimal reference to Enlargement (European Commission 1994).

12. It has been estimated that, in 2010, GDP per head in Slovenia would be nearly 80% of the EU average and in the Czech Republic nearly 75% of the EU average. However, in Romania and Bulgaria at the same date GDP would be only 29% and 36% respectively. In 1994, the poorest EU country (Greece) had a GDP per head just above half the EU-12 average.

13. If the MacSharry reforms and the implementation of the GATT agreement are successful, funds should be available which would otherwise have been needed for the CAP and which could now be diverted to other rural uses.

14. It is interesting to see how the titles of ministries have changed from some combination of agriculture with food/forestry/fisheries to (in the case of Belgium) the Middle Classes and Agriculture, and (in the Netherlands) to Agriculture, Nature Management and Fisheries. Even within the Commission, DGVI which is responsible for Agriculture now has sections dealing with Rural Development.

REFERENCES

1. Journal Articles, Conference Papers, Memoranda, and Books

Avery, G. (1985), 'Guarantee Thresholds and the Common Agricultural Policy', *Journal of Agricultural Economics*, 36, 355–64.

Berger, C. (1965), 'La place du F.E.O.G.A. dans la construction de l'Europe', *Revue du Marché Commun*, 8, 28–38.

Bergmann, D. (1980), 'Possible Alternatives to the CAP and Their Economic Consequences', Paper read at a conference of the Agricultural Economics Society (London, 2 Dec.).

Bourrinet, J. (1964), *Le problème agricole dans l'intégration européenne* (Paris).

Buckwell, A., J. Haynes, S. Davidova, V. Courboin, and A. Kwiecinski (1994), 'Feasibility of an agricultural strategy to prepare the countries of Central and Eastern Europe for EU Accession', Report to DGI of the European Commission (16 Dec.).

Butterwick, M., and E. N. Rolfe (1968), *Food, Farming and the Common Market* (London).

Camps, M. (1964), *Britain and the European Community 1955–1963* (London).

COPA/COGECA (1973), 'Comments on the situation of the CAP', PR (73) 18 fin. (Brussels, 12 Oct.).

—— (1975), 'First comments on the Commission's statement to Parliament and to the Council relating to the Stocktaking of the Common Agricultural Policy', (COM(75) 100), PR(75)11 (Brussels, 13 June).

Coppock, J. O. (1961), 'Land and Agricultural Resources', in J. F. Dewhurst *et al.*, *Europe's Needs and Resources*, ch. 15 (New York).

Corti, M. (1971), *Politique agricole et construction de l'Europe* (Brussels).

Dams, T. J. (1963), 'Co-ordination of Structural Policies for Agriculture: The Role of the European Economic Community', *International Journal of Agrarian Affairs*, 111, 319–30.

De Veer, J. (1979), 'The Objective Method: An Element in the Process of Fixing Guide Prices within the Common Agricultural Policy', *European Review of Agricultural Economics*, 6, 279–301.

ECE/FAO (1954), *European Agriculture: A Statement of Problems* (Geneva).

Fennell, R. (1968), 'Structural Change in Irish Agriculture', *Irish Journal of Agricultural Economics and Rural Sociology*, 1, 171–93.

—— (1979), *The Common Agricultural Policy of the European Community*, 1st. edn. (London)

—— (1982/3), 'Whatever Happened to Forestry Policy in the European Community?', *Journal of the Agricultural Society, UCW Aberystwyth*, 63, 191–212.

—— (1985), 'A Reconsideration of the Objectives of the Common Agricultural Policy', *Journal of Common Market Studies*, 23, 257–76.

—— (1987), *The Common Agricultural Policy of the European Community*, 2nd edn. (Oxford).

—— (1988), 'The Evolution of Rural Policies in the European Community: Agriculture, Forestry and the Environment', *Oxford Forestry Institute Occasional Papers*, no. 38, ed. P. S. Savill.

Hagenaars, A. J. M., K. de Vos, and M. A. Zaidi (1994), *Poverty Statistics in the Late 1980s: Research Based on Micro-Data* (Luxembourg).

Harris, S., A. Swinbank, and G. Wilkinson (1983), *The Food and Farm Policies of the European Community* (Chichester).

Hendriks, G. (1991), *Germany and European Integration: The Common Agricultural Policy, an Area of Conflict* (New York).

Hill, B. (1989), *Farm Incomes, Wealth and Agricultural Policy* (Aldershot).

—— (1991), *The Calculation of Economic Indicators: Making Use of FADN (RICA) Data* (Luxembourg).

—— (1993), *Farm Incomes in the European Community in the 1980s* (Luxembourg).

—— (1995), *Total Income of Agricultural Households: 1995 Report* (Luxembourg).

HMSO (1972), *Treaty Concerning the Accession of the . . . United Kingdom . . . to the European Community . . .* , Cmnd, 4862-I (London).

Holden, M. (1995), 'Biting the Hand that Feeds You', *Peatland News*, 9 (Winter).

Istituto Nazionale di Economia Agraria (1995), *Italian Agriculture in Figures 1995* (Rome).

Krause, L. B. (1968), *European Economic Integration and the United States* (Washington, DC).

Krohn, H.-B., and J. van Lierde (1963), 'Proposed Criteria for Fixing the Prices of Agricultural Products in the European Economic Community', *International Journal of Agrarian Affairs*, 111, 245–53.

Mahé, L.-P. avec la collaboration de J. Cordier, H. Guyomard, et T. Roe (1994), 'L'agriculture et l'élargissement de l'Union Européenne aux pays d'Europe Centrale et Orientale: transition en vue de l'intégration ou intégration pour la transition' (Ecole Nationale Supérieure Agronomique de Rennes).

Malgrain, Y. (1965), *L'intégration agricole de l'Europe des Six* (Paris).

Mansholt, S. L. (1959), 'Problèmes agricoles de la C.E.E.', *Revue du Marché Commun*, 2, 203–4.

—— (1962), 'La situation agricole dans le monde du point de vue de la Communauté Européenne', Paper read at the Institut de la CE pour les études universitaires (3 May).

Mayoux, J. (1962), 'L'établissement de la politique agricole commune', *Revue du Marché Commun*, 5, 7–19.

Muth, H. P. (1970), *French Agriculture and the Political Integration of Western Europe* (Leyden).

Nallet, H., and A. Van Stolk (1994), 'Relations between the European Union and the Central and Eastern European Countries in matters concerning agriculture and food production', Report to the European Commission (15 June).

Neville-Rolfe, E. (1984), *The Politics of Agriculture in the European Community* (London).

OECD (1987), *National Policies and Agricultural Trade* (Paris).

OEEC (1956), *Agricultural Policies in Europe and North America: First Report of the Ministerial Committee for Agriculture and Food* (Paris).

—— (1957), *Agricultural Policies in Europe and North America: Price and Income Policies—Second Report of the Ministerial Committee for Agriculture and Food* (Paris).

—— (1958), *Third Report of the Agricultural Policies in Europe and North America* (Paris).

—— (1961), *Trends in Agricultural Policies since 1955: Fifth Report on Agricultural Policies in Europe and North America* (Paris).

Pignot, P. (1969), 'Prise de position des organisations professionelles sur le memorandum concernant la réforme des structures agricoles', *Revue du Marché Commun*, 12, 637–42.

Ries, A. (1978), *L'ABC du Marché commun agricole* (Brussels).

Tangermann, S., and T. E. Josling, with W. Munch (1994), 'Pre-Accession Agricultural Policies for Central Europe and the European Union', Report to DGI of the European Commission (12 Dec.).

Tarditi, S., J. Marsh, and S. Senior-Nello (1995), 'Agricultural Strategies for the Enlargement of the European Union to Central and Eastern European Countries', DGI of the European Commission (Jan.).

Terluin, I. J. (1991), *Production, Prices and Income in EC Agriculture: An Analysis of the Economic Accounts for Agriculture 1973–88* (Luxembourg).

Tracy, M. (1989), *Government and Agriculture in Western Europe 1880–1988*, 3rd edn. (Hemel Hempstead)

Van Riemsdijk, J. F. (1973), 'A System of Direct Compensation Payments to Farmers as a Means of Reconciling Short-Run to Long-Run Interests', *European Review of Agricultural Economics*, 1, 161–89.

Wallon, A. (1958), 'Les origines des dispositions spéciales à l'agriculture dans le Marché Commun', *Revue du Marché Commun*, 1, 103–6.

Williamson, D. (1980), 'Future Direction of the CAP', Paper read at a conference of the Agricultural Economics Society (London, 2 Dec.).

Woods, Elizabeth J. (1980), 'Evaluation of the Socio-economic Advisory Service for Farmers Established in England and Wales under EEC Directive 72/161', D.Phil. thesis (Oxford).

Zeller, A. (1970), *L'imbroglio agricole du Marché Commun* (Paris).

2. Community Documents

Assemblée Parlementaire Européenne/European Parliament

—— (1958), *Rapport . . . sur le chapitre IV (problèmes agricoles) du premier rapport général sur l'activité de la Communauté Économique Européenne*, Rapporteur: Michele Troisi, Document No. 63 (décembre).

—— (1959), *Rapport . . . sur les problèmes de structure y compris les problèmes sociaux propres à l'agriculture, dans la Communauté Économique Européenne*, Rapporteur: H. Vredeling, Document No. 41 (juin).

—— (1960), *Rapport . . . sur la situation de l'agriculture et les principes de base d'une politique agricole commune*, Rapporteur: M. A. Lücker, Document No. 3 (mars).

—— (1979), *Report . . . on the conclusions to be drawn from the proceedings of the Seminar held by the Committee on Agriculture in Echternach*, Rapporteur: H. Caillavet, Working Documents 1979–80, Document 128/79 (4 May).

Comité Économique et Social/Economic and Social Committee

—— (1960), *Rapport général au sujet du 'Projet de propositions concernant l'élaboration et la mise en oeuvre de la politique agricole commune en vertu de l'article 43 du Traité instituant la Communauté Économique Européenne'*, Rapporteur Général: M. Luigi Anchisi, CES 55/60 fin. (juillet).

—— (1967), *Exposé de M. Mansholt . . . prononcé devant l'Assemblée plénière du Comité . . . , le 28 septembre 1967 au sujet des derniers développements de la politique agricole commune*, CES 363/67 annexe 3 bp.

—— (1974), *Study . . . on the progress report on the Common Agricultural Policy*, Rapporteur: F. Bourel, CES 1091/74 (28 Nov.).

Comité Intergouvernemental crée par la Conférence de Messine (1956), *Rapport des chefs de délégation aux Ministres des Affaires Etrangères* (le 21 avril).

Commission de la Communauté Économique Européenne/Commission of the European Economic Community (see also European Commission)

—— (1958), *Plan de travail pour la direction générale de l'agriculture*, COM(58)205 (le 24 septembre).

—— (1959), *Projet des propositions concernant l'élaboration et la mise en oeuvre de la politique agricole commune en vertu de l'article 43 du Traité instituant la Communauté Économique Européenne*, VI/COM(59)140 (le 2 novembre).

—— (1960) *Proposals for the Working-Out and Putting into Effect of the Common Agricultural Policy in application of Article 43 of the Treaty Establishing the European Economic Community* VI/COM(60)105 (30 June).

—— (1962), *Recueil des travaux de la conférence consultative sur les aspects sociaux de la politique agricole commune*, Rome, du 28 septembre au 4 octobre 1961 (Brussels [?]).

—— (1963*a*), *Proposition d'un Règlement du Conseil concernant le FEASA*, VI/COM(63) 19 final (le 27 février).

—— (1963*b*), *Proposition d'un Réglement du Conseil relatif aux conditions du concours du FEOGA*, VI/COM(63)34 final (le 27 février).

—— (1963*c*), *Proposition d'un Règlement financier concernant le FEOGA et le FEASA*, VI/COM(63)36 final (le 28 février).

—— (1963*d*), *Propositions de la Commission au Conseil concernant certaines mesures à prévoir dans le cadre de la politique commune en cas de formation d'excédents structurels sur le marché laitier*, VI/COM(63)229 final (le 10 juillet).

—— (1963*e*), *Programme d'action de la Commission en matière de politique sociale dans l'agriculture*, V/VI/COM(63)353 final (le 19 septembre).

—— (1963*f*), *Mesures en vue de l'établissement d'un niveau commun des prix des céréales*, VI/COM(63)430 final (le 20 novembre).

—— (1964), *Actions à entreprendre par priorité dans le cadre du 'Programme d'action de la Commission de la CEE en matière de politique sociale dans l'agriculture'*, S/O/1961/64 final (le 23 juillet).

—— (1966) *Ninth General Report on the activities of the Community (1 April 1965–31 March 1966)* (Brussels [?], June).

—— (1967*a*), *Proposition d'un Reglement du Conseil concernant les groupements de producteurs agricoles et leurs unions*, COM(67)68 final (le 21 février 1967).

—— (1967*b*), *Programmes Communautaires pour la Section Orientation du Fonds Europeen d'Orientation et de Garantie Agricole*, COM(67)194 final (le 12 juin 1967).

—— (1968*a*), *Memorandum sur la réforme de l'agriculture dans la Communauté Économique Européenne*, Partie A, COM(68)1000 (le 18 décembre).

—— (1968*b*), *Annexes au Memorandum sur la réforme de l'agriculture dans la Communauté Économique Européenne*, Partie B, COM(68)1000 (le 18 décembre).

—— (1968*c*), *Mesures à moyen terme pour différents marchés agricoles*, Partie C, COM (68)1000 (le 18 décembre).

—— (1968*d*), *Rapport sur la situation de l'agriculture et des marchés agricoles*, Partie D, COM(68)1000 (le 18 décembre).

—— (1968*e*), *Propositions de la Commission au Conseil concernant la fixation des prix pour certains produits agricoles*, Partie E, COM(68)1000 (le 18 décembre).

—— (1968*f*), *Rapport concernant les politiques nationales de structure agricole dans la Communauté*, Partie F, COM(68)1000 (le 18 décembre).

—— (1969), *L'équilibre des marchés agricoles*, COM(69)1200 (le 19 novembre).

428   *References*

Commission de la Communauté Économique Européenne/Commission of the European Economic Community (*cont.*)

—— (1970), *Réforme de l'Agriculture*, COM(70)500 (le 29 avril).

—— (1971*a*), *Communication et projet de Resolution du Conseil concernant la nouvelle orientation de la politique agricole commune*, COM(71)100 final (le 15 février).

—— (1971*b*), *Propositions de la Commission au Conseil concernant la fixation des prix pour certains produits agricoles et l'octroi d'aides au revenu à certaines categories d'exploitants agricoles*, COM(71)650 final (le 16 juin).

—— (1972), *Propositions de la Commission au Conseil concernant la fixation des prix pour certains produits agricoles et l'octroi d'aides aux revenus à certaines categories d'exploitants agricoles*, COM(72)150 final (le 2 février).

—— (1973*a*), *Proposal for a Directive on agriculture in mountain areas and in certain other poorer farming areas*, COM(73)202 final (21 Feb.).

—— (1973*b*), *Memorandum from the Commission to the Council on the future sugar policy of the Community . . .*, COM(73)1177 (12 July).

—— (1973*c*), *Proposal for a Council Regulation on the list of priority agricultural regions and areas . . .*, COM(73)1750 (10 Oct.).

—— (1973*d*), *Improvement of the Common Agricultural Policy*, COM(73)1850 final (31 Oct.).

—— (1973*e*), *First financial report concerning the European Agricultural Guidance and Guarantee Fund, Year 1971*, SEC(73) 1259 final (6 Apr.).

—— (1974*a*), *The Agricultural Situation in the Community: Report 1974, Volume III— Annex*, COM(74)2000 final (27 Nov.).

—— (1974*b*), *Commission proposal to the Council on the fixing of prices for certain agricultural products and connected measures*, COM(74)2001 final (27 Nov.).

—— (1974*c*), *Proposal for a Directive relative to the Community list of less-favoured farming areas . . .*, COM(74)2222 final (18 Dec.).

—— (1974*d*), *Special Measures to Deal with the Present Economic Situation in Agriculture*, SEC(74)3280 final (30 Aug.).

—— (1974*e*), *Report from the Commission to the Council on applying the premium system for the conversion of dairy cow herds to to meat production*, SEC(74)4852 (6 Dec.).

—— (1975*a*), *Stocktaking of the Common Agricultural Policy*, COM(75)100 (26 Feb.).

—— (1975*b*), *Fourth Financial Report on the European Agricultural Guidance and Guarantee Fund—Year 1974*, COM(75)396 final (24 July).

—— (1975*c*), *Proposal for a Regulation concerning common measures to improve the conditions under which agricultural products are marketed and processed*, COM(75)431 final (5 Aug.).

—— (1976*a*), *Proposal for a Council Directive amending Directives 72/159/EEC, 72/160/EEC, 72/161/EEC, 73/131/EEC and 75/268/EEC on the reform of agriculture*, COM(76)213 final (10 May).

—— (1976*b*), *Action programme (1977–80) for the progressive achievement of balance in the milk market*, COM(76)300 (9 July).

—— (1976*c*), *Fifth financial report on the European Agricultural Guidance and Guarantee Fund, Year 1975*, COM(76)553 final (25 Oct.).

—— (1976*d*), *Interdepartmental group on the coordination of Community Financial Instruments: Report on EAGGF Guidance Section*, SEC(76)2943 (date unknown).

—— (1977*a*), *Commission report to the Council on the foreseeable developments in the planting and replanting of vineyards in the Community and on the ratio between production and utilization in the wine sector*, COM(77)22 final (15 Feb.).

—— (1977*b*), *Commission proposals on the fixing of prices for certain agricultural products and on certain related measures*, COM(77)100 final (11 Feb.).

—— (1977*c*), *Mediterranean Agricultural Problems*, COM(77)140 final (1 Apr.).

—— (1977*d*), *Amended proposal for a Council Regulation concerning producer groups and associations thereof*, COM(77)228 final (27 May).

—— (1977*e*), *Commission proposals on the fixing of prices for certain agricultural products and on certain related measures*, vol. 1, COM(77)525 final (8 Dec.).

—— (1977*f*), *Guidelines concerning the development of the Mediterranean regions of the Community, together with certain measures relating to agriculture*, vol. 1 COM(77)526 final (9 Dec.).

—— (1977*g*), *Proposal for a Council Directive amending Council Directive 72/159/EEC . . . Directive 75/268/EEC . . . Directive 72/160/EEC . . . Proposal for a Council Directive on the programme to accelerate drainage operations in the less-favoured areas of the West of Ireland*, COM(77)550 final (28 Nov.).

—— (1977*h*), *Sixth Financial Report on the European Agricultural Guidance and Guarantee Fund—Year 1976*, COM(77)591 final (21 Nov.).

—— (1977*i*), *Financial consequences of the proposals for measures to assist Mediterranean agriculture*, COM(77)674 final (9 Dec.).

—— (1978*a*), *Guidelines concerning the development of the Mediterranean regions of the Community, together with certain measures relating to agriculture*, vol. II, COM(77)526 final (3 Jan. 1978).

—— (1978*b*), *Action Programme 1979–1985 for the progressive establishment of balance on the market in wine*, COM(78)260 final, vol. 1 (31 July).

—— (1978*c*), *Proposal for a Council Directive, relative to the programme for the acceleration and guidance of the collective irrigation works in Corsica*, COM(78)371 final (24 July).

—— (1978*d*), *Report on the situation in the milk sector*, COM(78)430 final (25 Sept.).

—— (1978*e*), *Seventh financial report on the European Agricultural Guidance and Guarantee Fund, Year 1977*, COM(78)633 final (24 Nov.).

—— (1978*f*), *Future development of the Common Agricultural Policy*, COM(78)700 final (7 Dec.).

—— (1979*a*), *Commission proposals on the fixing of prices for certain agricultural products and on certain related measures*, vol. 1, COM(79)10 final (31 Jan.).

—— (1979*b*), *Proposals on policy with regard to agricultural structures*, COM(79)122 final (19 Mar.).

—— (1979*c*), *Report from the Commission to the Council on the implemention of Council Regulation (EEC) No 794/76 . . . laying down further measures for reorganizing Community fruit production*, COM(79)350 final (3 July).

—— (1979*d*), *Third report on the implementation of the Council Directives on the reform of agriculture of 17 April 1972*, COM(79)438 final (27 July).

—— (1979*e*), *Changes in the Common Agricultural Policy to help balance the markets and streamline expenditure*, COM(79)710 final (30 Nov.).

—— (1980*a*), *Commission proposals on the fixing of prices for certain agricultural products and on certain related measures*, vol. 1: Explanatory Memorandum, COM(80)10 final (7 Feb.).

—— (1980*b*), *Ninth Financial Report on the European Agricultural Guidance and Guarantee Fund—1979—Guidance Section*, COM(80)639 final (3 Nov.).

—— (1980*c*), *Reflections on the Common Agricultural Policy*, COM(80)800 final (5 Dec.).

430 *References*

Commission de la Communauté Économique Européenne/Commission of the European Economic Community (*cont.*)

—— (1980*d*), *The Agricultural Structures Policy of the Community: Perspective and Evolution*, SEC(80)1471 (13 Oct.).

—— (1981*a*), *Commission proposals on the fixing of prices for certain agricultural products and on certain related measures (1981/82)*, vol. I, COM(81)50 final (20 Feb.).

—— (1981*b*), *Report from the Commission of the European Communities to the Council pursuant to the mandate of 30 May 1980*, COM(81)300 (24 June).

—— (1981*c*), *Guidelines for European agriculture: memorandum to complement the Commission's report on the Mandate of 30 May 1980*, COM(81)608 final (23 Oct.).

—— (1981*d*), *Study of the Regional Impact of the Common Agricultural Policy*, carried out for the Commission by Professor P. Henry, Regional Policy Series No. 21 (Brussels).

—— (1982*a*), *Commission proposals on the fixing of prices for certain agricultural products and on certain related measures (1982/83)*, vol. I: Explanatory Memorandum, COM (82)10 final (27 Jan.).

—— (1982*b*), *Differential rates of inflation and the common agricultural policy*, COM(82) 98 (11 Mar.).

—— (1982*c*), *Eleventh Financial Report on the European Agricultural Guidance and Guarantee Fund—1981—Guidance Section*, COM(82)446 final (26 July).

—— (1982*d*), *Fifth and final report on the operation of the system of premiums for the non-marketing of milk and milk products and the conversion of dairy herds under Regulation (EEC) No 1078/77*, VI/3760/82 (3 July).

—— (1983*a*), *The Commision's proposals for the Integrated Mediterranean Programmes*, COM(83)24 final (23 Mar.).

—— (1983*b*), *Further guidelines for the development of the common agricultural policy*, COM(83)380 final (20 June).

—— (1983*c*), *Proposal for a Council Regulation (EEC) instituting Integrated Mediterranean Programmes*, COM(83)495 final (16 Aug.).

—— (1983*d*), *Common Agricultural Policy—Proposals of the Commission*, COM(83)500 final (28 July).

—— (1983*e*), *Report and Proposals on ways of increasing the effectiveness of the Community's Structural Funds*, COM(83)501 final (28 July).

—— (1983*f*), *Proposal for a Council Regulation (EEC) on improving the efficiency of agricultural structures*, COM(83)559 final (10 Oct.).

—— (1983*g*), *Ten years of Community Environment Policy*, 1973–1983 (Nov.).

—— (1984), *Thirteenth Financial Report on the European Agricultural Guidance and Guarantee Fund—1983—Guidance Section*, COM(84)486 final (12 Sept.).

—— (1985*a*), *Commission proposals on the fixing of prices for agricultural products, and related measure (1985/86)*, vol. I: Explanatory Memorandum, COM(85)50 final (30 Jan.).

—— (1985*b*), *Perspectives for the Common Agricultural Policy*, COM(85)333 final (15 July).

—— (1985*c*), *Commission memorandum on the adjustment of the market organization for cereals*, COM(85)700 final (14 Nov.).

—— (1985*d*), *A future for Community agriculture: Commission guidelines following consultations in connection with the Green Paper*, COM(85)750 (18 Dec.).

—— (1986*a*), *Discussion paper on Community action in the Forestry sector*, COM (85) 792 (7 Jan. 1986).

—— (1986*b*), *Community action in the Forestry sector: complementary memorandum to the Commission's Discussion Paper COM(85)792*, COM(86)26 final (31 Jan.).

—— (1986*c*), *Proposal for a . . . Regulation . . . amending Regulations (EEC) No. 797/85, No. 270/79, No. 1360/78 and No. 355/77 as regards agricultural structures, the adjustment of agriculture to the new market situation and the preservation of the countryside*, COM(86)199 final/2 (31 July).

—— (1986*d*), *Biotechnology in the Community: stimulating agro-industrial development*, COM(86) 221 final (18 Apr.).

—— (1986*e*), *Fifteenth Financial Report . . . on the European Agricultural Guidance and Guarantee Fund—1985—Guidance Section*, COM(86)407 final (24 July).

—— (1986*f*), *Commission Report to the Council on foreseeable trends in the planting and replanting of vineyards in the Community and on the balance of production and consumption in the wine sector (1983/84)*, COM(86)482 final (22 Sept.).

—— (1986*g*), *Emergency action in the milk sector*, COM(86)510 final (11 Sept.).

—— (1986*h*), *Report to the Council concerning the application of the additional levy system in the milk sector*, COM(86)645 final (14 Nov.).

—— (1987*a*), *Commission proposals on the prices for agricultural products and on related measures (1987/88)*, vol. I: Explanatory Memorandum, COM(87)1 final (4 Mar.).

—— (1987*b*), *Making a success of the Single Act: a new frontier for Europe*, COM(87)100 (15 Feb.).

—— (1987*c*), *Report by the Commission to the Council and Parliament on the financing of the Community Budget*, COM(87)101 final (28 Feb.).

—— (1987*d*), *Proposal for a Council Regulation (EEC) establishing a Community system of aids to agricultural income*, COM(87)166 final/3 (3 June).

—— (1987*e*), *Sixteenth Financial Report . . . on the European Agricultural Guidance and Fund—1986—Guidance Section*, COM(87)357 final (31 July).

—— (1987*f*), *Report from the Commission on the implementation of Regulation (EEC) No. 389/82 on producer groups and associations thereof in the cotton sector*, COM(87) 362 final (15 July).

—— (1987*g*), *Reform of the Structural Funds*, *COM(87)*376 final (24 Aug.).

—— (1987*h*), *Review of action taken to control the agricultural markets and outlook for the Common Agricultural Policy*, COM(87)410 final (3 Aug.).

—— (1987*i*), *Implementation of Agricultural Stabilizers, vol. II-B: Milk Sector, Reports and Legal Texts*, COM(87)452 final (2 Oct.).

—— (1987*j*), *Proposition des Communautés Européennes pour les négociations commerciales multilaterales en ce qui concerne l'agriculture* (20–10–1987).

—— (1988*a*), *Commission proposals on the prices for agricultural products and on related measures (1988/89)*, vol. I: Explanatory memoranda, COM(88)120 final (28 Mar.).

—— (1988*b*), *Community Strategy and Action Programme for the Forestry sector*, COM (88), 255 final (11 Nov.).

—— (1988*c*), *Amended proposal for a Council Regulation (EEC) establishing a system of transitional aids to agricultural income*, COM(88)272 final (30 May).

—— (1988*d*), *Environment and Agriculture*, COM(88)338 final (8 June).

—— (1988*e*), *Seventeenth Financial Report . . . on the European Agricultural Guidance and Guarantee Fund—1987—Guidance Section*, COM(88)437 final (26 July).

—— (1988*f*), *The Future of Rural Society*, COM(88)501 final/2 (7 Oct.).

—— (1988*g*), *Proposal for a Council Regulation (EEC) laying down the conditions and procedures for the granting of aid for the conversion of agricultural production*, COM (88)553 final (21 Oct.).

Commission de la Communauté Économique Européenne/Commission of the European Economic Community (*cont.*)

—— (1988*h*), *Integrated Mediterranean Programmes: Progress report 1986/1987...*, SEC (88)335 final (27 Oct.).

—— (1989*a*), *Commission proposals on the prices for agricultural products and on related measures (1989/90)*, vol. I: Explanatory Memoranda, COM(89)40 final (31 Jan.).

—— (1989*b*), *Proposals for ... Regulations ... amending Regulations (EEC) No. 797/85, No. 1096/88, No. 1360/78, No. 389/82 and No. 1696/71 with a view to speeding up the adjustment of production structures, and on improving the processing and marketing of agricultural and forestry products*, COM(89)91 final (3 July).

—— (1989*c*), *Report from the Commission to the Council on the progress made in implementing the special measures for improving the production and marketing of Community citrus fruit*, COM(89)128 final (21 Mar.).

—— (1989*d*), *Report on the progress of the common measure instituted by Regulation (EEC) No 270/79 on the development of agricultural advisory services in Italy at 31 Dec. 1987*, COM(89)130 final (28 Mar.).

—— (1989*e*), *Report to the Council on the production refund system for users of starch manufactured from cereals, rice and potatoes*, COM(89)186 final (17 Apr.).

—— (1989*f*), *Report on the operation of the quota system in the milk sector*, COM(89)352 final (3 Aug.).

—— (1989*g*), *Report on the application of the Community scheme for the set-aside of arable land*, COM(89)353 final (12 Sept.).

—— (1989*h*), *Eighteenth Financial Report ... on the European Agricultural Guidance and Guarantee Fund—1988—Guidance Section*, SEC(89)1984 final (29 Nov.).

—— (1990*a*), *Use of agricultural commodities in the non-food sector*, COM(89)597 final (23 Jan. 1990).

—— (1990*b*), *Proposal for a Council Regulation (EEC) on the introduction and the maintenance of agricultural production methods compatible with the requirements of the protection of the environment and the maintenance of the countryside*, COM(90)366 final (2 Oct.).

—— (1991*a*), *Commission proposals on the prices for agricultural products and on related measures (1991/92)*, vol. I: Explanatory Memoranda, COM(91)72 final (1 Mar.).

—— (1991*b*), *The development and future of the CAP: Reflections paper of the Commission*, COM(91)100 final (1 Feb.).

—— (1991*c*), *The Development and Future of the Common Agricultural Policy: Follow-up to the Reflections Paper COM(91)100 of 1 February 1991—Proposals of the Commission*, COM(91)258 final/3 (22 July).

—— (1991*d*), *Reform of the Common Agricultural Policy-Legislation. Measures to accompany the reform of the market support mechanisms, Community aid scheme for forestry measures in agriculture, Community early retirement scheme for farmers*, COM(91)415 final (31 Oct.).

—— (1991*e*), *Report to the Council concerning aid for the formation of producer groups and associations thereof*, COM(91)438 final (14 Nov.).

—— (1991*f*), *Europe 2000: outlook for the development of the Community's territory*, COM(91)452 final (7 Nov.).

—— (1991*g*), *IMP—Progress Report for 1989*, SEC(91)553 final (5 Apr.).

—— (1992*a*) *Community Structural Policies: assessment and outlook*, COM(92)84 final (18 Mar.).

—— (1992*b*), *From the Single Act to Maastricht and beyond: the means to match our ambitions*, COM(92)2000 final (11 Feb.).

—— (1992*c*), *IMP—Progress Report for 1990*, SEC(92)690 final (15 Apr.).

—— (1992*d*), *Agricultural Income Aid: Commission report to the European Parliament and to the Council*, SEC(92)1864 final (16 Oct.).

—— (1992*e*), *Set-aside scheme for arable land: report on the implementation of the options relating to extensive livestock grazing and the cultivation of lentils, chick-peas and vetches*, SEC(92)1885 (9 Oct.).

—— (1992*f*), *Agriculture in the GATT negotiations and the reform of the CAP*, SEC(92) 2267 final (25 Nov.).

—— (1993*a*), *Commission proposals on the prices for agricultural products and on related measures (1993/94)*, vol. I: Explanatory Memorandum, COM(93)36 final (3 Feb.).

—— (1993*b*), *Development and Future of wine sector policy: Commission discussion paper*, COM(93)380 final (22 July).

—— (1993*c*), *Annual report on the implementation of the IMPs—1991–1992*, COM(93) 485 final (13 Oct.).

—— (1993*d*), *Recommendation for a Council Decision concerning the conclusion of an agreement on certain oilseeds between the European Economic Community and the United States of America within the framework of the GATT*, SEC(93)53 final (26 Jan.).

—— (1993*e*), *Report pursuant to Article 25 of Regulation (EEC) No. 2453/88: European Agricultural Guidance and Guarantee Fund, Guidance Section—1992*, VI/5954 93 (16 Dec.).

—— (1993*f*), Support for farms in mountain, hill and less-favoured areas, *Green Europe*, 2.

—— (1994*a*), *Proposal for a Council Regulation (EC) on reform of the Common organization of the market in wine*, COM(94)117 final (11 May).

—— (1994*b*), *Commission communication to the Council on coordination between the Community and the Member States concerning food security policies and practices*, COM(94) 165 final (4 May)

—— (1994*c*), *Development and future of Community policy in the fruit and vegetables sector*, (COM(94)360 final (27 July).

—— (1994*d*), *Interim review of implementation of the European Community programme of policy and action in relation to the environment and sustainable development*, COM(94) 453 final (30 Nov.).

—— (1994*e*), *Europe 2000+: cooperation for European territorial development* (Luxembourg).

—— (1994*f*), *Fifth annual report on the implementation of the reform of the Structural funds, 1993*.

—— (1995*a*), *Preparation of the Associated States of Central and Eastern Europe for Integration into the internal market of the Union, COM(95)163 final (3 May)*.

—— (1995*b*), *Preparation of the associated countries of Central and Eastern Europe for integration into the internal market of the Union: Addendum: Annex*, COM(95)163 final/2 (10 May).

—— (1995*c*), *Study on alternative strategies for the development of relations in the field of agriculture between the EU and the associated countries with a view to future accession of these countries*, CSE(95)607.

Communautés Européennes (1959), *Recueil des documents de la conférence agricole des*

États membres de la Communauté Économique Européenne à Stresa du 3 au 12 juillet 1958 (Brussels [?]).

Conseil de la Communauté Économique Européenne/Council of the European Communities:

—— (1964*a*), Actions à entreprendre par priorité dans le cadre du 'programme d'action de la Commission de la CEE en matière de politique sociale dans l'agriculture' (1110/64(SOC101/AGRI 312) (le 10 août).

—— (1964*b*), Actions à entreprendre par priorité dans le cadre du 'programme d'action de la Commission en matière de politique sociale en agriculture: note complémentaire' (1166/64(SOC107/AGRI 329) (le 16 septembre).

—— (1975*a*) Danish memorandum on the Common Agricultural Policy, R/348/75 (7 Feb.).

—— (1975*b*) German memorandum on the common agricultural policy, R/349/75 (7 Feb.).

European Commission:

—— (1994), EC agricultural policy for the 21st century: report of an expert group, *European Economy*: Reports and Studies No. 4.

—— (1995), Agricultural situation and prospects in the Central and Eastern European countries: Summary Report, DGVI Working Document.

European Community (1986), Agricultural incomes in the European Community in 1985 and since 1973, *Green Europe Newsflash*, Apr.

INDEX